Fulfilling the Sustainable Goals

This book contains an assessment of the progress, or lack thereof, in implementing the UN Sustainable Development Goals (SDGs). Through review of assessments and case studies, readers can draw lessons from the actions that could work to positively address the goals.

The 2030 Agenda for Sustainable Development is designed to catalyze action in critical areas of importance to humanity and the planet. The effort to implement the SDGs, however, demands a sense of urgency in the face of environmental degradation, climate change, emerging conflicts, persisting poverty and hunger, and growing inequality, among a number of other socio-economic problems. Five years after the launch of the 2030 Agenda, this book takes stock of how far the world has come and how we can position ourselves to achieve the global targets. This book is the first to assess how the implementation of each SDG is impeded by the onset of COVID-19. It contains a special chapter on COVID-19 and the SDGs, while many thematic chapters on different SDGs also assess how COVID-19 adversely affects implementation, and what measures could be taken to minimize the adverse effects.

This publication thus provides a fresh look at implementation of the SDGs highlighting impactful and creative actions that go beyond the business-as-usual development efforts. The volume reinforces this analysis with expert recommendations on how to support implementation efforts and achieve the SDGs through international and national strategies and the involvement of both the public and private sectors. The result is an indispensable textual tool for policy makers, academia, intergovernmental organizations (IGOs) and non-governmental organizations (NGOs), as well as the public, as we march toward the 2030 deadline.

Narinder Kakar is Director of the Sustainable Development Research Program and Distinguished Senior Fellow at the Global Center for Environmental Legal Studies, Elisabeth Haub School of Law at Pace University, USA, and Permanent Observer to the UN for the University of Peace, Costa Rica.

Vesselin Popovski is Professor and Vice Dean and Executive Director at the Center for the Study of United Nations, Jindal Global Law School, Sonipat, India.

Nicholas A. Robinson is University Professor for the Environment at the Elisabeth Haub School of Law at Pace University, USA.

Law, Ethics and Governance Series

Recent history has emphasised the potentially devastating effects of governance failures in governments, government agencies, corporations and the institutions of civil society. 'Good governance' is seen as necessary, if not crucial, for economic success and human development. Although the disciplines of law, ethics, politics, economics and management theory can provide insights into the governance of organizations, governance issues can only be dealt with by interdisciplinary studies, combining several (and sometimes all) of those disciplines. This series aims to provide such interdisciplinary studies for students, researchers and relevant practitioners.

Series Editor: Charles Sampford, Director, Institute for Ethics, Governance and Law, Griffith University, Australia

Recent titles in this series

Governing the Climate Change Regime
Institutional Integrity and Integrity Systems
Edited by Tim Cadman, Rowena Maguire and Charles Sampford

Positive Social Identity
The Quantitative Analysis of Ethics
Nick Duncan

Global Governance and Regulation
Order and Disorder in the 21st Century
Edited by Leon Wolff and Danielle Ireland-Piper

The Implementation of the Paris Agreement on Climate Change
Edited by Vesselin Popovski

Humanitarian Intervention, Colonialism, Islam, and Democracy
An Analysis Through the Human-Nonhuman Distinction
Gustavo Gozzi
Translated by Filippo Valente

For more information about this series, please visit:
www.routledge.com/Law-Ethics-and-Governance/book-series/LEAG

Fulfilling the Sustainable Development Goals
On a Quest for a Sustainable World

Co-editors:

Narinder Kakar,
Vesselin Popovski
and
Nicolas A. Robinson

This study on implementing the Sustainable Development Goals was conceived and directed by Narinder Kakar for the Global Center on Environmental Legal Studies of the Elisabeth Haub School of Law at Pace University.

LONDON AND NEW YORK

First published 2022
by Routledge
2 Park Square, Milton Park, Abingdon, Oxon OX14 4RN

and by Routledge
605 Third Avenue, New York, NY 10158

Routledge is an imprint of the Taylor & Francis Group, an informa business

© 2022 selection and editorial matter, Narinder Kakar, Vesselin Popovski, and Nicholas A. Robinson; individual chapters, the contributors

The right of Narinder Kakar, Vesselin Popovski, and Nicholas A. Robinson to be identified as the author[/s] of the editorial material, and of the authors for their individual chapters, has been asserted in accordance with sections 77 and 78 of the Copyright, Designs and Patents Act 1988.

All rights reserved. No part of this book may be reprinted or reproduced or utilised in any form or by any electronic, mechanical, or other means, now known or hereafter invented, including photocopying and recording, or in any information storage or retrieval system, without permission in writing from the publishers.

Trademark notice: Product or corporate names may be trademarks or registered trademarks, and are used only for identification and explanation without intent to infringe.

British Library Cataloguing-in-Publication Data
A catalogue record for this book is available from the British Library

Library of Congress Cataloging-in-Publication Data
Names: Kakar, Narinder, editor. | Popovski, Vesselin, editor. | Robinson, Nicholas A., editor.
Title: Fulfilling the sustainable development goals/edited by Narinder Kakar, Vesselin Popovski and Nicholas Robinson.
Description: Abingdon, Oxon; New York, NY: Routledge, 2021. | Series: Law, ethics and governance | Includes bibliographical references and index.
Identifiers: LCCN 2021006255 (print) | LCCN 2021006256 (ebook) | ISBN 9780367700256 (hardback) | ISBN 9780367700270 (paperback) | ISBN 9781003144274 (ebook)
Subjects: LCSH: Sustainable development–International cooperation. | Sustainable development–Law and legislation.
Classification: LCC HC79.E5 F837 2021 (print) | LCC HC79.E5 (ebook) | DDC 338.9/27–dc23
LC record available at https://lccn.loc.gov/2021006255
LC ebook record available at https://lccn.loc.gov/2021006256

ISBN: 978-0-367-70025-6 (hbk)
ISBN: 978-0-367-70027-0 (pbk)
ISBN: 978-1-003-14427-4 (ebk)

Typeset in Galliard
by Deanta Global Publishing Services, Chennai, India

Contents

Acknowledgments	ix
List of Contributors	xi
Foreword	xviii
Preface	xxi

I	**SDGs in Context**	1
1	**Special Introduction** AMINA J. MOHAMMED	3
2	**Multilateralism Under Challenge** MARÍA FERNANDA ESPINOSA GARCÉS	5
3	**COVID-19 and the SDGs** JOE E. COLOMBANO AND DAVID N. NABARRO	17
II	**Implementing the SDGs**	33
A	**People**	35
4	**Extreme Poverty Eradication: Conceptual Evolution and Policy Challenges** VESSELIN POPOVSKI AND KRASSEN STANCHEV	37
5	**Critical Assessment of the Latest Progress in Eradication of Extreme Poverty** AISHA MUHAMMED-OYEBODE	55
6	**Achieving Zero Hunger Using a Rights-Based Approach to Food Security and Sustainable Agriculture** SMITA NARULA	75

vi *Contents*

7   Health and Sustainable Development: Assessing Progress
    and Challenges   99
    OBIJIOFOR AGINAM

8   Gender Equality and Women's Empowerment: Critical
    Assessment of the Implementation of SDG 5   118
    AISHA MUHAMMED-OYEBODE

9   Sustainable Management of Water and Sanitation: A Long
    and Winding Road Ahead   137
    ZHOU DI

B   Prosperity   153

10 Inclusive, Safe, and Resilient Cities and Settlements   155
    DUAN CHECHE

11 Inclusive and Equitable Quality Education: Why Are We
    Missing the Mark?   168
    ANNA SHOSTYA

12 Environmental Education   185
    LYE LIN-HENG

13 STEM Education: Environmental Restoration Science in
    New York Harbor   201
    LAUREN BIRNEY AND DENISE MCNAMARA

14 Working Together toward Sustained and Inclusive Growth   211
    JOSEPH C. MORREALE

15 The Road to Sustainable Industrialization   224
    ANNA SHOSTYA

16 Reducing Inequality and Sharing Opportunities for All   240
    VESSELIN POPOVSKI

C   Planet   255

17 Accelerating the Energy Transformation   257
    MINORU TAKADA, DAVID KORANYI, RICHARD OTTINGER, BO FU, AND PIANPIAN WANG

18 Toward Sustainable Consumption and Production   274
    ANNA SHOSTYA AND NARINDER KAKAR

19 Missing Climate Action: Gaps in the Implementation of the
    Paris Agreement on Climate Change 294
    VESSELIN POPOVSKI

20 Climate Change and Small Islands 311
    TESSEL VAN DER PUTTE

21 Achieving SDG 14: Time for a Global
    Ocean Approach 329
    KRISTINA M. GJERDE AND MARJO VIERROS

22 Legal Tools in Combating Marine Pollution and Mitigating
    the Effects of Acidification 341
    ANNICK DE MARFFY-MANTUANO

23 Marine Pollution: Maximizing Synergies for
    Transformative Changes 357
    HIROKO MURAKI GOTTLIEB

24 Using Terrestrial Ecosystems Sustainably and Halting
    Biodiversity Loss 373
    JOHN G. ROBINSON AND FEDERICA PESCE

25 Restoration of Ecosystems and Land Degradation
    Neutrality 392
    BEN BOER AND IAN HANNAM

D   Peace 405

26 Peaceful Societies and Leaving No One Behind 407
    FATIMA AKILU

27 Nigeria's Alternative Pathway to Peace 417
    FATIMA AKILU

E   Partnership 423

28 Partnering for a Better World: Shift from Sustainable Finance
    to Financing Sustainable Development 425
    JOE E. COLOMBANO, MARCO NICOLI, AND ANIKET SHAH

29 Private Corporations and Environmental Social Governance:
    An Uneven Response 437
    MARK E. MEANEY

30 From Means of Implementation to Implementation of Means: Realizing the Sustainable Development Goals as If They Matter 449
MIHIR KANADE

III Integrating the SDGs 465

31 Interlinkages between Climate Change, Economic Inequality, and Human Migration 467
JOSEPH C. MORREALE

32 Indigenous Peoples, the SDGs, and International Environmental Law 485
ANXHELA MILE AND RAILLA PUNO

33 Codification and Implementation of Customary International Law 501
JUAN CARLOS SAINZ-BORGO

34 Integrating the SDGs through "One Health" 512
NICHOLAS A. ROBINSON

IV Conclusions 527

35 Pathways to 2030 529
VESSELIN POPOVSKI, NARINDER KAKAR, AND NICHOLAS A. ROBINSON

Index 541

Acknowledgments

The conceptualization of a complex project, comprising assessments of the implementation of all SDGs, requires contributions from academics and professional experts from diverse disciplines. We were fortunate to have had enthusiastic responses from many experts, whose papers are published here. We owe them a debt of gratitude. Their contributions enhance the capacity of all stakeholders—governments, civil society, academics, private sector, among others—to develop policies and plans to implement the SDGs. Without their dedication, commitment, and excellent work, this book would not have seen the light of day.

We are grateful to the Co-Directors of the Global Center for Environmental Legal Studies of the Elisabeth Haub School of Law at Pace University, our colleagues Dean Emeritus Professor Richard Ottinger and Prof. Smita Narula for the guidance in developing the framework of the book, as well as contributing their individual chapters. In the same vein, we are indebted to Pace University's former Provost and now Distinguished Professor Joseph Morreale, Chair of the Economics Department, and Associate Professor Anna Shostya, for their insights and guidance in shaping this book, in addition to their important individual chapters.

A number of experts and sustainable development practitioners have guided us in formulating the framework of this book. We are pleased to acknowledge the invaluable counsel provided by Mr. Joe E. Colombano, an international civil servant and an economist, who has devoted his career to development, and by Mr. Rob Haberman, LLM and a graduate of Elisabeth Haub School of Law, currently working on energy and climate policy as an associate counsel for the New York State Senate, who collaborated with us in the early phase of developing the framework of this book.

Essential to our project has been the team of young scholars who helped us. Ms. Anxhela Mile, JD and LLM, and Ms. Railla Veronica Puno, LLM, both graduates of the Elisabeth Haub School of Law at Pace University, provided superb professional skills in reading, editing, and formatting many chapters. Ms. Alexandra Horn, Esq., also a graduate of the Elisabeth Haub School of Law, was extremely helpful in the editing and formatting of most of the chapters into the manuscript. Our editorial team also benefitted considerably from the support of three student interns of the Center for the Study of the UN in O.P. Jindal Global University, India—Mr. Suhaas Putta, Mr. Tharun Rana Vuyurru, and Ms. Kirti Lohia—and their support has been invaluable.

We are grateful to H.E. Amina J. Mohammed for her special introduction of the book, and to H.E. Ms. Maria Fernanda Espinosa Garces, for her contribution on Multilateralism in the age of COVID-19. These two world-renowned female leaders have provided us with considerable inspiration. We are grateful for the chapter contributed by Mr. David Nabarro and Mr. Joe E. Colombano. Their insights on COVID-19 and the SDGs add special value.

Last but not least, our sincere thanks go to Ms. Alison Kirk and the team at Taylor & Francis Group for their guidance and support throughout the process.

Contributors

Obijiofor Aginam has held senior research positions at the United Nations University. He is Adjunct Research Professor of Law at Carleton University, Ottawa, Canada, and Visiting Professor at The Institute for Future Initiatives, University of Tokyo, Japan. He has been a fellow of the Social Science Research Council of New York, USA, on global security and cooperation, Global Health Leadership Fellow at the World Health Organization, and Visiting Professor at the University for Peace, Costa Rica. Dr. Aginam holds a PhD from the University of British Columbia. He is the author of *Global Health Governance: International Law and Public Health in a Divided World*.

Fatima Akilu is Executive Director of Neem Foundation, Nigeria. Akilu has had extensive experience working with forensic dually diagnosed mentally retarded women, violent offenders, and sex offenders. Previously Head of Communication for the Senior Special Assistant to the President on the Millennium Development Goals, she was Chairman of the Editorial Board Leadership Newspapers. Until recently, Akilu was Director of the Behavioral Analysis and Strategic Communication unit at the Office of the National Security Advisor which has developed a multi-pronged approach to countering violent extremism (CVE).

Lauren Birney is an urban science, technology, engineering, and mathematics (STEM) educator with a concentrated focus in providing opportunities for underrepresented students in STEM and Environmental Restoration Sciences through external funding sources. Currently, she is Director of the STEM Collaboratory NYC® and Professor of STEM Education at Pace University in New York City, USA. She earned a BA in Biology/Chemistry from the University of San Diego, USA, MA in Counseling and an EdD in Educational Leadership from the University of Southern California, Rossier School of Education, USA. She also serves as the Board Chair and President for The Biomimicry Institute.

Ben Boer was Distinguished Professor at Wuhan University, China from 2011 to 2020. He continues as Emeritus Professor in the University of Sydney Law School, Australia. He is a member of the Board of Governors of the International Council of Environmental Law and the Australian Academy of Law. He was Deputy Chair of the World Commission on Environmental Law of International Union for Conservation of Nature (IUCN) from 2012 to 2016 and co-founder with Dr. Ian Hannam of the Commission's Soil, Desertification, and Sustainable Agriculture Specialist Group. He is the Co-Editor-in-Chief of the *Chinese Journal of Environmental Law*.

xii *Contributors*

Duan Cheche is Assistant Professor at the Institute of Urban Governance, Shenzhen University, China. His research specialization is on urban governance and bureaucratic behavior. In the recent past, he has worked on issues related to urban community governance, urban street bureaucracy, and on technological governance. He prefers to use empirical methods to study urban micro-governance issues in China, such as official–civilian interaction, deliberative democracy, and bureaucratic behavior preferences. Duan received his PhD from National Chengchi University, Taiwan.

Joe E. Colombano is a senior international development executive with over 20 years of experience in the multilateral system. Formerly the Economic Advisor in the Executive Office of UN Secretary-General Ban Ki-moon, Colombano was instrumental in the definition and agreement of the SDGs. He recently served as Senior Advisor to the World Health Organization (WHO) Special Envoy on COVID-19. He built a career in development finance, first at the World Bank and later at the European Bank for Reconstruction and Development (EBRD). He is the author of *Learning from the World: New Ideas to Redevelop America* (Palgrave Macmillan). He graduated from Harvard University, USA.

Zhou Di is a lecturer at the School of Marxism of Wuhan University, China. She has done considerable research on the modern and contemporary history of environmental governance in China and the doctrine of "Ecological Civilization." She was a Fulbright visiting scholar at Elisabeth Haub School of Law at Pace University in the USA from 2016 to 2017. She received her PhD in Environmental Law from Wuhan University in December 2017. She is the winner of Green Talents Competition 2018 granted by the Federal Ministry of Education and Research of Germany.

Bo Fu has over six years of experience in international affairs on the topic of sustainable development. She currently works as a research consultant at the Department of Economic and Social Affairs, United Nations (UN DESA), supporting the overall review, follow-up, and implementation of SDG7 on energy. Fu holds a MS degree in Environmental Engineering from Columbia University, USA, and a BA degree in Mathematics and Statistics from Nanjing University, China.

Kristina M. Gjerde is Senior High Seas Advisor to IUCN's Global Marine and Polar Programme and Adjunct Professor at the Middlebury Institute of International Studies at Monterey, California, USA, where she teaches International Marine Law. Gjerde has authored or co-authored over 150 publications covering ocean governance, shipping, fishing, deep seabed mining, as well as tools and technologies for advancing marine biodiversity conservation and sustainable use. Kristina received her Juris Doctor from New York University School of Law, USA, with a focus on comparative and international law, and practiced admiralty law for several years in a New York City law firm.

Hiroko Muraki Gottlieb is an attorney with over 20 years of experience in law and policy on sustainability and international matters. As the Representative for the Ocean, International Council of Environmental Law (ICEL), Gottlieb leads the ICEL delegation on the high seas treaty negotiations at the United Nations. She is also an Associate of the Department of Organismic and Evolutionary Biology, Harvard University, USA, and an Adjunct Professor of Law at Elisabeth Haub School of Law, Pace University, USA. Her previous roles include Charge d'affaires/Senior Counselor, Permanent Observer

Mission of International Chamber of Commerce to the United Nations, and Counsel to IBM's Corporate Environmental Affairs.

Ian Hannam is Adjunct Associate Professor at the Australian Centre for Agriculture and Law, School of Law, University of New England, Australia. He is Chair Emeritus of the Specialist Group for Soil, Desertification, and Sustainable Agriculture of the IUCN World Commission on Environmental Law. He holds a B.Agr.Sc Dip, BA, MLitt, and a PhD. He has been consulted by governments and environmental institutions on law and policy of sustainable land management, specializing in land degradation and dryland agriculture. He has numerous book and journal publications on national and international environmental law and policy on land degradation and sustainable use of soil.

LYE Lin-Heng is Adjunct Professor and former Vice Dean and Director of Graduate Programs, Faculty of Law, National University of Singapore (NUS). She is Honorary Advisor and former Director of the Law Faculty's Asia-Pacific Center for Environmental Law (APCEL) (2013–2018); Special Advisor and former Chair of the NUS multi-disciplinary MSc in Environmental Management (MEM) Programme (2001–2018); Visiting Associate Professor at Yale's Environment School, USA (2003 to 2019). She was on the Board of Governors, IUCN Academy of Environmental Law and Co-Chair of its Teaching and Research Committee. She is a member of the Board of Directors, World Wide Fund (WWF) Singapore.

Narinder Kakar is Distinguished Senior Fellow at Elisabeth Haub School of Law at Pace University, USA, and has over 50 years' experience related to sustainable development activities. He worked for the United Nations Development Programme (UNDP) in Yemen, Guyana, Turkey, China, and Maldives, culminating in the position of UN Resident Coordinator/UNDP Representative. He represents the University for Peace, Costa Rica, as Permanent Observer to the UN and, as Professor Emeritus, teaches courses related to the UN and sustainable development. He has also represented IUCN at the UN. He participated in and contributed to the deliberations concerning sustainable development at various UN organs and conferences, inter alia, the General Assembly, the Intergovernmental Panel on Climate Change (IPCC),, the U N Conference on Sustainable Development—UNCSD (Rio+20), the Open Working Group on SDGs and the High-Level Political Forum (HLPF).

Mihir Kanade is Head of the Department of International Law at the University for Peace (UPEACE), Costa Rica, and Director of its Human Rights Centre. He currently serves as a member of the United Nations Human Rights Council's Expert Mechanism on the Right to Development. He also chairs the drafting group of international experts constituted by the United Nations to prepare a draft convention on the right to development. Kanade holds a LLB from Nagpur University (India) and an MA and Doctorate from UPEACE.

David Koranyi serves as Policy Advisor on Sustainable Energy at the United Nations Department of Economic and Social Affairs and as Senior Fellow for Energy Diplomacy at the Atlantic Council. Previously, he was Chief Foreign Policy Advisor to the Prime Minister of the Republic of Hungary. He edited a book on *Transatlantic Energy – Future Strategic Perspectives on Energy Security, Climate Change, and New Technologies in Europe and the United States* published by Brookings Institution Press. David has a MA in International Relations and Economics from Corvinus University Budapest, Hungary, and an Executive MA in Public Administration from Columbia University, USA.

Annick de Marffy-Mantuano is President of the Scientific Board of Institut du Droit Economique de la Mer (INDEMER) Monaco, Editor of *Annuaire du Droit de la Mer*, an annual review on international law of the sea, (INDEMER), Pedone publisher, Paris; Member of the Advisory Committee for the International Seabed Authority Secretary-General's Award for Deep-Sea Research Excellence; Lecturer at the Rhodes Academy of Oceans Law and Policy (9-25 July 2003 and July 7–24, 2004), (Greece); and former Director of UN/Division for Ocean Affairs and the Law of the Sea (DOALOS) (2001–2004). She has published a book and numerous articles on ocean affairs and the law of sea both in French and English.

Denise McNamara is Educational Consultant for the Curriculum and Community Enterprise for Restoration Science and a retired Director of Science for the New York City Department of Education. A former high school Chemistry teacher and Assistant Principal of Science, McNamara earned a BS in Chemistry from St. Joseph's College, an MS in Secondary Education from St. John's University, USA and a PhD in Urban Education from the City University of New York Graduate Center, USA.

Mark E. Meaney is Scholar in Residence for Social Responsibility and Sustainability at the Leeds School of Business, University of Colorado, Boulder, USA. Meaney also serves as the Chair of the United Nations Principles for Responsible Management Education (UN PRME) Chapter North America and on the UN PRME International Advisory Council. He also conducts education in leadership development for UN diplomats and staff through the United Nations Institute for Training and Research (UNITAR). Prior to his appointment with the Leeds School of Business, USA, Meaney held a faculty appointment at the Haas School of Business, University of California, Berkeley, USA.

Anxhela (Angela) Mile is an attorney and recent graduate of the Elisabeth Haub School of Law, Pace University, USA (JD and LLM). Anxhela specialized in global environmental law and has worked as a law clerk at the Department of Justice's Environmental and Natural Resources Division, as a legal intern with a Permanent Mission to the UN, and as a semester judicial clerk at the Southern District of New York. Her LLM thesis on emerging legal doctrines in climate change law and the movement seeking an advisory opinion from the International Court of Justice is forthcoming in the *Texas International Law Review*.

Joseph C. Morreale is Distinguished Professor and bi-campus Chair of the Economics Department at Pace University, NYC, USA. He holds a PhD in Economics and a MS in Higher Education Administration and Finance. He has extensive experience in administration, research, teaching, business, and government consulting. He has served as a Provost and Executive Vice President (VP) for Academic Affairs, Senior Associate Provost and Vice President for Academic Affairs. Morreale's specializations and published works include the pedagogy of quantitative undergraduate research, environmental economics, health economics, and public economics. He has also published books on senior faculty development and program assessment in higher education.

Aisha Muhammed-Oyebode is a development specialist and is currently a PhD researcher in Law with a focus on gender in conflict at the University of London, UK. She is CEO of the Murtala Muhammed Foundation and co-founder of the Bring Back Our Girls (BBOG) group. Muhammed-Oyebode is also on the Women's Leadership Board of the Harvard Kennedy School—Women and Public Policy Program and Advisor and Country

Expert to the University of Pennsylvania Law Global Women's Leadership Project, USA. She also advises the United States Institute of Peace (USIP) as a Member of its Senior Working Group on Northern Nigeria.

David N. Nabarro is Co-Director of the Imperial College Institute of Global Health Innovation and supports systems leadership for sustainable development through his Switzerland-based social enterprise 4SD (Skills, Systems and Synergies for Sustainable Development). Currently, Nabarro is Special Envoy of the WHO on COVID-19 and Senior Advisor to the United Nations Food Systems Summit. He secured his medical qualification in 1974 and has worked in over 50 countries in multiple positions. In October 2018, Nabarro received the World Food Prize together with Lawrence Haddad for their leadership in building coalitions for action for better nutrition across the Sustainable Development Goals.

Smita Narula is the Haub Distinguished Professor of International Law at the Elisabeth Haub School of Law, Pace University, USA. She is author of dozens of widely cited publications and has helped formulate policy, legal, and community-led responses to a range of human rights and environmental issues worldwide. Before joining Pace, she was Associate Professor of Clinical Law and Faculty Director of the Center for Human Rights and Global Justice at NYU School of Law, USA. Narula is former Legal Advisor to the UN Special Rapporteur on the Right to Food and has also worked at Human Rights Watch as their Senior Researcher for South Asia.

Marco Nicoli is currently Special Advisor to the Director of the Organization for Economic Cooperation and Development (OECD) Development Center, Senior Counselor at UNIDROIT Foundation, and Guest Lecturer at LUMSA University, Italy. Formerly, he was Sr. Project Manager at the World Bank and Economist at the Italian Central Bank. He has had experiences abroad in Mali with UNDP, in Belgium at the European Union (EU) Commission, in the USA with Rogers & Wells Law Firm, in the Slovak Republic as Visiting Professor at Comenius University, in Romania, Hungary, Bosnia, and Slovakia as Business Consultant. Nicoli has a Master's in International Law and Economics and other postgraduate degrees in International Organizations and European Law.

Richard Ottinger is Dean Emeritus of Elisabeth Haub School of Law at Pace University, USA, and served 16 years as a member of the United States House of Representatives, authoring a substantial body of energy and environmental laws. He chaired the Energy Conservation and Power Subcommittee of the House Energy and Commerce Committee. He was a founder of the Environmental and Energy Study Institute in Washington, DC, USA. He is author or co-author of five treatises and some 100 law review articles, frequently cited by the Courts. He is a graduate of Cornell University, USA, and Harvard Law School, USA.

Federica Pesce is currently Associate Expert at the UN Environment Programme—World Conservation Monitoring Centre (UNEP-WCMC) where she focuses on biodiversity and the 2030 Agenda for Sustainable Development. Before joining the UN, she worked for the European Commission and the Italian Development Agency on climate action and sustainability in the Mediterranean region. She holds a BA in Middle Eastern Studies from SciencesPo Paris, France, a double master's degree from SciencesPo and the Free University of Berlin, Germany, and a MA in Diplomacy from the College of Europe in Bruges, Belgium. In 2017, she was featured in Forbes 30 Under 30 Europe list for Law & Policy.

Vesselin Popovski is Professor and Vice Dean of the Jindal Global Law School in India, and Executive Director of its Centre for UN Studies. In 2004–2014, he was the Senior Academic Officer at UN University in Tokyo, Japan. Prior to that, he co-directed the EU project "Legal Protection of Individual Rights in Russia," was a lecturer at Exeter University, and a Bulgarian diplomat serving in Sofia, New York, and London. He has a PhD from King's College London, UK, MSc from London School of Economics, UK, and a BA/MA from the Moscow Institute of International Affairs, Russia. He has published numerous articles in peer-reviewed journals and written and edited over 20 books.

Railla Puno is a Philippine lawyer specializing in international environmental law. Puno has participated in the UNFCCC sessions in various capacities, including as a negotiator for the Philippines and as Policy Coordinator for the ENGO constituency focal point, Climate Action Network. She has a BS from the Ateneo de Manila University, a JD from the University of the Philippines, and she recently obtained her LLM degree in Global Environmental Law from Elisabeth Haub School of Law at Pace University, USA, with highest honors. She is currently working on various research pursuits with a particular focus on developing new policy and legal solutions for the climate crisis.

John G. Robinson joined the Wildlife Conservation Society in 1990, served as Chief Conservation Officer until 2020, overseeing the global programs, and today occupies the Joan L. Tweedy Chair in Conservation Strategy. Inducted into the Royal Order of the Golden Ark by Prince Bernhard of the Netherlands and given the Lifetime Achievement Award by the Zoological Society of London, he has served as President of the Society for Conservation Biology, Chair of the Foundations of Success, and Chairman of the Christensen Fund. Since 2012, he has been a Regional Councilor and Vice President of IUCN.

Nicholas A. Robinson is University Professor for the Environment at Pace University, USA. In 1978, he founded Pace's environmental law programs in The Elizabeth Haub School of Law (www.law.pace.edu). Elected Chair of the World Commission on Environmental Law of the International Union for the Conservation of Nature (IUCN), he led the establishment of the IUCN Academy of Environmental Law (www.iucnael.org). He has written widely on applications of environmental law for sustainability and resilience from both international and comparative perspectives. He is currently Executive Governor of the International Council of Environmental Law.

Juan Carlos Sainz-Borgo is Dean and Chair Professor of International Law at the University for Peace, Costa Rica, created by the UN General Assembly. He is a Tenure Researcher at the Institute of Public Law, Universidad Central de Venezuela; a Fulbright Visiting Scholar at Washington College of Law, American University, Washington DC; and an Adjunct Professor at the Universidad Alfonso X Madrid, Spain, Oregon State University, Universidad Javeriana, and Universidad del Rosario in Colombia, USA. He received his PhD in Law from Universidad Central de Venezuela and his MA from the University of Oxford, UK. He is the author of 10 books and more than 40 articles in international law and politics.

Aniket Shah has spent his career at the intersection of business, academia, and international institutions. He is currently Senior Fellow at the Columbia Center on Sustainable Investment (CCSI), where he works on a wide range of topics including Environmental, Social, and Corporate Governance (ESG) investing and global development finance. He previously worked at a wide range of institutions, including the UN Sustainable

Development Solutions Network and Oppenheimer Funds. Aniket is a graduate of Yale College, USA, and the University of Oxford, UK.

Anna Shostya received her PhD in Economics from New School University and MA in Economics from City University of New York, USA. She is Associate Professor and Associate Chair of the Economics Department at Pace University, NYC, USA. For ten years, she was a Visiting Lecturer at the University of Shanghai for Science and Technology in China. Her major fields of study are transition economies, Chinese economic studies, environmental economics, and economic development. She has numerous publications in these fields, and she is a member of the Oxford RoundTable for her research contributions to the area of higher education.

Krassen Stanchev teaches Public Choice, Macroeconomic Analysis, and Public Sector Economics at Sofia University, Bulgaria. He is also a Board Chairman, founder, and former (1993–2006) Executive Director of the Institute for Market Economics in Sofia and a former member and committee chairman of the Constitutional Assembly of Bulgaria (1990–1991), one of the most quoted Bulgarian observers. He was a principle drafter and leader of reforms from central planning to market economy in Bulgaria, "new" Europe, the Balkans, and former USSR.

Minoru Takada is Head of the Energy Team at the Division for Sustainable Development Goals, UN Department of Economic and Social Affairs. Prior to this position, he served in a number of senior positions with the United Nations, including at the Executive Office of the Secretary-General and the United Nations Development Program. He holds a PhD in Engineering from the University of Mie, Japan, and a Master's of Engineering from the University of Hokkaido, Japan.

Tessel van der Putte is a Dutch artist, researcher, and writer who focuses on Indigenous Peoples (land) rights, women's rights, as well as the right to development of Small Island Nations in the context of climate change. She holds an MA in International Law and Human Rights from the United Nations-Mandated University for Peace, USA, and a cum laude BA in Global Challenges of World Politics, from the International Honors University College of Leiden, the Netherlands. Tessel currently works for the International Committee of the Red Cross in Geneva.

Marjo Vierros is Director of Coastal Policy and Humanities Research, which undertakes interdisciplinary research on ocean issues. She is also Research Associate at the University of British Columbia Nereus Program, Canada, and Senior Fellow with the Global Ocean Forum. Previously, she coordinated the Global Marine Governance Project at the United Nations University, Tokyo, and the work program on marine and coastal biodiversity at the Secretariat of the Convention on Biological Diversity. With a background in marine science and policy, her research interests span ocean governance, traditional ecological knowledge, sustainable development, and environmental humanities.

Pianpian Wang is a Chinese Lawyer with multi-national education and experience focused on environmental law and international climate change policy. By working in the private and academic sectors, she has a wealth of knowledge in the areas of carbon markets, corporate environmental disclosure, and sustainability issues.She is a member of IUCN World Commission on Environmental Law, Legal Advisor of Carbon Credit Capital LLC, and Research Fellow to Pace Energy and Climate Center.

Foreword

A world beset by a long series of cascading crises and heart-rending events—and that is surely our world today—desperately needs roadmaps to guide us to a better place. We are blessed therefore to have the Sustainable Development Goals (SDGs). This international plan of action, agreed to by 193 countries in 2015, offers all of us a unique opportunity we must not fail to seize.

Stated most broadly, the SDGs provide pathways to end extreme poverty and hunger, reduce inequality across a broad front, and sustain natural resources of land, air, and water. The SDGs grew out of the most inclusive and comprehensive negotiations in United Nations (UN) history. The agreed target of 2030 for their achievement means that time is short. As the UN Foundation notes, "Achieving the goals by 2030 will require heroic and imaginative effort, determination to learn about what works, and agility to adapt to new information and changing trends."[1] The widespread persistence of social deprivations, the loss of two-thirds of the world's wildlife populations, the ongoing climate emergency, the gravity of the COVID-19 pandemic with the threat of more—these all underscore the need to galvanize efforts.

The SDGs comprise 17 areas of critical international concern, 169 sub-goals aimed at catalyzing action nationally and internationally, and indicators to measure progress. They will not be met with a mere escalation of business as usual, they "demand nothing short of a transformation of the financial, economic and political systems that govern our societies,"[2] as the UN Secretary-General Antonio Guterres has observed.

In light of the seriousness of these matters, the international community is fortunate that three of our most accomplished experts in international affairs combined forces to present us with this extraordinary and timely book. Narinder Kakar, Distinguished Senior Fellow with the Global Center for Environmental Legal Studies of the Elisabeth Haub School of Law at Pace University and Professor Emeritus at the University for Peace, has over 50 years of experience in the sustainable human development field, having worked for UNDP in Yemen, Guyana, Turkey, China, and the Maldives, and having represented organizations like the University for Peace and IUCN. He participated in a number of international forums, inter

---

1 *Sustainable Development Goals*, UNITED NATIONS FOUNDATION, https://unfoundation.org/what-we-do/issues/sustainable-development-goals/ (last visited Dec. 10, 2020).
2 U.N. Secretary General, *Foreword*, in THE SUSTAINABLE DEVELOPMENT GOALS REPORT 2020, DEP. OF ECON. & SOC. AFFAIRS (2020), https://unstats.un.org/sdgs/report/2020/The-Sustainable-Development-Goals-Report-2020.pdf.

alia, the UN Conference on Sustainable Development (Rio+20) and in the deliberations of the Open Working Group on SDGs.

Nicholas Robinson, a participant in both the 1972 UN Conference in Stockholm and 1992 Rio Earth Summit, contributed extensively to legal systems for environmental sustainability, both internationally among governments and through scholarly pathways such as the IUCN Academy of Environmental Law. He edited the *traveaux preparatoirs* for Agenda 21 and the proceedings of the Earth Summit. He is currently Executive Governor of the International Council of Environmental Law and Kerlin Professor of Environmental Law Emeritus at the Elisabeth Haub School of Law at Pace University.

Vesselin Popovski worked at the University of Exeter in the UK and at the UN University in Tokyo, and he is now in India as Professor and Vice Dean of the Jindal Global Law School and Executive Director of its Centre for the Study of the UN. He published numerous peer-reviewed journal articles and over 20 books, including *The Implementation of the Paris Agreement on Climate Change* (2018) and *Ethical Values and Integrity of the Climate Change Regime* (2015).

The three editors assembled an outstanding cast of experts to take stock of how far the world has come to achieve the global targets. The book shares the concern that governments and societies today are definitely behind where they should be to fulfill the promise of Agenda 2030. It provides a fresh look at ongoing implementation through the review and examination of various best practices. The book highlights impactful and creative actions that go beyond the usual development efforts and offers expert recommendations, forming an indispensable tool for policy makers, academia, IGOs, and NGOs, as well as the public, as we move toward 2030.

Many books have been written on the SDGs—on their origins, evolution, adoption, and assessment. This book is among the first to be courageous enough to tackle the most crucial task—the implementation. Our past experience tells us that states can negotiate and adopt agreements but can also lose momentum in implementing those agreements. Implementation requires adopting appropriate policies, developing a science-policy interface, allocating necessary financial resources, and none of these are easy.

This book speaks to the need to defy isolationism, populism, ignorance, and skepticism, and to re-build an alliance of multilateralism to achieve the 2030 Agenda. It is significant in combining overview papers with specific case studies and in bringing perspectives from various parts of both the South and the North. The presentation of the SDGs is carried out under five thematic "Ps" (People, Planet, Prosperity, Peace, and Partnership) as advocated by former Secretary-General Ban Ki-moon. This enables the readers to appreciate the interconnectedness of the SDGs.

Chapters are written during the COVID-19 pandemic and accordingly reflect in depth on the impacts of this formidable challenge to implementation of the Goals. An initial assessment is made of the adverse effect of COVID-19 on the ability and capacity to implement each SDG and what future actions need to be taken to mitigate those effects.

A strength of this publication is the effort at analyzing implementation of most targets, rather than presenting a general overview of the implementation of each goal. Relevant case studies from both developing and developed countries support the analyses presented. The assessment of implementation of all SDGs is followed by helpful concluding remarks.

My hope is that this book will help to spur action, will serve as a knowledge hub for proliferation of ideas that have worked around the globe, and readers will be able to draw lessons to positively address target goals. These lessons can be further distilled into international, national, and regional pathways to guide sustainable development. In the midst of the biggest pandemic crisis hitting the world in our lifetime, one danger is to over-focus on COVID-19 and deviate from fulfilling longer-term agendas, such as SDGs and climate change mitigation and adaptation. This book presents a strong argument that, in reality, an essential way to deal with this and future health crises is to speed up the implementation of Agenda 2030.

In my view, this book fills a big need for a mid-course assessment that is comprehensive and authoritative, and that explores how progress toward the Sustainable Development Goals can be greatly accelerated. I commend all those involved in this most important effort.

James Gustave Speth
Founder and President of the World Resource Institute (1982–1993)
Administrator of UNDP (1993–1999)
Former Dean of the Yale School of the Environment (1999–2009)

Preface

*Narinder Kakar, Vesselin Popovski,
and Nicholas A. Robinson*

Humanity has been on a centuries-long quest for a world in which prosperity is shared, progress leaves no one behind, and wars and armed conflicts are unimaginable. Yet, it was not until the last third of the 20th century that this ambition started to be given shape through consultations in intergovernmental forums, discussing economic growth, human development, and environmental protection together. The UN Conference on the Human Environment in Stockholm in 1972 was the first to address virtually all aspects of natural resources use, and to emphasize the threat to the environment posed by economic growth with resulting industrial pollution. The developing countries argued that poverty is a greater threat to both human welfare and the environment, and that economic growth in their case was not the problem, but the solution. The need for poverty alleviation for protecting the environment was thus broadly recognized. However, discussions at the Stockholm Conference still polarized the objectives of economic growth and environmental protection, which dominated the debate between rich and poor countries, and between interest groups within countries.

During the 1980s, a new political and developmental paradigm attempted to reconcile the conflicting objectives of economic growth and environmental conservation. During the 1980s, a new political and developmental paradigm attempted to reconcile the conflicting objectives of economic growth and environmental conservation. The World Conservation Strategy prepared by the International Union for Conservation of Nature, with the financial support of the UNEP and WWF, and in collaboration with the Food and Agriculture Organization of the United Nations (FAO) and the United Nations Educational, Scientific and Cultural Organization (UNESCO), was the first document to link the conservation of nature with the process of resource development for human needs, and to enunciate the concept of "sustainable development." Its Introduction stated:

> We must enable the earth to renew itself. We must aim to improve the material, intellectual, and spiritual circumstances of peoples. And we must nurture the values which enhance human possibilities. Our ancients believed in the unity of all things, even of life and non-life. We must rediscover this sense of identity and responsibility for fellow humans, other species, and future generations.

This vision was further elaborated in the Earth Charter, originated by Maurice Strong and Mikhail Gorbachev in 1987. Also in 1987, the World Commission on Environment and Development published its report "Our Common Future" (Brundtland Report) defining the concept of sustainable development as an integrated approach in policy-making, in which long-term environmental protection and economic growth are not incompatible but complementary and mutually dependent. The economic growth will produce the resources needed to solve the environmental problems, but this would not happen, if human health and natural resources are damaged by environmental degradation.

The Brundtland Report set in motion a process which culminated in 1992 with the UN Conference on Environment and Development (Earth Summit) held in Rio de Janeiro. Its Agenda 21 reaffirmed the Brundtland Report's central message, that socio-economic development and environmental protection are intimately linked and effective policy-making must tackle them together. The Earth Summit also adopted the far-reaching Rio Declaration on Environment and Development, which charted the course for global capacity building and cooperation and offered integrated strategies to promote human development through economic growth, based on sustainable management of natural resources. The Millennium Development Goals formulated at the Millennium UN Summit in 2000 included a goal on environmental sustainability, among other goals such as reducing extreme poverty and hunger, universal primary education, gender equality, reducing child mortality, improving maternal health, and combating preventable diseases.

The 2002 Johannesburg World Summit on Sustainable Development was the first to put sustainable development in its title (all previous conferences referred to environment and development separately). Based on inclusive ethical vision, this Summit acknowledged universally that environmental protection and social and economic advancement are the pillars of sustainable development. Its Declaration is the first in international law to recognize "the greater community of life," a value expressed in all religions and throughout the history of environmental ethics. These were giant steps forward to meet the needs of the world's most deprived. Many countries have made strides to raise people out of poverty; however, not enough has been done to end hunger, malnutrition, diseases, illiteracy, joblessness, inequality, and armed conflicts. More actions were needed to preserve the Earth's scarce resources and fragile ecosystems, reduce the escalating climate change, and ensure that the future generations could breathe clean air, have access to fresh water, and consume safe food.

Twenty years after the Earth Summit, the UN convened the Conference on Sustainable Development in Rio de Janeiro in 2012 and paved the way to develop the Sustainable Development Goals. The Open Working Group on Sustainable Development Goals worked for 17 months to formulate 17 goals with 169 targets. It was an arduous process, guided ably by the then-ambassadors of Kenya and Hungary. The 17 SDGs were adopted in 2015 and incorporated into the 2030 Agenda for Sustainable Development. Universal, inclusive, and indivisible, the Agenda 2030 calls for action by all countries—developing and developed—to improve the lives of people everywhere. Progress in one goal should be linked to progress in all other goals. Howsoever difficult and protracted the process for the formulation of the SDGs may have been, the task of implementing the SDGs will be much tougher, requiring strong commitment from all stakeholders—governments, civil society, international partners, the private sector, and others. The 2030 Agenda is a plan for action to empower *people*, protect a fragile *planet*, ensure all-inclusive *prosperity*, foster *peace*, and build solid *partnerships*. These 5 Ps represent a blueprint for inclusive and sustainable development and progress that should leave no one behind.

This book is published after a third of the way toward the target of 2030. How are we doing on building a sustainable future? What actions have been moving toward the SDGs fulfillment, and what areas are lagging behind and need help? What are the current challenges and how can we address them? What kind of threats does the COVID-19 pandemic pose and in what way will it hinder the progress toward the targets? The authors of this book present and analyze the progress, or the lack of it, toward achieving the SDGs. They share concerns that many of the targets may not be met by the deadline of 2030 and call for urgent and bold actions that all stakeholders—consumers and producers in both public and private sectors, as well as governments, civil society, and international organizations—need to take to meet the goals set by the global community. Fulfilling the SDGs highlights that inequalities of all kind are at the core of the issues we are facing: From persistent differences in incomes between and within countries, to social issues, conditions of minorities, migrants, women and girls, the poorest and most vulnerable. This is true in both developed and developing nations; therefore, it is essential to narrow considerably the gaps in equality.

At a time of challenge to multilateralism, competing priorities and growing nationalisms, this book assesses the state of global partnerships for sustainable development, including, inter alia, with the private sector, and for the need to reinforce financial support for the implementation of the SDGs. The chapters of this book demonstrate the progress in the relationship between peace and development, and between development, human rights, and rule of law. Neither can be achieved without the other. This book contains contributions from authors well recognized in their fields of competence, who have given rich in-depth perspectives on various goals, analyzing the level of progress made so far in implementing the targets, the challenges encountered, and what actions are needed to fulfil Agenda 2030. We were fortunate to secure excellent contributions from some well-known women leaders in sustainable development and multilateralism, as well as contributions from a number of young female scholars; as a result about half of the authors are female experts or professionals.

There is a famous saying: We do not inherit the Earth from our ancestors, we borrow it from our children. Ultimately, the importance of this book will be revealed in the coming years. How will the SDGs be fulfilled? Can stakeholders embrace the recommendations with firm commitment for constructive action, and will they progress in advancing the SDGs that lack action? These questions will reappear in the context of each SDG discussed in this book and the readers will find concrete answers, based on solid academic research.

I
SDGs in Context

1 Special Introduction

Amina J. Mohammed

Deputy Secretary-General of the United Nations

The 2030 Agenda and its 17 Sustainable Development Goals (SDGs) have been called a Declaration of Interdependence. In adopting the ambitious initiative in 2015, all nations affirmed not only their linkages with each other but also between the goals themselves. Failure to achieve progress on one goal would undermine progress in all the others.

We are now one-third of the way toward the target date of 2030 and the world is off track. The COVID-19 pandemic has made it far worse, exacerbating structural factors and exposing deep fragilities -including entrenched inequalities and vulnerabilities to shocks and the climate crisis.

The World Food Programme estimates that 265 million people face acute food shortages. The World Bank projects that up to 112 million more people could be pushed into extreme poverty. The United Nations Children's Fund (UNICEF) found that an additional 150 million children will be deprived of education, health, housing, or nutrition.

Clearly, we must intensify our efforts to achieve the SDGs. Now.

I commend the Global Center for Environmental Legal Studies of the Elisabeth Haub School of Law at Pace University for its focus on implementation of the Sustainable Development Goals.

This publication takes stock of efforts to achieve the global targets. It provides a glimpse of the difficult picture emerging from most parts of the world and highlights the daunting challenges ahead.

The publication analyzes where the world stands on the targets of each SDG with relevant case studies from both developing and developed countries. It helps illustrate the possibilities of building an alliance of multilateralism to implement the 2030 Agenda. As trillions of dollars are directed toward recovery from Covid-19, the world now has a window of opportunity to truly build a more sustainable and equitable future.

The papers contained here provide a unique combination of overview papers with specific case studies, bringing perspectives and expertise from various parts of both the South and the North, enriching both the community of knowledge and the voices of the practitioners.

The SDGs are presented under five thematic "Ps" (People, Planet, Prosperity, Peace, and Partnership) to allow readers to better understand how the goals and targets are expected to stimulate action in these areas and to highlights the interlinkages between the SDGs.

The book draws from many disciplines, most notably economics, politics, anthropology, geography, development studies, environmental studies, governance and public administration, international relations, and international law. It also provides in-depth insights on the likely impacts of the pandemic on sustainable development.

As we look ahead, we must work to avoid short-term and short-sighted decision-making. This challenge is an opportunity to recover better. That requires concerted action to strengthen, despite all the constraints, the multilateral system.

The contribution by Madame Maria Fernanda Espinosa, President of the 73rd Session of the UN General Assembly, offers excellent guidance in that respect. The chapter on COVID-19 by David Nabarro and Joe E. Colombano underscores how the SDGs must be at the core of the response to the COVID-19 crisis. Indeed, all the contributing authors have critically assessed the impact of COVID-19 on relevant SDGs and pointed the way forward.

Since the SDG agenda is universal, the publication reviews the situation in both developing and developed countries. Interlinkages between SDGs have been identified and interdependence of different dimensions of sustainable development are highlighted—all critical ingredients to policymaking since, of course, interventions in one sector may have unintended or unforeseen effects on another.

The assessment of the implementation of all the SDGs is followed by action points to guide future steps to ensure attainment of targets or objectives.

Both the format and the content of the book are aimed at informing a wider section of society. It is a useful guide not only to policy makers, but also to non-governmental actors, international organizations, financing institutions, the private sector, entrepreneurs, and civil society organizations. It also serves as an important reference for students of development and multilateral affairs.

Once again, my congratulations to the Global Center for Environmental Legal Studies of the Elisabeth Haub School of Law at Pace University for producing this vital and timely resource.

2 Multilateralism Under Challenge

María Fernanda Espinosa Garcés
President of the 73rd Session of the UN General Assembly

As I write this chapter, the Director-General of the World Health Organization (WHO), Dr. Tedros Adhanom, states in tears that worse than the SARS-CoV-2 (COVID-19) pandemic is the lack of leadership and cooperation. His broken voice warned us:

> My friends, make no mistake. The greatest threat we face now is not the virus itself. Rather, it is the lack of leadership and solidarity at the global and national levels ... we cannot defeat this pandemic as a divided world. ... The COVID-19 pandemic is a test of global solidarity and global leadership.[1]

Dr. Tedros cannot be more right. The COVID-19 pandemic has not only been a litmus test for our resilience and response capacity but has also put under scrutiny our international organizations. It highlights how the current multilateral architecture in place has and is responding to the crisis and challenges the present design of global governance arrangements.

In 1971, a path-breaking book on ecological thinking, *The Closing Circle*, by Barry Commoner outlined four laws of ecology to understand life on Earth. First, everything is connected to everything else; second, everything must go somewhere; third, nature knows best; and fourth, there is no such thing as a free lunch.[2] Almost 50 years after the publication of Commoner's book, humanity has been tested and the message is clear, we need to urgently rethink the way we approach life on Earth.

The pandemic has shown us how interconnected we are as human beings. Despite all the science and technological developments during the last decades, we are facing an unprecedented humanitarian crisis. The worst economic and social crisis since the Great Depression and a scenario not far from the end of the Second World War, due to a novel microscopic virus. The COVID-19 pandemic has shown us how fragile we are as a species and has magnified our weaknesses to face our common future.

Since the beginning of this century, common challenges continue to grow in number, complexity, urgency, and impact. Historical rates of poverty, inequality, discrimination, conflict, violence, and instability are common denominators of human society. Much more

---

1 Tedros Adhanom Ghebreysus, Director General, World Health Organization (WHO), Opening Remarks at the Member States Briefing on the COVID-19 Pandemic Evaluation (July 9, 2020).
2 BARRY COMMONER, THE CLOSING CIRCLE (1971).

serious, we are still fighting against the imminent threat of a climate crisis which, if unaddressed, will fuel further human insecurity.

As these challenges are enormous and no one country can tackle global issues alone, the COVID-19 human crisis has been a useful lens to better appreciate the virtues but also the limits of multilateralism.

Multilateralism is hard to pronounce but, more than ever, it plays a critical role in building back better our common future. Global dialog, international cooperation, multilateral and solidarity responses are irreplaceable instruments to address multifaceted and complex global challenges through collective action.[3]

This article is by no means a scholarly work, but it rather aims to share first-hand experience and analysis of current global governance challenges and how they affect performance in achieving the Sustainable Development Goals (SDGs). As a practitioner more than an academic, I also intend to identify some trends and bottlenecks in connecting the effectiveness of multilateral systems and their impact on policy-making and transformative action on sustainable development. I will close with some key questions and potential pathways for the retooling of our multilateral arrangements.

Are the Sustainable Development Goals Still Relevant?

Despite the fear and uncertainty, we are not lost. We do have a roadmap, a survival kit, and a global pact that we have agreed upon in 2015: the 2030 Agenda for Sustainable Development, the soul of which, and *raison d'être*, is the fight against poverty and inequalities while ensuring that we protect our planet and its ecosystems.

Even before the world was hit by the pandemic, we already knew that we were in trouble with achieving the SDGs. We realized that we were far behind our commitments to climate mitigation and adaptation, to combating inequalities, to gender equality and women's rights, and to achieving the zero-hunger objective, to cite a few. Things were not going well! For example, 2019 was the second warmest year on record and the end of the warmest decade (2010– 2019).[4]

The pandemic, of course, has not only brought to the surface inequalities, injustice, and the human rights and nature's rights crisis, but has also made more visible poor governance and leadership. It has put the 2030 Agenda further from our reach.

COVID-19 has kept 1.6 billion students out of schools[5] and the digital divide will widen education equality gaps. An estimated 71 million people were pushed into extreme poverty, causing the first increase in global poverty in more than 20 years.[6] Over 130 million more

---

[3] United Nations General Assembly (UNGA), *Resolution adopted by the General Assembly on 12 December 2018 on the International Day of Multilateralism and Diplomacy for Peace*, A/RES/73/127, at 1 (Dec. 19, 2018).

[4] *Copernicus: 2019 Was the Second Warmest Year and the Last Five Years Were the Warmest on Record*, COPERNICUS CLIMATE CHANGE SERVICE (Jan. 8, 2020), https://climate.copernicus.eu/copernicus-2019-was-second-warmest-year-and-last-five-years-were-warmest-record.

[5] Jason Milks & John McIlwaine, *Keeping the World's Children Learning through COVID-19*, UNITED NATIONS INTERNATIONAL CHILDREN'S FUND (UNICEF), www.unicef.org/coronavirus/keeping-worlds-children-learning-through-covid-19 (April 20, 2020).

[6] Daniel Gerszon Mahler et al., *Updated Estimates of the Impact of COVID-19 on Global Poverty*, WORLD BANK DATA BLOG, https://blogs.worldbank.org/opendata/updated-estimates-impact-covid-19-global-poverty (June 8, 2020).

people were estimated to have faced chronic hunger by the end of 2020.[7] The pandemic is pushing more than 300 million workers into unemployment, underemployment, and working poverty, especially young workers. More than one in six youths have stopped working since the onset of the pandemic.[8]

This crisis has touched every country, every economy, and every health system. However, the poorest and the most vulnerable people are disproportionally affected by the pandemic, including women, children, older persons, persons with disabilities, migrants, refugees, and the informal sectors.

Vulnerable countries such as Least Developed Countries (LDCs), Small Island Developing States (SIDs), Landlocked Developing Countries (LLDCs), and Middle-Income Countries (MICs), as well as countries in humanitarian or fragile situations, are suffering the most due to the fragility of their health systems, limited coverage of their social protection systems, limited financial resources, high debt servicing costs, vulnerability to external shocks, and excessive dependence on international trade.

Before the pandemic, it was estimated that the global gender gap could be closed in 100 years.[9] The promise of a world in which every woman and girl enjoys full gender equality and empowerment has melted. Globally, while women make up about 70% of the healthcare workforce, they are largely concentrated in lower-paid positions in comparison to their male counterparts.[10] Women in healthcare are also three times more exposed to the risks of COVID-19 but are losing 20% of their health and social service benefits because of the pandemic.[11]

Unpaid home care work has substantially increased, and reports confirm that domestic violence against women and girls is also rising during the global lockdown. Some countries have reported more than a five-fold increase in calls to helplines and women's support services are struggling.[12]

The 2020 Sustainable Development Report[13] is an eye-opener. Its findings are not very promising. While the 2030 Agenda helped States better prepare for the pandemic,

---

7 News Release, World Health Organization (WHO), As More Go Hungry and Malnutrition Persists, Achieving Zero Hunger by 2030 In Doubt, UN Report Warns (July 13, 2020), www.who.int/news/item/13-07-2020-as-more-go-hungry-and-malnutrition-persists-achieving-zero-hunger-by-2030-in-doubt-un-report-warns. *See also* Food and Agriculture Organization of the UN (FAO) et al., *The State of Food Security and Nutrition in the World 2020 Safeguarding against Economic Slowdowns and Downturns*, www.fao.org/3/ca5162en/ca5162en.pdf (July 2020).
8 INTERNATIONAL LABOR ORGANIZATION (ILO), ILO MONITOR: COVID-19 AND THE WORK OF WORK, FIFTH EDITION (June 30, 2020).
9 WORLD ECONOMIC FORUM, GLOBAL GENDER GAP REPORT 2020, (2019) [hereinafter "Gender Gap Report 2020"].
10 Mathieu Boniol et al., *Gender Equity in the Health Workforce: Analysis of 104 Countries*, WHO, https://apps.who.int/iris/bitstream/handle/10665/311314/WHO-HIS-HWF-Gender-WP1-2019.1-eng.pdf?ua=1 (March 2019).
11 UN SECRETARY-GENERAL'S INDEPENDENT ACCOUNTABILITY PANEL (IAP) EVERY WOMEN, EVERY CHILD, EVERY ADOLESCENT, CAUGHT IN THE COVID-19 STORM: WOMEN'S, CHILDREN'S, AND ADOLESCENTS' HEALTH IN THE CONTEXT OF UHC AND THE SDGS, at 8 (2020) [hereinafter "IAP Report"].
12 *Facts and Figures: Ending Violence against Women*, UN WOMEN, www.unwomen.org/en/news/in-focus/in-focus-gender-equality-in-covid-19-response/violence-against-women-during-covid-19 (last visited Nov. 25, 2020).
13 JEFFREY SACHS ET AL., THE SUSTAINABLE DEVELOPMENT GOALS AND COVID-19, SUSTAINABLE DEVELOPMENT REPORT 2020 (2020) [hereinafter "SDG Report 2020"].

growing inequalities are undermining worldwide progress toward the achievement of most SDGs.

Poorer countries and emerging economies will face devastating levels of poverty and challenges in refinancing their debts. COVID-19 will significantly delay progress toward the fulfillment of the SDGs, due to increasing levels of poverty, food insecurity, hunger, higher rates of mortality, and lack of decent work and unemployment, to name a few.[14] It is estimated that gender equality and women's rights will be some of the most negatively impacted elements because of greater exposure to labor market disruptions and the increase of domestic violence stemming from lockdowns.[15]

However, not everything is gray. The report highlights that "the only bright spot in this foreboding picture" is a short-term reduction in natural resources use due to reduced economic activity and consumption.[16] It also calls on the global community to restore economic activity without simply reestablishing old patterns of environmental degradation, to strengthen the resilience of health systems and prevention programs and to increase solidarity and international cooperation to address and prevent health, economic, and humanitarian crises in the wake of COVID-19.[17]

In consequence, the question is how to make sure that the world's shared goals for sustainable development can be achieved despite the devastating and multidimensional effects of the COVID-19 pandemic. We have less than a decade to deliver, to "walk the talk," on the commitments we have made.

We have undergone so many lessons these past few months. We have learned from our fragility and from our lack of preparedness. We have been made aware that fit and efficient public health and social protection systems are key to endure any crisis. It is clear that States with strong affirmative action and public policies, rather than markets and economic policies, have to take the driving seat in order to fight poverty and inequality.

We know that despite some "go it alone" responses, the only way is concerted global action, solidarity, and cooperation. These values are the core of multilateralism and at the epicenter of global multilateralism is the United Nations (UN) which we, humanity, established in 1945.

UN History and the Women's Rights Agenda

Seventy-five years have passed since the signing of the UN Charter in San Francisco. It was the birth of a new era and a pioneer political global pact to prevent and protect us from the scourge of war, defend our human rights, and promote development. But more importantly, it aimed to, and continues to, provide collective responses to global challenges based on cooperation and solidarity.

A Parliament of Humanity was established. It was the beginning of international architecture, as we know it today. The United Nations General Assembly (UNGA) occupies a central position as the chief deliberative, policy-making, and representative organ of the UN. The only international body where every country regardless of its respective size, gross domestic product (GDP), and population, has a seat, a voice, and a vote.

---

14 *Id.*
15 United Nations, Policy Brief: The Impact of COVID-19 on Women (April 9, 2020).
16 SDG Report 2020, *supra* note 13 at vi.
17 *Id.* at vi to vii.

At the United Nations Conference in San Francisco in 1945, there were only 8 women delegates out of 46 Member States, i.e., 8 out of 850 delegates.[18] Things have changed so much since then. Today, with 193 Member States, it is unimaginable that women do not hold frontline and decision-making posts in greater numbers. The fight for greater women's representation as Ambassadors or high-level officials at the UN has to continue. Let's recall that in 75 years of UN history, we have only had 4 women presidents of the General Assembly.[19] We need more.

Since the founding of the UN, the feminist movement has made sure to make its voice heard. Gender equality has been among the most fundamental guarantees of human rights. In 1946, the Commission on the Status of Women (CSW) was established as the principal global intergovernmental body exclusively dedicated to the promotion of gender equality and the empowerment of women. Later, in 1948, the Universal Declaration of Human Rights, under the leadership of Eleanor Roosevelt, was adopted and proclaimed the equal entitlements to the rights contained in it, "without distinction for any kind."[20]

Throughout the last quarter of the 20th century, the UN World Conferences on Women marked a point of no return on recognizing gender equality and women's rights. Successive international conferences have been landmarks for the advancement of the Women's Rights Agenda; the first Women's Conference in Mexico, in 1975; Nairobi, in 1985; Beijing, in 1995. More recently, the UNGA took a historic step when it created UN Women, the United Nations Entity for Gender Equality and the Empowerment of Women, in 2010. It has been a story of huge strides, struggles, and pushbacks.

UN history has also been women's rights history. Women's rights and dignity have been at the forefront of the global political agenda. A myriad of conventions and policies, including the sustainable development goals, the disarmament agenda, women, peace, and security, the human rights architecture, and, most recently, the COVID-19 pandemic effective responses, have included specific women's rights and equality provisions. The Women's Rights Agenda has made incremental progress along with some regressions, but we need to push forward and continue our struggle for equality. We need immediate action and a societal transformation.

The numbers are still staggering. Women 25–34 years old continue to be 25% more likely than men to live in extreme poverty,[21] especially indigenous women and women with disabilities. Before the pandemic, the global gender pay gap remained with women earning approximately 20% less than that of men[22] and 740 million women working in the informal economy.[23] While 35 million women need humanitarian aid and protection and at least 1 in 5 refugee women experience sexual violence, only 28% of assessments on humanitarian needs articulate the differentiated impact of crisis on women and girls.[24]

---

18 REBECCA ADAMI, WOMEN AND THE UNIVERSAL DECLARATION OF HUMAN RIGHTS 17 (1st ed, 2019).
19 *Woman Elected as Head of UN General Assembly for Fourth Time in 73 Years,* UN NEWS, https://news.un.org/en/gallery/534371 (last visited Nov. 25, 2020).
20 *See* Johannes Morsink, *Women's Rights in the Universal Declaration.* 13(2) HUM. RTS. Q. 229 (1991).
21 UN WOMEN AND THE UN DEPARTMENT OF ECONOMIC AND SOCIAL AFFAIRS, PROGRESS ON THE SUSTAINABLE DEVELOPMENT GOALS, THE GENDER SNAPSHOT 2019, at 2 (2019).
22 ILO, GLOBAL WAGE REPORT 2018/19, WHAT LIES BEHIND GENDER PAY GAPS, at 23 (2018).
23 ILO, WOMEN AND MEN IN THE INFORMAL ECONOMY: A STATISTICAL PICTURE, THIRD EDITION, at 20 (April 30, 2018).
24 United Nations Security Council, *Women and peace and security, Report of the Secretary-General,* S/2019/800, at 2 (Oct. 9, 2019) [hereinafter "UNSC Report"].

As mentioned before, the COVID-19 will likely produce serious regressions on gender equality and women's rights. The pandemic has magnified the structural inequalities and violence that disproportionately affect women and girls, which should directly translate into bolder action.

The Beijing+25 process, the Generation Equality Forum, together with the UN75 global dialog are golden opportunities to re-energize and retool the Women's Rights Agenda but also to strengthen our multilateral systems. We need more women in power.

Contested Multilateralism in a World of Paradox

We may believe that the United Nations is capable of solving every problem faced by humanity. However, reality, geopolitical dynamics, and power configurations pose serious hurdles. We live in an interconnected world of contradictions and paradoxes. We have the knowledge, the technologies, the resources, and the wealth to transform the world into a more just and sustainable place for everyone. What is holding us back? Why can we not remember our humanity? Our collective responsibility as a species? When I speak about paradoxes, let me briefly exemplify:

Firstly, as the latest FAO Report on *the State of Food Security and Nutrition in the World* highlighted, the decades-long decline in world hunger has unfortunately ended.[25] We produce enough food and yet, 2 billion people in the world do not have regular access to safe, nutritious, and sufficient food. Six hundred and ninety million people suffer from chronic hunger,[26] 381 million people are undernourished,[27] and 750 million people are exposed to several levels of food insecurity.[28] Meanwhile, adult obesity is expected to increase by 40% by 2025.[29] Forty and a-half million deaths have been attributable to non-communicable diseases (NCDs).[30] The shorthand is that while we produce enough food, one-third of that food— – approximately 1.3 billion tones—gets lost or wasted and hunger continues to grow.

Secondly, we are witnesses of revolutionary discoveries, advances in science and technology, and human knowledge at the highest levels, and yet, people still die from preventable diseases. During the COVID-19 pandemic, more than 20 countries reported vaccine shortages for other illnesses including hepatitis, measles, and rubella and 13.5 million people will miss vaccinations against life-threatening diseases.[31]

Thirdly, we have the technology and resources available to help fight climate change and shift to low-carbon economic models, such as circular economies, that would both boost economic productivity and increase GDP and simultaneously safeguard life on Earth and stay within the planetary boundaries. Yet, we are not able to comply with our commitments on mitigation and adaptation. From renewable energy alternatives to ecosystem restoration and sustainable agriculture, there is no shortage of solutions informed by science to fight the

---

25 FAO et al., THE STATE OF FOOD SECURITY AND NUTRITION IN THE WORLD 2020, TRANSFORMING FOOD SYSTEMS FOR AFFORDABLE HEALTHY DIETS (2020).
26 *Id.* at viii.
27 *Id.* at xviii.
28 *Id.* at xvi.
29 *Id.* at 32.
30 *Id.* at 94.
31 *COVID-19: Massive Impact on Lower-Income Countries Threatens More Disease Outbreaks*, GAVI THE VACCINE ALLIANCE, www.gavi.org/news/media-room/covid-19-massive-impact-lower-income-countries-threatens-more-disease-outbreaks (April 3, 2020).

climate crisis. The question that stands is, why have we not been able to use this knowledge and technology to act against the climate crisis?

Fourthly, women are agents of change and yet victims of discrimination, exclusion, and violence. Gender equality is the strongest predictor of a State's peacefulness.[32] When women are more empowered, the State is less likely to experience civil conflict or go to war. Despite this evidence, women make up only 4.2% of military personnel in the UN peacekeeping missions.[33] In 2018, less than 8% of peace agreements included gender-related provisions, a staggering decrease compared to 39% in 2015.[34]

Women's political participation remains the greatest gender disparity. Today, women do not make up even a quarter of all elected politicians in the world and they are doubly affected by record levels of harassment and/or political violence, which prevent women's effective political participation.[35] In 85 of 153 countries studied, a woman has never been the Head of State or Government.[36] Women also represent only 18.3% of ministers in government cabinets and in some countries, women are still not represented.[37] Globally, 243 million women and girls have experienced physical and/or sexual intimate domestic violence and every two hours a woman dies from gender-related issues.[38]

Fifthly, we have already created thousands of norms, resolutions, conventions, and policies, including the SDGs, to ensure we have the guidelines to build sustainable economies and societies. There is no scarcity of normative scaffolds and regulations, yet we experience a huge implementation deficit. Let's recall the hundreds of environmental agreements in place to limit environmental degradation - policies ranging from combating CO_2 and other greenhouse gas emissions to preserve freshwater and biodiversity. Still, our planet's health continues to deteriorate at an unprecedented pace. Experts say that we are witnessing a profound extinction crisis due to our overconsumption patterns and unsustainable economic development.

Sixthly, as the world has experienced the devastating effects of nuclear weapons new and emerging proliferating weapon technologies are configured as new threats to peace and security.[39] The UN was created precisely to protect humanity from the scourge of war. We know that nuclear weapons can wipe us all out and the nuclear nations spent a record of 73 billion dollars last year, a 10% increase from 2018 to 2019.[40] And yet, we know that nuclear weapons are not as effective as a deterrence strategy nor as a means of strategic stability. On the contrary, we know that they increase human insecurity and instability.

---

32 VALERIE M. HUDSON ET AL., SEX AND WORLD PEACE (2012).
33 UNSC Report, *supra* note 24 at ¶4(a).
34 *Id.* at ¶15.
35 UN WOMEN, VIOLENCE AGAINST WOMEN IN POLITICS. EXPERT GROUP MEETING REPORT & RECOMMENDATIONS (2018).
36 Gender Gap Report 2020, *supra* note 9 at 5.
37 *Id.* at 4.
38 *Shadow Pandemic: Violence against Women during COVID-19*, UN WOMEN, www.unwomen.org/en/n ews/in-focus/in-focus-gender-equality-in-covid-19-response/violence-against-women-during-covid-19 (last visited Nov. 25, 2020).
39 *Securing our Common Future, An Agenda for Disarmament*, UN OFFICE FOR DISARMAMENT AFFAIRS, at 4–5, https://s3.amazonaws.com/unoda-web/wp-content/uploads/2018/06/sg-disarmament-agenda -pubs-page.pdf#view=Fit (2018).
40 ICAN 2017 NOBEL PEACE PRIZE, ENOUGH IS ENOUGH: 2019 GLOBAL NUCLEAR WEAPONS SPENDING, at 10 (May, 2020).

Finally, and perhaps the most unexplainable paradox is inequality. On one hand, we are witnessing a staggering increase of poverty and extreme poverty, while on the other, we see that millionaires are piling up their earnings. The world's richest person since 2017, the Amazon CEO Jeff Bezos, has so far increased his fortune by about 40 billion dollars during the coronavirus pandemic to a net worth of over 186 billion dollars.[41] During a recent dialog on the role of parliaments in responding to the COVID-19 pandemic, Professor Jeffrey Sachs repeated a very bold phrase, "inequalities are killing us,"[42] and this statement cannot hold truer today.

The list is endless. The obvious consequences are public disenchantment and a deficit in trust and legitimacy regarding the capacity and ability of international organizations to respond effectively to these multiple crises, from climate to poverty, from hunger to insecurity. Individuals, citizens, and different stakeholders that feel dissatisfied by the performance of multilateral systems are therefore seeking to either reform, transform, or replace existing institutions.[43]

We can perhaps test some explanations for these paradoxes by addressing five areas of disconnect to which I will then provide some potential areas for transformation.

The Need to Reconnect

Amid this global unrest and public disenchantment and inspired by the path-breaking ecological thinking of Barry Commoner,[44] I propose five disconnects we need to address and reconnect to "build back better" our common future.

1. **The disconnect between the time of nature and its cycles and the time of politics and the decision-making cycles**. The first disconnect requires long-term vision, a holistic approach, structural responses, and sustainability. The immediate harvest of long-term planning and resilience building and of investing in strong and efficient public health and education systems may feel intangible.

   The time of politics is often dependent on short-term gains, sectoral approaches, and narrow, simple-minded cost–benefit analysis. We need the opposite. We need to recouple the times of nature with the time of our planning, policies, and action. We need to think about the next generations and not the next elections. Short-termism can truly harm decision-making processes both at the national and international levels and undermine the possibilities of acting and delivering on the SDGs.

   The SDGs require long-term predictable planning and policy. Therefore, social agency and public engagement are critical in improving accountability and transparency.

---

41 *Today's Winners and Losers, The Real-Time Billionaires List*, FORBES, www.forbes.com/real-time-billionaires/#5c276bb93d78 (last visited Nov. 26, 2020).
42 Jeffrey Sachs, President, Sustainable Development Solutions Network (SDSN), Expert Presentation at Webinar for Parliamentarians: COVID-19 and Gender Equality (July 7, 2020), *in* Inter-Parliamentary Union, SDSN, and Parliamentarians for the Global Goals, *COVID-19 Webinar July 7 Expert Presentations*, YouTube (July 7, 2020), www.youtube.com/watch?v=vXQZbUI-PO4&list=PLprXkx-4Du8LCsgpggDMTVxGH7TqNzqix&index=4.
43 Julia Morse & Robert Keohane, *Contested Multilateralism*, 9 Rev. Int. Organ 385, 389 (March 23, 2014).
44 Commoner, *supra* note 2.

2. **The disconnect between governments and people** (but also, the disconnect between international institutions and local needs). The urge for greater inclusion and participation that takes on a whole of society approach, where the private sector, society, governments, academia, and science all work together under the principle of co-responsibility. We need to listen more to the younger generations but also to the elders.

   During my tenure as President of the UNGA, I chose a theme to organize and spearhead the Assembly's work: "Making the UN relevant to all." The issue of relevance; the question of whether or not the organization was attentive, listening, and responding to people's needs, anxieties, and fears; whether or not the UN had any impact on people's lives, especially the lives of the most vulnerable, the poorest of the poor, persons with disabilities, trafficked girls and other victims of violence, refugees, and Indigenous Peoples. This question is perhaps even more relevant today than it was a year ago. The process leading to the commemoration of the seventy-five years of UN history is a unique opportunity to listen to peoples' voices and to engage in a global conversation on the UN we need.[45]

3. **The disconnect between the delivery capacity of institutions, laws, and policies and the expectations of society and public opinion**. There is a crisis of trust. The predictability and the efficacy of international law is a requisite to ensure strong democratic systems based on participation and engagement from all sectors of society. International law serves as social and political contracts to norm human coexistence in a transparent, just, and fair way. For example, in the specific case of Environmental Multilateral Agreements, the aim is to establish norms to share burdens and opportunities to manage and protect our commons. Common goods such as the atmosphere, oceans, and biodiversity require a strong multilateral system that is capable of governing the sustainable and fair use and the preservation of our commons.

4. **The disconnect between knowledge and action**. We have the science, the technologies, and the legal and policy frameworks and yet, we do not have the capacity or the willingness to act. We need wisdom, political will, and decisive action to do what is right. We can cite numerous examples. Scientists have alerted the world on the climate crisis for decades. We have seen and experienced the loss of human lives, food shortage, destruction of ecosystems, and the extinction of species. We have seen thousands of displaced persons or entire economies collapse in SIDs because of climate-related disasters, and still, we are not doing enough to reduce emissions, to retool our production and consumption patterns, or to transform our energy matrixes toward more sustainable models. It is imperative that decision-makers listen to science and make informed choices.

5. **The disconnect between scales of policy and action**. The disconnection between policy and decisions, between communities of practice and communities of knowledge, between first-hand local experiences and national, regional, and international decision-making may negatively impact the delivery capacity, the effectiveness, and the social ownership of decisions. Therefore, conscious and deliberate mechanisms to ensure that social agency and local practice connect to national and international policy and vice

---

45 The UN Secretary-General António Guterres launched a large and inclusive global conversation on the world's future to mark the 75th anniversary of the UN on the role of global cooperation in building the future we want.

versa are needed. This challenge is not easy to tackle and the connections do not happen naturally. This scale-wide connection has to be consciously built and institutionalized.

A Multilateral System That Delivers

The five areas of disconnect outlined above may be translated into tipping points for transformation:

1. **An inclusive, participatory, and intergenerational approach.** The future starts today. Intergenerational dialog and co-responsibility at national and international levels are critical. To reach the goals and targets of Agenda 2030 would be an impossible task if public opinion and people's needs were not connected to politics and politicians and to parliaments. A multi-stakeholder approach that includes youth and elders, women, and Indigenous Peoples is a prerequisite to overcome the disconnect between scales and actors. Social participation in multilateral decision-making should not be seen as a tokenistic, politically correct afterthought, but rather an indicator of effectiveness and impact. For decisions to be effective and transformative, there is a need for social ownership, public engagement, and a multi-scale architecture.
2. **A holistic and systemic approach.** The SDGs are inextricably interdependent. We have proven time and again that, for example, climate inaction deepens poverty, hunger, and displacement. Poverty also fuels conflict and women's empowerment is an antidote to food security, just to name a few interconnections. Sustainable development is a paradigm that requires not only concerted efforts and actions, but also comprehensive policy frameworks that encompass poverty eradication measures, while simultaneously providing guarantees for social and environmental protection nets. We also have proof that fighting inequalities and building fairer and inclusive societies do collide with climate mitigation and green economic choices.
3. **The need for a new social contract.** We need to recommit to the principles of cooperation and respect, enshrined in the UN founding Charter and the collective endeavor of building societies that are free from conflict and injustice, that are centered in human dignity and respect our planet.

    Today, there is a great impetus for promoting a "Global Green New Deal"[46] that goes beyond macroeconomic refurbishing. Green jobs, new energy matrixes, wise investments in sustainability, and poverty eradication are among the key proposals of this Green New Deal. There is a need for a new social contract for nature and people from an intergenerational perspective. In other words, we need a new social contract between society, the economy, and the planet. Truth be told, there has never been so much creativity, talent, think tanks, mobilized citizens, UN agencies, programs, and regional commissions that are working around the clock to propose new alternatives, ideas, and options.

---

46 *See* Kevin Gallagher and Richard Kozul-Wright, *A New Multilateralism for Shared Prosperity, Geneva Principles for a Global Green New Deal*, United Nations Conference on Trade and Development (UNCTAD) & Global Development Policy Center, www.bu.edu/gdp/files/2019/05/Updated-New-Graphics-New-Multilateralism-May-8-2019.pdf (April 1, 2019).

The menu is copious: From debt relief strategies and fiscal reordering to a global ceasefire, from a stronger drive toward greener economies and jobs, to a waiver on intellectual property rights on treatments and vaccines for COVID-19.

The great truth is that there is universal agreement that we cannot go back to the same old. A common understanding that we need to create a new normal, to "build back better." We need to craft a world that is more sustainable and more resilient. A world that is free of inequalities and injustice. We have the tools, we have the knowledge, and we have the resources to build one.

In sum, it is undeniable that the SDGs continue to be relevant, perhaps more than when they were adopted five years ago. They continue to be our roadmap for the present and the future. However, we need to revisit our commitments, not to dilute them or weaken them, but on the contrary to reassert its transformative power and relevance.

However, while the world addresses the immediate response to the current health emergency, we should work with the same impetus in addressing other related and protracted crises such as inequalities, women's rights, climate change, or the massive species extinction.

There is a minted phrase: "building back better" that is the task ahead. And of course, we have to guide our efforts using the SDGs as the paradigm. We should not take this challenge lightly because it requires an agreed checklist of the meaning and reaches of this new social, political, institutional, cultural, and economic infrastructure that we want and need, to rebuild our world.

This exercise of establishing a shared narrative, an agreed checklist needs the voices, experiences, and perspectives of the whole of society. Shared responsibilities and concerted action are the only way forward.

Conclusion

As mentioned, the catastrophic impact of the COVID-19 pandemic has brought enormous creativity, proposals, and ideas. We know what to do and even how to do it. The weak part of the equation, as stated by the Director-General of the WHO Dr. Tedros Adhanom, seems to be leadership and global governance arrangements. We need to deliver here and now.

Leadership is sorely needed, but it has to come from the whole of society. It is not only governments or messianic leaders, but also social activists, women, journalists, opinion-makers, scientists, and indigenous leaders. We all have a critical role to play in building a new social contract between society, the economy, politics, and nature.

We hear time and again that we need solidarity and cooperation. And here we have yet another paradox: A wealth of ideas and proposals and a shortage of political will and concrete decision-making to coordinate, to collaborate, and to have a shared vision that leads to transformative action.

We have the responsibility to collectively craft a new culture of multilateralism, which is a culture of cooperation, of coordination, of taking bold decisions to ensure that our global commons are managed, cared for, and preserved for future generations. Not only the conventional commons such as the oceans or the atmosphere but health, security, and human dignity should be considered global commons.[47] We need a multilateral system that is inclusive, efficient, relevant, accountable, and truly connected to peoples' needs and expectations.

---

47 *See* SUSAN J. BUCK, THE GLOBAL COMMONS: AN INTRODUCTION (1998).

Even if I have often insisted that the UN should use fewer acronyms and more synonyms, improve the way it communicates, reach out to society, local leaders, interest groups, and youth, I have allowed myself to use the DARE acronym, which stands for Delivery, Accountability, Relevance, and Efficiency. We should be daring, audacious, and creative and seize the moment of transformation for the betterment of our international architecture.

Some voices are calling for the creation of "something else," a plan B.[48] However, I strongly believe that there is so much that we have already created, established, and built, including the SDGs. It is perhaps time to "build back better" a multilateral system that goes beyond technocratic reforms. I am a strong believer that the UN is irreplaceable. Perhaps today we are witnessing the beginning of a new era—a new foundational moment for the UN. And the voice and the agency have to come to form all of us. We are the UN and the organization has to deliver for "We the Peoples," this powerful first phrase of the United Nations founding Charter.

---

48 Thomas Piketty, *Reconstructing Internationalism*, Le blog de Thomas Piketty, (July 14, 2020), www.lemonde.fr/blog/piketty/2020/07/14/reconstructing-internationalism/.

3 COVID-19 and the SDGs

Joe E. Colombano and David N. Nabarro[1]

The spread of the SARS-CoV-2 (COVID-19) pandemic, and the impact of the drastic measures introduced to contain it, represent a formidable challenge in meeting the Sustainable Development Goals (SDGs) and realizing the promise of the 2030 Agenda for Sustainable Development. When it jumped from the animal to the human world, the virus triggered a chain reaction with knock-on effects across all the interconnected dimensions of sustainable development, including the environmental, social, and economic ones. By taking a "system of systems" approach, our qualitative analysis finds a dynamic symbiosis between COVID-19 and the SDGs: Not only does the virus impact the chances of meeting the goals, but it also affects the extent to which progress has been made in achieving the goals and determines the level of societies' resilience to the crisis. We find that the virus's impact on the SDGs is profound and largely negative: Far from being the great equalizer it was initially thought to be, the virus hits the poor and most vulnerable the hardest. The only real positive is that this crisis has put the strengthening of the public health systems at the heart of the political debate. Going forward, policy solutions to the crisis will be most effective when globally coordinated and locally informed; when they are approached with a whole-of-system mindset, to manage complexity and build resilience; and when they put the SDGs at the center. Only this way will it be possible to turn the global reset caused by the pandemic into an opportunity to reject the original system with its persistent shortcomings and start anew to build a fairer and more sustainable world.

Introduction

If there is one lesson to be learned from the COVID-19 pandemic, it is that humanity and the planet it inhabits are tightly linked in sophisticated and interconnected systems. These systems encompass the reality of the biosphere and the constructs of our society, its politics, and the economy, and are all tied together in a dynamic symbiosis of interconnections and couplings of varying strength. Life, in every form, is at the center of such a "system of systems," from the microscopic of a virus to the macroscopic of the animal kingdom, the global commons, and the world economy. Because of its complexity however, such a structure is

---

1 The authors are grateful to Derek Chan of the Millennium Institute for his contribution to this chapter, including to section 3 and the diagram in Figure 3.1, adapted from the Millennium Institute's iSDG model.

vulnerable to sudden catastrophic collapse triggered by small, and at times insignificant, events in any one of the constituent systems.[2]

One such event occurred late last year, when an unknown virus jumped from a wild animal, probably a bat, to a human, possibly in a wet market in Wuhan, China, thus transmitting the Severe Acute Respiratory Syndrome Corona Virus 2 (SARS-CoV-2) responsible for the coronavirus disease 2019 (COVID-19). Since then, this zoonotic virus spread as a pandemic of unprecedented speed and reach, infecting over 3.5 million people, killing over 250,000, and causing a global recession of historical proportions.[3] At the time of writing in May 2020, these numbers are still increasing, as COVID-19 continues to wreak havoc around the world, at least until a vaccine or a therapy is found and made available to all.

The pain inflicted by the pandemic is likely to have deleterious effects on the pursuit of sustainable development, the concept that more than others reflects a "system of systems" approach in the way it combines and juxtaposes social, economic, and environmental aspects of human activity and their inter-linkages, co-benefits, and tradeoffs. In this chapter, we take a "system of systems approach" and consider how the COVID-19 virus impacts sustainable development as expressed through the 17 Sustainable Development Goals of the 2030 Agenda for Sustainable Development.[4] We do so by means of a qualitative analysis, on the basis of the people, planet, prosperity, peace, and partnership dimensions of the goals (the so-called "Five Ps"[5]). In addition, we look at the same question through a systems perspective, on the basis of a feedback-loop diagram developed by the Millennium Institute in Washington, DC.

The chapter is divided into three sections. The first section describes three main dynamics identified as part of the symbiosis between the virus and the goals. The second section focuses on the Five Ps to assess the impact of the virus on the goals and the main dimensions of sustainable development. The third section introduces feedback loops both as a diagnostic tool to explain how inter-linkages work, and as a reference to guide policymakers in the allocation of scarce public resources to respond to the COVID-19 crisis. The conclusion summarizes our findings and provides some preliminary suggestions for policymaking.

While we recognize that this is a very preliminary analysis that is largely based on qualitative and subjective interpretations and anecdotal evidence, we nevertheless believe it can be helpful in bringing some form of order and method to the analysis of the effects brought about by the COVID-19 pandemic, and the shocks that it inflicts to the complex network of relationships, co-benefits, and tradeoffs that constitute sustainable development.

The Virus and the SDGs: A Dynamic Symbiosis

Because of its exponential pace of growth and the consequences of the measures required to contain it, the COVID-19 pandemic is a formidable challenge to human progress and the realization of a more equitable and sustainable future envisioned by the 2030 Agenda for

---

2 Mahmoud Efatmaneshnik et al., *Complexity and Fragility in System of Systems*, 7 INT'L J. OF SYS. OF SYS. ENGINEERING 4, 294–312 (2016).
3 *A Crisis Like No Other, An Uncertain Recovery, World Economic Outlook Update,* INTERNATIONAL MONETARY FUND (IMF) (June 2020), www.imf.org/en/Publications/WEO/Issues/2020/06/24/WEOUpdate.
4 By considering the SDGs as an integrated and indivisible whole, in this chapter we refer interchangeably to them and the 2030 Agenda for Sustainable Development.
5 United Nations (UN) General Assembly (UNGA) Res. A/RES/70/01, *Transforming Our World: The 2030 Agenda for Sustainable Development,* (Sept. 15, 2015) [hereinafter "Agenda 2030"].

Sustainable Development. Like any phenomenon that concerns human beings, their relationship to the natural world and their interactions within social constructs, such as politics and the economy, are complex. Indeed, the way in which the pandemic and the resulting health care crisis is linked to financial, economic, and social crises forms a system of circular, interconnected, fast shifting, and highly complex elements. We see this system of interactions between the virus and the SDGs as an interconnected and dynamic symbiosis among living systems.

We recognize at least three main dynamics: First, the virus impacts each of the goals both directly, by way of its effects on health outcomes, and indirectly, due to the consequences of the extreme measures needed to contain it (i.e. lockdowns). We call this "first-order dynamics." Second, the relationship between the virus and the SDGs is two-ways: (1) The virus impacts on the achievement of the SDGs and (2) The extent to which progress has been made on the goals in any one society influences the severity of the COVID-19 impact on that society. In other words, the more progress we make in achieving the SDGs, the better equipped we are to cope with crises. We call this "resilience dynamics." And, lastly, the virus impacts not just each of the goals but also the inter-linkages among them, again not only directly in terms of SDG outcomes, but also indirectly, for example through the impact the pandemic has on public opinion and politics. We call this "inter-linkages dynamics."

First-Order Dynamics: Direct and Indirect Effects of COVID-19 on the SDGs

The virus impacts each of the goals both directly, by way of its effects on health outcomes, and indirectly, due to the consequences of the extreme measures needed to contain it (i.e. lockdowns). COVID-19 is a highly contagious virus, and the infectious phase can often be asymptomatic, with people unaware of being a danger to others.[6] As a result, the number of cases doubles every two and a-half days on average.[7] This makes it hard to suppress infections completely. A vaccine or a cure will help, but at present they remain under development, and it will be many months before they are made safe and widely available to everyone, including in the developing countries.

Direct Effects

The rates of morbidity and mortality of the virus exert a direct impact on the achievement of the SDGs. At the time of writing, the novel coronavirus COVID-19 is affecting 218 countries and territories around the world.[8] The total number of cases is estimated in excess of 3.5 million people, with around 250,000 deaths.[9] Out of 100 cases of COVID-19, on

---

6 *When Do Infected People Transmit the Virus?, Coronavirus Disease (COVID-19): How Is It Transmitted?*, WORLD HEALTH ORGANIZATION (WHO), www.who.int/news-room/q-a-detail/coronavirus-disease-covid-19-how-is-it-transmitted (last visited Nov. 12, 2020).
7 David Nabarro, *COVID-19 Narrative Eight*, SKILLS, SYSTEMS & SYNERGIES FOR SUSTAINABLE DEVELOPMENT, www.4sd.info/covid-19-narratives/narrative-eight/ (March 22, 2020).
8 *COVID-19 Coronavirus Pandemic*, WORLDOMETER, www.worldometers.info/coronavirus/ (last visited Nov. 10, 2020).
9 WHO, *Coronavirus Disease (COVID-19) Situation Report—107*, at 1, www.who.int/docs/default-source/coronaviruse/situation-reports/20200506covid-19-sitrep-107.pdf?sfvrsn=159c3dc_2 (May 6, 2020).

average, most are asymptomatic or have mild symptoms only.[10] Only around 15% require hospitalization including in Intensive Care Units, while around 5% become critical and can succumb to the virus.[11] These numbers risk reversing the global progress achieved on health outcomes as measured by SDG3 on healthy lives and well-being for all at all ages. The most vulnerable, including women, the elderly, and informal workers, are hit the hardest.

Mortality and morbidity rates of COVID-19 also translate into a direct effect on the size and health of the labor force and its productivity, which in turn impacts, for example, the fight against poverty (SDG1), the number of people at risk of famine (SDG2), education outcomes (SDG4), economic growth and employment (SDG8), and more. In addition, COVID-19 mortality rates also get compounded with the number of unnecessary deaths occurring because of the surge in demand for hospitalization that rapidly overwhelms health systems even in advanced countries with high level of capacity. When hospitals struggle or fail to accommodate demand, especially for Intensive Care Unit (ICU) beds, and resources get shifted to front the pandemic emergency, more deaths occur. Unnecessary deaths also occur when chronic patients with diseases other than COVID-19 postpone their treatment due to fear of coming into contact with COVID-19 patients in hospitals and health centers where they would otherwise go regularly.

Indirect Effects

In addition to the direct negative effects of the virus on health outcomes, the SDGs also suffer from the impact of the measures adopted to contain the pandemic. We refer to such impact as indirect effects of the virus. They are largely consequences from countries requiring their people to shelter in place, therefore effectively imposing a lockdown of their society and the stalling of their economy. Lacking a vaccine or a treatment for COVID-19, lockdowns are the only viable measure to interrupt the transmission of the virus. At the time of writing, around half of the world population is in some sort of lockdown.

While necessary, lockdowns have immediate and devastating consequences for all the SDGs. The artificial stop of the economy results in supply and demand shocks and a sudden drop in economic output: With estimates around negative 5% or worse,[12] the recession expected for the second quarter of 2020 is likely to be one of the most severe on record, "with historical levels of unemployment and deprivations."[13] Sectors such as transportation, retail trade, leisure, hospitality, and recreation have all been affected. A recent UN report on the crisis describes how supply chain disruptions have halted the manufacturing industry. This, combined with falling commodity prices, in particular oil, exacerbates the impact of

---

10 WHO, *Report of the WHO-China Joint Mission on Coronavirus Disease 2019 (COVID-19)*, at 12, www.who.int/docs/default-source/coronaviruse/who-china-joint-mission-on-covid-19-final-report.pdf (Feb. 2020).
11 *Id.*
12 IMF, *World Economic Outlook: The Great Lockdown*, at 7, www.imf.org/en/Publications/WEO/Issues/2020/04/14/weo-april-2020 (April 2020).
13 UN Sustainable Development Group, *Shared Responsibility, Global Solidarity: Responding to the Socio-Economic Impacts of COVID-19*, at 8, https://unsdg.un.org/sites/default/files/2020-03/SG-Report-Socio-Economic-Impact-of-Covid19.pdf (March 2020) [hereinafter "UNSDG Economics Impact Report"].

the pandemic, and rattles the financial markets. In the developing countries, this has tightened liquidity conditions, and created unprecedented outflows of capital.[14]

These lockdown consequences result in significant and pervasive negative effects on the SDGs. Almost all of the goals are affected, with negative effects on poverty and famine, education outcomes, gender, energy, employment, growth, climate action, social cohesion, and partnerships. Interestingly, some of these indirect effects of the pandemic on the SDGs can be positive, at least in the short term. The sudden stop in economic activity and the movement of people, for example, has had a positive impact on the environment, especially in terms of the count of fine particulate matter in the air and other measures of air, water, and soil pollution. There is an impact on CO_2 emissions but it is less significant, as sectors other than transport and industry remain active, for example to provide electricity and heath even during lockdowns. In any case, such improvements are destined to be short-lived, unless countries deliver on their commitment to sustainable development once the global economy restarts.

Resilience Dynamics: SDGs Progress as a Proxy for COVID-Readiness

The "resilience dynamic" effect is based on the consideration that societies that have made most progress on the achievement of the SDGs are also those that are likely to be less impacted by the virus and are better prepared to cope with it. In this sense, the level of SDGs achievement in a specific country or community can be considered a measure of the COVID-readiness of such a country or community. Put in other terms, the advancement on SDG implementation contributes to building resilient societies, which are able to better cope with the impact of the pandemic. The opposite is also true: Societies that are lagging behind in implementing the SDGs are also more likely to be more impacted by the spreading of the virus and are less able to cope with its consequences.

Take, for example, the first line of defense against the virus, as recommended by the World Health Organization: Frequent handwashing. This is explicitly included in SDG indicator 6.2.1 (b), which measures the proportion of the population that uses a handwashing facility with soap and water. While this is easily implementable and is part of daily hygiene measures for many, the latest SDGs Progress Report reminds us that 2 out of 5 people worldwide do not have a basic handwashing facility with soap and water at home.[15] In the least developed countries, it is less than one out of three people (28%). This means that, globally, an estimated 3 billion people are still unable to properly wash their hands at home and are therefore deprived of the most basic and effective prevention measure against COVID-19.[16] So countries that are lagging behind on implementing SDG6 are more at risk of being impacted by the pandemic.

Similarly, it can be argued that in general, the pandemic is more likely to affect those communities that are already at risk, as indicated by lack of progress on SDGs implementation. Examples include SDG3 on universal health coverage, as the virus is more likely to affect those whose health is already compromised, or on health emergency preparedness;

---

14 *Id.*
15 UN Department of Economic and Social Affairs, *The Sustainable Development Goals Report 2019*, at 9, https://unstats.un.org/sdgs/report/2019/The-Sustainable-Development-Goals-Report 2019.pdf (2019).
16 *Id.* at 34.

or SDG11, because people living in slums or densely populated urban areas are less able to adopt basic hygiene measures to prevent the virus; or SDG15, on the sustainable use of biodiversity, including to address the demand and supply of illegal wildlife products, which are considered to play a part in causing zoonotic diseases such as COVID-19; or SDG16, because population caught up in or fleeing war and persecution are left unable to adopt precautionary measures against the virus and lack access to basic social and political protections or any support system.[17]

Inter-linkages Dynamics: COVID-19 and the Integrated Nature of the 2030 Agenda

The integrated nature of the 2030 Agenda is of critical importance in the transition toward a sustainable future. The inter-linkages among each of the SDGs are a key part of the Agenda and one of the most valuable contributions to understanding the complexity of sustainable development and to leveraging resources and capabilities to realize it. The merit of the 2030 Agenda is to go beyond the traditional distinction of sustainable development as the sum of three distinct economic, environmental, and social dimensions. As put by the latest Global Sustainable Development Report, the biggest transformative potential of the 2030 Agenda is "not the pursuit of individual Goals and targets but the explicit consideration of their inter-linkages, co-benefits, and trade-offs."[18]

In recent years, and since the agreement of the 2030 Agenda in 2015 in particular, there has been a proliferation of models that have looked at the inter-linkages between the different dimensions of sustainable development. In practical terms, these typically consider potential synergies or tradeoffs to assess alternative paths toward sustainable development. While all models have limitations, the process to develop, validate, and use them enables the discussion of inter-linkages to become more concrete in the local context. In this respect, it is important to note that models and maps of inter-linkages are often value-laden and can reflect social and political priorities that influence operationalization.

With this in mind, it is important to consider the dynamic between the COVID-19 virus and the SDGs not just in terms of the effect that the former has on the latter, but in particular, with a view to assessing how the virus is affecting the co-benefits and tradeoffs that exists among each goal or set of goals. For example, it will be important to consider the link between food systems, the economy, nature, and health outcomes to assess the extent to which tradeoffs, say, between the existence of traditional trading practices such as wet markets—which provide livelihoods and food for many in the developing countries, and the risk that they could trigger the spreading of zoonotic viruses. Similarly, it will be important to look at the link between climate and health, to assess the co-benefit of eliminating fine particulate that pollutes the air, and the reduction in chronic pulmonary diseases.

The ultimate objective of such an exercise on the effect of the virus on SDGs inter-linkages is to understand: (i) If and how the inter-linkages among goals hold any responsibility, direct or indirect, for the emergence of viruses such as COVID-19; (ii) How non-medical

---

17 UNSDG Economics Impact Report, *supra* note 11 at 5.
18 Independent Group of Scientists 2019, *Global Sustainable Development Report 2019: The Future Is Now—Science for Achieving Sustainable Development*, UN DEPARTMENT OF ECONOMIC AND SOCIAL AFFAIRS, at 4, https://sdgs.un.org/publications/future-now-science-achieving-sustainable-development-gsdr-2019-24576 (2019).

measures may contribute to mitigate the chain of transmission of infections; (iii) How the inter-linkages can contribute to mitigate the social, economic, and environmental consequences of the crisis; (iv) How to prevent the reoccurrence of a similar crisis; and finally, (v) How to steer the new system toward a new and improved paradigm, in keeping with the 2030 Agenda. The next two sections consider in some detail two approaches to frame the impact of the virus on the interconnected dimensions of the SDGs: The Five-Ps approach and the feedback-loop approach.

Understanding the Impact of COVID-19 on the Integrated Dimensions of the 2030 Agenda: A "Five-Ps" Approach

One way to understand the impact of COVID-19 on the inter-linkages among the SDGs is to consider the integrated dimensions of sustainable development as presented in the Preamble of resolution A/RES/70/01, "Transforming our world: the 2030 Agenda for Sustainable Development." In the document, the Member States of the United Nations (UN) introduce the set of integrated and indivisible goals and targets by referring to five "areas of critical importance for humanity and the planet," which encompass and build upon the traditional economic, social, and environmental aspects of sustainable development. These are People, Planet, Prosperity, Peace, and Partnership (Box 3.1).[19]

Box 3.1 The Five Dimensions of the 2030 Agenda for Sustainable Development[20]

People

We are determined to end poverty and hunger, in all their forms and dimensions, and to ensure that all human beings can fulfil their potential in dignity and equality and in a healthy environment.

Planet

We are determined to protect the planet from degradation, including through sustainable consumption and production, sustainably managing its natural resources and taking urgent action on climate change, so that it can support the needs of the present and future generations.

Prosperity

We are determined to ensure that all human beings can enjoy prosperous and fulfilling lives and that economic, social and technological progress occurs in harmony with nature.

---

19 G.A. Res. A/RES/70/01, Transforming Our World: The 2030 Agenda for Sustainable Development, at 2 (Oct. 21, 2015).
20 Agenda 2030, *supra* note 4 at 2.

> *Peace*
>
> We are determined to foster peaceful, just and inclusive societies, which are free from fear and violence. There can be no sustainable development without peace and no peace without sustainable development.
>
> *Partnership*
>
> We are determined to mobilize the means required to implement this Agenda through a revitalized Global Partnership for Sustainable Development, based on a spirit of strengthened global solidarity, focused in particular on the needs of the poorest and most vulnerable and with the participation of all countries, all stakeholders and all people.

Crucially, in the intergovernmental process that led to the SDGs, Member States resisted the temptation to cluster the 17 goals under each of the dimensions identified, in the belief that sustainable development can only be achieved by working across sectors and fields and that progress, or lack thereof, toward achieving one of the goals has ripple effects on one or more of the others. In fact, the shortcomings of previous development agendas have often been attributed to the natural tendency of experts, practitioners, academics, policymakers, and politicians to work on each aspect of development separately, in part due to the primacy of specialized expertise. Instead, Member States pointed to the integrated nature of the goals as a critical aspect in ensuring that the purpose of the new Agenda is realized, as is the promise to leave no one behind.

It is important to underline that in the Five-Ps system, each of the five dimensions exists both on its own and as a part of a continuum with the others, without any order of priority or ranking. This, along with Member States' intuition that, depending on local conditions and preferences, each goal can fit under any of the dimensions or under more than one at the same time, introduces a dynamic element to the Five-Ps system that captures the ever-shifting relationships between people, the environment they inhabit, and the economy.

The Five-Ps approach can be helpful in understanding the effects that COVID-19 has on the interconnected dimensions of the 2030 Agenda, and indeed on the inter-linkages between the goals. Because of their circular and dynamic nature, we consider the Five Ps to be a reasonable proxy for the inter-linkages that exist among the goals. Hence, considering the effect of the virus on each of the dimensions provides an indication of the impact on the inter-linkages, albeit limited by the nature of each dimension. Unlike in the "First-Order Dynamics: Direct and Indirect Effects of COVID-19 on the SDGs" section, here we do not distinguish between the impact of the virus and the measures adopted to contain them—such as the lockdowns—but we take them as one combined effect that we call "COVID-19 crisis" or "crisis" for short. We consider direct effects those that the crisis has on each of the five dimensions of sustainable development (and, by proxy, on the goals inter-linkages). Indirect effects, on the other hand, are those brought about by the impact that the crisis has on the five dimensions and the inter-linkages through its impact on public opinion and politics. Both direct and indirect effects can be positive or negative.

Table 3.1 Impact of the COVID-19 crisis on the five dimensions of the 2030 Agenda.

5Ps		Direct effects		Indirect effects	
		Positive	Negative	Positive	Negative
People	End poverty and hunger		SDG1, 2		
	Ensure that all human beings can fulfill their potential		SDG3, 4, 8	SDG3	
	Ensure dignity and equality in a healthy environment	SDG11, 14, 15	SDG5, SDG10		
Planet	Protect the planet from degradation	SDG11 SDG3*		SDG14, 15	
	Sustainably manage its natural resources				
	Take action on climate change				SDG13
Prosperity	Ensure everyone enjoys prosperous and fulfilling lives	SDG9, 11, 12, 14, 15	SDG1, 2, 3, 4, 5 SDG10		SDG8, 12, 17
	Provide economic, social, and technological progress in harmony with nature		SDG8		
Peace	Foster peaceful, just, and inclusive societies		SDG5 SDG 10		SDG16
	Ensure freedom from fear and violence		SDG16		
Partnerships	Mobilize all means of implementation		SDG10		
	Foster a Global Partnership based on solidarity		SDG17		SDG16 SDG17
	Focus on the poorest and most vulnerable, with the participation of all		SDG1, SDG5, 8, SDG10	SDG3	

* This is only a theoretical effect, as in fact the lockdowns are not expected to last long enough for decreased pollution to result in improved health outcomes.

Table 3.1 shows the impact of the COVID-19 crisis on SDGs inter-linkages as approximated by the five dimensions of the 2030 Agenda. Let us take each dimension in turn.

- **People**: The crisis has had a direct negative impact on the People dimension (i.e. the inter-linkage between poverty, hunger, inequality, and environment) as evidenced by increasing poverty and famine (SDG1 and 2), decreasing health and education outcomes (SDG3 and 4), lower economic growth (SDG8), and increasing inequality, of gender and beyond (SDG5 and 10). The crisis has also had some direct positive effects, mostly attributable to the reduction in pollution resulting from the sudden stop of productive activities and transportation (SDG11, 14, and 15). About indirect effects, the crisis has brought about an increased public awareness of the importance of having resilient public health systems. The expectation therefore is that politicians will respond to this new sensitivity by increasing investments in public health (SDG3).

- **Planet**: The crisis has had some direct positive effects on the Planet dimension (i.e. the inter-linkage the planet, natural resources, and the climate). The lockdowns imposed in most countries result in a drop in pollution coming from transports and economic activity. This is mostly evident in cities, which see decreasing levels of fine particulate matter in the air (SDG11). In theory, this would also have direct positive effects on health outcomes (SDG3), although the expectation is that lockdowns will not last long enough for health outcomes to be significant and long lasting. About the indirect effects, these include positive ones, as people realize the importance of the natural world to their well-being and happiness and demand that these are protected (SDG12, 14, and 15), but also negative ones, as the primacy of the COVID-19 risk diverts political capital and financial resources away from climate change action (SDG13).
- **Prosperity**: In terms of direct effects, the inter-linkages between the individual, society, economy, technology, and environment is positively affected by the crisis in terms of incentivizing innovation and technology to make our societies COVID-ready (SDG9), with less harm to the environment (SDG11, 14, and 15). Such direct positive effects, however, less than compensate for the severe direct negative impact that the crisis has on economic growth and employment (SDG8), leading to higher levels of poverty, increased risk of famines (SDG1, 2, and 3) and lower social and equality outcomes (SDG5 and 10). Indirect effects are also predominately negative, as fear and uncertainty about the future may turn politics inward toward protectionism (SDG8) and isolationism (SDG17) or non-sustainable practices and policies (SDG12).
- **Peace**: The effects of the virus on the peace, justice, and inclusiveness dimensions are largely negative, both directly and indirectly. Far from being the great equalizer that it was initially thought to be, the virus impacts deeply into the fabric of our society (SDG16) and exposes violence—for example against those considered to be responsible for the contagions—and inequalities, as the poorest and most vulnerable, including women, are hit the hardest (SDG5 and 10). In some less democratic countries, the crisis has become the pretext for authoritarian leaders to strengthen their grip on power, in disregard of parliaments and the rule of law (SDG16).
- **Partnership**: The crisis has mostly negative effects, both directly and indirectly, on the partnership dimension. Faced with the speed and scale of an expanding pandemic, instead of considering a coordinated international response, world leaders turn inward and compete with each other (SDG17)—for example for medical supplies—at times by introducing protectionist measures (SDG8), leaving much to be desired in terms of global solidarity across nations, especially with those hardest hit, and the most vulnerable everywhere (SDG1, 5, and 10). The only positive effect is an indirect one, as the prominence of the crisis brings the issue of the resilience of public health systems to the center of the political debate (SDG3).

The limitation of the Five-Ps approach is that its explanation of the crisis on the integrated dimensions of the agenda and the inter-linkages is only partial, as it generally centers on the effects within each dimension but not across them. The approach also relies on a proxy for the inter-linkages among the goals, as it is based on qualitative observations and largely relies on subjective interpretations. Finally, in regard to the evolution over time of the interaction between COVID-19 and the SDGs, the Five-Ps approach is a rather static one: It only provides a snapshot in time rather than an understanding of short-, medium-, and long-term differences. At the same time, however, the approach can be helpful in bringing some form of order and method to the analysis of the effects brought about by introducing an external shock such as the COVID-19 virus to that complex network of relationships, co-benefits, and tradeoffs that characterizes sustainable development and the SDGs.

Understanding the Impact of COVID-19 on the SDGs Inter-linkages: A Dynamic Systems Approach

The analysis of the impact of the COVID-19 pandemic on an integrated system such as the SDGs requires exploring the inter-linkages between the goals. In a system of complex dynamics characterized by many feedback loops, time delays of varying durations, nonlinear patterns of growth and decline, and differing tipping points, any interruption affecting one SDG could result in cascading effects across the others. This calls for a dynamic systems-thinking approach to understand the complexity of the problem and suggest policies to solve it.

Figure 3.1 provides a system map of COVID-19 and its effect on the SDGs. The diagram is adapted from the Integrated Sustainable Development Goals (iSDG) Model, a policy simulation tool developed by the Millennium Institute to help policymakers make sense of the complex web of interconnections between the SDGs. The model integrates economic, social, and environmental factors and includes elements of complexity, such as feedback relationships, non-linearity, and time delays that are fundamental to fully understanding the

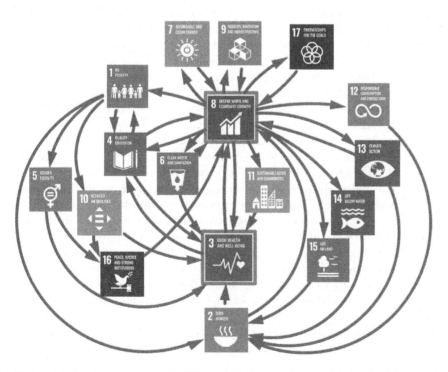

Figure 3.1 A systems map of COVID-19 and its effect on the SDGs. Figure adapted from Millennium Institute's iSDG model, *see* Millennium Institute, www.millennium-institute.org/isdg (last visited Nov. 15, 2020).

dynamics of development.[21] While not as sophisticated as a simulation, the diagram helps make sense of some of the dynamics triggered by the COVID-19 virus and their interactions with the SDG system.

The diagram illustrates some of the feedback loops resulting from the introduction of drastic lockdown measures adopted to contain the pandemic. A feedback loop is a process in which the outputs of a system are circled back and used as inputs. Most of the feedback loops we describe in this section stem from the effect on economic growth and unemployment (SDG8), which increases significantly in the short term, due to the sudden closure of the economy, but also persists over time, as economies are slow to restart once the lockdowns are gradually released.

A first simple feedback loop describes the relationship between unemployment (SDG8), poverty and hunger (SDG and 2), and health (SDG 3). In this case, individuals left without jobs become more prone to falling under the national poverty lines and are thus exposed to hunger and malnutrition. This in turn affects their health, which in turns prevents them from being able to rejoin the labor force.

Another feedback loop links together SDG8, 4, and 1. As jobs are lost due to the closure of the economy (SDG8), household incomes decline (SDG1), which in turn leads to an increase in school dropouts (SDG4), either because families can no longer afford school fees, or because the opportunity cost of keeping children in school is too high, as they can be more helpful in the short term at home. By not completing their education (SDG4) however, these children are less likely to get a well-paid job in the future (SDG8) and are therefore at higher risk of poverty (SDG1).

Often, it is possible to identify longer chains of feedback loops across SDGs. Consider, for example, that the jobs lost to the COVID-19 pandemic are disproportionately held by the working poor—whose job security is lowest—and by women, as they are forced to stay home to care for the children at home from school. Such effects of unemployment (SDG8) on gender (SDG5) and social inequalities (SDG10) are exacerbated by the lack of access to basic services such as health (SDG3) and education (SDG4) for the same groups, which in turn affects social cohesion (SDG16), therefore threatening economic stability (SDG8) and creating more unemployment (SDG8) and poverty (SDG1).

In addition to being an effective diagnostic tool, feedback loops are also useful in guiding government policy and expenditure allocation. Faced with the pandemic, governments have rightly invested in the strengthening of public health systems (SDG3). However, given the budget constraint under which most countries operate, especially in the developing world, and the pressures to restart the economy, governments may be tempted to divert public resources away from the social sector, and invest instead in key productive industries and infrastructure (SDG8 and 9) as is often done to boost productivity. Often, these decisions are at the expense of sectors such as education (SDG4), or water infrastructure (SDG6) and electricity (SDG7). In such cases, feedback loops such as those described above are helpful to clarify the impact of these choices, especially when they could weaken the response to COVID-19 and other diseases (for example by weakening water and sanitation infrastructure).

International cooperation and environmental policies may also become targets for cutting costs in the face of severe recessions, such as that triggered by the COVID-19 crisis.

---

21 *Millennium Institute*, SDG INTEGRATION—UN DEVELOPMENT PROGRAMME, https://sdgintegration.undp.org/partners/millennium-institute (last visited Nov. 10, 2020).

Such decisions may be taken more easily now that populist parties are in power, or because lockdowns have brought about cleaner air (SDG11) and more sustainable consumption patterns (SDG12). However, building climate resilience (SDG13) and increasing marine and land protection (SDG14 and 15) is dependent on continuous investment and would suffer greatly from such cuts. In these cases, feedback loops are helpful to illustrate the risk of severe economic losses (SDG8) coming from neglecting climate action (SDG13), or the risks of hunger (SDG2) and adverse health outcomes (SDG3) coming from weakened agricultural yields and fish stocks, if marine and land areas were to be neglected (SDG14 and 15). Similarly, cutting international aid (SDG17) would also have adverse economic effects by weakening trading partners (SDG8) and increasing poverty in the developing world (SDG1), hence increasing the likelihood of migration (SDG10) and preventing coordinated action to address global challenges such as climate change (SDG13).

Most of the feedback loops illustrated in the diagram above focus on the chains of effects triggered by the shutting down of the economy to contain the pandemic. While such a measure can be lifted relatively quickly, the economy will take time to rebound to pre-crisis level. Given the inherent inertia of the sustainable development system, any interruption is likely to severely set back progress toward the achievement of the SDGs. Understanding the complexity of the system and its fragility is the first step toward making the right decisions for planning for recovery and building more resilient, societies.

Conclusion

COVID-19 is not a "black swan," an unpredictable event with a massive impact on a global scale. On the contrary, many predicted the spreading of a respiratory infection caused by a coronavirus and warned us that the world was not going to be ready to deal with it. A non-exhaustive list includes infectious disease expert Dennis Carroll, former USAID Administrator Andrew Natsios, epidemiologist Michael Osterholm, Pulitzer Price-winner Laurie Garrett, epidemiologist Larry Brilliant, global-health expert Alanna Shaikh, philanthropist Bill Gates, virologist Robert G. Webster, and others.[22] Cassandras all of them, as their predictions were largely met, if not with incredulity, certainly with inaction. And yet it was not outlandish to foresee that the "system of systems" in which we live is complex enough that any unexpected event, even if small, can undo it. This is in accordance with the formula *complexity x uncertainty = fragility*, as every risk manager knows well.

In this chapter we looked at the complexity of the sustainable development systems and analyzed the relationships that exist between the COVID-19 virus and the SDGs. We found that these exist in a dynamic symbiosis in which not only does the virus affect the chances of achieving the goals, the extent to which progress has been made in achieving the goals also determines the level of COVID-19 resilience of societies. Countries that have made the most progress on the SDGs fare better during the pandemic. We also found that the virus' impact on the SDGs is profound and largely negative, with perhaps the most important lesson being about the level of inequality exposed by the virus. Far from being the great equalizer it was initially thought to be, COVID-19 hits the poor and most vulnerable the

---

22 David Ewing Duncan, *Prepare, Prepare, Prepare. Why Didn't the World Listen to the Coronavirus Cassandras?*, VANITY FAIR (Mar. 27, 2020), www.vanityfair.com/news/2020/03/why-didnt-the-world-listen-to-the-coronavirus-cassandras.

hardest. The only real positive effect of the crisis is that it has put the resilience of public health systems at the center of the political debate.

Summary Recommendations

While it would be wrong to make any precise recommendation for policy on the basis of the preliminary considerations outlined above, it is possible to indicate a number of general principles to keep in mind as we consider the actions to take in response to the COVID-19 crisis, while continuously learning about it and its impacts on sustainable development. These general principles include the following:

- **Managing complexity is a critical element of policy making for sustainable development**: Given the sophisticated interactions between the several dimensions of sustainable development, it is important to understand how complex such a system is, and how far it lies from its critical complexity limit, i.e. the threshold beyond which a system can unexpectedly fail. Because uncertainty cannot be controlled, the only alternative is to manage complexity.
- **Building resilience is key to sustainable development**: Building resilient societies will be critical to our ability to respond to the current COVID-induced crisis and achieve a sustainable future. Giovannini et al. put it best:

  > Being resilient means that we are able to stay on—or move towards—the sustainable development path, even if we are challenged away from it, as it is happening now with the COVID-19 pandemic. While sustainable development is related to the trend behavior of development (it answers the question of where we are going), resilience is about the fluctuations around and the transition towards it, and the dynamic mechanism that keeps us around the sustainable path, with as little well-being loss as possible. A society is resilient when it has the ability to face shocks and persistent structural changes without losing its ability to deliver well-being for its community in a sustainable way.[23]

- **Crisis response needs global coordination and local feedback**: COVID-19 is a multidimensional pandemic of global proportion. The response to it needs to be commensurate in scope and nature. Policy solutions to the crisis will be most effective when globally coordinated and locally informed, with a whole-of-system approach. As recommended by the United Nations,

  > a response needs to be multidimensional, coordinated, swift, and decisive. It needs to be a result of strong political leadership coupled with the buy-in of the population. It needs to foster public trust; be focused on human values; and supported by solid institutions, technical skills, and financial resources. Everyone needs to play their part in the response.[24]

---

23 Peter Benczur et al., Transition to a Sustainable Europe: The Importance of Resilience to Future-Oriented Policy-Making (March 2020) (unpublished manuscript) (on file with author).
24 UNSDG Economics Impact Report, *supra* note 11 at 13.

- **The SDGs must be at the core of the response to the COVID-19 crisis**: The global reset triggered by the crisis is an opportunity for a better recovery, to rebound forward toward realizing a sustainable world, rather than backward to the original system with its flaws, as we did, for example, after the 2008 financial crisis. For this to happen we need to strengthen our commitment to implement the 2030 Agenda and invest in meeting the 17 goals. This is how we can turn this global pandemic into the opportunity to start anew and realize the vision of a fairer and more sustainable world.

II
Implementing the SDGs

A People

4 Extreme Poverty Eradication
Conceptual Evolution and Policy Challenges

Vesselin Popovski and Krassen Stanchev

Fighting Poverty: Huge Progress and a Huge Challenge Ahead

Living in extreme poverty, defined by the World Bank in 1990 as surviving on $1.90 a day or less, is a reality for around 742 million people in the world today.[1] The number looks huge, and in fact, this is the total population of all countries in the European Union, plus all people in Russia and Japan together.[2] However, if we put this in a comparative perspective, today, 9.2% of the global population is in extreme poverty, which means that the other 90.8%, or almost 7 billion people, is outside of extreme poverty.[3] In another comparison, the number of people below extreme poverty in 1990 was 1.9 billion people[4] or 35.85% of the world's population at the time. In 1950 the number was 63.3%, or almost every two out of three people were extremely poor.[5]

Paradoxically, we can say that tremendous progress has been made in eradicating extreme poverty in the last few decades and simultaneously we can say that a tremendous challenge still remains to lift 742 million people out of extreme poverty. Jeffrey Sachs was correct in writing *The End of Poverty*[6] in 2006 and explaining the huge success in getting four billion out of poverty, as was Paul Collier in writing *The Bottom Billion*[7] in 2007, criticizing Sachs and explaining the rising gap between the rest of the world and the bottom billion below the poverty line. Hans Rosling explained this paradox in his book, *Factfulness*, defining the "size instinct" and cautioning how big numbers taken solely and separately can confuse, if they are not put into perspective, compared, and understood.[8] Such confusion can lead to two traps: (1) celebrating the success from the past and falling into complacency and (2) falling into despair from the huge burden remaining and developing a "negativity instinct."

---

1 WORLD POVERTY CLOCK, https://worldpoverty.io/ (last visited Dec. 8, 2020).
2 *Countries of the World by Population*, NATIONS ONLINE: POPULATION FIGURES FOR ALL COUNTRIES, www.nationsonline.org/oneworld/population-by-country.htm (last visited Dec. 8, 2020).
3 *Poverty Overview*, THE WORLD BANK, www.worldbank.org/en/topic/poverty/overview (last visited Dec. 8, 2020).
4 *World Population Living in Extreme Poverty, 1820–2015,* OUR WORLD IN DATA, https://ourworldindata.org/grapher/world-population-in-extreme-poverty-absolute?stackMode=relative (last visited Dec. 8, 2020).
5 *Share of the Population Living in Extreme Poverty, 2017,* OUR WORLD IN DATA, https://ourworldindata.org/grapher/share-of-the-population-living-in-extreme-poverty (last visited Dec. 8, 2020).
6 JEFFREY SACHS, THE END OF POVERTY:ECONOMIC POSSIBILITIES OF OUR TIME (Penguin 2006).
7 PAUL COLLIER, THE BOTTOM BILLION: WHY THE POOREST COUNTRIES ARE FAILING AND WHAT CAN BE DONE ABOUT IT (Oxford University Press 2007).
8 HANS ROSLING, FACTFULNESS: TEN REASONS WE'RE WRONG ABOUT THE WORLD AND WHY THINGS ARE BETTER THAN YOU THINK 128–31 (Sceptre 2019).

Considering poverty, Rosling asks whether we should have a "big party" because 91% of the world population "has escaped hell" or be "gloomy," watching on TV how many people still desperately live in extreme poverty.[9] The answer is to take positive inspiration from past successes and energetically commit to deliver efficiently on the goal of poverty eradication, especially knowing that COVID-19 and the resulting global recession will increase extreme poverty by about 100 million more people. This approach applies not only to the first Sustainable Development Goal (SDG 1), but to all other Sustainable Development Goals too. Reporting success is important, as we need to demonstrate all best practices, but these should not create complacency. We need to identify gaps and deficits, learn lessons, and come up with strategies on how to do better for the few remaining years until 2030 and fulfill—as much as possible—the SDGs.

Historical Context

The attention to reducing poverty as a global agenda started with Article 55a of the United Nations Charter in 1945 (the League of Nations was never a truly global organ), expressing the desire of the newly established world organization to create "conditions of stability and well-being to promote higher standards of living, full employment, and economic and social progress and development."[10] In 1948, Article 25 of the Universal Declaration of Human Rights (UDHR) set a qualitative definition of everyone's "right to a standard of living adequate for the health and well-being of himself and of his family" and listed 11 types of welfares—from food and clothing, to security in time of widowhood and old age.[11] The spirit of the UDHR was that no government-signatory shall act in violation of these rights. Accordingly, the economic and social progress and development of all people without discrimination became an internationally recognized policy goal of the United Nations (UN) member states.

For 75 years since, the desire and the quest to reduce poverty has relied on two major leverages: Growth and aid. The economic growth, or the idea that a rising tide would lift all the boats, was the preferred option for the conservatives, and the redistribution to the poor, either domestically by the state, or through foreign aid, was the preferred option for the left. However, growth and aid, at least as initially constituted, were insufficient tools to end extreme poverty. Remarkably, neither China nor India—the most successful stories of the late 20th century in cutting poverty—received much foreign aid, nor did they follow much advice from the World Bank. The problems with growth and aid were explained well by William Easterly in his book, *The Elusive Quest for Growth*.[12] Since the end of the Second World War, economists have tried to figure out how poor countries can attain standards of living approaching those of Europe and North America, and they proposed remedies such as foreign aid, investing in machines, fostering education, controlling population growth, making loans, and forgiving those loans on condition of reforms. None of these have delivered, and not because of the failure of economics, Easterly argued, but rather the failure to apply economic principles. All these "solutions" forgot the basic principle

---

9 *Id.* at 53.
10 U.N. Charter art. 55a.
11 Universal Declaration of Human Rights, G.A. Res. 217 (III) A, U.N. Doc. A/RES/217(III) (Dec. 10, 1948).
12 William Easterly, THE ELUSIVE QUEST FOR GROWTH: ECONOMISTS' ADVENTURES AND MISADVENTURES IN THE TROPICS (MIT Press 2002).

that private individuals and businesses, government officials, even aid donors, respond to incentives. Easterly, exposing the utter ineffectiveness of the Bretton Wood institutions to mitigate global poverty, was fired by his then-employer, the World Bank, and his "revenge" was the book, *The White Man's Burden*[13]—a blistering indictment of the West's economic policies for the world's poor. Dambisa Moyo in her book *Dead Aid*[14] also powerfully demonstrated that international aid did not work, and even worse, that it compounded the African economic problems. Collier, Easterly, and Moyo, among others, argued that the international development community should recalibrate the allocation of resources to increase accountability and state capacity to end extreme poverty in a sustainable manner. State institutions need to be strengthened and capacitated, leaders need to be made accountable to the needs of the poor, and the poor need to be empowered.

Two Schools on Poverty

The reduction of poverty as a global objective, therefore, swung between two schools of thought, which today tend to merge. To some extent this can be attributed to COVID-19. The first school of thought addresses well-being in terms of positive externality from economic development and growth, a context-inclusive approach linking development with human rights. Peter Bauer, out of his experience in Malaysia and West Africa, foresaw economic development gradually as "an extension of the range of choice …, an increase in the range of effective alternatives open to people," which is "both the core objective and the criterion of economic development."[15] The approach was advanced further by Amartya Sen, who was awarded a Nobel Prize for studying the links between social choice and poverty, and who expressed this school of thought well in his work, *Development as Freedom*.[16] Thomas Sowell argued that the randomness of incomes is not a direct causality between individual and/or collective intentions and goals; rather, it depends on a myriad of circumstances out of anyone's control. The task is to explain what created and sustained higher standards of living, because humanity began its development in a state of poverty that lasted for a very long time.[17]

The opposite approach is to understand poverty as a relatively separate phenomenon, theoretically distinguishable from other walks of economic life, and therefore subject to a purposeful policy action to limit and manage it as a social phenomenon. The post-Second World War economic models described economic growth through levels of saving and investment and the productivity of capital. Under this explanation, poverty should, theoretically, be dealt away by incentivizing savings and investment, debt relief, and other measures that help overcome the poverty trap, i.e. low incomes prevent saving and thus, investment. This approach helped monetization of policies and calculation of resources needed to lift populations out of poverty.

---

13 WILLIAM EASTERLY, THE WHITE MAN'S BURDEN: WHY THE WEST'S EFFORTS TO AID THE REST HAVE DONE SO MUCH ILL AND AND SO LITTLE GOOD (Penguin 2007).
14 DAMBISA MOYO, DEAD AID (Farrar, Straus & Giroux 2010).
15 Peter T. Bauer, *Economic Analysis and Policy in Underdeveloped Countries*, DUKE UNIVERSITY PRESS at 113 (1957).
16 AMARTYA SEN, DEVELOPMENT AS FREEDOM (Anchor 2000).
17 Thomas Sowell, *Chapter 1 and 13, in* WEALTH, POVERTY AND POLITICS: AN INTERNATIONAL PERSPECTIVE (New York, Basic Books, 2015).

Policies tend to induce complex, negative, and positive externalities to other walks of social life. Their analysis by economists, statisticians, and policymakers reformed the agenda of fighting poverty. Some policy instruments, like government debt relief assisted by the International Monetary Fund (IMF) and development banks, required redistribution of already produced income. This, however, led to unforeseen consequences, while many details of the real economic behaviors of the poor were left without attention. The consequences and the omissions were studied and explained by Abhijit V. Banerjee and Esther Duflo,[18] who along with Michael Kremer, received the Nobel Prize in Economics in 2019 for their in-depth experimental approach to alleviating global poverty. The discussion between economists and politicians of both schools led to better understanding of economic well-being and poverty.

Poverty and the Evolution of the Washington Consensus

The attention to quantitative policy objectives was raised in a UN document that was never implemented—the 1974 UN General Assembly's Declaration on the Establishment of a New International Economic Order (NIEO)—which recommended that industrial countries and other donors spend more on debt relief, support poorer countries' industrial policies, and relax existing rules of development and debt financing by the World Bank and the IMF.[19] The relief was required in order to meet the magnitude that is commensurate with the needs of the most affected countries. Politics aside, the microeconomic rationale behind this language was obvious: High government debts require high taxes, thus reducing the residual income and savings of the population. Therefore, the relief would expectedly increase the amount of public resources available for development and of private opportunities to work, consume, and save.

Over time, other measurable goals were formulated for many segments of well-being, such as poverty measured by income per person, food safety, hunger, infant mortality, life expectancy, etc. The incorporation of longevity, literacy, and health dimensions, or consequences of poverty, took place in the 1980s. The measure of poverty as one dollar a day per person was introduced in the 1990 World Development Report (WDR)[20] and Millennium Development Goal (MDG) One established a measurable target to halve the proportion of people who live below this income by 2015.[21]

---

18 ABHIJIT BANRJEE & ESTHER DUFLO, POOR ECONOMICS: A RADICAL RETHINKING OF THE WAY TO FIGHT GLOBAL POVERTY (New York, Public Affairs, 2011).
19 *See Programme of Action on the Establishment of a New International Economic Order*, G.A. Res. A/RES/3202(S-VI)-AR (May 1, 1974) (noting that the spirit and the letter of this document were hardly acceptable with an unclear rhetoric. It presumed responsibility of the "industrial nations" for economic backwardness and called for an autarchy of developing nations in terms of natural resources, trade, and economic institutions. In the next 10 years, the IMF and the World Bank promoted the so-called Washington Consensus that was accepted by most of the UN member states).
20 Ravi Kanbur & Lyn Squire, *The Evolution of Thinking about Poverty: Exploring the Interactions*, in FRONTIERS OF DEVELOPMENT ECONOMICS: THE FUTURE IN PERSPECTIVE 184–9 (Gerald M. Meier and Joseph E. Stiglitz eds., World Bank 2001). (The authors explain that (a) the measure leaves, without quantitative assessment, many important phenomena (differences in the cost of living between countries, non-markets transactions, intra family redistribution, etc.) and (b) concludes that including complex measures does not have a principal impact on sets of policies to end poverty.)
21 *Goal 1: Eradicate Extreme Poverty & Hunger*, WE CAN END POVERTY: MILLENNIUM DEVELOPMENT GOALS AND BEYOND, www.un.org/millenniumgoals/poverty.shtml (last visited Dec. 8, 2020).

The 1990s coincided with the collapse of communism and the Iron Curtain in Europe, and the former socialist countries embarked on the path of market reforms. The most successful followed a policy mix that became known, and sometimes misunderstood, as "the Washington Consensus:" Fiscal discipline, streamlining taxes, liberalization of interest rates, prices, trade, and investment, leveling the playground for domestic and foreign direct investment, securing property rights including privatization and bankruptcy, and deregulation. This was a reference to basic economic institutions that were restricted in indebted countries and destroyed by the communist system of central planning. The Consensus gave an extended formula of the above-mentioned theory of well-being as a positive externality of economic growth.

The 1994 Human Development Report (HDR) promoted the idea that human rights should be guaranteed by enhancing human security, in seven dimensions: Economy, food, health, environment, person, community, and political security; the economic security was thus statistically and politically linked to human development.[22] In 1995, The UN World Summit for Social Development in Copenhagen expanded previous definitions of poverty, underlining that, not only is income a factor, but also access to services.[23] Poverty was seen as a social and policy problem, along with unemployment and social exclusion, which further pointed at poverty as a "deprivation of basic human needs" (food, safe drinking water, sanitation, health, shelter, education, and information).[24] The Summit called for "stronger international cooperation and the support of international institutions to assist countries in their efforts to eradicate poverty and to provide basic social protection and services."[25] The Summit declared 1996 a Year for the Eradication of Poverty.[26] Later, this was expanded into the first UN Decade for the Eradication of Poverty (1997–2006)[27] and the Second UN Decade for the Eradication of Poverty (2008–2017).[28]

Seeing poverty as a social problem was an important paradigm shift: The task, henceforth, was to identify the most expedient policy mixes to deal with the problem. The understanding of poverty left the field of economics and human rights, and became a norm in international policy initiatives, incorporated eventually in both the MDGs and SDGs.

The 1974 NIEO policy targets, the 1994 HDR concept of human security, and the 1995 Copenhagen Summit added new institutional dimensions to the Washington Consensus, such as public and corporate governance, limiting corruption, observation of international standards in trade, finance, and central banking, existence of social safety nets, as well as targeted poverty reduction policy. These institutional requirements sought a greater efficacy of international and domestic development policies.

---

22 *Human Development Report 1994: New Dimensions of Human Security*, UNITED NATIONS DEVELOPMENT PROGRAM (UNDP) (Sept. 11, 2013), http://hdr.undp.org/en/content/human-development-report-1994 (HDR).
23 *Copenhagen Declaration on Social Development*, World Summit for Social Development, U.N. Doc. A/CONF.166/9 (Mar. 14, 1995).
24 *Id.* at 17.
25 *Id.* at 8.
26 *See* HDR, *supra* note 26 at ch. 2, p. 41; *see also*, Copenhagen Declaration, *supra* note 27, at ¶ 2,6 & Commitment 2.
27 G.A. Res. 51/178, 51st Sess. (Feb. 11, 1997).
28 G.A. Res. 62/205, 62nd Sess. (Mar. 10, 2008).

The 1996 Highly Indebted Poor Countries (HIPC) initiative was instrumentalized by the IMF and World Bank. In addition to offering criticism,[29] the IMF 2020 HIPC's review found that progress in poverty and inequality reduction accelerated thanks to the MDGs and SDGs, and in particular thanks to the 2005 Multilateral Debt Relief Initiative (MDRI). The latter gave an option of 100% of eligible debts to be written off if benefiting countries adopted (with civic participation) their own Poverty Reduction Strategy Papers (PRSP).[30] By 2015, when the MDRI was discontinued, the IMF and the World Bank had become involved in the effort with the African Development Fund (AfDF), Asian Development Bank (ADB), and International Development Bank (IaDB), helping altogether 35 countries, most of them in Africa but also in Latin America and Asia.[31] The MDRI was terminated in 2015.[32]

The 1997 WDR examined the role of the state and found it was too simplistic to assume that "good advisers and technical experts would formulate good policies, which good governments would then implement for the good of society."[33] The then-president of the World Bank, James Wolferson, noted that "building a more effective state to support sustainable development and the reduction of poverty will not be easy."[34] To supplement the role of the governments, a new institutional requirement was coined out: International organizations and national governments shall discuss, draft, and implement development programs in cooperation with non-governmental organizations (NGOs) and other stakeholders. It was the independent analysis of government failures that motivated the introduction of the above-mentioned PRSPs. A growing number of economists—David Dollar, Simeon Djankov, Miroslav Prokopijević, William Easterly, and Peter Bauer—to name just a few, studied how development funding is allocated, and questioned both its efficacy and integrity. In order to overcome irregularities, the IMF designed new instruments in an attempt to reformulate the missions of the IMF and the World Bank.

The Poverty Reduction and Growth Facility (PRGF) of the IMF, tasked with making the objectives of poverty reduction and growth more central to lending operations in the poorest countries, operated from 1999 to 2009, and extended loans to 78 African and Asian countries, including four ex-USSR states.[35]

In 1999, the US Congress commissioned a review of the Bretton Wood's institutions by the International Financial Institutions Advisory Commission (IFIAC), led by Allan Meltzer, and its core recommendation was that the IMF should primarily focus on crisis prevention, crisis management, improved quality and increased quantity of public information, and macroeconomic advice to developing countries.[36] Facilities like PRGF shall not deal with

---

29 *See Reducing Poverty: Is the World Bank's Strategy Working?*, 45 PANOS INST. REP. (2002).
30 *See MDRI Factsheet*, INTERNATIONAL MONETARY FUND (IMF) (Mar. 2016) (noting that the remaining funds were transferred to the Catastrophe Containment and Relief Trust, thus, assisting development of other SDGs).
31 *Id.*
32 *Id.* (noting that the remaining balance was transferred to Catastrophe Containment and Relief Trust, assisting other SDGs).
33 *World Development Report 1997: The State in a Changing World*, WORLD BANK GROUP (Oxford University Press 1997), https://openknowledge.worldbank.org/handle/10986/5980.
34 *Id.* at IV, 2.
35 *See PRGF Factsheet*, IMF (July 31, 2009).
36 For details *see* Allan Meltzer, *The Report of the International Financial Institution Advisory Commission: Comments on the c=Critics; Reform of the International Architecture*, 1(4) IFO INST. FOR ECON. RES. 9–17 (CESifo Forum 2000), www.cesifo.org/en/publikationen/2000/journal-complete-issue/cesifo-forum-4-2000.

long-term lending; rather, it is a competence of the International Bank for Reconstruction and Development (IBRD) and other development banks. If these banks did a better job, there would be no need for the PRGF. The development banks' programs, IFIAC stated, lack focus, are often loosely related, or unrelated, to their stated goals and all too frequently fail to accomplish their objectives.[37] Although the fault does not entirely lie with the development banks, they failed to find ways around the obstacles that some governments create, and they continue to lend despite the obstacles and the resulting failures.[38]

In this context it was logical that the 2006 WDR: Equity and Development analyzed global poverty as a systemic economic phenomenon that includes national, international, and social dimensions of equality, interrelations between well-being and equity, property rights, investment, justice, regulatory fairness, and longevity.[39]

Fulfilling Millennium Development Goal 1

The share of population in extreme poverty in 2005 was as follows:

- Sub-Saharan Africa—50.7%;
- Fragile and conflict-affected situations—44.7%;
- Low-income countries—33.3%;
- Low- and middle-income countries—25%;
- Latin America and the Caribbean—9.9%;
- Europe and Central Asia—4.9%;
- Middle East and North Africa—3%.[40]

It was upsetting that many continued to live in poverty and hunger, with limited to no access to healthcare, medicine, clean water, and other services. Similarly upsetting was that inequality remained between genders, households with different levels of income, urban and rural areas within countries and between countries, and the differences in environmental conditions between poor and rich. This was recognized on the eve of the 2012 UN Conference on Sustainable Development in Rio de Janeiro that decided to "make sustainable development a reality for seven billion people, and to define the future we want for nine billion by 2050."[41]

The poverty gap, or the amount of money that would be theoretically needed to lift the incomes of all people in extreme poverty up to the international poverty line of USD $1.90 a day, were predicted to go down to USD $161 billion in 2013, from $280 billion in 2005.[42] The global GDP in 2012 was estimated to be USD $71.2 trillion, of which the

---

37 *See generally id.*
38 *Id.*
39 *World Development Report 2006: Equity and Development*, WORLD BANK GROUP (Oxford University Press 2006), https://openknowledge.worldbank.org/handle/10986/5988.
40 *Global Extreme Poverty*, OUR WORLD IN DATA (2005), https://ourworldindata.org/extreme-poverty (last visited Dec. 8, 2020) (the figures account for differences in price levels, and for inflation; all estimates are in international dollars using 2011 purchasing power parities (PPP) conversion rates).
41 U.N. Conference on Sustainable Development, U.N. Doc. A/CONF.216/16 (Jun. 20–22, 2012).
42 *The Global Poverty Gap 1981–2013*, OUR WORLD IN DATA, https://ourworldindata.org/grapher/size-poverty-gap-world (last visited Dec. 10, 2020).

Sub-Saharan Africa region's share was barely 3%, while 96% belonged to regions which were unchallenged by extreme poverty.[43]

Given the global circumstances and comparatively moderate global GDP decline of 2.9%,[44] the 2008–2009 recession motivated the call to completely deal away with poverty and hunger. For the 2012 Rio Summit participants, it would have been an inexcusable political mistake not to take the lead.

When strategizing the Millennium Promise Alliance (with the mission to end extreme poverty and hunger), Jeffrey Sachs, then-UN-director overseeing the work on the MDGs, fortified the end-of-poverty goal and stretched the list of sustainable development objectives. In his work, *The End of Poverty: Economic Possibilities for Our Time* (2005) he proposed an annual spending of 0.7% of developed nations GDP per annum would be sufficient to end poverty in 15 years.[45] He encouraged debt relief for low-income countries (in 2005, the UN supported the aforementioned conduits to do so) and proposed immediate doubling (and then gradually increase to the quoted poverty gap assessments) of the annual development aid programs.[46] Similarly, the optimism was supported by the late Swedish statistician Hans Rosling, who by 2015 had become, if not a household name, a source of reference to political scientists from around the globe. His extrapolations made him a firm believer in ending poverty and as an advisor to the World Health Organization (WHO), UN High Commission for Refugees (UNHCR), and a collaborator of the UN Population Division, he managed to make others believe this objective was attainable. *Do Not Panic: How to End Poverty in 15 Years* (2015) was one of his last documentaries.[47] In this, summarizing his previous projections,[48] he closely linked poverty elevation to overcoming global demographic challenges.

Meanwhile, *Rethinking Poverty*, a 2010–2011 work by Sabina Alkirea and James Foster of the Oxford Poverty & Human Development Initiative (OPHI), proposed the Multidimensional Poverty Index (MPI).[49] The Multidimensional Poverty Index links monetary (consumption) measures of poverty with 10 human security indicators and HDRs, and is correlated with other SDG challenges.

The table below demonstrates the development by 2015.[50]

Population group	1990	2005	2015
Earth's population	5.31 bln	6.52 bln	7.35 bln
Not in extreme poverty	3.41 bln	5.17 bln	6.62 bln
In extreme poverty	1.9 bln	1.35	0.733 bln

43 Id.
44 See Ayhan Kose & Naotaka Sugawara, *Understanding the Depth of the 2020 Global Recession in 5 Charts*, WORLD BANK BLOG (Jun. 15, 2020), https://blogs.worldbank.org/opendata/understanding-depth-2020-global-recession-5-charts#.
45 JEFFREY SACHS, THE END OF POVERTY: ECONOMIC POSSIBILITIES FOR OUR TIME (Penguin Press, Dec. 30, 2005).
46 Id.
47 DON'T PANIC—HOW TO END POVERTY IN 15 YEARS (BBC 2015).
48 See Hans Rosling Ted Talks at www.gapminder.org; see also HANS ROSLING, FACTFULNESS: TEN REASONS WE'RE WRONG ABOUT THE WORLD—AND WHY THINGS ARE BETTER THAN YOU THINK (Flatiron Books 2018).
49 See Sabina Alkirea & James Foster, *Counting and Multidimensional Poverty Measurement*, 95(7–8) J. OF PUB. ECON. 476–87 (Aug. 2011) (note that the Annual MPI has been co-published by OPHI and UNDP since 2011).
50 Global Extreme Poverty, *supra* note 40.

The target of MDG 1—to halve the number of extreme poor—was therefore fully accomplished. This demonstrated that ambitious and aspirational global agendas can make a difference, irrespective of the global recession of 2008–2009.

Poverty Reduction in Ex-Communist Countries

It is well established that the population in extreme poverty has been declining globally mostly because China, since the 1980s, has promoted basic economic reforms that lifted a billion individuals out of extreme poverty. The unleashed growth in the last three decades in China reduced the number of extremely poor by 12–13 million per annum in China (India—by 2.7–2.8 million).[51] China is very likely to end extreme poverty in 2021or 2022. In 2020, its share of extremely poor is lower than that of the United States (1.6%).[52]

The Washington Consensus, despite very different country experience, was also the policy mix to bring down poverty in Eastern Europe and ex-USSR. In the last 20 years, the share of populations in extreme poverty (USD $1.90 per day) in some of these countries shrank by more than 10 times.[53] Today, only in Turkmenistan and Uzbekistan is it near 4%.[54] The other 27 countries have extreme poverty shares below 3%.[55] In all new EU member states (except for Romania –2%), ex-Yugoslav countries (except Macedonia –3%), and in Azerbaijan; Belarus; Kazakhstan; Kyrgyzstan; Moldova; Mongolia; Russia; and Ukraine, the extreme poverty headcount is below 1% of the population.[56] In 13 countries extreme poverty is practically extinguished.[57]

Below are the common economic policy denominators relevant for ex-communist countries:

- Definition, restoration, and protection of private property rights;
- Liberalization of trade, investment, and prices;
- No fancy industrial policies, keep public spending (most often) on track with revenues, streamlined and simplified taxes, adhere (with some exceptions) to sound monetary policies, and, except for the Eurasian Economic Union states and Ukraine, allow for completion in bank ownership;
- Globalize and integrate (politically and economically) with the EU and other centers of prosperity.

---

51 *See The Poverty Clock*, WORLDDATALAB (WDL), https://worlddata.io/ (demonstrating this effect per minute and tracks the progress of other SDGs in real time).
52 Zhao Hong, *China Is Set to End Absolute Poverty by 2020, What's Next?*, CGTN, (Oct. 17, 2020, https://news.cgtn.com/news/2020-10-17/China-is-set-to-end-absolute-poverty-by-2020-what-s-next--UF1rzv5WH6/index.html
53 Max Roser & Esteban Ortiz-Ospina, *Share of the Population Living in Extreme Poverty, 1977–2017*, OUR WORLD IN DATA (2013), https://ourworldindata.org/extreme-poverty; *Poverty Headcount Ratio at $1.90 a Day (2011 PPP) (% of Population)*, WORLD BANK, https://data.worldbank.org/indicator/SI.POV.DDAY (last visited Dec. 10, 2020) (Measures are most often available through the World Bank for the years after 1995, none of the countries had a statistical measure for the period before 1989 in Eastern Europe and before 1991 in ex-USSR. For the current situating we use WDL estimates.)
54 *Id.*
55 *Id.*
56 *Ibid.*
57 *Ibid.*

Similar policy mixes can be observed in China, or India, or such countries as Indonesia, Ghana, and Ethiopia, where the progress in reduction of poverty is also remarkable.

Most Eastern European countries kept their social safety nets unchanged but rationalized them instead (only Georgia abolished state pension and healthcare funds, and Kazakhstan introduced a Chilean-style pension reform). This is the key difference between China, India, and the fast-growing economies of East Asia and the Eastern European countries. Respectively, the governments' social spending differs substantially between the two groups of countries in transition. The labor markets are much freer in China and ex-USSR countries, respectively, youth unemployment was and still is lower.

What Eastern European countries spend on pensions, China spends on infrastructure. For the 2010–2015 period the average annual infrastructure investment here was 8.3% of the GDP, twice more than Russia, and three time more than the Organization for Economic Co-operation and Development (OECD) and East European countries.[58] Government spending on education is roughly the same in India, China, and Eastern Europe. Ten to fifteen years ago it was widely believed (by ADB, the International Labor Organization (ILO), UNDP, etc.) that such public investment would help in reducing poverty. The statistics suggest that there is a correlation, but there are no detailed recent studies.

The economic growth rates of all post-communist countries from the mid-1990s to 2009 was 2.5–3 times higher than growth rates in the EU or North America.[59] The global recession was sharp but short-lived, and then the pattern for these countries resumed in 2010–2011. Post-recession employment rates in Eastern Europe are at the highest historic levels, and wages grew relatively quickly. However, the East European growth rates, even for the boom period before 2008, were around 6% of GDP, far below China and India's growth in those years.[60]

The poverty reduction progress in individual ex-communist countries was as remarkable as in China: OUR WORLD IN DATA statistics reveal that the share of population in extreme poverty in Kyrgyzstan, Moldova, Georgia, and Kazakhstan 20 years ago was respectively 42.1, 38.5, 19.4, and 10.3%; now −1 or below 1%, in Georgia −3% at the beginning of 2020.[61]

There is one regularity evident from the experience of ex-communist countries: The faster economies liberalize, the faster the economic growth and poverty reduction.[62]

This is also evident in Bulgaria. In 1995 the share of the population in extreme poverty was 5.5%.[63] By March 1997 it grew to 36–37%, hardly affecting rural areas (about 47%), senior citizens and minorities (Roma—more than 80%; ethnic Turks—45%).[64]

The country was developing in the first half of the 1990s in parallel with Central European states. The trend was turned down by the 1995 government decision to support loss-making

---

58 See Raynor de Best, *Global Annual Spending on Infrastructure as Percent of GDP by Country 2010–2015*, STATISTA (Nov. 18, 2020), www.statista.com/statistics/566787/average-yearly-expenditure-on-econo mic-infrastructure-as-percent-of-gdp-worldwide-by-country/.
59 James Roaf et al., *25 Years of Transition Post-Communist Europe and the IMF*, INTERNATIONAL MONETARY FUND (IMF) (Oct. 2014).
60 *Id.* at 53.
61 Roser & Ospina, *supra* note 54.
62 IMF, *supra* note 66 (this was one of the key IMF findings in 2014).
63 BULGARIA: POVERTY DURING THE TRANSITION, WORLD BANK ii–v (1999).
64 *Id.*

state-owned enterprises. This led to a banking crisis[65] and hyperinflation. From April 1996 to March 1997 it was the highest in the world, ranking as the 17th highest inflation in the history of the 20th century.[66] From April to December 1996, real industrial wages were going down by 19% a month; in January 1997 the average monthly wage was USD $40 (the pension—$20).[67] In February, the average wage was USD $20 and $5 for pension.[68] Savings evaporated from 52% of GDP at the end of 1995 to 6% in March 1997.[69]

The economic crisis was resolved by stopping the printing press, reforming the central bank into a currency board, and, in a sense, returning to the original Washington Concusses – "growth is good for the poor."[70] The next poverty assessment found that by the end of 2001, the share of the population in extreme poverty shrank almost by two-thirds, to 12.8%.[71] "The improvement can be attributed to growth and the economic recovery, which has lifted the consumption levels of many households," pointed out the report.[72] "Despite the declining poverty rates, many Bulgarians feel that their living standards have not improved dramatically. Qualitative surveys suggest that nearly three-quarters of the population believe that they live in poverty."[73]

By 2017, the extreme poverty in Bulgaria had been gradually reduced to 1.3% and the multidimensional poverty measure was 1.7% of the population.[74] Before the COVID-19 pandemic hit the country, extreme poverty was already 1%.[75] The shock of 1996–1997, however, had a long-lasting stigma for the country—it is most often named in the press "the poorest EU country," and about 30% of Bulgarians are convinced they live in poverty.[76]

The trend of (non-extreme) poverty reduction was reversed in some countries even before the COVID-19 recession, irrespective of their economic potential. The case in point is Russia: Its national poverty rate is USD $3.20 a day (at 2011 international prices); in 2012 the share of the population under this threshold was 10.7%, in 2019—more than 14%—and this year, above 15%.[77] For the sake of comparison: Bulgaria's national poverty line is USD $5.50 a day, and in 2017, 7.5% of the population lived under this line.[78]

---

65 Helena Tang et al., *Banking Crises in Transition Countries: Fiscal Costs and Related Issues*, WORLD BANK 35 (2001) (in 1996 Bulgaria registered the costliest banking crisis in the transition –42% of GDP. Other countries had similar experiences: Macedonia –30% of GDP (due to a Greek blockade), Czech Republic –25% of GDP in 1998 (newly privatized firms stopped repaying credits), and Kyrgyzstan (18% of GDP) and Kazakhstan (10% of GDP) as an effect of the 1998 Russia government debt crisis).
66 *Id.*
67 *Id.*
68 *Ibid.*
69 *Ibid.*
70 David Dollar & Aart Kraay, *Growth Is Good for the Poor*, 7 J. OF ECON. GROWTH 195–225 (2002).
71 *Id.*
72 *Id.*
73 *Bulgaria: Poverty Assessment*, WORLD BANK (Oct. 29, 2002), https://openknowledge.worldbank.org/handle/10986/13868?locale-attribute=fr.
74 *Bulgaria: Poverty & Equity Brief*, WORLD BANK (Apr. 2020), https://databank.worldbank.org/data/download/poverty/33EF03BB-9722-4AE2-ABC7-AA2972D68AFE/Global_POVEQ_BGR.pdf .
75 *Id.*
76 *Id.*
77 *Id.*
78 *Bulgaria Poverty Rate 1992–20*, MACROTRENDS, www.macrotrends.net/countries/BGR/bulgaria/poverty-rate (last visited Dec. 9, 2020).

Progress in Implementing SDG 1 before COVID-19

In 2019, the SDG Report projected that the poverty line will go down to 8.2% of the global population.[79] The pace of progress had slowed down, and by 2030, the forecast is 6%.[80] It found, not only that the last margins are rather complex to be addressed in China and Eastern Europe, but the lack of social protection and insurance against natural disasters are especially visible in disparities between low-middle and low-income countries and the rest of the world.

If in the 1990s the extreme poverty was most visible in East and South Asia, now it is concentrated in Sub-Saharan Africa. The share of Sub-Saharan poor did not change between 2000 and 2015. It even grew after 2015, while other regions almost reached the point of ending extreme poverty.

As Duflo and Benerjee predicted in *Poor Economics*,[81] relying on general economic growth (the old Washington Consensus) for poverty reduction, turned out to be a low-hanging fruit. The World Bank forecasts that in 2030 almost 90% of the world's poorest will live in Sub-Saharan Africa if the last decade's pattern of economic growth is sustained.[82]

SDG 1 after COVID-19

COVID-19 swept away even the half-optimistic forecasts. The World Bank updated poverty projections for 2020 twice since the outbreak of the pandemic.

Latest projections, based on 2020 global economic growth assumptions,[83] show that the number of those living in poverty will increase by 71 to 100 million people. These are the unexpected "new poor," and they will move the poverty rate higher than the previously predicted 2020 level. These projections may well prove falsely optimistic. The 2020 multidimensional poverty line for the current poorest countries is 22%, and as the MPI states, this fact will negatively affect the progress in poverty elevation in 70 developing countries by bringing them back to the conditions of 2015 or even 2010.[84] Eighty-one million of the new poor could appear in Sub-Saharan Africa and South Asia; Europe and North America will be unaffected.[85]

The COVID-19 recession hit more countries than any other recession in the last 150 years with effects in 93% of the countries in the world.[86] The only precedent to compare this

---

79 *The Sustainability Development Goals Report 2019*, DEP. OF ECON. & SOC. AFFAIRS (DESA) (2019), https://unstats.un.org/sdgs/report/2019/ (SDG Report 2019).
80 *Id.* at 22.
81 Banjree & Duflo, *supra* note 19.
82 Divyanshi Wadhwa, *The Number of Extremely Poor People Continues to Rise in Sub-Saharan Africa*, WORLD BANK BLOGS (Sept. 19, 2018), https://blogs.worldbank.org/opendata/number-extremely-poor-people-continues-rise-sub-saharan-africa.
83 Daniel Gerszon Mahler et al., *Updated Estimates of the Impact of COVID-19 on Global Poverty*, WORLD BANK BLOG (Jun. 8, 2020), https://blogs.worldbank.org/opendata/updated-estimates-impact-covid-19-global-poverty; *see also Chapter 1, in* GLOBAL ECONOMIC PROSPECTS (GEP), WORLD BANK (June 2020).
84 Nishant Yonzan et al., *Projecting Global Extreme Poverty up to 2030: How Close Are We to World Bank's 3% Goal?*, WORLD BANK (Oct. 2020), https://blogs.worldbank.org/opendata/projecting-global-extreme-poverty-2030-how-close-are-we-world-banks-3-goal.
85 *Id.*
86 PAUL CORRAL ET AL., FRAGILITY AND VIOLENCE: ON THE FRONT LINES OF THE FIGHT AGAINST POVERTY (World Bank, 2020).

to is the Great Depression, with 84% of the world in 1933.[87] Historic reconstruction of the GDP dynamics suggests that all past recessions were not as sharp and deep as the world is experiencing now, and that underdeveloped regions suffered relatively modest declines in GDP.

"What began as a health crisis has quickly become the worst human and economic crisis in a lifetime," found the July 2020 session of the UN's Economic and Social Council (ESC).[88] In contrast to past losses of output due to pandemics, COVID-19's impact on developed economies will shrink more output than previously reconstructed GDP declines from the Spanish Flu (4.8%), the Asian Influenza (2% of GDP in 1957), or the Hong Kong Flu (1967–1969 –0.7%).[89] In July 2020, the European Commission estimated a 13.1% reduction in the European Union's GDP for the year, as well as decline in consumption and investment of 14.9% and 16.7%.[90] The poorest EU regions and households were most severely hit by lockdowns. EUROSTAT reported that on an annual basis the Eurozone GDP contracted by 12.1%, and that of the EU—by 11.9%.[91] The unprecedented economic slowdown in richer parts of the world will negatively affect the not so rich and the poorest regions.

Past recessions most often occurred for purely economic reasons: When people did not want to buy or could not afford to buy on a societal scale. The 2020 recession results from restrictions imposed on the human and physical factors of the economy. If the restrictions persist, the global economy could plunge even deeper, warned the June report on GEP.[92] For now, the baseline forecast is 5.2% contraction in global GDP in 2020.[93]

Lockdown policies depend on the perception of the threat, the inevitably limited knowledge about the virus, and the country's capacity to cope with the pandemic. All these factors are constantly subject to change. The UN, World Bank Group, OECD, EU, and regional and national institutions have updated their assessment of the situations at least three times since January.

According to the World Bank's June GEP, East Asia and Pacific, after a GDP decline of almost 8% since the beginning of the year, are expected to rebound by the year end.[94] Sub-Saharan Africa and South Asia, the regions of "old" and highest risk of "new" poor, will likely shrink by 2.8 and 2.7% of GDP, respectively.[95] For Eastern Europe and ex-USSR, a

---

87 *Id.*
88 *The Worst Crisis in a Lifetime*, *in* 33(65) SUMMARY OF THE 2020 MEETING OF THE HIGH-LEVEL POLITICAL FORUM ON SUSTAINABLE DEVELOPMENT, ECON. & SOC. COUNCIL (Jul. 20, 2020), https://enb.iisd.org/vol33/enb3365e.html.
89 *See* Andrew Burns et al., *Evaluating the Economic Consequences of Asian Influenza*, WORLD BANK (2009), www.researchgate.net/publication/237345628_Evaluating_the_Economic_Consequences_of_Avian_Influenza1.
90 *See European Economic Forecast, Summer 2020 (Interim)*, EUROPEAN COMMISSION, DIRECTORATE-GENERAL FOR ECONOMIC AND FINANCIAL AFFAIRS, EUROPEAN ECONOMY, Institutional Paper 132, https://ec.europa.eu/info/sites/info/files/economy-finance/ip132_en.pdf.
91 *GDP Down by 12.1% in the Euro Area and by 11.9% in the EU*, 121 NEWS RELEASE EURO INDICATORS (EUROSTAT Jul. 21, 2020), https://ec.europa.eu/eurostat/documents/2995521/11156775/2-3 1072020-BP-EN.pdf/cbe7522c-ebfa-ef08-be60-b1c9d1bd385b.
92 GEP June 2020, *supra* note 82.
93 *Id.* at 1.
94 *Id.* at 2.
95 *Id.* at 4.

decline by 4.7% is expected, and for the EU countries, more than 6% GDP.[96] The Middle East and North African economies look a bit worse with an average GDP decline of 6.2%.[97] The Latin American and Caribbean GDP forecast is a 7.2% decline.[98]

Like in previous pandemics, the poorer countries were less affected economically. The situation may change, however. For example, no 2020 GDP decline was expected in India, but mid-October statistics shows contraction of different sectors from between 9.2% (healthcare) to 23.1% (automotive industry).[99] These economies are expected to rebound in 2021. Sub-Saharan Africa (where the largest economies of Nigeria and South Africa were the hardest hit by the pandemic and experienced contracting economic activity) are forecasted to register the second-highest regional GDP growth in the world in 2021 (of 3.1%).[100] South Asia will, perhaps, grow modestly, because the largest economy of India is expected to decline by 3.2% in 2021.[101]

From historic pandemics, we know that they are socially "unbiased," and have killed princes and paupers, emperors and beggars with equal lack of mercy. The COVID-19 statistics so far paint a similar picture.

The 2019 Global Health Security Index (GHSI), a month before the outbreak of COVID-19, ranked "Best Prepared to Deal with a Pandemic;" the United States, the United Kingdom, and the Netherlands were at the top.[102] Poorer East European countries were far behind but still among the top 60 of 195 GHSI countries.[103] Nevertheless, according to the WHO Coronavirus Disease (COVID-19) Dashboard, the ex-communist countries registered less (typically around 10 per every 100,000 citizens) COVID-19 deaths compared to the "best" countries in the first 7 months.[104] Only Russia is an exception. There is a correlation between low number of deaths and historic specificities of these countries: Unreformed healthcare, high number of hospital beds per 100 thousand residents, long history of mass vaccinations, and high percentage of out-of-pocket payments, population density, and distanced lifestyles.[105] Except for Nigeria and South Africa, Sub-Saharan countries used to have as low rates of COVID-19 deaths as Eastern Europe.[106]

Some of these correlations are obviously valid for economically disadvantaged and poverty-distressed countries and regions. The John Hopkins University (JHU) COVID-19

---

96 *Ibid.*
97 *Ibid.*
98 *Ibid.*
99 Statista Research Department, *Estimated Impact from the Coronavirus (COVID-19) on India in 2020 by Market*, STATISTA (Oct. 18, 2020), www.statista.com/statistics/1111641/india-estimated-economic-impact-of-coronavirus-by-market/.
100 *WHO Coronavirus Disease (COVID-19) Dashboard*, WORLD HEALTH ORGANIZATION, https://covid19.who.int/?gclid=CjwKCAiAq8f-BRBtEiwAGr3DgUCMo7KYEKRVwwWoPV-pWS_utsZ5kMmpqIEp8Xjpc4CVIG7h1bnkcBoCn68QAvD_BwE (last visited Dec. 10, 2020); PANDEMIC, RECESSION: THE GLOBAL ECONOMY IN CRISIS, WORLD BANK GROUP FLAGSHIP REPORT (Jun. 2020), www.worldbank.org/en/publication/global-economic-prospects.
101 *Id.*
102 GLOBAL HEALTH SECURITY INDEX 2019: BUILDING COLLECTIVE ACTION AND ACCOUNTABILITY, NTI & JOHNS HOPKINS (2019), www.ghsindex.org/wp-content/uploads/2019/10/2019-Global-Health-Security-Index.pdf.
103 *Id.*
104 *See*, COVID-19 Dashboard, *supra* note 100.
105 Krassen Stanchev et al., *Health Security in Central Europe: Executive Summary*, VISEGRAD INSIGHT 34–43 (Marcin Zaborowski ed., Aug. 2020), https://visegradinsight.eu/human-security-in-central-europe/.
106 GEP June 2020, *supra* note 82.

database shows that confirmed infections (concentrated in five countries) are four times greater in Europe than in Africa (with a four times larger population).[107] And still the continent was the fastest growing economy of the world in the last five years and registered decent growth rates since 1990. The improvement of living standards is likely to be affected in the decades to come.

Still, the immediate future of poverty reduction remains at risk of deterioration due to the combined impact of the pandemic and the legacy of underdevelopment and missing safety nets. The July ESC report to the High-Level Political Forum of the UN summarized the following legacies and risks ahead of SDG 1:

- The poorest and the most vulnerable segments of the global population are being affected disproportionately by the pandemic;
- Seventy-one million such people are pushed back into extreme poverty in 2020; the 2020 and 2021 forecasts of extreme poor were downgraded to 8.8% and 8.7% of the population (from 7.7% and 7.4%, respectively);
- Vulnerable countries stand to be hit the hardest in the long term owing to the fragility of their health systems and due to the limited coverage of their social protection systems, limited financial and other resources, vulnerability to external shocks, and excessive dependence on international trade;
- Before the pandemic, the share of the world's workers living in extreme poverty fell, from 14.3% to 8.3% to 7.1% in 2010, 2015, and 2019, respectively, while progress was less encouraging for young workers. In 2019, 12.8% of the world's young workers lived in extreme poverty, compared with only 6% of all adult workers;
- Fifty-five percent of the world's population does not benefit from any form of social protection;
- Hurricanes, floods, earthquakes, wildfires, and other disasters exacerbate poverty. In 2018, 39 million were affected, 29 million of whom saw their livelihood disrupted or destroyed.[108]

COVID-19 is likely to bring about a synthesis of the recommendations of the two schools of thought about poverty, described above. This also includes the ESC conclusion that the data underscores the need for international solidarity and cooperation more than ever.

The good news is that even if the extreme poverty levels deteriorate, it is hardly possible that SDG 1 targets are back to the levels of before 2010. This expectation is justified by the fact that extreme poverty is concentrated in particular regions of the world, which have the potential to restore and sustain higher levels of economic growth than the rest of the world.

However, the main challenge is finding the policy mix that does not hamper economic growth. World Bank's GEP recommends massive but targeted government spending, and praises countries that seem able to mobilize resources for recovery of up to 10% of GDP

---

107 *Id.*; *Coronavirus Resource Center*, JOHNS HOPKINS UNIVERSITY OF MEDICINE, https://coronavirus.jhu.edu (last visited Dec. 10, 2020).
108 U.N. Secretary General, *Progress towards the Sustainable Development Goals*, U.N. Doc. E/2020/57 (Jul. 25, 2019–Jul. 22, 2020), https://documents-dds-ny.un.org/doc/UNDOC/GEN/N20/108/02/PDF/N2010802.pdf?OpenElement. (The report gives the following example about the differences between regions: "half of unemployed people in Australia and New Zealand receive unemployment payments, and 44% in Europe and Northern America. In contrast, just 3 per cent of the unemployed in sub-Saharan Africa and 12%in Latin America and the Caribbean receive such payments.")

or more, for expenditures that support and allow for economic freedom and innovation, productivity-driven growth, smart energy solutions, infrastructure and education spending with predicable if not inevitable positive externalities.[109]

When Benerjee and Duflo wrote that "low hanging fruits" in poverty reduction are over,[110] this was true for positive externalities from economic growth. In a sense we are back to the challenge to "inquire into the nature and causes of the wealth of nations."[111] The institutional requirement for good public governance and integrity remains even more valid than before COVID-19.

The problem here is two-fold. The pandemic blocked the human and physical factors of the economy and the government response everywhere is to peddle up the spending and monetary side of the economy. Irrespective of how one defines "targeted" spending policies, higher government expenditures to GDP entail risk of misrule and corruption. The entire criticism of foreign aid is not only still valid but reinforced. Easterly wrote that "foreign aid has on average probably no effect on long-run growth."[112] He echoed Sen's trust in democracy as a universal value, stating that "we need to convince many more that all people everywhere—women and men, black and white, rich and poor—deserve to be free at last."[113]

Benerjee, Duflo, and Kramer's experimental approach to poverty elevation is reiterated. The personal understanding and motivation for well-being is not a standard cost-benefit analysis. This is a well-established fact that values we assign to things are totally subjective and there is no objective accounting for individual preferences. Angus Deaton won a Nobel Prize in 2015 for his analysis of consumption, poverty, and welfare. Despite setbacks, this approach to ending poverty is practical, localized, and involves the endeavors of the poor themselves. It is likely to make a difference again.

Reversals of Fortune

The effects of the post-COVID-19 recession will be felt in many countries for many years, probably until 2030. There is no doubt that the zeroing of extreme poverty (SDG 1) will not be met. Even the less ambitious goal of bringing the absolute poverty rate to less than 3% by 2030 is also harder to reach. The World Bank Poverty and Shared Prosperity (PSP) Report 2018[114] showed the slowing pace of poverty reduction before the COVID-19 crisis. The sustained decline in extreme poverty was stalling between 2015 and 2017, when the number of people worldwide living below the poverty line fell from 741 million to 689 million.[115] Globally, extreme poverty dropped by an average of about 1 percentage point per year over the quarter of a century from 1990 to 2015, but the rate of decline slowed from

---

109 GEP June 2020, *supra* note 82.
110 Banjree & Duflo, *supra* note 19.
111 *Id.*
112 WILLIAM EASTERLY, ECONOMICS OF INTERNATIONAL DEVELOPMENT 16 (IEA, 2016).
113 *Id.*
114 *PSP Report 2018: Piecing Together the Poverty Puzzle*, WORLD BANK (2018), www.worldbank.org/en/publication/poverty-and-shared-prosperity-2018
115 *Id.*

2013 to 2015 to just 0.6% per year.[116] Between 2015 and 2017, the rate slowed further, to half a percentage point.[117]

The latest World Bank Poverty and Shared Prosperity Report 2020 under the title *Reversals of Fortune*[118] analyzed how poverty will be affected by three factors: (1) the COVID-19 pandemic and the associated global economic recession, (2) armed conflict, steadily growing in recent years,[119] and (3) climate change, a slowly accelerating risk that may potentially drive millions into poverty. COVID-19 alone is expected to increase extreme poverty by approximately 100 million people. Armed conflict is driving poverty up in some regions. In the Middle East and North Africa, extreme poverty rates nearly doubled between 2015 and 2018, from 3.8% to 7.2%, mainly spurred by the conflicts in Syria and Yemen.[120] Most worrisome, climate change may bring 132 million more people into poverty by 2030, exposed to the intertwined vulnerability to various climate-related threats such as extreme weather events (flooding, droughts, fires), land degradation, vector-borne diseases, fish scarcity, etc.

What lessons and recommendations can we summarize?

1. **Closing the gap between policy and capacity**. Sound policies are crucial but are not sufficient to tackle tough challenges. As challenges in reaching and responding to the poorest communities intensify, progress requires leadership fully committed not simply to financial support, but to build robust implementation systems and political accountability. Lucy Page and Rohini Pande explained well why money is not enough to end poverty,[121] pointing to the importance of providing complementary support factors (hungry children will struggle to learn even in well-equipped schools if they don't have food support). As the implementation capability in most low-income economies has been stagnant or declining in recent years, much more attention needs to be given not just to getting policies right, but to building the capability of the administrative systems tasked with implementing them.

2. **Enhancing learning and improving data**. With unprecedented scientific, organizational, and societal uncertainty provoked by COVID-19, governments need to learn—and quickly—how to identify, enact, and scale up effective, context-specific responses. Development experience itself can supply evidence on promising approaches and common pitfalls, so it is important to remain open to innovation, no matter where it comes from, and to share it. Diverse response and recovery strategies now unfolding around the world will generate vast quantities of data and opportunities for learning. Data limitations create doubt among the public, obstruct scientific progress, and hinder the implementation of sound, evidence-based policies. If captured and curated, data from the crisis response can guide rapid corrections in policy and inform future action on core development problems. Accessible, high-quality data is a public good whose importance increases during crises.

---

116 *Id.*
117 *Ibid.*
118 *PSP Report 2020: Reversals of Fortune*, WORLD BANK (2020), https://openknowledge.worldbank.org/bitstream/handle/10986/34496/211602ov.pdf
119 Corral et al., *supra* note 86.
120 *Id.*
121 Lucy Page & Rohini Pande, *Ending Global Poverty: Why Money Isn't Enough*, 32(4) J. OF ECON. PERSPECTIVES 173–200 (Fall 2018).

3. **Invest in preparedness and prevention**. COVID-19, armed conflict, and climate change underscore the need to invest in comprehensive preparedness and prevention. Multilateral agencies, including the Global Facility for Disaster Reduction and Recovery, are already active in this area. Successful international cooperation in disaster preparedness exists in the Indian Ocean Tsunami Warning and Mitigation System (IOTWMS). Following the 2004 earthquake and tsunami, Australia, India, Indonesia, Malaysia, and Thailand moved to set up their own warning centers but initially struggled to coordinate their work. After years of negotiations, technical challenges, and persistent shared efforts, IOTWMS became fully operational in 2013, and similar regional warning systems have also been created in the Mediterranean and the Caribbean.
4. **Expanding cooperation and coordination**. Cooperation and coordination are vital, not only to improve the empirical foundations of policy making, but to nurture social solidarity in affected countries and communities and ensure that decisions are both trusted and trustworthy. Strikingly different levels of cooperation and coordination are evident in the ways in which countries and local jurisdictions have responded to COVID-19 to date—some with decisive collective action from the outset, others hesitating or denying the threat until the pandemic has far advanced.

5 Critical Assessment of the Latest Progress in Eradication of Extreme Poverty

Aisha Muhammed-Oyebode

Introduction

The world entered the new millennium with ambitious global thinking fixated on extreme poverty eradication. This thinking dominated the agendas of international governance institutions, who successfully courted the attention of global powers to this end. The Millennium Development Goals (MDGs) of 2000 were the first tangible expression of this new collective effort and were implemented until 2015, when the Sustainable Development Goals (SDGs) replaced them. The SDG indicators presented a more robust approach but shared with the MDGs the focus on poverty eradication. This first agenda item of both goals underscored the singular importance of poverty eradication as a prerequisite to achieving a just and better world.

This chapter assesses the global progress or regress made with extreme poverty eradication through Sustainable Development Goal 1. The first section, "A Journey to End Poverty: Global Dynamics of the Sustainable Development Goals" provides a background to the study with emphasis on the features and trends of global extreme poverty. The second section, "Crossing the Poverty Line: Assessment of Global Regress" assesses Goal 1 using the targets and indicators, while the third section, "A Case for Africa Through Nigeria" presents a global assessment of targets 1.1, 1.3, and 1.5. These respectively cover the issues of global populations living below the international poverty line; social protection for the most vulnerable; and the unique susceptibility of poor people to extreme events and disasters. Further, the third section does a country-level assessment of targets 1.2, 1.A, and 1.B using Nigeria as a case study. The targets respectively provide for issues such as populations living in poverty according to national definitions and government spending on poverty programs, essential services, and sectors that disproportionately benefit vulnerable groups.

In both sections, the challenges facing the realization of Goal 1, both in Nigeria and at the international level are also examined. These challenges range from low economic growth and recession for Low-Income Countries (LICs); political instability; fragile statehood and conflicts; inadequate financing to fund social investment programs by national governments; inadequate political will; climate change; and the severe adverse effects of COVID-19 in LICS.

In addition, both sections conclude by offering policy recommendations and strategies to expedite the achievement of a world without extreme poverty. The concrete actions range from raising the income of farmers, expanding the coverage of social protection policies, increasing development aid targeted at the world's poorest, and building the resilience of the poor to extreme events and shocks. For Nigeria, specifically, it is important that the country structurally transforms and industrializes, expanding the existing social protection structures with a comprehensive legal framework that addresses systemic insecurity.

The findings show that, first, despite the significant progress made with extreme poverty eradication globally in the past three decades, current estimates still suggest that the world will not achieve the target of 3% extreme poverty reduction by 2030. Second, global social protection coverage for the most vulnerable groups is poor, and worse in Sub-Saharan Africa (SSA). Third, Nigeria will find it difficult to reduce by half, the proportion of its population living in extreme poverty by 2030. This is significant because Nigeria has one-sixth of Africa's population, as well as the highest proportion of the population of the extreme poor globally. With two-thirds of the world's extreme poor in SSA, not much progress can be recorded toward achieving Goal 1 if the macroeconomic situation in Nigeria does not improve. Financially, Nigeria's budgetary allocations to the health and education sectors declined in the first five SDGs years; however, the country has instituted a social investment program that targets vulnerable groups, and increased spending that disproportionately benefits women and the poor, though it might be too soon to observe the effects of these reforms.

A Journey to End Poverty: Global Dynamics of the Sustainable Development Goals

September 2000 witnessed the gathering of world leaders from 189 nations at the headquarters of the United Nations.[1,2] The purpose was the epochal signing of the Millennium Declaration. During that historic gathering, they identified eight measurable goals which included reducing extreme poverty by half; eliminating gender disparity in primary and secondary education; reducing by two-thirds the under-five mortality rate; and reducing by three-quarters the maternal mortality ratio. 2015 was the focus date and 166 Millennium Village Projects (MVPs) were established across the globe to realize this. Despite progress, the RIO+20 Conference commenced the process of developing new sets of Sustainable Development Goals to proliferate the global mandate of the MDGs beyond the terminal date of 2015. Tagged "The Future We Want," it gave coherence to the SDGs, amalgamating them with the United Nation's (UN's) post-2015 development agenda.[3]

The Millennium Development Goals had been criticized for being applicable only to developing countries, thus, history was once again made as the world witnessed the gathering of leaders at the headquarters of the United Nations, after one of the most robust and widespread consultative processes ever in history, for the signing of the SDGs. These new goals were as robust as they were ambitious. Seventeen broad goals covering most human development requisites as a lever to ensure their feasibility. Supreme on this broad global agenda again was poverty as Goal 1. The mandate was that by the year 2030, extreme poverty would have been totally eradicated for all people across the globe, living below that stipulated $1.90 a day.[4]

---

1 *Overview of Poverty, in* Poverty Reduction, JAPAN INT'L. COOPERATION AGENCY, (2002), www.jica.go.jp/jica-ri/IFIC_and_JBICI-Studies/english/publications/reports/study/topical/approaches/pdf/poverty_01.pdf.
2 Andy Haines & Andrew Cassels, *Can the Millennium Development Goals Be Attained?*, 7462 BRITISH MED. J. 139, 394–7 (2004).
3 *Goal 1: No Poverty*, UNITED NATIONS DEVELOPMENT PROGRAMME (UNDP), www.undp.org/content/undp/en/home/sustainable-development-goals/goal-1-no-poverty.html (last visited Dec. 2, 2020).
4 *The Sustainability Developmental Goals Report 2019*, DEP. OF ECON & SOC. AFFAIRS at 22 (2019), https://unstats.un.org/sdgs/report/2019/ (SDG Report).

What Does Poverty Really Mean?

Poverty as a concept is a highly contested socio-economic discourse, often defined by the philosophy and principles of the engagement of the term and as constructed by the subjectivities of the society's norms and values. Two major approaches to the definition of poverty are understood to include that of *income* poverty and *capability* poverty. The former lays emphasis on income and consumption, while the latter focuses on capability deprivation.[5] Following this, in the 1995 report of the World Summit for Social Development, the United Nations defined extreme poverty as a condition characterized by critical deprivation of basic human needs such as food, safe drinking water, health, shelter, sanitation facilities, education, and information.[6] According to this definition, the manifestation of poverty does not only depend on income but also on access to services, which converges with the capability thesis.

Quantitatively, and to provide universal measurement, the World Bank has continuously set an international poverty line (IPL). Updated in 2015, the IPL was pegged at \$1.90/day, which in 2011 prices is equivalent to \$2.16 in 2019.[7] Anyone living below the IPL benchmark is deemed extremely poor. Centuries ago, most of the world's population lived in extreme poverty;[8] however by 2006, this had fallen to 20%; a drastic reduction to a figure of over 80% in 1800.[9] In magnifying this, it is estimated that the numbers fell from 1.9 billion extremely poor people in 1990 to 1.2 billion in 2008, and then to 734 million in 2015.[10] The latest figure represents 9.6% of the global population, indicating that significant progress has been made globally in the fight against extreme poverty.[11] However, despite the fall in absolute figures of poverty, the pace of decline has decelerated sharply in recent years. After rates fell from 1990 to 2008 to 2015 of 36% to 16% to 9.6%, respectively, the assessment for 2018 was 8.6%.[12]

Geographic variations in extreme poverty remain pronounced (see Table 5.1).

Caveats at this juncture are essential. Firstly, the overall decrease is to be attributed to the sustained high rate of economic growth of countries such as China in the past three decades. Between 1981 and 2015, more than 850 million Chinese people have been lifted out of extreme poverty with the country's poverty rate falling from 88% to 0.7% within this

---

5 *See* Amartya Sen, *Assessing Human Development*, Human Development Reports, UNDP, www.hdr.undp.org/en/content/assessing-human-development (last visited Dec. 3, 2020). These deprivations could be political, socio-cultural, economic, human, and protective. They are based on the views of Amartya Sen. The UNDP focuses on capabilities while creating the Human Development Report: HDR.
6 *Report of the World Summit for Social Development*, UN A/CONF.166/9 (Mar. 6–12, 1995), https://undocs.org/pdf?symbol=en/a/conf.166/9 (World Summit).
7 *Poverty and Shared Prosperity 2020*, WORLD BANK, www.worldbank.org/en/publication/poverty-and-shared-prosperity.
8 *See generally* Jan Luiten van Zanden et al,. *The Changing Shape of Global Inequality— Exploring a New Dataset*, Working Papers 0001, UTRECHT U., CENTRE FOR GLOBAL ECON. HIST. (2011), https://ideas.repec.org/p/ucg/wpaper/0001.html.
9 Zach Beauchamp, *The World's Victory over Extreme Poverty, in One Chart*, VOX, (Dec. 14, 2014), www.vox.com/2014/12/14/7384515/extreme-poverty-decline.
10 *Principles and Practice in Measuring Global Poverty*, THE WORLD BANK (Jan. 13, 2016), www.worldbank.org/en/news/feature/2016/01/13/principles-and-practice-in-measuring-global-poverty.
11 *World Bank: Extreme Poverty "to Fall Below 10%,"* BBC NEWS WORLD (Oct. 5, 2015), www.bbc.com/news/world-34440567.
12 SDG Report, *supra* note 4, at 4.

Table 5.1 Numbers living in extreme poverty across global regions, 2013.

Number of people in extreme poverty $1.90/day	Regions
383 million	Africa
327 million	Asia
19 million	South America
13 million	North America
2.5 million	Oceania
0.7 million	Europe

Source: World Bank 2016 using 2013 household survey data. Max Roser & Esteban Ortiz-Ospina, *Global Extreme Poverty*, OUR WORLD IN DATA (2013), https://ourworldindata.org/extreme-poverty#the-evolution-of-extreme-poverty-country-by-country; *Poverty Headcount Ratio at $1.90 a Day (2011 PPP) (% of Population)—China*, THE WORLD BANK, https://data.worldbank.org/indicator/SI.POV.DDAY?locations=CN (last visited Dec. 2, 2020).

timeframe.[13] This juxtaposes with several other countries in other regions of the world, in particular SSA still has a vast majority of its populations living in extreme poverty, experiencing little alleviation. SSA alone accounts for over half of the world's extremely poor with 383 million of the 734 million figures of 2015.[14]

Further, women, people with disabilities, ethnic and linguistic minorities, children, and indigenous people are all disproportionately represented in extremely poor populations.[15] Even in cases where many have managed to escape extreme poverty, macro or micro-level shocks or setbacks can send poverty rates back up.[16] These shocks range from volatile capital flows, global market and commodities fluctuations, climatic patterns, natural disasters, pandemics, such as COVID-19, and prolonged conflicts, in particular unending insurgencies caused by terrorism. The consequences of these shocks are particularly dire for those with few resources or abilities to cope, as they progressively become risk challenged. Inequalities become exacerbated, even in countries with notable progress, as divisions based on class, gender, and geography continue to widen.

Crossing the Poverty Line: Assessment of Global Regress

The MDG goal of halving extreme poverty was met five years ahead of schedule;[17] with much of the credit being attributed to China's sustained economic growth, and the pace of growth in countries like Indonesia and Vietnam. The SDGs on the other hand, brought in new elements to the programming framework of the development agenda. Firstly, the

---

13 *Id.*
14 Divyanshi Wadhwa, *The Number of Extremely Poor People Continues to Rise in Sub-Saharan Africa*, WORLD BANK (Sept. 19, 2018), https://blogs.worldbank.org/opendata/number-extremely-poor-people-continues-rise-sub-saharan-africa.
15 *Ending Poverty by 2030: UNDP's Perspective and Role*, UNDP (Mar. 2016), www.undp.org/content/dam/undp/library/Sustainable%20Development/ISSUE_BRIEF_Ending_Poverty_by_2030.pdf.
16 Luis F. Lopez-Calva & Eduardo Ortiz-Juarez, *A Vulnerability Approach to the Definition of the Middle Class*, 12 J. OF ECON. INEQUALITY 23–47 (2014) (this 5-year study in Chile, Mexico, and Peru found that the probability of backsliding into poverty decreased as incomes rose but remained significant even at incomes twice the poverty line).
17 *See generally 2015 Millennium Development Goals Report*, THE UNITED NATIONS (2015), www.un.org/millenniumgoals/2015_MDG_Report/pdf/MDG%202015%20rev%20(July%201).pdf (MDG Report).

goals are interconnected with a list of goals measured against 169 targets and 232 indicators. These many-faceted measures lay emphasis on a multi- and transdisciplinary approach attempting to converge the economic, socio-political, and environmental sectors. Secondly, they prioritize gender equality and the empowerment of women with the forewarning that progress on all the SDGs will be stalled if gender equality and women's empowerment are not holistically given precedence by the diverse stakeholders involved.[18] In addition, while the MDGs were only applicable to developing countries, the SDGs apply to every country and region. This is partly because the goals included commitments that affect climate change and environmental degradation, which are primarily a product of greenhouse gas emissions by industries which are predominantly in the developed world.

SDG implementations began worldwide in January 2016. In localizing the goals, governments, individuals, civil society organizations, universities, institutions, and organizations at all levels began mobilizing at the same time. Governments began translating the goals into national legislation, developing plans of action, and establishing budgets while searching for implementation partners. In 2014, the United Nations Conference on Trade and Development (UNCTAD) estimated the annual costs of achieving the SDGs at $2.5 trillion per year.[19]

Unpacking SDG 1: Targets and Indicators

SDG Goal 1 is to achieve a target of less than 3% of the world's population living in extreme poverty by 2030.[20] As of 2018, this percentage was at 8.6%, which requires a global catch up of 5.6% in the next 9 years.[21] However, baseline projections already suggest that the 3% will not be met following estimations that 6% of the world population will still be living in extreme poverty by 2030.[22]

Target 1.1 focuses on extreme poverty eradication for all people everywhere by 2030 using the proportion of the population living below the poverty line while taking cognizance of the issues of gender, age, and geographical classifications. Following this, target 1.2 looks at the national definitions of poverty and its dimensionality,[23] and provides for the reduction of at least half the proportion of men, women, and children of all ages living in poverty in all its dimensions according to national definitions. Target 1.3 calls for the implementation of nationally appropriate social protection systems and measures for all, including floors, and to achieve by 2030, substantial coverage of the poor and the vulnerable.

This is to be achieved by enhancing the capacity of the poor and vulnerable to manage socio-economic risks, such as unemployment, exclusion, sickness, disability, and old age.[24]

---

18 *Gender Equality and Women's Rights in the Post-2015 Agenda: A Foundation for Sustainable Development*, 3(1) OECD, www.oecd.org/dac/gender-development/POST-2015%20Gender.pdf (last visited Dec. 2, 2020).
19 *Developing Countries Face $2.5 Trillion Annual Investment Gap in Key Sustainable Development Sectors, UNCTAD Report Estimates*, UNCTAD/Press/PR/2014/021 (Jun. 24, 2014), https://unctad.org/en/pages/PressRelease.aspx?OriginalVersionID=194.
20 Roser & Ortiz-Ospina, *supra* note 13.
21 *Id.*
22 SDG Report, *supra* note 4.
23 This is an improvement from MDG 1. This brings in the domestication effect for country-level planning on poverty reduction using national poverty lines.
24 *See generally Social Protection Sector Strategy: From Safety Net to Springboard*, WORLD BANK GROUP, THE INT'L BANK FOR RECONSTRUCTION & DEVELOP. (Jan. 2001), http://documents.worldbank.org/curated/en/299921468765558913/pdf/multi-page.pdf.

These risks critically affect the capability of those concerned to work and earn a living and provide for themselves and their dependents.

Target 1.4 focuses on ensuring that all men and women, in particular the poor and the vulnerable, have equal rights to economic resources, as well as access to basic services, ownership and control over land and other forms of property, including inheritance, natural resources, appropriate new technology, and financial services, as well as microfinance. Target 1.5 provides for building the resilience of the poor and those in vulnerable situations and reducing their exposure and vulnerability to climate-related extreme events and other economic, social, and environmental shocks and disasters. Finally, target 1.A[25] and 1.B[26] focus on resource allocation to poverty programs, essential services, and sectors that disproportionately benefit the poor.

Targets 1.1, 1.3, and 1.5 and their consequent indicators are used for the global assessment in the following subsection, while targets 1.2, 1.A, and 1.B are used for the country-level assessment in the next section using Nigeria as a case study. Target 1.4 is excluded from the analysis.[27]

Unpacking SDG 1: Global Performance against IPL

In the last 3 decades, the number of people living in extreme poverty fell from 1.9 billion in 1990 to 1.6 billion in 2002, 1.2 billion in 2008, 794 million in 2013, and then to 734 million in 2015.[28] Respectively, this is a fall from 36% in 1990, 26% in 2002, 18% in 2008, 11.2% in 2013, and 9.6% in 2015.[29] Although remarkable prima facie, the path remains rocky and the international community must remain vigilant. Using the 2015 IPL of $1.90/day adjusted to 2019 dollars, of $2.16, 600 million people still live in extreme poverty, with 70% of them residing in Africa.[30] Between 2002 and 2012, the populations living below the poverty line dropped by half, from 26% to 13%.[31] If such a commendable rate during those 10 years would hold sway for the next 15 years, the global extreme poverty rate would likely fall to 4% by 2030, close to the 3% target for Goal 1. This assumes that the growth process is inclusive and benefits all income groups of the population equally. However, if the rate over

---

25 Target 1.A: Ensure significant mobilization of resources from a variety of sources, including through enhanced development cooperation, in order to provide adequate and predictable means for developing countries and least developed countries, to implement programs and policies to end poverty in all its dimensions.
26 Target 1.B: Create sound policy frameworks at the national, regional, and international levels, based on pro-poor and gender-sensitive development strategies, to support accelerated investment in poverty eradication actions.
27 The exclusion is partly because of the SDGs' inter-connectedness: Target 1.4 elements are assessed/discussed in other chapters under SDGs (2—Zero Hunger, 6—Good Health and Well-being, 7—Quality Education and 9—Clean Water and Sanitation). Another reason for the exclusion is that the target could not have been successfully assessed using Nigeria as a case-study, because there is less explicit data on Nigerian households that have access to basic services. Also challenging is the non-availability of clear-cut land tenure and ownership demographics at both the global level and national level in Nigeria.
28 *See* MDG Report, *supra* note 18.
29 SDG Report, *supra* note 4, at 4.
30 Homi Kharas et al., *The Start of a New Poverty Narrative*, BROOKINGS (Jun. 19, 2018), www.brookings.edu/blog/future-development/2018/06/19/the-start-of-a-new-poverty-narrative/.
31 *Goal 1: End Poverty in All Its Forms Everywhere*, Dep. of Econ. & Soc. Affairs, https://unstats.un.org/sdgs/report/2016/goal-01/ (last visited Dec. 3, 2020).

the longer period of 20 years is extrapolated, the global poverty rate will likely be around 6%, farther away from the 2030 benchmark.[32]

The optimism gets more stilted when we move from globalized to localized poverty. Consider again SSA. There, the encouraging trends are reversed, as the number of extremely poor people living in SSA has actually been increasing, from 278 million in 1990 to 413 million in 2015, an increase of nearly 50%.[33] "In 2015, SSA was home to 27 of the world's 28 poorest countries and itself had more extremely poor people than did the rest of the world combined."[34] The average IPL rate for SSA in 2015 stood at 41%, whereas in all other regions combined it was below 13%.[35] Most recent evidence puts the SSA below-IPL rate at 70%.[36] The World Bank estimates that by 2030, 9 out of every 10 extremely poor people in the world will be living in SSA.[37]

Unpacking SDG 1: Resilience and Exposure to Vulnerability[38]

Disaster risk reduction and reducing the poor's exposure and vulnerability to climate-related events and other socio-economic and environmental shocks and disasters are essential to stimulating sustainable development and ending poverty. Disaster risk is disproportionally higher in poorer countries with weaker institutions and infrastructure. In low- and lower-middle-income countries experiencing rapid economic growth, the exposure of people and assets to natural hazards is increasing at a pace faster than that which risk-reducing capacities are being instituted and strengthened. This leads to increased disaster risk. In addition, populations in extreme poverty are increasingly found living in situations and fragile locations such as conflict zones that are difficult to reach. Indeed, conflict has continuously become the most overwhelming barrier to poverty eradication.

For indicator 1.5.2,[39] economic losses from globally reported disasters, primarily large-scale disasters, have grown steadily since 1990. In 2013, the annual cost was an estimated $200 billion.[40] In 2017, it reached $300 billion/year.[41] This was primarily because of the three major hurricanes that affected the United States of America[42] and several countries

---

32 SDG Report, *supra* note 4, at 4.
33 *Id.*
34 *Id.*
35 *Ibid.*
36 Kristofer Hamel et al., *Poverty in Africa Is Now Falling—but Not Fast Enough*, Brookings (Mar. 28, 2019), www.brookings.edu/blog/future-development/2019/03/28/poverty-in-africa-is-now-falling-but-not-fast-enough/.
37 Donna Barne & Divyanshi Wadhwa, *Year in Review: 2018 in 14 Charts*, WORLD BANK (last updated Dec. 12, 2018), www.worldbank.org/en/news/feature/2018/12/21/year-in-review-2018-in-14-charts.
38 Building the resilience of the poor and those in vulnerable situations and reducing their exposure and vulnerability to climate-related extreme events and other economic, social, and environmental shocks and disasters.
39 Indicator 1.5.2: Direct disaster economic loss in relation to global gross domestic product.
40 Statista Research Department, *Natural Disaster Losses Cost Worldwide 2000–2020*, STATISTA (Nov. 5, 2020), www.statista.com/statistics/612561/natural-disaster-losses-cost-worldwide-by-type-of-loss/.
41 *The Sustainable Development Goals Report 201*, DEP. OF ECON & SOC. AFFAIRS at 4 (2018), https://unstats.un.org/sdgs/files/report/2018/TheSustainableDevelopmentGoalsReport2018-EN.pdf.
42 The three big hurricanes of 2017 are Harvey, Irma, and Maria which brought widespread death and destruction to Texas, Florida, Puerto Rico, and the US Virgin Islands. According to the National Oceanic and Atmospheric Administration, the hurricanes are now three of the five costliest hurricanes in US history. Harvey ranks second with damage costs of $125 billion, Hurricane Maria ranks third at $90

across the Caribbean.[43] The result was damage to schools, homes, healthcare facilities, and agricultural production. In relation to economic sizes, small island states have borne a disproportionate impact.

In its 2019 Sustainable Development Goals Report, the United Nations estimated that from 1998 to 2017, economic losses from disasters were estimated at $3 trillion, of which climate-related disasters took 77% of this total.[44] This was a rise of 151% in comparison with the period from 1978 to 1997, when geophysical and climate-related disasters claimed an estimated 1.3 million lives.[45] These economic losses are also much higher in LICs, when measured as a percentage of their gross domestic product (GDP). Among the 10 worst disasters in terms of economic damage, 8 occurred in low- or middle-income countries.[46]

Under indicator 1.5.1,[47] the United Nations estimated that as of 2017, more than 90% of deaths reported globally were due to disaster events in low- and middle-income countries.[48] War, persecution, and violence worldwide led to the displacement of 65.6 million[49] people from their homes by the end of 2016.[50] This represents an increase of about 300,000 people since 2015, and the highest level recorded in decades.[51]

Lastly, examining the progress made under indicator 1.5.3,[52] the United Nations reported that in line with the Sendai Framework for Disaster Risk Reduction 2015–2030, country-level progress has been reported in the development and implementation of national and local disaster risk reduction strategies. As of 2019, 67 countries had reported progress in such alignment, from which 24 countries reported that their respective local governments had developed local strategies consistent with national strategies and plans.[53]

Global Challenges

The analysis in the previous section highlights a few challenges that affect the realization of target 1.5.[54] Firstly, statehood fragility, resulting from the pervasiveness of international conflicts and violence, displaced 65.6 million[55] people from their homes by the end of 2016. Secondly, climate change is a major constraint to extreme poverty eradication. Thirdly, the

---

billion, and Irma ranks fifth at $50 billion. *See* Office of Costal Mgmt., *Fast Facts: Hurricane Costs*, NAT'L OCEANIC & ATMOSPHERIC ADMIN., https://coast.noaa.gov/states/fast-facts/hurricane-costs.html (last visited Dec. 3, 2020).

43 Doyle Rice, *2017's Three Monster Hurricanes—Harvey, Irma and Maria—among Five Costliest Ever*, USA TODAY (Jan. 30, 2018), www.usatoday.com/story/weather/2018/01/30/2017-s-three-monster-hurricanes-harvey-irma-and-maria-among-five-costliest-ever/1078930001/.
44 SDG Report, *supra* note 4, at 23.
45 *Id*. at 16.
46 *Id*. at 21.
47 Indicator 1.5.1: Number of deaths, missing persons, and persons affected by disaster per 100,000 people.
48 SDG Report, *supra* note 4, at 21.
49 Of these, 22.5 million were refugees, 40.3 million were internally displaced, and 2.8 million were asylum seekers. *See Trends at a Glance*, UNHCR, www.unhcr.org/globaltrends2016/ (last visited Dec. 3, 2020).
50 *Id*.
51 *Id*.
52 Indicator 1.5.3: Number of countries with national and local disaster risk reduction strategies.
53 SDG Report, *supra* note 4, at 48.
54 Target 1.5: Resilience of the poor and those in vulnerable situations and their exposure to vulnerability.
55 UNHCR, *supra* note 50.

economic loss to climate and environmental disasters reached a record high of $300 billion/year according to the United Nations, with mostly low-income countries affected.[56] The implication of these shocks on livelihoods and incomes of the extreme poor remains high and threaten the realization of Goal 1.

In addition, low economic growth in the poorest countries of the world, a majority of which are primarily export dependent, are more susceptible to commodity price fluctuations. This primarily affects target 1.1. Adding to this challenge is the COVID-19 global economic crisis, which has affected commodity prices, occasioned job losses, halted livelihoods, considering the magnitude of the informal sector in LICs, and pushed more people down the extreme poverty bracket. This will directly affect SSA, the region with two-thirds of the world's most extreme poor.[57] Based on 2020 predictions, the economic effects of the pandemic are expected to plunge the region into recession, with economic growth contraction in that year estimated to be between −2.1% to as low as −5.1%.[58] This will dim the global goal of extreme poverty eradication by 2030 – for instance, the recessive reduction in government revenues will affect funding for poverty programs and essential sectors across many SSA countries.

Away from the pandemic's economic effects are also the adverse effects it is having on health and educational sectors—two essential sectors that directly affect the lives of the poor. In a bid to contain the pandemic's spread, educational activities have been halted globally and in most SSA countries, which will have adverse implications on learning outcomes, retention of pupils/students, and continuous learning. The impact of the pandemic on livelihoods and family incomes might also affect the ability of parents to send their children back to school when schools reopen since the latter might be needed for immediate household economic contributions through means such as street hawking. This makes the situation grave for LICs, especially SSA, which has more than half of the out-of-school primary children according to 2014 data[59] from the World Bank.

Furthermore, healthcare systems in many SSA countries are ill prepared for COVID-19, considering the low healthcare workers per capita, limited capacity, gross under-funding, and lack of efficient health systems. The pandemic has already added heavier strain on countries' health systems, while the current focus on containing the pandemic has limited access to routine, essential health services. In many of these countries, there are disruptions in measles vaccination programs with over 20 million children unprotected,[60] as well as other vaccination programs such as polio, measles, cholera, yellow fever, and meningitis, which would have covered an estimated 13 million people.[61] Resources meant for vaccination are

---

56 SDG Report 2018, *supra* note 42, at 4.
57 *See COVID-19 (Coronavirus) Drives Sub-Saharan Africa Toward First Recession in 25 Years*, Press Release 2020/099/AFR, WORLD BANK (Apr. 9, 2020), www.worldbank.org/en/news/press-release/2020/04/09/covid-19-coronavirus-drives-sub-saharan-africa-toward-first-recession-in-25-years (Noting that COVID-19 will cost the African region between $37 billion and $79 billion in output losses for 2020, through effects such as trade and value chain disruption; reduced foreign financing flows from remittances, tourism, foreign aid, foreign direct investment; capital flight etc. The institution also estimated agricultural production contraction of between 2.6% and 7% which would spark a food security crisis.)
58 *Id.*
59 Hannah Ritchie, *How Many Children Are Not in School*, OUR WORLD IN DATA (JAN. 23, 2019), https://ourworldindata.org/how-many-children-are-not-in-school.
60 Gaby Ooms, *COVID-19 and Its Far-Reaching Health Impacts in Sub-Saharan Africa*, HEALTH ACTION INTERNATIONAL (MAY 8, 2020), https://haiweb.org/covid-19-sub-saharan-africa/.
61 *Id.*

being directed toward COVID-19. This also implies that deaths caused by illnesses such as malaria, HIV, and tuberculosis might severely increase in SSA this year if their prevention and treatment programs are also disrupted. Adding to this are limited access to modern contraceptives, likely increasing sexually transmitted infections, and maternal and newborn deaths.

This calls for a more holistic conceptualization of healthcare, as billions of dollars are being directed to tackle the pandemic. While aid agencies and national governments mechanize approaches to addressing COVID-19, continued access to essential health services must be on their agenda. If not, there might be additional health crises in LICs (SSA in particular) in the immediate future, which would further complicate the realization of SDG 1.

Global Policy Recommendations

Expand the Coverage of Social Protection Schemes

Social protection coverage for the most vulnerable groups is globally lacking, with the situation being the worst in SSA. According to the United Nations, as of 2016 only 45% of the world's population was effectively covered by at least one social protection cash benefit;[62] meaning 4 billion people are excluded from such provisions. Ending poverty requires universal social protection schemes aimed at safeguarding the most poor and vulnerable populations. To achieve target 1.3, a more holistic approach is needed at the country level, especially in LICs, in providing social assistance to children, people with disabilities, and maternity benefits for women post-partum, while scaling up pension schemes. Partnerships should be explored with international donors and partners for the financial assistance to scale up social protection programs in LICs.

Targeted Measures to Reduce Vulnerability and Build the Resilience of the Poor and Most Vulnerable to Climate-Related Extreme Events and Conflicts:

Climate change has increased the severity and frequency of natural disasters. Ninety percent of all disasters were caused by floods, heatwaves, storms, droughts, or other extreme weather events.[63] Urban habitats in small island LICs are particularly vulnerable areas where natural disasters often have dire consequences. However, with sound urban planning and administration, cities can become resilient, safe, and sustainable. One hundred and fifty-two countries have domestic urban policies and frameworks in place to promote more coordinated urban development that sets the stage for sustainable urbanization.[64] However, more work must be done to ensure effective implementation of such policies.

Following these gloomy trends and estimates, to realize target 1.5, it is then imperative that more countries develop and implement national and local disaster risk reduction strategies in line with the Sendai Framework for Disaster Risk Reduction 2015–2030. As

---

62 *ILO: 4 Billion People Worldwide Are Left without Social Protection, in* World Soc. Protection Rep. 2017–2019, INT'L LABOUR ORG. (Nov. 29, 2017), www.ilo.org/global/about-the-ilo/newsroom/news/WCMS_601903/lang--en/index.htm.
63 SDG Report, *supra* note 4, at 23.
64 SDG Report 2018, *supra* note 42, at 15.

previously discussed, as of 2019, only 30% of countries globally have made alignments with such frameworks, consequently there is a need for more countries to do the same.[65]

Raising Income of Farmers

Almost 80% of the world's extreme poor live in rural areas and over 60% are dependent on agriculture.[66] There is a critical requirement for agricultural development to tackle poverty reduction and expedite the achievement of target 1.1. Increased efforts need to be made in boosting agricultural productivity to support poverty reduction through raising the income of farmers. Measures to achieve this range from providing access to high-yielding seeds, water, nutrients, and reliable markets for farmers, while making investment in transport infrastructure. This also calls for subsidizing farm inputs through pooled sales, pooled credit facilities, climate insurance, and increasing and supporting research on disease-resistant seed varieties.[67] Support for farmers to acquire information and communication technologies are also exceedingly important so that they can connect buyers, transfer money, and acquire valuable information regarding weather conditions and market prices.

Conclusion

In this section, Goal 1 has been globally assessed using targets 1.1, 1.3, and 1.5 and looking at the years 2016 to 2019. The targets respectively provide for the concerns of the global population living below the international poverty line; social protection systems for the most vulnerable; and reducing the poor's vulnerability to extreme events, shocks, and disasters.

Following the baseline projections which state that the 2030 target of 3% of the world's population living in extreme poverty will not be met, it is then crucial that existing efforts in realizing Goal 1 are scaled up with regards to financial resources, institutional capabilities, and political will to effectively address global poverty. To this end, the global community must increase its financing for LICs and specifically target social investment schemes and essential sectors. Following the adverse socio-economic effects of COVID-19, LICs need additional health financing to prepare for, respond to, and treat the pandemic. Furthermore, sufficient political will at the global level is increasingly important to make extreme poverty a thing of the past.

More than ever before, global partnerships are increasingly important in terms of resource mobilization, effective coordination, and cross-learning platforms on national successes.

---

65 *Id.* at 48.
66 *See generally* Laurence Chandy et al., *From a Billion to Zero: Three Key Ingredients to End Extreme Poverty, in* THE LAST MILE IN ENDING EXTREME POVERTY 6–17 (Brookings 2015).
67 *Id.*

A Case for Africa through Nigeria

Box 5.1 Framework for the Implementation of SDGs in Nigeria

Nigeria like most other countries successfully migrated from the implementation of the MDGs to the SDGs. Under the former, implementation in Nigeria revealed a mixture of results across the goals, geographic locations, and gender groups. While progress was recorded on some indicators such as reaching the threshold of eradicating polio, implementing a successful Conditional Grants Scheme (CGS), and mobilizing community utilization of health facilities, many of the goals and targets were not met. However, Nigeria embarked on this transition between the duo agendas, supposedly understanding the overwhelming nature of such and the underlying policy implications on planning, implementation, and monitoring; substantial multiplication of activities; and an expansion of partnerships and institutions.

The expansions of institutional and policy structures under the MDGs for the SDGs was an opportunity for Nigeria. Another opportunity was the consistency of the SDGs with some of the country's domestic socio-economic priorities such as poverty reduction, social inclusion, justice, and environmental sustainability issues. In addition to the series of opportunities is that the SDGs' timing corresponded with the inauguration of a new government, which should ensure political buy-in and integration of the goals into the new administration's broader agenda and development framework.

Furthermore, the Office of the Senior Special Assistant to The President (OSSAP) on MDGs was rebranded for the SDGs. The office is tasked with SDGs planning and coordination, representation and partnership development, resource mobilization, and Monitoring and Evaluation (M&E). The country also itemized ambitious plans in the transition that covers a large spectrum including institutional, policy, and legal framework, as well as partnerships, M&E, and human resource frameworks. Specifically, they included strengthening inter-governmental collaboration, repositioning local government as the SDGs tier of government, consolidating institutional platforms for M&E; creating SDGs legislation; establishing appropriate legislation for setting minimum expenditures for SDGs, Conditional Cash Transfers among other plans.

Source: UNDP[68]

Poverty Dimensions and Trends: A Race against the Poverty Clock

Six Nigerians become poor every minute.[69] As of June 2018, using the IPL benchmark, Nigeria's figure of 87 million overtook India's 73 million people as the country with the

---

68 *Nigeria's Road to SDGs—Country Transition Strategy.* UNDP (2015)
   www.undp.org/content/dam/nigeria/docs/IclusiveGrwth/Nigeria%20transition%20strategy%20to%20SDGs.pdf.
69 Emele Onu et al., *Six People Fall into Extreme Poverty in This Nation Every Minute*, BLOOMBERG (Feb. 21, 2019), www.bloomberg.com/news/articles/2019-02-22/six-people-fall-into-extreme-poverty-in-this-nation-every-minute.

highest number of people living in extreme poverty.[70] A year later, 4 million more Nigerians joined the poverty bracket bringing the figure to 91 million, which represents 46.5% of the country's population.[71] The rationale for this overtake is not implausible. Nigeria has been a rentier and primary-export dependent state that relies primarily on oil trade for foreign exchange and government revenues. As such, the country has been subject to international oil price fluctuations, such as the oil price collapse in 2014–2016. Following this, the country's gross domestic product growth rate dropped to 2.7% in 2015.[72] In 2016, the economy further contracted by 1.6% plunging the country into its first recession in 25 years.[73]

Comparably, at independence in 1960, only 15% of the Nigerian population was living below the IPL (see Table 5.2). This percentage rose to 53.3% in 1985 because of Nigeria's economic recession in the 80s, precipitated by again, the fall in oil prices; this dropped to 43% in 1990.[74] Subsequently, this increased to 63.5% in 1996 and 70% by 1999 because of a decade of slow economic growth, autarchic policies, high debt to GDP ratio from the early 80s economic downturn, and economic mismanagement.[75] Macroeconomic reforms since 1999 when Nigeria started its fourth democratic journey as well as years of sustained economic growth successfully brought down the rate to 53.5% in 2009 and 33.1% as of 2015.[76] This means that as of 2015 and as recent as 2019, there are proportionally poorer Nigerians than there were at the country's independence.

For a country that has the largest economy in Africa, with massive resource wealth, a huge population size,[77] and a surplus of natural resources with oil as its mainstay, such poverty levels at the different epochs of the country's history remain unfortunate. Factors that motivate this negative scenario are oil shocks, which automatically affect GDP growth for resource-dependent

Table 5.2 Percentage of Nigerians living below poverty line (1960–2019)

Years	1960	1985	1990	1996	1999	2009	2015	2019
Poverty rates (%)	15	53.3	43	63.5	70	53.5	33.1	46.5

Source: Nigeria National Bureau of Statistics (NNBS). Max Roser & Esteban Ortiz-Ospina, *GlobalExtreme Poverty*, Our World in Data (2013), https://ourworldindata.org/extreme-poverty#the-evolution-of-extreme-poverty-country-by-country; *Poverty Headcount Ratioat $1.90 a Day (2011 PPP) (% of Population)—China*, The World Bank, https://data.worldbank.org/indicator/SI.POV.DDAY?locations=CN (last visited Dec. 2, 2020).

70 Kharas (Poverty Institute), *supra* note 31.
71 Homi Kharas et al., *Rethinking Global Poverty Reduction in 2019*, BROOKINGS, www.brookings.edu/blog/future-development/2018/12/13/rethinking-global-poverty-reduction-in-2019/.
72 National Bureau of Statistics, Nigeria (2016), www.nigerianstat.gov.ng (last visited Dec. 3, 2020).
73 National Bureau of Statistics, Nigeria (2017), www.nigerianstat.gov.ng (last visited Dec. 3, 2020).
74 *Id.*
75 *Id.*
76 *Ibid.*
77 With approximately 200 million people in an area of 920,000 Km2 (360,000 sq mi), Nigeria is one of the most densely populated countries in Africa, the country with the largest population on the continent Africa and the seventh largest population in the world. *See* Africa: Nigeria *World Factbook*, CIA, www.cia.gov/library/publications/the-world-factbook/geos/print_ni.html (last visited Dec. 3, 2020).

countries, several years of high rates of unemployment, estimated at 23% in 2018,[78] a preponderance of income inequality, a higher population growth rate relative to GDP growth, political instability, weak agriculture sector performance, and political corruption.

As a rentier state, Nigeria's economy is not diversified and other sectors, such as manufacturing industries, have remained uncompetitive because of oil dependence. Considering political corruption, oil rents have mainstreamed political patronage and corruption. According to the UN Office on Drugs and Crimes, estimates show that Nigeria lost over $400 billion to corruption between 1960 and 1990.[79] Nigeria currently ranks number 146 on the Transparency International's 2019 Corruption Perception Index.[80] The pervasiveness of corruption in the country coupled with its oil rents dependence (with the prices volatility) all present a gloomy picture for the financial resources needed to address poverty.

Also worrisome is the uneven distribution of the poverty rate across regions in the country. By 2016, 87% of all the poor in the country were in Northern Nigeria, a historical trend with implications for social cohesion.[81] In addition, there is a significant degree of movement in and out of poverty in the country, evidence of significant household vulnerability.[82] The pervasiveness of low resilience and economic shocks, such as low GDP, easily translate into a reduction of welfare across the population. Furthermore, in examining other dimensions of poverty, it is estimated that as of 2019, 5.3 million Nigerians face acute hunger;[83] as of 2015, 20% of global maternal deaths happen in Nigeria;[84] as of 2018, Nigeria had 13.2 million out-of-school children,[85] the highest in the world; and as of 2019, 60 million Nigerians lack access to clean water.[86]

Although Nigeria does not have an official poverty line, the country will find it increasingly difficult to effectively address extreme poverty or halve it within the country by 2030 with several macroeconomic challenges looming; limited government revenues as a result of evolving global energy dynamics and the gloomy future of oil.[87] In fact, predictions suggest that oil prices will continue nosediving even after the COVID-19 pandemic has been

---

78 National Bureau of Statistics, *supra* note 73.
79 *Nigeria's Corruption Busters*, UNODC, www.unodc.org/unodc/en/frontpage/nigerias-corruption-busters.html (last visited Dec. 3, 2020).
80 *Corruption Perception Index*, TRANSPARENCY INT'L, www.transparency.org/en/cpi/2019/results (last visited Dec. 3, 2020).
81 *Nigeria: A Short Update on Poverty and Shared Prosperity*, THE WORLD BANK, http://documents.worldbank.org/curated/en/636531549879664295/pdf/NIGERIA-Poverty-Briefing-Note.pdf (last visited Dec. 3, 2020).
82 *Id*.
83 Samson Toromade, *Nigerians among World's Hungriest People in 2018, UN Report Says*, THE PULSE.NG (Apr. 3, 2019), www.pulse.ng/news/local/nigerians-among-worlds-hungriest-people-in-2018-un-report-says/hz62ts4.
84 Amarachi Nasa-Okolie, *Nigeria's Maternal Healthcare Crisis*, STEARS NG (Mar. 3, 2020), www.stearsng.com/article/nigerias-maternal-healthcare-crisis.
85 *UN: In Nigeria More Than 13 Million School-Age Children Out of School*, VOA NEWS, (Dec. 11, 2018), www.voanews.com/africa/un-nigeria-more-13-million-school-age-children-out-school#:~:text=UN%3A%20In%20Nigeria%20More%20Than%2013%20Million%20School,age%20Children%20Out%20of%20School&text=ABUJA%2C%20NIGERIA%20%2D%20A%20survey%20conducted,the%20highest%20in%20the%20world.
86 Voice of America, *Millions in Nigeria Lack Access to Clean Water*, RELIEFWEB (Mar. 1, 2019), https://reliefweb.int/report/nigeria/millions-nigeria-lack-access-clean-water.
87 Dianna Games, *Uncertain Outlook for Nigerian Economy*, AFRICA BUSINESS MAGAZINE (Mar. 30, 2020), https://africanbusinessmagazine.com/region/west-africa/uncertain-outlook-for-nigerian-economy/.

contained. This would bring along more economic challenges for Nigeria in terms of further shortages in government revenues and foreign exchange earnings.

Combating Poverty, Assessing Target 1.A

While Nigeria has been able to increase budgetary allocations to poverty programs, it has performed poorly in terms of allocation to essential sectors using its federal government expenditures.

An Attempt to Fund Poverty: The Performance of Nigeria's Social Investment Programmes

Nigeria's allocation to poverty programs can be grouped under its federal government's Social Investment Programmes (SIP) which were launched by Buhari's administration in 2016. The SIP seeks to tackle poverty and hunger across the country through ensuring a more equitable distribution of resources to vulnerable populations. The programs, which supported more than 4.5 million beneficiaries[88] across the country in 2018[89] include:

- The N-power program which assists young Nigerians between the ages of 18 and 35 to acquire and develop life-long skills with which to become changemakers in their communities. It provides them with a stipend of ₦30,000 ($78) monthly[90] with 500,000 young Nigerians on its payroll.[91]
- The Conditional Cash Transfer (CCT) program which directly supports those within the lowest poverty bracket through cash benefits to various categories of the poor and vulnerable. They are provided with a monthly stipend of ₦5,000 ($13). As of 2018, payment had covered over 250,000 beneficiaries.[92]

---

88 INVESTING IN OUR PEOPLE: A BRIEF ON THE NATIONAL SOCIAL INVESTMENT PROGRAMMES IN NIGERIA, SOCIAL INVESTMENT PROGRAMMES (SIP) & NIGERIA (Jun. 2018), www.npower.gov.ng/nsip.pdf.
89 *Id.*
90 *Id.*
91 *See* N-Power Program, GOVERNMENT OF NIGERIA, www.npower.gov.ng (last visited Dec. 3, 2020). The N-Power Program was built to address the issue of youth unemployment and help increase social development. The program targets Nigerians between the ages of 18 and 35 to acquire and develop life-long skills for becoming changemakers in their communities. By deploying a force of 500,000 trained graduates in their communities, the N-Power Program is a community-sourced solution to the nation's underdeveloped public services such as education, healthcare, and civic engagement.
92 *See National Cash Transfer Office*, GOVERNMENT OF NIGERIA, https://ncto.gov.ng (last visited Dec. 3, 2020). Nigeria's Conditional Cash Transfer program provides targeted cash transfers to the most vulnerable households with the goal of lifting millions out of poverty. A monthly stipend of ₦5,000 ($13) is given to households in poverty-stricken communities along with an additional ₦5,000 for families designated as priorities or extreme cases. Along with the cash transfers, the program beneficiaries are supported, mentored, and coached by Community Facilitators who visit them weekly to help them take ownership of their lives. Savings groups are formed, beneficiaries are provided with training for employment and life skills, as well as improve nutrition, hygiene, and sanitary conditions. Part of the requirement is that households with school-age children enroll in school to promote educational enrollment.

- The Home-Grown School Feeding Programme (HGSF)[93] delivers school food to young children with a specific focus on increasing school enrollment; reducing malnutrition; empowering community women as cooks (estimates of 44,000 as of 2018); and supports small farmers that help stimulate economic growth.[94] The program has fed over 4 million pupils in 26 Nigerian states as of 2018.[95]

While the Nigerian government is yet to formally evaluate these programs, they signify progress, considering the levels of extreme poverty in the country. While the Nigerian government is yet to formally evaluate these programs, they signify progress, considering the levels of extreme poverty in the country. As of April 2019, the National Social Investment Office (NSIO) estimates that ₦300 billion ($800 million) have been spent on the programs in the past 3 years.[96]

The Poverty Slice: Health and Education

Nigeria's national health budget allocation remains below 6% annually for the past 10 years. This falls abysmally below the 2001 African Union 'Abuja Declaration' of 15% annual budgetary allocation to the health sector.[97] The highest percentage recorded in the past decade in the country was 5.8% in 2012 and 2015.[98] During the SDGs' years (2016–2020), the highest allocation so far was in 2017 at 5.1%.[99] The remaining 4 years had a percentage ceiling of 4.1%.[100] In the education sector, the scenario is mirrored. The country's annual education budget allocation in the past decade also did not meet the United Nations Educational, Scientific and Cultural Organization (UNESCO) Declaration of 26% budgetary allocation to the education sector. The highest allocation so far was 10.7% in 2014.[101] For the SDGs' years, the highest allocation was in 2018 at 7.04%.[102] In 2019, it declined to 7.02%, and in 2020, it further declined to 6.7%.[103]

---

93 *See* National Home Grown School Feeding Program, GOVERNMENT OF NIGERIA, www.nhgsfp.gov.ng (last visited Dec. 3, 2020). The HGSF was created to provide a nutritious and balanced meal to 5.5 million school children grades 1 to 3. The Program aims to improve the enrollment of primary school children and reduce the drop-out rate, estimated at over 30%. Most of this shortage is due to poverty and this program is built to address the most important basic need of schoolchildren and provide the nutrition needed to engage successfully with their education. By linking the program to local food supply chains, the community is engaged to create a social support beyond simply providing meals to certain children. Over 44,000 cooks are engaged in the program, feeding over 4 million students in 26 Nigerian States.
94 Nigeria Social Investment Programmes, *supra* note 90.
95 *Id.*
96 Vanguard News, *FG Spends N300bn on Social Investment Programme—Presidency*, VANGUARD NEWS (Apr. 2, 2019), www.vanguardngr.com/2019/04/fg-spends-n300bn-on-social-investment-programme-presidency/.
97 Budget Documents 2010—2020, Budget Office of the Federation, FEDERAL REPUBLIC OF NIGERIA, https://budgetoffice.gov.ng/index.php/resources/internal-resources/budget-documents?layout=columns (last visited Dec. 3, 2020).
98 *Id.*
99 *Id.*
100 *Ibid.*
101 *Ibid.*
102 *Ibid.*
103 *Ibid.*

Target 1.B As the Standard[104]

The Nigerian government's spending on sectors that specifically target women and vulnerable groups have been minimalized by a sequence of "frivolous, unclear and inappropriate" federal government spending. On the country's 2015 Appropriation Bill, for instance, budgetary provisions for the Presidency had a hiked expenditure for food and catering services estimated at ₦257 million ($663,000), welfare packages of ₦162 million budgeted, and upgrades, construction, or renovation of presidential villa facilities of ₦676 million.[105] In addition, earmarked spending included ₦378 million for pilgrimage, ₦500 million for constructing the Vice President's residence, ₦2 billion for designing and constructing the National Assembly Presiding Officers' residence.[106] Such wasteful and unclear figures were estimated at ₦227 billion in the 2015 Appropriation Bill. In 2017, the estimate was at ₦151 billion.[107] In 2018 it had jumped to ₦219 billion[108] and by 2020 it was at ₦150 billion.[109] The 4 years cumulatively have a figure of ₦747 billion ($2 billion), which is almost equivalent to what was budgeted for the entire health sector in 2019 and 2020.[110]

Local Challenges: Nigeria

Following the analysis in the section "Poverty Dimensions and Trends: A Race against the Poverty Clock",[111] the most pressing challenge that affects Nigeria's ability to halve the proportion of its population in extreme poverty (target 1.2) is first, low economic growth and recession, triggered by plummeting oil prices. With this, the country would find it difficult to provide jobs for millions of its unemployed population to raise its per capita income, the implication being that millions would slide into the extreme poverty category. Second, slowed growth would affect the government's revenues and foreign exchange earnings. Estimates have it that 65% of government revenues in the country are from oil rents.[112] Revenue shortage currently being experienced in the country makes it difficult for the gov-

---

104 Target 1.B and the proportion of Nigeria's government recurrent and capital spending to sectors that disproportionately benefit women, the poor, and vulnerable groups.
105 Eze Onyekpere, *Inappropriate, Unclear and Wasteful Expenditure in the 2015 Appropriation Bill*, CENTRE FOR SOCIAL JUSTICE & CITIZENS WEALTH PLATFORM (Jun. 2015), http://csj-ng.org/wp-content/uploads/2018/06/INAPPROPRIATE-UNCLEAR-AND-WASTEFUL-EXPENDITURE-IN-THE-APPROVED-2015-BUDGET-.pdf.
106 Id.
107 Eze Onyekpere, *Inappropriate, Unclear and Wasteful Expenditure in the 2017 Appropriation Bill*, CENTRE FOR SOCIAL JUSTICE & CITIZENS WEALTH PLATFORM (2017), http://csj-ng.org/wp-content/uploads/2018/06/INAPPROPRIATE-UNCLEAR-WASTEFUL-EXPENDITURE-IN-2017-FEDERAL-BUDGET.1.pdf.
108 Eze Onyekpere, *Inappropriate, Unclear and Wasteful Expenditure in the 2018 Appropriation Bill*, CENTRE FOR SOCIAL JUSTICE & CITIZENS WEALTH PLATFORM (2018), http://csj-ng.org/wp-content/uploads/2018/06/RECOMMENDATIONS-ON-THE-LINE-ITEMS-OF-FRIVOLOUS-INAPPROPRIATE-UNCLEAR-AND-WASTEFUL-ESTIMATES-IN-THE-2018-FEDERAL-APPROPRIATION-BILL.pdf.
109 Eze Onyekpere, *Inappropriate, Unclear and Wasteful Expenditure in the 2020 Appropriation Bill*, CENTRE FOR SOCIAL JUSTICE & CITIZENS WEALTH PLATFORM (2020), http://csj-ng.org/wp-content/uploads/2019/11/2020-FRIVOLOUS-EXPENDITURE.pdf.
110 Id.
111 *See* Indicator 1.A.1—Nigeria's social investment programs' performance.
112 *Nigeria—Overview*, NIGERIA EXTRACTIVE INDUSTRIES TRANSPARENCY INITATIVE (last updated Jun. 10, 2020), https://eiti.org/es/implementing_country/32.

ernment to build schools and hospitals, pay teachers and health personnel, fund its poverty programs, etc. (targets 1.A and 1.B).

A further challenge is that of political instability. The North Eastern region of the country has faced Boko Haram terrorism for several years. Economies are devastated in the region, livelihoods are destroyed, poverty is metastasizing, and many are internally displaced.[113] Regardless of the insurgency, there is banditry in northern western states[114] and farmer-herder clashes in the north central region.[115,116] These crises will significantly raise the figures of the extreme poor in the country if they are not holistically arrested.

Each One, Reach One, Lift One: Policy Recommendations for Nigeria

Ending poverty in Nigeria is a long journey which requires a combination of many efforts by various stakeholders. To begin, the political will of government to tackle poverty is the fundamental basis for any level of success and the importance of a robust social protection scheme aimed at safeguarding poor and vulnerable populations cannot be overemphasized. To achieve targets 1.2 and 1.3, a more holistic approach at the country-level must be urgently considered and scaled up. These include providing access to qualitative education for children; inclusive policies for people with disabilities and other vulnerable groups; increased spending on healthcare development in order to reduce maternal and child mortality; comprehensive pension coverage for the majority of the country's workforce; and broad-based multi-stakeholder partnerships are to be considered for sustained, widespread social impact.

This section is an attempt to critically assess the progress Nigeria has made toward the total eradication of extreme poverty by 2030; in line with the UN mandate of Goal 1 of the SDGs. Using the target indicators 1.A.1[117] and 1.A.2[118] as a framework for analysis, it is evident that Nigeria has a long way to go if the stipulated targets are to be realized. Although some measures of progress have been recorded, especially in the social investment schemes, a more robust socio-economic framework needs to be deployed urgently. The current national efforts must be geared at ensuring diligent and grounded commitment in pursuit of policies that will leave no one behind. These should include the following:

---

113 *See Nigeria Emergency*, UNHCR, www.unhcr.org/en-us/nigeria-emergency.html (last visited Dec. 3, 2020). According to the UNHCR, over 3.3 million people have been displaced from the instability, including an estimate of 2.5 million internally displaced persons (IDPs) in the region, over 550,000 IDPs in Cameroon, Chad, and Niger, as well as 240,000 refugees in the four countries.

114 Chukwuma Okoli, *What Can Be Done to Fight Rural Banditry in Northern Nigeria*, THE CONVERSATION (*Sept.* 12, *Nigeria*,2019), https://theconversation.com/what-can-be-done-to-fight-rural-banditry-in-northern-nigeria-122776.

115 Ugwumba Eguta, *Understanding the Herder-Farmer Conflict in Nigeria*, Conflict Trends 2018/3, THE ACCORD, www.accord.org.za/conflict-trends/understanding-the-herder-farmer-conflict-in-nigeria/ (last visited Dec. 3, 2020).

116 *Herders against Farmers: Nigeria's Expanding Deadly Conflict*, Report 252/Africa, INTERNATIONAL CRISIS GROUP (Sept. 19, 2017), www.crisisgroup.org/africa/west-africa/nigeria/252-herders-against-farmers-nigerias-expanding-deadly-conflict.

117 Indicator 1.A.1: Proportion of resources allocated by the government directly to poverty reduction programs.

118 Indicator 1.A.2: Proportion of total government spending on essential services.

Structural Transformation and Industrialization

Nigeria, and by extension SSA, should, as a matter of urgency, structurally transform, industrialize, and diversify its economy. This is one of the most important ways it could effectively address extreme poverty through ensuring sustained economic growth, job creation, and raising per capita income. There are many models such as the Growth Facilitation and Identification Framework (GIFF) that lay down steps through which developing countries with traditional firm growth constraints can still jump-start industrialization.[119] This would also enable the country to raise the necessary government revenues to expand its poverty alleviation programs and allocate more resources to essential sectors.

Expand, Sub-Nationalize, and Legislate the Social Investment Programs

The global goal of ending poverty requires universal social protection schemes aimed at mostly safeguarding the poor. At the onset of the breakout of the COVID-19 pandemic, the distribution of palliatives to the most vulnerable populations in Nigeria was marred by irregularities and the absence of an updated social register. Although the government has demonstrated a compelling political will to end poverty through an unprecedented budgetary allocation to social protection programs through the Office of Social Investment Programs (OSIP) domiciled at the Presidency, the implementation of these policies, such as mass skill acquisition schemes, conditional cash transfers, among others, have been plagued by irregularities in data integrity and corruption.

For targets 1.A and 1.B to be achieved in Nigeria, it is imperative that the existing social investment and protection programs are expanded through increased partnerships with international donors, as well as sub-nationalized for increased ownership, and improved service delivery and accountability. In this light, it has then become imperative that the country reduces the cost of governance through cutting down frivolous and unnecessary budgetary expenditures. This would enable the channeling of more resources to social protection and essential sectors. Four years into the administration of President Buhari, the OSIP was restructured into a Ministry for Humanitarian Affairs and Disaster Management to deepen governance, provide a stronger legal framework, and better coordinate the scope of areas covered by the targets and indicators under Goal 1. Consequently, in order to manage the risk of a policy somersault by a change in government, a more feasible governance structure and ease in implementation is recommended by making the OSIPs law, and not a mass welfare program so that it would not be affected by a change in government.

Address Insecurity

The high level of political instability across the country in the shape of inter-state conflicts such as the herdsmen clashes, banditry, and proliferation of arms and small weapons, remains a threat to the dividends of democratic governance. Through a coordinated approach and the cooperation of citizens, the security agencies must approach insecurity, not just as a threat to poverty eradication, but as a panacea for peace and security. In addition to this, the lingering fight against the Boko Haram insurgency in the North East continues to claw

---

119 Justin Lin, *New Structural Economics—A Framework for Rethinking Development and Policy*, THE WORLD BANK (2012).

at the socio-economic development of the zone. With a steady increase in the number of internally displaced persons particularly in the North; other efforts by government, private sector, and international donors or multilateral agencies will continue to be thwarted by counter-efforts as well as non-cooperation by citizens who do not trust the commitment of government. Finally, through more effective military strategies and courting more international support, insecurity can be curbed to levels that do not undermine the attainment of the goal indicators.

Concluding Thoughts for Nigeria

This section presents a country-level assessment of targets 1.2, 1.A, and 1.B, using Nigeria as a case study, targets of which respectively provide for issues such as population living in poverty according to national definitions; government spending on poverty programs, essential services, and sectors that disproportionately benefit vulnerable groups. In line with its analysis, Nigeria must dedicate more financial resources to the education and health sectors and should scale up its social investment schemes for the most vulnerable. While Nigeria has successfully launched a framework for the domestication of the SDGs through the Office of the Senior Special Assistant to The President on SDGs, there is still much to be done in terms of ensuring that the established frameworks, strategies, and processes are cascaded down to relevant subnational governance structures with the requisite capacity building schemes for these structures to effectively implement the SDGs. In addition, the country must systematically address insecurity while mechanizing coherent and long-term strategies for industrial restructuring and diversification, for sustained economic growth.

6 Achieving Zero Hunger Using a Rights-Based Approach to Food Security and Sustainable Agriculture

Smita Narula[1]

The 2030 Agenda for Sustainable Development was adopted by the United Nations (UN) General Assembly in September 2015 and signed by 193 countries. Its 17 Sustainable Development Goals (SDGs) and 169 Targets are intended to guide global development action from 2016 to 2030. Described as "the blueprint to achieve a better and more sustainable future for all,"[2] the SDGs collectively represent an urgent and universal call to action to end poverty, address inequality, protect the planet, and secure peace and justice.

The second Sustainable Development Goal—SDG 2 or the "Zero Hunger Goal"—seeks to end hunger and achieve food security for all by 2030. SDG 2 recognizes that achieving this Goal requires a dual and inter-related focus on improving access to nutritious food while promoting sustainable agriculture. This, in turn, "entails improving the productivity and incomes of small-scale farmers by promoting equal access to land, technology and markets, sustainable food production systems and resilient agricultural practices."[3] As noted in the 2017 High Level Political Forum (HLPF) Thematic review of SDG 2, the Zero Hunger Goal "links the eradication of hunger and of malnutrition to a transformation in agriculture and food systems, and to the empowerment of rural people, women and men alike, as critical agents of change."[4]

SDG 2's linking of food security and nutrition to sustainable agricultural production, and its associated call for the empowerment of rural communities, is significant in at least three respects: First, it is a reminder that the majority of those who live in poverty and suffer from food insecurity live in rural areas and rely on agriculture as their primary source of livelihood.[5] Second, it is a tacit acknowledgment of the enormous social, environmental, and health-related costs of our industrial food system. And third, it points to the fundamental

---

1 The author thanks, with great appreciation, Cassandra Jurenci, Taylor Keselica, and Claire McLeod for their research support.
2 *About the Sustainable Development Goals*, U.N. SUSTAINABLE DEVELOPMENT GOALS, /www.un.org/sustainabledevelopment/sustainable-development-goals/, (last visited May 18, 2020).
3 *Goal 2: End Hunger, Achieve Food Security and Improved Nutrition and Promote Sustainable Agriculture*, U.N. DEP'T OF ECON. & SOC. AFF., STATISTICS DIVISION, https://unstats.un.org/sdgs/report/2016/goal-02/ (last visited May 18, 2020).
4 2017 HLPF THEMATIC REVIEW OF SDG 2: END HUNGER, ACHIEVE FOOD SECURITY AND IMPROVED NUTRITION, AND PROMOTE SUSTAINABLE AGRICULTURE, HIGH-LEVEL POLITICAL FORUM ON SUSTAINABLE DEVELOPMENT 1 (2017) [hereinafter "2017 HLPF THEMATIC REVIEW"].
5 U.N. Special Rapporteur on the right to food, *Critical Perspective on Food Systems, Food Crises and the Future of the Right to Food*, ¶ 14, U.N. Doc A/HRC/43/44 (Jan. 21, 2020) [hereinafter "*Critical Perspective on Food Systems*"].

imbalance of power in that food system, underscoring both the vulnerability and resiliency of rural communities therein.

This chapter brings into view the transformative changes that are needed to build food systems that are sustainable, nourishing and just—which in turn can help achieve SDG 2 and related Goals. The first part of the chapter provides an overview of the many costs and consequences of our industrial food system—the fragility of which has been brought into sharp relief by the COVID-19 pandemic. The second part then turns to a review of SDG 2 targets and assesses the lack of progress in achieving these targets on multiple fronts. I argue that this lack of progress can be attributed in part to the SDGs' continued embrace of a productivist approach that fails to center the human rights of those made most vulnerable by our industrial food system. In the third part of the chapter, I argue that we must reject destructive agricultural practices and embrace a rights-based approach to food security and to sustainable food production. This, in turn, requires shifting from industrial agriculture to diversified agroecological food systems. It also requires global recognition of the rights of peasants and other small-scale food producers who, ironically, also form the majority of the world's food insecure. The chapter concludes with a look at emerging data and case studies that illuminate the viability and potential of these alternative agroecological models.

The Costs and Consequences of our Industrial Food System

The causes and consequences of hunger and food insecurity are many and include both urban and rural poverty, widening income and wealth inequality, conflict, climate change, and myriad issues surrounding the inequitable distribution of, and access to, land and other productive resources. This chapter focuses in particular on the role that the industrial food system plays in exacerbating hunger, rural dispossession, and environmental degradation.

Our shift from complex, diverse, and decentralized food systems toward a homogenous, extractive, and centralized industrial food system began far before the mid-20th century but deepened considerably with the advent of the so-called Green Revolution.[6] Beginning in the 1960s, the Green Revolution ushered in a new era of food production that combined high-yielding plant varieties with increased irrigation, highly mechanized production processes, and the use of nitrogen-based fertilizers and pesticides.[7] These innovations increased the production volumes of major cereals (particularly maize, wheat, and rice) and of soybean,[8] but also entailed significant environmental and social costs.[9]

In the decades following the Green Revolution, structural adjustment programs mandated by international financial institutions encouraged developing countries to focus on

---

6 The Catholic Health Association of India [CHAI], *Exploring the Potential of Diversified Traditional Food Systems to Contribute to a Healthy Diet*, at 21, (2018), https://foodsovereigntyalliance.files.wordpress.com/2018/12/Report-1.pdf.
7 U.N. Special Rapporteur on the right to food, *The Transformative Potential of the Right to Food*, ¶ 6, U.N. Doc A/HRC/25/57 (Jan. 24, 2014); *see also*, Bryan Newman, Development Report No. 15: *A Bitter Harvest: Farmer Suicide and the Unforeseen Social, Environmental and Economic Impacts of the Green Revolution in Punjab, India*, Food First Institute for Food and Development Policy 1 (2007).
8 Over recent decades, however, yields have either failed to improve, stagnated, or collapsed in 24–39% of the world's production zones for these crops. *See* International Panel of Experts on Sustainable Food Systems [IPES-Food], *From Uniformity to Diversity: A Paradigm Shift from Industrial Agriculture to Diversified Agroecological Systems*, at 3, (June 2016) [hereinafter "*From Uniformity to Diversity*"].
9 U.N. Special Rapporteur on the right to food, *The Transformative Potential of the Right to Food*, *supra* note 7, at ¶ 6.

the production and export of cash crops over basic food crops. These shifts in production, along with the liberalization of trade in agricultural products in the 1990s, turned a number of food-exporting developing countries into net food-importers,[10] making them particularly vulnerable to price volatility and supply chain disruptions. Moreover, as highly subsidized developed-country producers glutted markets, peasant farming was undermined across the Global South, fueling waves of migration.[11]

The focus on integrating food producers into global markets that are now dominated by mega-sized agribusiness actors has decidedly come at the expense of sustainable and diversified local food systems. As the COVID-19 pandemic has shown, the industrial food system's complex and specialized food supply chains are also ill-equipped by design to handle disruptions such as closed borders, reduced labor mobility, trade restrictions, and lockdowns.[12] Ultimately, when measured against the Goal of ending hunger, achieving food security, improving nutrition, and promoting sustainable agriculture, the food systems we have inherited from the 20th century fall dramatically short. As described below, "food and agriculture are now deeply implicated in the climate crisis and loss of biodiversity, the erosion of rural livelihoods, and the contamination of land and water."[13]

Environmental Costs

The natural resource base on which food production depends is being rapidly degraded. A hyper-focus on increasing agricultural production, including from the time of the Green Revolution, has led to a host of environmental problems including accelerated soil erosion, deforestation, extension of monocultures, and a loss of biodiversity. The industrial food system—which relies on long petrochemical-based supply chains—causes massive deforestation in order to make way for large-scale plantations to produce food commodities and animal feed, and to secure land for animal grazing.[14] Such changes in land and water use and management have been cited by the UN Food and Agriculture Organization (FAO) as a key driver of biodiversity loss, along with the attendant "transition to intensive production of a reduced number of species, breeds, and varieties."[15] A 2019 FAO study—which was based

---

10 Smita Narula, *Reclaiming the Right to Food as a Normative Response to the Global Food Crisis*, 13 YALE HUM. RTS. & DEV. L.J. 403, 411 (2010) [hereinafter "*Reclaiming the Right to Food*"].
11 U.N. Special Rapporteur on the right to food, *The Transformative Potential of the Right to Food*, supra note 7, at ¶¶ 10–12.
12 Jennifer Clapp, *Spoiled Milk, Rotten Vegetables and a Very Broken Food System*, N.Y. TIMES (May 8, 2020), www.nytimes.com/2020/05/08/opinion/coronavirus-global-food-supply.html.
13 COLIN ANDERSON ET AL., CENTRE FOR AGROECOLOGY, WATER & RESILIENCE, BUILDING, DEFENDING AND STRENGTHENING AGROECOLOGY: A GLOBAL STRUGGLE FOR FOOD SOVEREIGNTY, at 2, (2015) www.gaiafoundation.org/wp-content/uploads/2017/04/Building-defending-strengthening-agroecology-2015-3.pdf.
14 *See* FAO, WORLD LIVESTOCK: TRANSFORMING THE LIVESTOCK SECTOR THROUGH THE SUSTAINABLE DEVELOPMENT GOALS 100 (2018) (stating that "[t]he expansion of pastures and croplands to feed livestock is a major driver of land-use change and deforestation."); *see also* FAO, STATE OF THE WORLD'S FORESTS 2016: FORESTS AND AGRICULTURE: LAND-USE CHALLENGES AND OPPORTUNITIES 88 (2016) (noting that cattle ranching has been a major driver of deforestation in the Amazon region since the 1990s); *see also* ETC GROUP, WHO WILL FEED US? THE PEASANT FOOD WEB VS. THE INDUSTRIAL FOOD CHAIN 32 (3rd ed. 2017) [hereinafter "WHO WILL FEED US?"] (noting that the industrial food chain "dominates more than 75% of global agricultural land … and 80% of the Chain's agricultural land is used for livestock production").
15 COMMISSION ON GENETIC RESOURCES FOR FOOD AND AGRICULTURE, FAO, THE STATE OF THE WORLD'S BIODIVERSITY FOR FOOD AND AGRICULTURE 65 (2019) [hereinafter "FAO BIODIVERSITY REPORT"] (adding

on 91 country reports—found that "many key components of biodiversity for food and agriculture [BFA] at genetic, species and ecosystem levels are in decline,"[16] including many species that contribute to vital ecosystem services, such as pollinators.[17]

According to some estimates, approximately one-fourth of human-made greenhouse gas emissions can be attributed to industrial modes of agricultural production when combined with the resource requirements to transport, package, and conserve food.[18] In turn, "increased climate variability and weather-related disasters affect agriculture and threaten the stability of food prices."[19] The FAO estimates that one-third of all the food that is produced globally goes to waste, wasting with it the immense resources that went into the food's production.[20] As industrial farming methods are further introduced into nonindustrial settings, soil depletion, petrochemical fertilizers, eutrophication, and coastal dead zones are also increasingly becoming commonplace in regions where such environmental degradation was previously unseen.[21]

Social Costs

Our industrial food system also generates hunger and malnutrition, impoverishes farmers, and displaces rural communities and Indigenous Peoples from their lands. Studies reveal that, "[a]n estimated 80 percent of the poorest people live and work in rural areas, half of whom are small-scale and traditional farmers, 20 percent are landless and 10 percent subsist through fishing, hunting, and activities."[22] The extreme vulnerability of food producers to hunger and food insecurity—and to the current COVID-19 crisis—is a result of the deep imbalance of power in our food system and the systematic denial of food producers' basic rights.[23]

---

that "the maintenance of traditional knowledge related to BFA is negatively affected by the loss of traditional lifestyles as a result of population growth, urbanization and the industrialization of agriculture and food processing, and by overexploitation and overharvesting").

16 *Id.* at xxxviii.
17 *Id.* The report further notes that in 2014, fewer than 200 of cultivated plant species were produced at significant levels, and just 9 crops—sugar cane, wheat, maize, potatoes, soybeans, oil-palm fruit, sugar beet, cassava, and rice—constituted more than 66% of world crop production by weight. Additionally, as of 2015, nearly one-third of fish stocks were overfished and as of 2018, nearly 26% of the 7,745 local livestock breeds were at risk of extinction. *Id.* at 114.
18 Joseph Poore and Thomas Nemecek, *Reducing Food's Environmental Impacts through Producers and Consumers*, 360 (6392) Science, 987, 987 (2019); *see also* 2017 HLPF Thematic Review, *supra* note 4, at 6 (estimating that "20–25 percent of total greenhouse gas emissions are directly caused by agriculture, including deforestation").
19 2017 HLPF Thematic Review, *supra* note 4, at 6.
20 *Food Loss and Food Waste*, Food & Agriculture Org., www.fao.org/food-loss-and-food-waste/en/ (last visited May 19, 2020).
21 Eli D. Lazarus, *Land Grabbing as a Driver of Environmental Change*, 46.1 Area.74, 79 (2014). *See also* Intergovernmental Panel on Climate Change (IPCC), *Climate Change and Land: An IPCC Special Report on Climate Change, Desertification, Land Degradation, Sustainable Land Management, Food Security, and Greenhouse Gas Fluxes in Terrestrial Ecosystems*, Table 4.1 at 356–8, and Findings 4.2.1 at 354–6, 4.3.1 at 366, 4.4.1.3 at 372–3, and 4.7.2 at 379–80 (2019).
22 U.N. Special Rapporteur on the right to food, *Critical Perspective on Food Systems*, *supra* note 5, at ¶ 14 (internal citations omitted).
23 *See, e.g., id.* at ¶¶ 22–5 (describing the exploitation of agricultural workers, their exposure to dangerous pesticides, and the prevalence of child labor in the agricultural sector).

The increasing corporate consolidation of the food chain means that a mere handful of agribusiness companies now exert immense control over and reap tremendous profit from the production, processing, and retailing of our food.[24] Small-scale farmers are hungry because the profits of their labor are being captured by agribusinesses along the food chain, and because they cultivate plots of lands that are often very small, making the vast majority of them net food buyers.[25] They also face significant barriers to markets due to infrastructural deficiencies and technical trade requirements.[26] Most smallholder farmers are women, but few hold titles to land. The land they do own is often infertile or lacks water. Many women also face wage inequities and sexual violence in the fields.[27]

In most countries, peasants and rural workers have no right to form unions, earn a living wage, or receive social security.[28] Peasant farmers struggle to access productive resources or save their seeds, and are highly vulnerable to climate shocks.[29] Price volatility and a lack of proper supports for small-scale agriculture are also putting peasant farmers in a dire situation, as is evident by the high incidence of farmer suicides in multiple countries.[30]

Rural communities throughout the world, including peasant farmers, landless rural workers, Indigenous Peoples, pastoralists, fisherfolk, and their families, also bear the brunt of the large-scale land and water grabs that prop up the industrial food chain. In 2016, and 8 years since publishing its first and influential report on the subject of land grabs,[31] GRAIN published a new dataset documenting nearly 500 land deals around the world that were exclusively for food and agriculture and covered roughly 30 million hectares. In early 2016, a similar data-pooling initiative known as the Land Matrix included about 1,100 land deals

---

24 *See generally* IPES-Food, *Too Big to Feed: Exploring the Impacts of Mega-Mergers, Consolidation and Concentration of Power in the Agri-Food Sector* (2017).
25 U.N. Special Rapporteur on the right to food, *Report of the Special Rapporteur on the Right to Food*, U.N. Doc. A/65/281 (Aug. 11, 2010). The industrial food chain also generates hunger in urban areas. *See, e.g.*, Sylvia A. Allegretto et al., *UC Berkeley Center for Labor Research and Education, Fast Food, Poverty Wages: The Public Cost of Low-Wage Jobs in the Fast-Food Industry*, U.C. BERKELEY LABOR CENTER (Oct. 15 2013), http://laborcenter.berkeley.edu/fast-food-poverty-wages-the-public-cost-of-low-wage-jobs-in-the-fast-food-industry/ (noting that workers in the fast food industry in the United States work for poverty wages and are often food insecure).
26 U.N. Special Rapporteur on the right to food, *Critical Perspective on Food Systems, supra* note 5, at ¶ 14.
27 *See* Maryellen Kennedy Duckett, *Empowering Female Farmers to Feed the World*, NAT'L GEOGRAPHIC, www.nationalgeographic.com/culture/2019/03/partner-content-empowering-female-farmers/ (asserting that, among other barriers, women face farm land ownership barriers that negatively affects their ability to seek "higher earnings and reliable sources of income"); *see also* SARA KOMINERS, OXFAM AMERICA, WORKING IN FEAR: SEXUAL VIOLENCE AGAINST WOMEN FARMWORKERS IN THE UNITED STATES 15–16 (2015) (stating that women farmworkers in the United States face sexual violence in many forms, including verbal abuse and rape).
28 Peter Hurst et al., *Agricultural Workers and Their Contribution to Sustainable Agriculture and Rural Development*, Food and Agriculture Organization et. al., 19, Point 1.4 at 25, 32, 3.4 at 35, 2.21 at 58 (2007), www.fao.org/3/a-bp976e.pdf.
29 2017 HLPF THEMATIC REVIEW, *supra* note 4, at 1.
30 *See Farmer Suicides: A Global Phenomenon*, PRAGATI (May 6, 2015), http://pragati.nationalinterest.in/2015/05/farmer-suicides-a-global-phenomena/; Paméla Rougerie, *Quiet Epidemic of Suicide Claims France's Farmers*, N.Y. TIMES (Aug. 20, 2017), www.nytimes.com/2017/08/20/world/europe/france-farm-suicide.html; and Debbie Weingarten, *Why Are America's Farmers Killing Themselves?*, THE GUARDIAN (Dec. 11, 2018), www.theguardian.com/us-news/2017/dec/06/why-are-americas-farmers-killing-themselves-in-record-numbers.
31 *See Seized: The 2008 Landgrab For Food and Financial Security*, GRAIN (Oct. 24, 2008) www.grain.org/article/entries/93-seized-the-2008-landgrab-for-food-and-financial-security.

representing 38 million hectares, 74% of which were for food and agriculture.[32] These land deals often lack transparency, disregard land users' rights, and are concluded without the consent of or meaningful consultation with affected communities.[33] The impact of these deals and of industrial agriculture on a region's water supply is another major concern. According to the HLPF, "A growing number of regions are facing water scarcity due to excessive water use in agriculture. Groundwater is being depleted, polluted, or salinized in ways disproportionately affecting the poor and vulnerable."[34]

The industrial food system has also stripped our diet of its nutritional content. Agribusiness companies have flooded markets with processed, calorie-dense, and nutrient-poor foods. Inadequate diets are a major contributing factor to the increase of non-communicable diseases occurring now in all regions of the world. Worldwide, the prevalence of obesity is on the rise, heightening the risk for type 2 diabetes, heart disease, and gastrointestinal cancers.[35] Industrial agriculture also creates the conditions for future pandemics in two respects. First, as a key driver of habitat destruction, commercial agriculture removes essential protective barriers and enhances human–wildlife interaction.[36] Second, intensive livestock production, "amplifies the risks of diseases emerging and spreading" through the "confinement of large numbers of animals in small spaces, narrowed genetic diversity, fast animal turnover, and habitat fragmentation through expansion of livestock production."[37]

In sum, our industrial food system "generates food loss and waste, mistreats animals, emits greenhouse gases, pollutes ecosystems, displaces and abuses agricultural and fishery workers, and disrupts traditional farming communities. Put simply, the human rights of food system actors, including agricultural workers, smallholder farmers, and consumers, are often ignored or worse, violated."[38]

Tracking Progress on SDG 2

As evidenced above, how we produce our food—and how we treat those who feed us—has profound implications for food security, climate change, agro-biodiversity, public health, and human rights. SDG 2 therefore clearly intersects with other Sustainable Development Goals, including but not limited to: SDG 1 (poverty eradication), SDG 3 (good health and well-being), SDG 5 (gender equality), SDG 6 (clean water and sanitation), SDG 7 (clean energy), SDG 8 (decent work), SDG 10 (reduced inequalities), SDG 12 (responsible consumption and production), SDG 13 (climate action), SDG 15 (life on land), and SDG 16 (peace, justice, and strong institutions). That the implementation of SDG 2 has implications for multiple SDGs is, of course, unsurprising given the interdependent and holistic nature of all the Goals and the fact that food security and food production implicate social, political,

---

32 GRAIN, *The Global Farm Land Grab in 2016: How Big, How Bad?*, Resilience (July 13, 2016), www.resilience.org/stories/2016-07-13/the-global-farm-land-grab-in-2016-how-big-how-bad/.
33 Smita Narula, *The Global Land Rush: Markets, Rights, and the Politics of Food*, 49 Stan. J. Int'l L. 101, 107 (2013) [hereinafter "*The Global Land Rush*"].
34 2017 HLPF Thematic Review, *supra* note 4, at 6.
35 U.N. Special Rapporteur on the right to food, *Critical Perspective on Food Systems*, *supra* note 5, at ¶¶ 31, 33.
36 IPES-Food, *COVID-19 and the Crisis in Food Systems: Symptoms, Causes, and Potential Solutions*, at 2 (April 2020) [hereinafter "*COVID-19 and the crisis in food systems*"].
37 *See Id.* at 2.
38 U.N. Special Rapporteur on the Right to Food, *Critical Perspective on Food Systems*, *supra* note 5, at ¶ 6.

economic, environmental, cultural, and human rights concerns. This section begins with an overview of the SDG 2 targets and then looks at how the global community is faring in achieving the Zero Hunger Goal, especially in light of the COVID-19 pandemic.

SDG Targets

To help actualize SDG 2, the UN has set multiple ambitious targets. The first four targets, which are to be achieved by 2030, are as follows:

Target 2.1: "end hunger and ensure access by all ... to safe, nutritious and sufficient food all year round."

Target 2.2: "end all forms of malnutrition, including achieving, by 2025, internationally agreed targets on stunting and wasting in children under [five]."

Target 2.3: "double the agricultural productivity and incomes of small-scale food producers, in particular women, indigenous peoples, family farmers, pastoralists and fishers, including through secure and equal access to land, other productive resources and inputs, knowledge, financial services, markets and opportunities for value addition and non-farm employment."

Target 2.4: "ensure sustainable food production systems and implement resilient agricultural practices that increase productivity and production, that help maintain ecosystems, that strengthen capacity for adaptation to climate change, extreme weather, drought, flooding and other disasters and that progressively improve land and soil quality."[39]

A fifth target (2.5), which is indexed to the year 2020, is to "maintain the genetic diversity of seeds, cultivated plants, and ... animals[,]" and to "promote access to and fair and equitable sharing of benefits arising from the utilization of genetic resources and associated traditional knowledge, as internationally agreed." Finally, an additional three targets call for: Increasing investments in agricultural and rural economies "in order to enhance agricultural productive capacity in developing countries" (Target 2.A); correcting and preventing "trade restrictions and distortions in world agricultural markets" (Target 2.B); and ensuring "the proper functioning of food commodity markets and their derivatives ... in order to limit extreme food price volatility" (Target 2.C).[40]

Progress toward achieving each target is measured using specific indicators. Target 2.1 on ending hunger, for example, is assessed by looking at the prevalence of undernourishment and of moderate or severe food insecurity in the world today. Target 2.2 on ending all forms of malnutrition looks at the prevalence of stunting and malnutrition (both wasting and overweight) among children under 5 years of age.[41] A look at several indicators reveals a lack of progress toward achieving SDG 2.

A Troubling Lack of Progress and the Impact of COVID-19

The annual "State of Food Security and Nutrition in the World" (SOFI) report is widely viewed as a critical measure of global progress toward the achievement of SDG 2 as it provides updated estimates on the prevalence of hunger and malnourishment in the world

---

39 *Goal 2: Zero Hunger*, U.N. SUSTAINABLE DEVELOPMENT GOALS, www.un.org/sustainabledevelopment/hunger/ (last visited May 19, 2020).
40 *Id.*
41 *Id.*

today.[42] The most recent SOFI report, which was published in July 2020, continues to paint a worrying picture. Critically, the report found that "The number of people affected by hunger globally has been slowly on the rise since 2014 .... In 2019, close to 750 million—or nearly one in ten people in the world—were exposed to severe levels of food insecurity."[43]

The SOFI report additionally estimated that around 2 billion people experienced some level of food insecurity in 2019 in that they lack regular access to safe, nutritious, and sufficient food.[44] Moreover, the "gender gap in accessing food increased from 2018 to 2019," with women experiencing a greater prevalence of moderate and severe food insecurity at the global level.[45] More than 1 in 5 children under five (144 million) were stunted in 2019—so malnourished that they will not reach their full physical and cognitive potential. Although progress has been made on this front, the world is not on track to achieve the 2025 target for stunting in children under five.[46] Meanwhile, the prevalence of overweight and obesity—another form of malnutrition—continues to rise in all regions.[47] With regard to the SDGs and the impact of COVID-19, the report concludes that

> The world is not on track to achieve Zero Hunger by 2030. If recent trends continue, the number of people affected by hunger will surpass 840 million by 2030, or 9.8 percent of the population. This is an alarming scenario, even without taking into account the potential impacts of the COVID-19 pandemic .... A preliminary assessment suggests the pandemic may add between 83 and 132 million people to the total number of undernourished in the world in 2020 depending on the economic growth scenario.[48]

The COVID-19 pandemic is accelerating hunger and nutrition-related crises, hitting poor and vulnerable communities the hardest and dealing a profound blow to efforts to achieve the SDGs.[49] Worldwide lockdowns are further straining people's ability to access food as is a widespread loss of income. UN agencies have warned that projected global economic downturns and disruptions to food supply chains could unleash widespread food-related crises.

In April 2020, the World Food Programme (WFP) estimated that without concerted action, 265 million people in low- and middle-income countries would suffer from acute hunger by the end of the year as a result of the COVID-19 pandemic[50]—up from the 135 million people who already faced acute hunger, largely as a result of conflict, climate change,

---

42 *See* FAO, IFAD, UNICEF, WFP & WHO, THE STATE OF FOOD SECURITY AND NUTRITION IN THE WORLD 2020. TRANSFORMING FOOD SYSTEMS FOR AFFORDABLE HEALTHY DIETS (2020). [hereinafter "FAO SOFI REPORT"].
43 *Id.* at xvi.
44 *Id.*
45 *Id.*
46 *Id.*
47 *Id.*
48 *Id.*
49 A Resolution adopted by the U.N. General Assembly on April 2, 2020 recognized that, "the poorest and most vulnerable are the hardest hit by the pandemic and that the impact of the crisis will reverse hard-won development gains and hamper progress towards achieving the Sustainable Development Goals." G.A. Res. A/RES/74/270, at 1 (Apr. 3, 2020).
50 Paul Anthem, *Risk of Hunger Pandemic as COVID-19 Set to almost Double Acute Hunger by End of 2020*, WORLD FOOD PROGRAM INSIGHT (Apr. 16, 2020), https://insight.wfp.org/covid-19-will-almost-double-people-in-acute-hunger-by-end-of-2020-59df0c4a8072.

and economic crises.[51] Those living in conflict zones and refugee camps are particularly vulnerable as are countries that rely heavily on food imports should trade flows be affected.[52] The FAO too has sounded the alarm on the pandemic's devastating impacts on efforts to reduce hunger and food insecurity, especially in net food-importing countries.[53]

With regard to other SDG 2 targets, the FAO concluded pre-pandemic that it was "too early to call" whether we are on track to meeting Target 2.3 on doubling the agricultural productivity and incomes of small-scale food producers.[54] It did, however, note that the "productivity of small-scale producers is systematically lower on average than for larger food producers and, in most countries, the incomes of small-scale food producers are less than half those of larger food producers."[55] In a more recent post-COVID-19 briefing paper the FAO drew attention to the fact that the "poorest and most vulnerable groups will experience the most negative effects of the current pandemic," a demographic that "includes subsistence farmers as well as smallholder farmers' enterprises"[56] who in the most immediate term are being affected by the disruption of markets and related services and by reduced labor mobility, which in turn means lower incomes for farming households.[57]

Progress toward Target 2.5 on maintaining the genetic diversity of seeds, cultivated plants, and their related wild species—as indicated by the number of plant genetic resources secured in medium- or long-term conservation facilities—is decidedly "off track"[58] as is progress toward Target 2.C which seeks to limit extreme food price volatility.[59] Government spending on agriculture declined by 37% from 2001 to 2017,[60] contravening Target 2.A's goal of increasing investments in agricultural and rural economies. A continuous downward trend in export subsidy outlays, however, has decreased distortions in world agricultural markets (Target 2.B).[61]

Target 2.4 on ensuring sustainable food production systems and implementing resilient agricultural practices is of particular relevance to this chapter, and to ensuring progress

---

51 Global Network against Food Crises, *2020 Global Report on Food Crises* (2020), www.wfp.org/publications/2020-global-report-food-crises.
52 *See* Paul Anthem, *Risk of Hunger Pandemic as COVID-19 Set to almost Double Acute Hunger by end of 2020*, *supra* note 50 (noting that "Sub-Saharan African countries such as Somalia and South Sudan imported more than 40 million tons of cereals from around the world in 2018 to plug gaps in local food production." The WFP notes that countries with large public debt will also struggle to mobilize the resources needed to respond to the crisis).
53 *See* FAO, COVID-19 GLOBAL ECONOMIC RECESSION: AVOIDING HUNGER MUST BE AT THE CENTRE OF THE ECONOMIC STIMULUS 1 (2020) [hereinafter "FAO COVID-19 STIMULUS REPORT"]; A June 2020 report prepared by teams of independent experts at the Sustainable Development Solutions Network and the Bertelsmann Stiftung similarly concluded that COVID-19 will have "severe negative impacts on most SDGs" including SDG 2. J. SACHS, ET AL. SUSTAINABLE DEVELOPMENT REPORT 2020: THE SUSTAINABLE DEVELOPMENT GOALS AND COVID-19 vi, 4 (2020).
54 FAO, TRACKING PROGRESS ON FOOD AND AGRICULTURE-RELATED SDG INDICATORS 10 (2019) [hereinafter "FAO PROGRESS REPORT"].
55 *Id*. at 10.
56 FAO, SUSTAINABLE CROP PRODUCTION AND COVID-19 1 (2020).
57 *Id*. at 2.
58 FAO PROGRESS REPORT, *supra* note 54, at 12.
59 *Id*. at 18 (stating that during the 2016–2017 period, for example, the "high volatility of general food prices affected a quarter of countries in Africa and Western Asia, and a fifth of countries in Central and Southern Asia").
60 U.N. Secretary-General, *Special Edition: Progress towards the Sustainable Development Goals*, ¶ 23, U.N. Doc. E/2019/68 (July 24, 2019).
61 *Id*.

on other SDG 2 targets. The 2017 HLPF review of SDG 2 concluded that better tools are "urgently needed" to monitor progress toward Target 2.4 on sustainable agriculture and resilient food systems.[62] Under the custodianship of the FAO, progress has been made toward the development of SDG Indicator 2.4.1, which intends to measure the proportion of agricultural area under productive and sustainable agriculture. The main measurement instrument—farm surveys—are being piloted in several countries and are intended to capture the environmental, economic, and social dimensions of sustainable production.[63]

A look at the list of themes and sub-indicators that inform indicator 2.4.1 suggests that there may now be a concerted attempt to shift away from simply focusing on net calorie production and yield per hectare toward inclusion of other important indicators such as soil health, water use, use of practices that support agro-biodiversity, wage rates for agricultural workers, and secure tenure rights to land.[64] This shift to more holistic forms of measurement that can capture the inequities of our food system is a welcome development. The prevailing political climate, however, continues to favor and support industrial agriculture, which exacerbates inequalities and undermines the achievement of multiple SDG 2 targets. Indeed, efforts to reduce hunger, support small-scale food producers, ensure sustainable food production systems, and maintain the genetic diversity of seeds, plants, and animals, will decidedly fail if States continue to invest in large-scale industrial agriculture.[65]

Taken together, the reports cited above do not paint an optimistic picture. On the contrary, they suggest that if we proceed with business as usual, we will continue to witness a rise in hunger and food insecurity, as well as a profound loss of biodiversity and increasingly unsustainable agricultural practices. Lifting billions out of food insecurity, addressing the impending COVID-19 food crisis, and averting future pandemics requires nothing short of a fundamental paradigm shift in how we grow our food and how we treat those who feed us. Even prior to COVID-19, the UN acknowledged as much, asserting that

> It is time to rethink how we grow, share and consume our food .... A profound change of the global food and agriculture system is needed if we are to nourish the 821 million people who are hungry today and the additional 2 billion people expected to be undernourished by 2050.[66]

These calls for a transformative paradigm shift have only gotten louder in the context of the COVID-19 pandemic,[67] which is placing food and farmworkers in a particularly precarious position[68] and laying bare "the underlying risks, fragilities, and inequities in global food

---

62 2017 HLPF THEMATIC REVIEW, *supra* note 4, at 6.
63 FAO, SDG INDICATOR 2.4.1 PROPORTION OF AGRICULTURAL AREA UNDER PRODUCTIVE AND SUSTAINABLE AGRICULTURE 11 (2019).
64 *Id.* at 25–28, 33–36, 39–40.
65 U.N. Special Rapporteur on the right to food, *Interim Report of the Special Rapporteur on the Right to Food*, ¶ 38, U.N. Doc A/74/164 (July 15, 2019) [hereinafter "*Interim Report*"].
66 *Goal 2: Zero Hunger*, *supra* note 39.
67 *See, e.g.*, FAO, SUSTAINABLE CROP PRODUCTION AND COVID-19, *supra* note 56, at 4 (advocating for more local food distribution with shorter and more simplified food supply chains).
68 COVID-19 has laid bare the precarious situation of food- and farmworkers who in addition to working in poor conditions at very low pay are now facing major health risks as they work to keep food supplies flowing. *See, e.g.*, Leah Douglas, *Mapping COVID-19 Outbreaks in the Food System*, FOOD & ENV'T REPORTING NETWORK (Apr. 22, 2020), https://thefern.org/2020/04/mapping-covid-19-in-meat-and

systems."[69] But despite reaching these conclusions, States continue to advance large-scale industrial agriculture.[70] Moreover, the mainstream prescriptions for how to achieve SDG 2 remain rooted in a productivist approach[71] that fails to center the human rights of those made most vulnerable by our industrial food system.

The Fallacies of the Productivist Paradigm

The dominant paradigm used to organize, measure, and evaluate our food system, is a market-based and profit-driven productivist paradigm that reduces the host of issues we are facing to a production problem. Put simply, the productivist paradigm focuses on the supply of food commodities and the efficiency of food production. The narrative that we must increase food production by 50% by 2050 in order to meet the needs of a growing population[72] is a case in point. Increasing food production is offered as a unidimensional solution to a problem that is in fact complex, multidimensional, and structural. A narrow and short-sighted focus on increasing the global production of food commodities conveniently sidesteps key questions related to poverty, access to food and food-producing resources, and social equity and power relations in the food system.[73] In other words, it is not enough to simply ask how much food we can produce. We must ask *how* and *for whom* and with what *nutritional content*.

Although the SDGs place great value on the need for inclusion and sustainability in achieving the 17 Goals, SDG 2 does not challenge embedded assumptions that continue to correlate increased food production with a decrease in food insecurity, when in fact food insecurity is not a production problem but a distribution problem tied to impoverishment and the denial of access to food-producing resources such as land, water, and seeds. Indeed, the number of hungry people in the world has grown since 2014, despite the fact that we have increased global food production.[74] As articulated by Food First Information and Action Network (FIAN) International,

> Mainstream monitoring of food security and nutrition fails to address the critical questions around the social control of the food system, and in particular natural resources,

---

-food-processing-plants/ (noting that as of May 26, 2020, at least "17,893 meatpacking workers, 1,189 food processing workers, and 703 farmworkers" had tested positive for COVID-19 in the United States).

69 *See* IPES-Food, *COVID-19 and the Crisis in Food Systems*, *supra* note 36, at 1.

70 U.N. Special Rapporteur on the right to food, *Critical Perspective on Food Systems*, *supra* note 5, at ¶ 41 (noting that "States continue to invest in production practices and industrial agriculture that have detrimental environmental impact" and citing the expansion of the palm oil industry as an example).

71 *See Goal 2: End Hunger, Achieve Food Security and Improved Nutrition and Promote Sustainable Agriculture*, *supra* note 3 (noting that "increased investments through international cooperation" are required to "bolster the productive capacity of agriculture in developing countries").

72 *See Food Production Must Double by 2050 to Meet Demand from World's Growing Population, Innovative Strategies Needed to Combat Hunger, Experts Tell Second Committee*, U.N. MEETINGS COVERAGE & PRESS RELEASES (Oct. 9, 2009), www.un.org/press/en/2009/gaef3242.doc.htm; *see also* FAO, SUSTAINABLE CROP PRODUCTION AND COVID-19, *supra* note 56, at 1 (noting this need for food production increases).

73 *See* IPES-Food, *From Uniformity to Diversity*, *supra* note 8, at 8.

74 FAO, THE FUTURE OF FOOD AND AGRICULTURE: TRENDS AND CHALLENGES 2 (2018) (noting that "[g]ains in productivity and technological advances have contributed to more efficient resource use and improved food safety. But major concerns persist. Some 795 million people still suffer from hunger, and more than two billion from micronutrient deficiencies or forms of overnourishment").

and proposes solutions based on the current industrial model of production that feeds a global, and inherently unequal economy.[75]

Prescriptions to "invest in agriculture" will not work until and unless we pursue a rights-based approach that centers the agency and authority of peasants and other rural communities in decision-making processes, and prescriptively puts a thumb on the scale in favor of shorter supply chains, of more equitable land distribution, of food sovereignty and sustainable labor-intensive food systems, and of using agro-ecological methods and traditional knowledge that helps protect agro-biodiversity. As noted by the UN Special Rapporteur on the right to food,

> The right to food extends beyond productivism, the paradigm in which Goal 2 (zero hunger) is rooted. Realizing this right requires tackling the historical and structural inequalities that undermine availability, adequacy, accessibility and sustainability of food systems ... States, as the primary duty bearers, must create environments conducive to the enjoyment of the right to food.[76]

The Right to Food and Rights-Respecting Food Systems

Ensuring Food as a Human Right

The right to food has been part of the international human rights legal framework since its inception. The right first found expression in Article 25 of the Universal Declaration of Human Rights (UDHR), which states that "[e]veryone has the right to a standard of living adequate for the health and well-being of himself and of his family, including food."[77] The right was subsequently codified by Article 11 of the International Covenant on Economic, Social and Cultural Rights (ICESCR), which encompasses two separate but related norms: The right to adequate food (Article 11(1)) and the right to be free from hunger (Article 11(2)).[78]

Under international human rights law, States-parties to the ICESCR must progressively ensure that food is *accessible*, both physically and economically; that food is *adequate*, meaning safe, nutritious, and culturally appropriate; that food is *available* to purchase or that people have the means to produce it themselves, including through secure access to land and other productive resources; and that food is produced *sustainably*, preserving the right to food for future generations.[79]

As part of their obligations, States must take steps to *respect*, *protect*, and *fulfill* the right to food. Respecting the right to food means refraining from enacting laws, policies, or programs that would interfere with people's ability to exercise their right to food. Protecting the right to food means ensuring that third party actors such as corporations do not interfere with people's ability to exercise their right. The duty to fulfill the right to food is a positive obligation that requires states to pro-actively engage in, *inter alia*, "activities intended to strengthen people's

---

75 Emily Mattheisen, FIAN International, *SDG 2: Approaching SDG 2 through the Right to Food and Nutrition*, *in* Spotlight on Sustainable Development 2018, 109, 109. (Civil Society Reflection Group on the 2030 Agenda for Sustainable Development, 2018.)
76 U.N. Special Rapporteur on the right to food, *Interim Report*, *supra* note 65, at ¶ 3.
77 Universal Declaration of Human Rights, G.A. Res. 217 (III) A, art. 25, U.N. Doc. A/RES/217 (III) (Dec. 10, 1948).
78 G.A. Res. 2200A (XXI), art. 11, U.N. Doc. A/6316, at 4 (Dec. 16, 1966).
79 ECOSOC, U.N. CHR, General Comment No. 12, The Right to Adequate Food, U.N. Doc. E/C.12/1999/5 ¶¶ 7, 12, 13 (1999).

access to and utilization of resources and means to ensure their livelihood."[80] In situations where people are unable to provide food for themselves, the State must implement effective social programs that directly provide adequate food to those in need.[81]

SDG 2 does not explicitly recognize the human right to adequate food, but its goals can be seen as aligning with the obligations of States to ensure this right. The SDGs also promise to "leave no one behind"[82]—a nod to the human rights principles of equality and non-discrimination which in turn are highly relevant to ending hunger, the root cause of which is the inequitable distribution of food and productive resources.[83] But SDG 2 does not pursue a rights-based approach—either to ensuring food security or to transitioning to sustainable food systems. As noted above, the Zero Hunger Goal is rooted in a productivist paradigm that fails to hold either State or corporate actors accountable.

If we are to achieve the goal of ending hunger, achieving food security, improving nutrition, and promoting sustainable agriculture, then States' actions must be informed by their human rights obligations. In short, States must ensure food as a human right and they must invest in a radical transformation of our food system to move away from industrial practices toward diversified agroecological systems.[84]

Although the ICESCR has been widely ratified, it does not enjoy universal ratification.[85] There is also a significant gap between recognizing the right and ensuring its implementation.[86] A rights-based approach to the SDGs recognizes that the fulfillment of human rights are a precondition for sustainable development.[87] A rights-based approach also reminds States to focus on the most vulnerable and marginalized sections of the population,[88] and ensure that the policy-making process integrates the human rights principles of participation, accountability, non-discrimination, transparency, and the rule of law.[89]

In addition to fulfilling substantive rights such as the right to adequate food in a non-discriminatory manner,[90] States must also fulfill multiple procedural rights as expressed in both international human rights law and international environmental law. Namely, they must ensure that individuals have the right to receive information about policies and projects that affect their rights; the right to participate in decision-making related to these policies; and the right to an effective remedy when their rights are violated.[91] In short, a rights-based

---

80 *Id.* at ¶ 15.
81 *Id.*
82 *The Sustainable Development Goals Report: Leaving No One Behind*, U.N. DEP'T OF ECON. & SOC. AFF. (2016), https://unstats.un.org/sdgs/report/2016/leaving-no-one-behind.
83 U.N. Special Rapporteur on the right to food, *Interim Report, supra* note 65, at ¶ 2.
84 *See, e.g., id.* at ¶ 37 (calling on States to "restructure policies that reinforce inequality, such as those that favour large-scale land acquisitions over small farm development").
85 The United States, for example, where 1 in 9 households are food insecure and whose trade and agricultural policies have outsized impacts on rural communities worldwide, has signed but not ratified ICESCR. ALISHA COLEMAN-JENSEN, ET AL., HOUSEHOLD FOOD SECURITY IN THE UNITED STATES IN 2018, 6 (2019).
86 U.N. Special Rapporteur on the right to food, *Interim Report, supra* note 65, at ¶ 59.
87 *See* Yesudas Choondassery, *Rights-Based Approach: The Hub of Sustainable Development*, 8(2) DISCOURSE & COMM. FOR SUSTAINABLE EDUC., 17 (2017).
88 U.N. Special Rapporteur on the right to food, *Critical Perspective on Food Systems, supra* note 5, at ¶ 65.
89 *See* United Nations Sustainable Dev. Grp., Human Rights Working Grp., The human rights-based approach to development cooperation: towards a common understanding among United Nations agencies, (2003); U.N. Special Rapporteur on the right to food, *Interim Report, supra* note 65, at ¶ 50.
90 *Id.*
91 *See* Sumudu Atapattu and Andrea Schapper, *Procedural Rights, in* HUMAN RIGHTS AND THE ENVIRONMENT: KEY ISSUES, 129 (Routledge, 2019) (summarizing these procedural rights in the context of explaining States' obligations to uphold environmental rights). *See also Sustainable Development Goal 16*, U.N.

approach and the human rights instruments that underpin such an approach, provide a set of tools to hold governments accountable. They also provide a framework for transitioning to a rights-respecting food system.

Building Rights-Respecting Food Systems

In addition to the ICESCR and other human rights treaties that codify the right to food,[92] several soft law instruments can help ensure food as a human right and support the transition to sustainable rights-respecting food systems. Most notable among these instruments are the Voluntary Guidelines on the Responsible Governance of Tenure of Land, Fisheries and Forests (Tenure Guidelines) and the UN Declaration on the Rights of Peasants and Other People Working in Rural Areas (UNDROP).

The Tenure Guidelines, which were adopted by the 125 member countries of the Committee on World Food Security in 2012,[93] represent a landmark international agreement that provides practical guidance to States on how to "improve the governance of tenure of land, fisheries and forests based on human rights, with an emphasis on vulnerable and marginalized people."[94] The Guidelines are of particular significance for Target 2.3 and more generally for small-scale food producers who have been dispossessed of land or denied access to or control over food-producing resources. The Tenure Guidelines also represent a clear repudiation of the philosophy that land distribution should be purely market-driven, or that large-scale industrialized agricultural production can ensure the developmental and food security needs of the planet in a sustainable and equitable way.[95]

UNDROP is the most recent addition to the human rights toolkit. It was adopted by the UN General Assembly in December 2018 following six years of intensive inter-governmental negotiations and extensive inputs from those whose rights are directly at stake. UNDROP makes visible the widespread and often egregious violations of peasants' rights.[96] It also makes visible the profound role that rural women play in the economic survival of

---

SUSTAINABLE DEV. GOALS (expressly stating that access to justice must be achieved in order to provide "security, rights and opportunities").

92 *See, e.g.,* Convention on the Elimination of All Forms of Discrimination against Women [CEDAW], U.N. GAOR, 34th Sess., G.A. Res. 34/180, Supp. No. 46 at 193, U.N. Doc. A/34/46 (Dec. 18, 1979), art. 12(2) (requiring States Parties to ensure adequate nutrition for women during pregnancy and lactation); and Convention on the Rights of the Child [CRC], G.A. Res. 44/25, annex, U.N. GAOR, 44th Sess., Supp. 49 at 167, U.N. Doc. A/44/49 (Nov. 20, 1989), arts. 24(2)(c), 27 (requiring States Parties to take appropriate measures to combat disease and malnutrition through, *inter alia*, the provision of adequate nutritious foods and clean drinking water).

93 *See generally* FAO, VOLUNTARY GUIDELINES ON THE RESPONSIBLE GOVERNANCE OF TENURE OF LAND, FISHERIES AND FORESTS IN THE CONTEXT OF NATIONAL FOOD SECURITY (2012).

94 Emily Mattheisen, FIAN International, *SDG 2: Approaching SDG 2 through the Right to Food and Nutrition, supra* note 75, at 110.

95 Narula, *The Global Land Rush, supra* note 33, at 169.

96 *See* Preamble of UNDROP, which notes the disproportionate impacts of poverty, hunger, and malnutrition faced by peasants, and further acknowledges the prevalence of forcible evictions and displacement, gender discrimination and violence, hazardous and exploitative work environments, violence and intimidation, and lack of meaningful access to institutional and procedural protections as the conditions under which a disproportionate number of peasants work and live. Human Rights Council Res. 39/12, U.N. Doc. A/HRC/RES/39/12, at 3 (Oct. 8, 2018).

their families and in rural and national economies, as well as the financially and legally precarious (and often violent) circumstances in which they carry out this work.[97]

UNDROP, which aligns with several SDG 2 targets, reaffirms that "peasants and other people working in rural areas have the right to the full enjoyment of all human rights and fundamental freedoms,"[98] including the right to adequate food.[99] The Declaration also fills key normative gaps in rights protections under international law. Notably, the Declaration asserts peasants' rights to land, seeds, and food sovereignty.[100] UNDROP also affirms peasants' rights to maintain biological diversity[101] which is highly relevant to SDG Target 2.5, as well as their right to contribute to the design and implementation of climate change adaptation and mitigation policies, including through the use of traditional practices and knowledge.[102]

Ensuring peasants' rights can help States reduce hunger and malnutrition, in line with SDG Targets 2.1 and 2.2, while increasing incomes for small-scale producers and securing access to food-producing resources for women, Indigenous Peoples, family farmers, pastoralists, and fisherfolk (Target 2.3).[103] Importantly, UNDROP upholds peasant farming as a sustainable and viable alternative to industrial agriculture thereby advancing Target 2.4.

Transnational peasant movements—led by *La Via Campesina*—have been advocating for a peasants' rights declaration since at least 2001 on the premise that small-scale farmers, pastoralists, fisherfolk, and farmworkers are a vulnerable group increasingly subject to forced displacements from their lands, denied access to water and seeds, impoverished by trade and agricultural policies, and attacked and criminalized by State actors acting in collusion with the private sector.[104] *La Via Campesina* is a transnational grassroots peasants' movement that promotes and defends food sovereignty and small-scale sustainable agriculture "as a way to promote social justice and dignity."[105] Most significantly, they have framed their demands

---

97 *See* Preamble of UNDROP, "Stressing that peasant women and other rural women play a significant role in the economic survival of their families and in contributing to the rural and national economy, including through their work in the non-monetized sectors of the economy, but are often denied tenure and ownership of land, equal access to land, productive resources, financial services, information, employment or social protection, and are often victims of violence and discrimination in a variety of forms and manifestations." Human Rights Council Res. 39/12, U.N. Doc. A/HRC/RES/39/12, at 3 (Oct. 8, 2018).
98 *Id*. at art. 3.
99 *Id*. at art. 15.
100 *Id*. at art. 15(4)(5), 17, 19 (Oct. 8, 2018).
101 *Id*. at art. 19, 20.
102 *Id*. at art. 18(3).
103 The Committee on the Elimination of All Forms of Discrimination against Women's general recommendation No. 34 (2016) on the rights of rural women provides additional guidance on resource access for rural women. Comm. On the Elimination of Discrimination against Women, General Recommendation No. 34 (2016), U.N. Doc. CEDAW/C/GC/34 (Mar. 7, 2016). Likewise, the UN Declaration on the Rights of Indigenous Peoples (UNDRIP) calls on States to ensure indigenous peoples' right to free, prior, and informed consent on development projects as well as properly valuing Indigenous Peoples' knowledge and practices through closing education gaps and expanding work opportunities. U.N. Special Rapporteur on the right to food, *Interim Report, supra* note 65, at ¶¶ 40, 42.
104 La Via Campesina, Declaration on the Rights of Peasants—Women and Men (2009). *See also* Marc Edelman, *Linking the Rights of Peasants to the Right to Food in the United Nations*, 10(2) L., Culture & The Humanities, 196 (2014) (analyzing the efforts of *La Via Campesina* to have the United Nations adopt an instrument on peasants' rights).
105 *What Is La Via Campesina? The International Peasant's Voice*, Via Campesina. https://viacampesina .org/en/international-peasants-voice/ (ostensibly the largest social movement in the world, *La Via*

90   *Smita Narula*

using the language and framework of food sovereignty as a means of reclaiming control over food and agricultural systems.

Food sovereignty—defined as the right of people to determine their own food and agricultural systems, and to healthy food that is sustainably produced[106]—is a transformative political project that seeks to decentralize power, restore ecological balance, and put forward an alternative rights-respecting agricultural paradigm.[107] As stated by *La Via Campesina*,

> The alternative exists .... Small farmers and social movements from all over the world promote a model based on food sovereignty and orientated towards peasant-based agriculture and artisan fisheries, prioritising local markets and sustainable production methods. This model is based on the right to food and on the rights of peoples to define their own agricultural policies.[108]

Collectively, the human rights instruments cited above call for structural shifts in power. They create a foundation for a policy framework to help ensure the right to food and the rights of food producers. They also provide the building blocks for a transformative shift in our food systems. As such, their implementation must be front and center to any SDG 2 strategy. The next section looks at data and emerging case studies that help make the case for a transition to diversified agroecological food systems.

Making the Case for an Agroecological Transition

Peasant movements around the world are both defending and bringing into view viable alternatives to our industrial food system—namely, diverse and small-scale agroecological food systems that, provided proper supports, have the potential to strengthen rural livelihoods, conserve biodiversity, help cool the planet through carbon sequestration, and support global food production.[109] This section looks at available evidence to support the assertion that a transition to diversified agroecological food systems is not only necessary but also viable. It takes as its premise the notion that in addition to being able to feed a growing population, food systems must be socially and ecologically viable and must support human and planetary health. Only then can all the dimensions of SDG 2 be achieved.

Campesina is comprised of about 182 organizations in 81 countries and claims to represent around 200 million farmers worldwide).
106 *See The Declaration of Nyéléni*, born *in* Nyéléni 2007 Forum for Food Sovereignty, 8, (2007) https://nyeleni.org/DOWNLOADS/Nyelni_EN.pdf.
107 *See* Priscilla Claeys, Human Rights and the Food Sovereignty Movement: Reclaiming Control (2015) (providing an in-depth analysis of the vision and strategies of the food sovereignty movement).
108 La Via Campesina, *Farmers and Social Movements Call for a Fundamental Restructuring of the Global Food System*, (Jan. 27, 2009) https://viacampesina.org/en/farmers-and-social-movements-call-for-a-fundamental-restructuring-of-the-global-food-system/.
109 *See Food Sovereignty Now!, At Global Climate Talks, La Via Campesina Calls for Peasant Agroecology*, Climate and Capitalism (2017), https://climateandcapitalism.com/2017/11/09/climate-talks-via-campesina-peasant-agroecology/ (noting that as articulated by peasant activists, peasant farmers and indigenous peoples "feed the world and cool the planet").

Peasant Agriculture Feeds the World and Protects Biodiversity

As a starting point, it is important to make clear that peasant agriculture, not industrial farms, feeds the world and protects biodiversity. Although trade and agricultural policies heavily favor large industrial farms, peasants are the main or sole food providers for more than 70% of the world's population. Moreover, they produce this food using less than 25% of the world's agricultural land (and even less water and fossil fuels), while inflicting far less damage to soils and forests.[110] By contrast, the industrial food chain—which as noted above is a significant source of greenhouse gas emissions and a major cause of topsoil degradation and deforestation—uses at least 75% of the world's agricultural resources to produce food for less than 30% of the world's population.[111]

The so-called "peasant food web" also nurtures 9 to 100 times the biodiversity used by the industrial food chain, across plants, livestock, fish, and forests.[112] The FAO reports that "[m]uch of the world's BFA is managed in, or associated with, smallholder cropping or mixed systems, pastoralist systems or small-scale forest, aquaculture or fishing systems."[113] As stated by the ETC Group, "Peasants have the knowledge, innovative energy and networks needed to respond to climate change; they have the operational scope and scale; and they are closest to the hungry and malnourished."[114] While these statistics provide reason for hope, the "peasant food web" has for decades been under sustained attack—displaced by destructive industries, undermined by trade policies, and denied necessary infrastructural and State support. As such, peasant agriculture is in desperate need of protection and fortification. As outlined below, the potential benefits of the agroecological strategies employed by peasant agriculture also merit far greater study and support.

The Benefits and Potential of Diversified Agroecological Food Systems

Agroecology is a science, a set of principles and practices, and a socio-political movement that stands in sharp contrast to industrial agriculture.[115] As a practice, agroecology is characterized by "diversifying farms and farming landscapes, replacing chemical inputs with organic materials and processes, optimizing biodiversity, and stimulating interactions between different species, as part of holistic strategies to build long-term soil fertility, healthy agroecosystems and secure and just livelihoods."[116] Agroecology also promotes "fair, short distribution networks rather than linear distribution chains and builds a transparent network of relationships … between producers and consumers."[117] As a political framework, agroecology highlights the connections between food sovereignty, locally adapted agricultural

---

110 ETC Group, Who Will Feed Us?, *supra* note 14, at 17; *see also Putting Family Farmers First to Eradicate Hunger*, FAO (Oct. 16, 2014), www.fao.org/news/story/en/item/260535/icode/ (stating that "family farms produce about 80 percent of the world's food").
111 ETC Group, Who Will Feed Us?, *supra* note 14, at 17.
112 *Id.* at 6.
113 FAO Biodiversity Report, *supra* note 15, at 380.
114 ETC Group, Who Will Feed Us?, *supra* note 14, at 6.
115 *See* Colin Anderson et al., Centre for Agroecology, Water & Resilience, Building, Defending and Strengthening Agroecology: A Global Struggle for Food Sovereignty, *supra* note 13.
116 *Agroecology*, IPES-Food, www.ipes-food.org/topics/Agroecology (last visited May 28, 2020).
117 CIDSE,*Economic Dimension of Agroecology, The Principles of Agroecology—Towards Just, Resilient and Sustainable Food Systems* (Mar. 30, 2018), https://agroecologyprinciple.atavist.com/the-principles-of-agroecology-#chapter-3408922.

systems, and the right to food.[118] As asserted in the *Declaration of the International Forum for Agroecology, 2015*—a social movement-led initiative—agroecology is

> [A] key form of resistance to an economic system that puts profit before life .... Our diverse forms of smallholder food production based on Agroecology generate local knowledge, promote social justice, nurture identity and culture, and strengthen the economic viability of rural areas. As smallholders, we defend our dignity when we choose to produce in an agroecological way .... Families, communities, collectives, organizations and movements are the fertile soil in which agroecology flourishes.[119]

In addition to promoting social justice and nurturing identity and culture, there is growing evidence to suggest that diversified agroecological systems "keep carbon in the ground, support biodiversity, rebuild soil fertility and sustain yields over time, providing a basis for secure farm livelihoods."[120] The ETC Group asserts that,

> [w]ith the right policies, land and rights, peasant-led agroecological strategies could double or even triple rural employment, substantially reduce the pressure for urban migration, significantly improve nutritional quality and availability, and eliminate hunger while slashing agriculture's greenhouse gas (GHG) emissions by more than 90%.[121]

Notably, the Intergovernmental Panel on Climate Change (IPCC) 2019 Special Report on Climate Change and Land states with high confidence that agricultural practices that include indigenous and local knowledge can help overcome the combined challenges of climate change, food insecurity, and biodiversity conservation.[122]

Diversified agroecological food systems can also improve resilience to global crises such as the COVID-19 pandemic.[123] As noted above, the vulnerability of the industrial food system stems in part from its long supply chains and its dependence on external inputs.[124] The agroecological principles of replacing external chemical inputs with organic materials and processes, and of creating short distribution networks that bring producers and consumers closer together, can help turn small-scale farms into vital assets for providing food while protecting the environment and promoting food sovereignty.

---

118 U.N. Special Rapporteur on the right to food, *Interim report*, *supra* note 65, at ¶ 38.
119 La Via Campesina, *Declaration of the International Forum for Agroecology*, (Mar. 4, 2015), https://viacampesina.org/en/declaration-of-the-international-forum-for-agroecology/.
120 IPES-Food, *From Uniformity to Diversity*, *supra* note 8, at 2.
121 ETC Group, Who Will Feed Us?, *supra* note 14, at 48.
122 Intergovernmental Panel on Climate Change [IPCC], Summary for Policymakers, *Climate Change and Land: An IPCC Special Report on Climate Change, Desertification, Land Degradation, Sustainable Land Management, Food Security, and Greenhouse Gas Fluxes in Terrestrial Ecosystems*, Finding C.4.3 at 31 (2019).
123 *See* Brooke Porter, *Pandemic Challenges the Global Food System and Brings Us Closer to Agroecology*, Over Grow the System (Apr. 17, 2020), https://webcache.googleusercontent.com/search?q=cache:2fwMqRleGpgJ:https://overgrowthesystem.org/pandemic-challenges-global-food-system-brings-us-closer-agroecology/+&cd=1&hl=en&ct=clnk&gl=us.
124 Food Sovereignty, Friends of the Earth Int'l et al., *Statement to the Extraordinary Meeting of G20 Agriculture Ministers*, (April 21, 2020) https://fian.org/files/files/G20_agricultural_workers_and_peasant_farmers_COVID-19.pdf.

Case studies from around the globe suggest that agroecological transitions are succeeding, at least at the local level. In 2018, the International Panel of Experts on Sustainable Food Systems (IPES-Food) published the results of its investigation of 7 case studies that showed that "in spite of the many barriers to change, people around the world have been able to fundamentally rethink and redesign food systems around agroecological principles."[125] These case studies—which looked at localized initiatives in the United States, Nicaragua, Mexico, Tanzania, China, France, Spain, and Cuba—revealed that "it is possible for communities, regions, and whole countries to fundamentally redesign their food and farming systems. The change process can be initiated from a variety of entry points, and does not always begin on the farm with input substitution."[126]

With changes in "production practices, in knowledge generation and dissemination, in social and economic relations, and in institutional frameworks," the report concludes, "the multiple 'lock-ins' of industrial food systems can be overcome and new sustainable food systems can start to emerge."[127] Moreover, IPES-Food adds, "diversified agroecological systems can also pave the way for diverse diets and improved health."[128] An in-depth study undertaken by the Food Sovereignty Alliance, India and the Catholic Health Association of India in the southern Indian states of Telangana and Andhra Pradesh provides a case in point. The study analyzed the traditional food systems of marginal farmers and agropastoralists from several marginalized communities and found that traditional food systems that are embedded in local ecological and cultural contexts were sufficiently rich and diverse in nutrients so as to counter malnutrition, including deficiencies of micronutrients, such as Vitamin A.[129]

On the question of whether agroecological systems can improve yields, IPES-Food concludes that indeed they can and that they perform "particularly strongly under environmental stress, and deliver production increases in the places where additional food is desperately needed."[130] The next section looks at Tanzania's Chololo Ecovillage project—a case study developed by IPES-Food and the Alliance for Food Sovereignty in Africa—as a case in point.[131]

The Chololo Ecovillage Project

Situated in the semi-arid drylands of Central Tanzania, the 5,500-person village of Chololo faces food insecurity, recurrent drought, and deep vulnerability to climate change.[132] Led by Tanzania's Institute for Rural Development Planning, the Chololo Ecovillage project was undertaken by a partnership of six organizations with the aim of adopting a holistic approach

---

125 IPES-Food, *Breaking Away from Industrial Food and Farming Systems: Seven Case Studies of Agroecological Transition* 2 (October 2018) [hereinafter "*Breaking Away from Industrial Food and Farming Systems*"].
126 *Id.*
127 *Id.*
128 IPES-Food, *From Uniformity to Diversity*, *supra* note 8, at 2.
129 *See* CHAI, *Exploring the Potential of Diversified Traditional Food Systems to Contribute to a Healthy Diet*, *supra* note 6.
130 *See* IPES Food, *From Uniformity to Diversity*, *supra* note 8, at 2.
131 IPES-Food, *Breaking Away from Industrial Food and Farming Systems*, *supra* note 125, at 47.
132 *Id.* at 39.

to address the multiple challenges that the community faced.[133] The first phase of the project, which spanned from 2011 to 2014, worked with the community to identify, introduce, and evaluate a range of agroecological innovations spanning agricultural, livestock, water, energy, and forestry sectors.[134]

The project began with a participatory process to assess the village's specific vulnerabilities, revealing the following concerns:

- Increasing drought, which makes the rain less frequent and less predictable, thereby affecting agricultural productivity and household incomes;
- Deforestation, which leads to a loss of vegetation and animal pasture and a shortage of fuel wood and timber, which in turn increases women's workload;
- Flooding and strong winds that lead to soil erosion, crop losses, and land degradation;
- Human diseases, livestock diseases, and crop pests; and
- Inadequate ground water recharge, leading to a shortage of water for domestic use, livestock, and crop production.[135]

These problems were exacerbated by the traditional dependency on rain-fed agriculture, a limited awareness of climate change issues, and the use of "slash and burn" agriculture, among other factors.[136] Food shortages that resulted from the above were also leading villagers to migrate to urban areas or travel to other districts to seek work as agricultural laborers.[137]

Having identified the villagers' main concerns, the project then built on local knowledge and traditional practices to encourage villagers to adopt a series of agroecological "technologies" which were "aimed at making the most of the limited rainfall, improving soil fertility, reducing farmers' workload, and improving the quality of local seeds."[138] These technologies included

> the use of ox-drawn tillage implements which reduced farmers' workloads and improved rainwater harvesting; water conservation measures such as contour ridges, *fanya juu* bunds, grass strips and gully healing to capture rainwater and prevent soil erosion; the use of farmyard manure to improve soil fertility; the use of improved early-maturing, high-yielding seed varieties of maize, sorghum, millet, cowpeas and groundnuts; and the adoption of optimal planting, spacing, thinning and weeding practices as well as intercropping and crop rotation in order to control weeds and improve yields.[139]

The beneficial impacts of Chololo's agroecological transition were significant. The agricultural innovations successfully increased crop yields in the range of 37.5 to 70% for crops

---

133 Institute of Rural Development Planning, *Chololo Ecovillage: A Model of Good Practice in Climate Change Adaptation and Mitigation* 4 (2014) [hereinafter "*Chololo Ecovillage*"]. The Chololo Ecovillage is part of the EU's Global Climate Change Alliance. *Id.*
134 *Id.* at 5.
135 *Id.*
136 IPES-Food, *Breaking Away from Industrial Food and Farming Systems*, supra note 124, at 39.
137 *Id.*
138 *Id.* at 41.
139 *Id.*

such as maize, sorghum, pearl millet, sunflower, and groundnuts.[140] Increased yields in turn meant more household food security and greater income from the sales of cash crops.[141] The following impacts were also noted by the end of the project's first phase (2011–2014):

- Fifty-four percent of farmers and livestock keepers were using climate adaptation innovations (an increase from 19% during year one of the project);
- Ninety-seven percent of the community had a good understanding of climate change;
- Sixty-two percent of households were eating three meals per day (an increase from 29 percent);
- Households experienced an average income increase of 18%; and
- The average period of food shortage decreased 62% (from 7.3 to 2.8 months).[142]

The project also engendered changes in social and economic relations. The need to improve livelihoods was central to the project, as were approaches that allowed women to take a leading role and become income providers.[143] Women's growing earning capacities, and their reduced financial dependency on their husbands, were a documented impact.[144] Significantly, the project also led to more women holding leadership positions in village institutions and committees.[145]

These beneficial outcomes of the project have in large part been attributed to its multi-sectoral approach[146] and to its "participatory approach to knowledge generation and dissemination," which included a series of community workshops to "explore the village's background and history, livelihood resources and hazards, climate vulnerability and capacity."[147] Farmer-to-farmer outreach, farmers' field days, and community assessment meetings were used to disseminate knowledge, evaluate and reflect on the technologies used, and ensure an uptake of good practices.[148] The holistic design of the project was also intentionally aligned with Tanzania's climate adaptation policy to help ensure the greatest impact.[149]

In March 2015, a 54-month long second phase of the project was launched. The so-called Eco-Act (Ecovillage Adaptation to Climate Change in Central Tanzania) project, or Chololo 2.0, aims to build on Chololo Ecovillage's success by scaling out its practices to three more villages and increasing their capacity to adapt to climate change while reducing

---

140 *Id*. at 40, 42. The data collected compared the yields between transitioning farmers and a control group during a normal rain year. The research adds that, "Participants that had a high technology uptake achieved significantly higher yields (ranging from 100% to 157% increase over the control group) in a drought year." *Id*. at 40.
141 Institute of Rural Development Planning, *Chololo Ecovillage*, *supra* note 133, at 10.
142 IPES-Food, *Breaking Away from Industrial Food and Farming Systems*, *supra* note 124, at 40.
143 *Id*. at 45. Chicken rearing and dairy cattle and goats were identified as the most beneficial sub-sectors for women. *Id*. at 46. The chicken and goat keeping improvements introduced by the project led to on average a 64% increase in women's incomes. *Id*. at footnote 39.
144 *Id*. at 46.
145 *Id*. (noting that, "By 2014, 50% of village leadership positions were held by women, compared to 40% in 2012").
146 *See* Institute of Rural Development Planning, *Chololo Ecovillage*, *supra* note 133, at 31 (noting while discussing the reasons for the project's success that "Working across agriculture, livestock, water, energy and forestry, the project touches every key aspect of people's lives").
147 IPES-Food, *Breaking Away from Industrial Food and Farming Systems*, *supra* note 124, at 43.
148 *Id*. at 39–40.
149 *Id*. at 40.

poverty.¹⁵⁰ Chololo 2.0 also aims to build the capacity of local authorities to implement climate change strategies and create a knowledge management system to share the project's learnings nationally.¹⁵¹

Case studies such as the Chololo Ecovillage project suggest that a shift toward diversified agroecological systems—when accompanied by processes that center the agency, knowledge, and priorities of community members—can yield benefits on multiple fronts and put food systems on a more sustainable and just footing. Moreover, and as IPES-Food notes,

> [w]hile industrial systems often improve one outcome (e.g. productivity) at the expense of others (e.g. environmental degradation, nutrient availability), diversified agroecological systems are showing major potential to reconcile the various priorities. The evidence is particularly impressive given how little funding and support has been dedicated to the agroecological alternative to date.¹⁵²

Conclusion

The achievement of SDG 2 is critical to the health of our communities and our planet. Regrettably, we are falling far short of achieving this paramount Goal, as revealed by the lack of progress across multiple targets and indicators. As this chapter has shown, how we produce our food and how we treat those who feed us has profound implications for food security, climate change, agro-biodiversity, public health, and human rights. For SDG 2 and related Goals to succeed, States must ensure food as a human right and they must invest in a radical transformation of our food system to move away from destructive industrial practices and toward diversified agroecological food systems.

The goals of ensuring food security, sustainable production methods, and farmer livelihoods may not always be easy to reconcile, but these interdependent goals can be achieved by a deep structural shift to food systems that are sustainable, resilient, nourishing, and just. The creation of these food systems will in large measure be context-specific and actualized at the local or regional level.¹⁵³ They will also require supporting public policies and investments. The human rights instruments cited in this chapter provide the building blocks for this transition and their implementation must be central to any SDG 2 strategy.

---

150 *Breaking News: Chololo 2.0 Gets the Go Ahead*, CHOLOLO ECOVILLAGE (Mar. 26, 2015), https://chololoecovillage.wordpress.com/2015/03/26/breaking-news-chololo-2-0-gets-the-go-ahead/; IPES-Food, *Breaking Away from Industrial Food and Farming Systems*, *supra* note 125, at 39.

151 IPES-Food, *Breaking Away from Industrial Food and Farming Systems*, *supra* note 124, at 39; Biovision, *Climate-Resilient "Ecovillage" in Chololo, Tanzania* 2 (2018).

152 *See* IPES-Food, *From Uniformity to Diversity*, *supra* note 8, at 11. *See also* Biovision, IPES-Food, Institute of Development Studies, *Money Flows: What Is Holding Back Investment in Agroecological Research for Africa?* 4 (April 2020) (noting that while "[a]pproximately 30% of farms around the world are estimated to have redesigned their production systems around agroecological principles," funding for agroecology-focused research in Africa remains marginal).

153 *See, e.g.*, Jennifer Blesh et al., *Development Pathways Toward "Zero Hunger,"* 118 World Development J. 1 (2019) (arguing that "the pathway to achieving Zero Hunger should center on place-based, adaptive, participatory solutions that simultaneously attend to local institutional capacities, agroecosystem diversification and ecological management, and the quality of local diets").

With great urgency, States must also take immediate steps to protect those who are most vulnerable to food insecurity, including as a result of the COVID-19 pandemic. As the World Food Programme notes, the pandemic is pushing millions of people to the brink of starvation.[154] In line with their human rights obligations, States must "urgently establish or strengthen social protection mechanisms and emergency food assistance programs that protect the most vulnerable" while ensuring that "food- and farmworkers—including migrant labourers and those in the informal sector—have access to safe and dignified working conditions."[155]

In this vein, the FAO has called for States to ensure that economic stimulus initiatives target health, agriculture, and food sectors with a view to building the resiliency of food systems.[156] The agency notes that if economic stimulus measures fail to ensure that

> all people at all times have physical, social and economic access to sufficient, safe and nutritious food ... the pandemic will not only kill people due to the viral disease, but lives will be lost and health severely impaired due to hunger.[157]

In many ways, the COVID-19 pandemic is a "wakeup call for food systems that must be heeded."[158] As artfully stated by FIAN International, "The world can lurch from crisis to crisis, or we can begin now to start building the resilient, sustainable food system the world desperately needs."[159] But this transition cannot succeed unless it is supported by institutional and governance structures that ensure the right to food and support the rights of peasants and other people working in rural areas to access productive resources and define their own food systems. Even in this catalytic moment of multiple and intersecting crises, we have all the tools we need to achieve the Zero Hunger Goal. All that remains is the political will to do so.

Summary Recommendations

To achieve the Goal of ending hunger, achieving food security, improving nutrition, and promoting sustainable agriculture:
- States' actions must be informed by their human rights obligations.
  - This includes respecting, protecting, and fulfilling the right to food, and ensuring the rights of peasants and other people working in rural areas;
  - It also includes taking immediate steps to protect those who are most vulnerable to food insecurity, including as a result of the COVID-19 pandemic.

---

154 *See supra* notes 50–51 and accompanying text.
155 IPES-Food, *COVID-19 and the Crisis in Food Systems, supra* note 36, at 7–8.
156 FAO COVID-19 STIMULUS REPORT, *supra* note 53, at 3, 8.
157 *Id.* at 3–4.
158 IPES-Food, *COVID-19 and the Crisis in Food Systems, supra* note 36, at 1. COVID-19 is not the first wake-up call. The food and financial crises of 2007–2008 saw basic food prices shoot up, pushing millions more into food insecurity. The international community did not, however, learn the lessons offered by the crisis then. Narula, *Reclaiming the Right to Food, supra* note 10, at 120.
159 Food Sovereignty, Friends of the Earth Int'l et al., *Statement to the Extraordinary Meeting of G20 Agriculture Ministers, supra* note 124.

- States and non-State actors must invest in a radical transformation of our food system to move away from destructive industrial practices and toward diversified agroecological food systems.
  - These transitions must uphold the right of people to determine their food and agricultural systems, also known as the right to food sovereignty, which in turn entails advancing more just and equitable trade policies and dismantling the corporate capture of the food chain.[160]

---

160 *See also* HLPF, FOOD SECURITY AND NUTRITION: BUILDING A GLOBAL NARRATIVE TOWARDS 2030, EXECUTIVE SUMMARY (2018) for a comprehensive set of recommendations to guide decision-makers as they develop policies to ensure the right to food and achieve the SDGs, especially SDG 2.

7 Health and Sustainable Development
Assessing Progress and Challenges
Obijiofor Aginam

Introduction

This chapter explores the progress and challenges for achieving the Sustainable Development Goal (SDG) 3 "Ensure healthy lives and promote well-being for all at all ages." While countries have made progress on increasing life expectancy, reducing maternal and child mortality, and fighting leading communicable diseases, as part of the Millennium Development Goals (MDGs) agenda, challenges remain ahead of the journey to 2030. The chapter focuses on two SDG 3 targets: (i) addressing the growing burden of non-communicable diseases (NCDs) through a health-trade policy coherence framework and (ii) supporting the research and development of vaccines and medicines for communicable and non-communicable diseases, providing access to affordable essential medicines and vaccines, in accordance with the Doha Declaration on the TRIPS Agreement and Public Health. Doha affirms the right of developing countries to use the provisions in the Agreement on Trade-Related Aspects of Intellectual Property Rights to protect public health and provide access to medicines for all. The relevance of these two case studies is underpinned by the emergence of NCDs as the leading cause of death globally, and the impact of intellectual property rights (patents) on availability of new vaccines and medicines in a time of global pandemic like COVID-19.

Health and Well-Being in Agenda 2030

The definition of health by the 1948 Constitution of the World Health Organization as "a state of complete physical, mental and social well-being and not merely the absence of disease or infirmity" underscores the centrality of health on the sustainable development agendas of nation-states and multilateral institutions.[1] The SDG 3 "Ensure healthy lives and promote well-being for all at all ages" has 13 ambitious targets:

- By 2030, reduce the global maternal mortality ratio to less than 70 per 100,000 live births.
- By 2030, end preventable deaths of newborns and children under 5 years of age, with all countries aiming to reduce neonatal mortality to at least as low as 12 per 1,000 live births and under-5 mortality to at least as low as 25 per 1,000 live births.

---

1 *Constitution*, WORLD HEALTH ORGANIZATION (WHO), www.who.int/about/who-we-are/constitution (note that this definition has not changed since the establishment of the WHO Constitution in 1948).

- By 2030, end the epidemics of AIDS, tuberculosis, malaria, and neglected tropical diseases, and combat hepatitis, water-borne diseases, and other communicable diseases.
- By 2030, reduce by one-third premature mortality from non-communicable diseases through prevention and treatment, and promote mental health and well-being.
- Strengthen the prevention and treatment of substance abuse, including narcotic drug abuse and harmful use of alcohol.
- By 2030, halve the number of global deaths and injuries from road traffic accidents.
- By 2030, ensure universal access to sexual and reproductive healthcare services, including for family planning, information and education, and the integration of reproductive health into national strategies and programs.
- Achieve universal health coverage, including financial risk protection, access to quality essential healthcare services and access to safe, effective, quality, and affordable essential medicines and vaccines for all.
- By 2030, substantially reduce the number of deaths and illnesses from hazardous chemicals and air, water, and soil pollution and contamination.
- Strengthen the implementation of the World Health Organization Framework Convention on Tobacco Control in all countries, as appropriate.
- Support the research and development of vaccines and medicines for the communicable and non-communicable diseases that primarily affect developing countries, provide access to affordable essential medicines and vaccines, in accordance with the Doha Declaration.
- Substantially increase health financing and the recruitment, development, training, and retention of the health workforce in developing countries, especially in least developed countries and small island developing States.
- Strengthen the capacity of all countries, in particular developing countries, for early warning, risk reduction, and management of national and global health risks.

To achieve these health-related targets, States have a duty to cooperate individually and collectively, nationally and internationally. Related to the duty of States to cooperate internationally to implement the SDGs is the need to create a policy space for all countries, especially the developing and least developed ones to pursue their development priorities within an international system that promotes the right to development for all.

Overview of Progress in the Implementation of SDG 3 Targets

It is a daunting task to comprehensively assess progress in the implementation of all 13 SDG 3 targets across the policy terrain of United Nations (UN) member states because of the differential levels of socio-economic development, resilience, and capacity of national health systems. Implementation can be assessed globally, where possible, by aggregating data and figures from different countries. Assessing the progress of Goal 3, the UN Sustainable Development Goals Report stated that

> Major progress has been made in improving the health of millions of people. Maternal and child mortality rates have been reduced, life expectancy continues to increase globally, and the fight against some infectious diseases has made steady progress. In the case of other diseases, however, progress has slowed or stalled, including global efforts to eradicate malaria and tuberculosis. Far too many deaths occurred because trained health workers or routine interventions, such as immunizations, were not available. In

Health and Sustainable Development 101

fact, at least half the world's population, many of whom suffer financial hardship, are still without access to essential health services. In rich and poor countries alike, a health emergency can push people into bankruptcy or poverty. Concerted efforts are required on these and other fronts to achieve universal health coverage and sustainable financing for health; address the growing burden of non-communicable diseases, including mental health; and tackle antimicrobial resistance and environmental factors contributing to ill health, such as air pollution and the lack of safely managed water and sanitation.[2]

Reduce Global Maternal Mortality to Less than 70 per 100,000 Livebirths

Despite significant progress made on improving maternal health in 2017, the UN and World Health Organization (WHO) estimated that 300,000 women, over 90% of them in low- and middle-income countries, died from complications relating to pregnancy and childbirth in 2018.[3] Globally, sub-Saharan Africa remains the epicenter of maternal mortality with two-thirds of the world's maternal deaths occurring in the region and only an estimated 60% of births assisted by skilled birth attendants and trained health professionals.[4] The major challenge is how to sustain the critically needed human and financial investment, as well as timely policy interventions, to ensure that all births are assisted by skilled health professionals in order to reach the global target of fewer than 70 maternal deaths per 100,000 live births by 2030.

End Preventable Deaths of Newborns and Children under 5 Years of Age

Infant mortality has improved significantly in all regions. The UN observed that under-5 mortality rate has fallen by 49%—from 77 deaths per 1,000 live births in 2000 to 39 deaths in 2017, while the total number of under-5 deaths dropped from 9.8 million in 2000 to 5.4 million in 2017.[5] Half of those deaths occurred in sub-Saharan Africa, and another 30% in Southern Asia.[6] Almost half (2.5 million) of the total number of under-5 deaths took place in the first month of life—the most crucial period for child survival.[7] The global neonatal mortality rate fell from 31 deaths per 1,000 live births in 2000 to 18 deaths in 2017—a 41% reduction.[8] One critical intervention that is needed to improve infant mortality at the global level is increased immunization and access to life-saving vaccines. The UN stated that in 2017, 116.2 million children were immunized, the highest number ever reported.[9] At the same time, pockets of low coverage have led to outbreaks of measles and diphtheria, resulting in many deaths—a clear demonstration of the importance of reaching full coverage. The

---

2 *The Sustainable Development Goals Report 2019*, UN DEP. OF ECON. & SOC. AFFAIRS (DESA) 29 (2019), https://unstats.un.org/sdgs/report/2019/ [hereinafter, "SDG Report 2019"].
3 *Id.*; *See also, Progress towards the SDGs: A Selection of Data from World Health Statistics 2018*, WHO (2018), www.who.int/gho/publications/world_health_statistics/2018/EN_WHS2018_SDGhighlights.pdf?ua=1.
4 *Id.* at 26.
5 *Id.* at 27.
6 *Ibid.*
7 *Ibid.*
8 *Ibid.*
9 *Ibid.*

proportion of children who have received the required three doses of the diphtheria-tetanus-pertussis (DTP3)-containing vaccine increased from 72% in 2000 to 85% in 2015, but remained unchanged between 2015 and 2017.[10] An estimated 19.9 million children did not receive the vaccine during the first year of life, putting them at serious risk of potentially fatal diseases.[11] Governments and philanthropic organizations should incentivize public–private partnerships, such as the Geneva-based Global Alliance for Vaccines and Immunization (GAVI), to address the gaps in immunization.

End the Epidemics of AIDS, Tuberculosis, Malaria, and Neglected Tropical Diseases, and Combat Hepatitis, Water-Borne Diseases and Other Communicable Diseases

The global HIV/AIDS response targeting evidenced-based programs for prevention, testing, and treatment has led to a decline in the incidence of HIV. The UN reports that the incidence of HIV among adults (15 to 49 years of age) in sub-Saharan Africa declined by around 37% from 2010 to 2017, representing a drop from 3.39 infections per 1,000 uninfected people in 2010 to 2.14 in 2017.[12] However, some sub-regions have even seen an increase in HIV incidences, including Western Asia (53%), Central Asia (51%), and Europe (22%).[13]

According to the UN, no significant advances were made in reducing the number of malaria cases worldwide from 2015 to 2017. While malaria incidence rates declined by 18% between 2010 and 2015— from 72 cases per 1,000 people at risk to 59—it remained unchanged from 2015 to 2017.[14] In 2017, an estimated 219 million cases of malaria and 435,000 deaths from the disease were reported.[15] Sub-Saharan Africa continues to carry the heaviest burden, accounting for more than 90% of global malaria cases, and the toll is rising.[16] From 2016 to 2017, approximately 3.5 million more malaria cases were reported in the ten most affected African countries.[17] Children under 5 years of age are the most vulnerable to the disease, and account for 61% (266,000) of malaria deaths worldwide.[18] Funding for malaria has been increasing since 2000, but recently stalled. Increased support directed to the most affected countries is urgently needed.

In 2017, an estimated 10 million people were infected by tuberculosis.[19] Although the incidence of tuberculosis declined by 21% since 2000, and tuberculosis mortality rate among HIV-negative people fell by 42% over the same period,[20] the UN observed that large gaps in detection and treatment persist, and the current pace of progress is not fast enough to meet the target of ending the epidemic by 2030. Drug-resistant tuberculosis continues to

---

10 *Ibid.*
11 *Ibid*; *See also* World Health Organization, *Children: Reducing Mortality*, WHO (Sept. 8, 2020), www.who.int/en/news-room/fact-sheets/detail/children-reducing-mortality.
12 *Id.* at 6.
13 *Id.* at 28.
14 *Ibid.*
15 *Ibid.*
16 *Ibid.*
17 *Ibid.*
18 *Ibid.*
19 *Ibid.*
20 *Ibid.*

be a threat. In 2017, there were 558,000 new cases with resistance to rifampicin, the most effective first-line drug, of which 460,000 had multidrug-resistant tuberculosis.[21]

Neglected tropical diseases (NTDs) are a diverse group of communicable diseases found in 149 tropical and subtropical countries. They affect billions of people—particularly those who live in poverty, lack adequate sanitation, and are in close contact with infectious vectors and domestic animals—costing developing economies billions of dollars each year. Available data from the UN and WHO suggest that the number of people requiring treatment from NTDs has been declining steadily in recent years. In order to control and eliminate NTDs, current measures must be sustained.

Strengthen the Prevention and Treatment of Substance Abuse, Including Narcotic Drug Abuse and Harmful Use of Alcohol

The WHO estimates that

> Alcohol consumption contributes to 3 million deaths each year globally as well as to the disabilities and poor health of millions of people. Harmful use of alcohol is responsible for 5.1% of the global burden of disease. Alcohol is the leading risk factor for premature mortality and disability among those aged 15 to 49 years, accounting for 10 percent of all deaths in this age group. Disadvantaged and especially vulnerable populations have higher rates of alcohol-related death and hospitalization.[22]

Substance abuse and harmful use of alcohol are risk factors for non-communicable diseases and mental health. To accelerate progress toward strengthening the prevention and treatment of substance abuse and harmful use of alcohol, the WHO—building on past Resolutions of the World Health Assembly—launched the SAFER initiative in 2018, "a new initiative and technical package outlining five high-impact strategies that can help governments to reduce the harmful use of alcohol and related health, social and economic consequences."[23] The five high-impact strategies captured by the SAFER acronym are

S—Strengthen restrictions on alcohol availability (enacting and enforcing restrictions on commercial or public availability of alcohol through laws, policies, and programs).

A—Advance and enforce drink driving counter measures (enacting and enforcing strong drink-driving laws and low blood alcohol concentration limits via sobriety checkpoints and random breath testing).

F—Facilitate access to screening, brief interventions, and treatment (the role of health professionals in helping people reduce or stop their drinking to reduce health risks, and health services to provide effective interventions for those in need of help).

E—Enforce bans or comprehensive restrictions on alcohol advertising, sponsorship, and promotion (enforcing bans and comprehensive restrictions on alcohol advertising, sponsorship, and promotion as impactful and cost-effective measures).

---

21 *Ibid.*
22 *Alcohol*, WHO, www.who.int/health-topics/alcohol#tab=tab_1 (last visited Dec. 10, 2020).
23 *SAFER: Preventing and Reducing Alcohol-Related Harms Harmful Use of alcohol: A Health and Development Priority*, WHO, www.who.int/substance_abuse/safer/msb_safer_framework.pdf?ua=1.

R—Raise prices on alcohol through excise taxes and pricing policies (an increase in excise taxes on alcoholic beverages as measures to reduce harmful use of alcohol and provide governments revenue to offset the economic costs of harmful use of alcohol).

According to the WHO, the SAFER initiative is "the newest WHO-led roadmap to support governments in taking practical steps to accelerate progress on health, beat noncommunicable diseases (NCDs) through addressing the harmful use of alcohol, and achieve development targets."[24]

By 2020, Halve the Number of Global Deaths and Injuries from Road Traffic Accidents

Available data from the WHO establishes several key facts. An estimated 1.35 million people die each year as a result of road traffic accidents.[25] Road traffic crashes cost most countries 3% of their Gross Domestic Product (GDP).[26] More than half of all road traffic deaths are among vulnerable road users: Pedestrians, cyclists, and motorcyclists. Ninety-three percent of the world's fatalities on the roads occur in low- and middle-income countries, even though these countries have approximately 60% of the world's vehicles.[27] Road traffic injuries are the leading cause of death of children and young adults aged 5–29 years.[28] In the Global Status Report on Road Safety 2018, the WHO stated that

> The progress that has been achieved in a number of countries to stabilize the global risk of dying from a road traffic crash has not occurred at a pace fast enough to compensate for the rising population and rapid motorization of transport taking place in many parts of the world. At this rate, the SDG target to halve road traffic deaths by 2020 will not be met.[29]

The challenges that lie ahead for countries would entail a holistic and comprehensive review of key risk factors to sustain progress being made "in improving key road safety laws, making infrastructure safer, adopting vehicle standards, and improving access to post-crash care."[30]

By 2030, Ensure Universal Access to Sexual and Reproductive Health-Care Services, Including for Family Planning, Information and Education, and the Integration of Reproductive Health into National Strategies and Programs

The SDGs addressed sexual and reproductive health in two of the Goals: The health Goal (SDG 3.7) and the Gender Goal (SDG 5.6). SDG 5.6 complements SDG 3.7 by striving to "ensure universal access to sexual and reproductive health and reproductive rights as agreed

---

24 *Id.*
25 *Road Traffic Injuries*, WHO (Feb. 7, 2020), www.who.int/news-room/fact-sheets/detail/road-traffic-injuries.
26 *Id.*
27 *Id.*
28 *Ibid.*
29 *Global Status Report on Road Safety 2018*, WHO (Jun. 17, 2018), www.who.int/publications/i/item/9789241565684.
30 *Id.*

in accordance with the Programme of Action of the International Conference on Population and Development and the Beijing Platform for Action and the outcome documents of their review conferences." The United Nations Population Fund (UNFPA), the United Nations sexual and reproductive health agency observed that

> the Sustainable Development Goals mark tremendous progress in addressing women's sexual and reproductive health and reproductive rights. For the first time, an international development framework includes not only targets on services (Targets 3.1 and 3.7), but also targets that address the barriers and human rights-based dimensions (Target 5.6).[31]

Two indicators are used to measure progress on sexual and reproductive health: The proportion of women aged 15–49 who make their own informed decisions regarding sexual relations, contraceptive use, and reproductive health care, and the number of countries with laws and regulations that guarantee full and equal access to women and men aged 15 years and older to sexual and reproductive health care, information, and education. While progress has been made by some countries, UNFPA, in a recent survey of the key elements of these indicators across countries and regions, stated that

> Data on each core element reflect the enormous heterogeneity of access to sexual and reproductive health education and services, and to reproductive rights. To achieve the Goal by 2030, unnecessary legal, medical, clinical and regulatory barriers to the utilization of sexual and reproductive health services must be removed, and changes in social norms and government policies that allow women and girls to fully exercise their reproductive rights must be prioritized.[32]

Achieve Universal Health Coverage, Including Financial Risk Protection, Access to Quality Essential Health-Care Services and Access to Safe, Effective, Quality, and Affordable Essential Medicines and Vaccines for All

According to the WHO,

> Universal health care (UHC) means that all individuals and communities receive the health services they need without suffering financial hardship. It includes the full spectrum of essential, quality health services, from health promotion to prevention, treatment, rehabilitation, and palliative care. UHC enables everyone to access the services that address the most significant causes of disease and death and ensures that the quality of those services is good enough to improve the health of the people who receive them.[33]

---

31 *Ensure Universal Access to Sexual and Reproductive Health and Reproductive Rights*, UN POPULATION FUND (UNFPA) (Feb. 2020), www.unfpa.org/sites/default/files/pub-pdf/UNFPA-SDG561562Combined-v4.15.pdf.
32 *Id.* at 7.
33 *Universal Health Coverage (UHC)*, WHO (Jan. 24, 2019), www.who.int/news-room/fact-sheets/detail/universal-health-coverage-(uhc).

Based on available data and information, the WHO has established the following key facts on UHC: (i) at least half of the world's population still does not have full coverage of essential health services; (ii) about 100 million people are still being pushed into extreme poverty (defined as living on 1.90 USD or less a day) because they have to pay for health care; and (iii) over 930 million people (around 12% of the world's population) spend at least 10% of their household budgets to pay for health care.[34] Because UHC, as the WHO observed, "does not mean free coverage for all possible health interventions, regardless of the cost, as no country can provide all services free of charge on a sustainable basis,"[35] assessing the progress in achieving UHC entails assessing policy interventions on all components of the health system. These components include health service delivery systems, the health workforce, health facilities, and communications networks, health technologies, information systems, quality assurance mechanisms, and governance and legislation. Although many countries are making progress toward improving these components of UHC, serious challenges remain on the road to 2030. These challenges, according to WHO, require policy interventions aimed at strengthening health systems in all countries by developing robust financing structures, pooling funds from compulsory funding sources (such as mandatory insurance contributions), improving health service coverage and health outcomes based on the availability, accessibility, and capacity of health workers to deliver quality people-centered integrated care, investing in quality primary health care (including the primary health care workforce), good governance, sound systems of procurement and supply of medicines and health technologies, and well-functioning health information systems.[36]

By 2030, Substantially Reduce the Number of Deaths and Illnesses from Hazardous Chemicals and Air, Water, and Soil Pollution and Contamination

According to the UN,

> Household and ambient air pollution increase the risk of cardiovascular and respiratory diseases, and are major risk factors for non-communicable diseases. Exposure to household air pollution, mainly due to polluting fuels and technologies for cooking, led to around 4 million deaths in 2016.... Ambient air pollution from traffic, industry, power-generation, waste-burning and residential fuel combustion resulted in around 4.2 million deaths in 2016.[37]

The WHO estimates that there were "13.7 million deaths per year in 2016, amounting to 24% of the global deaths, [which] are due to modifiable environmental risks. This means that almost 1 in 4 of total global deaths are linked to environment conditions."[38] To create a healthy environment to achieve this SDG target, the WHO recommends that countries invest in leadership to guide transitions such as in energy and transport; knowledge generation and dissemination for evidence-based norms and efficient solutions, steering research and

---

34 *Id.*
35 *Id.*
36 *Universal Health Coverage Partnership: A Country-Level Resource for UHC 2030*, WHO, www.uhcpartnership.net/ (last visited Dec. 10, 2020).
37 SDG Report 2019, *supra* note 3, at 29.
38 *Environmental Health*, WHO, www.who.int/health-topics/environmental-health#tab=tab_3 (last visited Dec. 10, 2020).

monitoring change in risks to health and implementation of solutions; and building capacity for emergency preparedness and response in case of environment-related incidents.[39] Some of these policy recommendations are part of the WHO's comprehensive global assessment of the global burden of disease from environmental risks with linkages and pathways to the SDGs.[40]

Strengthen the Implementation of the World Health Organization Framework Convention on Tobacco Control in All Countries, as Appropriate

The WHO Framework Convention on Tobacco Control (WHO FCTC) is the first international treaty negotiated under the auspices of the WHO. Adopted by the World Health Assembly on May 21, 2003, it entered into force on February 27, 2005. According to the WHO FCTC Secretariat, the Convention

> was developed in response to the globalization of the tobacco epidemic and is an evidence-based treaty that reaffirms the right of all people to the highest standard of health. The Convention represents a milestone for the promotion of public health and provides new legal dimensions for international health cooperation.[41]

Currently, the Convention has 182 parties covering more than 90% of the world population. While the WHO FCTC has been widely accepted by countries, the Convention's Protocol to Eliminate Illicit Trade in Tobacco Products has only 61 Parties. While the WHO FCTC covers a wide range of tobacco control measures on which countries have made progress ranging from cross-border effects, such as trade liberalization and direct foreign investment, tobacco advertising, promotion, and sponsorship beyond national borders, and illicit trade in tobacco products, many countries still face difficult challenges in implementing the Convention, including the powerful influence of the tobacco industry, especially in low- and middle-income countries. Article 5.3 of the FCTC requires Parties to protect their tobacco control and public health policies from "commercial and other vested interests of the tobacco industry."[42] In order to address these challenges, the WHO FCTC Conference of the Parties, in October 2018, adopted *The Global Strategy to Accelerate Tobacco Control: Advancing Sustainable Development through the Implementation of the WHO FCTC 2019–2025* (GS2025).[43] Among others, GS2025 aims to "empower Parties to work multi-sectorally, with the health and non-health sectors and other stakeholders engaged in the fight against tobacco at the global, regional and country levels."[44] GS2025 is aligned with the FCTC 2030 Project which aims to provide intensive support to a selected number of low- and middle-income countries (LMICs) that have demonstrated considerable motivation to

---

39 *Id.*
40 A Prüss-Ustün et al., *Preventing disease through healthy environments: a global assessment of the burden of disease from environmental risks*, WHO (2016).
41 WHO Framework Convention on Tobacco Control, May 21, 2003, 2302 U.N.T.S. 166, https://www.who.int/fctc/cop/about/en/.
42 *Id.* at art. 5.3.
43 *Global Strategy to Accelerate Tobacco Control: Advancing Sustainable Development through the Implementation of the WHO FCTC 2019–2025*, WHO (2019), https://apps.who.int/iris/bitstream/handle/10665/325887/WHO-CSF-2019.1-eng.pdf?ua=1.
44 *Id.*

advance tobacco control through (i) the achievement of the general obligations and the time-bound measures of the WHO FCTC; (ii) strengthening tobacco taxation; (iii) implementing other articles of the Convention according to national priorities; and (iv) promoting treaty implementation as part of the 2030 Agenda for Sustainable Development.

Substantially Increase Health Financing and the Recruitment, Development, Training, and Retention of the Health Workforce in Developing Countries, especially in Least Developed Countries and Small Island Developing States

A resilient Primary Health Care system anchored on an adequate, available, and motivated health workforce is a critical and indispensable component of UHC. Achieving UHC for all is virtually impossible without an adequate and available workforce. As the UN stated,

> Available data from 2013 to 2018 indicate that close to 40 per cent of all countries have fewer than 10 medical doctors per 10,000 people, and around 58 per cent of countries have fewer than 40 nursing and midwifery personnel per 10,000 people.... Evidence shows that health workers are unevenly distributed across the globe and even within countries. Not surprisingly, regions with the highest burden of disease have the lowest proportion of health workers to deliver services. All of the least developed countries have fewer than 10 medical doctors per 10,000 people, and 98 per cent have fewer than 40 nursing and midwifery personnel per 10,000 people. It is estimated that around 18 million additional health workers will be needed globally by 2030 to ensure healthy lives for all.[45]

In order to assist countries progressing toward meeting the critical health workforce shortages by 2030, the WHO's Global Strategy on Human Resources for Health: Workforce 2030 incorporates the following guiding principles: Provision of integrated, people-centered health services devoid of stigma and discrimination; fostering empowered and engaged communities; upholding the personal, employment, and professional rights of all health workers, including safe and decent working environments and freedom from all kinds of discrimination, coercion, and violence; elimination of gender-based violence, discrimination, and harassment; promotion of international collaboration and solidarity in alignment with national priorities; ensuring ethical recruitment practices in conformity with the provisions of the WHO Global Code of Practice on the International Recruitment of Health Personnel; and mobilization and sustainability of political and financial commitment and fostering of inclusiveness and collaboration across sectors and constituencies.

Strengthen the Capacity of All Countries, in Particular Developing Countries, for Early Warning, Risk Reduction, and Management of National and Global Health Risks

The International Health Regulations (IHR) is one of the oldest regulatory mechanisms for the detection, prevention, and control of global health risks. IHR is a legally binding agreement on 196 countries, including the 194 WHO Member States. IHR requires

---

45 SDG Report 2019, *supra* note 3; *see also Health Workforce*, WHO, www.who.int/health-topics/health-workforce#tab=tab_1 (last visited Dec. 10, 2020).

countries to report certain disease outbreaks and public health events to the WHO. The Regulations outline the criteria to determine whether or not a particular event constitutes a "public health emergency of international concern."[46] According to the UN,

> Since 2010, all 196 States Parties have sent reports to WHO on their capacity to implement the Regulations, and on their preparedness to deal with health emergencies more generally. In 2018, 190 States Parties submitted reports, compared to 167 in 2017. An analysis of 182 reports shows that, globally, progress has been made in all 13 of the Regulations' core capacities. Almost all States Parties are performing better in detection (e.g., surveillance and laboratory detection) than in emergency preparedness and response. Bigger gaps have been observed in capacity at points of entry (e.g., ports, airports and ground crossings) and in chemical safety and radiation emergencies.[47]

Although countries have made steady and remarkable progress toward implementing the IHR, many low- and middle-income countries lack robust and resilient surveillance systems for a timely detection of acute public health events and response to public health risks and emergencies. To address these challenges, the WHO offers technical assistance to countries, based on priorities identified by the WHO Country and Regional Offices, toward strengthening and maintaining their capacities for ensuring rapid detection, verification, and response to public health risks to meet their core obligations under the IHR.

Two Case Studies

Case Study: Reducing Premature Mortality from Non-Communicable Diseases (NCDs) through a Health-Trade Policy Coherence Framework

The mortality and morbidity burdens of non-communicable diseases constitute a major crisis that undermines the social and economic development of many countries, particularly the low- and middle-income countries. In its Global Action Plan for the Prevention and Control of NCDs, the WHO stated that,

> an estimated 36 million deaths, or 63% of the 57 million deaths that occurred globally in 2008, were due to noncommunicable diseases, comprising mainly cardiovascular diseases (48% of noncommunicable diseases), cancers (21%), chronic respiratory diseases (12%) and diabetes (3.5%).[48]

These four major NCDs "share four behavioral risk factors: tobacco use, unhealthy diet, physical inactivity, and harmful use of alcohol."[49] As observed by the WHO, "although morbidity and mortality from non-communicable diseases mainly occur in adulthood, exposure

---

46 *IHR Procedures Concerning Public Health Emergencies of International Concern (PHEIC)*, Strengthening Health Security by Implementing the International Health Regulations (2005), WHO, www.who.int/ihr/procedures/pheic/en/ (last visited Dec. 10, 2020).
47 *SDG Report 2019*, *supra* note 3, at 29.
48 *Global Action Plan for the Prevention and Control of Non-Communicable Diseases, 2013–2020*, WHO (2013), 7; https://apps.who.int/iris/bitstream/handle/10665/94384/9789241506236_eng.pdf?sequence=1.
49 *Id.* at 7.

to risk factors begins in early life."[50] Children are vulnerable to death from treatable non-communicable diseases (such as rheumatic heart disease, type 1 diabetes, asthma, and leukemia) "if health promotion, disease prevention and comprehensive care are not provided."[51] The Commission on Ending Childhood Obesity developed a set of policy recommendations to tackle childhood and adolescent obesity in different contexts around the world.[52]

Dietary habits and changes in industrial food processing systems are among the leading causes of the increase in the mortality and morbidity burdens of NCDs. Trade and corporate investment opportunities create opportunities for the globalization of harmful substances, such as tobacco and processed foods, with limited nutritional content; high in salt, sugar, and fats which lay the foundations for high blood pressure, increased blood glucose, obesity, and consequently, diabetes, cardiovascular disease, and other chronic illnesses. While good for economic growth, the globalization of the world economy driven by trade and investment opportunities, also paradoxically, leads to the unintended consequence of creating a super-highway for the globalization of unhealthy lifestyles, and marketing of unsafe food and harmful products.

While governments and multilateral institutions like the WHO and the Food and Agriculture Organization of the UN (FAO) have developed policies, recommendations, and regulatory instruments on NCD risk factors, the effectiveness of these policies is often undermined by commercial interests, and powerful corporate lobbyists, especially in low- and middle-income countries. In many countries, the Ministry of Health is often marginalized in the decision-making processes and negotiation of trade and investment agreements by the more powerful and influential Ministries of Finance, Trade, and Investment. This leads to lack of coherence between the policies of the Trade, Finance, and Investment Departments and the Ministry of Health. This incoherence is due to the fact that the Finance, Trade, and Investment Departments are driven by economic motives of attracting foreign direct investment, creating jobs, and pursuit of economic growth often measured by Gross Domestic Product, while the Ministry of Health is driven by access to Universal Health Coverage, and health promotion to address the short, immediate, and long-term emerging and re-emerging NCDs.

What is policy coherence? According to the Organization of Economic Co-operation and Development (OECD), policy coherence for development entails the following:

- Ensuring that the interactions among various policies in the economic, social, environmental, legal, and political domains support countries on their pathway toward inclusive sustainable growth.
- Putting in place institutional mechanisms, processes, and tools to produce effective, efficient, sustainable, and coherent policies in all sectors.
- Developing evidence-based analysis, sound data, and reliable indicators to inform decision-making and help translate political commitments into practice.

---

50 *Id.* at 7.
51 *Ibid.*
52 *Report of the Commission on Ending Childhood Obesity: Implementation Plan–Executive Summary*, WHO (2017), https://apps.who.int/iris/bitstream/handle/10665/259349/WHO-NMH-PND-ECHO-17.1-eng.pdf?sequence=1.

- Fostering multi-stakeholder policy dialog to identify the barriers to, and the catalysts for, change.[53]

Policy coherence promotes mutually reinforcing policies across government departments to create synergies. In 2006, responding to the demand for information on the possible implications of international trade and investment agreements for health and health policy at the national, regional, and global levels, the World Health Assembly, the highest policy-making organ of the WHO adopted Resolution WHA 59.26[54] on international trade and health. The Assembly, among other measures, urged Member States to do the following:

- Promote multi-stakeholder dialog at the national level to consider the interplay between international trade and health.
- Adopt, where necessary, policies, laws, and regulations that deal with issues identified in that dialog, and to take advantage of the potential opportunities, and address the potential challenges, that trade and trade agreements may have for health, considering, where appropriate, using their inherent flexibilities.
- Apply or establish, where necessary, coordination mechanisms involving *ministries of finance, health, and trade, and other relevant institutions*, to address public-health related aspects of international trade.
- Create constructive and interactive relationships across the public and private sectors for the purpose of generating *coherence in national trade and health policies*.
- Continue to *develop capacity at the national level* to track and analyze the potential *opportunities and challenges* of trade and trade agreements for health-sector performance and health outcomes.

If countries, especially the low- and middle-income countries, are to achieve the SDG 3 target of reducing by 2030, one-third of premature mortality from non-communicable diseases through prevention and treatment, they must endeavor to develop an effective trade–health coherence framework by aligning their development policies toward ensuring that short-term benefits from trade–investment opportunities do not undermine health in the long run, since most non-communicable diseases would take decades to peak.

Case Study: Access to Vaccines and Medicines, and the Trade-Related Intellectual Property Agreement (TRIPS)

The TRIPS Agreement[55] epitomizes the tensions between the neo-liberal trade liberalization agenda of the World Trade Organization (WTO), and the right to "the enjoyment of the highest attainable standard of health" codified by the Constitution of the WHO.[56] The TRIPS Agreement, among other things, sets a minimum standard of intellectual property

---

53 *Policy Coherence for Inclusive and Sustainable Development*, Element 8(1), OECD and Post-2015 Reflections, www.oecd.org/gov/pcsd/POST-2015%20PCD.pdf (last visited Dec. 10, 2020).
54 World Health Assembly Res. 59.26 (2006).
55 TRIPS: Agreement on Trade-Related Aspects of Intellectual Property Rights, Apr. 15, 1994, Marrakesh Agreement Establishing the World Trade Organization, Annex 1C, 1869 U.N.T.S. 299, 33 I.L.M. 1197 (1994) [hereinafter, "TRIPS"] (TRIPS is one of the trade agreements enforced by the WTO).
56 WHO Constitution, *supra* note 2.

protection (including pharmaceutical patents) for all WTO member states through their national legislation. Patent protection for pharmaceuticals, under TRIPS, is set for a minimum of 20 years. Although TRIPS provides for certain flexibilities, and time-bound exceptions for developing and least developed countries, efforts to deploy these flexibilities in the first few years after the establishment of the WTO were opposed by Big Pharma and some industrialized countries.[57]

On November 14 2001, following sustained agitation by developing countries, and advocacy by a coalition of civil society groups, the WTO ministerial conference in Doha, adopted the Declaration on the TRIPS Agreement and Public Health.[58] The Declaration affirmed that TRIPS can and should be interpreted and implemented in a manner supportive of WTO Members' right to protect public health, and in particular, to promote access to medicines for all.[59] The Declaration recognized that WTO Members with insufficient or no manufacturing capacities in the pharmaceutical sector could face difficulties in making effective use of compulsory licensing under the TRIPS Agreement.[60] On August 30, 2003, the General Council of the WTO adopted a decision on the Implementation of Paragraph 6 of the Doha Declaration on the TRIPS Agreement and Public Health.[61] The decision provides for the criteria aimed at facilitating access to essential medicines by vulnerable populations in the least developed and developing countries.

Complex interlinked trade-health-development-human rights issues in the international trade governance architecture catalyzed the launch of The Doha Round of trade negotiations among the WTO member states in 2001. Known semi-officially as The Doha Development Agenda (DDA), it aims to achieve major reform of the international trading system with a fundamental objective to improve the trading prospects of developing countries. What is urgently needed for the DDA to make progress is a recognition of the stark disparities and inequalities between countries followed by an adaptable policy space and package of incentives to enable countries at different stages of development to strengthen their institutional capacities in line with the "special and differential treatment" provisions codified in many WTO agreements.

Given the complexity of these trade issues and their impact on public health, it is not surprising that issues of Research and Development and access to vaccines and medicines in the context of patents and the Doha Declaration are included in the SDG 3 targets. As the world deals with the COVID-19 pandemic, there is now a race for a vaccine by scientists around the world. Who gets the vaccine first? If a vaccine is found to be safe and produced, would it be accessible and affordable to all who need it? Who gets priority? Should populations in low- and middle-income countries be prioritized over those of industrialized countries? From an ethical perspective, should a COVID-19 vaccine be subject to a patent?

---

57 Caroline Thomas, *Trade Policy and the Politics of Access to Drugs* 23 THIRD WORLD QUARTERLY 251(2002); Naomi A. Bass, *Implications of the TRIPS Agreement for Developing Countries: Pharmaceutical Patent Laws in Brazil and South Africa in the 21st Century*, THE GEORGE WASHINGTON INT'L LAW REV. 191 (2002); Ellen 't Hoen, *TRIPS, Pharmaceutical Patents, and Access to Essential Medicines: A Long Way from Seattle to Doha*, 3 CHICAGO J. OF INT'L LAW 27 (2008).
58 *Declaration on the TRIPS Agreement and Public Health*, World Trade Organization, Nov. 14, 2001, WT?MIN(01)/DEC/2 [hereinafter, "The Doha Declaration"].
59 *Id.* at ¶ 4.
60 *Id.* at ¶ 6.
61 *Implementation of Paragraph 6 of the Doha Declaration on the TRIPS Agreement and Public Health*, General Council, Aug. 30, 2003, WT/L/540.

Although, in principle, some countries have pledged to treat a COVID-19 vaccine as a "global public good" to be made available to people that need it most, it remains to be seen how these ethical dilemmas will be resolved given the human and material costs of producing a new vaccine.

COVID-19 and SDG 3

On December 31, 2019, the country office of the WHO in the People's Republic of China picked up a media statement by the Wuhan Municipal Health Commission from their website on cases of "viral pneumonia" in Wuhan, the People's Republic of China. On January 30, 2020, following a confirmation of 98 cases in 18 countries outside China, including 8 cases of human-to-human transmission confirmed in Germany, Japan, the United States of America, and Viet Nam, the Director-General of the WHO accepted the advice of the IHR Emergency Committee and declared COVID-19 a "public health emergency of international concern" under the International Health Regulations.[62] Although most people infected with the COVID-19 virus, according to the WHO, might experience mild to moderate respiratory illness and recover without requiring special treatment, older people and those with underlying health conditions, like cardiovascular disease, diabetes, chronic respiratory disease, and cancer, are more likely to develop serious illness. Given its rapid worldwide spread, severity, morbidity, and mortality burdens, the WHO declared COVID-19 a pandemic on March 11, 2020, and called on all countries to "take a whole-of-government, whole-of-society approach, built around a comprehensive strategy to prevent infections, save lives and minimize impact."[63] In its Situation Report-190, published on July 28, 2020, the WHO estimated that there are 16,341,920 cases of COVID-19 globally resulting in an estimated 650,805 deaths.[64]

The COVID-19 pandemic is not simply a health crisis. It is a developmental crisis that threatens to scale back gains made by countries toward achieving the SDGs. In the framework for immediate socio-economic response to COVID-19, the UN stated that,

> The COVID-19 pandemic is far more than a health crisis: it is affecting societies and economies at their core. While the impact of the pandemic will vary from country to country, it will most likely increase poverty and inequalities at a global scale, making achievement of SDGs even more urgent. Without urgent socio-economic responses, global suffering will escalate, jeopardizing lives and livelihoods for years to come. Immediate development responses in this crisis must be undertaken with an eye to the future. Development trajectories in the long-term will be affected by the choices countries make now and the support they receive.[65]

---

62 *Timeline of WHO's Response to COVID-19*, WHO (Jun. 29, 2020), www.who.int/news-room/detail/29-06-2020-covidtimeline.
63 *Id.*
64 Situation Report 190, *Coronavirus Disease 2019 (COVID-19)*, WHO (Jul. 28, 2020), www.who.int/emergencies/diseases/novel-coronavirus-2019/situation-reports.
65 *A UN Framework for the Immediate Socio-Economic Response to COVID 19 APRIL 2020*, UN Sustainable Development Group 13 (Apr. 2020), https://unsdg.un.org/resources/un-framework-immediate-socio-economic-response-covid-19.

COVID-19 has exposed the fault lines of the fragile SDG architecture of countries. As the UN noted,

> the virus is exposing structural fragilities that would have been attenuated through more rapid, effective and universal development responses in the past. The pandemic is exacerbating and deepening pre-existing inequalities, exposing vulnerabilities in social, political, economic, and biodiversity systems, which are in turn amplifying the impacts of the pandemic.[66]

Numerous proposals have been put forward to address COVID-induced SDG challenges in countries. The Elders, an independent group of global leaders working together for peace, justice, and human rights, currently chaired by Mary Robinson, have called on the G-20 leaders to immediately agree to commit $8 billion—as set out by the Global Preparedness Monitoring Board—to fill the most urgent gaps in the COVID-19 response targeting the following three major interventions:[67]

- **$1 billion this year urgently needed by WHO**: This would enable WHO to carry out its critically important mandate in full. While it has launched a public appeal—200,000 individuals and organizations have generously donated more than $100 million—it cannot be expected to depend on charitable donations.
- **$3 billion for Vaccines**: The Coalition for Epidemic Preparedness Innovations (CEPI) is coordinating the global research effort to develop and scale up effective COVID-19 vaccines. In addition, GAVI, the Vaccine Alliance, will have an important role procuring and equitably distributing vaccines to the poorest countries, and requires $7.4 billion for its replenishment. This should be fully funded.
- **$2.25 billion for Therapeutics**: The COVID-19 Therapeutics Accelerator aims to deliver 100 million treatments by the end of 2020 and is seeking these funds to rapidly develop and scale up access to therapeutics.

If these and other interventions are fully funded, the UN has rightly advocated that its Development System

> must respond urgently to stem the impact, and it must do so by helping governments and populations respond in a way that builds a better future.... The responses should aim to protect people and planet; preserve gains across all the SDGs; ensure equality; promote transparency, accountability, and collaboration; increase solidarity; and place the voice, rights and agency of people at the center.[68]

Based on past experience concerning the duplication of multiple funding of vertical programs in countries, the UN Development System must devise a framework that prevents unnecessary duplication to avoid waste of resources. In a recent study on funding effective UN Responses to COVID-19, the Uppsala-based Dag Hammarskjöld Foundation raised

---

66 *Id.*
67 *COVID-19: A Joint Call to the G20 for Coordination on Health and the Economy*, THE ELDERS, (Apr. 6, 2020) www.theelders.org/news/covid-19-joint-call-g20-coordination-health-and-economy.
68 UN COVID-19 Framework, *supra* note 66, at 31.

awareness of the Funding Compact, its key principles and the expected commitments at the country-level so as to inspire and influence smart funding decisions. Making the collective COVID-19 response part of the existing strategy of achieving the SDGs at the country-level reduces the risk of duplication and waste of resources and reinforces efforts for the strongest possible response.[69] As the Foundation observed, three major global UN appeals/trust funds have been launched: (i) The COVID-19 Solidarity Response Fund initiated by the World Health Organization; (ii) The Consolidated Global Humanitarian Response Plan (GHRP) administered by the UN Office for the Coordination of Humanitarian Affairs (OCHA); and (iii) The UN COVID-19 Response and Recovery Fund administered by the Multi-Partner Trust Fund Office. Within the UN system, other existing pooled funds, such as the Peacebuilding Fund, the Joint SDG Fund, and the Spotlight Initiative are

> repurposing, adjusting and expanding activities, to adapt to COVID-19-related needs. In addition to these three major UN initiatives, the majority of UN agencies have also appealed for funding in their own agency capacity in order to mitigate the effects of the pandemic at country level in line with their respective mandates.[70]

These instruments and funding mechanisms will require a "joint, integrated and multi-sectoral approach in order to best address the magnitude of the crisis."[71]

Conclusion

It is now widely accepted that the SDGs are 17 integrated and interdependent goals. Goal 3 (health) is meaningless without Goal 2 (ending hunger and achieving food security). Neither will Goal 4 (ensuring inclusive and equitable quality education) make much sense if children are too sick or hungry to attend school. Given the definition of health as "a state of complete physical, mental and social well-being and not merely the absence of disease or infirmity," and the codification of the "highest attainable standard of health" as a fundamental right in the Constitution of the WHO, some commentators have argued that

> the significance of the SDGs lies in their ability to move beyond a biomedical approach to health and healthcare, and instead to seize the opportunity for the realization of the right to health in its fullest, widest, most fundamental sense: the right to a health-promoting and health protecting environment for each and every one of us.[72]

Achieving most of the SDG 3 targets would entail "utilizing the full range of commitments, conventions and covenants already in existence that promote, protect and ultimately realize rights in relation to the determinants of health."[73] There is a litany of such human rights covenants, conventions, and declarations including the UN Declaration on the Right to

---

69 John Hendra et al. (eds.), *Staying the Course: Funding Effective UN Responses to COVID-19 While Protecting the 2030 Agenda*, THE DAG HAMMARSKJÖLD FOUNDATION (Jun. 2020), www.daghammarskjold.se/wp-content/uploads/2020/07/stay-the-course-final.pdf.
70 *Id.* at 23.
71 *Id.*
72 Sarah Hawkes & Kent Buse, *Searching for the Right to Health in the Sustainable Development Agenda*, 5(5) INT'L J. OF HEALTH POL'Y AND MGMT. 337–39 (May 2016).
73 *Id.* at p.338.

Development. Using the 1966 International Covenant on Economic, Social and Cultural Rights as an example, Hawkes and Buse point to the codification of the rights to fair wages within a safe and healthy working environment, education, safe portable water, adequate sanitation, adequate and safe nutrition, and non-discrimination as indispensable to health.[74]

The legacy of the SDGs for the right to health "lies in the possibility that the ambition of the global goals reaches far beyond rolling out of Universal Health Coverage to one that gives impetus to action on the range of social determinants of health."[75] This proposal, albeit unassailable, is not radically new. Going back to the socially ambitious definition of health in the WHO Constitution, signed in 1946, the WHO-UNICEF Declaration of Alma-Ata on Primary Health Care 1978, Ottawa Charter for Health Promotion (1986), the reports of two important commissions by the WHO: the Commission on Social Determinants of Health (2008) and the Commission on Macroeconomics and Health (2001), health has never been confined to the biomedical sphere. In the context of the 2030 Agenda, it is important that countries place health and well-being at the center of their development agendas. This expansive and holistic approach promotes a right to health framework, which includes two things: Access to affordable health care and the underlying social and economic determinants of health.

A pragmatic realization of the right to the highest attainable standard of health in the 2030 Agenda requires two things: (i) effective accountability mechanisms for the review of the social determinants of health taking into consideration the benchmarks that are already working in some existing human rights treaty obligations;[76] and (ii) sustained use of workable human rights impact assessment practices in the development sector.[77] If meticulously developed and applied, policies developed under these two pragmatic pathways will connect with existing international human rights instruments and have measurable impacts on most of the SDG 3 targets: Maternal and child mortality, epidemics of AIDS, tuberculosis, and malaria, substance abuse, UHC, road traffic accidents, tobacco control, prevention and control of non-communicable diseases, training and retention of a health workforce in developing countries, risk reduction and management of national and global health risks.

It is important to note that some of the targets, like tobacco control and prevention and control of non-communicable diseases, would require states to regulate the operations and activities of non-state actors, notably businesses and transnational corporations. Innovative policies are needed post-Doha to address situations where, for instance, pharmaceutical patents held by multinational corporations impede access to health care and keep the prices of essential medicines artificially high for the poor and vulnerable groups who are in most need of the drugs.[78] In their struggles to roll out generic anti-retroviral drugs for HIV/

---

74 *Id.*
75 *Id.*
76 Paul H. Hunt, *SDGs and the Importance of Formal Independent Review: An Opportunity for Health to Lead the Way*, HEALTH AND HUMAN RIGHTS J. (Sept. 2, 2015), www.hhrjournal.org/2015/09/sdg-series-sdgs-and-the-importance-of-formal-independent-review-an-opportunity-for-health-to-lead-the-way/.
77 Paul H. Hunt & Gillian MacNaughton, *Impact Assessments, Poverty and Human Rights: A Case Study Using the Right to the Highest Attainable Standard of Health*, UNESCO (2006).
78 James Orbinski, *Creating a World of Possibility: The Fight for Essential Medicines*, in AN IMPERFECT OFFERING: DISPATCHES FROM THE MEDICAL FRONTLINE 351–80 (London: Rider, 2008); *See also* Obijiofor Aginam, *Between Life and Profit: Global Governance and the Trilogy of Human Rights, Public Health and Pharmaceutical Patents*, 31(4) N.C. J. OF INT'L LAW AND COMMERCIAL REG. 901–22 (2006).

AIDS, the experiences of Brazil, South Africa, Kenya,[79] and a few other countries in the post-TRIPS era, have shown that invoking the human rights argument can be a tortuous and complicated adventure because of corporate lobbyists. How this will play out if and when a COVID-19 vaccine is developed is open to debate. Related to this is the need for low- and middle-income countries to develop effective trade-health policy coherence along the lines discussed in the case study. Trade and health objectives need not be mutually exclusive. The challenge however is the development of strategies to ensure that trade and health are mutually reinforcing through coherent policy actions across government departments and agencies by creating synergies to ensure that short-term economic growth does not undermine health in the long term.

Concrete Actions

- Countries should move beyond a biomedical approach to health and healthcare, and position health at the center of their developmental policies in order to fully capture the social determinants of health.
- Countries should develop a policy coherence framework to address the tensions between trade-investment objectives and health promotion to ensure that short-term economic growth does not undermine public health in the long term.
- Countries should pursue an effective regulatory framework to address private sector interests and corporate determinants of health, especially in dealing with tobacco, alcohol, and the food industry.
- Countries should steadily increase their health budget in order to fund the critical components of UHC.

---

[79] *Id.* at 25; John Harrington, *Access to Essential Medicines in Kenya: Intellectual Property, Anti-Counterfeiting, and the Right to Health*, 16 LAW AND GLOBAL HEALTH: CURRENT LEGAL ISSUES (Michael Freeman et al. (eds.), Oxford U. Press, 2014).

8 Gender Equality and Women's Empowerment
Critical Assessment of the Implementation of SDG 5

Aisha Muhammed-Oyebode

Introduction

Background

Women still occupy only 25.1% of political positions in parliaments worldwide.[1] In the 49 countries of sub-Saharan Africa, approximately 73% of women believe domestic violence by a partner is warranted, and 21% of women are married as children.[2] Perpetuating extreme gendered social norms, boys are still recruited as child soldiers and sent out to men who exude toxic masculinity.[3] Measured by the Sustainable Development Goal (SDG) 5 indicators, the pace of achieving equality remains arduous because of constraining social norms and the lack of institutional capacity, political will, insufficient financing, and conflicting regulations. Renewed effort and strengthening collaborations between state and non-state actors, including the general public are essential to fast-tracking SDG 5 success.

In the wake of the global pandemic caused by COVID-19, the corresponding realities and consequent progress made on the construct was further amplified bringing back to the front burner conversations about inclusion, equity, and social justice, which had seemingly been fully understood and embraced by most stakeholder groups. This chapter takes a cursory look at the implementation timeline for the SDG 5 on Gender Equality and interrogates the linkages between equality, women's empowerment, and identity among other areas covered by the goal. This chapter also investigates the progress and regress made under SDG 5 in line with the following categorizations: (1) legal framework, rule of law, and national policies regarding indicators 5.1.1, 5.A.2, and 5.C.1; (2) economic empowerment, which refers to indicators 5.4.1, 5.5.1, 5.5.2, 5.A.1, and 5.B.1; (3) gender-based violence and harmful cultural practices as assessed by indicators 5.2.1, 5.2.2, 5.3.1, and 5.3.2; and (4) sexual and reproductive health rights of women, which concern indicators 5.6.1 and 5.6.2. The rights of nonbinary gender persons through cis-normative binary constructs were also examined using Nigeria as a case study.

---

1 *Global and Regional Averages of Women in National Parliaments*, IPU Parline, https://data.ipu.org/women-averages (Oct. 1, 2020).
2 *Child Marriage: Latest Trends and Prospects*, United Nations Children's Fund, (UNICEF), at 1, https://data.unicef.org/resources/child-marriage-latest-trends-and-future-prospects/ (July, 2018).
3 *Promoting Gender Equality: An Equity-Focused Approach to Programming*, UNICEF, at 7, www.unicef.org/gender/files/Overarching_Layout_Web.pdf (2011) [hereinafter "UNICEF Approach"].

Global Outlook on Gender and Women's Empowerment

In 2000, world leaders signed the Millennium Development Goals (MDGs). The MDGs were a set of eight measurable international goals for ending poverty, with 21 targets to be achieved by 2015. Goal 3 intended to promote gender equality and empower women.[4] Evaluation of the MDGs did show progress in the advancement of gender equality. Women in the paid formal workforce excluding agriculture increased from 35% in 1990 to 41% globally in 2015 and more girls now attend school compared to 15 years ago.[5] Despite these gains, in 2015, only 50% of women were in paid labor compared to 75% of men, and despite the average proportion of women in parliament almost doubling in the years leading up to 2015, four-fifths remain marginalized.[6] Underscoring the efforts was inspired ambition that was unattainable within entrenched international, national, and regional agendas.

The creation of the MDGs was criticized for being exclusive because there was very little involvement of developing countries and civil society, and less than 25% of national parliaments reviewed or considered its scope. After 2015, the eight MDGs were replaced by 17 new SDGs, with a deadline set for 2030. SDG 5 seeks to mobilize the United Nations (UN) Member States with the expressed intent to achieve equality of rights, responsibilities, and opportunities for women and girls and men and boys.[7] SDG 5's success is measured by specific targets and indicators.[8] The nine targets and 14 indicators are categorized thematically: (1) legal framework, rule of law, and national policies; (2) economic empowerment, (3) gender-based violence and harmful cultural practices; and (4) sexual and reproductive health rights of women. These targets and indicators are identified and categorized in Table 8.1.

At one-third of the target for the SDGs by the end of 2020, an appraisal of policies and interventions is significant.

Global Assessment of Progress

Are Legal Frameworks in Place?

Gender equality has been a focus of the United Nations since its inception. The UN General Assembly's 1993 Declaration on the Elimination of Violence against Women (DEVAW), which augmented its bedrock 1979 Convention on the Elimination of all Forms of Discrimination against Women (CEDAW), brought gender-based violence (GBV) prevention to the forefront of international efforts. DEVAW defined violence against women and girls for governments with emphasis on criminalization including for purported private domestic matters.[9] The Declaration established the Special Rapporteur on Violence against Women to evaluate the impact of violence on the lives of women worldwide.[10]

---

4 G.A. Res. A/RES/55/2, *United Nations Millennium Declaration* (Sept. 18, 2000).
5 *The Millennium Development Goals Report 2015*, UNITED NATIONS (UN), at 5, www.un.org/millenniu mgoals/2015_MDG_Report/pdf/MDG%202015%20rev%20(July%201).pdf (2015).
6 *Id.* at 8.
7 *Concept and Definitions*, UN WOMEN, www.un.org/womenwatch/osagi/conceptsandefinitions.htm (last visited Dec. 2, 2020).
8 G.A. Res. A/RES/70/1, *Transforming Our World: The 2030 Agenda for Sustainable Development*, at 18 (Oct. 21, 2015).
9 Mary Treuthart, "*No Woman, No Cry*" *Ending the War on Women Worldwide and the International Violence against Women Act*, 33(1) BOSTON U. INT'L L. J. 73, 88 (2015); *See also* Elizabeth Defeis, *The United Nations and Women—A Critique*, 17(2) WM. & MARY J. WOMEN & L. 395 (2011).
10 Defeis, *id.* at 414.

Table 8.1 SDG 5 at a glance.

SDG 5: Achieve gender equality and empower all women and girls

Targets	Indicators	Category
5.1: End all forms of discrimination against all women and girls everywhere.	5.1.1: Whether or not legal frameworks are in place to promote, enforce, and monitor equality and non-discrimination on the basis of sex.	Legal framework, rule of law, and national policies.
5.2: Eliminate all forms of violence against all women and girls in the public and private spheres, including trafficking and sexual and other types of exploitation.	5.2.1: Proportion of ever-partnered women and girls aged 15 years and older subjected to physical, sexual, or psychological violence by a current or former intimate partner in the previous 12 months, by form of violence and by age.	Gender-based violence and harmful cultural practices.
	5.2.2: Proportion of women and girls aged 15 years and older subjected to sexual violence by persons other than an intimate partner in the previous 12 months, by age and place of occurrence.	Gender-based violence and harmful cultural practices.
5.3: Eliminate all harmful practices, such as child, early, and forced marriage and female genital mutilation.	5.3.1: Proportion of women aged 20–24 years who were married or in a union before age 15 and before age 18.	Gender-based violence and harmful cultural practices.
	5.3.2: Proportion of girls and women aged 15–49 years who have undergone female genital mutilation/cutting, by age.	Gender-based violence and Harmful cultural practices.
5.4: Recognize and value unpaid care and domestic work through the provision of public services, infrastructure, and social protection policies and the promotion of shared responsibility within the household and the family as nationally appropriate.	5.4.1: Proportion of time spent on unpaid domestic and care work, by sex, age, and location.	Economic opportunities, decision-making, and technological progress.
5.5: Ensure women's full and effective participation and equal opportunities for leadership at all levels of decision-making in political, economic, and public life.	5.5.1: Proportion of seats held by women in national parliaments and local governments.	Economic opportunities, decision-making, and technological progress.
	5.5.2: Proportion of women in managerial positions.	Economic opportunities, decision-making, and technological progress.

(*Continued*)

Table 8.1 Continued

SDG 5: *Achieve gender equality and empower all women and girls*

Targets	Indicators	Category
5.6: Ensure universal access to sexual and reproductive health and reproductive rights as agreed in accordance with the Program of Action of the International Conference on Population and Development and the Beijing Platform for Action and the outcome documents of their review conferences.	5.6.1: Proportion of women aged 15–49 years who make their own informed decisions regarding sexual relations, contraceptive use, and reproductive health care.	Sexual and reproductive health rights.
	5.6.2: Number of countries with laws and regulations that guarantee women aged 15–49 years access to sexual and reproductive health care, information, and education.	Sexual and reproductive health rights.
5.A: Undertake reforms to give women equal rights to economic resources, as well as access to ownership and control over land and other forms of property, financial services, inheritance, and natural resources, in accordance with national laws.	5.A.1: (a) Proportion of total agricultural population with ownership or secure rights over agricultural land, by sex and (b) share of women among owners or rights-bearers of agricultural land, by type of tenure.	Economic opportunities, decision-making, and technological progress.
	5.A.2: Proportion of countries where the legal framework (including customary law) guarantees women's equal rights to land ownership and/or control.	Legal framework, rule of law, and national policies.
5.B: Enhance the use of enabling technology, in particular information and communications technology, to promote the empowerment of women.	5.B.1: Proportion of individuals who own a mobile telephone, by sex.	Economic opportunities, Decision-making and technological progress.
5.C: Adopt and strengthen sound policies and enforceable legislation for the promotion of gender equality and the empowerment of all women and girls at all levels.	5.C.1: Proportion of countries with systems to track and make public allocations for gender equality and women's empowerment.	Legal framework, rule of law, and national policies.

Source: UN SDGs *Goal 5: Achieve Gender Equality and Empower all Women and Girls*, UN DEPARTMENT OF ECONOMIC AND SOCIAL AFFAIRS, https://sdgs.un.org/goals/goal5 (2020).

However, the adoption of DEVAW was voluntary for UN Member States and neglected the role of dogmatic religious and harmful cultural practices in perpetuating violence against women.[11] The UN attempted to enhance individual states' accountability by endorsing the Beijing Declaration and Platform for Action (BPfA) during its Fourth World Conference on Women in 1995. The BPfA demanded clear-cut obligations and deliverables by states and

---

11 Treuthart, *supra* note 10, at 88.

organizations in several core areas: education, decision-making, health, violence, and socio-economic rights.[12] Annually, data is reviewed, with best practices and challenges shared at the Commission on the Status of Women. However, the BPfA was not legally binding[13] and lacked any mechanism for enforcement; demands with neither carrots nor sticks.[14]

Echoing CEDAW, DEVAW, BPfA, the MDGs, and the SDGs, the sole indicator for target 5.1. is "whether or not legal frameworks are in place to promote, enforce and monitor equality and non-discrimination based on sex,"[15] as legal frameworks can provide a foundation for ending all forms of gender discrimination. Globally, 189 states have ratified CEDAW.[16] The United States and Palau are the only two signatory countries, while the Holy See, the Islamic Republic of Iran, Somalia, Sudan, and Tonga remain independent.[17]

To implement international gender equality standards within national frameworks, countries opt for autonomous laws for gender equality, as did Armenia's 2013 Equal Rights and Equal Opportunities of Women and Men Act.[18] Others opt for constitution review, as did Tunisia in 2014 with improved complementarity and equality between men and women.[19] Canada has adopted both strategies.[20] Also, 52 out of the 57 Member States in the Organization for Security and Co-operation in Europe (OSCE) all domesticated gender equality.[21]

When Do-Not-Discriminate Becomes Law

Indicator 5.1.1: Whether Legal Frameworks Are in Place to Promote, Enforce, and Monitor Equality and Non-Discrimination Based on Sex

The 2019 Social Institutions and Gender Index (SIGI) report[22] in monitoring SDG indicator 5.1.1. posits that all countries have made progress in legal reforms in advancing gender equality. Regionally, however, about 45% of Asian countries analyzed in the report have increased levels of discrimination based on gender.[23]

---

12 *The Beijing Declaration and Platform for Action, 4th World Conference on Women*, UN WOMEN, www.un.org/en/events/pastevents/pdfs/Beijing_Declaration_and_Platform_for_Action.pdf (1995).
13 Defeis, *supra* note 10, at 399.
14 Petra Debusscher et al., *Evaluation of the Beijing Platform for Action +20 and the Opportunities for Achieving Gender Equality and the Empowerment of Women in the Post-2015 Development Agenda*, at 10–11, EUROPEAN PARLIAMENT (2015).
15 Goal 5, *supra* note 9.
16 *Convention on the Elimination of all Forms of Discrimination against Women*, UN TREATY COLLECTION, https://treaties.un.org/Pages/ViewDetails.aspx?src=TREATY&mtdsg_no=IV-8&chapter=4&lang=en (last visited Dec. 11, 2020).
17 *Id.*
18 *Armenia, Country Gender Assessment*, ASIAN DEVELOPMENT BANK, at xii, www.adb.org/sites/default/files/institutional-document/162152/arm-country-gender-assessment.pdf (July 2015).
19 *Tunisia's Constitution of 2014.*
20 *See Gender Equality, Canada*, LEGISLATIONLINE, www.legislationline.org/topics/topic/7/country/38 (last visited Dec. 11, 2020).
21 *See Gender Equality: Legislation*, LEGISLATIONLINE, www.legislationline.org/legislation/topic/7 (last visited Dec. 11, 2020).
22 *About the SIGI*, SOCIAL INSTITUTIONS AND GENDER INDEX, www.genderindex.org/sigi/ (last visited Dec. 12, 2020).
23 *2019 Regional Analysis*, SOCIAL INSTITUTIONS AND GENDER INDEX, www.genderindex.org/2019-regional-analysis/ (last visited Dec. 12, 2020).

The Social Institutions and Gender Index reveals clear regional trends: approximately 14% of African countries ranked as having "high" levels of discrimination based on existing legal frameworks, and none of them achieved the "very low level" ranking.[24] However, close to 80% and about 25% of the countries analyzed in Europe and the Americas, respectively, have a "very low level" of gender discrimination. Progress is not uniform across regions.[25] South Africa is ranked as having the lowest level of gender discrimination in Africa, while Guinea ranks the highest.[26] The effect of social structures on gender equity is proportional, as involvement in paid labour often correlates with gender discrimination. Inequality is not proportional to per capita income with the Middle East rating high.[27] Interestingly, it seems the higher the percentage of women who can read and write, the lower the percentage of them that suffer discrimination in social institutions[28] making education a strong promoter of women's rights. In both legal frameworks and social norms, the lowest-performing countries communicate the reality of a woman being measured by reproductive and caring responsibilities.

At three times higher than the global average, less than two-thirds of the lowest-performing countries recognize women as heads of household.[29] Sixty-four percent of these populations indicate that children whose mothers work outside the home are gravely disadvantaged and 70% suggest men are preferred as political leaders over women.[30] Twenty-two percent of their adolescent girls are in informal relationships or have been married compared to 15% globally, and men spend five times less time than women in unpaid care and domestic work, at one-third of the global level.[31] These obvious forms of legal discrimination create loopholes globally and sustain weak law enforcement and discriminatory social practices by communities, including women, hampering advancement toward global progress in gender equality.[32]

Indicator 5.A.2: Proportion of Countries Where the Legal Framework (Including Customary Law) Guarantee Women's Equal Rights to Land Ownership and/or Control

Legal backing to support women's access to and control of land varies across countries and regions. The Food and Agriculture Organization of the United Nations (FAO) has created measuring proxy tools to assess frameworks on women's equal rights to land. Their findings show that Paraguay and Colombia both score the highest for securing the land rights of women, while Jordan and Qatar score lowest.[33] Of 182 countries reviewed, 164 or 90% have legal frameworks protecting the rights of women with land.[34] Such progress must be matched with equivalence in very low performing countries. Plural customary laws may

---

24 *Id.*
25 *Id.*
26 *Id.*
27 *See Social Institutions and Gender Index 2019 Global Report*, ORGANIZATION FOR ECONOMIC AND COOPERATION AND DEVELOPMENT (2019) [hereinafter "SIGI 2019 Report"].
28 *Id.*
29 *Id.* at Ch. 1.
30 *Id.*
31 *Id.*
32 *Id.*
33 *Sustainable Development Goals,* Food and Agriculture Organization of the UN, (FAO), www.fao.org/sustainable-development-goals/indicators/5a2/en/ (last visited Dec. 11, 2020).
34 SIGI 2019 Report, *supra* note 29, at Ch. 5.

counteract national laws as analysis shows that 123 countries still have traditional, religious, and customary laws in operation that inhibit women's freedom to claim and protect land.[35]

Tracking Public Spending on Gender and Women—Indicator 5.C.1: Proportion of Countries with Systems to Track and Make Public Allocations for Gender Equality and Women's Empowerment

Achieving gender equality requires adequate planning, financing for implementation, and applying a results-based approach. Indicator 5.C.1 aims to ensure that national governments have made provisions supporting accountability in gender-responsive budgeting with designated host institutions. Budgets are gender-responsive when computed interventions tackle gender gaps from a multi-sector, multi-level perspective. Measuring the accountability and transparency of funding for gender equality using sex-disaggregated data seeks to counteract disproportionate systems for tracking public allocations for gender equality and is currently at 19%.[36] In sub-Saharan Africa, this proportion is 11%, calling for conscientious action, including adequate planning, tracking, financing, and implementation with development actors to catalyze achieving the SDGs.[37]

Where international frameworks are implemented at the national level, gender discrimination still pervades due to poor transfer as well as plurality of other discriminatory laws and social norms and poor policies and regulations.[38]

What Is the Progress in Economic Opportunities, Decision-Making, and Technology for women?

Indicator 5.4.1: Proportion of Time Spent on Unpaid Domestic and Care Work by Sex, Age, and Location

Unpaid domestic and care work is vital for the survival and quality of life of people worldwide. Over the past decade, much emphasis has been placed on the disproportionate levels of unpaid domestic care work carried out by women and girls, and the inverse relationship between this and their economic advancement.[39] Globally, women conduct 75% of unpaid domestic and care work,[40] and women dedicate an average of 3.2 times more time to unpaid care work than men.[41] A regional breakdown indicates that the ratio of time women spend on unpaid domestic and care work in comparison to men is 1.7 in the Americas, 2.1 in

---

35 *Id.*
36 *Achieve Gender Equality and Empower All Women and Girls,* DESA, https://unstats.un.org/sdgs/report/2019/goal-05/ (last visited Dec. 15, 2020).
37 *Id.*
38 *Approaches to Gender Equality,* UNITED NATIONS RESOURCES ON GENDER, www.un.org/womenwatch/resources/goodpractices/approach.html#capacity (last visited Dec. 11, 2020).
39 *Global Gender Gap Report 2020,* WORLD ECONOMIC FORUM, at 11, http://www3.weforum.org/docs/WEF_GGGR_2020.pdf (2020).
40 Jorge Silva, *Why You Should Care about Unpaid Care Work,* OECD, https://oecd-development-matters.org/2019/03/18/why-you-should-care-about-unpaid-care-work/ (March 18, 2019).
41 Jacques Charmes, *The Unpaid Care Work and the Labour Market. An Analysis of Time Use Data Based on the Latest World Compilation of Time-Use Surveys,* INTERNATIONAL LABOR ORGANIZATION (ILO), www.ilo.org/wcmsp5/groups/public/---dgreports/---gender/documents/publication/wcms_732791.pdf (2019).

Europe and Central Asia, 3.4 in Africa, 4.1 in Asia and the Pacific, and 4.7 in the Arab States.[42]

Trends across a decade and a half (1997–2012) in 23 countries show that the average time spent by women on unpaid care work has only slightly reduced by 23 minutes, from 4 hours and 23 minutes to 4 hours.[43] Based on the current trend, parity in unpaid and domestic care work will only be achieved by the year 2228 unless the adoption of best practices for recognizing, reducing the amount of time through the use of technology, redistributing, rewarding, and ensuring the inclusive representation of care workers in social dialog are adopted.[44]

Indicator 5.5.1: Proportion of Seats Held by Women in National Parliaments and Local Governments

The need for women in parliament cannot be overstated, as women in parliament tend to prioritize socioeconomic matters such as healthcare, education, and other gender-inclusive agendas.[45] Progress has been made in the fight to improve women's participation in politics and the participation of women in parliament has increased by over 11.4%, from 13.1% in 2000 to 24.5% in 2019.[46] Rwanda is now the highest-ranking country, where 61.3% of the lower house parliament is comprised of women.[47] The Pacific region has the highest number of women in the upper parliament at 48%.[48] Following the Pacific is the Americas, with an average of 31% women in political affairs.[49] The region with the least representation of women in parliament is the Middle East and North Africa, which has an average of 17%.[50] These figures remain below the gender parity mark for women in legislative government. Challenges such as misogynistic social norms and attitudes and violence against women participating in politics remain obstacles in achieving gender parity in political positions.

REGIONAL AVERAGE PERCENTAGES OF WOMEN IN PARLIAMENT

Male domination in all spheres of life has impeded women's involvement in present-day Nigerian politics. For instance, in the legislative house, out of 360 house of representative members and 106 senate members seats, those held by women in 2019 accounts for

---

42 *Care Work and Care Jobs for the Future of Decent Work*, ILO, at 54, www.ilo.org/wcmsp5/groups/public/---dgreports/---dcomm/---publ/documents/publication/wcms_633135.pdf (2018).
43 *Id.* at 68.
44 *Id.*
45 Sandra Pepera, *Why Women in Politics?*, WOMEN DELIVER, https://womendeliver.org/2018/why-women-in-politics/ (Feb. 28, 2018).
46 *Women in Parliament: 20 Years in Review*, INTER-PARLIAMENTARY UNION, http://archive.ipu.org/pdf/publications/WIP20Y-en.pdf (2015).
47 *Women in National Parliaments: Country Averages*, INTER-PARLIAMENTARY UNION, http://archive.ipu.org/wmn-e/classif.htm (Feb. 1, 2019).
48 *Women in National Parliaments: Regional Averages*, INTER-PARLIAMENTARY UNION, http://archive.ipu.org/wmn-e/world.htm (Oct. 1, 2019).
49 *Id.*
50 *Id.*

only 3.38%.[51] This is the lowest value in 19 years with the highest in 2010 being 7%.[52] This under-representation extends to ministerial, director, special advising, and even secretarial positions. Many political parties in Nigeria have little or no accessible data on women's representation in their affairs, and this has also restricted women's opportunities in general elections.

Indicator 5.5.2: Proportion of Women in Managerial Positions

The level of female participation in paid work is challenged by limited gender-inclusive policies in the corporate world and national governments and the core issues of unpaid care work, unpaid maternity leave, and social attitudes and norms.[53] A critical look at the economies reveals that the proportion of women in managerial positions has risen from 13.8% in 2016 to 17.6% in 2019.[54] This proportion varies across regions, with North America at the top with over 20%, followed by Asia-Pacific excluding Japan, which has the lowest proportion of women in managerial positions in the developed world.[55] Although limited data is available at the global level, country-level data ranks Eswatini as the country with the highest number of women in middle and senior management.[56] By contrast, 2017 data from Afghanistan shows their share of women in managerial positions to be 4%.[57] Beyond gender parity in managerial leadership positions, there is also the issue of patriarchal ingenuity where, although women occupy leadership and managerial positions, their leadership is undermined and challenged, and in many cases, their male subordinates make the critical decisions while women are subjected to "softer" roles with "institutional trappings or titles."[58]

5.A.1: (a) Proportion of Total Agricultural Population with Ownership or Secure Rights over Agricultural Land by Sex and (b) Share of Women among Owners or Rights-Bearers of Agricultural Land by Type of Tenure

Women living in rural areas account for 20% to 50% of the agricultural labor force worldwide.[59] However, they have limited access to assets to boost productivity that would significantly empower them. If land ownership is a vital sign of economic empowerment, there is a crucial need to measure the level of ownership by women, particularly as it relates to access to and control of resources. There is limited data available to measure progress. However, from the data of 10 countries (Burkina Faso, Cambodia, Ethiopia, Peru, Nigeria, India, United Republic of Tanzania, Malawi, Niger, and Uganda) the highest proportion of

---

51 Gender Data Portal: Nigeria, *Public Life and Decision Making*, The WORLD BANK, www.worldbank.org/en/data/datatopics/gender/country/Nigeria (last visited Dec. 15, 2020).
52 *Id.*
53 Richard Kersley et al., *The CS Gender 3000 in 2019: From Boardroom to "C-Suite"*, at 43 and 47, CREDIT SUISSE RESEARCH INSTITUTE (CSRI) (2019).
54 *Id.* at 31.
55 *Id.* at 13.
56 *Female Share of Employment in Senior and Middle Management (%)*, WORLD BANK, https://data.worldbank.org/indicator/SL.EMP.SMGT.FE.ZS?most_recent_value_desc=false (June 21, 2020).
57 *Id.*
58 Jill Blackmore & Judyth Sachs, *Paradoxes of Leadership and Management in Higher Education in Times of Change: Some Australian Reflections*, 3(1) INT'L J. LEADERSHIP EDUC. 1, 1–16 (Nov. 10, 2010).
59 Terri Raney et al., *The Role of Women in Agriculture*, ESA Working Paper No. 11-02, Agricultural Dev. Econ. Div., FAO (Mar. 2011), www.fao.org/3/am307e/am307e00.pdf.

people with ownership or secure rights over agricultural land, out of the total agricultural population, by sex is Ethiopia with 65.3% of women as opposed to 69.4% of men.[60] By contrast, Burkina Faso has a staggering discrepancy of 5.9% for women and 35% for men.[61] Peru, the only country with multi-year data, has fluctuated with low figures from 8.2% in 2014, 7.7% in 2016, and 8.0% in 2018.[62]

Malawi's figures for women landowners stand at 58%, followed by Ethiopia and Cambodia at 51%, with Niger at 11%.[63] These results may have been further impacted by land and agricultural laws, financing and credit policies, and inheritance laws. Addressing these constraints through adequate policymaking and institutional support may increase the likelihood of significant improvements by 2030.

5.B.1: Proportion of Individuals Who Own a Mobile Telephone by Sex

The success of the #MeToo movement, leading to the prosecution of several sexual assault perpetrators, was supported by technology through social media platforms. Technology aids in the advancement of the protection of women's rights through advocacy. A thriving technology ecosystem also enhances women's economic empowerment. Globally, 80% of women now have access to a mobile phone; however, this is not commensurate with their ownership of phones.[64] The gender gap in mobile telephone ownership is highest in South Asia (28%), followed by Sub-Saharan Africa (15%).[65] Affordability, literacy, and access to mobile networks in hard-to-reach communities are the major barriers to gender parity in mobile telephone ownership.[66]

Progress and Regress on Sexual and Reproductive Health Rights

Indicator 5.6.1—Proportion of Women Who Make Their Own Informed Decisions Regarding Sexual Relations, Contraceptive Use, and Reproductive Health Care

Sexual and reproductive health rights for women have improved worldwide. More women now have a say in the timing and number of children they want to have and in the use of contraceptives. For instance, in Albania, the proportion of women who make informed decisions regarding sexual relations, contraceptive use, and reproductive health care went from 61.5% in 2009 to 69% in 2018, and in the Democratic Republic of Congo, this figure rose from 19.3% in 2007 to 30.7% in 2014. In the Philippines, 2017 data shows that 81% of women make informed choices regarding sexual and reproductive health rights, while in Senegal this figure is only 7% for the same year. Issues of access to sexual healthcare services, health financing, and cultural beliefs and practices continue to create obstacles in the

---

60 *Gender and Land Rights Database*, FAO, www.fao.org/gender-landrights-database/data-map/statistics/en/ (last visited Dec. 15, 2020).
61 *Id.*
62 *Id.*
63 *Id.*
64 *The Mobile Gender Gap Report 2019*, GSMA, at 3, www.gsma.com/mobilefordevelopment/wp-content/uploads/2019/02/GSMA-The-Mobile-Gender-Gap-Report-2019.pdf (Feb. 2019).
65 *Id.*
66 *Id.*

advancement of adolescent girls and women's agency regarding their sexual and reproductive rights.⁶⁷

Indicator 5.6.2—Number of Countries with Laws and Regulations that Guarantee Women Aged 15–49 Years Access to Sexual and Reproductive Health Care, Information, and Education

The UN Women's database indicates that of 59 constitutional provisions that specifically guarantee women's rights to sexual and reproductive healthcare and information, 44% of them refer to access to healthcare for women. Also, in an analysis carried out by the UN Population Fund (UNFPA), 73% of laws in 75 countries have provisions ensuring sexual and reproductive health rights (SRHR).⁶⁸ Sweden scored 100% according to the criteria used to measure the laws.⁶⁹ These criteria include legal provisions on maternity care, contraception and family planning, comprehensive sexuality education, health, and well-being.⁷⁰

However, of the countries with laws that promote access to contraceptives, 28% have a minimum age of 21, thereby excluding adolescent girls.⁷¹ Only 79% of countries have laws that promote access to post-abortion care, and 20% have counter laws that imperil women's SRHR.⁷² Furthermore, countries like the Maldives, South Sudan, and Mauritania scored below 30% in the ranking of adequate laws that promote women's SRHR.⁷³ Several constraints play strong roles in the adoption of laws regarding the SRHR of women. The strongest is the knowledge, attitudes, and beliefs of members of parliament toward sensitive issues such as abortion and contraceptives as well as widespread community acceptance of SRHR.

*Global Policy Recommendations*⁷⁴

Beyond global averages, countries like Rwanda have fared well regarding women's political participation in the lower senate. Malawi and Ethiopia have furthermore achieved gender parity in the percentage of landowners and right bearers. Based on the nuances and trends at regional and national levels, the chance that SDG 5 will be achieved by 2030 is low. It is against this context that this chapter makes the following policy recommendations:

---

67 *See Unfinished Business, The Pursuit of Rights and Choices for All*, UN POPULATION FUND (UNFPA), www.unfpa.org/sites/default/files/pub-pdf/UNFPA_PUB_2019_EN_State_of_World_Population.pdf (2019).
68 *Legal Commitments for Sexual and Reproductive Health and Reproductive Rights for All*, UNFPA, at 4, www.unfpa.org/sites/default/files/resource-pdf/19-321_UNFPA-SDG562-A4-Brochure-v3.7-2020-03-06-09491.pdf (Feb. 2020),
69 *Id*. at 2 and 5.
70 *Id*.
71 *Id*. at 3.
72 *Id*. at 2–3 and 9.
73 *Supra* note 76.
74 SIGI 2019 Report, *supra* note 29, at 23–25.

Funding Development

There is a need to return to the drawing board regarding financing, as funding development is one of the challenges hindering progress in gender equality and has impeded the ability of national governments to implement gender equality laws and programs. Political will and institutional capacity must be mobilized to promote financing for gender responsiveness for all arms and tiers of government in concert with regional and global platforms to enhance resource mobilization and knowledge sharing. The economics of gender which involves budgeting for gender priorities into programs remain limited, as indicated by the progress on target 5.C.

Technology and Innovation

There are strong reasons for applying technology and innovation and fostering intersectional and multi-faceted approaches to addressing gender inequality. Innovation and technology for use in planning, implementing, and monitoring gender equality interventions is vital to achieving SDG 5 by 2030. With the process of digitalization occurring worldwide, it is necessary to also include the use of technology in programmatic approaches. However, this will require a contextual analysis of the present knowledge of technical skills and the target audience of interventions.

Review of Legal Frameworks and Capacity Building

Capacity building on gender equality in all arms of government, including the executive, parliamentary, and judiciary branches at the national and sub-national levels, is also crucial. Despite high ranking on the SIGI by South Africa, the occurrence of intimate partner violence is higher there than in Nigeria. South Africa's implementation and enforcement of legal frameworks are not vibrant. This challenge may either be due to limited financing, the limited capacity of custodian ministries, departments, and agencies, or conflicting laws that promote discrimination such as legalized spousal rape. Unwritten customary laws endorsed by custodians and gatekeepers such as religious and traditional leaders heighten conservativism. Limited data also hampers development. It is important to build upon the datasets made available by national governments, UN Women, UN Children's Fund (UNICEF), UN Population Fund, and other coordinating institutions.

Advocacy against Harmful Social Practices

Harmful social practices stemming from social norms mitigate the impact and extent of implementation of gender equality laws and interventions across national levels. The change in power dynamics resulting from gender-targeted programs has led to violence against women and girls. To begin to change the narratives of gender in societies, it is important to create programs directly targeted at engaging traditional and religious leaders as well as other influencers. This may require the promotion of laws which highly influence attitudinal and behavioral change.

Journey to Equal Opportunities

The SDGs emphasize leaving no one behind. Therefore, the voices of women and girls with disabilities must be represented in the discourse. Prioritizing the needs of the over 1.2

million women and girls with disabilities is crucial to the realization of the SDGs. Their disabilities leave them highly susceptible to GBV as well as discrimination with regard to access to education, healthcare, and political and economic representation.[75] Furthermore, women are often underrepresented and marginalized in the fight for gender equality by development actors.[76] There is further limited capacity for understanding and creating evidence-based interventions for women due to limited disaggregated data.

The rural–urban divide also poses a challenge to gender equality. Girls in rural areas are twice as likely to get married early than girls living in urban areas.[77] Moreover, because some rural communities are in hard-to-reach areas, access to justice for many women and girls is limited.[78] Furthermore, women and girls in conflict-affected areas are at greater risk of violence.[79] Solutions include adequate mapping of needs including for women in remote locations, and the provision of infrastructure.

Interventions that include a multidimensional strategy, covering immediate needs and long-run beneficial needs are likely to yield results. Wage discrimination, unpaid care work, and the high participation of women in the informal sector, particularly agriculture, further expands unequal opportunities for women and girls from lower-income households.[80]

Due to historical disadvantages, women's issues represent the core of gender discourses. However, marginalized men and boys must be captured in the gender equality conversation. Social norms that promote gender stereotypes and roles are said to increase toxic masculinity in men and boys.[81] In Bangladesh, 12.1% of boys are classified by the Global Multidimensional Poverty Index as multidimensionally poor.[82] Furthermore, boys are less likely to continue with upper secondary and post-secondary education in Europe, North America, and Latin America and the Caribbean.

---

75 *Achieving Gender Equality and Empowering all Women and Girls with Disabilities (Goal 5)*, UNITED NATIONS, www.un.org/development/desa/disabilities/wp-content/uploads/sites/15/2020/01/GenderEquality_Brief_Final_20191203.p (last visited Dec. 11, 2020).
76 *The Empowerment of Women and Girls with Disabilities: Towards Full and Effective Participation and Gender Equality*, UN WOMEN, at 7–10, www.unwomen.org/-/media/headquarters/attachments/sections/library/publications/2018/empowerment-of-women-and-girls-with-disabilities-en.pdf?la=en&vs=3504 (2018).
77 Jennifer McCleary-Sills et al., *Child Marriage: A Critical Barrier to Girls' Schooling and Gender Equality in Education*, 13(3) REV. FAITH & INT'L. AFF. 69, 69–80 (Oct. 23, 2015).
78 *A Girl's Right to say No to Marriage: Working to End Child Marriage and Keep Girls in School*, PLAN INTERNATIONAL, at 6 and 13, https://plan-uk.org/file/en-a-girls-right-to-say-no-to-marriage-fullreport-web-32000722pdf/download?token=BE80wUlB (2013).
79 *Violence against Women and Girls in Humanitarian Emergencies*, DEPARTMENT FOR INTERNATIONAL DEVELOPMENT, https://assets.publishing.service.gov.uk/government/uploads/system/uploads/attachment_data/file/271932/VAWG-humanitarian-emergencies.pdf (Oct. 2013).
80 HUMANITY DIVIDED: CONFRONTING INEQUALITY IN DEVELOPING COUNTRIES, UN DEVELOPMENT PROGRAMME (UNDP) 87 (Nov. 2013).
81 UNICEF Approach, *supra* note 3.
82 GLOBAL MULTIDIMENSIONAL POVERTY INDEX 2019: ILLUMINATING INEQUALITIES, UNDP 8 (2019).

Are We Making Progress?—Gender Violence in Nigeria

Is There a Reduction in Gender-Based Violence and Harmful Cultural Practices?

Indicator 5.2.1: Proportion of Ever-Partnered Women and Girls Aged 15 Years and Older Subjected to Physical, Sexual, or Psychological Violence by a Current or Former Intimate Partner in the Previous 12 Months by Form of Violence and by Age

There is a high prevalence of intimate partner violence in Nigeria. In a 2018 survey, 35% of women aged 15 to 49 affirmed experiencing physical violence.[83] Of the 9% who experienced sexual violence, 4% experienced it before the age of 18.[84] Relationship inequality is often a key indicator of violent relationships. Out of the women who have experienced physical, sexual, and emotional violence, women who are employed with no earned cash, but in-kind payments were more likely to experience violence (49%) than women who earned cash from employment (36%) and unemployed women (32%).[85]

Indicator 5.2.2: Proportion of Women and Girls Aged 15 Years and Older Subjected to Sexual Violence by Persons Other than an Intimate Partner in the Previous 12 Months by Age and Place of Occurrence

Although there is extensive research on the violence of former and current intimate partners, limited data and research are available on non-intimate partner violence. However, as a result of the insurgency in the North East which is rapidly spreading to the North West of Nigeria, sexual violence by "non-intimate" partners has grown disproportionately. A report by the United Nations on sexual violence in conflict issued in June 2020 documented that 88% of examples of conflict-related sexual violence documented by the UN from the end of 2018 were attributed to Boko Haram and the Civilian Joint Task Force.[86] The Security forces were responsible for the remaining 12%.[87] Thirty-four percent of the incidents occurred when Boko Haram abducted women and girls from their communities.[88] This had also fostered an increased number of forced and child marriage within the communities largely to prevent further abductions by armed groups.[89] Access to other multi-year and recent data for indicators 5.2.1 and 5.2.2 is limited.

Indicator 5.3.1: Proportion of Women Aged 20–24 Years Who Were Married or in a Union before Age 15 and before Age 18

In Nigeria, 43% of girls are married before they are 18 years old, and 16% are married before they turn 16, with some as young as 12 years of age.[90] The occurrence is highest in the North

---

83 *Nigeria Demographic and Health Survey 2018*, NATIONAL POPULATION COMMISSION, at 429, https://dhsprogram.com/pubs/pdf/FR359/FR359.pdf (Oct. 2019).
84 *Id.* at 430.
85 *Id.* at 433.
86 U.N. Secretary General, *Conflict-Related Sexual Violence*, UN (Jun. 2020), www.un.org/sexualviolenceinconflict/wp-content/uploads/2020/07/report/conflict-related-sexual-violence-report-of-the-united-nations-secretary-general/2019-SG-Report.pdf.
87 *Id.*
88 *Id*
89 *Nigeria*, GIRLS NOT BRIDES, www.girlsnotbrides.org/child-marriage/nigeria/ (last visited Nov. 30, 2020).
90 *Id.*

West and North East at 68% and 57%, respectively.[91] The high occurrence in the North East and North West has been exacerbated by conflict, civil strife, increased gendered crimes, and internal displacement.[92] Poverty, limited education, and harmful religious and social norms and practices are further exacerbated by conflicting legal and policy frameworks. A noteworthy example is the legal minimum age for marriage under the Marriage Act 1990 and the Child Rights Act of 21 and 18 years, respectively being contradicted by the Sexual Offense Bill, which sets the age of consent at 11 years.[93] Customs, religious practices, and by-laws that controvert the positive gains of progressive frameworks usually find adherence at the community level and are common in regions of high occurrence.[94]

Indicator 5.3.2: Proportion of Girls and Women Aged 15–49 Years Who Have Undergone Female Genital Mutilation/Cutting by Age

Nigeria has the highest absolute number of women who have undergone female genital mutilation (FGM) in the world, with higher occurrences for women in Igbo and Yoruba ethnic groups.[95] With attitudes and beliefs as key drivers of FGM in some ethnic groups, only 52% of the sampled population think FGM should be discontinued.[96] Often FGM and cutting and child marriage tend to correlate. The Nigerian government is a signatory to the CEDAW and Maputo Protocols. Furthermore, the National Gender Policy,[97] the 1999 constitution,[98] and the recent Violence Against Person's Prohibition Act (VAPP),[99] as well as other laws criminalize gender-based violence. At the sub-national level, however, 11 states mostly based in Northern Nigeria and 23 states across the country have yet to domesticate the Child Rights Act and VAPP laws, respectively.[100]

The lack of robust support for laws that empower women has been largely blamed on the poor gender distribution of persons in governance and national leadership.[101] Although Nigeria is the most populous country in Africa,[102] it ranks 122 out of 129 countries in the 2019 SDG Gender Index rankings by country.[103]

---

91 *Id.*
92 *Id.*
93 *Id.*
94 *Id.*
95 *Harnessing the Power of Data for Gender Equality: Introducing the 2019 EM2030 SDG Gender Index*, EQUAL MEASURES 2030, at 44 (2019) [hereinafter "2019 EM2030 Index"].
96 *Id.*
97 National Gender Policy (2006) (Nigeria).
98 CONSTITUTION OF NIGERIA (1999).
99 Violence Against Persons (Prohibition) Act (2015) (Nigeria).
100 Nike Adebowale, *Why Every Nigerian State Must Domesticate, Implement the Child Rights Act*, PREMIUM TIMES, www.premiumtimesng.com/health/health-features/336790-why-every-nigerian-state-must-domesticate-implement-child-rights-act.html (June 24, 2019).
101 Damilola Agbalajobi & Leke Oluwalogbon, *The Nigerian Senate and the Politics of the non-passage of the Gender Equality Bill*, 13(3) AFR. J. POL. SCI. & INT'L. REL. 17 (April 4, 2019).
102 *Population, Female (% of Total Population)—Nigeria*, WORLD BANK, https://data.worldbank.org/indicator/SP.POP.TOTL.FE.ZS?locations=NG&view=chart (2018).
103 2019 EM2030 Index, *supra* note 101.

Rethinking Gender Equality: Are We Missing Gender Minorities?

COVID-19

Recently, the COVID-19 pandemic compelled many countries to enforce a lockdown to better respond to and contain the spread of the new coronavirus. For many women, the implication has been dire and life-threatening due to an alarming increase in reported cases of violence against women and girls worldwide.[104] Labeled a shadow pandemic by the UN, gendered violence during lockdowns portend long-term and severe consequences for the future opportunities and life trajectories of these women and girls.[105] Between March and April 2020, a 56% increase in gender violence was reported in Nigeria alone in the 23 states for which data exists in two weeks of lockdown.[106]

There are also simultaneous reports of an alarming increase in violence against trans and non-binary gendered persons worldwide.[107] This coincides with an ongoing national conversation in Nigeria on how to be inclusive of different identities and promote the rights and recognition of those who live on the margins of gender. At the core of the conversation is the emergence and rapid rise of Bobrisky, a young Nigerian internet personality and transgender woman who was born Okuneye Idris Olanrewaju and is based in Lagos.[108] With over 300 unique ethnic groups, Nigeria's diversity is also reflected in the fluid expression of gender in certain parts of the country. Gender identity that is nonbinary is not new in Nigeria but has been a dominant feature for many centuries. In the northern region of Nigeria, for instance, this author grew up with the concept of Yan Daudu; men who dressed up as women. They were reified for more than a century, "as part of an unremarkable but fringe subculture in the Muslim north."[109] Similarly, during the initiation ritual of priests to the deity in traditional Yoruba religion, Yorùbá priests in the final preparatory stage, would dress in women's clothing. This was regarded by many "as a mark of transvestitism."[110]

The Rise of Bobrisky

The emergence and rapid rise of Bobrisky has come with a mix of shock and awe. Bobrisky is one of many fast-rising internet sensations who are vocal about their transgender status and publicly document their lives and their challenges dealing with the putative cis-normative binary constructs of gender. Bobrisky currently attracts about 25,000 daily views on social

---

104 *Gender-Based Violence in Nigeria During the COVID-19 Crisis: The Shadow Pandemic*, UNITED NATIONS NIGERIA, https://nigeria.un.org/sites/default/files/2020-05/Gender%20Based%20Violence%20in%20Nigeria%20During%20COVID%2019%20Crisis_The%20Shadow%20Pandemic.pdf (May 4, 2020).
105 *Id.*
106 *Id.* at 4.
107 Phumzile Mlambo-Ngcuka, *Violence against Women and Girls: The Shadow Pandemic*, UN WOMEN, www.unwomen.org/en/news/stories/2020/4/statement-ed-phumzile-violence-against-women-during-pandemic (April 6, 2020).
108 Woju Aderemi, *Who Is Bobrisky, Nigeria's Controversial Transgender Social Media Queen?*, GAL-DEM, https://gal-dem.com/who-is-bobrisky-nigerias-controversial-transgender-social-media-queen-%EF%BB%BF/ (Jan. 3, 2020).
109 Monica Mark, *Nigeria's Yan Daudu Face Persecution in Religious Revival*, THE GUARDIAN, www.theguardian.com/world/2013/jun/10/nigeria-yan-daudu-persecution (June 10, 2013).
110 Mojúbàolú Olúfúnké Okome, *African Women and Power: Labour, Gender and Feminism in the Age of Globalization*, 30(2) SAGE RACE REL. ABSTRACTS 3, 3–26 (May 2005).

media by documenting her transition, sex life, and sales of skin-bleaching products.[111] After being arrested and escaping a police raid on her 28th birthday, Bobrisky was subjected to sporadic physical and emotional attacks by various members of society, including those in authority.[112] These attacks include a notorious internet brawl with a government official, the Director-General of the National Council of Arts and Culture, who threatened her freedom of movement and personal safety.[113] According to the official, young people like Bobrisky portray an idea that conflicts with Nigeria's traditions and culture.[114]

The normative discourse on gender in Nigeria remains binary and people like Bobrisky are rendered invisible within the law. If they choose to be visible, their reality is criminalization. This is because gender identity is conflated with sexual orientation.

Goodluck Jonathan signed the Same-Sex Marriage Prohibition Bill (SSMPA) into law on January 7, 2014.. The notional purpose of the bill is to prohibit marriage between persons of the same sex. However, its scope is much wider. The law creates a situation of double jeopardy for those who might exist outside binary sex and gender norms, neglecting in particular intersex persons whose duality of gender is a function of biology. Speculation is rife as to whether Bobrisky falls into the latter category as in July 2020, Bobrisky announced that she is pregnant.

"Leave No One Behind"

Unfortunately, Bobrisky is also an interesting anomaly if viewed within the context of SDG 5. A major criticism of SDG 5 in the attempt to build inclusion and sustainability is that its focus on women and girls marginalizes gender minorities, which is contrary to its dictum of no one be left behind." Liberty Matthyse suggests that

> despite an increase in visibility of trans and gender-diverse persons in Western media, globally, dominant narratives remain those of discrimination, marginalisation, invisibilisation, violence, and erasure. Rarely are trans and gender-diverse persons represented as people that belong, able to exercise self-determination as autonomous beings, and/or positioned as positive builders and shapers of societies.[115]

In sum, SDG 5 goals summarily omit gender minorities from its targets and indicators.

"Are We Getting Our Girls Back?"

Any conversation about gender in the 21st century would be incomplete without a discussion on the "Bring Back Our Girls" Movement, and the kidnappings on the night of April 14, 2014, of 276 female students from their secondary school in the town of Chibok in Borno State, Nigeria.[116] Over the next several days and weeks, a fervent and agonizing campaign by

---

111 Aderemi, *supra* note 114.
112 *Id.*
113 *Id.*
114 *Id.*
115 Liberty Matthyse, *Achieving Gender Equality by 2030: Transgender Equality Concerning Sustainable Development Goal 5*, 34(1) AGENDA 124, 124 (June 2020).
116 Ewan Watt, *Celebrities Join Worldwide Calls to #BringBackOurGirls*, THEIRWORLD, https://theirworld.org/news/celebrities-join-worldwide-calls-to-bringbackourgirls (May 20, 2014).

Nigeria's mothers in support of the parents of the children of Chibok would grow into a mass movement that would come to be known worldwide as the #BringBackOurGirls campaign.[117] Despite the international outcry and the eventual escape, release, and negotiation for 164 of the girls, six years later 112 girls remain with the terrorist group Jama'atu Ahlis Sunna Lidda'awati wal-Jihad, commonly known as Boko Haram.[118]

At the core of the #BringBackOurGirls campaign was dissent against the scourge of rape, sexual violence, forced marriage, transborder kidnapping, and the widespread appropriation of female bodies.[119] Abubakar Shekau was irreverent as his rhetoric tapped into radicalized notions of masculine supremacy, linking medieval sensibilities with present-day patriarchy and worldwide gender-based violence. Unfortunately, the rise of Boko Haram in Northern Nigeria has set back an already educationally disadvantaged region by at least a decade, if not more. At the peak of the insurgency, all public schools in Borno State were shut, and most have not reopened. To date, at least 2,295 teachers have been killed since the conflict began in 2009, and over 1,400 schools have been destroyed.[120] As with geography and poverty, gender plays a significant role in educational marginalization. Today, most of the states in the north-east and north-west regions of the country record attendance rates that are below average hovering between 47.7% and 47.3%, respectively, which means that more than half of the girls in these areas are not in school.[121] According to UNICEF, about 10.5 million children within the age bracket of 5–14 years are not in school nationwide.[122] 35.6% of children receive only early education with the most disadvantaged region recording a net attendance rate of 53%.[123]

Education deprivation worldwide is driven by factors such as economics, social norms, and practices that discourage education. Accordingly, providing education to girls in a safe environment is critical to reversing the stark prospects and current statistics for basic education in Nigeria. The linkages between safety, peace and security, and basic education at scale are a useful empirical study focus for policy makers. The overall goal to build inclusive institutions and provide access to justice for all cannot be overemphasized just as the need to end all forms of violence against children, especially girls.

Conclusion and Policy Recommendations for Nigeria

In 2014, the African Commission of Human and People's Rights acknowledged gender identity in its Resolution 275, which prohibits violence against gender minorities.[124] To

---

117 *Id.*
118 *Id.*
119 *Spotlight on Sustainable Development 2019*, 2030 SPOTLIGHT, at 117–121, www.2030spotlight.org/en/book/1883/chapter/sdg-5-advancing-womens-rights-and-strengthening-global-governance-synergies (2019).
120 Morgan Winsor, *Boko Haram Has Abducted over 1,000 Children, Killed More than 2,000 Teachers*, ABC-NEWS (Apr. 14, 2018), https://abcnews.go.com/International/boko-haram-abducted-1000-children-killed-2000-teachers/story?id=54442518.
121 *Education*, UNICEF, www.unicef.org/nigeria/education (last visited Dec. 12, 2020).
122 *Id.*
123 *Id.*
124 *African Commission on Human and Peoples' Rights Adopts Resolution Condemning Violence and Discrimination against LGBTI Persons*, INTERNATIONAL JUSTICE RESOURCE CENTER, https://ijrcenter.org/2014/06/10/african-commission-on-human-and-peoples-rights-adopts-resolution-condemning-violence-and-discrimination-against-lgbti-persons/ (June 10, 2014).

promote gender diversity, it might be useful to begin to examine within the broad context of SDG 5 the concept of gender identity. Without an identity, the journey to inclusion might be hindered. The case study of Nigeria analyzed invisibility and the lack of identity for gender minorities, which could pose a challenge to long-term gender equality and empowerment.

The linkage between legal frameworks and the occurrence of GBV and harmful cultural practices can be traced to drivers such as poverty, gender imbalance in political participation, harsh legislation, and a lack of inclusion especially within the global development agendas of the SDGs. Using several approaches, for instance, cash transfer programs (to address poverty), capacity building, and sensitization to religious and traditional rules (to address social norms), same-sex community dialogs (to provide safe spaces for discourse), the provision of learning materials, and free sexual and reproductive education and healthcare services (to mitigate teenage pregnancy) are likely to engender greater opportunities.

This chapter shows that Nigeria will be far from achieving SDG 5 unless accelerated efforts are made to address the obstacles mentioned. The following points highlight these challenges and recommendations that can be adopted to accelerate the process in Nigeria:

- The need for political will, institutional capacity, and legislation for social justice cannot be overemphasized. This can be heralded by a review of legislation and legal frameworks that protect women and a national gender policy to be implemented at all levels in the country.
- Aggressive, widespread advocacy should be kickstarted and sustained especially in rural areas and local communities until there is a shift in perception and cultural norms regarding harmful social practices and stereotypes that impact gender. This should include capacity building and workshops on gender across all arms of government in particular, the executive, parliamentary, and judiciary branches while the traditional grassroots and religious leaders remain crucial.
- The designated department or division for gender affairs, which is domiciled in the respective ministries for women's affairs throughout the country should play a leadership role in implementing a robust reform agenda, while ensuring that access to data for national planning and development is required by both federal and state governments to ensure gender mainstreaming at all levels.
- Gender studies should be a new curriculum subject in Nigerian early childhood education rather than only being taught at the tertiary level as currently practiced. More profoundly from a young age, students, in particular girls should be taught to recognize and classify traditional notions around gender and educated to understand the influence of gender in socio-political life.

9 Sustainable Management of Water and Sanitation

A Long and Winding Road Ahead

Zhou Di

Introduction

Water is the essence of life. Water plays a key role in food security, energy production, ecosystem development, economic growth, social stability, and poverty reduction. In the United Nations World Water Development Report 2020, the potential of water in becoming a part of a solution to climate change is further explored.[1] Ensuring availability and sustainable management of water and sanitation for all has been a topic at the United Nations (UN) for a long time. The 2030 Agenda for Sustainable Development adopted at the UN Summit in September 2015 includes Sustainable Development Goal (SDG) 6 on water and sanitation. In support of the achievement of SDG 6 and other water-related targets, the UN General Assembly adopted the resolution "International Decade for Action—Water for Sustainable Development" (2018–2020). Now the priority is on making SDG 6 and other water-related targets a reality.

The section "Assessment of SDG 6 Implementation and Fragmentation of Water Resource Management System" of this chapter will firstly provide an assessment of progress during the last four years toward the implementation of the SDG 6 globally. Despite progress made since the turn of the millennium across various fields, much remains to be done to achieve SDG 6 and succeed in sustainable water resource management. The section "Innovative Water Resource Management Mechanism after 2015: Case Study of China" will look into the situation of water resource management in China. Water resource management is one of the main battlefields in moving toward the "ecological civilization" in China, as well as in fulfilling China's commitment to implementing the 2030 SDGs. In the section "Risk of Unsustainability and the Way Forward", the question on the risk of unsustainability of the River Chief Mechanism will be raised and analyzed. This section will offer recommendations for substantial transformation in order to achieve sustainable water resource management in China. On the basis of the case study of China, the concluding part will further analyze the uncertainty of implementing the SDGs globally and will provide some recommendations in actions taken to ensure the implementation.

---

1 *The United Nations World Water Development Report 2020: Water and Climate Change*, UN Water, UNITED NATIONS EDUCATIONAL, SCIENTIFIC AND CULTURAL ORGANIZATION (2020), https://unesdoc.unesco.org/ark:/48223/pf0000372985.locale=en [hereinafter "World Water Development Report 2020"].

Assessment of SDG 6 Implementation and Fragmentation of Water Resource Management System

The UN Sustainable Development Goals include 17 goals and 169 targets. In practice, the SDGs are critically important to development initiatives, focusing political attention and financial resources on meeting the specific targets and timetables articulated in the SDGs.[2] Given the focus of this chapter, we mainly assess SDG 6: Ensure availability and sustainable management of water and sanitation for all. The SDGs are not isolated objectives, but prerequisites to achieve all the others.[3] Among the 169 targets in the framework of 17 SDGs, SDG 6 on clean water and sanitation should be regarded as one of the central SDGs, considering the vital functions of water relating to the ecological system and human health. In SDG 6,[4] the UN sets the following specific targets:

- Universal and equitable access to safe and affordable drinking water for all.
- Access to adequate and equitable sanitation and hygiene for all and end open defecation.
- Improve water quality.
- Increase water-use sufficiency, ensure sustainable withdrawals and supply of freshwater and reduce the number of people suffering from water scarcity.
- Protect and restore water-related ecosystems.
- Expand international cooperation and capacity-building support to developing countries in water- and sanitation-related activities and programs and support and strengthen the participation of local communities.

As illustrated in the above specific targets, SDG 6 focuses on water supply (resource), water quality (environment), as well as water-related ecosystems. Water resources must be carefully managed to ensure sustainability and equitable sharing among users.[5]

The Progress toward Implementing SDG 6

Significant progress has been made, mainly in the following fields:[6]

- Reliable water supply: Between 2000 and 2017, the proportion of the global population using safely managed drinking water increased from 61% to 71%.
- Sanitation services: The global population using managed sanitation services increased from 28% in 2000 to 45% in 2017, and the proportion lacking even a basic sanitation service decreased from 44% to 27% between 2000 and 2017.

---

2 *Environmental Rule of Law: First Global Report 2019*, UNITED NATIONS ENVIRONMENT (2019), https://wedocs.unep.org/bitstream/handle/20.500.11822/27279/Environmental_rule_of_law.pdf?sequence=1&isAllowed=y.
3 *The United Nations World Water Development Report 2019: Leaving No One Behind*, UN WATER, UNITED NATIONS EDUCATIONAL, SCIENTIFIC AND CULTURAL ORGANIZATION (2019), https://unesdoc.unesco.org/ark:/48223/pf0000367306 [hereinafter "World Water Development Report 2019"].
4 *See also* United Nations G.A. Res. A/RES/70/1, *Transforming Our World: The 2030 Agenda for Sustainable Development*, (Sept. 25, 2015) [hereinafter "Agenda 2030"].
5 *The Sustainable Development Goals Report*, UNITED NATIONS (2019), https://unstats.un.org/sdgs/report/2019/The-Sustainable-Development-Goals-Report-2019.pdf [hereinafter "2019 SDG Report"].
6 *Id.*

- Handwashing facility: In 2017, three out of five people worldwide had a basic handwashing facility with soap and water on the premises, compared with less than one out of three in the world's least developed countries.
- Official Development Assistance (ODA) commitments to the water sector jumped by 36% between 2016 and 2017.

The Remaining Threats

Water Availability and Safety

Water use has been increasing worldwide by about 1% per year since the 1980s. Global water demand is expected to continue increasing at a similar rate until 2050, accounting for an increase of 20 to 30% above the current level of water use.[7] Yet over 2 billion people live in countries experiencing high water stress. Although the global average water stress is only 11%, 31 countries experience water stress between 25% and 70%, and 22 countries are above 70% and are therefore under serious water stress.[8] Additionally, according to the Food and Agriculture Organization and World Water Council, globally, water resources will be sufficient to produce the food required in 2050, but many regions will face substantial water scarcity.[9]

Water Quality and Water-Related Ecosystem

Water quality problems persist worldwide. Water quality interacts with the problem of water availability in the fact that poor water quality impacts people who rely directly on the sources as their main supply by further limiting the access to water.

Water and water-related ecosystems, even in water-rich countries, are still under threat. Even in terms of water supply and sanitation services where steady improvement has been achieved, coverage of safely managed water services varies considerably across regions (from only 24% in sub-Saharan Africa to 94% in Europe and Northern America), wealth quintiles, and subnational regions.[10] Of all the people using safely managed drinking water services, only about one out of three (1.9 billion) lived in rural areas.[11]

In the fields of water quality and water-related ecosystem protection, an estimated 50–70% of the world's natural wetland area has been lost over the last 100 years.[12] Estimates suggest that if the degradation of the natural environment and the unsustainable pressures on global water resources continue, 45% of the global gross domestic product (GDP), 53%

---

7 P. Burek et al., *Water Futures and Solution: Fast Track Initiative (Final Report)*, International Institute for Applied Systems Analysis (IIASA) (May 2016), http://pure.iiasa.ac.at/13008/.
8 *UN World Water Assessment Programme 2018*, UNITED NATIONS EDUCATIONAL, SCIENTIFIC AND CULTURAL ORGANIZATION (2018), www.unesco.org/new/en/natural-sciences/environment/water/wwap/wwdr/2018-nature-based-solutions/.
9 *Towards a Water and Food Secure Future: Critical Perspectives for Policy-Makers* (2015), United Nations FOOD AND AGRICULTURE ORGANIZATION & WORLD WATER COUNCIL, www.fao.org/3/a-i4560e.pdf.
10 World Water Development Report 2019, *supra* note 3.
11 World Health Organization, *Safely Managed Drinking Water—Thematic Report on Drinking Water* (2017), https://data.unicef.org/wp-content/uploads/2017/03/safely-managed-drinking-water-JMP-2017-1.pdf [hereinafter "WHO Drinking Water Report"].
12 2019 SDG Report, *supra* note 5.

of the world's population, and 40% of the global grain production will be at risk by 2050.[13] Poor water quality continues to impact people both in developed and developing countries. Worldwide, over 80% of all wastewater returns to the environment without being treated.[14]

Regional Discrepancy

The availability and quality of water resources vary from country to country and from region to region, which makes water one of the key influencing elements on local social and economic development. According to the 2019 SDG Report, almost all countries that have registered high water stress are located in North Africa and West Asia or in Central and South Asia.[15] Additionally, coverage of safely managed water services varies considerably across regions, from only 24% in sub-Saharan Africa to 94% in Europe and Northern America.[16] Of the 159 million people still collecting untreated (and often contaminated) drinking water directly from surface water sources, 58% lived in sub-Saharan Africa.[17] Similarly, a large level of variability can be observed in terms of access to basic sanitation among countries.

Estimates suggest that if the degradation of the natural environment and the unsustainable pressures on global water resources continue, 45% of the global GDP, 52% of the world's population, and 40% of global grain production will be at risk by 2050.[18] Poor and marginalized populations will be disproportionately affected, further exacerbating already rising inequalities.[19]

An Overall Assessment

Although progress has been made in water supply and sanitation service, the achievement in SDG 6 and its targets lacks balance between regions. If the current pace of progress remains unchanged, the world will not achieve SDG 6 by 2030.[20] The UN Global Sustainable Development Report illustrates that the implementation of target 6.2 (Access to safe sanitation) stays within the interval of 5–10%, while that of target 6.1 (Access to safely managed drinking water) and 6.2 (Access to safely managed sanitation services) is above 10%.[21]

Data suggests that "achieving universal access to even basic sanitation service by 2030 would require doubling the current annual rate of progress."[22] While in terms of water qual-

---

13 World Water Development Report 2019, *supra* note 3.
14 *Water: The Untapped Resource*, UN World Water Assessment Programme UNESCO (2017), www.unesco.org/new/en/natural-sciences/environment/water/wwap/wwdr/2017-wastewater-the-untapped-resource/ [hereinafter "UN World Water Assessment Programme"].
15 2019 SDG Report, *supra* note 5.
16 *Id*.
17 WHO Drinking Water Report, *supra* note 11.
18 UN World Water Assessment Programme, *supra* note 14.
19 *Nature-Based Solutions for Water*, UN World Water Development Work UNESCO (2018), https://unesdoc.unesco.org/ark:/48223/pf0000261424_eng.
20 *Id*.
21 *The Future Is Now: Science for Achieving Sustainable Development*, UN Global Sustainable Development Report (2019), https://sustainabledevelopment.un.org/content/documents/24797GSDR_report_2019.pdf.
22 U.N. Secretary-General, *Special Edition: Progress towards the Sustainable Development Goals. Report of the Secretary-General*, E/2019/68 (May 8, 2019), https://unstats.un.org/sdgs/files/report/2019/secretary-general-sdg-report-2019--EN.pdf [hereinafter "Secretary-General SDGs Special Edition Report"].

ity and water-related ecosystem, considering the growing integration of the world economy concerning water contamination and environmental degradation in the coming decade, there is a stronger need for accelerated progress to achieve the targets by 2030.

However, lack of human and financial resources will constrain the implementation of SDG 6. Given the accelerated pace of technological development and the commitment to increasing the financial support to the water sector, the biggest issue for the next decade remains the slow pace of social developments, including legal, institutional, political, and cultural aspects of water management. In the process of achieving sustainable and integrated water resource management, legal, institutional, and political barriers can be greater obstacles than financial or technical challenges.

Integrated Water Resources Management (IWRM)

To prevent a severe water management crisis, we need to be creative.[23] A global framework for a water resources management approach is known as integrated water resources management.[24] The IWRM is defined as "a process which promotes the coordinated development and management of water, land and related resources, in order to maximize the resultant economic and social welfare in an equitable manner, without compromising the sustainability of vital ecosystems."[25] The conventional change model for IWRM has been based on four practical elements:[26]

- Policies, laws, and plans.
- An institutional framework.
- Use of management and technical instruments.
- Investments in water infrastructure.

It has been criticized that countries over-emphasize planning and reforms to policies, laws, and institutions, and under-emphasize pragmatic problem solving. With the expected adoption of the SDGs, it is a critical moment to re-evaluate the IWRM. Hence, an agenda for operationalizing IWRM as an adaptive strategy for change needs to combine four basic strategies:[27]

- High-level policy and strategy setting.
- Pragmatic problem solving that complements strategy setting.
- Operating mechanisms that bridge strategy setting and problem solving.
- Monitoring of progress and achievement of goals and targets.

---

23 William J. Cosgrove & Daniel P. Loucks, *Water Management: Current and Future Challenges and Research Directions*, 51 AGU (Jun. 02, 2015), https://doi.org/10.1002/2014WR016869.
24 World Water Development Report 2019, *supra* note 3.
25 *Integrated Water Resources Management: Global Water Partnership Technical Advisory Committee (TAC)*, Tac Background Papers (March 2000), www.gwp.org/globalassets/global/toolbox/publications/background-papers/04-integrated-water-resources-management-2000-english.pdf.
26 Mark Smith & Torkil Jønch Clausen, *Integrated Water Resource Management: A New Way Forward*, Global Water Partnership Technical Advisory Committee (2015), www.worldwatercouncil.org/sites/default/files/Initiatives/IWRM/Integrated_Water_Resource_Management-A_new_way_forward%20.pdf.
27 *Id.*

In pursuit of this adaptive integrated water resource management, the interaction between sectors and stakeholders at different levels and particularly the participation at community levels are strongly recommended. For example, FAO leads programs to help water governance achieve more efficient, transparent, and equitable use of water for agriculture. In recognizing the interaction between food, energy, environment, and resources, it addresses competition for water between sectors through the water-food-energy nexus approach, building upon multi-sectoral policy dialog and conflict resolution work. FAO also presents an integrated multi-sectoral approach to integrated water resources management under the One Water One Health concept of water, reflected in SDG 6.[28]

Of the 172 countries that reported their implementation of IWRM in 2018, 80% had a medium-low level of implementation or higher;[29] however, 60% of countries are still unlikely to reach full implementation of IWRM by 2030.[30] In terms of transboundary basins, according to data from 67 of 153 countries that share transboundary waters, the average percentage of national transboundary basins covered by an operational arrangement was 59% in the period of 2017–2018, with only 17 countries reporting that all their transboundary basins were covered by such arrangements.[31]

Fragmentation of Water Resource Management System

The lack of implementation of IWRM in most countries should not be neglected. Traditionally, responsibilities for water policy design and implementation are distributed between authorities. There are at least two elements that have aggravated the risk of fragmentation. First, the increasing complexity of water resources planning at various layers has made the implementation of water policies more difficult and less cooperative. Second, water distinguishes itself from all other natural elements and resources by its mixed functions as both an environmental element and a natural resource. For instance, under certain circumstances, there exist conflicts between water protection and water supply. The contradiction between the integration of water resources and the legal and institutional fragmentation has for a long period been impeding the efficiency of water resource management.

Indeed, for equitable and sustainable management of water and sanitation, it is key to have inclusive institutional devices in place for dialog, multi-stakeholder involvement and cooperation, and the fundamental connectivity between multiple layers of government, as well as the private sector and civil society.[32] Creating coherence between the various institutional levels is essential to ensure that policies deliver on their objectives.[33]

---

28 *See* Seminar *Lessons from COVID-19 for One Water One Health*, FOOD AND AGRICULTURAL ORGANIZATION OF THE UNITED NATIONS, www.fao.org/land-water/news-archive/news-detail/en/c/1272240/ (last visited Nov. 5, 2020)
29 World Water Development Report 2020, *supra* note 1.
30 Secretary-General SDGs Special Edition Report, *supra* note 22.
31 2019 SDG Report, *supra* note 5.
32 World Water Development Report 2019, *supra* note 3.
33 *Id.*

General Recommendations of Actions to Implement SDG 6 at the Global Level

- Recommendation 1: Global or regional platforms such as high-level conferences and regular meetings of government officials and experts should be set up by the UN, regional organizations, or individual countries with the aim of enhancing exchange, interaction, and collaboration in the field of water resource management and sanitation. The sharing of experience would not only expand the beneficiaries but also reduce policy inconsistencies.
- Recommendation 2: The coordination of SDG 6 with relevant SDGs such as SDGs 3, 7, 8, 11, and 13 should be fully identified. In recognizing this inter-goals relevance, each country could design a package plan to strengthen coordination among competence authorities. At the global level, basic principles should be set on coordination and on how to fix the priority under specific circumstances, in case of conflicts.
- Recommendation 3: It is necessary for the UN to make new arrangements for implementing regular epidemic prevention and control measures and to establish an SDGs 2030 implementation plan in response to the new situation of COVID-19. Focus should be put on adjusting some of the targets in order to be more flexible and adaptive to the new situation.

An Innovative Water Resource Management Mechanism after 2015: Case Study of China

Policy Background

The river chief mechanism, as a local initiative, derived from the outbreak of a cyanobacteria pollution incident in Lake Taihu in Jiangsu Province in 2007. Responding to the emergency of the water pollution and water supply crisis, the local government of Wuxi City began a river basin governance mechanism, within the jurisdiction of the river, to designate river chiefs from all levels of Party and government leaders to be responsible for the implementation of water management regulations.

In 2017, the river chief mechanism was included in the revised Water Pollution Prevention Act for the first time. As of July 2018, more than 300,000 river chiefs in a four-tier system, from provincial to township levels, have been appointed in the 31 provinces in China, according to the Minister of Water Resources.[34] There are four levels of river chiefs, which are provincial, urban, county, and township, in descending order of power. For each province, the position of the principal river chief is undertaken by principal leaders of the provincial government or Party committee. The river chiefs are assigned to take charge of rivers in their jurisdiction. The performance of river chiefs, which depends mainly on the water quality in the jurisdiction, is an important criterion for the overall assessment of officials.

Vertical and Horizontal Collaborations

Figures 9.1 and 9.2 illustrate vertical and horizontal collaborations in selected provinces.

---

34 Hou Liqiang, *Government Implements River Chief System across the Country*, CHINA DAILY (July 17, 2018), www.chinadaily.com.cn/a/201807/17/WS5b4d9664a310796df4df6f21.html.

144 Zhou Di

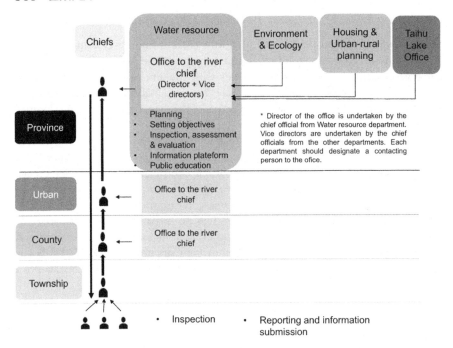

Figure 9.1 Collaboration mechanism of Jiangsu Province.

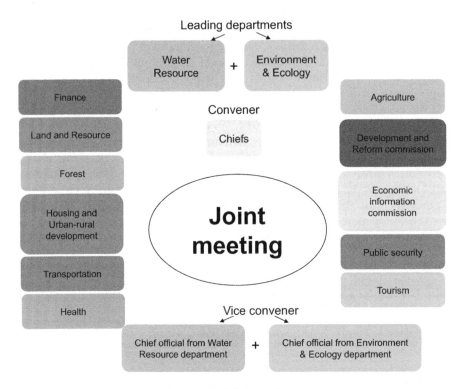

Figure 9.2 Collaboration mechanism of Hubei Province.

Assessment and Accountability

Performance assessment of the river chiefs and accountability are core issues in implementing the mechanism. In Jiangsù Province, the assessments including daily assessment, yearly assessment, and assessment led by the provincial principal river chief are initiated by the river chiefs and organized by the office of the river chiefs, with the supervision by an independent third party. The results depend on the effect of the working mechanism, completion of main tasks, and water quality management. All the assessment results should be reported to the provincial government and the provincial party committee and should be disclosed to the public. The assessment criteria should be updated once a year. In the example of Hubei Province, the one-vote veto is applied in the assessment for failure to meet the frequency to take routine inspections specification (once a year for provincial river chiefs, once every six months for urban river chiefs, once a quarter for county river chiefs, once every two months for township river chiefs).

The "Opinions on Fully Promoting the River Chief Mechanism" explains that superior river chiefs are in charge of assessing inferior river chiefs.[35] It further explains that river chiefs who contribute to environmental damage will be put on record and subject to a lifelong accountability system.[36] In the framework of the stipulations, the details should be determined by working plans at the local level. Table 9.1 illustrates the selected provisions on the accountability system and cases in Jiangsu and Hubei. According to the Ministry of Water

Table 9.1 Selected provisions on the accountability system and cases in Jiangsu and Hubei.

Jiangsu Province Hubei Province
(1) The assessment result is included in the government target responsibility system. The assessment result is linked with annual financial allocation, performance, and appointment of government officials.
(2) The performance of the river chiefs will be scored and graded. In case of failure to meet the assessment, the river chiefs should submit a report explaining the situation and complete the rectification within a prescribed time. They will also be summoned for persuasion and admonition and face disciplinary punishment within the CPC.
Cases of river chiefs being held accountable
(1) 21 river chiefs in Jiangsu Province were summoned for persuasion in April 2018 due to the poor water quality of the rivers/lakes within their jurisdiction which was graded as inferior V class.[a]
(2) 2 Township river chiefs from Zhijiang River of Hubei Province were summoned for persuasion by their county river chief in October 2018 for failing to meet the water quality requirement for five consecutive months.[b]

[a] Ni Min, 21 *River Chiefs in Jiangsu Are Summoned for Persuasion and Admonition by the Provincial Government*, JIANGSU CHINA (Apr. 12, 2017), http://jsnews.jschina.com.cn/jsyw/201704/t20170412_343098.shtml.
[b] *See* Department of Water Resource of Hubei Province, Workshop of River Chief Mechanism and River Protection held in Zhijiang, Hubei Province, www.hubei.gov.cn/zhuanti/2017zt/ztjslggjxdd/201908/t20190801_1404908.shtml.

---

35 *See* The Ministry of Water Resources: Opinions on Fully Promoting the River Chief Mechanism. http://www.mwr.gov.cn/ztpd/gzzt/hzz/zyjs/201708/t20170811_973312.html
36 *Id.*

Resources, since 2017, 694 river chiefs have been held accountable for their performance, including 5 urban chiefs, 85 county chiefs, and 604 township chiefs.[37]

Effect on Water Quality Improvement

Under the direction of the river chiefs, much action has been taken by local governments. For example, over ten million tons of blue algae have been salvaged during the past 10 years in promoting the river chief mechanism in the whole Taihu lake basin.[38] In the case of Honghu Lake, over 2667 hectares of water hyacinth have been cleaned out, and the wooden poles and nets used by the fishermen for enclosure aquaculture have been permanently removed from a water surface of over 9700 hectares all within one year.[39] A huge amount of work has been done over a very short period of time, and some of the long-standing historical problems have been finally resolved. However, water management is a long-term process. Therefore, long-term monitoring is required in order to explore the effectiveness in the long run.

Questions

The following questions could be raised on the basis of the case study: (1) What is the legal basis for the policy documents on promoting the river chief mechanism?; (2) Why are the officials from the different departments willing to take orders from their river chiefs?; (3) How can a scientific and appropriate assessment system for each river/lake be guaranteed?; (4) Will the accountability of persuasion and admonishment really impact the political future of the river chiefs?; (5) Is it possible that the provincial river chiefs are held accountable?; and (6) With a large amount of work being completed, why has the water quality not significantly improved?

With all these pending questions, I argue that, instead of serving as a mature water management mechanism, the current river chief mechanism should be characterized as an experimental exploration at various local levels within the central policy framework. The great importance attached to environmental and ecological protection by Chinese political leaders since 2013 is the main driving force of the rapid popularization of this policy. The existing laws and policies cannot keep up with China's ever-growing need to develop ecological civilization. In this sense, the issue of water management is actually "chosen" as a typical experimental field for the successful transition in environmental and ecological governance. However, at this stage, many details still need to be clarified. It is too early to conclude that the river chief mechanism will come as a storm but will disappear in the near future. The future of this mechanism lies in itself. In the next section, I will analyze whether an internal rationale exists in this mechanism. Three features have

---

37 *See* The Ministry of Water Resources: *Implementation of River-Lake Chief Mechanism*, http://www.xinhuanet.com/fortune/2018-07/17/c_1123140400.htm.

38 Yongping Zhao, *The Story of Rejuvenation of Lake Taihu*, PEOPLE'S DAILY (2018), http://www.mwr.gov.cn/ztpd/gzzt/hzz/mtjj/201801/t20180103_1019210.html.

39 *Note*: Interviews with the urban river chief, county river chief, representatives of township river chiefs of Honghu Lake and the director of Bureau of Water Resource, the director of bureau of Ecology and Environment and the director of bureau of agriculture of Honghu during a three-day field survey in July 2018 at Honghu Lake.

been identified: Competence integration, contracting responsibility system, and the risk of uncertainty.

The Rationale of the River Chief Mechanism in China

Competence Integration

In China, water management has been artificially split into different levels and authorities. From a vertical perspective, governments at all levels act at the same time as a competent authority in water management, without consideration for the content of their competence. Without a clear specification of their competence, the macro-management from the central government and the micro-management from the local government fully overlap.

The departmental division creates much more trouble. The Department of Environment and Ecology and the Department of Water Resources are the leading departments, with collaboration from other relevant departments. However, the so-called leading departments have actually no leading power since they enjoy the same administrative rank as their collaborative departments. Therefore, the relevant subsidiary departments opt for getting rid of such collaboration considering the need to reduce administrative costs and avoid the potential risk of shouldering more responsibility. Substantial collaboration is unrealistic due to the lack of legal obligation and political willingness.

Considering all this, the designer of the river chief mechanism intends to solve the problem by providing competence integration. Powerful intervention from higher ranking officials makes this integration possible in practice.

The first step is replacing the leading departments with a government or Party leader in organizing collaboration. The chief official, who is usually the government or Party leader at the same level, undertakes the position of river chief and is powerful enough to mobilize the relevant departments under his general leadership. The river chief mechanism does not change the function of different departments but establishes a platform for collaboration, such as the office of the river chiefs and regular joint meetings under the leading officials.

Now that a network has been established, the separated administrative resources in water management must be brought together. Both horizontal and vertical collaboration are explored to a large extent, as all the related departments could be involved.

Contracting Responsibility System

The contracting responsibility system was a considerably successful policy experiment in the modern history of China.[40] The success of the experiments of the contracting responsibility system in agriculture lies in the idea of linking the peasants' personal income to their

---

40 *Note*: The contracting responsibility system was first adopted in China in the early 1980s. It was an agriculture production system that allowed households to contract land, machinery, and other facilities from collective organizations. Households could make decisions independently within the limits set by the agreement and could freely dispose of surplus production over and above national collective quotas. The aim was to preserve the unified management of the collective economy, while stimulating the enthusiasm of the peasants, in order to achieve a higher efficiency of agricultural productivity. The experiments began in Anhui and Sichuan Provinces, both saw dramatic increases in agricultural productivity, and the system was adopted nationwide in 1981.

personal contribution, which therefore vigorously motivates them to increase production.[41] A similar logic exists in the establishment of the river chief mechanism, with the linkage of the officials' performance as river chiefs to their personal promotion. The river chiefs of multiple levels have contracting responsibility in the water management of their assigned water sections. They also enjoy comprehensive and independent power in using resources and taking measures within their jurisdiction. Good performance will help them with promotions, while failures may lead to punishments, resulting in a negative impact on their political future. The river chief mechanism should be considered as an incentive and responsibility mechanism.

The co-responsibility of Party and government officials provides a guarantee for the implementation of the river chief mechanism. Chief officials of local governments usually shoulder dual responsibility, both from the Party and the government. This explains why the river chiefs are commonly undertaken by the main leadership of the local governments as well as the Party committees. This means that the top pyramid of the local administrative and Party power is now directly connected with the issue of water management.[42] The responsibility has been transformed from the general local government to specific individual officials. In practice, as the river chief does not act in a formal administrative position, political legitimacy actually aids the mechanism.

Risk of Unsustainability and the Way Forward

The High Risk of Unsustainability

The dual responsibility and the centralized Party and administrative system have, to some degree, assured the feasibility of the river chief mechanism in practice. However, a high risk of unsustainability derived from an emergency responding system exists for this mechanism.

The first risk is over-reliance on political willingness and personal capacity of individual officials or Party leaders. The importance of water management has continuously been emphasized in recent years. However, it is undeniable that water management remains to be a small part of the officials' overall performance. Instead, issues such as public security and economic growth still have the overriding weight in the general assessment system. Government leaders have to make a choice on which should be prioritized. What if the preference of the central government changes from water management to soil management? After all, the political willingness changes frequently, just as the high mobility of the local government officials.

Second, formalism, which goes along with the assessment-centered measures, exists in the framework of the river chief mechanism. In Jiangsu and Hubei, salvaging cyanobacteria and removing garbage are actions that have widely been taken up, while in-depth and long-term measures have rarely taken place. According to Shen and Jin's research on the water pollution data nationwide, after the full implementation of the river chief mechanism, the mechanism has achieved the preliminary control of water pollution by increasing the

---

41 Deng Xize, *From "Mercenary" to "Justice and Benefit-Compatible": The Reasons for the Success of Household Responsibility System, Its Universal Mechanism and Trend*, at 74–87 ISSUES IN AGRICULTURAL ECONOMY (2014), 10.13246/j.cnki.iae.2014.09.011.
42 Zhou Jianguo & Xiong Ye, *"The River Chief System": How Is Continuous Innovation Possible? A Two-Dimension Analysis on the Basis of Both Policy Text and Reform Oractice*, at 38–47 JIANGSU SOCIAL SCIENCE (2017), 10.13858/j.cnki.cn32-1312/c.2017.04.006.

dissolved oxygen but did not significantly reduce the main water pollutants.[43] A scientific and personalized assessment system of each river/lake goes beyond the budget and capability of most local governments. Due to the unclear assessment, local governments tend to take measures that may easily be accepted by the public. This becomes a common choice for many river chiefs.[44] In terms of the deep-rooted pollutants and accumulated ecological damage, it seems that the river chief mechanism is not able to provide enough personnel and financial support to deal with them.

Way Forward

Fragmentation poses the biggest obstacle to water resource management. In China's case, the essence of establishing the river chief mechanism is realizing competence and responsibility integration in water management. The theoretical suitability of the key problem and the proposed mechanism proves its potential for acting as a resolution. The uncertainty lies mainly in the river chiefs themselves as individuals. It is also exacerbated by the instability of China's long-term development strategy in relation to whether the country will maintain its emphasis on the issue of environmental protection, including water management. Transformation is absolutely needed in order to overcome the high risk of unsustainability. If the status quo remains, sustainable water management will be utopian in the framework of the river chief mechanism. A fixed resource support system and an integrated political-legal accountability system are indispensable conditions for overcoming the unsustainability of the mechanism.

In terms of the fixed resource support system, the river chiefs and their affiliated personnel should be integrated with the existing administrative system in an appropriate way. First, the office of the river chiefs should be established within the general office of the river chiefs, instead of staying within the department of water resources, in order to avoid being regarded as an internal office to the department of water resources, with very limited power to initiate the collaborations.[45] Further, besides mobilizing officials from the relevant departments as part-time office members, there should be full-time personnel, with government staff status. Second, a fixed financial allocation should be guaranteed, especially for the work of river chiefs at the county and township levels.

There should also be an appropriate allocation of working issues between the four levels of river chiefs in order to match their power, capabilities, and affiliated resource. For example, issues, such as the overall planning and water quality survey, which requires high-level coordination and administrative and technical resources, should be the responsibility of relatively high-level river chiefs, while specific measures and actions, such as preventing non-point pollution and clearing out waste in the watercourse, should be the responsibility of river chiefs at the grass-roots levels.

---

43 Shen Kunrong & Jin Gang, *The Policy Effects on Local Governments' Environmental Governance in China–A Study Based on the Evolution of the River-Director System*, at 92–114 CHINA SOCIAL SCIENCE (2018).

44 Yan Feng, *Great Leap Forward of Pei County of Jiangsu Province under the Support of the River Chief Mechanism*, JIANGSU CHINA (Jul. 4, 2016), http://js.people.cn/n2/2016/0704/c360304-28609847.html; Zheng Jingxia, *River Chief Mechanism in Tianjin: From Out of Control to Good Management*, XINHUANET (29 August 2016), http://www.xinhuanet.com//politics/2016-08/29/c_129260629.htm.

45 Li Yuansheng & Hu Yi, *On the Integrated Governance of River Basin Environment: Research Based on the River Chief Mechanism*, at 73–77 STUDIES ON THE SOCIALISM WITH CHINESE CHARACTERISTICS (2017).

An integrated political-legal accountability system could, to a large extent, reduce the risk of the unstable performance of the river chiefs, especially those of higher levels. Weak accountability, observed in the case studies, has exacerbated the uncertainty of the future of the river chief mechanism. The weakness is mainly reflected by the absence of legal responsibility, the lack of variety of Party responsibility, and the unbalanced accountability between different levels of river chiefs. In 2015, the Communist Party of China (CPC) Central committee and the State Council jointly released the Measures for the Accountability of Party and Government Leaders for Damage to the Ecological Environment (for Trial Implementation).

According to the document, officials will be held responsible over their lifetime for the damage caused to the environment during their terms in office, whether they have moved to other posts, been promoted, or retired. Four forms of accountability have been stipulated in ascending order, from persuasion, admonishment, and issuance of public apology to dismissal and demotion as well as punishment, according to Party and administrative discipline. The lifetime accountability system and the various forms of accountability have been integrated into the policy documents of promoting the river chief mechanism. However, in order to avoid using only persuasion and admonishment as the lightest punishment on particularly the lower-level river chiefs, the realization of the accountability system should be combined with the implementation of the current administrative environmental public interest litigation.

Legalization of political responsibility is the first step in realizing this combination. The legal responsibility of the local governments, including the leaders in water management, has been explicitly stipulated in the amended Environment Protection Act and Water Pollution Prevention Act. China is now experiencing reforms in environmental public interest litigation, involving the procuratorate (prosecutor), non-governmental organizations (NGOs) and the general public in supervising government enforcement. By enhancing access to justice in the field, the court, procuratorate, and the general public will all be involved. Moreover, only through this multi-participation could the "Dual political-legal responsibility" really be realized.

Assessment constitutes the basis for accountability. Considering the demanding expertise and neutrality required in the process of assessment, I argue that independent third-party assessment should be introduced through government tender projects. The public tendering process should be structured and must follow certain procedures. Sample surveys and public satisfaction surveys also need to be involved. The results of the third-party assessment should be integrated as important indicators of the overall performance of the river chiefs.

Conclusions: Uncertainties and Actions Taken to Strengthen Implementation of SDG 6

Uncertainties

Lack of Clarification of Targets

The river chief mechanism in China represents an individual country's efforts in establishing innovative institutions at a national level under the framework of implementing SDGs 2030. However, as is shown in the section "Risk of Unsustainability and the Way Forward", a high risk of uncertainty occurs and will probably undermine the sustainability of the mechanism. This uncertainty is not exclusively existing in China. The achievement of SDGs 2030 requires substantial changes to the business-as-usual mode. And the reforms would bring about both positive and negative impacts. The uncertainty is further increased by two factors. First, the diversity of objects and targets, as well as the relevance among them could be very controversial, as some of the specific targets themselves are conflicting with each other in their respective implementation. Of all the 169 targets, more than two-thirds of them still need to be clearly defined. The lack of clarification of the targets generally and globally would exacerbate the complexity of implementation at the local level. In practice, how to balance the conflict between economic growth and environmental protection is still a question to be answered, especially in developing countries. Second, with the different levels of development and various structures of different countries, it is hard to guarantee whether the individual efforts would finally join together in realizing the overall goals.

COVID-19 Pandemic

It is worth noting that the outbreak and worldwide spread of COVID-19 will add further uncertainties to the achievement of the SDGs by 2030. The possible impacts of COVID-19 on the implementaiton of the SDGs vary depending on the linkage of the specific SDGs with the coronavirus. For example, SDG 3 (Good health and well-being), SDG 1 (poverty eradication), and SDG 8 (employment) may experience more support. However, COVID-19 has further disrupted the balance between economic growth and environmental protection. While it will reaffirm the importance of SDGs 2030, it will likely deeply influence the specific strategies and pace of implementation.

The COVID-19 pandemic has magnified the problem of water. More water will be needed for handwashing, cleaning, and disinfecting. More emphasis should be put on water contamination prevention in order to block the spread of the disease. More importantly, with the increasing demand for water resource protection, the disparity among different regions and countries will become larger, as the basis of water and sanitation availability for each region and country varies significantly. Rich or poor, the virus could attack everyone equally. However, people from regions where clean water and sanitation are in pressing demand are exposed to a higher risk of infection by the virus. Even worse, presumably, they lack the basic medical and financial resources to battle against the virus. This is the reason why the COVID-19 pandemic has indeed strengthened the importance of water and integrated water resource management.

Regarding SDG 6, implementation will most likely be slowed down due to the current shortage of various resources. However, with increasing awareness of the importance of ecological security, the protection of water resources will remain a focus of the global community. This may possibly accelerate the pace of water resource protection after the pandemic. Additionally, water, as the core element of nature which connects ecosystems as a whole, can help fight the virus and safeguard global health in the future.

Actions to Strengthen Implementation

Recommendations to help ensure the implementation of SDG 6 at the national level

- **Recommendation 1**: Establish an overarching plan at the national level to integrate the various and fragmented elements in water management, including water pollution prevention, water resources management and sanitation, and the conservation of the aquatic ecosystem. The national integrated plan will serve as a top design in the aim of

avoiding the possible conflicts between different dimensions, especially the use of water as a national resource and the protection of water as an environmental element.
- **Recommendation 2**: Adjust the institutional system in water management. Institutional innovations should be made in the water basin management in order to break the administrative obstacles between local governments. Setting up the cross-regional special administrative department and special courts for the water basin would be considered an effective effort.
- **Recommendation 3**: Create a strict responsibility system and strong incentive mechanism to explore the potential of local governments in the field of water management. Financial and official promotion incentives would stimulate the inherent willingness. And the accountability and responsibility system would serve as external pressure forcing the local governments to focus on sustainable water management.
- **Recommendation 4**: Set up national and local scientific databases based on long-term water quality and quantity monitoring, which will provide the basis for making reasonable policies and regulations.

B
Prosperity

10 Inclusive, Safe, and Resilient Cities and Settlements

Duan Cheche

Introduction

This chapter will firstly provide an overall assessment on the implementation of SDG 11. Then, in the section "Four Important Dimensions Selected for Assessing the General Implementation of SDG 11 Globally", four dimensions will be used to analyze the remaining problems that need to be solved. The section "National Urban Policy: a 'Package' Strategy to Deal with the Challenges of 'Urbanization'" will discuss strategies to implement SDG 11 at the national level. The section "Impacts of COVID-19 on the Implementation of SDG 11" will focus on the special impacts of COVID-19 on SDG 11, as cities are on the frontline in response to the pandemic. The section "Case Study: Beijing—A Successful Example of Collaborative Control of Air Pollution" will assess a case study on the successful management of 2.5PM in Beijing city, which can provide a reference model for cities in developing countries deeply affected by smog. This chapter will end with several recommendations.

Four Important Dimensions Selected for Assessing the General Implementation of SDG 11 Globally

Reasons For Selecting The Four Dimensions

In the framework of SDG 11, the overarching goal is divided into 7 specific targets:

- Develop adequate, safe, and affordable housing.
- Develop safe, affordable, accessible, and sustainable transport system.
- Planning and management capacity enhancement.
- Reduce the number of deaths and people affected by disasters.
- Reduce the adverse per capita environmental impact of cities.
- Provide universal access to safe, inclusive, and accessible, green, and public spaces.

In the following four sections, four aspects will be discussed on States' practices including (1) slum improvement; (2) public transportation; (3) environmental pollution; and (4) open public space. These dimensions of city governance are interconnected with each other, and each has a significant impact on ensuring equitable housing, de-congesting urban areas, reducing greenhouse gas emissions, and improving the quality of life for city residents.

Slum Improvement

In the past few years, the global urban slum population proportion has continued to increase. Slums are increasing faster than they are improving, and there is a high risk of failing to achieve SDG 11 by 2030.

In the past few years, the proportion and absolute number of slum populations in the world have increased. In 2019, the total global population was 7,579,238,198, with a projection of 8.363–8.733 billion in 2030.[1] The global urbanization rate has increased from 54.37% in 2016 to 55.27% in 2018, at a disproportionate rate of population increase in more rural areas.[2] Therefore, rapid urbanization brings great challenges to the global urban belt, as millions of people will pour into regions that are doing their best to feed the existing population.

Housing affordability has become a global challenge affecting almost all families. According to the 16th Annual Demographia International Housing Affordability Survey in 2020, over the past year, housing prices increased in some of the least affordable major markets.[3] However, the trends were insufficient to materially improve housing affordability. On the worldwide scale, people who want to buy a house have to save more than five times their annual income in order to afford a standard house.[4] Rental households often spend more than 25% of their monthly income on rent.[5] The serious situation of unaffordability means that inadequate housing, informal settlements, and slums are still the only housing options for low-income people. Up to 24% of the world's urban population lived in slums in 2018, an increase of 1% over 2016, with more than 1 billion people living in slums and informal settlements.[6]

The global slum distribution presents regional heterogeneity and can be divided into three categories related to the targets of SDG 11 and aiming to lower the proportion of slum-dwellers:

- Met or likely to be met by 2030/substantial progress: Europe and Northern America, Australia and New Zealand.
- Moderate proportion of slum-dwellers and fair progress of SDG 11.1, but acceleration is still needed: Northern Africa and Western Asia, Central and Southern Asia, Eastern and South-Eastern Asia.
- Very high proportion of slum-dwellers and limited or no progress: Sub-Saharan Africa, Latin America, and the Caribbean, Oceania (except Australia and New Zealand).

---

1 Population Division, *Prospects of World Urbanization*, WORLD BANK (2018), https://data.worldbank.org.cn/indicator/SP.URB.TOTL.IN.ZS?end=2018&start=1960&view=chart.
2 *Id.*; *68% of the World Population Projected to Live in Urban Areas by 2050, Says UN*, Dep. of Econ. & Soc. Affairs (DESA) (May 16, 2018), www.un.org/development/desa/en/news/population/2018-revision-of-world-urbanization-prospects.html.
3 Wendell Cox et al., *16th Annual Demographic International Housing Affordability Survey: 2020*, DEMOGRAPHIC & PERFORMANCE URBAN PLANNING (2019), www.demographia.com/dhi.pdf.
4 *Id.*
5 *Id.*
6 *Progress in the Implementation of the New Urban Agenda and the 2030 Agenda for Sustainable Development*, UN HABITAT (Feb. 22, 2019), https://papersmart.unon.org/sites/default/files/HSP_HA_1_4_C.pdf.

Generally speaking, housing affordability is a great challenge in the process of urbanization in developing countries, and some regions show a worsening trend, such as North Africa and West Asia. Sub-Saharan Africa is still the region with the most inadequate housing for its urban population, with more than half of its urban residents living in slums.

The sustained growth of slum populations is the result of the urbanization rate, the polarization between the rich and the poor, and the population growth rate in developing countries exceeding the response capacity of urban governments. Although governments around the world, and intergovernmental institutions such as UN-Habitat, have paid attention and tried to solve the slum problem, much remains to be done. Countries have steadily improved urban slums and are committed to ridding millions of people of poor living environments and further providing them with appropriate housing conditions. These measures are mainly divided into two aspects: (1) Government-led slum upgrading and (2) promoting the "urban renewal" campaign. Governments can renovate city centers and clean up slums, demolish all the slums, and transfer their residents. Auction of land to the public will replace those items that can provide high taxes. The government should guide and involve multiple subjects in the housing supply plan to improve the overall housing supply in the city. The main body of the market provides market-oriented housing supply, and the government is responsible for providing low-rent housing or affordable housing. In the process of rapid population gathering, if the urban construction and management cannot keep up with the rapidly growing demand, a series of contradictions will be triggered, which will result in a shortage of housing and lead to numerous slums. Renewed political and business leaders' attention, increased investments, and multi-level, multi-agent participation housing supply systems are needed to ensure affordable and adequate housing for all by 2030.

Public Transportation

Traffic has always been one of the most important problems in big cities. Rapid urbanization and rapid population expansion in big cities have made the contradiction between urban traffic demand and traffic supply increasingly prominent, mainly manifested in traffic congestion and the resulting pollution and safety issues, among others. Private car travel causes congestion. With the development and expansion of the city and the rise in housing prices, many young families have to migrate from the suburbs to work in the urban areas. While driving is often the only feasible way to commute, taking public transportation becomes very complicated and time-consuming. What is more serious is that some cities adopted the policy of "adapting to car development"(适应小汽车发展) in the second half of the 20th century.[7] As a result, the number of private cars is increasing day by day, causing serious traffic congestion in urban areas. Soon after the opening of the ring expressway in different cities, there was continuous congestion. Traffic congestion will not only lead to the decline of various economic and social functions but will also lead to the continuous deterioration of the city's living environment and become a "persistent urban disease" which hinders development.

In order to meet this challenge, different countries have instilled two measures: (1) increasing the supply of public transportation and (2) implementing smart transportation.

---

7 Jun Wang, *The Pain of a City That Relies Heavily on Car Traffic*, Xinhua (2017), www.xinhuanet.com/comments/2017-01/06/c_1120255167.htm.

Regarding the supply of public transportation, with the rise of "internet" technology, cities with a large number of private cars began to consider how to optimize the use of private cars. For example, Paris made significant progress in controlling single-driver vehicles. The city took the lead in launching the bicycle sharing program in 2007 and the electric vehicle sharing program in 2011.[8] Uber, Didi, and other online car-sharing companies operate globally.[9] Car sharing and carpooling use privately owned vehicles as part of the mobile travel service solution, helping to control or even reduce the private car ownership rate and improve traffic accessibility. In addition, some local governments in cities are trying to reduce the cost of public transportation. Shenzhen, China, uses the "rail+real estate" model to finance infrastructure projects and reduce the cost of public transport operations.[10] This model can attract private investment, create revenue sources for rail transport enterprises through land premiums, reduce land costs, and reduce dependence on government funds by 50%, but it also introduces market risks. Economically developed cities, such as Dubai, are trying to implement a driverless strategy, trying to convert 25% of the city's total traffic—involving 5 million daily trips—into autonomous travel by 2030.[11] According to estimates, this measure will reduce transportation costs by 44%.[12]

"Smart transportation" has been promoted in cities around the world to improve the efficiency of public transportation. With the rise of "smart city" construction in the world, "smart transportation" has become an important component. By arranging edge cloud facilities on the roadside, collected data can be processed and transmitted locally, greatly reducing the time delay and being suitable for fast decision-making on businesses such as emergency braking and safe parking. The central cloud platform is mainly responsible for gathering all kinds of information to realize the overall dynamic planning, control, and driving behavior analysis of the route. The application of these related technologies will significantly optimize intelligent traffic control systems, and further ensure travel safety and improve traffic efficiency. According to calculations, cities with intelligent transportation facilities such as the "comprehensive transportation system" established in Seoul, South Korea, can reduce attendance time by 15–20% on average.[13]

According to 2019 data from 467 cities, in 90 countries, 49% of urban residents had convenient access to public transport,[14] a 53% decline compared to 2018. Sub-Saharan Africa lagged behind, with only 35% of its residents having convenient access to public transport.[15] In some regions with low access, informal transport modes are widely available and, in many

---

8 Simon Dixon et al., *The Deloitte City Mobility Index*, DELOITTE (Aug. 10, 2018), www2.deloitte.com/cn/en/pages/consumer-business/articles/city-mobility-index-2018.html.

9 *Entering Online Car-Hailing: Toyota Invests $600 Million in Didi*, CHINATIMES (Aug. 1, 2019), http://finance.eastmoney.com/a/201908011194749329.html.

10 Deloitte, *supra* note 8.

11 Damian Radcliffe, *Driverless Air Taxis, Drones, Pods: Dubai Puts Future Tech at Heart of Transportation*, ZD NET (Jan. 23, 2019), www.zdnet.com/article/driverless-air-taxis-drones-pods-dubai-puts-future-tech-at-heart-of-transportation/.

12 *Id.*

13 Qiuhong Mao, *Smart City, the Future Is Here*, 5G CENTER (2020), http://5gcenter.people.cn/n1/2020/1111/c430159-31926764.html.

14 *Progress in the Implementation of the Strategic Plan for the Period 2020–2023: Draft Results Framework*, UN HABITAT (2010), https://unhabitat.org/sites/default/files/2020/09/english-9-rev1.pdf. (Also note that public transport is defined as residing within 500 meters walking distance of a bus stop or a low-capacity transport system or within 1,000 meters of a railway and/or ferry terminal.)

15 *Id.*

cases, there are regional differences—Australia and New Zealand (75%), North America and Europe (72%), Latin America and the Caribbean (54%), West Asia and North Africa (48%), sub-Saharan Africa (35%), Central and South Asia (37%), East and South-East Asia (41%).[16]

Although efforts have been made to obtain public traffic accessibility, faster progress is still needed globally, especially for developing countries.

Environmental Pollution

Residents in many big cities are deeply affected by air pollution. Many recent studies have shown that actions to mitigate greenhouse gas emissions can quickly have a positive impact on economic and social welfare by improving public health and ecosystem sustainability. In order to meet this cross-regional challenge, United Nations organizations, private organizations, and governments have taken cooperative measures to reduce air pollution caused by urban activities. There are mainly two aspects.

The first aspect involves reducing emission of air pollutants. Many cities in the world have begun to implement "clean energy plans." Countries are taking measures to solve and reduce the air pollution caused by particulate matter. Although the latest data shows that environmental air pollution levels in most parts of the world are still high, some positive progress has been made through (1) expansion of renewable energy and electricity; (2) elimination of coal; (3) decarbonizing transportation; (4) decarbonizing industry; (5) avoiding future emissions; and (6) implementing renewable energy sources (wind, electricity, and solar). These measures have made remarkable progress in some cities. For example, in a short period of two years, India's Pradhan Mantri Ujjwala Yojana Plan has provided free liquefied petroleum gas connections to 37 million women living below the poverty line to support the switch to clean household energy. Mexico City has promised to implement cleaner vehicle standards, including switching to smoke-free buses and banning private diesel vehicles by 2025.

The second aspect involves optimizing urban ecological space and improving air quality. "Forest City,"[17] "Garden City,"[18] and "Ecological City"[19] have become the planning concepts of some city authorities around the world. Most cities around the world regard "greening rate" as an important goal of ecological construction. Research shows that every tree can reduce the carbon emissions of power plants by about 10kg through reducing the demand for air conditioners, increasing the quantity and quality of green spaces, and reducing short-term climate pollutants. To this end, the governments of various countries have implemented measures to improve the rate of urban greening. Examples include vertical three-dimensional greening, such as Singapore's skyscraper greening project, construction of urban forest parks, such as New York's Central Park, and the expansion of urban green belts, such as London's construction of a national park city.

In order to cope with increasingly complex environmental challenges, local governments around the world have begun to promote coordinated climate and environment governance.

---

16 *Id.*
17 The Forest City pattern is where forests are brought into cities and where cities are located in forests. It is regarded as the most economic and effective means of improving urban environmental quality.
18 The Garden City is an urban development pattern that is based on natural and geographic features, distributional character, and social economic status.
19 The Ecological Economics pattern requires full recognition of the ecological benefits of urban forests and, at the same time, the need for economic benefits.

This governance model coordinates global temperature rise targets with local/national policy priorities, reduces greenhouse gas emissions, realizes sustainable development, and controls air pollution within the framework of coping with climate change. Air pollution and climate change have different temporal and spatial ranges. The impact of air pollution on human health and ecosystems is local and short-term, but the impact of climate change is global, medium, long-term, and cumulative. At present, many countries are evaluating the benefits of coordinating climate and air pollution strategies and measures. For example, in 2017 Canada promulgated the world's first "Short-Living Climate Pollutants"[20] to jointly address climate and air quality issues. China also implemented air pollution control policies. These policies are some of the most important driving forces for China to deal with climate change, promote the green transition to cleaner energy and economic structure, and achieve other SDGs.

Although local governments have made some positive progress in tackling the challenge of air pollution, this problem is still a great challenge for urban residents in developing countries around the world. Three billion people still rely on burning wood, coal, crop residues, feces, and kerosene for cooking, heating, and lighting, and have the highest exposure to air pollution, especially fine particles. The elderly, children, the sick, and the poor are more vulnerable to air pollution. In 2016, 9 out of 10 urban residents still breathe air that does not meet the particulate matter value stipulated in the World Health Organization's (WHO) air quality guidelines,[21] and more than half of the world's population has experienced an increase in fine particulate matter between 2010 and 2016. More than half of the urban population was exposed to outdoor air pollution levels at least 2.5 times above the safety standard set by WHO.[22]

Over 90% of air pollution-related deaths occur in low- and middle-income countries, mainly in Asia and Africa.[23] In 2019, the top 10 countries with the worst air pollution in the world are all in Asia.[24] In 2016, 97% of the cities with more than 100,000 residents in low- and middle-income countries did not meet the air quality standards, compared with 49% in high-income countries.[25] Air pollution from transportation, industry, power generation, garbage incineration, and residential fuel combustion, combined with household air pollution, poses a major threat to human health and the containment of climate change. Air pollution causes nearly 7 million deaths each year, 650,000 of which are of children.[26]

Especially concerning is that 2019 air quality data show that climate change will increase the frequency and intensity of forest fires and sandstorms. Forest fires and open-air burning

---

20 *Climate Change*, GOVERNMENT OF CANADA, www.canada.ca/en/services/environment/weather/climatechange.html (last visited Dec. 8, 2020).
21 *9 out of 10 People Worldwide Breathe Polluted Air, but More Countries Are Taking Action*, WORLD HEALTH ORGANIZATION (WHO) (May 2, 2018), www.who.int/news/item/02-05-2018-9-out-of-10-people-worldwide-breathe-polluted-air-but-more-countries-are-taking-action (also noting that fine particulate matter (PM2.5) is defined as having a diameter less than or equal to 2.5 microns, not exceeding the annual average of 10 micrograms per cubic meter or the daily average of 25 micrograms per cubic meter).
22 Statistics Division, *Goal 11: Make Cities and Human Settlements Inclusive, Safe, Resilient and Sustainable*, DESA, https://unstats.un.org/sdgs/report/2016/goal-11 (last visited Dec. 8, 2020).
23 Doyle Rice, *90% of People Breathe Polluted Air; New Delhi Is World's Most Polluted Big City*, USA TODAY (May 2, 2018), www.usatoday.com/story/news/world/2018/05/02/world-health-organization-air-pollution-affects-90-population/572825002/.
24 Bangladesh is ranked first.
25 *Id.*
26 *Goal 11, supra* note 22.

agricultural operations have a significant impact on air quality in cities, like Singapore, Kuala Lumpur, Bangkok, Chiang Mai, and Los Angeles, and countries around the world, thus directly increasing the risk of air pollution, including in Australia, Indonesia, Brazil, and the United States. As air quality declines, the risk of stroke, heart disease, lung cancer, and chronic and acute respiratory diseases, including asthma, increases for the people who live in them. Air pollutants not only affect our health, but also affect the ecosystem and food production, and are related to climate change. These environmental challenges have seriously affected the realization of the SDGs.

Open Public Space

Open public space is becoming more and more important to city residents. However, the walkability of certain cities may not be safe for many residents.

Public open spaces in cities, such as parks, boulevards, gardens, amusement parks, and streets, can provide an interactive place for people, play an important role in social and economic life, and are also beneficial to the physical and mental health of urban residents. In recent years, the walkability of urban public creative space (UPRS) has become one of the most respected concepts in urban planning space. Building a community life circle that covers the accessibility of daily living service facilities has become the planning goal set by some city governments. The successful transformation of street space into a walkable and dynamic place with the dual attribute of "traffic space-public space" is helpful to promoting the development of humanization. In order to make up for the shortage of urban public space, some city leaders have begun to think about how to redevelop existing assets to serve new purposes and a growing population. The activation of cities' existing facilities has transformed abandoned elevated railways, factories, and other facilities into parks and commercial areas for public activities and has successfully brought about the revival of the entire region. For example, a railway line in New York City changed from disuse to a park called the High Line.[27] Some cities in developing countries carry out an "urban gardening" plan. This plan attempts to combine urban design, planning, architecture, landscape design, and other means to supplement and reconstruct the city's external public space in order to stimulate the emergence of a new layer of urban life. These urban plans have effectively provided a large amount of urban public space and improved the welfare of urban residents.[32]

Although cities all over the world have realized that urban public space can create urban value and have made some efforts toward this goal, they are limited by the financial pressure of cities and the impulse of commercial development, in which public space is inadequate, poorly designed, or privatized. The cities become increasingly segregated. Based on the data from 467 cities in 90 countries in 2019, few cities have been able to implement a system of open public spaces that covers entire urban areas—that is, within easy reach of all residents.[28] The results show that the average share of the population within 400 meters walking distance of an open public space is around 35%, which is smaller than the data in 2018 (53%) and the data in 2014 (59%), with huge variations among cities[29] and a decline over time. A low percentage does not necessarily mean that the share of land in open public space is

---

27 S. Lang & J. Rothenberg, *Neoliberal Urbanism, Public Space, and the Greening of the Growth Machine: New York City's High Line Park*, 49(8) ENV'T AND PLANNING A: ECON. AND SPACE 1743–61 (2017).[37]
28 UN HABITAT, *supra* note 14.
29 *Id.* (Noting that this information is from a low of 22% to a high of 67%.)

inadequate. In addition, there are regional differences—Australia and New Zealand (67%), North America and Europe (67%), Latin America and the Caribbean (46%), West and North Africa (40%), sub-Saharan Africa (26%), Central and South Asia (26%), East and South-East Asia (22%).[30]

National Urban Policy: A "Package" Strategy to Deal with the Challenges of "Urbanization"

Clear national urban policies have played an important role in the process of setting the direction of action to eliminate inequality and promote development, and have been well demonstrated in Brazil, China, South Africa, and other countries. There has been global consensus to foster National Urban Policies (NUPs) as key vehicles to achieve the New Urban Agenda. A NUP is a coherent set of decisions derived through a deliberate government-led process of coordinating and rallying various actors for a common vision and goal that will promote more transformative, productive, inclusive, and resilient urban development for the long term.

First, state and government institutions are primary change agents for implementing urban policy. While objectives may differ between more socially or economically driven motives, NUPs can predominantly be conceived as a policy vehicle for improved planning and service delivery by the state, which is Private-led, place-based, and Public–Private Partnership (PPP). Second, some countries integrate national urban policies with other urban policies in the country, such as integrating "smart city," "urban development plan," and "sustainable urban development plan." These policies and plans link up the policies of various departments at different levels that affect national, regional, and local governments, thus promoting the links between cities, urban–rural fringe areas, and villages, and providing comprehensive solutions to the challenges posed by "urbanization." Finally, most urban policies link them with the SDGs and subdivide them according to the important themes of the sustainable development agenda as a way of combining national policies with local actions.

In recent years, the number of countries carrying out national urban policies has gradually increased. In 2015, 142 countries had implemented city policies at the national level.[31] In 2017, 149 countries implemented city policies at the national level.[32] In 2019, 150 countries implemented the national urban policy, which is a policy strategy specifically aimed at today's urbanization challenges.[33] Nearly half of them have been fully implemented. National urban policies can provide a good example of effective implementation for the rest of the world and enhance the enthusiasm of regional and local governments to participate in national urban policies or regional development planning. They also ensure the joint efforts of all levels of government and provide the best strategy for sustainable urbanization.

---

30 *Id.*
31 *The Sustainable Development Goals Report 2019*, DESA (2019), https://unstats.un.org/sdgs/report/2019/. Eighty-two countries were in the implementation phase and 23 countries were in the detection and evaluation phase.
32 *Id.* (Noting that 56 policies were fully implemented.)
33 *Id.*

Impacts of COVID-19 on the Implementation of SDG 11

The global outbreak of the novel coronavirus (hereinafter "COVID-19") is the worst and most important public health emergency of the 21st century. By April 20, 2020, the virus spread to major countries on all continents, challenging the public governance capacity of governments at all levels. The pandemic has had unprecedented effects, including severe disruption to societies and economies, global travel and commerce, and on the livelihoods of people, particularly the poorest. The impact of the crisis will reverse hard-won development gains and hinder progress toward achieving the SDGs. Stagnation of economic activities has resulted in a sharp drop in government revenue and a decrease in citizens' personal income, affecting the progress of urban housing, transportation facilities, and public space construction. Therefore, as COVID-19 continues to spread around the world, it will have a great impact on the global economy which may delay the realization of the SDGs.

COVID-19 has a short-term positive effect on SDG 11.6. According to the 2019 air quality report released by IQAir, which has been testing global air pollution data for several decades, due to the global epidemic, the air pollution level in 10 major cities in the world dropped by 9% to 60% during the period of city closure by governments.[34] The annual average of fine particulate matter (such as PM2.5 and PM10) in cities around the world may be better than expected in 2020. However, this positive effect is temporary. With the recovery of economic activities, air pollution is still a great challenge to the physical and mental health of urban residents around the world.

Overall, despite progresses made in the SDG 11 targets, achieving these goals by 2030 is still a huge challenge facing the world, especially for developing countries with insufficient public financial resources. These countries are more likely to lack effective means to achieve the expected targets. The challenges require countries to take a proactive approach, and there is also a need to establish some global coordination mechanisms to assist the developing countries to cope with common governance problems.

Case Study: Beijing—A Successful Example of Collaborative Control of Air Pollution

The Threat of Air Pollution in the Capital City

In the past 20 years, China has experienced rapid economic development. The urbanization rate has increased from 30% in 1996 to 61% in 2018.[35] Rapid economic growth and urbanization have brought great challenges to urban environmental governance. Among them, the issue that attracts the most public attention is smog. In 2017, Beijing's Gross Domestic Product (GDP), population, and vehicle ownership were 11.78 times, 1.74 times, and 4.35 times that of 1998, respectively,[36] of which the per capita GDP has exceeded US$20,000, the resident population is 21.7 million and the vehicle ownership is 5.99 million.[37] The rapid development of the urban economy led to the deterioration of air

---

34 *2019 World Air Quality Report: Region & City Ranking*, IQAIR (2019), www.iqair.com/blog/report-over-90-percent-of-global-population-breathes-dangerously-polluted-air.
35 *Id.*
36 UN Environment Report–A Review of 20 Years' Air Pollution Control in Beijing, UNEP CLIMATE & CLEAN AIR COALITION (2019), www.ccacoalition.org/en/resources/review-20-years'-air-pollution-control-beijing.
37 *Id.*

quality, and the daily life of urban residents facing the "smog" problem dominated by PM2.5. Beijing established 35 monitoring PM2.5 stations in 2012 and began to release pollutant monitoring data from January 1, 2013. In 2013, the annual average concentration of PM2.5 in Beijing was 89.5μg/m3, exceeding the national air quality standard of 35μg/m3 and far exceeding the standard of 10μg/m3 set by the WHO.[38] However, after many years of efforts, through coordination at the national level, successful coordination with neighboring cities and regions, and scientific and systematic methods, the concentration of PM2.5 in the air has decreased by 53% (2013–2019) in five years.[39] In 2020, Beijing dropped out of the list of 200 cities with the worst pollution in the world. The Swedish company, IQAir, considered Beijing as an example of successful policy implementation leading to air quality improvement at a press conference on the release of testing data in 2020.[40] The 2019 report released by the United Nations Environment Program also gives the same conclusion, even praising Beijing's experience in air pollution control as "a model that can be used for reference" for the world.[41]

Beijing's policies are mainly reflected in the following aspects:

Measures Taken in the Fight against Air Pollution

First, the top-level system design of the central government sets environmental governance objectives from top to bottom. In 2016, China's National Plan on Implementation of the 2030 Agenda for Sustainable Development was released. The national plan is the overall guidance and practical guide to realizing the SDGs. The construction of the evaluation index system should be consistent with the plan's logic. In December 2016, the State Council issued the document "China's Implementation of the 2030 Agenda for Sustainable Development Innovation Demonstration Zone Construction Plan," which clearly defined the main construction tasks of the innovation demonstration zone.[42] It has become one of China's important strategies for implementing the 2030 Sustainable Development Agenda to promote provinces, cities, and regions to effectively link their own development strategic goals with the country's overall plan.

The "Five-Year Plan for National Economic and Social Development" is China's most important national strategic plan. According to the overall requirements of the national "13th Five-Year Plan" (2016–2020), 31 provinces, autonomous regions, and municipalities directly under the Central Government in mainland China have formulated their own 13th Five-Year Plan.[43] Cities and counties have also formulated implementation action road maps and annual plans, implemented various specific tasks, effectively implemented the unified plan for national sustainable development, and achieved effective coordination between the central and local authorities in implementing the 2030 Agenda. In particular, considering the urgent need to improve air quality, the Chinese Government has added two new indicators

---

38 *Id.*
39 *Ibid.*
40 IQAir, *supra* note 35.
41 UNEP, *supra* note 37.
42 *China's Implementation of the 2030 Agenda for Sustainable Development Innovation Demonstration Zone Construction Plan*, THE STATE COUNCIL, CHINA (2016), www.gov.cn/zhengce/content/2016-12/13/content_5147412.htm.
43 *Outline of the 13th Five-Year Plan for National Economic and Social Development of the People's Republic of China*, XINHUA NEWS AGENCY (Jul. 3, 2016).

into the 13th Five-Year Plan (2016–2020): "the ratio of days with good air quality in cities at prefecture level and above (%)" and "the concentration drop (%) in cities at prefecture level and above where PM 2.5 is not up to standard."[44] Setting the PM2.5 target reflects the central government's idea of strengthening the coordinated control of air pollution and climate, and also provides an incentive mechanism for local government to make good behavior choices.

Second, the Chinese government has actively promoted Beijing-Tianjin-Hebei coordinated governance to provide a good surrounding environment for Beijing. "Beijing-Tianjin-Hebei and its surrounding areas (including Beijing, Tianjin, Hebei, Shanxi, Inner Mongolia and Shandong) are the regions with the most serious air pollution in China."[45] The annual average PM2.5 concentration in the Beijing-Tianjin-Hebei region in 2013 was about 106μg/m3 or about three times the national air quality standard.[46] As air pollutants will be transported and diffused between different regions, Beijing, Tianjin, and Hebei need to cooperate to solve the serious air pollution problems they face. In order to achieve the goal of environmental improvement in Beijing, it is necessary to improve the air quality in the urban areas around Beijing simultaneously. The "Air Pollution Prevention Action Plan" published by the State Council in September 2013 pointed out that by 2017, the concentration of PM2.5 in the Beijing-Tianjin-Hebei region will be 25% lower than that in 2012, of which the average annual concentration of PM2.5 in Beijing will be controlled at about 60μg/m3.[47] With the detailed rules for the implementation of the air pollution prevention and control action plan in Beijing, Tianjin, and Hebei and its surrounding areas, the air pollution prevention and control action plan has been launched, and a number of control measures have been uniformly deployed and implemented in the region.

These measures mainly include three types. The first measure is to reduce coal consumption. Beijing, Tianjin, and Hebei have reduced coal consumption by 71 million tons at the end of 2017 compared with 2012, exceeding the target set by the local governments strictly implemented the policies of eliminating small coal-fired boilers and phasing out the use of scattered coal by residents ("coal to electricity" and "coal to gas"). The second measure is to adjust the industrial structure. The Beijing-Tianjin-Hebei region actively cultivates strategic emerging industries, including but not limited to a new generation of information technology, biology, high-end equipment manufacturing, new energy, and other low energy-consuming industries. Moving forward, the surplus production capacity of major energy-intensive industries should be eliminated. The third measure is to reduce motor vehicle fuel consumption. Many measures have been taken to eliminate low energy efficiency and high pollution vehicles. New energy vehicles have been promoted, including providing subsidies for car purchase, building charging piles, and expanding the number of new energy buses. In 2017, the average annual concentration of PM 2.5 in the Beijing-Tianjin-Hebei region has been reduced to 64μg/m3, 39.6% lower than that in 2013,[48] and the average annual

---

44 *Id.*
45 Ministry of Environmental Protection et al., *Beijing, Tianjin, Hebei and Surrounding Areas Implementation Rules for Implementation of Air Pollution Prevention and Control Action Plan*, MINISTRY OF ECO. & ENV'T (Sept. 17, 2013), www.mee.gov.cn/gkml/hbb/bwj/201309/t20130918_260414.htm.
46 *Id.*
47 *Id.*
48 *Breakthroughs Chinas Path to Clean Air*, CLEAN AIR ASIA (Dec. 27, 2018), www.allaboutair.cn/a/reports/2018/1227/527.html.

concentration of PM2.5 in Beijing has been reduced to 58µg/m3, achieving the goal set by the State Council.[49]

Third, Beijing has taken comprehensive air pollution control measures. Beijing's practices can be divided into two categories: (1) Government-led measures that attach equal importance to project emission reduction and (2) management of emission reductions. Since 1998, Beijing has drawn up a series of air improvement plans based on scientific research by universities and research institutes. Relevant measures have been incorporated into local legislation. Meanwhile, real-time data from more than 1,000 air monitoring stations in the city are used to assess its implementation in a timely manner. Based on the testing data and the setting goals, Beijing has established a number of local environmental economic policies, including subsidies, fees, pricing, and other financial practices to provide economic incentives for the comprehensive air pollution control measures. These measures are divided into seven categories: (1) coal-fired boiler renovation, (2) clean-up of civil fuels, (3) industrial structure adjustment, (4) emission control of mobile sources, (5) upgrading of industrial standards, (6) comprehensive dust control, and (7) treatment of volatile organic compounds.[50]

Valuable Experience in the Pollution Control at City Level

To expand participants and achieve co-governance, market-oriented tools of "carbon trading" are used to encourage market players to reduce emissions. In October 2011, China launched a carbon emissions trading pilot in Guangdong, Hubei, Beijing, Tianjin, Shanghai, Shenzhen, and Chongqing. Since July 2013, Beijing has started trading carbon emissions. The whole city is mobilized through information disclosure and public participation. Beijing has put forward the plan of "common governance and sharing," that is, common governance and common enjoyment of the blue sky. Beijing has gradually enhanced its environmental promotion and education agencies. It worked to set up all media communications platforms that feature interactions of traditional and new media, including newspaper, radio, television, internet, Weibo, and WeChat, and foster online and offline brand activities with public participation. An environmental petition and complaint system have been established, which includes an environmental protection hotline and an online complaint mailbox.[51] Incentives up to 50,000 Yuan per case are offered to encourage the public to actively report violations related to environmental pollution.

Public participation and support in Beijing have been very strong. In general, since the PM2.5 monitoring was carried out in 2013, the PM2.5 concentration level in Beijing has shown a gradual downward trend and achieved remarkable results. However, it is still higher than the minimum standard set by the WHO (35µg/m3). The change of air quality mainly depends on the total emission of air pollutants in the region. Therefore, through adjusting the industrial structure, optimizing the energy structure, changing lifestyles, and through the joint efforts of the whole society, Beijing has continuously reduced the atmospheric pollutants in the city. However, improving the air quality thoroughly is still a long-term and arduous task, which requires the participation of all citizens. Beijing's PM2.5 governance

---

49 *Id.*
50 UNEP, *supra* note 37.
51 *Environmental Pollution Complaints*, MINISTRY OF ECO. & ENV'T (Oct. 10, 2019), www.mee.gov.cn/ywgz/hjwrjb/.

process and experience can provide a reference model for urban air pollution control in developing countries around the world.

Conclusion and Recommendation for the Way Forward

Conclusion

With SDG 11, the task is to make cities inclusive, safe, resilient, and sustainable. Instead of widening the gap between the rich and the poor, creating congestion and pollution, and isolating the urban residents from nature, the existence of cities should make people's lives better. The common goals of city governance can be achieved using various solutions. People should be put at the center of city governance, and cities should be locally tailored for their residents. Hence, the steps taken by the cities toward the final goal of SDG 11 will be heterogeneous. Yet, there are some common lessons that cities could adopt. As is shown in the case study of Beijing, public participation is important in the process of policy making, enforcement, and implementation of city governance. Public participation could not only improve the quality of decision-making, but also strengthen its enforceability. Public participation could be widely applied in other issues beyond pollution control to improve city governance within SDG 11.

Recommendations to Speed up Implementation on SDG 11

To improve implementation of SDG 11 at the global level:

- **Establish a collaborative governance mechanism to alleviate the problem of insufficient governance resources.** These collaborations include regional coordination, central and local coordination, public and private coordination, and citizen and government coordination.
- **Apply and promote new technologies to reduce energy consumption and improve governance efficiency.** To use Information Communication Technology (ICT) to promote shared transportation, improve the efficiency of urban transportation, and reduce pollutant emissions. To promote new energy technologies and reduce overall energy consumption.
- **Promote "urban renewal" and reduce slums through cooperation between the "visible and invisible hand."** The government should guide and involve multiple subjects in the housing supply plan to improve the overall housing supply in the city. The main body of the market provides market-oriented housing supply, and the government is responsible for providing low-rent housing or affordable housing.
- **Appraise and promote the best practices of urban policy packages and promote the spread of best practices in urban governance around the world.**

11 Inclusive and Equitable Quality Education

Why Are We Missing the Mark?

Anna Shostya

Introduction

Education is one of the fundamental objectives of development and has the potential to improve economic and social quality of life. Together with improvements in health, another type of human capital, investment in education helps people escape poverty and hunger and expands human "capability to function."[1] Education is also a driving force behind self-sustaining economic growth and prosperity. It improves workers' skills and knowledge and makes their labor more productive. It also advances workers' ability to absorb technology and generate new knowledge, thereby boosting the productivity of complementary physical capital. Finally, education often leads to something that economists' term as *positive externalities*—spillover effects that benefit society.[2] Studies show, for example, that more educated societies tend to have lower crime rates.[3] On a family level, more educated parents, especially mothers, tend to have better educated and healthier children,[4] consequently, contributing to long-term self-sustaining economic growth.

Since the end of the 20th century, the international community has been troubled by stagnating educational attainment and the educational gender gap that hinders economic growth and fosters social inequality, especially in low-income and developing countries. Efforts by national governments and international organizations undertaken during the last several decades have produced significant results, but they lack much coordination and monitoring. Recognizing the pivotal role that education plays in human development and sustainability, the United Nations (UN) addressed urgent educational issues in its 2030 Agenda that was adopted by Member States in 2015. Sustainable Development Goal (SDG) 4 that calls for *inclusive and equitable quality education* and *life-long learning opportunities for all*, is a universal goal that is interlinked with other development goals.[5] It is an ambitious attempt to ensure that education systems around the world that face similar challenges can

---

1 Amartya Sen, *Development and Thinking at the Beginning of the 21st Century*, LSE STICERD RESEARCH PAPER (Mar. 1997), https://ssrn.com/abstract=1126934.
2 WALTER W. MCMAHON, EDUCATION AND DEVELOPMENT: MEASURING THE SOCIAL BENEFITS (Oxford University Press 2000).
3 Laura Chioda et al., *Spillovers from Conditional Cash Transfer Programs: Bolsa Família and Crime in Urban Brazil*, 54 ECONOMICS OF EDUCATION REVIEW 306–20 (2016).
4 Abdul Ghafoor Awan & Kauser Dahmina, *Impact of Educated Mother on Academic Achievement of her Children: A Case Study of District Lodhran-Pakistan*, 12 J. OF LITERATURE, LANGUAGES AND LINGUISTICS 57–65 (2015).
5 *See* United Nations G.A. Res. A/RES/70/1, *Transforming our world: the 2030 Agenda for Sustainable Development*, at 14, 17–18 (Sept. 25, 2015) [hereinafter "Agenda 2030"].

achieve quality education outcomes in the most efficient way and, thus, align with sustainable development.

This chapter evaluates the progress achieved toward implementing SDG 4. We begin with a brief overview of the conceptual development of this goal during the last several decades. We proceed with the analysis of interlinkages between SDG 4 and other SDGs, and we show how education plays an integral role within the sustainable development framework. The next part of the chapter is devoted to assessing the progress toward SDG 4. We provide quantitative and qualitative evaluation of selected targets, based on regional comparisons as well as gender and age disaggregation of indicators. Four case studies of Finland, Burundi, China and Mexico further offer insights into the role of institutional factors that may curb or foster quality education. We devote the next section to the effect of the ongoing novel COVID-19 pandemic on SDG 4 by 2030. The follow-up section draws conclusions based on the lessons learned from the experiences of countries used as case studies as well as from the regional comparisons. The last section is a summary of the urgent actions that are needed to address the current challenges and ensure a more robust movement toward ensuring inclusive and equitable quality education for all.

Inclusive and Equitable Quality Education as a Universal Developmental Goal

The international community had not actively pursued education as a universal developmental goal until the end of the 20th century, when social science findings and empirical evidence had started to indicate stagnating schooling rates and startling gender disparities, especially in poorer regions. As a result, governments and international organizations, such as the UN and the World Bank, initiated tremendous efforts to improve access to education for all children and close educational gaps. A formal international agenda on these goals was first established in 1990, at the World Conference Education for All in Thailand, an important step in building a vision. Unfortunately, the vision was void of coordination and a monitoring framework.

The 2000 World Education Forum in Dakar initiated another major attempt to bring positive change to global education. The Dakar Framework for Action was designed to amend the flaws of the former agenda and ensure international, regional, and national commitment and accountability. It became a foundation for the Millennium Development Goals (MDGs) that were approved five months later. In 2002, the World Summit on Sustainable Development adopted the Johannesburg Plan of Implementation which reaffirmed MDG 2 in achieving universal primary education by 2015 and the Dakar Framework's goal of eliminating gender disparity in primary and secondary education by 2005 and at all levels of education by 2015.[6]

Two and a half decades since the 1990 conference, these deliberate efforts of the international community to accelerate educational attainment of the world's poor have resulted in historically unprecedented advances in literacy rates and basic education enrollment. Participation in primary and lower secondary education and literacy rates have increased substantially. By 2016, less than 10% of the world's youth lacked basic literacy skills, compared

---

6 *Education*, SUSTAINABLE DEVELOPMENT GOALS KNOWLEDGE PLATFORM, https://sustainabledevelopment.un.org/topics/education [hereinafter "SDG Knowledge Platform"].

to almost one-quarter of illiterate youth in the 1980s.[7] Despite this visible progress, learning outcomes tended to be low, especially in low-income and middle-income countries. This suggested that while a growing number of children attended school, *quality* education and gender inequality remained some of the pressing challenges that desperately needed to be addressed.

There were several reasons as to why these early efforts were not producing desirable outcomes. First, the MDGs placed too much emphasis on universal primary education and literacy, which were attractive only to the countries furthest from these goals, as well as high-income countries that were supposed to finance their achievement.[8] Second, the MDGs framework did not emphasize the link between quality education and sustainable development that was envisioned by Agenda 21 (Chapter 36) at the UN Conference on Environment and Development in 1992.[9]

Fortunately, both the Muscat Agreement adopted at the Global Education for All Meeting in 2014 and the proposal for SDGs developed by the Open Working Group of the UN General Assembly on SDGs included education as an integral component of and key catalyst for sustainable development.[10]

Interlinkages between Education and Development

Economists have long recognized the multipronged returns on education, perhaps since 1964, when Gary Becker, a Nobel Laureate in economics, published his influential *Human Capital* treatise. Becker's work initiated the discussion of both private and social rates of return to human capital, based on gender, race, and age differences.[11] More recent social science studies have improved our understanding of the role of education in development, especially in developing and less developed countries.[12] The interconnections between education and other aspects of human development are reflected in the SDGs framework.[13]

Perhaps the strongest and the most important link in this framework is between education and poverty (SDG 1). People with more education have a greater capacity to pull themselves and their families out of poverty. This is because an increase in human capital

---

7 *Literacy Rates Continue to Rise from One Generation to the Next*, UNESCO INSTITUTE FOR STATISTICS, FS/2017/LIT/45, (Sep. 2017), http://uis.unesco.org/sites/default/files/documents/fs45-literacy-rates-continue-rise-generation-to-next-en-2017_0.pdf.
8 *Beyond Commitments: How Countries Implement SDG 4*, UNESCO (2019) https://unesdoc.unesco.org/ark:/48223/pf0000369008/PDF/369008eng.pdf.multi.
9 *United Nations Conference on Environment & Development Rio de Janerio, Brazil*, UNITED NATIONS SUSTAINABLE DEVELOPMENT (1992), https://sustainabledevelopment.un.org/content/documents/Agenda21.pdf.
10 SDG Knowledge Platform, *supra* note 6.
11 GARY BECKER, HUMAN CAPITAL: A THEORETICAL AND EMPIRICAL ANALYSIS, WITH SPECIAL REFERENCE TO EDUCATION (New York Bureau of Economic Research 1964).
12 *See* for example, Erin Murphy-Graham & Cynthia Lloyd, *Empowering Adolescent Girls in Developing Countries: The Potential Role of Education*, 14 POLICY FUTURES IN EDUCATION 556–77 (2016); Alejandro J. Ganimian & Richard J. Murnane, *Improving Education in Developing Countries: Lessons from Rigorous Impact Evaluations*, 86 REVIEW OF EDUCATIONAL RESEARCH 86, 719–55 (2016); J.P. Robinson & R. Winthrop, *Millions Learning: Scaling up Quality Education in Developing Countries*, Center for Universal Education at The Brookings Institution (2016).
13 Katia Vladimirova & David Le Blanc, *Exploring Links between Education and Sustainable Development Goals through the Lens of UN Flagship Reports*, 24 SUSTAINABLE DEVELOPMENT (Mar. 30, 2016).

investment increases labor productivity and thus leads to a greater earning potential. The relationship is reciprocal, that is people with higher incomes are more likely to invest in their children's education. Hence there is a clear link between education and inequality (SDG 10), as more educated people not only have higher income, but also have a greater capacity to assert their rights. Education also can affect values and norms that shape society. As such, education has a potential to achieve greater gender equality (SDG 5). Gender equality prevents an intergenerational poverty by breaking the cycle of early marriage and childbearing, poor health, and other risks associated with these events.[14]

Another powerful link that is well documented by the literature is the link between education and economic growth.[15] Education raises innovation capacity and entrepreneurship, the backbones of industrial transformation (SDG 9) and job-building and economic progress (SDG 8). At the same time, higher Gross Domestic Product (GDP) growth can translate into more resources for the education system, while the industrial transformation boosts the demand for skilled labor. Education also helps increase farm productivity and agricultural outcomes (SDG 2), which can improve nutrition and health outcomes (SDG 3). Specialized skills are very valuable for sustainable management, which is a necessary element in achieving the goal on green energy (SDG 7), water and sanitation (SDG 6), ecosystem conservation (SDG 15), and climate change (SDG 13). More educated people are also more aware of environmental damage that may be associated with unsustainable consumption. Such awareness can help to achieve the goal of sustainable consumption and production (SDG 12). Education also increases resilience to adverse shocks, improves disaster preparedness (SDG 11), and helps build more peaceful societies (SDG 16).[16]

Because education is so tightly intertwined with other aspects of human development, solutions to educational deficiencies that haunt many countries, and especially developing and least developed countries (LDCs), often lie within a broader framework. This framework includes improvements in political stability, strengthening of human rights, facilitating an inclusive social safety net, creating a sound financial system, and building a resilient economy based on an adequate incentive/reward structure. Without these crucial elements, a truly inclusive equitable quality education cannot be achieved.

Assessing the Progress toward SDG 4

The SDG 4 framework consists of 10 targets and 11 indicators. In this section, we provide an assessment to the core targets (4.1, 4.5, 4.6, and 4.c) that fall short of desired outcomes and call for urgent actions. SDG Target 4.1 aims to "ensure that all girls and boys complete free, equitable and quality primary and secondary education leading to relevant and effective learning outcomes" by 2030.[17] Target 4.6 calls for "all youth and a substantial proportion

---

14 *Global Monitoring Report 2014/2015: Ending Poverty and Sharing Prosperity*, World Bank & International Monetary Fund (2015).
15 R. J. Barro, *Economic Growth in a Cross Section of Countries*, 106 QUARTERLY JOURNAL OF ECONOMICS 407–43 (May 1991), http://piketty.pse.ens.fr/files/Barro91.pdf.
16 B. Desai et al., *Making Development Sustainable. The Future of Disaster Risk Management, Global Assessment Report on Disaster Risk Reduction*, Global Assessment Report UNISDR (2015).
17 *Ensure Inclusive and Equitable Quality Education and Promote Lifelong Learning Opportunities for All*, UNITED NATIONS DEPARTMENT OF ECONOMIC AND SOCIAL AFFAIRS, https://sustainabledevelopment.un.org/sdg4.

of adults, both men and women, achieve literacy and numeracy" by 2030.[18] Target 4.5 is a call to "eliminate gender disparities in education and ensure equal access to all levels of education and vocational training for the vulnerable, including persons with disabilities, indigenous peoples and children in vulnerable situations."[19] And Target 4.c aims to "substantially increase the supply of qualified teachers, including through international cooperation for teacher training in developing countries, especially least developed countries (LDCs) and Small Island Developing States" (SIDs) (internal abbreviations added).[20] These targets are intertwined with other targets of SDG 4. Therefore, they give good insight into a learning crisis that the world is currently facing.

Missing the Mark on Inclusion

Global and regional data strongly suggest that the world most likely will not achieve Target 4.1 in 10 years. It is true that the number of children, adolescents, and youth who are excluded from education fell steadily in the decade following 2000, but this progress has basically stopped in recent years. Shockingly, in 2018, more than a-quarter of a billion children, adolescents, and youth were still out of school, representing one-sixth of the global population of this age group.[21] After an initial decline in the years after 2000, the primary out-of-school rate has decreased only slightly since 2008, reaching 8% in 2018, and the lower secondary out-of-school rate has been at 16% since 2012.[22]

Low-income countries are particularly at risk in meeting this target. According to the United Nations Educational, Scientific and Cultural Organization (UNESCO) 2019 Global Education Monitoring Report, to achieve universal secondary school completion by 2030, all children need to enroll in primary school by 2018. However, the intake rate in low-income countries was only 73% in 2016.[23] Just 79% of children will complete primary school, 53% will complete lower secondary, and 26% will complete upper secondary by 2030.[24] Sub-Saharan Africa, where the out-of-school rates remain stubbornly high, has accounted for an increasing share of out-of-school populations since 2000. In this region, only 63% of primary school age children and 38% of 12–14-year-old youths complete their levels of educations.[25] In Africa, as in other low-income regions, upper secondary school-age youths are much more likely to be out of school as children of primary school age. This is because most youths have never had a chance to enter school when they were younger, or because in some countries upper secondary education is not compulsory. Additionally, upper secondary school-age youths staying in school have higher opportunity cost (the cost of alternatives

---

18 *Id.*
19 *Id.*
20 *Id.*
21 *New Methodology Shows That 258 Million Children, Adolescents and Youth are out of School*, UNESCO Fact Sheet No. 56 UIS/2019/ED/FS/56 (Sep. 2019), http://uis.unesco.org/sites/default/files/documents/new-methodology-shows-258-million-children-adolescents-and-youth-are-out-school.pdf.
22 *Id.*
23 *Target 4.1: Primary and Secondary Education*, UNESCO & GLOBAL EDUCATION MONITORING REPORT (2018), http://gem-report-2019.unesco.org/chapter/monitoring-progress-in-sdg-4/primary-and-secondary-education-target-4-1/ [hereinafter "UNESCO Target 4.1 Report"].
24 Silvia Montaya & Manos Antoninis, *"Business as Usual" Will Not Achieve Global Education Goals*, WORLD ECONOMIC FORUM (Jul. 9, 2019), www.weforum.org/agenda/2019/07/business-as-usual-will-not-achieve-the-global-education-goals/.
25 UNESCO Target 4.1 Report, *supra* note 23.

forgone), primarily due to their need to help generate more income for their cash-strapped families. As a result, they may choose employment over continuing their education.

Ensuring that children have access to school is necessary but is only one condition for achieving equitable and quality education for all. One of the most important elements of this goal is for all children to actually complete their education. Data indicates that if current trends continue, the global completion rate will be 93% in primary education, 85% in lower secondary education, and 60% in upper secondary education by 2030.[26] Another element is the *quality* of education, which is rather subjective and difficult to quantify. The indicators for quality education are typically based on national curricular standards for knowledge and skills, processes and methods, and attitudes and values. Standardized tests, like the Program for International Student Assessment (PISA),[27] though being in existence for a while, are rarely used in low-income countries. The picture would be clearer if SDG 4 provided measurable indicators that could be used to compare the progress in quality of education in different countries and regions, especially for poorer countries.

Setting the Example of Inclusive and Equitable Quality Education: The Case of Finland

Finland has gained reputation for being one of the highest-ranking countries in terms of education. Finnish 15-year-olds do exceptionally well on PISA tests, and its 4th-graders and 8th-graders perform just as well on Trends in International Mathematics and Science Study (TIMSS).[28] It is also one of the best education systems in terms of equity, the achievement gaps between pupils and regions are among the narrowest in the world.[29] What critical ingredients are included in the Finnish "educational equation" that produced such successful outcomes? And most importantly, can other countries, especially the LDCs imitate these ingredients?

The first critical ingredient is qualified, trusted, and respected teachers. Finnish teachers are high-quality, extremely well-trained, and committed. They often teach the same children in multiple grades and as a result, build a trusted bond with students and their parents.[30] Finnish teachers also have substantial social prestige. They are perceived not "as technicians whose work is to implement strictly dictated syllabi, but rather as professionals who know how to improve learning for all.... Teachers are ranked highest in importance because educational systems work through them." [31]

The second ingredient is government's willingness to reform an inequitable, mediocre education system into an inclusive and equitable one. In the 1970s, Finland made teacher education more rigorous, making a Master's degree a prerequisite for teaching. It also created a highly centralized and closely monitored system with uniform curricula, which later,

---

26 Montaya, *supra* note 24.
27 *What Is PISA*, OECD, www.oecd.org/pisa.
28 Hani Morgan, *Review of Research: The Education System in Finland: A Success Story Other Countries Can Emulate*, 90 J. CHILDHOOD EDUCATION 453–57 (2014), https://doi.org/10.1080/00094056.2014.983013.
29 Mike Colagrossi, *10 Reasons Why Finland's Education System Is the Best in the World*, WORLD ECONOMIC FORUM (Sep.10, 2018), www.weforum.org/agenda/2018/09/10-reasons-why-finlands-education-system-is-the-best-in-the-world.
30 SECOND INTERNATIONAL HANDBOOK OF EDUCATIONAL CHANGE (Hargreaves, A., Lieberman, A., Fullan, M., Hopkins, D. Eds. 2010).
31 Reijo Laukkanen, *Finnish Strategy for High-Level Education for All*, *in* GOVERNANCE AND PERFORMANCE OF EDUCATION SYSTEMS, at 306–24 (2007).

in 1985 was replaced with a decentralized framework that increased the freedom and the sovereignty of municipal governments. By 1994, the National Board of Education designed a national core curriculum, which only gave broad guidelines and recommendations, giving the municipalities the right to make decisions based on local needs.[32]

Finally, the reforms needed time and consistency. Finnish education policies are a result of almost four decades of "systematic, mostly intentional, development that has created a culture of diversity, trust, and respect within Finnish society in general, and within its education system in particular."[33] Three ingredients in the Finnish equation have helped produce quality and equitable results: (1) empowerment of high-quality teachers; (2) government's commitment to fix the entire education system (instead of just patching its ineffective components); and (3) time and consistency. While it may be impractical to implement the entire package, some of these strategies can be applied in the countries that need to improve their education systems.

Missing the Mark on Achieving Literacy and Numeracy

The second half of the 20th century and the beginning of the 21st century have witnessed a historically unprecedented growth of literacy rates. In 1970, 63% of people were literate,[34] compared to 86% in 2017, with the youth rate being 91%.[35] Some regions have made significant progress toward achieving Target 4.6 in the past several decades. Adult literacy rates are at or near 100% in most countries in Central Asia, Europe, and Northern America, and Eastern and South-Eastern Asia. Youth literacy rates are highest in the same three regions and in Latin America and the Caribbean. The youth literacy rate increased the most in Southern Asia (from 59% in 1990 to 89% in 2016), Northern Africa and Western Asia (from 80% to 90%), and sub-Saharan Africa (from 65% to 75%).[36]

Despite this progress, 750 million adults still cannot read and write a simple statement, and two-thirds of those adults are women, according to the latest available data for 2016. More than 100 million of the illiterate population are between 15 and 24 years old. Southern Asia is home to almost one-half of the global illiterate population (49%) and more than a quarter of all illiterate adults live in sub-Saharan Africa. Only one in six children in Sierra Leone, for example, had foundational literacy skills.[37] These two regions also reported the lowest literacy rates.[38] In India alone, more than 252 million people were illiterate in 2018.[39] This is the world's largest illiterate body (about 34% of the global total). While India made headway in improving access to education (its primary school enrollment is around 100% and its literacy rate did rise drastically from less than 50% in 1990 to more than 70% by

---

32 *Id.*
33 Second International Handbook of Educational Change, *supra* note 31, at 10.
34 *Confronting the Challenges of Gender Equality and Fragile States*, Global Monitoring Report (2007), www.imf.org/external/pubs/ft/gmr/2007/eng/gmr.pdf.
35 UNESCO Target 4.1 Report, *supra* note 23.
36 *Literacy Rates Continue to Rise from One Generation to the Next*, Unesco Fact Sheet No. 45 FS/2017/LIT/45 (Sept. 2017), http://uis.unesco.org/sites/default/files/documents/fs45-literacy-rates-continue-rise-generation-to-next-en-2017_0.pdf [hereinafter "UNESCO Literacy Rates Continue to Rise"].
37 UNESCO Target 4.1 Report, *supra* note 23.
38 UNESCO Literacy Rates Continue to Rise, *supra*, note 37.
39 *India: Education and Literacy*, UNESCO Institute for Statistics, http://uis.unesco.org/en/country/in (last accessed on Dec. 6, 2020).

2018), population growth has cancelled these gains. India is also a prime example of how primary school enrollment does not guarantee advances in literacy and numeracy. In India, even youth with basic numeracy skills cannot perform simple daily tasks needed at work, like telling time, measuring length, and adding weights.[40] This may be because many children may drop out of school or may not receive quality education.

A Regional Exception: The Case of Burundi

Burundi is a small, resource-poor, landlocked country of slightly over 11 million people.[41] With annual per capita income of roughly $800 and a largely agricultural economy,[42] it is one of the poorest countries in sub-Saharan Africa. It is ranked second to last in the World Economic Forum's Network Readiness Index that draws international comparisons based on countries' information and communication development.[43] Torn by bouts of violent conflicts and years of political instability, the country, as many of its neighbors, has inadequate infrastructure, insufficient school supplies, overcrowded classrooms, and poorly built schools that often lack windows, doors, and desks.[44]

Surprisingly, Burundi has substantially higher average (Program for the Analysis of Education Systems) scores[45] on reading and mathematics tests in both second and sixth grades than other participating sub-Saharan African countries do. It also did relatively better than its neighbors in two rounds of the Early Grade Reading Assessment.[46] In fact, it has been showing remarkable progress over the last several decades. Its literacy rates among 15–24-year-old students had jumped from 31% in 1979 to 88% in 2017, with an impressive improvement among young women whose literacy rates soared from around 20% to more than 85% during the same period. Primary education is free since 2005 and the primary to secondary transition rate of 76% is relatively high for a sub-Saharan African country.[47] According to the United Nations International Children's Emergency Fund (UNICEF), the proportion of children in school increased from about 60% in 2005 to 96% in 2011.[48]

What accounts for Burundi's success and its regional exception? There are multiple explanations, including trained teachers (over 90% of primary teachers have undergone two years of training), high community participation (school infrastructure and teacher training often is co-funded by religious organizations), and "structured pedagogy," a holistic, participative,

---

40 UNESCO Target 4.1 Report, *supra* note 23.
41 *Burundi At-A-Glance 2018*, THE WORLD BANK (Sept. 14, 2020), www.worldbank.org/en/country/burundi/overview.
42 *Id.*
43 *Global Information Technology Report 2016: Networked Readiness Index*, WORLD ECONOMIC FORUM https://reports.weforum.org/global-information-technology-report-2016/networked-readiness-index/ (last accessed on Dec. 6, 2020).
44 Joyce Sambira, *Burundi's Push for Universal Education*, UNITED NATIONS AFRICA RENEWAL, www.un.org/africarenewal/web-features/burundi%E2%80%99s-push-universal-education (last accessed on Dec. 6, 2020).
45 *The Performance of Education Systems in Francophone Sub-Saharan Africa*, PASEC (2015), www.pasec.confemen.org/wp-content/uploads/2015/12/RE_Pasec2014_GB_web21.pdf.
46 Sajitha Bashiret et al., *Facing Forward: Schooling for Learning in Africa*, THE WORLD BANK (2018), https://openknowledge.worldbank.org/bitstream/handle/10986/29377/9781464812606.pdf?sequence=14&isAllowed=y.
47 Burundi at a Glance, *supra* note 42.
48 The Performance of Education Systems in Francophone Sub-Saharan Africa, *supra* note 46.

and student-friendly approach.[49] What has made the most difference, however, is a fairly consistent and comprehensive education policy with a focus on universal education and its quality.[50] The Ministry of Education accepted the recommendations of an international team of educational experts, included educational goals into its National Plan, and initiated much needed reforms.[51]

Burundi still faces enormous challenges. Many students perform poorly on tests and consequently are held back, often repeatedly. Dropout rates, especially among teenagers, remain a serious problem. Girls, when they reach puberty, are more likely to drop out than boys because of the lack of gender-based bathrooms, early marriages, and pregnancies. Closer to the borders with Tanzania, boys are more likely to drop out as they seek lucrative jobs across the border. Poor infrastructure often leads to a long commute to school. Nevertheless, Burundi's ambitious efforts to revamp the failing educational system has been bearing fruit and thus sets a model that other countries in the region can emulate.

Missing the Mark on Equity

Achieving equitable education that leaves no one behind is at the core of SDG 4. Unfortunately, the world is not on track to meet this goal. Primary school-age girls face a disadvantage in most regions, with the exception of Europe, Northern America, Latin America and the Caribbean. The widest gender disparities at the primary level are observed in Central Asia.[52] In 2018, no region had achieved gender parity among children of primary school age, and there is evidence that 15 million girls of primary school age will never get the chance to learn to read or write in primary school compared to 10 million boys.[53]

For lower secondary out-of-school rates, the widest gender disparity is observed in Central Asia, where there are 137 female adolescents out of school for every 100 male adolescents not in school. Regional variation is much larger at the upper secondary level. In sub-Saharan Africa, adolescent girls (48.1%) are more likely to be out of school than adolescent boys (43.6%). In Northern Africa and Western Asia, 25.7% of girls are out of school compared to 21.7% of boys.[54]

For parity in literacy, data show that in Central Asia, Europe, and Northern America, Eastern and South-Eastern Asia, and Latin America and the Caribbean, there is no or little difference between male and female adult literacy rates. On the other hand, there are relatively large gender gaps in Northern Africa and Western Asia, Southern Asia, and sub-Saharan Africa. Additionally, there are large age variations. While gender disparities in literacy skills among youths are generally smaller and improving more quickly over time, almost 90% of women aged 15 to 24 years globally had basic literacy skills in 2016, compared with only 73% of women from the older cohort. Improvements in female youth literacy are

---

49 Bashiret, *supra* note 47.
50 *Id.*
51 J. Greenland, *The Reform of Education in Burundi: Enlightened Theory Faced with Political Reality*, 10 Comparative Education 57–63 (1974), https://doi.org/10.1080/0305006740100107.
52 UNESCO Literacy Rates Continue to Rise, *supra* note 37.
53 *Turning Promises into Action: Gender Equality in the 2030 Agenda for Sustainable Development*, UN Women (2018), www.unwomen.org/-/media/headquarters/attachments/sections/library/publicati ons/2018/sdg-report-summary-gender-equality-in-the-2030-agenda-for-sustainable-development -2018-en.pdf?la=en&vs=949 [hereinafter "UN Women (2018)"].
54 *Id.*

significantly greater than for young men in all regions of the world, except in Central Asia and Europe and Northern America, where parity in youth literacy was reached about 50 years ago.[55]

The causes for such a persistent gender gap in education are complex and are often a result of broader gender inequality that is embedded in a given culture. In some countries, girls are discriminated against both by their families and society at large. When this is the case, parents tend to invest less in their daughters' education. Additionally, in developing and LDCs, girls and women are more likely to face "time poverty" due to multiple domestic work burdens that fall disproportionally on their shoulders. This curtails their opportunities for education and decent employment.[56]

Besides the gender gap, there are other disparities that stem from income and rural/urban inequalities and that raise serious concerns. There are severe differences in educational attainment between poor and better-off children within countries and between countries, but this gap is particularly large in the sub-Saharan African region that suffers from extreme poverty.[57] In many low- and middle-income countries, rural students have, at best, around half the chance of their urban peers to complete upper secondary, and often much less than that.[58] Children with disabilities are most vulnerable in these countries. In Sierra Leone, for example, children with walking difficulties were three times as likely not to attend school as those without such difficulty.[59]

Children living in slums, where at least 800 million people reside worldwide,[60] are also among the most vulnerable because slum dwellers are more likely to be evicted or relocated. A study of those displaced by the Sabarmati River Front Project, an urban project in Ahmedabad, India, found that about 18% of relocated students dropped out and 11% had lower attendance, mostly because they had difficulty commuting to their schools.[61] Children of displaced parents, refugees, and undocumented migrants are more likely to have the lowest educational attainments, though global and regional indicators on these groups are virtually nonexistent.[62] In some countries, constitutions and laws limit the right to education to citizens.[63] In others, laws that more explicitly deny rights for undocumented migrants may undermine a constitutional right to education.[64] Migrants and refugees face multiple challenges, from lack of academic counseling to lack of financial support (see the case study

---

55 UNESCO Literacy Rates Continue to Rise, *supra* note 37.
56 *Progress of the World's Women 2019–2020: Families in a Changing World*, UN WOMEN (2019) www.unwomen.org/-/media/headquarters/attachments/sections/library/publications/2019/progress-of-the-worlds-women-2019-2020-en.pdf?la=en&vs=3512.
57 UN Women (2018), *supra* note 54.
58 UNESCO Target 4.1 Report, *supra* note 23.
59 *Sierra Leone Multiple Indicator Cluster Survey 2017*: Survey Findings Report, UNICEF (2017), www.statistics.sl/images/StatisticsSL/Documents/sierra_leone_mics6_2017_report.pdf.
60 *Urbanization and Development: Emerging Futures*, UN-HABITAT (2016), https://unhabitat.org/sites/default/files/download-manager-files/WCR-2016-WEB.pdf.
61 Tanvi Bhatkal et al., *Towards a Better Life? A Cautionary Tale of Progress in Ahmedabad*, OVERSEAS DEVELOPMENT INSTITUTE (2015), www.odi.org/publications/9621-towards-better-life-cautionary-tale-progress-ahmedabad.
62 *EU Regional Trust Fund in Response to the Syrian Crisis*, European Commission (Dec. 2018) [hereinafter "EU Regional Trust Fund (Response to Syria)"].
63 UNESCO Target 4.1 Report, *supra* note 23.
64 *Id.*

below).⁶⁵ The "Leaving no one behind" principle at the core of SDG 4 implies that broader political and societal changes, especially the ones dealing with human rights, immigration policies, and social protection are needed so most vulnerable demographic groups can gain access to quality education.

Working toward More Equitable Education: The case of China

With about 260 million students and about 514,000 schools (excluding higher education institutions), China has the largest education system in the world. It provides diversified education services for people of various ages, education levels, and income levels. Yet the system fosters different types of inequalities. For instance, to qualify for Chinese tertiary education, students need high scores on a competitive university entrance examination, the *gaokao*. Candidates from wealthier households start preparing since pre-school years and have access to private tutoring, expensive after-school programs, and secondary school education abroad. In 2015, more than 43,000 Chinese students were enrolled in US secondary schools, and they had a large presence in Australia, Canada, and the United Kingdom.⁶⁶ Thus, they are more likely to get into highly ranked domestic universities or foreign universities than their less fortunate peers.

Another major education gap in China is a result of the administrative, economic, and social divides between rural and urban areas. One of the main drivers of China's phenomenal economic growth during the past several decades is the large-scale rural-to-urban migration.⁶⁷ As a result of this "greatest migration in human history," more than half of China's almost 1.4 billion people now live in cities, as compared to only 20% in the early 1980s.⁶⁸ A core aspect of the challenges migrants face is found in China's *hukou* household registration system,⁶⁹ which classifies China's citizens as either rural or urban residents. This system ensures that rural-to-urban migration is under control and only takes place to meet the growing demand for labor in urban areas. It is nearly impossible for rural *hukou* holders to acquire urban residence rights.⁷⁰ This often excludes them from full access to pension, health care, social benefits, and above all, education.

Children who remain in rural areas, while their parents leave to work in cities, are known as "left-behind children." As most of their rural counterparts, they have limited access to quality education and may suffer from anxiety and mental disorders due to long-term separation.⁷¹ This is why, despite the challenges they face in the urban centers, an increasing

---

65 EU Regional Trust Fund (Response to Syria), *supra* note 63.
66 Christine Farrugia, *Charting New Pathways to Higher Education: International Secondary Students in the United States*, INSTITUTE OF INT'L CENTER FOR ACADEMIC MOBILITY RESEARCH (July 2014).
67 Yuanyuan Chen & Shuaizhang Feng, *Access to Public Schools and the Education of Migrant Children in China*, 26 CHINA ECONOMIC REVIEW (Jan. 2012), 10.1016/j.chieco.2013.04.007; BARRY NAUGHTON, THE CHINESE ECONOMY: TRANSITIONS AND GROWTH (MIT Press 2007).
68 C. Textor, *Urban and Rural Population of China 2009-2019*, STATISTA (Nov. 20, 2020) https://www.statista.com/statistics/278566/urban-and-rural-population-of-china.
69 BARRY NAUGHTON, THE CHINESE ECONOMY: TRANSITIONS AND GROWTH (MIT Press 2006).
70 John Knight & Sai Ding, *China's Remarkable Economic Growth*, JOURNAL OF CHINESE POLITICAL SCIENCE (Dec. 2015), 10.1007/s11366-015-9380-0.
71 Kara Liu, *No Child Left Behind: Deficiencies in the Education of China's Migrant Children*, CHINA HANDS (Dec 1, 2019), https://chinahandsmagazine.org/2019/12/01/no-child-left-behind-deficiencies-in-the-education-of-chinas-migrant-children/.

number of migrants have begun bringing their children to the cities.[72] These children are China's so-called migrant children. Together, these "children of migrants" comprised nearly 40% of all children in China in 2015.[73]

China's central government mandated local authorities provide basic education to migrant children; yet urban public schools have been unable to accommodate the growing number of migrant children. As a result, some of these children are pushed into privately operated migrant schools.[74] In Beijing alone, there are over 250 of such schools, all privately owned and operated for profit. Because these schools are not funded by the government, they have poor conditions, inadequate resources, and under-qualified teachers.[75] Studies show that the low quality of school resources and teachers in migrant schools have reduced the academic progress of the migrant students. Students' academic performance also diminishes the longer students stay in migrant schools.[76]

In the past several years, numerous international organizations have worked with the Chinese government to improve conditions for these migrant children. UNICEF, for example, has started a pilot program to improve migrant children's access to education and healthcare in Beijing and Shanghai.[77] Yet, there is still much to be done, especially in the area of educational infrastructures (to absorb a large body of students) and the regulation of privately owned profit-seeking schools (to make the learning environment more inclusive and equitable).

Missing the Mark on Qualified Teachers

According to the Target 4.C, developing countries, and especially LDCs and SIDs should see a substantial increase in the supply of qualified teachers by 2030 through international cooperation on teacher training in developing countries. Unfortunately, there has been little progress toward this goal globally. In fact, according to the 2019 SDG Report, the percentage of trained primary school teachers has been stagnating at about 85% since 2015.[78] In Southern Asia, 72% of primary teachers were trained in 2018 compared to 78% in 2013.[79]

The situation is particularly alarming in sub-Saharan Africa, where too many schools lack the very basic elements of a good quality education: (1) trained teachers and (2) adequate facilities. Only 64% of primary and 50% of secondary school teachers were trained in 2018–17, compared to 71% and 79%, respectively, in 2005. One of the reasons for such a dire situation in this region deals with demographic trends. The rising demand for education

---

72 Shu Zhou & Monit Cheung, *Hukou System Effects on Migrant Children's Education in China: Learning from Past Disparities*, INTERNATIONAL SOCIAL WORK (2017), https://doi.org/10.1177/0020872817725134.
73 Liu, *supra* note 72.
74 Chen, *supra* note 68.
75 Lisa Yiu & Luo Yun, *China's Rural Education: Chinese Migrant Children and Left-Behind Children*, 50 CHINESE EDUCATION & SOCIETY 307–14, (Dec. 2017), https://doi.org/10.1080/10611932.2017.1382128.
76 Fang Lai et al., *The Education of China's Migrant Children: The Missing Link in China's Education System*, 37 INT'L J OF EDUCATIONAL DEV. 68–77 (2014).
77 Liu, *supra* note 72.
78 *Ensure Inclusive and Equitable Quality Education and Promote Lifelong Learning Opportunities for All*, UNITED NATIONS, https://sustainabledevelopment.un.org/sdg4.
79 *World Teachers' Day 2019 Fact Sheet*, UNESCO Institute of Statistics (Oct. 5, 2019), http://uis.unesco.org/sites/default/files/documents/world-teachers-day-2019-fact-sheet.pdf.

from a growing school-age population presses countries to hire teachers, often unqualified, on a contractual basis.[80] Teachers' absenteeism is rampant, and there is often minimal effort in educating children, especially in the poorest areas.[81]

Even trained and qualified teachers may not be able to deliver quality education where there is a critical shortage or absence of resources. Teachers need decent classroom conditions, and in many low-income countries, this means having textbooks and access to the internet, and also blackboards, desks, and electricity. In sub-Saharan Africa, only 34% of primary schools had access to electricity in 2018–2017. Forty-five percent of the world's primary schools had access to computers for pedagogical purposes in 2017. This was the case for 66% or less of schools in Eastern and South-Eastern Asia, Latin America and the Caribbean, Northern Africa, and Oceania in 2018.[82]

The solution to meeting Target 4.c is government investment in qualified teachers. Many developing and LDCs are unable to cover the cost of qualified teachers, and teachers are severely underpaid. Therefore, the governments in these countries have to provide a stable and robust incentive structure and certification system that can be strictly enforced. In high-income countries, all teachers must receive the required certification. This is often not the case in developing, LDCs, and SIDSs.[83] Lack of training has a negative effect on education quality and hinders the progress toward the achievement of all other targets of SDG 4.

One Step Forward, Two Steps Backward: The Case of Mexico

Whether or not students receive inclusive and equitable quality education depends on how a nation's educational system is designed and financed. Because public benefits of education exceed private benefits (the concept that is associated with positive externalities), the architecture of educational systems in most countries, and especially in developing and LDCs is typically government's responsibility. The wrong kinds of government policies may lead to distortions in the education system or reverse the progress that has been achieved thus far. This is exactly what has happened in Mexico. Since 1997, when Santiago Levy, a development economist, led the design and introduction of the innovative federal program, Progresa/Oportunidades, Mexico has been desperately trying to improve its education system as part of the integrated poverty program.[84] Under this program, participating families were given different incentives, such as grants for school supplies, food subsidies, conditional monthly cash payments, etc. Although the program has sometimes been criticized for its "top down" approach, it has effectively impacted enrollment and performance per dollar spent.

In 2017, Mexico's Secretariat of Public Education released the New Educational Model, with implementation starting in 2018/2019. The model envisioned reforms in the national education system around five pillars: (1) curriculum; (2) schools; (3) inclusion and equity;

---

80 Silvia Montoya & Manos Antoninis, *"Business as Usual" Will Not Achieve Global Education Goals*, WORLD ECONOMIC FORUM (Jul. 9, 2019), www.weforum.org/agenda/2019/07/business-as-usual-will-not-achieve-the-global-education-goals/.
81 GERALD ROLAND, DEVELOPMENTAL ECONOMICS (PEARSON Series 2014).
82 *Id.*
83 *Id.*
84 SANTIAGO LEVY, PROGRESS AGAINST POVERTY: SUSTAINING MEXICO'S PROGRESA-OPORTUNIDADES PROGRAM (Brookings Institution Press 2007).

(4) governance of the education system; and (5) teacher training and professional development.[85] The latter one was a serious challenge because for decades, the powerful teachers' union, has virtually had a monopoly on education. Before the reforms, the union had controlled the hiring process, so teaching positions and promotions were often made on the basis of union participation, not performance. Lack of monitoring and government supervision allowed teachers to transfer their positions at will to almost anyone they chose. According to the 2014 census, there were almost 40,000 unaccounted teachers who were paid from the federal budget.[86] The reform was supposed to make a radical change and make teachers more accountable and student-oriented and improve the country's education system and students' learning outcomes that had been lagging by global standards. However, Mexico's 15-year-olds' scores on the PISA test, which measures proficiency in science, reading, and math, lag far behind some of the European countries (like Bulgaria and Romania), where education expenditures per student are similar to those in Mexico. Even compared to its neighbors in Latin America, Mexico scores are only slightly better than those of Colombia, where per-student spending is 45% lower.[87]

On May 8, 2019, the school reform was scrapped by the new President, Lopez Obrador, much to the pleasure of the union leaders. Yet the short-lived program[88] did leave a mark. A study published in 2019 by the Development Bank of Latin America found that teachers hired on merit not only had better high-school grades than union-picked ones, but they also helped their pupils learn faster.[89] The next round of PISA tests may not see any improvement, however. It may take more than just one round of hiring qualified teachers, which depends on the government's commitment to quality education and the boldness of its actions, to make this commitment a reality.

The Great Reversal: The Effect of COVID-19 on the Achievement of the SDG 4

Historically, wars, civil conflicts, famines, and natural disasters have disrupted education in regions affected by these events. None of them have probably endured the scale and magnitude of the ongoing coronavirus (COVID-19) pandemic. The virus, that started in December 2019 in China and over the next several months (to date), has spread around the entire world and led to mass lockdowns, bans on commercial activities, and travel restrictions. The resulting immense economic shock threw hundreds of millions of workers out of their jobs, back into destitution. Although the final numbers are yet to be seen, preliminary estimates show that the number of extremely poor people could increase by 420 million, which would virtually eliminate all the gains in the fight against poverty made during the last

---

85 Carlos Iván Moreno Arellano, *The Educational Reform in Mexico and Some Public Policy Lessons*, 1 LATIN AMERICAN REVIEW 40–56 (2017), http://iippg.cucea.udg.mx/sites/default/files/Journal_N%C3%BAmero%2005_con%20portada.pdf.
86 *Id*.
87 *Mexico's Crucial Education Reform Risks Being Unwound*, THE ECONOMIST, (May 31, 2018), www.economist.com/the-americas/2018/05/31/mexicos-crucial-education-reform-risks-being-unwound.
88 *Note*: Just 171,000 teachers, less than 10% of the total, were hired on merit and 36,000 head teachers and supervisors were promoted on ability rather than loyalty to union bosses.
89 *In Mexico, AMLO Seeks to Expel Merit from Schools*, THE ECONOMIST (May 2019), www.economist.com/the-americas/2019/05/18/in-mexico-amlo-seeks-to-expel-merit-from-schools.

decade.[90] Among those who are severely impacted by the outbreak are about 1.57 billion children (90% of all students) who have been barred from their classrooms.[91] What is the expected effect of this massive "lost learning"?

In the developed world, where a three-month hiatus from education usually leads to 20%–50% loss of skills that the children gained over the school year, the education pause will most likely lead to a slowdown in development, especially in critical thinking, perseverance, and self-control.[92] In developing countries and LDCs, both the demand for and supply of child labor will increase. Children, especially those of the secondary school age are more likely to go to work to support their cash-strapped families. Employers may want to hire cheap young labor to cut down their costs. Experiences with the Ebola outbreak in West Africa, about 6 years ago, showed that when schools reopened after the 9-month quarantine, many students did not return. Many adolescent girls were banned from schools due to their pregnancies.[93] The COVID-19 pandemic may produce similar, if not worse, dynamics.

It is expected that the long-term consequences of this pandemic in low- and middle-income countries will actually be more calamitous than the effects of Ebola in West Africa.[94] School closures and interrupted education all over the world will affect the future productivity of today's youth and doom them to earn less in the future. In well-off families, such depreciation of human capital may not be as drastic since well-educated parents are more likely to do home schooling. Additionally, rich countries are more technologically equipped to provide distance learning (though younger children may not learn as much, especially if left unsupervised). In fact, nearly nine in ten rich countries affected by COVID-19 school closures have been able to provide some form of distance learning, compared to only one in four low-income countries.[95]

Lessons Learned and Conclusions

The global and regional assessment of the progress toward SDG 4 reveals a critical truth about the global education crisis. Recent data reveal low proficiency rates in reading and mathematics, stalled progress in reaching out-of-school children, and remaining illiteracy. Additionally, many schools around the world lack the basic elements of a good quality of education—qualified teachers and adequate school supplies. Although remarkable progress in primary and secondary school enrollment and literacy rates has been made in the second half of the 20th century, critical issues in educational achievements on regional and country-specific levels make it improbable that the world will attain the targets of SDG 4 in ten years, as it is envisioned by the UN's 2030 Agenda.

The crisis is most severe in the regions and countries that have been disadvantaged in all areas of economic and social life. The educational gap is significant between the poor and their better-off counterparts, both within and between countries. Among all the regions,

---

90 *Closing Schools for Covid-19 Does Lifelong Harm and Widens Inequality*, THE ECONOMIST (Apr. 30, 2020) [hereinafter "Economist, Closing Schools"].
91 *See The Sustainable Development Goals Report*, UNITED NATIONS (2020) [hereinafter "2020 SDG Report"], https://unstats.un.org/sdgs/report/2020/The-Sustainable-Development-Goals-Report-2020.pdf.
92 *The Experience of Ebola: Lessons Learned*, THE ECONOMIST (May 2, 2020), www.economist.com/international/2020/04/30/school-closures-lessons-from-the-ebola-pandemic.
93 *Id.*
94 *Id.*
95 Economist, Closing Schools, *supra* note 91.

sub-Saharan Africa is the farthest from reaching SDG 4. Poverty creates severe constraints for families to invest in education, and this lack of educational investment among the poor perpetuates poverty and social inequality. Those living in slums suffer the most. Cultural and social barriers contribute to females' exclusion, often from their birth. The educational attainments in rural areas are lagging behind urban areas. Children of migrant workers and refuges, as well as children with disabilities, are most vulnerable. The ongoing COVID-19 pandemic has further exacerbated the gaps and posed new challenges.

Education-based issues are too large and much too complex to be solved by cash programs and educational subsidies, which, though important, make only a marginal difference. Trained teachers, remedial programs for children, early childhood programs, and free school meals are necessary but not sufficient conditions for ensuring *inclusive and equitable quality education* and *life-long learning opportunities for all*. The global education crisis demands government action and a coordinated international response. It also calls for greater recognition by *all* countries that free, equitable, quality education is a pathway to prosperity and sustainable development. Developed countries that have achieved substantial progress in educational attainments in the last century, can show stronger commitment to raising their gains and sharing their knowledge and educational technology and resources with less developed countries. Just the same way as the Ebola outbreak in West Africa in 2014–2015 highlighted the flaws in West African education systems,[96] the COVID-19 pandemic may become a catalyst for galvanizing efforts in developing and LDCs to improve their schooling in the future. But given the depth and the breadth of the pandemic, as well as the pre-outbreak trends in educational attainment, these positive changes may not materialize soon enough to meet the SDG 4 by 2030.

Actions Needed

Much needs to be done to improve education in developing and LDCs, eliminate the inefficiencies of education systems in developed ones, and reduce the education gaps within and between countries. We propose some urgent actions that must be taken to get on track toward achieving the UN's 2030 Agenda:

- **More precise measurement for some targets of SDG 4**: Real progress in learning can be hidden by enrollment and a narrow focus on students achieving a minimum proficiency level. While the current definition of indicator 4.1.1 provides a clear measure of progress toward the learning outcomes dimension of the target, it omits the completion dimension.
- **Foster building stronger technical capacity to improve the current education data**, particularly the capacity to drive innovation within individual countries allowing them to adapt and innovate practices at the regional or global level—A weak technical capacity in a country exposes national assessment systems to political interference. Country-level capacity building would benefit if a broader list of competences were included.
- **Promote an inclusion of education rights in all national constitutions**: In some countries, laws that more explicitly deny rights for undocumented migrants may undermine a constitutional right to education.[97]

---

96 Economist, Closing Schools, *supra* note 91.
97 UNESCO Target 4.1 Report, *supra* note 23.

- **Ensure that governments and formal-sector public and private educational institutions maintain quality of education through strictly enforced teachers' certification**: Greater investment is needed for the training and recruitment of teachers, in addition to new pedagogical approaches to support quality education. In developed countries, all teachers receive the required certification. This is often not the case in developing and LDCs. Developed countries can help developing and LDCs build capacity for the training and re-training of teachers and the establishment of merit standards for hiring and promotions.
- **Encourage the inclusion of SDG 4 in national plans**: Low proficiency levels, illiteracy, and low school enrollment and school completion rates often are not isolated problems but rather outcomes of broader development issues, such as poverty, lack of employment opportunities, and stagnant economic growth and thus have to be addressed simultaneously with those issues.
- **Patching pavement** is a temporary solution to roads that would benefit the most from being replaced with new asphalt. The same analogy can be applied to the issues in some LDCs, where cash transfers and free training for existing teachers may only have short-term, marginal effects. There is often a need to overhaul the flawed education systems, but this requires governments' commitment, consistency, and time.

12 Environmental Education

LYE Lin-Heng

Introduction

The 17 Sustainable Development Goals (SDGs) were adopted by the United Nations (UN) General Assembly in September 2015. They built on the eight Millennium Development Goals (MDGs) signed by 189 countries at the UN Millennium Summit in September 2000 "to secure a sustainable, peaceful, prosperous and equitable life on earth for everyone now and in the future."[1] Its foremost aspiration was to "Leave no one behind."[2]

While the MDGs[3] were aimed at developing countries, to eradicate extreme poverty, hunger, and disease by 2015, the SDGs are an urgent call for action by all countries—developed and developing—in a global partnership for a sustainable world. The SDGs recognize that ending poverty and other deprivations must be integrated with strategies that improve health and education, reduce inequality, provide job opportunities, and facilitate economic growth while preserving our forests and oceans and tackling climate change.[4] A holistic approach must be taken, and many synergies can be found in the 17 goals. The timeline for achieving these goals is 2030. SDG 4, with its focus on education, is a clear recognition by the global community that education is a powerful driver for sustainable development.[5]

This chapter seeks to analyze the implementation of SDG 4 in the year 2020, ten years before this 2030 deadline. SDG 4 states: "Quality Education—Ensure inclusive

---

1 *See Education for Sustainable Development Goals*—LEARNING OBJECTIVES, UNESCO 6 (2017), www.unesco.de/sites/default/files/2018- 08/unesco_education_for_sustainable_development_goals.pdf (Education for SDGs).
2 *See generally* Committee for Dev. Pol'y, *Leaving No One Behind*, UNITED NATIONS (2018) https://sustainabledevelopment.un.org/content/documents/2754713_July_PM_2._Leaving_no_one_behind_Summary_from_UN_Committee_for_Development_Policy.pdf.
3 The eight MDGs were (1) Eradicate extreme poverty and hunger; (2) Achieve universal primary education; (3) Promote gender equality and empower women; (4) Reduce child mortality; (5) Improve maternal health; (6) Combat HIV/AIDs, malaria, and other diseases; (7) Ensure environmental sustainability; and (8) Global partnership for development. *See 2013: MDG Acceleration and Beyond 2015, We can End Poverty: Millennium Development Goals and Beyond 2015*, UNITED NATIONS, www.un.org/millenniumgoals/bkgd.shtml (last visited Dec. 6, 2020).
4 *See The 17 Goals*, Dep. of Econ. and Soc. Affairs: Sustainable Development, UNITED NATIONS, https://sdgs.un.org/goals (last visited Dec. 6, 2020).
5 "Education is key to the global integrated framework of sustainable development goals. Education is at the heart of our efforts both to adapt to change and to transform the world within which we live." *See* Irina Bokova, *Foreword*, *in* RETHINKING EDUCATION: TOWARDS A GLOBAL COMMON GOOD?, UNESCO 3 (2015).

and equitable quality education and promote lifelong learning opportunities for all." It focuses on Environmental Education (EE) in particular, and its evolution into Education for Sustainable Development (ESD). It will look at some examples of ESD implementation in various parts of the world and will make recommendations as to how its implementation, both globally and nationally, may be strengthened.

Environmental Education—Meaning, History, and Evolution

Environmental education in the twentieth century appears to have been first conceptualized in 1969 by a group of scholars in the School of Natural Resources, University of Michigan. Their paper entitled "The Concept of Environmental Education"[6] asserted that "There is a vital need for an educational approach that effectively educates man regarding his relationship to the total environment," and called for environmental education to "reach citizens of all ages." It declared that "Environmental education is aimed at producing a citizenry that is knowledgeable concerning the biophysical environment and its associated problems, aware of how to solve these problems and motivated to work toward their solutions."[7] It emphasized that education for conservation of the environment must be transformed to community-based environmental education.

At the global level, the environment first appeared in the education agenda at the Stockholm Conference on the Human Environment in 1972. Principle 19 of the *Stockholm Declaration on the Human Environment* (1972) declared that

> Education in environmental matters, for the younger generation as well as adults, giving due consideration to the underprivileged, is essential in order to broaden the basis for an enlightened opinion and responsible conduct by individuals, enterprises and communities in protecting and improving the environment in its full human dimension. It is also essential that mass media of communications avoid contributing to the deterioration of the environment, but, on the contrary, disseminates information of an educational nature on the need to project and improve the environment in order to enable man to develop in every respect.[8]

Recommendation 96 of the Conference Report[9] called on the UN Educational, Scientific and Cultural Organization (UNESCO) and other international agencies to

> take the necessary steps to establish an international programme in environmental education, interdisciplinary in approach, in-school and out-of-school, encompassing all levels of education and directed towards the general public, in particular the ordinary citizen living in rural and urban areas, youth and adult alike, with a view to educating him as to the simple steps he might take, within his means, to manage and control his environment.

---

6 William B. Stapp et. al, *The Concept of Environmental Education*, 1(1) THE J. OF ENVTL. EDU. 30-31, (1969).
7 *Id.*
8 Stockholm Declaration on the Human Environment, UNEP, 21st plenary mtg., at principle 16 (Jun. 16, 1972).
9 *See Report of the UN Conference on the Human Environment*, A/CONF.48/14/Rev.1, UNEP, (Jun. 5–16, 1972).

Three years later, the *Belgrade Charter: A Framework for Environmental Education* (UNESCO, 1975)[10] called for a new global ethic, listing six objectives of environmental education: Awareness; knowledge; attitude; skills; evaluation ability; and participation.

In 1977, the Tbilisi Declaration[11] emphasized that Environmental Education should constitute a comprehensive lifelong education for all persons, to prepare the individual for life through a holistic understanding of the major problems of the contemporary world, including its biological, physical, social, economic, cultural, and ethical aspects. Thus, environmental education seeks to create new patterns of responsible behavior of individuals, groups, and society as a whole, toward the environment.

Environmental educators led by UNESCO and the United Nations Environment Program (UNEP) implemented the International Environmental Education Program in 1975. The UNESCO-UNEP program does not call for environmental education to be made a specific subject. Rather, it seeks to integrate and co-relate environmental education within existing educational systems and programs. Educators who attended these international meetings sought to implement EE in their home countries. Developed economies also emphasized a need for understanding the political process so that individuals can push politicians, government agencies, and corporations to make the right decisions in the context of the environment.[12]

A useful and aspirational guide is found in the 2011 *Treaty on Environmental Education for Sustainable Societies and Global Responsibility*, drafted in preparation for the Rio+10 Summit.[13] It contains 65 principles, which emphasize *inter alia* that environmental education must be holistic and inter-disciplinary, must recognize, respect, reflect, and utilize indigenous history and local culture, develop an ethical awareness of all forms of life, respect all life cycles, and impose limits on humans' exploitation of other life forms. It calls for the media to be one of the main channels of education, and for the creation of interdisciplinary centers for the environment in each university.

In the context of the use of the media for environmental education, mention must be made of India and the very laudable judgments by India's Supreme Court, in advancing environmental education and in protecting the environment.[14] India started its Center for

---

10 *The Belgrade Charter: a Framework for Environmental Education*, UNEP (Oct. 22, 1975), https://unesdoc.unesco.org/ark:/48223/pf0000017772.
11 *First International Conference on Environmental Education*, ED/MD/49 UNEP (Apr. 1978), https://unesdoc.unesco.org/ark:/48223/pf0000032763.
12 *See What is Environmental Education?*, UNITED STATES ENVIRONMENTAL PROTECTION AGENCY, www.epa.gov/education/what-environmental-education (last visited Dec. 6, 2020) (emphasizing "skills to identify and help resolve environmental challenges, and participation in activities that lead to the resolution of environmental challenges"); EVERY STUDENT SUCCEEDS ACT (ESSA), 20 U.S.C. ch. 28 § 1001 et seq. (Dec. 10, 2015) (Provides funding for environmental education as an enrichment activity that supports a 'well rounded education' and student health and safety programs, as well as environmental literacy programs and STEM (Science, Technology, Engineering and Mathematics) activities).
13 *Treaty on Environmental Education for Sustainable Societies and Global Responsibility*, RIO+20 Portal: Building the Peoples Summit Rio+20, (August 1, 2011), http://rio20.net/en/documentos/treaty-on-environmental-education-for-sustainable-societies-and-global-responsibility/.
14 *See* Sylvia Almeida & Amy Cutter-Mackenzie, *The Historical, Present and Future-ness of Environmental Education in India*, 27(1) AUSTRALIAN J. OF ENVTL. EDU 122–33 (2011); *see also Environmental Education*, INDIAN INST. OF ECOL. AND ENV'T, www.ecology.edu/environmentaleducation.html (last visited Dec. 6, 2020).

Environmental Education in 1984. In the 1991 decision of *MC Mehta v. Union of India*,[15] the Supreme Court, convinced by the petitioner MC Mehta (an environmental lawyer) of the importance of public education on the environment, ordered that as from February 1, 1992, all cinema halls, touring cinemas, and video parlors must exhibit at least two slides/messages on the environment in each show. The Ministry of Information and Broadcasting was also ordered to start producing documentaries on various aspects of the environment and pollution, and one such film should be shown, as far as practicable, in each cinema venue, each day. There must also be daily radio programs of five to seven minutes on the environment and once a week, a longer program.

Education for Sustainable Development (ESD)

The concept of sustainable development came to the forefront in 1987 with the World Commission on Environment and Development's Report entitled *Our Common Future*,[16] commonly known as "The Brundtland Report." This defines sustainable development as "development that meets the needs of the present without compromising the ability of future generations to meet their own needs."[17] Following the Brundtland Report, there was a slow but perceptible shift in environmental education, from a focus on the environment to a focus on sustainable development.[18]

In 1992, at the Earth Summit in Rio de Janeiro, *Agenda 21*, a non-binding Action Plan for the Earth, was introduced.[19] It contained very detailed statements on education. Chapter 36—*Promoting Education, Public Awareness and Training* has 26 paragraphs on education, focusing on three areas:

(1) Re-orienting education toward sustainable development.
(2) Increasing public awareness.
(3) Promoting training.

Paragraph 36(3) cogently expresses the aims and methods of education for sustainable development, emphasizing that both formal and informal forms of education are important and that ethical values and awareness are needed, together with the need for public participation.[20]

---

15 *M.C. Mehta v. Union of India*, WP 860/1991 (1991) (Environmental Education Case), ELAW, https://elaw.org/content/india-mc-mehta-v-union-india-wp-8601991-19911122-environmental-education-case.
16 *Report of the World Commission on Environment and Development: Our Common Future*, (1987), https://sustainabledevelopment.un.org/content/documents/5987our-common-future.pdf.
17 *Id.* at 17.
18 Jo-Ann Ferrera et al., *Learning to Embed Sustainability in Teacher Education (2019)*, Springer Briefs in Education, 12 (2019).
19 Earth Summit: Agenda 21, *UN Conference on Environment and Development* (Jun. 3–14, 1992), https://sustainabledevelopment.un.org/outcomedocuments/agenda21.
20 *Id.* at ¶ 36.3. "36.3. Education, including formal education, public awareness and training should be recognized as a process by which human beings and societies can reach their fullest potential. Education is critical for promoting sustainable development and improving the capacity of the people to address environment and development issues. While basic education provides the underpinning for any environmental and development education, the latter needs to be incorporated as an essential part of learning. Both formal and non-formal education are indispensable to changing people's attitudes so that they have

Sustainable Development Goal 4.7

It is clear that the 17 SDGs can only be achieved if all countries ensure that the education of its population is linked with education on environmental sustainability. Thus, SDG 4.7 reads:

> Ensure that all learners acquire the knowledge and skills needed to promote sustainable development, including, among others, through education for sustainable development and sustainable lifestyles, human rights, gender equality, promotion of a culture of peace and nonviolence, global citizenship and appreciation of cultural diversity and of culture's contribution to sustainable development.[21]

UNEP implemented a Global Action Plan on Sustainable Development from 2015–2019. ESD is reinforced in the 2017 UNESCO Report *Education for Sustainable Development Goals–Learning Objectives*, which emphasized that "People must understand the complex world in which they live. They need to be able to collaborate, speak up and act for positive change."[22] Education for Sustainable Development seeks to help them develop "key competencies for sustainability."[23] Again, the Report emphasized that each nation must strive to address these issues. As each country seeks to implement ESD, much has been written on the many challenges.[24]

So, what then, is the difference between Environmental Education and Education for Sustainable Development? There is a continuing debate on this, but it can be said that ESD goes beyond a focus on the biophysical environment and its inter-connection with humans.[25]

---

the capacity to assess and address their sustainable development concerns. It is also critical for achieving environmental and ethical awareness, values and attitudes, skills and behaviour consistent with sustainable development and for effective public participation in decision-making. To be effective, environment and development education should deal with the dynamics of both the physical/biological and socio-economic environment and human (which may include spiritual) development, should be integrated in all disciplines, and should employ formal and non-formal methods and effective means of communication."

21 *Indicators and a Monitoring Framework—Target 4.7*, SUSTAINABLE DEVELOPMENT SOLUTIONS NETWORK (SDSN), https://indicators.report/targets/4-7/ (last visited Dec. 6, 2020).
22 Education for SDGs, *supra* note 2, at 10 ¶ 1.1.
23 *Id.*
24 These include J. Salmon, *Are We Building Environmental Literacy?*, 31(4) J. OF ENVTL. EDU. 4–10 (2000); Stewart J. Hudson, *Challenges for Environmental Education: Issues and Ideas for the 21st Century*, 51(4) BIOSCIENCE 283–88 (Apr. 1, 2001); David Grunewald, *A Foucauldian Analysis of Environmental Education: Toward the Socioecological Challenge of the Earth Charter*, in 34(1) CURRICULUM INQUIRY 71–107, (Mar. 2004); John C. Smyth, *Environment and Education: A View of a Changing Scene*, 1(1) ENVTL. EDU. RES. 3–20 (2005); D.T. Blumstein & C. Saylan, *The Failure of Environmental Education (and How We Can Fix It)* 5(5) PLOS BIOLOGY 973–77 (May 2007); R.B. Stevenson, *Schooling and Environmental Education: Contradictions in Purpose and Practice*, 13(2) ENVTL. EDU. RES. 139–53 (Apr. 2007); Arjen E. J. Wals et al., *Convergence Between Science and Environmental Education*, 344 SCIENCE (May 9, 2014).
25 *See eg.*, D. Tilbury, *Environmental Education for Sustainability: Defining the New Focus of Environmental Education in the 1990s*, 1(2) ENVTL. EDU. RES. (1995); M. Bonnett, *Education for Sustainable Development: A Coherent Philosophy for Environmental Education?*, 29(3) CAMBRIDGE J. OF EDU. 313–24 (1999); Bob Jickling & Arjen E. J. Wals, *Globalization and Environmental Education: Looking Beyond Sustainable Development*, 40(1) J. OF CURRICULUM STUD. 1–21 (2008), II. Kopnina, *Education for Sustainable Development (ESD): The Turn Away from "Environment" in Environmental Education?*, 2(5) ENVTL. EDU. RES. 699–717 (2012).

It seeks to improve the capacity of the people to address environment and development issues, enhance their awareness of environmental and ethical issues as well as develop their values, attitudes, skills, and behaviors so that they can play an effective role and make the right decisions in their work and in the way they live, to ensure a sustainable planet. Each nation will have to craft its education on the environment to ensure that it addresses the issues of sustainable development. It is best expressed in the Bonn Declaration (2009):

ESD helps to change societies to address different priorities and issues, *inter alia*, water, energy, climate change, disaster and risk deduction, loss of biodiversity, food crisis, health risks, social vulnerability, and insecurity. It is critical for the development of new economic thinking. ESD contributes to creating resilient, healthy, and sustainable societies through a systemic and integrated approach. It brings new relevance, quality, meaning, and purpose to education and training systems. It involves formal and informal education contexts, and all sectors of society in a lifelong learning process.[26]

Some examples of ESD projects and programs taken from around the world include the following:

(1) The Global Schools Program

This initiative was led by the UN Sustainable Development Solutions Network—Youth Initiative (*SDSN Youth*) in support of UNESCO's Global Action Program on Education for Sustainable Development (GAP-ESD).[27] The program provides the necessary tools and resources for schools and teachers to educate their students on the SDGs. In working with educators, the program aims to transform learning environments globally to empower students to prioritize sustainable development in their lifestyles, behaviors, education, and professional careers. Currently, the Global Schools Program is being conducted in North America, South America, Asia, Africa, Europe, the Middle East, and Australia with hundreds of schools participating.[28]

(2) Australia, New Zealand, the United Kingdom, and the United States

Various jurisdictions have started to promote sustainable or green schools. The United Kingdom has a *Green Schools* project.[29] Australia started its Australian Sustainable Schools Initiative.[30] This is a partnership of the Australian Government and the States and Territories that supports schools to develop a whole school approach to *Education for Sustainability* (EfS). This program encourages schools to be "sustainable schools," so as to embed sustainability within the culture of the school, as well as connect with other cultures, including aboriginal cultures. New Zealand has an Environmental Education for Sustainability Strategy

---

26 *Bonn Declaration on Education for Sustainable Development*, UNESCO World Conference on Education for Sustainable Development ¶ 7 (2009).
27 *Network of Schools*, GLOBAL SCHOOLS, www.globalschoolsprogram.org/current-schools.
28 *Id.*
29 GREEN SCHOOLS PROJECT, www.greenschoolsproject.org.uk/about-us/ (last visited Dec. 6, 2020); *see also* NATIONAL ASSOCIATION FOR ENVIRONMENTAL EDUCATION (NAEE), http://naee.org.uk/ (last visited Dec. 6, 2020).
30 This followed the Federal Government's 2009 National Action Plan for Education for Sustainability, *see Australian Sustainable Schools Initiative ACT* (AuSSI Act), CERES Education—Outreach Team (May 1, 2013), https://sustainability.ceres.org.au/resource/australian-sustainable-schools-initiative-act/.

and Action Plan 2017–2021[31] with a strong focus on understanding indigenous (Maori) culture and ethics on the environment. Green schools are just starting in New Zealand.[32]

In the United States, the National Association for Environmental Education (NAEE) was established in 1971 and later renamed the North American Association for Environmental Education (NAAEE), with members from the United States, Canada, and Mexico.[33] Environmental education is strongly supported by the Environmental Protection Agency (EPA), which was mandated by the National Environmental Education Act (1990) to provide national leadership to increase environmental literacy.[34] The EPA established the Office of Environmental Education to implement the National Environmental Education Training Program for teachers.[35] The United States also passed the Every Student Succeeds Act (2015) which provides funding for environmental education.[36]

(3) The Philippines

The Philippines is a developing country that has made considerable effort in environmental education. In 2008, the National Environmental Awareness and Education Act (2008)[37] was passed "to promote environmental awareness through environmental education." November of every year is "Environmental Awareness Month" throughout the Philippines. The Philippines also passed its Climate Change Act (2009) "mainstreaming climate change into government policy formulations."[38] Encouraged by these very supportive laws and policies, many environmental education programs and activities have been initiated

---

31 *See Environmental Education for Sustainability Mahere RautakiStrategy and Action Plan 2017–2021*, ENVIRONMENTAL EDUCATION FOR SUSTAINABILITY STRATEGY AND ACTION PLAN 2017–2021 (2017), www.doc.govt.nz/about-us/our-policies-and-plans/education-strategies/environmental-education-for-sustainability-strategy-and-action-plan/strategy-and-action-plan-20172021/. *See also Guidelines for Environmental Education in New Zealand Schools*, NZ CURRICULUM ONLINE, https://nzcurriculum.tki.org.nz/Curriculum-resources/Education-for-sustainability/Tools-and-resources/Guidelines-for-Environmental-Education-in-New-Zealand-Schools#collapsible4 (last visited Dec. 6, 2020).

32 Education Central, *Green School Is Coming to New Zealand*, EDUCATION CENTRAL: POKAPU MATAURANGA (Feb. 19, 2019), https://educationcentral.co.nz/green-school-is-coming-to-new-zealand/.

33 *See* North American Association for Environmental Education (NAAEE), https://naaee.org/ (last visited Dec. 6, 2020).

34 *Environmental Education* (EE), EPA (2020), www.epa.gov/education (last visited Dec. 6, 2020); *The Center for Green Schools*, US GREEN BUILDING COUNCIL, www.centerforgreenschools.org/about (last visited Dec. 6, 2020); *see also* Doris Zhang, *The Roots of Environmental Education in the US*, EDUC 300: EDUCATION REFORM, PAST AND PRESENT (May 5, 2017), https://commons.trincoll.edu/edreform/2017/05/the-roots-of-environmental-education-in-the-us/.
 Treaty on Environmental Education, *supra* note 14.

35 *National Environmental Education Training Program*, EPA (2018), www.epa.gov/education/national-environmental-education-training-program (last visited Dec. 6, 2020).

36 *Stockholm Declaration*, *supra* note 8.

37 *An Act to Promote Environmental Awareness through Environmental Education and for Other Purposes*, Republic Act No. 9512, 14th Congress 2nd Sess., Congress of the Philippines (Dec. 12, 2008), https://lawphil.net/statutes/repacts/ra2008/ra_9512_2008.html.

38 *An Act Mainstreaming Climate Change into Government Policy Formulations, Establishing the Framework Strategy and Program on Climate Change, Creating for this Purpose the Climate Change Commission, and for Other Purposes*, Republic Act 9729, Congress of the Philippines (Oct. 23, 2009), www.officialgazette.gov.ph/2009/10/23/republic-act-no-9729/.

in the Philippines.³⁹ The non-governmental organization (NGO) Fostering Education & Environment for Development, Inc. (FEED) supports sustainable education and tree-planting/nurturing, aims for inclusive growth, preservation, and protection of Philippine biodiversity—marine and terrestrial—through integrated social forestry programs, community development, and livelihood initiatives, and scientific and practical research into agricultural, environmental, farming, forestry, fisheries, and sustainability studies.⁴⁰

(4) India

In the 1991 decision of *MC Mehta v. Union of India*,⁴¹ the Supreme Court gave directions that the environment should be taught as a compulsory subject at every level of education and that all universities should prescribe a compulsory course on the environment. The National Policy on Education of 1986 states the "paramount need to create a consciousness of environment which must permeate all ages and all sections of society beginning with the child" and recommends the integration of environmental consciousness into the entire educational process.⁴² The National Council for Educational Research and Training confirms that Environmental Studies has been inducted into primary, secondary, and higher secondary stages.⁴³

The UNEP has showcased five landmark and diverse ESD Initiatives from India, set in five different locations across the country, and culled from five different organizations—Center for Environment Education (CEE), The Energy Research Institute (TERI), Wildlife Institute of India (WII), Dusty Foot Productions, and the World Wildlife Fund (WWF).⁴⁴ The Report concluded that

> Hunters were now wildlife educators in Chizami, Nagaland; village boys and girls from Sagar Islands, Sunderbans turned fearless filmmakers as they staunchly defended their vision of sustainability; school children in Mysore, Karnataka turned untiring saviours of their lake; in Chandigarh, Punjab a young girl took the message of recycling to semi-urban areas, and in Bharatpur, Rajasthan the son of a rickshaw puller now aspires to be a nature guide. The one guiding force: the ESD approach being followed in their

---

39 A. Galang, *Environmental Education for Sustainability in High Education Institutions in the Philippines*, 11(2) Int'l J. of Sustainability 173–83 (2010); *see also* Gaudencio M. Alaya-ay et al., *Teaching Environmental Education in Raising Pupils' Environmental Awareness: A Process Approach*, 2(1) IAMURE Int'l J. of Soc. Sci. (2012); Annelies Andringa-Davis, *Environmental Education at Local Schools*, MARINE CONSERVATION PHILIPPINES (Jan. 30, 2016), www.marineconservationphilippines.org/environmental-education-local-schools/.
40 *Philippine (Environmental) Education*, FOSTERING EDUCATION & ENVIRONMENT FOR DEVELOPMENT, INC. (FEED) (2013), https://feed.org.ph/directory-of-environmental-education-institutions-in-the-philippines/philippine-environmental-education/ (last visited Dec. 6, 2020).
41 *M.C. Mehta v. Union of India*, *supra* note 15.
42 Pratik Phadkule, *Facilitate Learning about Environment*, DECCAN HERALD (Feb. 20, 2020), www.deccanherald.com/opinion/panorama/facilitate-learning-about-environment-806638.html.
43 *Id*.
44 Alka Tomar, *Good Practice Stories on Education for Sustainable Development in India*, UNESCO Office New Delhi, IN/2014/SC/67 (Oct. 2014).

respective schools and communities which empowered them to make a change in their lives and surroundings so that nature could be nurtured.[45]

Regional Initiatives—Association of South-East Asian Nations (ASEAN)

An example of a regional initiative on environment education is the Association of South-East Asian Nations.[46] It has established an ASEAN Working Group on Environmental Education (AWGEE). Three Environmental Education Action Plans were developed for the periods 2000–2005, 2008–2012, and 2014–2018. Key activities included the ASEAN Eco-Schools Program, the ASEAN Green Higher Education Program (led by the Philippines), and Regional Communication, Education and Public Awareness Initiatives—these include the ASEAN Plus Three Youth Environment Forum, the ASEAN Youth Eco-Champions Award, and the ASEAN Environment Year which is celebrated every three years.

UNESCO Awards for ESD

The UNESCO-Japan Prize on ESD started in 2015 to recognize the role of education in connecting the social, economic, cultural, and environmental dimensions of sustainable development.[47] There are three winners each year, each receiving US$50,000. The first award was made in 2015.

One of the most interesting winners was the Kalabia Foundation's program "Environmental Education for the Heart of the Coral Triangle" (2018 winner).[48] The Kalabia is a 34-meter long ship that brings interactive marine conservation education to more than 100 remote coastal villages of Raja Ampat, West Papua, Indonesia. Its rich marine resources are under threat from destructive fishing and poaching, compounded by the effects of climate change, as well as emerging threats, such as improper waste disposal. The Kalabia teaches whole communities that by using unsustainable practices, they are undermining their own future. Staffed with local educators, this innovative floating platform tours the islands offering four-day intensive education programs to children, while involving the communities.

Evaluation

Notwithstanding the above examples of laudable implementation of ESD, the 2009 meeting at Bonn reported that "The progress of ESD remains unevenly distributed and requires different approaches in different contexts."[49] In 2016, a special report on Target 4.7 commissioned by UNESCO examined 94 country reports and concluded that "sustainable

---

45 *Id.* at 9; *see also* UTTARAKHAND SEVA NIDHI ENVIRONMENTAL EDUCATION CENTRE, UEEC, www.sevanidhi.org/aboutus.html (last visited Dec. 6, 2020) (another laudable initiative is the Uttarakand Seva Nidhi Environmental Education Center, which has worked with village communities in Uttarakhand since 1987, undertaking environmental education in schools and villages in these mountain districts).
46 *ASEAN Cooperation on Environmental Education*, ASEAN COOPERATION ON ENVIRONMENT, https://environment.asean.org/awgee/ (last visited Dec. 6, 2020).
47 *Japan Prize on Education for Sustainable Development*, UNESCO (2020), https://en.unesco.org/prize-esd (last visited Dec. 6, 2020).
48 Kalabia Foundation (Indonesia), UNESCO (2018), https://en.unesco.org/prize-esd/2018/kalabia (last visited Dec. 6, 2020).
49 Agenda 21, *supra* note 20, at ¶ 15.

development" is a growing concept in education policies, reported by only 51% of member states.[50] Only 12% prioritized sustainable development with a dedicated or stand-alone policy, plan, or law as a guiding framework.[51] This is a most disappointing record. This chapter advocates the following actions to strengthen efforts at attaining SDG 4.7 in ESD by 2030:[52]

(1) Constitutional Protection for the Right to Education

It is firstly essential that everyone has access to education. The right to education has been recognized as a human right in Article 26 of the Universal Declaration of Human Rights (1948)[53] and Articles 13 and 14 of the International Covenant on Economic, Social and Cultural Rights (1966).[54] This right should be enshrined in the constitution of each country, so that all persons, especially females and the disadvantaged, will have equal access to education. This must be reinforced with a clear statement in the constitution for gender equity.

(2) Government Policies and Integration with Civil Society

Governments must prioritize ESD into national policies on education to increase public awareness and understanding about ESD through formal and informal learning. The Ministries of Education worldwide must work together with teachers to ensure the incorporation of ESD into mainstream education in both formal and informal programs, at all levels, from pre-primary to university levels. ESD policies and training should be implemented through government and inter-agency policies that involve civil society, including non-government organizations, unions, religious and community groups, as well as the business and corporate sectors.

(3) The Media as Partners in ESD

More efforts should be made to use the media (television, radio, the internet, etc.) to reach all sectors of society and provide on-going education in environmental issues.

---

50 Claire McEvoy, *Historical Efforts to Implement the UNESCO 1974 Recommendation on Education in light of 3 SDG Targets*, ED/IPS/ESG/2017/01, UNESCO (2016), https://unesdoc.unesco.org/ark:/48223/pf0000247275 (this report also focused on SDGs 12.8 and 13.3).
51 *Id*.
52 *See also* Bonn Declaration, *supra* note 27.
53 *Universal Declaration of Human Rights*, G.A. Res. 217 (III) A, U.N. Doc. A/Res/217(III) (Dec. 10, 1948).
54 International Covenant on Economic, Social and Cultural Rights, Dec. 16, 1966, 993 U.N.T.S. 3; *see also What You Need to Know About the Right to Education*, UNESCO (Nov. 26, 2020), https://en.unesco.org/news/what-you-need-know-about-right-education (noting that this right has also been affirmed in the UNESCO Convention against Discrimination in Education (1960), the Convention on the Elimination of All Forms of Discrimination Against Women (CEDAW) (1981), the Convention on the Rights of Persons with Disabilities (2006), and the African Charter on Human and Peoples' Rights (1981)).

(4) Transforming the Learning Environment

The learning environment provides an ideal first setting for the practice of ESD. Thus, governments should encourage and support sustainable learning environments such as eco-schools and green campuses, incorporating sustainability practices into campus operations, policy, and management. These reduce the institution's ecological footprint and serve as a practical model for students. Ideally, tertiary institutions should have a dedicated School for the Environment, but where this is not possible, efforts should be made for the effective collaboration of different faculties to mount multi-disciplinary and inter-disciplinary programs on the environment. The learning environment should also go beyond the classroom. Outdoor classes and field trips to nature sites or even to a field nearby should be mandated. This is especially important for students in the urban environment.

(5) Building Capacities of Educators

Educators and trainers are agents that facilitate ESD. Each nation must, therefore, invest in first educating their educators and trainers in ESD. Capacity building of teachers must be a continuous process to ensure they keep abreast of new teaching tools and technology. The international community should provide scholarships for teachers from developing countries as well as assist in building schools and facilities for a sound learning environment. Participation at international and regional workshops and conferences, and collaboration with other institutions should be encouraged and facilitated by international funding for developing states.

Challenges Presented by COVID-19

The coronavirus (COVID-19) has shown the world's vulnerability to global pandemics. Offices and schools have had to be closed, and classes have been conducted remotely via video-conferencing and the use of virtual platforms. This requires students to possess computers and laptops in their homes. However, these are not available to many developing states, some of which even lack access to electricity. These are glaring inequities in the global community and call for effective national and international governance and management to help developing states build the infrastructure as well as provide students with the hardware for e-learning.

Conclusion

ESD has an extremely important role to play in the achievement of the SDGs as it ensures that all persons will understand the fragility of the Earth and will be inspired to be its stewards, even as each nation seeks economic development. Traditional systems of education must be revised to ensure the incorporation of environmental perspectives and changes in pedagogy, as well as a constant upgrading of skills in technology and innovation. The environment can be restored through sustainable education programs that are cross-disciplinary, involving science, technology, social studies, economics, public policy, culture, and ethics. The multi-disciplinary Masters in Environmental Management (MEM) program at the National University of Singapore is one such model. Emulating such programs through inclusive education will secure a more sustainable future for all.

Actions Needed

1 **Constitutional protection for the Right to Education**—The right to education has been recognized as a human right in many international law instruments. Ideally, it should be enshrined in the constitution of each country to ensure that all sectors of society have an equal right to be educated.
2 **Cogent and consistent government policies and integration with civil society**—Governments play a major role in the success of the implementation of all 17 SDGs as the goals are inter-connected. All goals must be linked to the overall objective of education for sustainable development, which must be a priority for all governments.
3 **The media as partners**—The media can be a very effective tool for ESD and governments should make full use of the many facets of media to educate all sectors of society in ESD.
4 **Transforming the learning environment**—There is a need to build and upgrade education facilities to ensure access to modern technology and the internet so as to provide inclusive and effective learning environments for all. Governments must make this a priority and ensure the allocation of funds, as an investment in the nation's future.
5 **Building capacities of educators**—Considerable funding is needed to assist developing countries to build capacity in education. This should be met with Official Development Assistance (ODA) and prudent fiscal policies and priorities set by national governments. Scholarships should be given to the best candidates on the basis of merit. This requires a sound, fair, and transparent process for evaluation of candidates. It should also be a condition of the scholarship that the candidate must return home to help build capacity in his/her home country.

Case Study: Implementing SDG 4—Education in Sustainable Development, the Master's in Environmental Management (MEM) Program, National University of Singapore

The Master of Science (Environmental Management) [MEM][55] program at the National University of Singapore (NUS) is a unique and innovative program involving the collaboration of nine faculties/schools at NUS. These are the Faculties of Arts and Social Sciences; Engineering; Law; and Science; the Lee Kuan Yew School of Public Policy; the NUS Business School; the Saw Swee Hock School of Public Policy; the Yong Loo Lin School of Medicine; and the School of Design and Environment (SDE), which hosts the program. It was the result of the realization of a core group of teachers from different disciplines, that while each faculty/school had specific courses on the environment in their discipline, there was no one program to put these specialities together to form a coherent and integrated whole. As the environment has many dimensions, it is essential that students from different disciplines are

---

55 Ideally, this program should not be an MSc as it traverses other disciplines beyond the sciences. However, an industry survey was conducted prior to its launch, as part of preliminary studies on its marketability, and it was found that while the MSc degree was well recognized and readily acceptable, the title "Masters in Environmental Management" was unfamiliar to most at that time (2001). A decision was made to call it the MSc (Environmental Management) but we refer to it as the Masters in Environmental Management or MEM for short. Nineteen years later, it is now an opportune time to discuss whether to rename this program, the Masters in Environmental Management without ascribing a Science focus, which in fact, is rather misleading.

well informed and educated on the many components that comprise the environment, their inter-dependence, and their synergies. This is particularly important as countries acknowledge the need for development to be integrated with a sustainable environment. The MEM program seeks to provide students with both a multi-disciplinary perspective as well as an inter-disciplinary perspective. This will ensure that graduates from this program can play a leading role in protecting the environment as well as enhancing Earth's natural resources, while engaged in development and economic activities.

The program is targeted at senior and mid-level managers and officers in corporations, government and non-government organizations in Singapore, South-East Asia, the Asia-Pacific region, and beyond. It focuses on managing the environment sustainably from the perspective of different disciplines, as well as from the national, international, and regional perspectives. As this is a graduate program, students must first have a college degree at the Bachelor level, with Honors, from a reputable university. They can come from any discipline—this in itself is a strength of the program, as students can learn from each other in class discussions and projects. Many students have a first degree in engineering or the sciences (especially biological science), but there are also graduates from law and the arts (geography, economics, English), business, computer science, and even veterinary science. Thus, the program has engineers, scientists, lawyers, journalists, teachers, and even a veterinary surgeon among its graduates.

Program Structure

The program can be undertaken either full-time (two semesters—one academic year) or part-time (four semesters—two academic years). Those who work in Singapore often choose to do it part-time. The program facilitates this by conducting all classes in the evenings, from 6.30 pm to 9.30 pm. Classes are taught by academic staff members, senior persons in the industries, the professions and government, as well as visiting professors from partner institutions, particularly the Yale School of Forestry & Environmental Studies.[56]

The main components of the program are a group of seven core modules taught by staff members from six of the nine faculties/schools. These are

(1) *Environmental Science*—taught by professors from the Faculty of Science.
(2) *Environmental Law*—taught by professors from the Faculty of Law.
(3) *Environmental Technology*—taught by professors from the Faculty of Engineering.
(4) *Business and the Environment*—jointly taught by a team comprised of professors from the School of Design and Environment, the Business School, leading practitioners, and a professor from the Yale School of the Environment.
(5) *Environmental Economics and Public Policy*— taught by a professor from the Lee Kuan Yew School of Public Policy; previously taught by a professor from the Department of Economics, Faculty of Arts and Sciences.
(6) *Environmental Management and Assessment*—taught by specialists from the private sector.
(7) *Environmental Planning*—taught by professors from SDE.

---

56 The program has signed Memoranda of Understanding (MOUs) with Yale's School of the Environment (formerly called the School of Forestry & Environmental Studies) and Duke University's Nicholas School for the Environment.

Students who have a background in one or more of these modules in their earlier studies may not be allowed to do a similar module, and will be required to pick another module relating to the environment—e.g., a graduate from environmental engineering, may not be allowed to do the module on Environmental Technology.

Apart from these seven modules, there is a compulsory research component. Each student must complete either a Dissertation of 20,000 words or a Study Report of 10,000 words. Students who opt for the shorter Study Report must do an elective module from any of the nine partner-faculties and schools. This includes modules from the other partners in this program—the Medical School, School of Public Health, and the Faculty of Arts and Social Sciences. Students must also attend a non-examinable module on Environmental Ethics as well as a series of Seminars held every fortnight which features talks on various themes related to the environment, conducted by guest speakers from different professions, non-government organizations, and industry, including visitors from abroad. Indeed, teachers and faculty representatives take special pains to invite interesting persons that they meet socially or at networking sessions, to speak at these seminars. The seminars are open to the NUS community as well as members of the public, as part of the program's efforts to educate the general community and raise awareness on environmental issues.

Pedagogy

Classes are taught using various pedagogies, including interactive lectures, case studies, seminars, workshops, and field trips to relevant environmental sites and projects in Singapore and overseas. Each teaching session is three hours in duration and classes are held in the evening.

Assessment

The performance of a candidate on each of the modules of the MEM program is assessed through a combination of continuous assessments and a final examination.

Continuous assessment may take the form of assignments or projects, on which reports are prepared, and presentations made by individual candidates or groups of students, term papers, and tests. There is also a strong research component, as mentioned earlier, with supervisors coming from the different disciplines depending on the topic chosen. It is not unusual for students to write on an area that traverses different disciplines, in which case co-supervisors would be appointed from different faculties/schools. The best student papers are published every few years in the series *Environment Matters*. To date, there are six volumes in this series, edited by staff members from the different disciplines.[57]

Program Management

The program's Director and Deputy Director are from the School of Design and Environment, which hosts the program. The program is administered by a Program Management Committee (PMC), which comprises a representative from each of the nine faculties and schools that are involved in this program.[58] The PMC meets from time to time

---

57 The latest volume was published in 2018, entitled Sustainability *Matters: Environmental Management in the Anthropocene*. It comprises 15 chapters in the fields of Biodiversity and Conservation, Environmental Science, Environmental Governance and Management, Energy, and Urban Studies; Lye Lin-Heng, Harvey Neo, Sekhar Kondepudi, Yew Wen-Shan, & Judy Sng GK (eds), World Scientific, xlv 468 pp.
58 This writer, from the Law Faculty, has chaired the program since its inception in 2001, until 2019. The new chair is a professor from the Business School.

to discuss policies and future directions for the program. Its individual members participate in the interview process to select students for admission, as well as help find supervisors and examiners for the research papers, which are a core component of this program.

Evaluation

The program draws on the strength of Singapore's experience as a city-state in an urban environment. It focuses on managing the urban environment in a sustainable way, to ensure that all development processes and projects are implemented without damaging the environment. In the course of some 18 years, some 330 students have graduated, coming from some 28 countries. While about half are from Singapore, the other students have come from India (51), China (including Hongkong) (20), Malaysia (12), Vietnam (12), Philippines (10), Bangladesh (10), Indonesia (6), Sri Lanka (6), Pakistan (5), Myanmar (5), United States of America (USA) (5), England (4), Thailand (2), Japan (2), Korea (2), Germany (2), and one student each from Norway, Canada, Maldives, Mauritius, Iran, Greece, Serbia, the Czech Republicc, France, and Sweden.

These graduates came from different disciplines and different parts of the world. They are now capable environmental managers and, being possessed of a keen understanding of the many dimensions and perspectives that relate to the environment, are in a position to take leadership roles in their organizations. Our graduates are now employed in government ministries and institutions in a multitude of countries, as well as in international, regional, and national organizations, corporations, non-governmental organizations, universities, schools, and other institutions of learning. Many of our graduates from abroad have joined international NGOs, such as the World Wildlife Fund (WWF) and Trade Records Analysis of Flora and Fauna in Commerce (TRAFFIC—which monitors wildlife trade), the International Union for Conservation of Nature (IUCN) in Pakistan, the United Nations Development Program (UNDP) in Jakarta, Nepal, and Vietnam, and the United States Agency for International Development (USAID) and Freeland in Bangkok, Thailand, which works with ASEAN's Wildlife Enforcement Network to monitor wildlife trade in the region. Those who have obtained PhDs are teaching environment-related courses at leading universities in the region.

The Bachelor in Environmental Studies (BES) program, NUS

The success of the MEM program led to the conceptualization of a new multi-disciplinary and inter-disciplinary program at the undergraduate level in NUS, with the collaboration of the same nine faculties/schools. This is the Bachelor in Environmental Studies (BES) program,[59] launched in 2011. The BES program is jointly hosted by the Faculty of Arts & Social Sciences (FASS), and the Faculty of Science, with the collaboration of the other seven faculties/schools as those that are involved in the MEM program. It is a four-year direct honors program. Its inter-disciplinary nature requires students to acquire a strong foundation in environmental issues through a two-year, broad-based curriculum, as they complete modules in biology, chemistry, economics, geography, law, management, math, policy, public health, and statistics.[60] Students then choose to specialize in either the Science

---

[59] *Bachelor of Environmental Studies*, NATIONAL UNIVERSITY OF SINGAPORE, http://envstudies.nus.edu.sg/ (last visited Dec. 6, 2020).
[60] *Id*. at *Requirements*.

or Social Studies theme in their 3rd and 4th years, whereupon they go to the Department of Biological Sciences at the Faculty of Science or the Department of Geography at the FASS, respectively. Some BES students have proceeded to the MEM program after graduation.

The Future—Lifelong Learning

As the MEM program is approaching its 20th year (in 2021), the current review of the program is timely. We see clear synergies with the UN's Education for Sustainable Development. In recent years, Singapore has moved to facilitate "lifelong learning," which is emphasized in SDG 4, to ensure it remains competitive in a globalized interconnected world. This requires its workforce to be nimble and able to adapt to new challenges by developing new skills and mindsets.[61] NUS has established a School of Lifelong and Continuing Education (SCALE).[62] Its vision is "To provide opportunities for lifelong learners to stay relevant and competitive in the global workplace, through innovative continuing education offerings." Courses in both the BES and MEM programs may be open to the public in the near future, but this is currently under discussion. Indeed, new modules should be developed, such as data analytics, the internet of things, public health and the environment ("well and green"), sustainable finance, smart and sustainable urban environments, climate change justice, human rights and policies, religion and the environment, etc.

Finally, returning to the SDGs and environmental education, it is submitted that multi-disciplinary and inter-disciplinary programs like the MEM and the BES should be taught in every college and every country, at both undergraduate and postgraduate levels. While it is difficult for a tertiary institution to have a dedicated school for the environment, most institutions of higher learning would have various faculties and schools in the different disciplines, and courses/modules relating to the environment in their respective fields. The teachers in each discipline should combine their efforts and start a program that takes a holistic look at the environment. This requires initiative on the part of individual staff members, as well as support from the deans and the university's administration. This was found in the NUS team that started the MEM program, and the administration was supportive. In turn, the teachers have found their lives enriched by the warm friendships built across disciplines, and both staff and students have enhanced their knowledge and understanding of the vastness and intricacies of the Earth and its environment and the interconnection of the different disciplines. Indeed, there should be more partnerships with other tertiary institutions for staff and student exchanges, and NUS should expand their partnership links. This then, is the way forward for environmental education in the 21st century.

---

61 *See* Robert Kamei, *How Singapore Encourages Lifelong Learning and Workforce Resilience*, The Diplomat (Oct. 12, 2017), https://thediplomat.com/2017/10/how-singapore-encourages-lifelong-learning-and-workforce-resilience/; *see* MINISTRY OF TRADE AND INDUSTRIES, https://www.mti.gov.sg/FutureEconomy/Resources (last visited Dec. 6, 2020) (noting that a Committee for the Future Economy was established in January 2016 to develop strategies for long-term economic growth); *see About SkillsFuture*, SkillsFuture, www.skillsfuture.sg/AboutSkillsFuture#section2. (Educational institutions are now encouraged to work closely with industry to ensure that programs are matched to market needs, and to encourage "modular" programs based on short courses or targeted certifications, using new technologies and pedagogical methods, such as flipped classrooms. The Singapore Ministry of Education's *Skills Future Singapore* offers direct financial subsidies of SGD $500 to all Singapore citizens above 25 years of age, to pursue a pre-approved list of courses.)

62 *FAQs*, National University of Singapore, https://scale.nus.edu.sg/programmes/faq (last visited Dec. 6, 2020).

13 STEM Education

Environmental Restoration Science in New York Harbor

Lauren Birney and Denise McNamara

Introduction

Evidence of Need

There are nearly 8.6 million Science, Technology, Engineering, and Mathematics (STEM) jobs in the United States (median annual salary of $84,880)[1] suggesting that STEM employment is booming. However, the reality is that the state of STEM education in the United States is sorely lacking. Currently, STEM skills and experience are scarcer relative to workforce demands. For example, STEM positions are some of the most challenging to fill—often taking more than twice the duration than other positions.[2] The President's Council of Advisors on Science and Technology (PCAST) has called for a 34% increase in the number of STEM bachelor's degrees yearly making recommendations toward achieving that goal.[3] These include increasing active learning to improve critical thinking skills, engaging students in authentic STEM experiences, and encouraging partnerships among stakeholders to diversify pathways to STEM careers with an emphasis on the inclusion of non-traditional STEM students.

Curriculum and Community Enterprise for Restoration Science (CCERS)

Although the report to the president intimated that more work is needed to bolster the US educational system in STEM-related coursework, the National Science Foundation has been continually investigating thousands of proposals and funding those that "focus on educational developments," earmarking advancements in STEM Education at the K–12 level. Through this opportunity, an ambitious and multifarious project began in the harbor, once called "a safe haven wherein a thousand ships may ride in safety."[4]

---

1 Stella Fayer et al., *STEM Occupations: Past, Present and Future*, U.S. BUREAU OF LABOR STATISTICS (2017) www.bls.gov/spotlight/2017/science-technology-engineering-and-mathematics-stem-occupations-past-present-and-future/pdf/science-technology-engineering-and-mathematics-stem-occupations-past-present-and-future.pdf.
2 Jonathan Rothwell, *Job Vacancies and STEM Skills*, BROOKINGS (Jul. 1, 2014) www.brookings.edu/still-searching-job-vacancies-and-stem-skills/.
3 Report to the President, *Engage to Excel: Producing One Million Additional College Graduates with Degrees in Science, Technology, Engineering and Mathematics*, PCAST STEM UNDERGRADUATE WORKING GROUP, at 1 (Feb. 2012) https://obamawhitehouse.archives.gov/sites/default/files/microsites/ostp/pcast-engage-to-excel final_2 25 12.pdf.
4 ADRIAEN VAN DER DONK, DESCRIPTION OF THE NEW NETHERLANDS, 6 (University of Nebraska Press, Jan. 1, 2010).

The project augments another environmental initiative begun at a unique NYC public high school located on Governor's Island in New York Harbor. The New York Harbor School is located in the heart of the island, with a number of specialized buildings sprinkled along the coast. The mission of the school is to ensure the restoration and improvement of New York Harbor. The Billion Oyster Project ("BOP") grew from this mission.

In a seemingly direct response to PCAST, an NSF grant entitled Curriculum and Community Enterprise for New York Harbor Restoration in NYC Schools ("BOP CCERS") was awarded in 2014. The focus of this grant was to extend the restoration of the harbor through the reintroduction of the oyster and include an educational program with an enhanced middle school environmental STEM curriculum, dedicated professional learning for teachers, and the inclusion of several key stakeholders. The point of convergence for all was and still is the magnificent harbor of NYC.

Waterfront STEM Education Classroom The New York Harbor

The geography of New York Harbor is one of the major contributors to its historical, financial, and environmental importance. A tidal estuary that spills into New York Harbor and ebbs and flows with the ocean's tide, supports a plethora of ecologically communities: Aquatic, amphibious, and terrestrial. One of the key species in the estuary is the Eastern oyster. At the time of Henry Hudson's arrival in 1609, there were approximately 220,000 oyster reefs in the harbor.[5] The oyster had been an essential of the Lenape diet, and the Dutch and English newcomers quickly adopted this cuisine. Waves of European immigrants continually teemed into NYC throughout the 17th and 18th centuries, and this radical and continual increase to the population placed an enormous stress on the city's natural resources which were being depleted through overuse. With an insatiable populace, indigenous species such as the oyster and the beaver were reduced to the point of annihilation.

Oysters are considered to be "ecosystem engineers" because of the multiple functions they perform to shape their environment.[6] Oysters have the unique ability to filter sediments, pollutants, and microorganisms from the water and assimilate most of the organic matter that they filter.[7] By creating this ecological niche, oysters improve the quality of the water and provide the environment for increased biodiversity. Once the oyster population declined to the point of eradication, so did the ability of the harbor to support the other aquatic life. The decline of the oyster population in New York Harbor also had a dire effect on the human population in NYC. The polluted waterways were hosts to water-borne illnesses, such as cholera, dysentery, and typhoid, and remained so until the onset of environmental policies such as the Clean Water Act of 1972.[8]

It became apparent that ecological restoration and sustainability was needed to revitalize New York Harbor. To that end, an informed and dynamic citizenry was needed to understand

---

5 Tom Perrottet, *How New York City Is Rediscovering Its Maritime Spirit*, SMITHSONIAN (May 2017) www.smithsonianmag.com/travel/new-york-rediscovering-maritime-spirit-180962769/.
6 Robert D. Brumbaugh et al., *A Practitioners Guide to the Design and Monitoring of Shellfish Restoration Projects: An Ecosystem Services Approach*, THE NATURE CONSERVANCY (2016) www.oyster-restoration.org/wp-content/uploads/2012/06/tnc_noaa.pdf.
7 *See* S. Gregory Tolley et al., *Influence of Salinity on the Habitat Use of Oyster Reefs in Three Southwest Florida Estuaries*, 24(1) J. OF SHELLFISH RES. 127, (Jan. 1, 2005).
8 *Summary of the Clean Water Act 33 U.S.C. §1251 et seq. (1972)*, U.S. EPA, www.epa.gov/laws-regulations/summary-clean-water-act (last visited Nov. 19, 2020).

the underpinnings of our past mistakes and alter the course of human intervention. Through citizen science and stewardship, the children in the NYC public schools are becoming the stakeholders in this endeavor. Several studies strongly suggest that students are in need of a stronger connection between the natural world and the classroom setting, and that experiences of nature boost academic learning, personal development, and environmental stewardship.[9] The time and place were ripe for the BOP CCERS Project to begin work.

New York Harbor is accessible to all NYC residents, making it an ideal setting for community-based, hands-on education. Connecting the school subject matter and the world around them by restoring the native oyster to the harbor rouses student interest and concern by using their own community as a source of learning and action.[10] Oyster Restoration field stations (ORS) are sprinkled on the shore of each of the five boroughs, and it is there that the students are able to make the connections between their classroom curriculum and the real world by monitoring and nurturing the oysters that have been entrusted to them. Through this situated learning, they become stewards of the environment in which they live and environmentally conscious stakeholders of their community.

Phase I of the BOP CCERS Project

Overview

The collaboration between the CCERS and BOP in 2014 created a union that encompassed the restoration of the Eastern Oyster into New York Harbor with hands-on, problem-based learning for NYC's urban middle school students. Research has shown that this form of learning increases the level of student engagement, heightens interest in the content, and is a powerful motivator for all students, but particularly students who are historically underrepresented populations in the area of STEM.[11] The conceptual framework of the project is based on five interrelated components or pillars and several key partnerships. These pillars are fluid in that the partners in the project are associated with one or more of the pillars and freely collaborate across all of the pillars.

NYC has a plethora of stakeholders grounded in the environmental stability of the city and the education of its populace. Pivotal partners in the project include Pace University, the Columbia University Lamont-Doherty Earth Observatory, the New York Academy of Sciences, the New York Harbor Foundation, the New York Aquarium, the River Project, Good Shepherd Services, the University of Maryland's Center for Environmental Sciences, and the New York City Department of Education (NYCDOE) which is the largest and most diverse public school system in the United States. It is composed of 1,843 schools and 1.1 million students (72.8% economically disadvantaged and 66.1% underrepresented minorities). Research indicates that the partnership value to a project is crucial and helps to involve the community as a whole.[12] The success of the restoration of New York Harbor

---

9 *See generally* Michael Barnes et al., *Do Experiences with Nature Promote Learning? Converging Evidence of a Cause-and-Effect Relationship*, FRONT. PSYCHOL. (Feb. 19, 2019).
10 *See generally* Amy C. Berg et al., *Community Based Learning: Engaging Students for Success and Citizenship*, 40 PARTNERSHIPS/COMMUNITY (2006).
11 Margaret Holm, *Project-Based Instruction: A Review of the Literature on Effectiveness in Prekindergarten through 12th Grade Classrooms*, 7(2) INSIGHT: RIVIER ACADEMIC J. (Nov. 2018).
12 Mavis G. Sanders, *The Role of "Community" in Comprehensive School, Family and Community Partnership Programs*, 102 THE ELEMENTARY SCHOOL J. 19–34 (Number 1, 2001).

through the seeding of oysters relies on the synergy created through these partnerships and the five explicitly defined pillars.

Pillar I—Teacher Training Curriculum

The environmental STEM curriculum was created by CCERS staff and experts in marine biology and environmental science and then shared with the Title I school NYCDOE teachers participating in a fellowship conducted by Pace University. Teachers participated in science workshops and professional development classes, on-site coaching, and instructional support to create dynamic and evolving activities to accompany the lessons.

Pillar II—Student Learning Curriculum

The Next Generation Science Standards (NGSS)-aligned environmental STEM lessons were then implemented in the middle school classrooms in the NYCDOE along with field science-based curriculum from the Oyster Restoration Manual. This allowed students to engage in trans-disciplinary learning by connecting the classroom to the community, increasing academic achievement, enhancing students' appreciation for the natural world, and creating a heightened commitment to serving as active, contributing citizens.[13]

Pillar III—Digital Platform for Project Resources

The digital platform is an interactive open-source application containing lesson plans, environmental data, project metrics, events and workshops, student research publications, and locations of the ORS in New York Harbor. It is accessible to all stakeholders in the project—students, teachers, parents, school community members, and citizen scientists. The NSF Task Force on Cyberlearning recommends that a "platform perspective" should be instilled into NSF's cyber-learning activities.[14]

Pillar IV—After-School and Summer STEM Mentoring Program

Through the collaboration of three of the partners in the project—Good Shepard Services, the New York Academy of Science, and the NYCDOE, students have the unique opportunity to extend their engagement in STEM activities in both after-school and summer programs. Research indicates that participants in after-school STEM programs learn essential STEM-relevant life and career skills and come to understand the value of STEM in contributing to society and solving global and local issues.[15]

---

13 *See generally* DAVID SOBEL, PLACE-BASED EDUCATION: CONNECTING CLASSROOMS AND COMMUNITIES (The Orion Society, 2005).
14 *See generally* NSF Task Force on Cyberlearning, *Fostering Learning in the Networked World: The Cyberlearning Opportunity and Challenge*, NAT'L SCI. FOUNDATION (June 24, 2008).
15 *See generally* Melissa Ballard et al., *Examining the Impact of Afterschool STEM Programs*, AFTER-SCHOOL ALLIANCE (July 2014).

Pillar V—Community Restoration-Based Exhibits

Exhibits at the Hudson River Project and the New York Aquarium are presented to the public to highlight the Oyster Restoration work that is being done throughout New York Harbor and in the middle school classrooms in the NYC public school system. The exhibits also provide family enrichment and public awareness about the state of the waterways in New York Harbor and the sustainability measures being taken to restore the oyster reefs in the harbor.

Outcomes

The initial BOP CCERS Project exists in 78 public middle schools in NYC, 96% of which are Title I funded and located in low-income neighborhoods. More than 5,600 marginalized students are reaping the benefits of the BOP CCERS Project—students who are typically underrepresented in the STEM fields. Research has shown that low socio-economic status students who participate in these programs tend to score higher in achievement, motivation, and affinity to school than similar students who do not participate in STEM professional programs.[16] The BOP CCERS digital platform now contains more than 168 environmental datasets collected by students and citizen scientist volunteers working at 118 unique waterfront field locations across New York Harbor.

The students showed marked gains in content knowledge (7%) but still showed little interest in STEM content and exploring STEM career options. It was clear that more work had to be done to promote greater student agency to make students aware of their capacity to be scientists. Thus, like any well-developed design plan, modifications would have to be made to the BOP CCERS Project to address the inconsistencies and strengthen the project.

Phase II and Phase III of the BOP CCERS

In direct response to the challenges encountered in the original project, Phase II—The Curriculum and Community Enterprise for Restoration of a Keystone Species in New York Harbor was launched in March 2018. The inclusion of the Innovative Technology Experiences for Students and Teachers (ITEST) program will serve to broaden the appeal of the CCERS restoration curriculum, increasing students' motivation and competence to explore careers in STEM. As with the original CCERS Project, this project also targets students in low-income communities with high populations of English language learners and students from groups underrepresented in STEM fields and educational pathways. The goal is to directly involve 97 schools, 300 teachers, and approximately 15,000 K–12 students over the duration of the project.

The long-term objective of the model aims at a systemic approach whereby students are both encouraged to pursue meaningful, viable STEM career pathways beginning in elementary school and continuing through middle and high school. To achieve this outcome, four additional programmatic pillars have been added as can be seen in Figure 13.1.

---

16 *See* Peter C. Scales, *Reducing Academic Achievement Gaps: The Role of Community Service and Service-Learning*, 29(1) J. OF EXPERIENTIAL EDUC. 38 (Mar. 1, 2006).

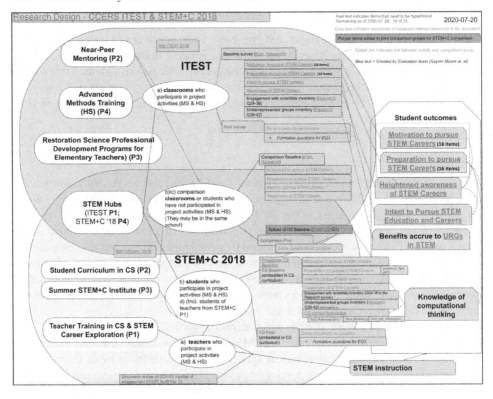

Figure 13.1 Additions of Phase II and Phase III to the BOP CCERS Project.

Community-Based Restoration Science Hubs

Four regional oyster reef restoration sites in New York Harbor where NYC middle and high school students work alongside professional scientists and researchers, learning environmental monitoring methods and the technologies. Place-based education engages students in cross-curricular or multidisciplinary methods, where knowledge is co-constructed through hands-on, real world learning experiences.[17]

Near-Peer Mentoring Program

Cohorts of highly motivated students participate in small cohorts and are formally mentored by a STEM professional. In addition, a select number of 11th and 12th graders peer-mentor middle school cohorts. Peer-mentor research has shown gains in content knowledge and college readiness by both the student and the peer-mentor.[18]

---

17 *See* David A. Gruenewald, *Foundations of Place: A Multidisciplinary Framework for Place-Conscious Education*, 40(3) AM. EDUC. RES. J. 619 (Jan. 1, 2003).
18 *See generally* Sarah M. Bonner et al., *Leveraging the Power of Peer-Led Learning: Investigating Effects on STEM Performance in Urban High Schools*, 21(7–8) EDUC. RES. AND EVALUATION 537 (Mar. 8, 2016).

Restoration Science Professional Development Programs for Elementary Teachers

The inclusion of elementary teachers is paramount to the STEM continuum for students in at-risk communities. Teacher self-efficacy and teachers' beliefs about their abilities impact the implementation of inquiry-based STEM practices in the classroom.[19]

Advanced Methods in Restoration Science for High School Students

Teachers will select one or more of four topics in environmental monitoring utilizing standardized protocols, enabling them to guide their students in environmental monitoring and data collection. Teachers need to incorporate knowledge derived from experimental and practical experiences.[20]

Concurrently, Phase III—Integrating Computational Science with Environmental Sciences Associated with Habit Restoration and Education in New York Harbor also began in March 2018. Perceived as a vital addition to the ongoing and ever-changing project, Phase III addresses the area of computation in STEM education and occupations. Computational thinking and reasoning have become one of the preeminent 21st-century skills. Computational thinking combines critical thinking with computing power as the foundation for innovating solutions to real-world problems.[21] Phase III is addressing this issue by embedding computational thinking and computing activities into the field-based environmental restoration curriculum model for students and teachers in the K–12 NYCDOE. The two additions to the original project serve to augment the on-going real world, community-based science restoration project by embedding data science and literacy into the primary project and adding substance to the already robust efforts.

Phase IV—Modeling the Human Harbor—Applying Computational Thinking and Computer Science Core Practices to Environmental Restoration Science in New York Harbor

In Phase IV of the project, computer science will be embedded into the environmental restoration-based STEM educational model. Embedding the technology and computational tools into the existing curriculum allows learners to reflect on their experiences and this continuity of engagement can lead to increased retention of STEM knowledge and skills.[22] The focus will be on incorporating computational thinking into the existing student curriculum. Computational thinking is considered to be the 5th "C" in 21st--century skills, added to the original four (communication, critical thinking, collaboration, and creativity).[23] The end

---

19 Isha DeCoito & Philip Myszkal, *Connecting Science Instruction and Teachers' Self-Efficacy and Beliefs in STEM Education*, 29(6) J. OF SCI. TEACHER EDUC. 485 (Jun. 5, 2018).
20 Sonia Guerriero, *Teachers' Pedagogical Knowledge: What It Is and How It Functions*, in PEDAGOGICAL KNOWLEDGE AND THE CHANGING NATURE OF THE TEACHING PROFESSION 99–118 (OECD Publishing, Feb. 21, 2017).
21 Yahya Tabesh, *Computational Thinking: A 21st Century Skill*, 11 Special Issue OLYMPIADS IN INFORMATICS 65 (IOI Vilnius U. 2017).
22 Susan M. Land &Heather Toomey Zimmerman, *Facilitating Place-Based Learning in Outdoor Informal Environments with Mobile Computers*, 58(1) TECH TRENDS 77 (Dec. 5, 2013).
23 Jeanette M. Wing, *Computational Thinking*, 49(3) COMM. OF THE ACM 33 (Mar. 2006).

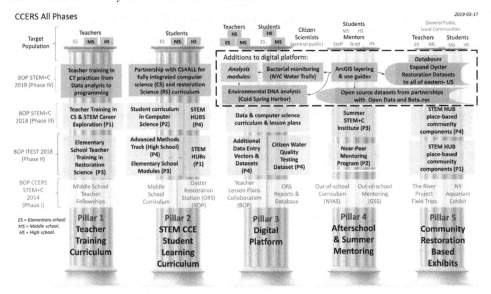

Figure 13.2 The BOP CCERS Project—Phases I–IV.

product will be a fully articulated Computer Science/Restoration Science curriculum with the goal of training students to develop, design, and implement their own computational models focused on human health and environmental issues. Research has found that students demonstrate stronger engagement, self-efficacy, and skill development when they are engaged in high levels of interactivity and engagement with data science.[24] See Figure 13.2.

The Future—"All Is in Flux, Nothing Stays Still"—Plato

A proposal for the Living Breakwaters was made in direct response to the devastation on the shores of NYC by Super Storm Sandy. Its partially submerged rubble mound structures lining the southeast coast of Staten Island are designed to attenuate shoreline erosion and enhance ecosystems by increasing the diversity of aquatic habitants in the harbor. The project will also help to demonstrate the ecological, social, and economic benefits that can be provided by restoring natural ecosystems as a method for reducing flood risks.[25] Because the BOP CCERS is the signature grant of NYC, implementation of the reintroduction of the native oyster species and an educational programming done at the water hub—a floating vessel and an onshore site will be handled by the project. Civic and educational activities will also occur, such as beach clean-up, shore birding walks, and citizen science monitoring and research.[26] The synergy that will be created with this combination will focus on the

---

24 *See generally* Linda Darling-Hammond et al., *Using Technology to Support At-Risk Students' Learning*, Alliance for Excellent Education & SCOPE (Sept. 2014).
25 A. Michael Pappalardo, *Walls beneath the Waves*, Am. Anthropological Assoc.: Anthropology News (Nov. 25, 2019) www.anthropology-news.org/index.php/2019/11/15/walls-beneath-the-waves/.
26 *Learn More about the Living Breakwaters Project*, N.Y. State Governor's Office of Storm Recovery (GOSR) https://stormrecovery.ny.gov/learn-more-about-living-breakwaters-project (last visited Nov. 19, 2020).

engagement of the community service as a model for any community-based environmental restoration project, be it local or global. Longevity, sustainability, and inclusive and equitable education to promote life-long STEM learning are paramount and give this project its universal appeal and application.

On a Global Scale

Although the BOP CCERS Project is a localized community environmental project, the SDGs outlined in the United Nations Department of Economic and Social Affairs (UNSDESA) have been and continue to be addressed and refined through this multi-faceted restoration effort. Points of convergence between the SDGs and the BOP CCERS Project are as follows:

SDG 4—Ensure Inclusive and Equitable Quality Education and Promote Lifelong Learning Opportunities for All

By increasing the interest and motivation in students living in areas of high poverty, CCERS is promoting equitable lifelong learning and broadening the STEM pipeline. Equity in science learning occurs when individuals from diverse backgrounds participate in science as practiced in the established scientific community and centers on making science accessible, meaningful, and relevant for diverse students by connecting their home and community cultures to science.[27]

SDG 8—Promote Sustained, Inclusive, and Sustainable Economic Growth, Full and Productive Employment, and Decent Work for All

A component of the BOP CCERS Project is a summer STEM institute which will provide secondary school students with opportunities to connect with STEM industry professionals and explore STEM career pathways. Research on the effect of high school STEM summer programs on students' STEM career interests found program participation was linked to increased science career motivation and increased interest in pursuing a science career.[28]

SDG 11—Make Cities and Human Settlements Inclusive, Safe, Resilient, and Sustainable

The development of this urban plan to restore the oysters to New York Harbor has national and international potential. Bivalve habitat restoration for ecosystem services has been scaling up in the United States and is increasingly being undertaken worldwide as a way to improve estuary conditions and bring back imperiled ecosystems.[29]

---

27 *See generally* NATIONAL RESEARCH COUNCIL, LEARNING SCIENCE IN INFORMAL ENVIRONMENTS: PEOPLE, PLACES AND PURSUITS (The National Academies Press, 2009).
28 Marino De Leon et al., *Underrepresented Minority High School and College Students Report STEM Pipeline Sustaining Gains After Participating in the Loma Linda University Summer Health Disparities Research Program*, 9(9) PLoS ONE (Sept. 24, 2014) https://doi.org/10.1371/journal.pone.0108497.
29 Philine S.E. zu Ermgassen et al., *Can Bivalve Habitat Restoration Improve Degraded Estuaries?*, in COASTS AND ESTUARIES: THE FUTURE 427–42 (Humphries Lab 2019).

SDG 14—Conserve and Sustainably Use the Oceans, Sea, and Marine Resources for Sustainable Development

By reintroducing the oyster to the waterways of the harbor of NYC, the amount of industrial waste is being diminished and the water is being cleansed. NYC Harbor is counted among the 104 of 220 coastal regions that improved their coastal water quality.[30]

SDG 17—Strengthen the Means of Implementation and Revitalize the Global Partnership for Sustainable Development

The BOP CCERS Phase IV intends to integrate computer science in all aspects of the grant, infusing data literacy into each of the five pillars. The internet helps to bring sustainability to the entire population, with up-to-date information and day-to-day solutions. In this way, we can communicate globally, without borders.[31]

The BOP CCERS Project will continue to grow along with the needs of the community in which it serves. Building on the leverage in the NYC public school system, and the multitude of stakeholders who benefit from this project—including the communities in and around NYC, the potential for expansion and ongoing modification to improve the model seems endless.

The Challenges Presented by COVID-19

The world is currently in the throes of the coronavirus (COVID-19) pandemic which spread internationally in a matter of months, infected more than 7.5 million persons, and to date has claimed almost 424,000 lives worldwide.[32] The consequences have been apocalyptic in many areas of the world, with life-altering modifications in daily existence. Businesses have shuttered as well as educational systems throughout the world. The impact on the educational community is palpable.

The overwhelming response to the crisis was to close the schools (as of May 24, 2020, approximately 1.725 billion learners worldwide are affected by school closures) and move to a remote learning environment. This represents 98.6% of the world's student population.[33]

The remote emergency plan relies on the virtual communication of teachers, students, administrators, and parents through video conferencing and online lessons using a variety of virtual platforms. These facilities, however, are not available to many developing states, some of which do not even have access to electricity, let alone possess computers and laptops for e-learning. Once again, this brings to the fore, the inequities that exist in the global community. It calls for better planning at the international level and a fresh call for funding and capacity building in education to ensure that effective learning can still take place despite the shuttering of school buildings.

---

30 Independent Group of Scientists appointed by the Secretary-General, *Global Sustainable Development Report 2019: The Future is Now—Science for Achieving Sustainable Development*, 50, U.N. Dep. of Econ. & Soc. Affairs (2019).
31 *How Does the Internet Help with Sustainability?*, Acciona: Sustainability for All www.activesustainability.com/sustainable-life/how-does-the-internet-help-with-sustainability/ (last visited Nov. 19, 2020).
32 *WHO Coronavirus Disease (COVID-10) Dashboard*, WORLD HEALTH ORGANIZATION (last updated Nov. 19, 2020) https://covid19.who.int/?gclid=CjwKCAjw8pH3BRAXEiwA1pvMsZkC6-2UpY2901VFvYI6aPyL9gLTFE45zNgXppRfnwyb3yaWLT-BABoCro0QAvD_BwE.
33 *Education and COVID-19*, UNICEF, (Sept. 2020), https://data.unicef.org/topic/education/covid-19 (last visited Nov. 23, 2020).

14 Working Together toward Sustained and Inclusive Growth

Joseph C. Morreale

Introduction

In 2015, when the United Nations (UN) adopted its historic 2030 plan for sustainable development, almost 10% of the Earth's 7.34 billion population lived in extreme poverty, on less than US$1.90. About 95% of the world's poor were concentrated in three regions only—East Asia and Pacific, South Asia, and sub-Saharan Africa. This is not to say that there had been no improvement. Since the 1970s, encouraging news has emerged from developing countries. Life expectancy and school enrollment have increased, child mortality and malnutrition have declined, and per capita Gross Domestic Product (GDP) has more than doubled, lifting millions of people out of extreme poverty.[1] Much of these encouraging trends resulted from unprecedented economic growth, particularly in East Asia and Latin America and the Caribbean.[2] Yet, even though global poverty has been declining for several decades, the concentration of the remaining poverty, as well as its depth and breadth, became a serious concern for the international community.[3] With the expected global population to reach 8.6 billion by 2030 and slowing global economic growth, especially in the conflict-ridden and disaster-prone states,[4] there was an urgent need for national and international efforts to ensure that strong economic growth reduces poverty and generates prosperity, that an increase in standard of living does not come at the cost of environmental degradation, and that employment opportunities and economic gains reach the most disadvantaged and most vulnerable parts of the world.

Sustainable Development Goal (SDG) 8 of the UN's 2030 Agenda to "promote sustained, inclusive and sustainable economic growth, full and productive employment, and decent

---

1 *Human Development Report 2015: Work for Human Development* (UNDP), http://hdr.undp.org/sites/default/files/2015_human_development_report.pdf.
2 *HLPF Background Note—Implementing the SDGs: Lessons from the Regions*, High-level Political Forum on Sustainable Development, at 2–3 (2018), https://sustainabledevelopment.un.org/content/documents/198562018_background_notes_Key_regional_trendswith_original_header.pdf.
3 Press Release, *World Bank Forecasts Global Poverty to Fall Below 10% for First Time; Major Hurdles Remain in Goal to End Poverty by 2030*, THE WORLD BANK (2015), www.worldbank.org/en/news/press-release/2015/10/04/world-bank-forecasts-global-poverty-to-fall-below-10-for-first-time-major-hurdles-remain-in-goal-to-end-poverty-by-2030.
4 *The Sustainable Development Goals Report*, United Nations, at 2 (Jul. 19, 2019) [hereinafter "2019 SDG Report"], https://unstats.un.org/sdgs/report/2019/The-Sustainable-Development-Goals-Report-2019.pdf.

work for all"[5] is the commitment of the international community to address this call.[6] As all other goals, SDG 8 is universal—its targets are applicable to developed, developing, and least developed regions. The UN, however, places more emphasis on the latter ones. One of the main foci of this goal is to rethink economic and social policies to foster economic growth and create decent employment opportunities in the Least Developed Countries (LDCs). SDG 8 is also one of the most central goals because economic growth can play a catalytic role for human development in conjunction with other SDGs. At the same time, other SDGs can affect economic growth.

This chapter provides an assessment of the progress on SDG 8. We begin with some important definitions of sustained, inclusive economic growth and sustainability. We discuss different theories of economic growth and explain how SDG 8 targets are related to these theories and to each other. We then evaluate the global progress toward these goals and use case studies of developing nations to illustrate how different policies implemented in these countries have affected the speed and nature of their progression. We devote one section to the projected impact of the ongoing COVID-19 pandemic on achieving SDG 8 by 2030. In the last section, we offer policy proposals that would advance more effective implementation of this goal. We provide additional insights in our concluding section.

Why Sustained, Inclusive, Sustainable Growth?

Traditionally, economic growth has been defined as a long-term rise in total output of goods and services. It is growth based on supply-side factors, such as labor productivity, population and size of the work force, and real capital accumulation. Growth in this case is endogenous—it results from increasing returns to scale from expansion of production and specialization of labor and capital. It presumes that the desires and wants of the population will drive ongoing productivity and economic growth. International trade is important because it leads to greater specialization and thus greater output. Capital deepening, defined as an increase in a country's stock of fixed capital per worker, plays an important role in this context, and it is a result of technological progress and investment in machinery and equipment.

These are the basics of the neoclassical theory of economic growth that is rooted in the Industrial Revolution and the first (classical) thinkers who described the many factors that foster economic growth—Adam Smith, David Ricardo, and Thomas Malthus. Neoclassical theory has evolved over time and included more factors, such as human capital and the role of the financial system. Population growth can lead to greater economic growth only if labor is more productive. Labor productivity depends on skills and knowledge of workers, which can be increased through education and training (human capital). Real investment (investment in machinery and technology) comes from savings; therefore, a strong and stable financial system is needed to facilitate the transfer of funds from those with savings to those who need funds for investing.

Most of the historical growth of today's developed countries can be explained by this theory which is based on several important assumptions: Private ownership of resources, free markets, and the rule of law. Some of the former Soviet bloc countries, like Poland,

---

5 *Id.*
6 *See also* United Nations G.A. Res. A/RES/70/1, *Transforming Our World: The 2030 Agenda for Sustainable Development*, at 19–20 (Sept. 25, 2015) [hereinafter "Agenda 2030"].

Latvia, Lithuania, and Estonia, were successful in promoting economic growth during their transition from socialism to capitalism because they restructured their economies according to this framework. In the late 1980s and early 1990s, they introduced private property, deregulated their markets, and opened their borders to international flows of goods, services, credit, and labor.[7] The framework was formalized in 1989 by economist John Williamson who first conceived of the economic and policy recommendations known as the *Washington Consensus*.[8] By the 1990s, this Consensus became generally accepted as the most effective model by which developing nations could spur growth. By embracing ideals of free-market capitalism, which included open trade policies, privatization, and deregulation, the Washington Consensus provided a prescription for development to the rest of the world.

Nevertheless, implementations of the Washington Consensus have had mixed results. In fact, it led to multiple currency crises, stagnation, and recession during the financial turmoil of the 1990s and was mostly responsible for the severe financial crisis and the Great Recession of 2007–2009. It also did not perform well in developing and underdeveloped nations, many of which have been suffering from weak and corrupt legal systems, armed conflict, and the lack of a strong government capable of protecting its citizens from crime, violence, and economic hardship. Even resource-rich developing countries were often unable to sustain economic growth that could result from a sudden increase in demand for their exports. Many fell into what economists call a "natural resource trap," a situation in which focus on exporting of natural resources diverts human and physical capital from other industries and reduces diversification.[9]

Relying on the export of natural resources sets in motion several factors that affect economic growth negatively. First of all, such reliance will make the economy particularly vulnerable to outside demand shocks. A good example of this is Russia's dependence on oil and gas. During the novel COVID-19 pandemic, the Russian economy was hit much harder than its better diversified neighbors. Second, resource exports crowd out other exports that can drive growth. Finally, and perhaps most importantly, such resource-intensive growth leads to resource depletion and environmental degradation. This means that such economic growth is not sustainable and thus it puts the future of the Earth and its many billions of inhabitants in jeopardy.

As a result, alternative models and strategies of economic growth have come forward. One of them, dubbed the "Beijing Consensus"[10] developed by China, is in sharp contrast to the Washington Consensus.[11] Instead of prescribing rigid recommendations for the problems of distant nations, the Beijing Consensus is pragmatic and recognizes the need for flexibility in solving economic problems. It is inherently focused on individual nations being innovative in their approach to economic growth, while simultaneously emphasizing ideals

---

7 Anna Shostya, *The Effect of the Global Financial Crisis on Transition Economies*, 42 ATLANTIC ECON. J. 317–32 (2014).
8 John Williamson, *Democracy and the "Washington Consensus,"* 21 WORLD DEVELOPMENT 1329–36 (1993).
9 Anthony J, Venables, *Using Natural Resources for Development: Why Has It Proven So Difficult?* 30 J. OF ECONOMIC PERSPECTIVES, 161–183 (2016).
10 JOSHUA COOPER RAMO, THE BEIJING CONSENSUS (Foreign Policy Centre, 2004), https://fpc.org.uk/publications/the-beijing-consensus/.
11 Dustin R. Turin, *The Beijing Consensus: China's Alternative Development Model*, INQUIRIES JOURNAL (2010), www.inquiriesjournal.com/articles/134/the-beijing-consensus-chinas-alternative-development-model.

such as equitable development and a "Peaceful Rise."[12] This development strategy has been highly successful, especially in China, with its average annual growth rate of more than 9% over a 25-year period.

Since the early 21st century, the Chinese model has gained appeal within the developing world, especially in the Southeast Asian region, and influenced a reassessment of Washington's policies. As a prominent Indonesian scholar, Ignatius Wibowo, writes, "Southeast Asian nations have shifted their development strategy from one based on free markets and democracy to one based on semi-free markets and an illiberal political system."[13] Another region that has been influenced by this new growth strategy has been resource-rich Africa. The size of trade between China and Africa has soared from $10 billion in 2000 to $200 billion in 2018.[14] China's tapping into Africa's natural resources, however, raises concerns about the pursuance of economic growth (as measured by an increase in GDP and GDP per capita) that does not necessarily advance human development.

Until very recently economists believed that economic growth and economic development go hand in hand. Both are continuous processes with stimulating effects on the economy; both involve the allotment and utilization of resources and the increase of efficiency; and both can improve the standard of living. The empirical experiences, however, indicated that some countries that exhibited strong economic growth saw little progress in human development and other countries that achieved rather moderate growth were enjoying above-average human development.[15] This is because development is a much broader, more inclusive, and more multidimensional concept. It involves acceleration of economic growth, the reduction of inequality and poverty, greater employment opportunities, and more decent work.

It was the empirical evidence from the developing countries and LDCs that led economists, policymakers, national leaders, and the UN to look beyond GDP growth. SDG 8, the way it is defined, is a serious attempt to ensure that economic growth is sustained, which implies that there is macroeconomic stability with only moderate fluctuations in GDP over a long-term trend and that economies are well diversified and development-oriented (Targets 8.1, 8.2, 8.3, 8.10, 8.a).[16] It is an attempt to ensure that economic growth is inclusive, that it creates equal opportunities for all, and promotes equity and equality (Targets 8.5, 8.6, 8.7, 8.8, 8.b).[17] Finally, it is an attempt to promote sustainability, so that the global economy uses its scarce recourses efficiently, in such a way that the improvement in the quality of life of today's generations does not come at a cost of the standard of living of our children and grandchildren (Targets 8.1, 8.2, 8.4, 8.9).[18] SDG 8 contains 12 targets that reflect this thinking.

---

12 Ramo, *supra* note 10.
13 Joshua Kurlantzick, *China's Model of Development and the "Beijing Consensus,"* CHINA-UNITED STATES FOCUS (Apr. 29, 2013), www.chinausfocus.com/finance-economy/chinas-model-of-development-and-the-beijing-consensus.
14 *Id.*
15 2019 SDG Report, *supra* note 4.
16 *Id.*
17 *Id.*; *See also* Agenda 2030, *supra* note 6.
18 *Id.*

Assessment of Progress toward SDG 8

So where does the world stand in terms of the SDG 8? The UN's 2019 Sustainable Development Goals Report found that real GDP per capita increased globally by 1.9% in 2017, a slight (0.6 percentage points) increase from the previous year.[19] The growth was expected to be around 2%, but it has been greatly affected by the novel COVID-19 virus that has been holding the world hostage in a lockdown since the beginning of 2020.[20] Economic growth in LDCs was on the upswing in recent years, but the 7% target set out by the SDG 8 is still out of reach.[21] In Africa, "infrastructure deficits undermine industrial development," and though the region has enjoyed a high rate of economic growth in the past decade, the benefits of this progress have been very uneven. The Latin American and the Caribbean region has been experiencing a disappointingly low economic growth rate of around 1%.[22] Asia and the Pacific still need a lot of improvement in the area of decent work and inclusion. The European region is also not performing well with regard to economic growth, employment, and infrastructure. The Arab region has shown lots of commitment but not statistics, making it difficult to assess the progress in this region.[23]

Labor productivity, measured by GDP per worker, is rising but wide disparities among LDCs can be found across regions. In 2017–2018, the highest gains in labor productivity were in the Central and Southern Asian region (4.8%) and the Eastern and South-Eastern Asian region (4.2%).[24] Little has changed in Latin America and the Caribbean and sub-Saharan Africa. The global unemployment rates have persisted in 2017 at 5.7%.[25] The UN reported that informal employment remains a major challenge to the goal of decent work.[26] Of 54 developing countries, more than half of those with jobs in non-agricultural sectors are informally employed.[27] Informal employment has a negative impact on earnings of these workers and also does not carry the social and economic protections workers in the regular employment sector have.[28]

There are statistically significant measured gender and youth employment differences in the LDCs. In very poor regions of the world (Western Asia and Northern Africa), women suffered an unemployment rate of 8% higher than men in 2018.[29] In Latin America and the Caribbean region, the rate for women was 3% higher than men.[30] Furthermore, the gender gap between men and women exacerbated this unemployment differential. Men's median hourly pay was 12% higher than that of women.[31] The youth unemployment rate was also 3

---

19 *Id.*
20 *Id.* (*Note*: There will be more about the impact of the virus on SDG 8 further in the chapter.)
21 *Id.*
22 2018 HLPF Background Note, *supra* note 2.
23 *Id.*
24 2019 SDG Report, *supra* note 4, at 38.
25 *Id.* at 38.
26 *Id.* at 39.
27 *Id.*
28 *What Is the Informal Economy?* WEIRGO, www.wiego.org/informal-economy (last accessed on Nov. 30, 2020).
29 2019 SDG Report, *supra* note 4, at 39.
30 *Id.*
31 *Id.*

times that of adult workers. In 2018, the youth unemployment rate was 12% as compared to 4% for adults.[32]

A final issue centers on access to education, employment, or training. One-fifth of the world's youth were not engaged in these opportunities and young women particularly were left out of these opportunities. Similar patterns in gender disparities were seen across developing nations around the globe. The lack of such opportunities for education, skill development, employment, and training greatly reduces the potential productivity of labor of these young people, especially women, and hinders their ability to add to the growth and development of their countries' economies.

Case Studies

Three countries have been selected as case studies of the ability (or inability) of developing countries to achieve economic growth in a sustained, inclusive, and sustainable way. Two countries, Singapore (Southeast Asia) and Kenya (Africa), have been making remarkable progress. Even though still much has to be done in these countries to achieve the targets set by the UN, they each offer important lessons that other developing and LDCs can learn from. The third country, Brazil (Latin America), has experienced diminished progress and will most likely not achieve SDG 8, as well as other SDGs by 2030. Brazil is an example of how weak institutions, political instability, and lack of commitment can encumber economic growth and lead to environmental degradation.

Singapore

The transformation of the city-state of Singapore over the past five decades has been impressive. Rapid economic growth delivered extraordinary improvements in social welfare and standard of living. During that period, Singapore has evolved into one of the world's most important financial and transportation centers, and it is the location for regional or global headquarters of major corporations. Its robust manufacturing base is involved primarily in high value-added activities and is a key link in the complex supply chain that wraps around East Asia. In 2017, Singapore was ranked the world's top maritime capital and as the key international airport center in the Association of Southeast Asian Nations (ASEAN) region. As a global financial center, Singapore ranks only behind London, New York, and Hong Kong, and ahead of Tokyo in the 2018 Global Financial Centers Index.[33] Singapore is also a popular investment destination as shown by an impressive share of global flows of Foreign Direct Investment (FDI).[34]

However, during recent years, the Singapore economy has been facing significant challenges that may delay the country's achievement of SDG 8 by 2030. In 2017, its per capita GDP growth of 3.6% was almost half of the Agenda 2030 target (8.1) and it has

---

32 *Id.*
33 *The Global Financial Centres Index 24*, Financial Centre Futures (Sept. 2018), www.longfinance.net/media/documents/GFCI_24_final_Report.pdf.
34 Manu Bhaskaran, *Getting Singapore in Shape: Economic Challenges and How to Meet Them*, Lowy Institute (Jun. 15, 2018), www.lowyinstitute.org/publications/getting-singapore-shape-economic-challenges-and-how-meet-them-0.

plummeted by almost one percentage point in 2018.[35] The annual changes in value-added per worker (Target 8.2) also declined during this period. Labor markets, on the other hand, showed some improvement in terms of inclusion (8.5 and 8.6).[36] The average unemployment rate has declined for all genders and young people.[37]

Some of these challenges are associated with domestic changes (such as rising business costs and demographic trends discussed above), while others stem from a number of external sources, such as disruptions caused by new technologies and changing structures of international competitiveness. These could not only threaten Singapore's position as a key global and regional economic hub, but also slow down its progress toward the achievement of the 2030 goals. Rising competition from other countries, such as China, India, and Mexico could have a significant impact on Singapore's ability to maintain its past rapid economic growth and competitive position in Asia.

In conclusion, Singapore's economy, while still robust and possessing considerable strengths, faces growing challenges. However, Singapore's ability to adjust effectively to these challenges may have weakened compared to the past. The major reason for this diminished capacity is that the policy responses required to support a successful adjustment may not be evolving quickly enough. If policymakers in Singapore are committed to the SDG 8, they need to seriously consider two intermediate objectives. First, Singapore needs to build greater resilience into Singapore's economy. In a world that is likely to be marked by volatility and frequent economic and financial shocks, Singapore's economy needs to be able to absorb shocks and bounce back rapidly. One of the ways to achieve this resiliency is to foster innovations and new technology. An increase in government-sponsored R&D may be beneficial in doing so. Second, Singapore needs to respond to an aging population and slowing population growth, rising costs, and slower productivity growth. Empirical analyses assessing Singapore's future point to two main adjustment mechanisms for dealing with such challenges: The government's top-down policy intervention and more spontaneous bottom-up adjustments by companies. Unless bolder changes are made to overcome these challenges, Singapore's extraordinary economic performance may prove difficult to sustain.[38]

Kenya

Kenya has introduced significant political, structural, and economic reforms that helped the country meet some Millennium Development Goals (MDGs) targets, including reduced child mortality, near universal primary school enrollment, and narrowed gender gaps in education.[39] While economic activity slowed down following the 2007–2008 Global Financial Crisis and the Great Recession, growth resumed in the last five years reaching 5.7% in 2019 (Target 8.1).[40] This placed Kenya as one of the fastest growing economies in sub-Saharan Africa.

---

35 *Sustainable Development Goals*, DEPARTMENT OF STATISTICS SINGAPORE, www.singstat.gov.sg/find-data/sdg/goal-8 (last accessed on Nov. 30, 2020).
36 *Id.*
37 *Id.*
38 *Id.*
39 Lily Kuo, *What's Holding Back Kenya's Economy?*, WORLD ECONOMIC FORUM (Mar. 16, 2016), www.weforum.org/agenda/2016/03/whats-holding-back-kenyas-economy.
40 *Id.*

Kenya's government has been committed to the SDGs, is a pioneer in partnerships, and has raised awareness among all stakeholders to engage in partnerships to achieve the SDGs. The UN and the government have been working together to develop the Kenya SDG Partnership Platform, called the Partnership Accelerator to develop capacity for SDG partnerships at the national or sub-national levels.[41] These partnerships build on the skills and resources available locally, and together, they are expected to have a transformative impact. The recent economic expansion has been boosted by a stable macroeconomic environment, positive investor confidence, and a resilient services sector.[42] Kenya is one of the leaders among African countries to foster mobile phone-use (Target 8.10). More than 80% of adults have an account at a bank or other financial institution or with a mobile-money-service provider.[43] Kenya also promoted access to financial services for farmers for agribusiness and assisted women-farmers with cash grants to diversify their livelihood options and become micro-entrepreneurs (Target 8.3).[44]

Although Kenya's commitment to the UN's Agenda 2030 is noteworthy, the country still faces many challenges and may not be able to reach the targets of SDG 8 in time. For example, under Kenya's "Vision 2030" plan, the country aims to reach the World Bank's second highest grouping of countries (upper middle income) by gross national income (GNI) within the next 15 years.[45] To meet its goal of becoming a developed economy by 2030, the country will need to jumpstart stagnating industries, provide more jobs for its youth, and reduce corruption. These aims may be difficult to achieve. As much as 80% of jobs are in the low-paying and less productive informal sector and only 75,000 formal jobs are being created each year.[46] Kenya's GNI would have to increase five-fold from $1,160 per capita to $5,600 to meet the World Bank's threshold for upper middle-income status.[47] Even if incomes grew at historically high rates, Kenya would still be far from this ambitious goal. Poverty is still a major problem. In 2019, about 57% of Kenya's population was among the poorest 20% of the global population.[48] As the World Economic Forum report concludes, "Looking in the rearview mirror, that is, at Kenya's past performance, the Vision 2030 goal seems farfetched."[49]

Kenya has the potential to be one of Africa's success stories from its growing youthful population, a dynamic private sector, highly skilled workforce, improved infrastructure, a new constitution, and its pivotal role in East Africa. The major goals for Kenya to continue to achieve sustainable growth center on addressing the challenges of poverty, inequality, governance, climate change, low investment, low firm productivity, and the skills gap between market requirements and the education curriculum.

---

41 *Id.*
42 *Id.*
43 *Sustainable Development Report 2019: Transformations to Achieve the Sustainable Development Goals*, Bertelsmann Stiftung, The Sustainable Development Solutions Network, at 53 (Jun. 28, 2019) [hereinafter "SDSN Report"].
44 *The Second Progress Report on Implementation of SDGs in Kenya: Civil Society Report 2019*, SDGS KENYA FORUM FOR SUSTAINABLE DEVELOPMENT, at 11 (Jun. 2019), https://sdgkenyaforum.org/content/uploads/documents/6c1e1bb60b0902e2.pdf.
45 Kuo, *supra* note 39.
46 *Id.*
47 *Id.*
48 *Id.*
49 Kuo, *supra* note 39.

Brazil

As the 9th largest economy in the world, Brazil has been a remarkable success story in the Latin American region. It has been rather successful in achieving MDGs, especially in the area of poverty reduction. It also reformed its labor markets. The country has advanced in creating national mechanisms for monitoring SDGs and established an online platform with available data on the international targets and indicators.[50] The advances, however, started to disappear, due to a series of harmful and severe austerity measures that were put in place by the Brazilian government in 2015–2017. Moreover, all government information regarding SDG efforts ended abruptly in December 2018. A recent report concluded that "nothing prepared civil society for the kind of setback that is undergoing since the new government took office in January 2019."[51]

During the last several years, the country has been suffering from sharp societal divisions and political upheavals. Growth has been affected by government instability fostered by the impeachment of President Dilma in 2016 and the election of far-right Jair Bolsonaro in 2018. GDP decreased by 3.5% in 2015 and 3.6% in 2016.[52] By 2019, the rate of growth was −4.7%.[53] One year after the labor reform approval, the average unemployment rate in 2018 was 12.3%, the highest in seven years.[54] In 2019, it was 12.7%, amounting to more than 13.4 million Brazilians. For young people, the unemployment rate was around twice the national average.[55] Over 60% of the unemployed were black or mixed race and around 51% were women.[56] Gender wage discrepancies are prevalent, with employed women making 20.5% less than men, with the same role and responsibilities at work.[57]

Perhaps the biggest challenge that Brazil is facing is the lack of commitment to preserve its valuable natural resources. It has 40% of the world's tropical forests and 20% of the planet's fresh-water supply, and the Brazilian economy relies heavily on their utilization.[58] As a result, economic growth in Brazil has not de-coupled from economic degradation and the situation has become more alarming. Dramatic fires and deforestation in the Amazon made global headlines in 2019. In fact, data indicate that deforestation rates in Brazil have been at the highest levels in two decades.[59] If deforestation persists at current rates, the Amazon could transform from one of the world's largest tropical forests into its largest desert with few trees. This would release up to 140 billion tons of stored carbon into the atmosphere,[60] effectively halting efforts to meet most of the Agenda 2030 goals, including SDG 8. Most

---

50 Grazielle Custódio David, *The Unreality of Promoting the SDGs without a Sufficient Budget*, SOCIAL WATCH, www.socialwatch.org/node/18072 (last accessed on Nov. 30, 2020).
51 *Id.*
52 Ana Cernov et al., *When Dismantling Democracy Becomes a Government Priority*, SOCIAL WATCH (2019), www.socialwatch.org/node/18297.
53 SDSN Report, *supra* note 43.
54 Cernov, *supra* note 52.
55 *Id.*
56 *Id.*
57 Cernov, *supra* note 52.
58 Sue Branford & Mauricio Torres, *As 2019 Amazon Fires Die Down, Brazilian Deforestation Roars Ahead*, MONGABAY (Oct. 23, 2019), https://news.mongabay.com/2019/10/as-2019-amazon-fires-die-down-brazilian-deforestation-roars-ahead/.
59 *Id.*
60 *Id.*

importantly, Brazil's failure to protect the Amazon can then have far-reaching consequences for global survival.

To tackle the big challenges and to move closer to the SDG 8 targets, Brazil needs to transform its institutional framework, restore political stability, and bring in accountable and responsible leadership that is committed to the goals set by the 2030 Agenda. This means that Brazil needs an all-inclusive transformative strategy. This is a task that is not easy to accomplish and yet, is absolutely necessary in order to increase the living standards of its millions of inhabitants, and at the same time, ensure the survival of future generations.

A Novel Global Challenge

Perhaps one of the most serious challenges that the world has been facing recently, which impacts the achievement of SDGs 8, comes from the novel coronavirus (COVID-19) pandemic that has triggered a global downturn of the scale similar to that of the Great Depression. Massive shut downs and quarantine measures across the globe, with restricted movement of people and goods, have cut business revenues and disrupted supply chains. Unemployment is skyrocketing while policymakers across many countries race to implement fiscal and monetary measures to alleviate the financial burden on citizens and shore up economies under severe strain.

None of the regions of the world have been spared as even the strongest and most diversified economies have been drastically affected by COVID-19. On April 15, 2020, the International Monetary Fund (IMF) warned that economies in Asia would see no growth this year for the first time in 60 years, with the service sector particularly under pressure.[61] Official data recently showed that the Chinese economy, the world's second largest economic superpower, had contracted 6.8% in the first quarter, the first time since quarterly records began in 1992.[62] The Chinese economy is likely to be hit further by reduced global demand for its products. According to a Reuters poll, the country's economic growth is expected to fall by 2.5% in 2020, its slowest in almost 50 years.[63] As for the impact on the US economy, around 4.4 million Americans filed unemployment claims in the week ending April 18, 2020, showing the continued impact of COVID-19 on the US economy.[64] That means more than 26 million people have lost their jobs in the United States over five consecutive weeks. Meanwhile, Bloomberg reports that around half the jobs in Africa are at risk as a result of the outbreak, according to the United Nations Economic Commission for Africa.[65]

A recent UN study has analyzed three scenarios for projecting the economic impact of the COVID-19 pandemic on the 2030 SDGs and the long-term future (through 2050).[66] The

---

61 Rosamond Hutt, *The Economic Effects of COVID-19 Around the World*, WORLD ECONOMIC FORUM (Feb. 17, 2020), www.weforum.org/agenda/2020/02/coronavirus-economic-effects-global-economy-trade-travel.
62 *Id.*
63 *Id.*
64 *Id.*
65 Alonso Soto, *Coronavirus May Weigh on African Economies for Three Years*, BLOOMBERG (Apr. 1, 2020), www.bloomberg.com/news/articles/2020-04-01/coronavirus-may-weigh-on-african-economies-for-three-years.
66 U.N. Secretary General, *Long-Term Future Trends and Scenarios—Impacts in the Economic, Social and Envrionmental Areas on the Realization of the Sustainable Devleopment Goals*, E/HLS/2020/5 (May 7, 2020).

three scenarios put forth are (1) Best Case Scenario (BC), (2) Business-as-Usual (BAU), and (3) Worst-case (WC).[67] The first one (BC) assumes a low-energy demand, reinforced global cooperation, higher level of scientific and technological engagement, and a quick pandemic end and economic recovery.[68] This scenario predicts that all SDGs are achieved by 2030, as planned, and there is a sustainability built into a high-tech interconnected world.[69] The second scenario (BAU) assumes a continuation of today's governance systems, continuation of rapid technological progress amid great socioeconomic and technological divides, with mainly national responses and lingering effects until 2021.[70] Progress is made toward the SDGs but major gaps remain. The third (WC) scenario envisions a fragmented world, unable to deal with its larger global challenges and a collapse of the multilateral political system with barriers to access to advancing knowledge and technologies.[71] There is a protracted health disaster and economic depression.[72] There is progress in a few of the SDGs, but regress in others, resulting in major sustainable development disasters.[73]

It is too early to make a full assessment of the COVID-19 effect on the global economy. In the last few months, governments of many countries passed legislation to address the economic impact of the pandemic and more initiatives to mitigate the damage are probably on the way. Yet, there are alarming signs that the world may not be able to reach SDG 8 and many other SDGs by 2030.

Policy Recommendations

So what do we do to help achieve SDG 8 of "sustained, inclusive and sustainable economic growth and decent employment for all"? Here are five suggestions to try to maintain the momentum of sustaining higher levels of economic growth and fostering economic sustainability and inclusion:

Encourage Stable and Well-Planned Monetary and Fiscal Policies in Developing Countries Based on Fiscal Responsibility and a Sound Financial System

Among the main targets of monetary policy are targets designed to achieve price stability, maximum output, and full employment. In this sense, monetary policy can be considered, by design, a policy compatible with sustainable economic growth. The other principal stabilization policy is fiscal policy. Several factors must be considered for the development of a sustainable fiscal policy. First, fiscal policy implicitly includes mechanisms acting as automatic stabilizers of short-run fluctuations. These automatic stabilizers are a fundamental characteristic of autonomous fiscal instruments, and they should be developed to further reduce the impact of the business cycle on low-income people. Second, fiscal instruments can be used to limit the negative effects of production activities on the environment by promoting energy efficiency and energy-related technological change, as basic pillars of sustainable economic growth.

---

67 *Id.* at 3.
68 *Id.* at 6.
69 *Id.* at 6.
70 *Id.* at 6.
71 *Id.*
72 *Id.*
73 *Id.*

Encourage Stable, Secure, and Continuous Government Upholding of the Principles of the Rule of Law, Private Property Rights, and Entrepreneurship

The rule of law is critical for economic growth. The importance of contracts in the buying and selling of goods and services and the borrowing and lending of financial assets, including loans, are heavily dependent on a firm legal system that enforces the contracts. This also hinges on the legal rights of property ownership and the upholding of those rights. There is a positive relationship between the rule of law index and the accumulation of physical and human capital.[74] The UN should establish a set of principles of good government and influence regional organizations to establish standards of good government in these regions.

Promote the Use of Environmentally Friendly Energy Resources Such as Solar and Wind Energy through Transfers of Renewable Energy Technology

This policy could be achieved through promotion of "Technology" bonds (similar to Disaster Recovery bonds). These could attract investors in developed countries to invest in programs in developing countries to adopt renewable energy technology. The UN could also work more with regional organizations and help them set a multilateral program of grants to promote renewable energy technology transfers.

Facilitate the Introduction of National Minimum Wages That Allow for the Working Poor to Earn a Decent Wage at 50% of the Median Household Income, Especially in Developing and LDCs

Motivations for introducing a statutory minimum wage in developing countries include reducing poverty, advancing social justice, and accelerating growth. Only about 50% of low-income and lower-middle-income countries have a statutory minimum wage.[75] One of the reasons governments in these countries are hesitant to introduce wage floors is their concerns about the effect of such floors on labor costs and overall competitiveness. This is the reason why regional partnerships and cooperation is crucial. The UN could set up a series of regional Roundtables to promote the idea that minimum wages can reduce poverty and accelerate growth without compromising each country's competitiveness.

Encourage Incorporating Contingency Plans into National Frameworks to Cope with Large-Scale Economic or Natural Disasters

As the world economy continues to grapple with the ongoing consequences and uncertainty of the novel COVID-19, we have to keep an eye on the hazards that could threaten the achievement of the 2030 Agenda. One of the key lessons of the COVID-19 is that countries

---

74 The WJP Rule of Law Index measures rule of law performance in 128 countries and jurisdictions across eight primary factors: Constraints on Government Powers, Absence of Corruption, Open Government, Fundamental Rights, Order and Security, Regulatory Enforcement, Civil Justice, and Criminal Justice. *See WJI Rule of Law Index*, https://worldjusticeproject.org/rule-of-law-index/.
75 T. H. Gindling, *Does Increasing the Minimum Wage Reduce Poverty in Developing Countries?*, I Z A WORLD OF LABOUR (Nov. 2018), https://wol.iza.org/articles/does-increasing-the-minimum-wage-reduce-poverty-in-developing-countries/long.

must act with urgency and build into their national framework plans for large-scale/long-term challenges, including the threat of a global pandemic.

Conclusions

This chapter provides an assessment of global and regional progress toward sustained, inclusive, and sustainable economic growth, one of the core SDGs of the 2030 Agenda. We found that despite recent progress, many regions struggle to reach the targets set by SDG 8, especially in the area of sustainability. Economic growth in all parts of the world, and especially in developing countries, is still linked to the use of resources and non-renewable energy sources. Industrialization, financial capacity growth, and promotion of new technologies in LDCs are also slow, inhibiting the meeting of the SDG 8 by 2030. In addition, in many regions/countries, the progress toward these goals has been hindered by political instability and weak economic institutions. COVID-19, with its global shut downs of air travel and commerce and restriction of movement of people, has exacerbated the problems that existed in many countries and created an unprecedented threat to the entire Agenda 2030.

More ambitious steps in the direction of SDG 8 need to be taken to move toward economic prosperity and social equality for the current generation and a better future for the ones to come. It is also important to remember that economic growth cannot be targeted alone, but rather has to be targeted as part of the entire development package. Traditional drivers of economic growth (industrialization, financial development, international trade, and specialization, technological advance, etc.) are necessary but not sufficient conditions to ensure broad-based human development and sustainability. The policy recommendations offered in this chapter touch upon a broader set of transformations that have been suggested originally in SDG 8. This is because economic growth has to be targeted together with other crucial components and structures, such as an accountable and transparent legal system, government stability, a sound monetary and fiscal framework, and inclusive institutions. It needs the "right" mixture of market forces and government policies. Economic growth also needs a commitment from all stakeholders, and especially from the national governments to improve our world and preserve the planet for future generations.

15 The Road to Sustainable Industrialization

Anna Shostya

Going Back to Where IT All Began

In 1769, James Watt patented his invention of the separate condenser for the Newcomen steam engine.[1] Seven years later, in partnership with Matthew Boulton, he began commercial production of steam engines,[2] thus marking a major turning point in the history of human civilization. Steam engines became a major source of mechanical power, dramatically improving cotton textile production and iron manufacture. The Industrial Revolution, however, was not the Age of Cotton or the Age of Steam,[3] but rather "the age of improvement."[4] Changes in textile and metallurgical technologies paved the road for a torrential increase in the rate of patenting and the technical improvements that were feasible only after advances in related fields.[5] The scale of the spillover effects was unparalleled, both in terms of the breadth and depth. By the mid-19th century, railway construction had transformed the landscape of Britain and became what economic historians call "the most important single stimulus to industrial growth in western Europe."[6] The changes were widespread and all of western Europe, and later the United States (US) profited by improvements in transportation, which included not only the railroads, but also road building, river work, canal construction, and vehicles. The Industrial Revolution initiated a cumulative, self-sustaining advance in technology, with repercussions felt in all aspects of economic life. It fostered unprecedented urbanization, mechanization, and modernization and promoted a multifaceted array of economic, social, political, and cultural changes, which in turn influenced the rate and course of technological development in today's developed countries.[7]

More than 250 years have passed since Watt's invention and many parts of the world have witnessed technological progress, mechanization, and advances in infrastructure that have increased productivity of labor, stimulated economic growth, and initiated the most significant structural change from a predominantly agricultural, labor-intensive economy to a predominantly industrial, capital-intensive one. Yet, the gains have not been ubiquitous.

---

1 LARRY NEAL AND RONDO CAMERON, A CONCISE ECONOMIC HISTORY OF THE WORLD, FROM PALEOLITHIC TIMES TO THE PRESENT (4th ed., 2003).
2 *Id.*
3 RODERICK FLOUD & DEIRDRE MCCLOSKEY, THE ECONOMIC HISTORY OF BRITAIN SINCE 1700 118 (1987).
4 JOEL MOKYR, THE LEVER OF RICHES: TECHNOLOGICAL CREATIVITY AND ECONOMIC PROGRESS 83 (1990).
5 *Id.*
6 DAVID LANDES, THE UNBOUND PROMETHEUS: TECHNOLOGICAL CHANGE AND INDUSTRIAL DEVELOPMENT IN WESTERN EUROPE FROM 1750 TO THE PRESENT 153 (1999).
7 Simon Kuznets, *Modern Economic Growth: Findings and Reflections*, 63(3) AM. ECON. REV. 247 (1973).

Today's advanced countries underwent this process between the 18th and 20th century and have been enjoying the benefits of the high-tech service-based economies. Many developing countries, especially Asian ones, have been going through this process since the end of the 20th century. Overall, manufacturing employs more than half a billion people worldwide and every job creates 2.2 jobs in other sectors, according to 2013 estimates.[8] Many developing and least developed countries (LDCs), however, have been lagging behind, both in terms of technological progress and industrialization.

Historical experience and modern empirical evidence suggest that much of economic growth, especially in developing and underdeveloped areas can be explained by technological advance, advances in infrastructure, and industrialization. These are the three pillars of the Sustainable Development Goal (SDG) 9, one of the 17 SDGs framework put forth in 2015 by the United Nations (UN).[9] The framework is called Agenda 2030 and it is an urgent call to transform the global community and to achieve sustained, inclusive, and sustainable development that leaves no one behind by 2030. This chapter provides global and regional assessments of the progress on SDG 9 and uses empirical evidence from three countries to draw recommendations for policy makers to ensure that the world is on the way toward "building resilient infrastracture, promoting industrialization and fostering innovation."[10] We start with a brief historical and theoretical justification of the interlinkages between these three pillars and economic growth. We then explain how these interlinkages became part of the 2030 vision. The section that follows utilizes available data to assess the regional progress toward SDG 9 and uses South Korea and the Democratic Republic of Congo (DRC) as case studies. We then discuss the effect of the short-term and long-term impacts of the ongoing Covid-19 pandemic on SDG 9. The last section concludes and offers policy recommendations.

Resilient Infrastructure, Sustainable Industrialization, and Widespread Innovation as Drivers of Economic Growth: Theoretical Framework

It has been long recognized that investment in infrastructure, machinery, and technology can foster economic growth. After all, much of the historical economic growth in Europe and North America during the 18th, 19th, and 20th centuries was due to important technological innovations, investment in transport, irrigation, and machinery. Classical economists (e.g. Adam Smith, David Ricardo, Alfred Marshall), therefore, believed that economic growth and development were "natural" processes that resulted from free markets and competitive forces and necessarily involved a transition from rural, agricultural, labor-intensive economy to an urban, industrial, and capital-intensive one. One of the most influential modern advocates of this model of development was the American economic historian Walt W. Rostow. According to his doctrine, the transition from underdevelopment to development can be described in terms of a series of steps or stages through which all countries must proceed: (1) the traditional society, (2) the pre-conditions for take-off into self-sustaining growth, (3) the take-off, (4) the drive to maturity; and (5) the age of

---

8 *Goal 9 Targets*, UNITED NATIONS DEVELOPMENT PROGRAMME (UNDP), www.undp.org/content/undp/en/home/sustainable-development-goals/goal-9-industry-innovation-and-infrastructure/targets.html (last visited Nov. 6, 2020) [hereinafter "UNDP Goal 9"].
9 *Id.*
10 *Id.*

high mass consumption.[11] A required feature of the "take-off" stage was the mobilization of domestic (or foreign) saving in order to generate adequate investment to accelerate economic growth. The traditional ("Old") neoclassical model viewed economic growth as a result of increases in labor quantity, increases in physical capital, and improvement in technology. In fact, Robert Solow, the Nobel Prize laureate, estimated that roughly 50% of historical growth in the industrialized nations was a result of technological change and assumed its level, together with other growth theorists, to be determined exogenously, that is, independently of other factors.[12]

Neoclassical theory offered an appealing explanation of economic growth and development: Liberalization (opening up) of national markets draws additional domestic and foreign investment and thus increases the rate of capital accumulation. Yet, it failed to recognize that saving and investment is a necessary but not a sufficient condition for economic growth. The theory's major oversight was its negligence of the role of government reforms, political stability, a sound financial system, and other institutional factors that are necessary to establish the environment conducive to innovation and technological advance. Deliberate thinking about the role of these drivers of economic growth and the framework that fosters these drivers, came about rather recently, at the end of the 20th century, when the New Growth economic theory, led by Romer and Lucas, offered a new look at the endogenous factors that promote economic prosperity.[13] Endogenous models placed greater focus on the concept of human capital and the idea that workers with greater knowledge, education, and training are more productive and thus help to increase the rates of technological development. New Growth advocates also argued that scientific knowledge could not only lead to a greater quantity and quality of goods and increase employment but also foster further knowledge and development. A good example that supports this argument comes from the development of computers and the internet that have had an ever-increasing return to scale and brought radically improved working conditions and quality of life for millions of people. Thus, increased application of new scientific knowledge in the form of inventions and innovations in both physical and human capitals can lead to more and better roads, railways, waterways, airways, and other transportation and communication systems.

The end of the 20th century, however, has brought a lot of evidence from developing and the least developed regions of the world that did not support the theoretical framework, and was rather different from the historical evidence that came from today's most advanced economies. Most of those developing and LDCs experienced a technological and scientific vacuum and struggled to develop a reliable, sustainable, and resilient infrastructure. Relying mostly on resource extraction for revenues, their economies were not well diversified to mitigate external shocks, such as a disaster, a major conflict, or a financial crisis. Part of the vacuum was a result of a lack of savings (or the so-called "savings gap"), in turn a result of their underdeveloped financial systems. Studies have suggested that increases in the share of Foreign Direct Investment (FDI) or the relative productivity of the foreign firms lead to a higher additional growth in financially developed economies compared to those observed in

---

11 Walt Rostow, *The Stages of Economic Growth*, 12 (1) ECON. HIST. REV. 1 (1959).
12 Robert Solow, *A Contribution to the Theory of Economic Growth*, 70 (1) Q. J. OF ECON. 65 (1956).
13 Paul M. Romer, *Increasing Returns and Long-Run Growth*, 94(5) J. POL. ECON. 1002 (1986). *See also* Robert E. Lucas, *On the Mechanisms of Economic Development*, 22 J. MONETARY ECON. 3 (1988).

financially underdeveloped ones.[14] Foreign Direct Investment levels were also catastrophically low, mostly because of the uncertainty and volatility that drenched those regions.

From Agenda 21 to Agenda 2030

The role of infrastructure, industrialization, and technology in sustainable development was first recognized at the 1992 UN's Earth Summit in Rio de Janeiro.[15] Agenda 21, the summit's outcome document, and the Rio Declaration on Environment and Development provided the fundamental framework for policy discussion and actions related to these three interrelated sources of sustainable development.[16] The relationship between industrial development and social objectives, such as poverty eradication, job creation, and greater access to education and health care were also identified in Chapter 2 of the Johannesburg Plan of Implementation (JPOI) at the 2002 World Summit on Sustainable Development.[17] The JPOI also advanced the dialog on sustainable transportation and its role in promoting economic growth.[18]

The global community continued this discussion at the 2012 United Nations Conference on Sustainable Development (Rio +20). The importance of the transport sector has also been linked to climate action as a-quarter of energy-related global greenhouse gas emissions come from transport and these emissions are anticipated to grow substantially in the future.[19] The year after the Rio +20 conference, the Lima Declaration: Toward Inclusive and Sustainable Industrial Development addressed the relevance of inclusive and sustainable industrial development as the basis for sustainable economic growth. Paragraph 2 of the Lima Declaration states,

> industrialization is a driver of development. Industry increases productivity, job creation, and generates income, thereby contributing to poverty eradication and addressing other development goals, as well as providing opportunities for social inclusion, including gender equality, empowering women and girls and creating decent employment for the youth.[20]

Li Yong, Director General of the UN's Industrial Development Organization, forcefully argued at the conference,

---

14 Parash Upreti, Factors Affecting Economic Growth in Developing Countries, 17 MAJOR THESES IN ECON. 37 (2015).
15 *Id.* at 7.
16 Chapters 7 and 9 of the Agenda focus on the role of transport; chapter 30 focuses on the role of business and industry; and chapter 34 addresses the issues of transfer of environmentally sound technology to be adopted in specific international instruments. *See* United Nations Sustainable Development (UNSD), *United Nations Conference on Environment & Development, Rio de Janeiro, Brazil, 3 to 14 June 1992*, https://sustainabledevelopment.un.org/content/documents/Agenda21.pdf (1992).
17 *Industry*, UN SUSTAINABLE DEVELOPMENT GOALS KNOWLEDGE PLATFORM (UNSDGKP), https://sustainabledevelopment.un.org/topics/industry (last visited Dec. 2, 2020).
18 *Sustainable Transport*, UNSDGKP, https://sustainabledevelopment.un.org/topics/sustainabletransport (last visited Dec. 2, 2020).
19 *Id.*
20 *Lima Declaration 2013*, UN Industrial Development Organization (UNIDO), www.unido.org/who-we-are/inclusive-and-sustainable-industrial-development/lima-declaration (last visited Nov. 6, 2020).

> Industry is at the core of any development path. In order to eradicate poverty and to achieve higher levels of prosperity for all peoples, we will need to accelerate economic growth, driven by industrial development in all our countries. We need to do more to advance the industrialization of all countries, so they can create decent jobs and opportunities for all of their people. The entire world wants, and needs, to grow its industries.[21]

This call for the structural transformation that enhances productivity, promotes transfer and absorption of environmentally sound technologies, encourages inclusive and sustainable industrial development, and improves connectivity and infrastructure was at the heart of the UN's 2030 Agenda. SDG 9 is the world's commitment to "build resilient infrastructure, promote inclusive and sustainable industrialization and foster innovation" to ensure sustainable and all-inclusive economic growth in all parts of the world. The UN has identified 8 Targets and 12 Indicators for SDG 9. Five of the Targets are universal (which means they apply to *all* countries), while some (Targets 9.3 and 9.5) place a special emphasis on developing countries.

The last three targets (Targets 9.a, 9.b, and 9.c) focus specifically on developing, LDCs and in some cases small island states. The UN's SDG 9 is strongly linked to the SDG 8 and has a special focus on the countries that have been in desperate need to promote crucial drivers of economic growth. Four of the targets (Targets 9.1, 9.2, 9.3, and 9.c) have a direct impact on social development and inclusion and thus are linked to SDG 5 (on gender equality) and SDG 10 (on inequality within and between countries). SDG 9 targets also underscore the link between technology, the environment, and development and call for building sustainable infrastructure and industrialization (Target 9.1 and 9.2) and a "greater adoption of clean and environmentally sound technologies and industrial processes" (Target 9.4). Therefore, SDG 9 is linked to SDG 7 (on access to affordable, reliable, sustainable, and modern energy), SDG 12, (on sustainable consumption and production patterns), and SDG 13 (on climate change).

Assessment of Progress toward SDG 9

Since 2015, the world has seen the most rapid progress toward three SDGs and SDG 9 (Industry, Innovation, and Infrastructure) is among them.[22] There have been some impressive advances made in economic infrastructure in developing countries (an increase of more than 30% in real terms since 2010) and in mobile connectivity (by 2018, 90% of the world's population had 3G internet or higher-quality network). The recent trends in manufacturing value added (MVA) per capita[23] indicate strong growth trends in all country groups. Global investment in research and development has also been growing. Manufacturing is the most important sector and a major driver of economic growth for

---

21 *Id.*
22 The other two are SDG 1 (No Poverty) and SDG 11 (Sustainable Cities and Communities). *See* JEFFREY SACHS, ET AL., THE SUSTAINABLE DEVELOPMENT GOALS AND COVID-19, SUSTAINABLE DEVELOPMENT REPORT 2020 (2020) [hereinafter "SDG and COVID-19 2020"].
23 MVA is a widely recognized indicator of Target 9.2, on the role of manufacturing production and employment in sustainable industrial development. *See* UNIDO, *Statistical Indicators of Inclusive and Sustainable Industrialization. Biennial Progress Report 2019*, at 13, https://www.unido.org/sites/default/files/files/2020-07/SDG_report_final.pdf (2019) [hereinafter "UNIDO Biennial Report"].

developing economies in general, accounting for the largest share of total exports in Africa (58.0%), Latin America (75.8%), developing Asia-Pacific (89.1%), and developing Europe (91.3%) in 2016.[24] In 2017, the five major developing economies—China, India, Brazil, Indonesia, and Mexico—accounted for almost 70% of manufacturing employment in the developing and the emerging world and about 10% of total global employment.[25] In LDCs, the number of manufacturing jobs doubled between 2000 and 2017, reaching 30 million.[26]

Gender-disaggregated data and data on marginalized demographic groups have been sparse, particularly in LDCs. Even though significant improvement has been achieved in data availability during recent years, it is still very difficult to make an assessment toward the SDGS in the Arab region, sub-Saharan Africa (SSA), and Oceania. There are significant data gaps and time lags in official statistics. Nonetheless, available gender-disaggregated data show that global female employment in manufacturing rose from 41.0% to 43.7% in the period 2000–2017, with the largest growth in female participation in Africa, Asia-Pacific, and Latin America.[27] Most women, however, are employed in low-tech industries, such as food and beverages, textiles, and wearing apparel.[28]

And how about the sustainability aspect of industrial development? Some indicators of Target 9.4 that address this aspect and call for increased resource-use efficiency and greater adoption of environmentally friendly technologies display encouraging signs. The total amount and relative intensity of CO_2 emissions from manufacturing industries have been showing a declining trend since 2015. China, the top emitter of CO_2 among developing and emerging industrial economies, has seen the relative value of its emissions per unit of MVA dropping from 1.65 kg/USD in 2005 to 0.95 kg/USD in 2015.[29]

At the same time, SDG 9 exhibits the largest inequality between top and bottom performers.[30] High-income European and North American countries rely on high-tech industries and are making some, albeit marginal, progress toward resource-efficient production. The Organization for Economic Cooperation and Development (OECD) region, the club of mostly wealthy countries, tops the SDG 9 Index score dashboard.[31] The overall picture in these regions, however, is rather mixed. There are still severe shortcomings regarding progress toward SDG 9.[32] According to the Sustainable Development Report 2020, the SDG 9 Index score for East and South Asia is more than twice of that for SSA and five times more than that in Oceania.[33] The disparities in industrial productivity between developed and LDCs are particularly troubling. In 2018, MVA per capita was only $114 in LDCs,

---

24 *Id.* at 19.
25 *Id.* at 24.
26 *Id.*
27 *Id.* at 27.
28 *Id.*
29 *Id.* at 40.
30 The SDG Index tracks country performance on the 17 SDGs, as agreed by the international community in 2015 with equal weight to all 17 goals. The score signifies a country's position between the worst (0) and the best or target (100) outcomes. There is also a score calculated for each individual SDG. For methodology and recent Index data *see* SDG and COVID-19 2020, *supra* note 22 at 30.
31 SDG and COVID-19 2020, *supra* note 22 at 32.
32 High-Level Political Forum on Sustainable Development, *HLPF Background Note— Implementing the SDGs: Lessons from the regions,* https://sustainabledevelopment.un.org/content/documents/1985 62018_background_notes_Key_regional_trendswith_original_header.pdf (2018) [hereinafter "HLPF Background Note"].
33 SDG and COVID-19 2020, *supra* note 22 at 30.

compared to almost $5,000 in Europe and Northern America.[34] Although LDCs more than doubled their MVA in the period 2007–2017, their share in global manufacturing production increased only slightly during this period (from 0.5% to 0.8%).[35] The progress in LDCs that has been recorded to date remains below the targets identified by the 2030 Agenda.

There are wide disparities among regions in terms of spending on research and development as well. In 2017, in Europe and Northern America, 2.25% of GDP was spent on research and development (R&D), compared to only 0.54% in Central and Southern Asia and 0.38% in SSA.[36] Basic infrastructure, like roads, information and communication technologies, and electrical power are still limited in many developing countries. At least a billion people still do not have access to reliable phone services and about 2.6 billion people in the developing world are facing difficulties in accessing electricity full time.[37]

Below, we offer the assessment of three selected regions: Asia and the Pacific, Latin America and the Caribbean, and Africa. We focus on these regions because, even though they exhibit a wide country-based variation of the level of industrial development and technological achievement, each of these regions provides a different perspective on the progress made toward SDG 9.

Asia and the Pacific

Overall, the countries in this region have been showing significant progress in the area of innovation, new industries, and infrastructure, with East and South Asia topping the overall 2020 SDG 9 Index scores after OECD countries.[38] Asian economies produce the largest share of manufacturing output (more than 60% in 2017), with China heading the list of the ten largest manufacturing producers worldwide since 2010 and almost a quarter of the world MVA in 2017.[39] China alone employs more than 80 million people in the manufacturing sector.[40] There is an overall upward trend in manufacturing in Asian LDCs, with an annual growth rate of 8.4%.[41] The region's (excluding China) female employment as a proportion of manufacturing employment has been rather low but has increased slightly from 31.7% in 2010 to 32.4% in 2017.[42] China's relative female employment in manufacturing has been on a decline, reflecting a shift to a service-based economy, and was 46.6% in 2017.[43] At the same time, this rapid growth in manufacturing in this region is responsible for most of the world's growth in CO_2 emissions, which more than doubled in the period from 2000 to 2015.[44]

The region's success in building a strong industrial base and emphasizing technological advance can be particularly seen in East Asian economies that became known as the four Asian

---

34 *SDG Goals: SDG 9 Industry, Innovation and Infrastructure*, UN STATISTICS DIVISION, https://unstats.un.org/sdgs/report/2019/goal-09/ (last visited Dec. 2, 2020).
35 UNIDO Biennial Report, *supra* note 23 at 14.
36 *The Sustainable Development Goals Report* (2020), at 45, https://unstats.un.org/sdgs/report/2020 [hereinafter, "SDG Report 2020"].
37 UNDP Goal 9, *supra* note 8.
38 SDG and COVID-19 2020, *supra* note 22 at 32.
39 UNIDO Biennial Report, *supra* note 23 at 16.
40 *Id*. at 26.
41 *Id*. at 20.
42 *Id*. at 57.
43 *Id*.
44 *Id*. at 41.

Tigers (South Korea, Singapore, Hong Kong, and Taiwan).[45] Since the 1980s, these countries promoted robust export-driven manufacturing push, coordinated by the government, and motivated by strong financial incentives. Recently, however, some of these economies have been facing structural challenges. In Singapore, for example, although the share of MVA as a proportion of Gross Domestic Product (GDP) (Indicator 9.2.1) has been exhibiting a strong growth trend (from 17.6% in 2016 to 18.4% in 2017 to 20.7% in 2018), the MVA per capita (Indicator 9.2.1) has declined from 10.3% in 2017 to 6.5% in 2018,[46] reflecting perhaps an aging population, declining workforce growth and productivity growth.[47] Private R&D expenditure (Indicator 9.5.1) as a proportion of GDP has still been disappointedly low, despite several decades of the government's effort to boost it.[48] Nevertheless, East Asian economies and China have been moving successfully toward achieving most of the targets of SDG 9. Among these countries, the Republic of Korea has been recognized as a leader of high-tech industry and is one of the most prominent examples of how industrialization and technology can lead to strong economic growth and human development. Below, we discuss the sources of its recent success in more details.

Case Study: The Republic of Korea (South Korea)

In the 1960s, the Republic of Korea was a low-income, capital-intensive, low-tech country that specialized mainly in steel and chemicals.[49] In the 1980s and 1990s, South Korean government embraced free market reforms, fostered an industrial strategy, and communicated this strategy with industry leaders. Industrial targeting was pragmatic, consistent, and flexible, with the government supporting infant industries only at their early stages of growth.[50] Following in the footsteps of Japan, South Korea developed strong automobile and electronics industries and invested in infrastructure. Another reason South Korea has advanced its high-tech sector is because of its investment in human capital. The country has a well-developed primary and secondary school system, which is among the best in the world. [51]

Since 2013, the South Korean government has been on a mission to establish what is termed as "the creative economy."[52] The government has set three goals:

- To create new jobs and markets through creativity and innovation;
- To strengthen its global leadership through a creative economy; and
- To create a society where creativity is respected and manifested.[53]

---

45 THE WORLD BANK, THE EAST ASIAN MIRACLE: ECONOMIC GROWTH AND PUBLIC POLICY 1 (1993).
46 The World Bank Data https://data.worldbank.org/indicator/NV.IND.MANF.ZS?locations=SG.
47 Manu Bhaskaran, *Getting Singapore in Shape: Economic Challenges and How to Meet Them*, LOWY INSTITUTE, www.lowyinstitute.org/publications/getting-singapore-shape-economic-challenges-and-how-meet-them-0 (June 15, 2018).
48 *Id.*
49 GÉRARD ROLAND, DEVELOPMENT ECONOMICS (2016).
50 SANJAYA LALL, COMPETITIVENESS, TECHNOLOGY AND SKILLS (2001).
51 *Id.* at 46.
52 UN Conference on Trade and Development (UNCTAD), *Strengthening the Creative Industries for Development in the Republic of Korea*, UNCTAD/DITC/TED/2017/4, at 6 (2017).
53 *Id.* at 7.

The policy is aimed at the reduction of reliance on large corporations (like Samsung and Hyundai) and instead promotes support and expansion of small-to-medium businesses to create jobs. In 2013 alone, the government allocated about $3 billion to support startup companies as the new growth engines.[54] By 2015, 17 Centers for Creative Economy & Innovation (CCEI) were open across the country to function as regional innovation hubs to support startup ventures. Each center has an online Creative Economy Town that serves as a core off-line platform for the promotion of people's ideas and technologies and suggesting them to local businesses.[55] Anyone can publicly propose ideas, exchange opinions, and participate in evaluation and mentoring. This collective intelligence is then provided to the government and businesses as ways of solving social, economic, and environmental issues. These centers have been supported jointly by local governments and major Korean companies. Such government-driven strategy utilizes the country's strengths—science, information, and communication technology capacity, culture, and education—to ensure progress toward achieving SDG 9.

Latin America and the Caribbean

As a region, Latin America and the Caribbean (LAC) has been unable to transform its production structure and build technological capacity similar to those in Asia and particularly in East Asian countries. The region still mainly relies on natural-resource exports and resource-intensive low-tech manufacturing for economic growth. The decline in investment in machinery and equipment is particularly worrisome because it has very serious repercussions for productivity growth and technological upgrading. This means that the region is not building the capacity or infrastructure needed to change its development pattern.[56] Investments in technological innovation and infrastructure have also been on decline, which indicates the weakness of domestic capacity building.[57] This affects the region's international competitiveness, as well as the achievement of other SDGs, especially the ones related to poverty (SDG 1) and economic growth (SDG 8).

The region also suffers from harsh inequalities. Differences in internet access, for example, persist between rural and urban areas, with the difference in penetration of about 27 percentage points.[58] The Caribbean infrastructure is lagging behind that of Latin America. In 2016, only four Caribbean countries had port infrastructures that were of an adequate or high standard. The others were either in a poor state with immediate need for reinvestment or were ports with poor infrastructure layout.[59] Among all countries, only Brazil has Research and Development capacity comparable to dynamic emerging market

---

54 *Id.* at 33.
55 *See Creative Economy*, Creative Korea, www.creativekorea.or.kr (last visited October 14, 2020).
56 Economic Commission for Latin America and the Caribbean (ECLAC), *Annual Report on Regional Progress and Challenges in Relation to the 2030 Agenda for Sustainable Development in Latin America and the Caribbean*, LC/L.4268(FDS.1/3)/Rev.1, at 22 (2017) [hereinafter "LAC Annual Report"].
57 *Id.*
58 *SDG 9: Build Resilient Infrastructure, Promote Inclusive and Sustainable Industrialization and Foster Innovation in Latin America and the Caribbean*, ECLAC, at 1, /www.cepal.org/sites/default/files/static/files/sdg9_c1900691_press.pdf (2019) [hereinafter "ECLAC SDG 9 2019"].
59 *Id.*

economies.⁶⁰ Other countries are lagging far behind with no more than 1% of GDP spent on R&D.⁶¹ Most spend half of that.

Another type of inequality that hinders the region's progress toward SDG 9 is gender inequality. A high proportion of women are employed in micro- and small enterprises, which constitute between 70% and 85% of enterprises in the Caribbean, contribute between 60% and 70% of GDP, and account for about 50% of employment.⁶² These enterprises, however, often face disproportionately high overheads and low operating margins,⁶³ which limit earning potential and opportunities to advance for women.

Even though progress has been slow in many indicators, there are some encouraging signs, especially in the area of clean energy use. Many countries have introduced regulatory frameworks and fiscal incentives to promote renewable energy and related research.⁶⁴ There is also a significant improvement in terms of regional cooperation. The Caribbean Community Climate Change Center Plan (2011–2021), for example, promotes regional initiatives to facilitate technology transfer and absorption, and is complemented by a first regional Strategic Plan for the Caribbean Community (2015–2019).⁶⁵ This plan is a vision to foster innovation and creativity, entrepreneurship, digital literacy, and inclusiveness.

Another regional cooperation project is the "Developing Sustainable Industrial Parks in Latin American and Caribbean Countries" initiative, which is supported by the UN Industrial Development Organization LAC Trust Fund, and involves eight participating countries (Argentina, Bolivia, Chile, Costa Rica, El Salvador, Guatemala, Peru, Panama, and Paraguay).⁶⁶ The initiative's objective is to strengthen cooperation and potential synergies for promoting social development and sustainable industrial growth and minimizing their environmental impacts. The project began at the end of 2015 and seeks to improve cooperation within the region and develop technical experience in planning, developing, and managing sustainable industrial parks.⁶⁷ Such regional cooperation is essential to strengthen and update the region's technological capacity and gradually reduce its dependence on natural resources. The region still has a long way to go however, if it is to meet SDG 9 by 2030, especially in the area of inclusion and equity.

Africa

Due to high poverty rates and insecurity and conflict in some countries, performance on most socioeconomic and developmental goals in Africa (with the exception of North Africa)

---

60 *Regional Overview: Latin America and the Caribbean*, UN Educational, Scientific and Cultural Organization (UNESCO), https://en.unesco.org/unesco_science_report/lac (last visited Dec. 1, 2020) [hereinafter "UNESCO Regional Overview"].
61 *Id.*
62 ECLAC SDG 9 2019, *supra* note 58 at 2.
63 *Id.*
64 UNESCO Regional Overview, *supra* note 60.
65 *Strategic Plan for the Caribbean Community 2015–2019: Repositioning Caricom Vol. 1—The Executive Plan*, CARICOM, https://caricom.org/documents/strategic-plan-caribbean-community-2015-2019/ (July 3, 2014).
66 *Development of Sustainable Industrial Parks in Latin America and Caribbean*, UNIDO, www.unido.org/sites/default/files/files/2018 (May 2017).
67 *Id.*

has been poor compared to other world regions.[68] African's MVA added share in GDP (at constant 2010 US$) has been the lowest among all regions and has been only about 10.4% from 2015 on.[69] The MVA added per capita that rose from $159 in 2000 to $197 in 2015,[70] has been stagnating. The trend in manufacturing employment has been even more disappointing, showing a slight increase (from 7.6% to 8.2% of total employment) from 2000 to 2010 and then a reversal to the initial level by 2017.[71] At 44.4%, female employment as a proportion of manufacturing employment is one of the highest among regions yet it has not changed since 2015.[72] The proportion of medium high- and high-tech value added in total manufacturing has declined from 20.9% in 2005 to 18.7% in 2015 and no recent data are available.[73] Total emissions from manufacturing have been rising very slowly but are rather minimal in comparison to other parts of the world.

There is an acute deficit of infrastructure that undermines industrial development in the region.[74] Even though there has been some progress during 2010–2015, airfreight and air travel remain extremely low, representing only 1.3% and 1.5% of the world air travel and air shipping, respectively.[75] Rail transportation is not well developed either and represents only 6% of the total rail in the world, compared to 10% in Latin America and the Caribbean and 12% in Asia and the Pacific.[76] Some countries, however, are making significant strides in this area. In Kenya, for example, there has been a major effort to improve infrastructure and enhance connectivity and trade. The Lamu Port South Sudan Ethiopia Transport (LAPSSET) Corridor Project is considered to be the largest integrated transformative infrastructure project in Africa (Target 9.1).[77] In 2017, the government outlined the "Big Four" development priority areas and one of them prioritized manufacturing (Target 9.2). One of the countries that has been lagging severely behind even its regional neighbors and yet has been recently displaying a welcomed promise is the Democratic Republic of Congo (DRC). We offer here some insights into its historical trends and recent developments.

Case Study: The Democratic Republic of Congo

The DRC is one of the world's poorest countries, with an annual GDP per capita of about $800 in 2017.[78] The country failed to meet any Millennium Development Goals by 2015 and much-needed economic reforms have been slow because of years of bloody conflicts, political upheavals, and systemic corruption.[79] Another reason for DRC's stagnant economic growth is what economists call a "resource curse," a phenomenon associated

---

68 *See* AFRICAN UNION ET. AL., 2017, *Africa Sustainable Development Report:Tracking Progress on Agenda 2063 and the Sustainable Development Goals* 88 (2017) [hereinafter "2017 Africa Report"].
69 *Id.* at 88.
70 UNIDO Biennial Report page 55.
71 *Id.* at 56.
72 *Id.* at 57.
73 *Id.* at 60.
74 2017 Africa Report, *supra* note at 94.
75 *Id.* at xiv.
76 *Id.* at 88.
77 Ngala Chome, *Land, Livelihoods and Belonging: Negotiating Change and Anticipating LAPSSET in Kenya's Lamu County*, 14(2) J. E. AFR. STUD. 310, 310–31 (2020).
78 *The World Factbook: Congo, Democratic Republic of the*, CENTRAL INTELLIGENCE AGENCY, www.cia.gov/library/publications/the-world-factbook/geos/cg.html (last visited Dec. 3, 2020).
79 Roland, *supra* note 49 at 537.

with an overdependence on mineral deposits and lack of diversification. Studies show that countries with wealthy resource endowments fail to grow more rapidly than those without.[80] The DRC is endowed with a vast amount of natural resources that include tropical woods, diamonds, copper, and coltan (a rare metal that is used in electronics) and yet the economy has been in decline since the 1980s. The country's power infrastructure is inadequate and inefficiently operated and the DRC lags well behind peer countries in electrification.[81]

In recent years however, the DRC government has initiated a quest to diversify its economy and reduce poverty. Upgrading infrastructure is at the core of this ambitious plan. Since mid-2000, when most of the spending on infrastructure (less than half a billion dollars per year) was financed from domestic sources,[82] the country has made significant strides. It now enjoys the new 34-km road, which directly links the Kamoa-Kakula copper project, a mining project in the DRC and the Kolwezi airport in Zambia. This corridor offers endless opportunities and is only part of the grand vision.[83] Another part is the Ruzizi III, a 147-megawatt (MW) hydropower project being developed on the Ruzizi River that flows along the borders of the DRC, Burundi, and Rwanda.[84] The implementation of this project, as well as the proposed Grand Inga project (the world's largest hydropower scheme that is anticipated to generate about 40,000 megawatts of power from water sourced at the mouth of the Congo River)[85] however, depends on regional and international support. The Ruzizi III is being developed as a public–private partnership between the three countries, a consortium of Industrial Promotion Services and SN Power through a 25-year concession agreement.[86] The proposed Build, Own, Operate, Transfer (BOOT) structure is beneficial to all countries, as each of the three contracting states will have a stake of 10% with an equal off-take share in the project and the rest going to the consortium.[87] International financial institutions such as the World Bank, the EU, the European Investment Bank, the African Development Bank, and a few others will fund 60% of the project cost.[88] The EU-Africa Infrastructure Trust Fund approved a total technical assistance grant of €4.2M ($4.6M) for this project, which is being developed with an estimated investment of $650M to $700M, and is expected to be operational by 2026.[89] Although the progress is slow in other areas of SDG 9, there is hope that these partnerships, together with the government commitment to overhaul the

---

80 See Jeffrey A. Frankel, *The Natural Resource Curse: A Survey of Diagnoses and Some Prescriptions*, HKS Faculty Research Working Paper Series, JOHN F. KENNEDY SCHOOL OF GOVERNMENT, HARVARD UNIVERSITY (2012) https://dash.harvard.edu/bitstream/handle/1/8694932/RWP12-014_Frankel.pdf.
81 Nataliya Pushak & Cecilia Briceño-Garmendia, *The Republic of Congo's Infrastructure: A Continental Perspective*, THE INTERNATIONAL BANK FOR RECONSTRUCTION AND DEVELOPMENT AND THE WORLD BANK, at 1 https://openknowledge.worldbank.org/bitstream/handle/10986/27259/630990WP0P12420 0Box0361499B0PUBLIC0.pdf?sequence=1&isAllowed=y (2010),
82 *Id*. at 2.
83 Koketso Lediga, *How Infrastructure and Energy Are Key to a New Economic Journey in the Democratic Republic of Congo*, AFRICANEWS, www.africanews.com/2019/10/01/how-infrastructure-and-energy-are-key-to-a-new-economic-journey-in-the-democratic-republic-of-congo-drc-by-koketso-lediga-managing-director-infra-afrika-advisory// (last visited Nov. 6, 2020).
84 *Id*.
85 *Id*.
86 *Id*.
87 *Id*.
88 *Id*.
89 *Id*.

DRC's infrastructure will bear short-term benefits that may have spillover effects onto other SDG 9 targets and overall development.

A Bump in the Road: The Effect of Covid-19 on the SDG 9 Progress

External shocks, like armed cross-border conflicts, natural disasters, and epidemics can have profound implications on the progress toward the 2030 Agenda. This is why the ongoing Covid-19 pandemic presents a grave threat, both in terms of human health and other socioeconomic dimensions of development. The world is still in the early phase of the outbreak and at the time of this writing, cases have been increasing drastically in many countries. Early lockdown and quarantines have somewhat flattened the curve and helped to curb the spread, yet they put hundreds of millions of people out of work and thus without income to feed their families. Even though official statistics record a large majority of cases in the United States, Brazil, and India (as of July 10, 2020), it is LDCs that are affected the most.[90] Authorities in these countries lack the ability to track the outbreak and very often are unwilling to.[91] They are also the least prepared for a pandemic and while in high-income countries, governments extended unprecedented support to their jobless masses, many developing and LDCs had to lift nation-wide lockdowns early or ignore them in the first place, to bring relief to their battered economies.[92] As a result, by June 2020, infections were rising especially rapidly in South Asia and Latin America, the regions that had a slow infection rate during the first months of the outbreak.[93]

It is too early to estimate the full effect of the Covid-19 outbreak on progress toward SDG 9, yet there are alarming signs that it is having what the recent Sustainable Development Report termed a "mixed or moderately negative impact."[94] All around the world the work on infrastructure projects has been limited or halted and industrial production has suffered from imposed quarantines and mobility restrictions. In Hanoi, Vietnam, such impediments delayed a test of a new metro line because more than 100 Chinese engineers involved in building it were unable to re-enter the country.[95] China's most massive global infrastructure project, the Belt and Road Initiative (BRI) that involved hundreds of billions of dollars in loans and grants for power plants, ports, railways, and roads in Africa, Latin America, South-East Asia, and Europe, came to almost a complete halt.[96] Airline industries around the globe have been severely impacted by quarantines and cross-border mobility restrictions and while governments in Europe and the US have supported their cash-strapped airlines with billions of dollars, their counterparts in developing regions have less funds and different priorities.

---

90 SDG Report 2020, *supra* note 36 at 3.
91 *Id*. at 3.
92 *Id*. at 3.
93 *Covid-19 Infections Are Rising Fast in Bangladesh, India and Pakistan*, THE ECONOMIST (Jun. 6, 2020), www.economist.com/asia/2020/06/06/covid-19-infections-are-rising-fast-in-bangladesh-india-and-pakistan. (last visited Nov. 6, 2020).
94 SDG and COVID-19 2020, *supra* note 22 at 4.
95 *The Belt and Road Initiative: Break Time*, THE ECONOMIST (Jun. 4,2020), www.economist.com/china/2020/06/04/the-pandemic-is-hurting-chinas-belt-and-road-initiative (last visited Nov. 6, 2020).
96 *Id*.

They first have to support millions of their citizens who are dealing with a sudden onset of hunger, poverty, and unemployment.[97]

Yet, the pandemic may be also responsible for some positive effects on SDG 9 progress. First, the outbreak has fostered scientific collaboration, especially in developed nations to find the treatment and vaccine for the virus. Second, it has promoted digital technologies for e-health, e-education, e-governance, and e-payments.[98] This digital revolution, combined with plummeting industrial output, has also been producing positive spillover effects on climate change and the environmental crisis. And even though many jobs have been lost and many enterprises have already gone or will go out of business around the world, there is hope that most of the world's nations will be able to build back their economies, resume their interrupted projects, and benefit from the long-term developmental effects of the digital revolution.

Conclusions and Recommendations

The experience of the last several decades strongly indicates that economic growth can reduce poverty and generate prosperity. Yet, it can come at a cost of increased inequality and environmental degradation. It is vital then that the global community pursues all-inclusive, sustainable, and sustained growth and sustainable development that leave no one behind, the main objective of the UN's 2030 Agenda. This objective cannot be achieved without the development of resilient infrastructure, promotion of inclusive and sustainable industrialization, and fostering new technologies.

The assessment of the progress toward SDG 9, provided in this chapter, suggests that although there is an improvement in many parts of the globe, especially in the Asian region, the world still has a long way to go. There are still a lot of challenges and opportunities for action to accelerate progress on the implementation of the 2030 Agenda. The technology gap often hinders diversification into other sectors and activities and lack of adequate infrastructure limits some regions, especially Africa's, capacity to create decent jobs. The progress has been still rather slow in terms of including women and traditionally marginalized groups. The ongoing Covid-19 pandemic has exacerbated these challenges and in the short-run stalled the progress toward SDG 9.

Another troubling issue associated with the achievement of the SDG 9 by 2030 is the large spread between top and bottom performers. Thus, there is a need to accelerate the dissemination of technologies and innovation globally and build regional and country-based capacities and skills. Strong government commitment and government-driven industrial policies can foster innovative utilization of existing skills and talents and stimulate progress toward SDG 9, as it has in South Korea. Another area that indicates the continued need for strong government policies in the LDCs is in promoting resilient infrastructure, an important engine of economic growth. Developing countries and LDCs often function in an environment of instability and uncertainty and are unable to provide funds and technological expertise for large-scale infrastructure projects. Regional cooperation and partnership, such as seen in the DRC, can provide local companies with much sought-after credit, generate employment, and stimulate economic growth.

---

97 *Latin America's Empty Skies*, THE ECONOMIST (Jun. 4, 2020), www.economist.com/the-americas/2020/06/04/latin-americas-empty-skies (last visited Nov. 6, 2020).
98 SDG Report 2020, *supra* note 22 at 4.

Policy Recommendations

Based on the regional assessment and a more detailed analysis of several countries, we believe that the following policy approaches applied in the regions that are lagging behind will yield positive results in addressing the SDG 9 targets:

Improve technical capacity for producing data in all countries and establish an International Data Bank for SDGs.

Some parts of the world, particularly the Arab region, SSA, and Oceania, have shown lots of commitment but not lots of statistics, making it difficult to assess their progress.[99] There is an urgent need to build technical capacity in these regions and ensure the uniformity of assessment methods. An International Data Bank for SDGs sponsored by major international organizations, such as the UN, the World Bank, and an International Monetary Fund, could help countries that lack technical capacity and financial infrastructure to develop their progress reports.

Encourage the development of small businesses and local credit systems in LDCs through microfinance and strenthening local financial services.

Obtaining credit or attracting FDI in LDCs is challenging due to their weak and inefficient financial systems. Building a financial system from bottom up may be easier in LDCs, and it can yield significant direct and indirect benefits. In particular, an increase in microfinancing may promote entrepreneurship and thereby reduce the informal labor market. It can also stimulate FDI as it creates more investment opportunities. The UN should provide a small business development fund financed by developed nations to encourage more microfinance and the development of local financial services.

Promote Industrial Diversification and Reduce Reliance on Natural Resources in Countries That Suffer from a "Resource Curse"

One way to promote industrial diversification is through facilitating infant industry protection in LDCs as a first phase before launching the export-drive. South Korea, for example, is a long-term success story that started with a small number of industries that were protected initially, and the effects of protection were offset by strong export activities.

Promote Regional and International Cooperation and Partnerships

Joint action at the international level can provide lagging regions with the opportunities to build more modern infrastructure, which will lead to job creation and stronger economic growth. The UN could also lead the efforts to improve technical capacity and transfer of technologies. This would help countries that either lack technical capacity or have financial constraints to initiate large cross-border projects.

---

99 *See* HLPF Background Note, *supra* note 32.

Embrace Entrepreneurship and Technological Acumen as Part of the Multifaceted Developmental Strategy

Entrepreneurial interest in industrial development and capacity to innovate are strongly linked to material incentives and profit opportunities, which have to be part of the overall developmental strategy. Entrepreneurship and technological acumen therefore require a stable political environment, a sound financial system that channels the funds from lenders to borrowers, a legal framework that protects human rights and property rights, and a government that is committed to inclusion, diversity, and equity. This means that achieving progress toward SDG 9 is impossible without the progress in many other SDGs.

16 Reducing Inequality and Sharing Opportunities for All

Vesselin Popovski

Introduction

Inequality has been recognized as a universal challenge having profound economic, social, and environmental impacts. It is a multidimensional phenomenon with both income and non-income aspects. There are millennia of years of history of inequality[1] going through the extreme inequality of the slave societies, the domination and segregation in the colonialist societies, the labor exploitation in capitalist societies, which gave birth to Marxist ideological dreams for full and complete equality, tragically materializing in the communist economic collapses and human tragedies of the 20th century.

This chapter will not engage in the humongous task to deliberate as to what society, or model of economy, is best for reducing inequality, or whether the future of capitalism is a kind of hypercapitalism, zigzagging between archaism and modernity, or a participatory socialism, with tax on inherited wealth and progressive income tax to finance universal basic income and capital endowment for every citizen.[2] Inequalities in income and wealth may adversely affect politics, by giving fiscal power over to elected officials or by attenuating their connections to the common good. These arguments operate under the assumption that inequality does not undermine individual freedom and democracy. Indeed, one can maintain that inequality normally would enhance individual freedom. By expanding the options of affected agents, inequalities may reflect mutually beneficial transactions between consenting traders.

However, the opposite argument can also be made, that the effect of income inequality on economic freedom is negative and associated with those components, related to international trade, domestic market regulation, rule of law, and property rights protection. The negative effect of inequality on freedom is due to elites, converting their economic power into de facto political power to defend their economic interests, or what can be described as political capitalism or captured democracy. The elites' interests run counter to economic freedom, discouraging innovation and competition, and as a result the economic freedom decreases and even in democratic countries, the institutions cannot prevent the erosion of economic freedom. This explains why inequality—both external between countries, and internal within countries and communities—persists. The inequality has been rising over the last several decades in different ways and in different regions. Even in rich countries there are parents who cannot afford healthcare and school lunches for their children, women who are

---

1 *See* THOMAS PICKETTY, THE CAPITAL OF THE 21ST CENTURY (Harvard University Press 2017).
2 *See generally* THOMAS PICKETTY, CAPITAL AND IDEOLOGY (Harvard University Press 2020).

not paid equally to their male coworkers, and people who are treated differently because of race, religion, age, or where they come from.

This chapter reflects on the debates about the inclusion of inequality as a separate Sustainable Development Goal (SDG) 10, discusses the various targets adopted to reduce inequality globally, and proposes how to achieve those targets.

Should Inequality Reduction Be a Development Goal?

Inequality was not regarded as a separate goal when the United Nations (UN) Millenium Declaration, adopted with the General Assembly Resolution 55/2 in September 2000 led to formulating the Millenium Development Goals (MDGs). Equality was simply listed as a principle, among others, emphasizing that no individual and no nation should be denied the opportunity to benefit from development.[3] If we go back to the UN Charter, adopted in 1945, we will see a general emphasis on the "equal rights of men and women and of nations large and small" in the Preamble, and that the Organization will be "based on the principle of the sovereign equality of all its members" in Art. 2, listing the principles of the UN.[4] However, nobody had any desire to put any emphasis on inequality of incomes for 70 years until the inclusion of inequality as a separate goal, number 10, among the 17 SDGs in 2015.

The adoption of SDG 10 was a complex and challenging process, preceded by a significant debate with arguments both in favor and against. The debate on inequality was put in the agenda of the World Economic Forum at Davos in 2014, and some significant academic writings on inequality described it as a systemic and overpowering world phenomenon.[5] During the discussions on the post-2015 Development Agenda, criticisms pointed to a lacuna and lack of accountability mechanisms and defective concepts of inequality.[6]

Arguments for inclusion as a separate goal were advanced by civil society groups, UN agencies, the UN Secretary-General, and backed by data from economists including the keynote address by Joseph Stiglitz in the Roundtable "The Threat of Growing Inequalities: Building More Just and Equitable Societies to Support Growth and Sustainable Development."[7] Stiglitz noted that from 2009 onward, 95% of all economic gains in the United States (US) had gone to only the wealthiest 1% of the population.[8] This and other presentations played a considerable role in convincing the G77 countries in the UN that inequality was not just a socio-economic problem, but rather one of politics and policies.

There were several arguments against inequality as a separate development goal. The redundancy argument was based on thinking of inequality as a matter of inefficiency, not of underutilization of human capital and of corroding standards of democracy.[9] Inequality for too long was not regarded as a purely economic problem; instead, the focus was limited

---

3 G.A. Res. 55/2, *Millennium Declaration*, Sept. 8, 2020.
4 U.N. Charter, *Preamble*, art. 2.
5 Sakiko Fukuda-Parr, *Keeping Out Extreme Inequality from the SDG Agenda—The Politics of Indicators*, 10 GLOB. POLICY 61–69 (2019), https://onlinelibrary.wiley.com/doi/abs/10.1111/1758-5899.12602 (last visited Sept. 2, 2020).
6 *Id.*
7 Heike Kuhn, *Reducing Inequality Within and Among Countries: Realizing SDG 10—A Developmental Perspective*, *in* SUSTAINABLE DEVELOPMENT GOALS AND HUMAN RIGHTS 137–53 (Markus Krajewski & Heike Kuhn eds., 2020).
8 *Id.*
9 Fukuda-Parr, *supra* note 5.

to merely lack of financial resources and failing to consider inequality as a broader systemic problem concerning social, economic, legal, and financial parameters.[10] The opponents of including SDG 10 considered it to be redundant because all sustainable development goals battled inequality to a certain degree, be it SDG 1 (Poverty), SDG 2 (Hunger), SDG 3 (Health), SDG 4 (Education), SDG 5 (Gender), and so on.

The second argument against including inequality as a separate goal was that of poverty. The roots of the argument stem from the narrative of "leave no one behind," elucidated by the High-Level Panel of Eminent Persons appointed by the UN Secretary-General in 2012, ensuring that "no person—regardless of ethnicity, gender, geography, disability, race or other status—is denied basic economic opportunities and human rights."[11] The principle of leave no one behind was in itself criticized by scholars as being indifferent and insensitive to the concept of inequality.[12] Leave no one behind portrayed poverty as an all-pervasive issue without recognizing extreme inequalities.

The third argument, well presented for example by Edward Conard, is more provocative: That our current obsession with income inequality is misguided and will only slow growth further.[13] The argument tracks the implications of an economy constrained by both its capacity for risk-taking and by shortage of properly trained talent—rather than by labor or capital, as was the case historically. This perspective challenges liberal economists by arguing that the growing wealth of successful billionaires is not to blame for the stagnating incomes of the middle and working classes. If anything, the success of the top 1% has put upward pressure on employment and wages, and the high payoffs for success motivate talent to get the training and take the risks that gradually loosen the constraints to growth. Attempts to decrease inequality through redistribution would damage these incentives, gradually hurting not just the 1%, but everyone else as well. The better way is to grow middle- and working-class wages with a near infinite supply of labor that is shifting from capital-intensive manufacturing to knowledge-intensive, innovation-driven fields.

At the end of the day, the arguments to include a separate goal on inequality prevailed and we now have SDG 10. The decision was crucial because it reflected the difference between inequality and poverty, and inequality and extreme inequality of the most vulnerable and marginalized groups. SDG 10 was among the last SDGs to be introduced as a means to tackle the growing income disparities across the world.[14]

Inequalities of various types, be it economic, social, or cultural, are deeply entrenched; therefore, SDG 10 pledges to provide a vision of a shared future with equality and opportunities for all. The objective of reducing inequality is both a stand-alone goal and a cross-cutting issue, closely linked with eradication of extreme poverty and hunger, with health, education, gender equality, and other SDGs. When inequality persists, the growth and developmental prospects of significant sections of societies remain hindered. The rationale behind the pronouncement and adoption of SDG 10 was to reduce inequality with the aid of the international community, where developed nations provide assistance to developing

---

10 *Id*.
11 *A New Global Partnership: Eradicate Poverty and Transform Economies through Sustainable Development*, High Level Panel on the Post-2015 Development Agenda, THE POST-2020 DEVELOPMENT AGENDA (2013), www.post2020hlp.org/the-report/.
12 Fukuda-Parr, *supra* note 5.
13 EDWARD CONARD, THE UPSIDE OF INEQUALITY (Portfolio 2016).
14 Joel E. Oestreich, *SDG 10: Reduce Inequality in and among Countries*, 37(1) SOCIAL ALTERNATIVES 34–41 (2018).

and least developed countries to contribute to eradication of, not only poverty and hunger, but also inequality.[15] The adoption of SDG 10 manifested the consistent acknowledgement that while the extent of economic inequalities between countries has reduced, inequalities within the countries have risen. The UN realized that an increase in national income would not necessarily reduce poverty and advanced a three-dimensional model of reducing inequality by ensuring sustainable development policies that fall in line with economic, social, and environmental aspects.[16]

Rising Inequalities

In December 2018, the first World Inequality Report (WIR)[17] alarmingly showed how over several decades the inequality has grown all over the world in different ways. The World Inequality Lab, chaired by Thomas Piketty, Facundo Alvaredo, and Lucas Chancel, with more than 100 researchers constructed an accessible database with 175 million data points, giving the first worldwide comprehensive picture of inequality.[18] The report demonstrated that the worst inequality exists in the Middle East, a region hugely polarized between those who tremendously profit from industries (mostly oil), and the poor who work in the service of the wealthy.[19] The inequality rises in the United States, where the top 1% hold 20% of the wealth, is much higher than 12% in Europe.[20] Inequality in Europe is weaker as a result of national institutions, taxation policies, and public services, which play an important role in managing inequality.[21] The authors of the WIR projected that if inequality follows the patterns of the last three decades, the inequality will continue to grow wider in the years to come, exposing capitalism's structural tendency to widen the wealth gap.[22]

The global inequality has increased in nearly all regions at different speeds[23] and this highlights the important roles that national policies and institutions play in shaping inequality.

> The rise was particularly abrupt in Russia, moderate in China, and relatively gradual in India, reflecting different types of deregulation and policies. The divergence in inequality has been particularly visible between Western Europe and the U.S., which had similar [inequality levels] in 1980 but today are radically different[.] While the top 1% income share was close to 10% [in 1980,] it rose only slightly to 12% in 2016 in Western Europe, [but] shot up to 20% in the U.S. Meanwhile, the [income of the] bottom 50% [in the U.S.] decreased from more than 20% in 1980 to 13% in 2016. The income-inequality trajectory in the [U.S.] is largely due to massive educational inequalities, combined with a tax system that grew less progressive despite a surge in top labor compensation since the 1980s, and in top capital incomes in the 2000s. Europe

---

15 Fukuda-Parr, *supra* note 5.
16 *Ibid.*
17 *See generally Facundo Alvaredo et al.*, WORLD INEQUALITY REPORT 2018 (World Inequality Lab 2017), https://wir2018.wid.world/files/download/wir2018-summary-english.pdf.
18 *See generally id.*
19 *Id.* at 5.
20 *Id.* at 8.
21 *See id.* at 5–6.
22 *Id.* at 13–16.
23 In 2016, the share of total national income accounted for by top 10% earners was 37% in Europe, 41% in China, 46% in Russia, 47% in US–Canada, and around 55% in sub-Saharan Africa, Brazil, and India. In the Middle East, the world's most unequal region, the top 10% capture 61% of national income. *See id.* at 5–6.

meanwhile saw a lesser decline in its tax progressivity, while wage inequality was also moderated by educational and wage-setting policies that were relatively favorable to middle-income groups. In both regions, income inequality between men and women has declined but remains particularly strong at the top of the distribution.[24]

At the global level, the WIR showed that

> inequality has risen sharply since 1980, despite strong growth in [Asia.] The poorest half of the global population has seen income increase significantly thanks to high growth, particularly in China and India. However, because of rising inequality within countries, the top 1% richest individuals in the world captured twice as much growth as the bottom 50% individuals since 1980. Income growth has been sluggish or even zero for individuals with incomes between the global bottom 50% and top 1% groups. This includes all North American and European lower- and middle-income groups. The rise of global inequality has not been steady. While the global top 1% income increased from 16% in 1980 to 22% in 2000, it declined slightly thereafter to 20%.[25]

The high inequality is problematic not simply in terms of justice and fairness, but also as it affects the pace of upward mobility, economic growth, and sustainable economic development.[26] Extreme income inequality leads to economic inefficiency, because low-income individuals lack collateral and cannot obtain credit or save because of low incomes.[27] Those who have accumulated substantial collateral typically spend their money on luxury goods, mostly abroad, and their savings do not add to the nation's productivity and lead to capital flight, exacerbating the inequality within the country and between countries further.[28]

Targets in SDG 10

SDG 10 is a loosely worded and broad goal. It lists ten targets for implementation, seeking to promote socio-political, legal, and economic inclusion, irrespective of peoples' sex, gender, race, ethnicity, disability, religion, etc. Let us see how these targets are reflected in the latest 2020 report of the High-Level Political Forum (HLPF):

> Target 10.1—By 2030, progressively achieve and sustain income growth of the bottom 40% of the population at a rate higher than the national average

The "40% of the population," called a "*built-in*" indicator, has been subject both to praise and criticism.[29] While the 40% is more ambitious than the 20% indicator in the MDGs, it does not indicate the changes in income disparities between the wealthiest 10% and the

---

24 *Id.* at 6.
25 *Id.* at 7.
26 Era-Dabla-Norris et al., *Causes and Consequences of Income Inequality: A Global Perspective*, INT'L MONETARY FUND at 6–9 (June 2015), www.imf.org/external/pubs/ft/sdn/2015/sdn1513.pdf.
27 *Id.* at 6–9, 18.
28 *Id.*
29 Edward Anderson, *Equality as a Global Goal*, 30(2) ETHICS & INT'L AFFAIRS 189–200 (June 2016), www.ethicsandinternationalaffairs.org/2016/equality-global-goal/.

bottom 10% of the population.³⁰ The 2020 HLPF Report notes that from 2012 to 2017, 73 out of 90 countries experienced real income growth.³¹ Out of these 73 countries, 49 saw an increase in income for the bottom 40% of the population as higher than the overall national average.³² Although this is a step forward to achieving equality, there remains substantial ground to cover. In all these countries the bottom 40% of the population received less than 25% of total income as opposed to the wealthiest 10% that received nearly 20% of the total income.³³ The HLPF report concludes that the bottom 40% of the population is making considerable progress in Eastern and South-Eastern Asia as opposed to negligible growth in sub-Saharan African countries.³⁴

> Target 10.2—By 2030, empower and promote the social, economic and political inclusion of all, irrespective of age, sex, disability, race, ethnicity, origin, religion or economic or other status.

The indicator for this target measures the proportion of people living below 50% of median income, by sex, age, and persons with disabilities.³⁵ Women, children, disabled, and other marginalized communities have been facing systematic oppression for years. Existing social, political, economic, and legal policy interventions have barely managed to dive into the root causes of such discrimination. The 2020 HLPF Report 2020 points out that every 2 out of 10 people have faced discrimination on at least one of the grounds mentioned in the International Human Rights Laws, as per data collected from 31 countries from 2014 to 2019.³⁶ The 2020 HLPF Report also mentions that while women are more prone to facing discrimination than men, they are further discriminated against on the grounds of disability, religion, and ethnicity.³⁷ Thus, there is a need to have concrete provisions regarding the intersectional approaches toward ensuring the inclusion of all. A mandate to follow a development-rights based approach over a moral or ethical approach would ensure that states do not violate their obligations to various human rights bodies by engaging in discrimination and subjugation. A development-rights based approach values the right to development for all, and this has been discussed repeatedly in the UN since 2013.³⁸

> Target 10.3—Ensure equal opportunity and reduce inequalities of outcome, including by eliminating discriminatory laws, policies and practices and promoting appropriate legislation, policies and actions in this regard.

A global survey by the United Nations Development Program (UNDP) found that discriminatory law-making process threatens long-term socio-economic development of

---

30 *Id.*
31 *Sustainable Development Goals Report* 2020, Dep. of Econ. And Soc. Affairs 44 (2020), https://unstats.un.org/sdgs/report/2020/ (hereinafter "SDG Report 2020").
32 *Id.*
33 *Id.*
34 *Ibid.*
35 *SDG Indicators: Metadata Repository*, U.N. Statistics Division, https://unstats.un.org/sdgs/metadata/ (last visited Nov. 25, 2020).
36 *Id.*
37 *Id.*
38 Oestreich, Joel E, *supra* note 14.

the vulnerable and marginalized people.[39] The inclination of policymakers toward short-term rapid developmental prospects severely impacts on the financial system, mainly because women remain unrepresented and excluded from financial opportunities.[40] The indicator for this target measures the proportion of the population that felt discrimination on the grounds prohibited under the Human Rights Laws.[41] The limitation of this indicator is that it does not account for a general prevalence of discrimination in a country as it is only based on the data for what people personally feel. Additionally, it does not consider that not everyone would be aware that they faced discrimination, and if they were, not everyone would necessarily disclose it when being surveyed.[42]

> Target 10.4—Adopt policies, especially fiscal, wage and social protection policies, and progressively achieve greater equality.

The first indicator for this target, 10.4.1., also known as "Labor share of GDP," states that the total compensation of all employees within a country is a share of its gross domestic product (GDP).[43] "Compensation to employees" is any remuneration, be it in-cash or in-kind, whereas GDP is the measure of the monetary value of final goods and services produced, and employees are all individuals holding explicit or implicit employment contracts.[44] This indicator measures equality by evaluating the extent of increase in the income of employees with the increase in the national income of the country.[45] However, it needs improvement/modification, as initially it did not cover the labor income of the self-employed, which might be a significant source of income in countries with self-employment. The 51st session on the data and indicators for the 2030 Agenda for Sustainable Development decided to correct the indicator 10.4.1 to measure the "Labor share of GDP" without the "comprising wages and social protection transfers," so that the calculation of global labor income now takes into account the earnings of both the employed and the self-employed.[46] It indicates whether an increase in national income would lead to a rise in the material living standards for the workmen.[47] The wage and social protection policies aim to combat social inequalities by ensuring that the laborer gets to reap the benefit of their work by receiving a substantial share of the output they help produce.[48] Global labor income had reduced significantly from 54% in 2004 to 51% in 2017.[49]

---

39 *Goal 10: Reduced Inequalities—SDG Tracker*, OUR WORLD IN DATA, https://sdg-tracker.org/inequality (last visited Nov. 25, 2020).
40 Muhammad Abdul Mazid, *SDG 10: Reducing Iinequality within and among Countries*, THE FINANCIAL EXPRESS (Jun. 4, 2018), https://thefinancialexpress.com.bd/views/sdg-10-reducing-inequality-within-and-among-countries-1527864339.
41 Goal 10, *supra* note 39.
42 *SDG Indicators*, supra note 35.
43 *Id*. at Target 10.4.1: Labor share of GDP.
44 Ze Yar Min, *E-Handbook on SDG Indicators: Indicator 10.4.1*, UN STATISTICS WIKI, https://unstats.un.org/wiki/display/SDGeHandbook/Indicator+10.4.1 (last visited Nov. 24, 2020).
45 *SDG Indicators*, *supra* note 35.
46 *Report of the Inter-Agency and Expert Group on Sustainable Development Goal Indicators*, ECON. AND SOC. COUNCIL., 51st Sess., E/CN.3/2020/2* (Mar. 3–6, 2020).
47 *SDG Indicators*, *supra* note 35 at 10.4.1.
48 *Id*.
49 SDG Report 2020, *supra* 31, at 44.

The second indicator 10.4.2 is the "Redistributive Impact of Fiscal Policy." The Gini Coefficient is reported as an additional component of indicator 10.4.2.[50] With respect to indicator 10.4.1, in 2017 the labor income was 58% of the total national GDP in Europe and Northern America and 36% of the total national GDP in Northern Africa and Western Asia, reported by the International Labor Organization (ILO).[51] However, indicator 10.4.2 is only available in 82 countries, and hence, there is no regularized data/schedule available to map the progress under this indicator.[52]

> Target 10.5—Improve the regulation and monitoring of global financial markets and institutions and strengthen the implementation of such regulations.

The indicator 10.5.1, also known as the "Financial Soundness Indicator" (FSIs), is a combination of 7 FSIs that measure capital assets, weighted assets, loans, gross loans, return on assets, short-term liabilities, and foreign exchange to capital.[53] As of 2018, 138 FSIs were reported.[54] Most countries report all the core FSIs and also data that can be used to interpret these FSIs.[55] While some countries report on a monthly or quarterly basis, a few report annually.[56] The concern is not with the regularity of this reporting, rather with differences between countries in the availability of resources, ease of access to food, health, shelter, the standard of living, and improved life chances.

While equality within and between the countries has been deliberated upon time and again, the discussion on "equity" within and between countries has remained neglected. This target makes an implicit assumption that the inequality between the countries arises only because of insufficient regulation and monitoring of global financial markets, when it could also be because of the legacy of colonialism and other historical factors.[57] Therefore, it is necessary for equity to be kept on par with that of equality.

> Target 10.6—Ensure enhanced representation and voice for developing countries in decision-making in global international economic and financial institutions in order to deliver more effective, credible, accountable and legitimate institutions.

This target is based on the principle of sovereign equality of all UN Member States. The indicator 10.6.1 shows the proportion of members and voting rights of developing countries in eleven international organizations and is calculated by taking the number of developing country members and dividing it by the total number of members.[58] The economic and financial havoc caused by the global recession in 2008 led to immense pressure on the developmental aid organizations.[59] The 2020 HLPF Report warned that a second wave

---

50 *SDG Indicators*, supra note 35 at 10.4.2.
51 *Decent Work and the SDGs: 11 charts that tell the story*, ILO STAT, https://ilostat.ilo.org/decent-work-and-the-sdgs-11-charts-that-tell-the-story/ (last visited Nov. 25, 2020).
52 *SDG Indicators*, *supra* note 35 at 10.4.2.
53 *Id.* at 10.5.1.
54 *Id.*
55 *Id.*
56 *Ibid.*
57 Oestreich, Joel E, *supra* note 14.
58 *SDG Indicators*, *supra* note 35 at 10.6.1.
59 SDG Report 2020, *supra* note 31, at 45.

of the COVID-19 pandemic could seriously jeopardize the amount of development aid.[60] Before the pandemic, the aid from the Development Assistance Committee of the Organization for Economic Co-operation and Development (OECD) donors, multilateral agencies, and other key providers was $314 billion in 2015 and $420 billion in 2017.[61] The aid was reduced by $149 billion in 2018, and can be expected to drop again in 2020 due to the COVID-19 crisis.[62]

> Target 10.7—Facilitate orderly, safe, regular and responsible migration and mobility of people, including through the implementation of planned and well-managed migration policies.

The implementation of this target is measured by the "Recruitment cost borne by employee as a proportion of monthly income earned in the country of destination."[63] This first indicator was developed in collaboration between the Population Division of the UN Department of Economic and Social Affairs (DESA) and the International Organization for Migration (IOM).[64] The target requires global solidarity between the countries to ensure an extensive set of policies that facilitate orderly, safe, regular, and responsible migration and mobility of people.

The next indicator 10.7.2. is an internationally accepted standard that measures the number of countries that facilitate orderly, safe, regular, and responsible migration and mobility of people through six policy domains.[65] The six domains are Migrant rights; Whole-of-government/ Evidence-based policies; Cooperation and partnerships; Socio-economic well-being; Mobility dimensions of crises; and Safe, orderly, and regular migration.[66] For each domain, one proxy measure containing a question is identified to inform five sub-categories that aim to assess the migration and mobility policies.[67] The indicator 10.7.2. detects variations in policies across countries and is obtained by calculating the unweighted average of 30 sub-categories under these six policy domains.[68] An earlier version of indicator 10.7.2. looked out solely for the number of countries that have well-constructed and well-implemented migration policies.[69] After the refinement of the global indicator framework as proposed under the Fiftieth Session of the Statistical Commission Report of the Inter-Agency and Expert Group on SDGs Indicators, this indicator has been reformed.[70] Currently, this indicator does away with the broad ambit of "well-managed migration policies," as in

---

60 *Id.*
61 *Id.*
62 *Ibid.*
63 *Policy Brief: SDG Indicator* 10.7.2, DESA-IOM-OECD 1 (Oct. 2019), www.un.org/en/development/desa/population/publications/pdf/technical/Policy%20Brief_10.7.2.pdf (last visited Aug Nov. 25, 2020).
64 *SDG Indicators*, supra note 35, at 10.7.1.
65 Policy Brief, *supra* note 63.
66 *Id.* at 3.
67 *Id.* at 2.
68 *Id.*
69 IOM Res. C/106/RES/1310, 106th Sess., Migration Governance Framework, IOM (Dec. 4, 2015).
70 Policy Brief, *supra* note 63.

the above definition, by specifying that well-managed migration policies are the ones that necessarily allow for a safe, orderly, and regular migration.[71]

The available data up to 2019 provides that 54% of the states fully meet the criteria of indicator 10.7.2 in providing safe, orderly, and regular migration and mobility to people.[72] Central and Southern Asia along with Latin America and the Caribbean, have the highest percentage for abiding by the criteria with 80% and 79%, respectively.[73]

The indicator 10.7.3. takes into account the number of migrants killed while attempting to cross maritime, land, and air borders, and the indicator 10.7.4 shows the proportion of the population who are refugees, by country of origin.[74]

> Target 10.a—Implement the principle of special and differential treatment for developing countries, in particular least developed countries, in accordance with WTO agreements.

The indicator 10.a.1 specifies the percentage of National Tariff Lines (NTL) codes that correspond to zero tariff rate on products imported from least developed and developing countries.[75] NTL codes can be customized by countries, and hence, are used to find out the ease of market access through evaluating the differential treatment for developing and least developed countries.[76] The data is collected through the International Trade Center, the World Trade Organization (WTO), and the United Nations Conference on Trade and Development (UNCTAD) databases.[77] While the scope of tariff-based measures is disputed for their accuracy, any alternative is currently unavailable.[78]

> Target 10.b—Encourage official development assistance and financial flows, including foreign direct investment, to States where the need is greatest, in particular, the least developed countries, African countries, small island developing States and landlocked developing countries, in accordance with their national plans and programmes.

The indicator 10.b.1 measures the type and amount of development aid flow from the donor to the recipient countries, including foreign direct investments.[79] It is defined as the total of all resource flows for development, be it Official Development Assistance (ODA), other official flows, or foreign direct investments.[80] ODA includes aid provided by state and local authorities to promote and ensure economic development and welfare of developing countries, such that at least 25% of the assistance is calculated at a 10% discount.[81]

---

71 *Report of the Inter-Agency and Expert Group on Sustainable Goal Indicators,*, ECON. AND SOC. COUNSIL, 50th Sess., E/CN.3/2019/2 (March 5–8, 2019).
72 Policy Brief, *supra* note 63, at 2.
73 *Id.*
74 ECON. AND SOC. COUNCIL, 2020, supra note 46.
75 Ze Yar Min, *E-Handbook on SDG Indicatior 10.a.1*, UN STATISTICS WIKI, https://unstats.un.org/wiki/display/SDGeHandbook/Indicator+10.a.1 (last visited Nov. 26, 2020).
76 *Id.*
77 *Id.*
78 *Ibid.*
79 Ze Yar Min, *E-Handbook on SDG Indicator 10.a.1*, UN STATISTICS WIKI, https://unstats.un.org/wiki/display/SDGeHandbook/Indicator+10.b.1 (last visited Nov. 26, 2020).
80 *Id.*
81 *Id.*

Target 10.c—By 2030, reduce to less than 3% the transaction costs of migrant remittances and eliminate remittance corridors with costs higher than 5%.

The rationale behind this target is to measure the cross-border payments to cater to the goal of reducing the global average total cost of migrant remittances by five percentage points in five years.[82] It measures the remittance costs as a proportion to the amount remitted.[83] For a successful implementation under this target, the governments had to comply with the General Principles for International Remittances Services introduced by the World Bank on Payment and Settlement Systems.[84] According to the World Bank statistics, the data collected for this target is generally free of significant discrepancies.[85] As of June 2020, South Africa (5.7%) is the most expensive country to remit to, followed by Brazil, China, and Turkey at 5.42, 5.02, and 4.90, respectively.[86] There are no upcoming or existing alternatives for indicator 10.c.1, other than countries establishing a remittance database according to the World Bank minimum requirements.[87]

The analysis of the targets and indicators above suggests a pressing need for multi-pronged approaches toward reducing inequalities. There needs to be a significant overhaul of the existing mechanism for accounting payments and incomes. Payment mechanisms usually focus on conventional forms of 'work' leading to short-sighted results. A gendered analysis of governmental policies on income and payments reveals that women and other marginalized groups face structural discrimination and remain poor despite an increase in the National GDP of their respective countries. The UN GA Resolution dated April 2, 2020, which appealed for a global solidarity to fight inequality post-COVID-19, emphasized, among other things, the urgent need to exchange information including relevant statistics.[88]

Inequality and the Rise of the South

One serious tension of globalization was the different speed of development of the North and the South. The economic growth of the middle class in the South far exceeded that of the Northern middle class and as a result, the growth gap between the two has increased. But if global inequality continued to trend downward, it did so for a new set of reasons. China, from the beginning of its market reforms in the late 1970s, has played an enormous role in lowering global inequality. The economic growth of its population of 1.4 billion people has reshaped the distribution of wealth around the world. But now China has become sufficiently wealthy that its continued growth no longer plays such an important role in lowering global inequality. In 2008, the median Chinese income was just slightly higher than the world's median income; 5 years later, China's median income was 50% higher than

---

82 SDGCounting, *SDG 10 Indicators—2017 Updates*, MEDIUM—SDG Resources (May 25, 2017), https://medium.com/sdgs-resources/sdg-10-indicators-2017-updates-f241dfbf961.
83 *Id.*
84 World Bank, *Indicator: 10.c.1*, SDG METADATA TRANSLATION PROJECT, https://worldbank.github.io/sdg-metadata/documents/en/10-c-1.pdf (Nov. 26, 2020).
85 *Id.*
86 *Remittance Prices Worldwide*, WORLD BANK (last updated Oct. 28, 2020), https://remittanceprices.worldbank.org/sites/default/files/rpw_annex_q2_2020.pdf (last visited Nov. 26, 2020).
87 Indicator: 10.c.1, *supra* note 84.
88 GA Res. 74/270, 74th Sess., *Global solidarity to fight the coronavirus disease 2019 (COVID-19)*, (Apr. 2, 2020).

the world's—and it is probably even higher now. High growth in China, in global terms, is ceasing to be an equalizing force. Soon, it will contribute to rising global inequality. India, with a population that may soon surpass China's and that is still relatively poor, now plays an important role in making the world more equal. In the last 20 years, China and India have driven the reduction in global inequality. Africa, which boasts the world's highest rates of population growth, will become increasingly important. But if the largest African countries continue to trail behind the Asian giants, global inequality will rise.

COVID-19 has so far not disrupted these trends and in fact might lead to their intensification. The remarkable deceleration of global growth will not be uniform. Chinese economic growth, while much lower now than in any year since the 1980s, will still outpace economic growth in the North. This will accelerate the closing of the income gap between the South and the North. If China's growth continues to exceed the North by 2–3% annually, within the next decade many middle-class Chinese will become wealthier than their middle-class counterparts in the North. For the first time in two centuries, the North middling incomes within their own nations will no longer be part of the global elite, or in the top 20% of global incomes. This will be a truly remarkable development.

From the 1820s onward—when national economic data began being collected—the North has consistently been wealthier than any other part of the world. In the long run, the most optimistic scenario would see continued high growth rates in Asia and an acceleration of economic growth in Africa, coupled with a narrowing of income differences within rich and poor countries alike through more activist social policies (higher taxes on the rich, better public education, and greater equality of opportunity). Economists from Adam Smith onward hoped that this scenario of growing global equality would follow from the spread of technological progress around the globe and the increasingly rational implementation of domestic policies.

Unfortunately, much gloomier forecasts seem more plausible: Trade and technology wars between China and the US, perhaps understandable from narrow strategic points of view, are fundamentally pernicious from the global point of view and will prevent the spread of technology and hamper improvements in living standards across large swaths of the world. The development aid was $420 billion USD in 2017 and fell by $149 billion USD in 2018.[89] It will certainly fall further because of COVID-19, significantly impacting the global economy and hitting the vulnerable groups, such as women, children, people with disabilities, migrants, and refugees the hardest.

Slowing growth will make it harder to eradicate poverty and likely preserve current levels of global inequality. The opposite of the initial dynamic of globalization might happen: The gap between American and Chinese middle classes may be preserved, but at the cost of the slower or negative income growth in both the US and China. Improvements in real income would be sacrificed in order to freeze the pecking order of the global income distribution. The net real income gain for all concerned would be zero

By the middle of the 19th century, even members of the working class in the North were well-off in global terms. That period is now coming to an end. The US remains a richer country than China. However, in 2013, the gap between the median income of an American and a Chinese person was 4.7 to 1. That gap has shrunk and will further diminish. If China

---

89 SDG Report 2020, supra note 31, at 15.

continues to outperform the US by about 2–3% per capita income growth every year, the average income gap between the two countries will take about two generations to close.[90]

Institutions like the World Bank sought to promote a socio-economic rights-based approach toward the right to development aims to reduce inequalities in a twofold manner.[91] They aim to reduce inequality "within" the countries and "among" the countries. Before 2020, income inequality fell considerably in 38 out of 84 countries between the years 2010–2017 and Slovenia and the Czech Republic recorded the lowest income inequalities.[92] The statistics are evaluated using the Gini Coefficient that measures economic inequality through income and wealth distribution, using a scale of 0 to 100, where values closer to 0 indicate that income is shared equally, whereas values closer to 100 denote inequality in income distribution.[93]

Inequality and Discrimination

The primary goal of SDG 10 is to reduce inequality, be it economic or social. It implies that the goal should work against community-based discrimination and ensure that financial disparity is kept under check as much as possible. The UN has pushed for eradication of social and economic inequality through various welfare schemes, acknowledging that although it is not always practical to achieve income parity, there can always be welfare schemes for the low-income groups to ensure that they do not suffer in the process. In a vastly capitalist world, the onus of implementation of welfare schemes for the poor depends on high-income groups along with the government. There are two means to achieve that, either to tax the rich to help the poor, or to place hope in philanthropy. The concept of Corporate Social Responsibility (CSR) has been brought in for that reason to ensure that companies will give something back to society.[94] The fact is that many rich businessmen, such as Bill Gates, Ratan Tata, etc., immensely contribute to social welfare. They may be among the top 1%, but they make it a point to give back to society.

However, at the social level we see a rampant rise in discrimination against marginalized communities in many countries. In Pakistan, the non-Muslim population is discriminated against pretty severely. Recently, many Hindus in Pakistan were forced to convert to Islam for the sake of making a livelihood.[95] Further, in some parts of the Northeast in India, non-tribal people are often discriminated against and are often subject to communal violence.[96]

---

90 Branko Milanovic, *The World Is Becoming More Equal*, Majalla (Sept. 4, 2020), https://eng.majalla.com/node/101761/the-world-is-becoming-more-equal.
91 *See generally Reducing Inequalities: SDG 10 Progress and Prospects*, World Bank (Apr. 2–3, 2019), www.worldbank.org/en/events/2018/12/17/reducing-inequalities-progress-and-prospects (last visited Nov. 26, 2020).
92 SDG Report 2020, *supra* note 31, at 48.
93 *Who, What, Why: What Is the Gini Coefficient?*, BBC News (Mar. 12, 2015), www.bbc.com/news/blogs-magazine-monitor-31847943.
94 *See generally* Uma Kambhampati et al., *Overview of Corporate Social Responsibility*, in Sustainable Development and Corporate Social Responsibility 7–45 (Research Gate 2017), www.researchgate.net/publication/336327454_Overview_of_Corporate_Social_Responsibility.
95 Maria Abi-habib & Zia ur-Rehman, *Poor and Desperate, Pakistani Hindus Accept Islam to Get by*, New York Times (Aug. 4, 2020), www.nytimes.com/2020/08/04/world/asia/pakistan-hindu-conversion.html.
96 *Hidden Apartheid: Caste Discrimination against India's "Untouchables,"* Human Rights Watch, www.hrw.org/report/2007/02/12/hidden-apartheid-caste-discrimination-against-indias-untouchables# (last visited Nov. 26, 2020).

The same applies to Muslims in India, one of the largest minority groups in the world under severe discrimination.[97] Therefore, it is important to stop discrimination, resolve communal conflicts, and realize that each and every person, irrespective of their caste, creed, sex, or religion, is a human being and has to be treated with dignity. This attitude needs to be imbibed into people in the best manner possible. Primary education must put great emphasis on this. The move should be toward promoting communal harmony and encouraging people to live peacefully. These steps are crucial to promoting communal harmony.

Inequality within countries is not attributable to a specific stage of development or geography. Rather, it is a challenge faced by least developed, middle-income, and developed countries alike and hence is universal in scope. Inequality trends are affected strongly by national and global policymaking. Some countries have reduced trends of inequality amidst an opposite trend of rising global inequality. They have shown that universal social policies, including social protection, universal access to essential services, effective employment policies, and robust institutions are critical. Policy approaches need to recognize inequality as a cross-cutting issue, as sustained inequality reduction requires integrated policymaking that combines the economic, social, and environmental dimensions at all levels. At the regional level, countries can benefit from cooperation, particularly the exchange of lessons learned with regard to addressing the drivers of inequality, including physical barriers, such as infrastructure and geographic location, as well as intangible barriers, such as cultural norms.

Policy priorities at the global level to address inequalities between countries remain a formidable challenge. Inequality between countries has not improved for large parts of the developing world outside of Asia. Among the several drivers of these gaps is the globalization of finance and trade, including phenomena such as illicit financial flows and tax evasion. In view of the variety of experiences in inequality, there is a need to analyze policy approaches to address inequalities and find pathways toward inclusive growth that could be universally applied. The failure to address this phenomenon at a global level could endanger the success of the 2030 Development Agenda and would represent a major roadblock on the path to shared prosperity for all.

Recommendations to Fulfill SDG 10

The implementation of SDG 10 and its related targets should build upon the fundamental values of equality, non-discrimination, "leave no one behind," and the right to development. The rising inequality in all regions in the last decades, as reported consistently, requires immediate action. The COVID-19 crisis exemplified many already existing deep inequalities everywhere, it should serve as an alarm bell, mobilizing force, and a galvanizing moment for action.

It is crucial to effectively address the root systemic causes of inequality within countries, recognizing its broad, cross-cutting, and multi-dimensional nature. Also, national and international drivers of inequality should be addressed, together with the necessary institutional requirements for reducing it. Let us remember that we need to reduce horizontal

---

97 *"Shoot the Traitors", Discrimination Against Muslims under India's New Citizenship Policy,* HUMAN RIGHTS WATCH, www.hrw.org/report/2020/04/09/shoot-traitors/discrimination-against-muslims-under-ind ias-new-citizenship-policy (last visited Nov. 26, 2020).

inequalities as significant sources of conflict. The focus needs to be made on healthcare and education as two crucial sectors in reducing inequality.

It is also crucial to strengthen institutions at all levels to support the reduction of inequality. States should review progress regularly, including through the use of disaggregated data, invite and engage with high-level participatory expertise for current and quality substantive information. They must always be action-oriented and impactful, and highlight the strong interconnectedness between the national, regional, and international levels. The interrelated nature of inequality should be addressed as a cross-cutting issue affecting all the SDGs, in addition to recognizing its reduction as a stand-alone goal.

States must immediately address tax evasion, illicit financial flows, and money laundering. These are global threats and challenges and cannot be solved without close international cooperation, information sharing, and robust international institutions.

C
Planet

17 Accelerating the Energy Transformation

Minoru Takada, David Koranyi, Richard Ottinger, Bo Fu, and Pianpian Wang

The Centrality of Energy for Sustainable Development: A Global Overview

Energy is at the very heart of the 2030 Agenda for Sustainable Development. Delivering on Sustainable Development Goal (SDG) 7 has the potential to spur progress across virtually all the other SDGs: poverty eradication, achieving gender equality, progress on climate change mitigation and adaptation, ensuring food security, improving health and education, building sustainable cities and communities, delivering clean water and sanitation, creating jobs, and boosting innovation are all dependent on sustainable energy solutions. The Global Sustainable Development Report published in 2019 identified energy transformation with universal access as one of the six required transformative pathways for sustainable development.[1]

Reliance on fossil fuels for energy is also a major cause of air, water, and chemical pollution that is deadly to humans and the major cause of greenhouse gas emissions responsible for record species extinction, making it unsustainable, unreliable, and unsafe and thus in direct conflict with achievement of the SDG 7 goals. They also are expensive fuels, unaffordable by many of the low-income people of the world, especially when health costs and early deaths caused by the pollution are accounted for. For example, a pioneer study by the Pace Energy & Climate Center, confirmed by studies by the US Department of Energy and the European Union, found that coal is the most expensive energy resource due to these externality costs, paid by consumers, but not reflected in the coal price.[2]

Achieving the SDG 7 objectives is essential for meeting the climate change mitigation goals of the Paris Climate Change accords. Lack of progress toward SDG 7 could contribute to the destructive impacts of climate change—heating of the planet, increased frequency and intensity of hurricanes, floods, droughts, and forest fires, among others—and will impair the ability of countries to meet the Paris Agreement goals.

Significantly, climate change, through heating of the planet, has been found to be a major cause of coronaviruses, such as those presently plaguing the globe, through the accelerated

---

1 Independent Group of Scientists 2019, *Global Sustainable Development Report 2019: The Future Is Now—Science for Achieving Sustainable Development*, UN DEPARTMENT OF ECONOMIC AND SOCIAL AFFAIRS, at 76 (2019). https://sdgs.un.org/publications/future-now-science-achieving-sustainable-development-gsdr-2019-24576.
2 RICHARD OTTINGER ET. AL., ENVIRONMENTAL COSTS OF ELECTRICITY (1991).

destruction of forests that cause increased exposure of humans to wild animals that carry the viruses.[3]

Currently, the world is not on course to meet the well-below 2°C climate objective, and even further from attaining the aspirational target of limiting warming to 1.5°C. Energy-related CO_2 emission growth from 2014 to 2016 was flat, but estimated emission levels increased by 1.7% in 2018 to reach a historic high of 33.1 Gt, with the power sector accounting for nearly two-thirds of the emissions growth.[4] While these results have been greatly reduced by the global economic shutdown resulting from SARS-CoV-2 (COVID-19), the virus-caused improvements will only be temporary unless countries reject the use of fossil fuels to power energy upon economic recovery, and instead adopt clean energy alternatives.

Only through delivering on the SDG 7 goals can the objectives of the Paris Agreement be met. The rapid deployment of renewables, coupled with energy efficiency, could achieve around 90% of the emission reductions in the energy sector needed by 2050, while also advancing economic growth and development.[5]

Encouraging progress has been recorded in reaching several SDG 7 targets. The global population without access to electricity fell from about 1.2 billion in 2010 to around 789 million in 2018.[6] Accelerating electrification growth between 2016 and 2018 delivered access to 137 million people on average each year as compared to 127 million between 2010 and 2016.[7] There has also been rapid progress for renewables in electricity generation—close to 25% came from renewables in 2016, and for five consecutive years, more than half of new investments have gone into modern renewables, with renewable energy investments exceeding $300 billion annually.[8]

Yet serious difficulties remain in adopting clean decarbonized energy sources at scale. Progress has been uneven in many areas, and urgent reinforced action is needed to achieve SDG 7 by 2030. With current trends, 620 million people, living predominantly in rural settlements in sub-Saharan Africa, are projected to remain without electricity in 2040.[9] The share of renewables in final energy consumption increased from 16.3% in 2010 to only 17.2% in 2016.[10] Close to 3 billion people do not have access to clean cooking solutions, resulting in close to 4 million premature deaths annually, with a disproportionate toll among women and children.[11]

---

3 Emma Newburger, *Wildlife Habitat Destruction and Deforestation Will Cause More Deadly Pandemics Like Coronavirus, Scientists Warn*, CNBC (May 9, 2020), www.cnbc.com/2020/05/09/coronavirus-wildlife-habitat-destruction-will-cause-more-pandemics.html.
4 *Climate Change and Renewable Energy—National Polices and the Role of Communities, Cities and Regions*, International Renewable Energy Agency (IRENA), at 10, 16 (June 2019), www.irena.org/publications/2019/Jun/Climate-change-and-renewable-energy [hereinafter "Climate Change and Renewable Energy"].
5 *Id*. at 7.
6 International Energy Agency (IEA) et al., *Tracking SDG7—The Energy Progress 2020*, at 1 (2020) https://irena.org/publications/2020/May/Tracking-SDG7-The-Energy-Progress-Report-2020 [hereinafter "Tracking SDG7"].
7 *Id*. at 4.
8 *Id*. at 30, 133–36.
9 *Id*. at 4.
10 *Id*. at 8.
11 *Id*. at 59.

To achieve universal electricity access, especially in sub-Saharan Africa, significant further efforts are required. Despite impressive growth in the use of modern renewables in the power sector, deployment is lagging well behind in end use sectors, with special regard to transport, industry, heating, and cooling. The rate of energy efficiency improvements is still below the required 2.6% per year to meet the global target.[12] Improvement in global primary energy intensity has fallen over the last few years. Global primary energy intensity was 5.01MJ/USD (2011) on purchasing power parity (PPP) in 2017, a 1.7% improvement from 2016—the lowest rate of improvement since 2010.[13] Technologies already exist to move toward a cleaner, decarbonized energy pathway. The price for solar photovoltaics (PV) dropped by 77% and for onshore wind by 38%.[14]

Despite the progress in the power sector, smart-grid management challenges and long-term electricity storage remain major bottlenecks to a full transition to clean energy. Moreover, direct and indirect fossil fuel subsidies still by far exceed subsidies to renewable energy, slowing the spread of renewable energy sources. The transport sector remains massively reliant on fossil fuels. Global oil use may drop for personal vehicles, but fossil fuel demand for heavy duty road vehicles, ships, and aircrafts continues to push overall oil demand for transport on an upward trajectory. Global passenger demand is expected to increase the use of oil more than twofold between 2015 and 2050, with the bulk of growth occurring in developing economies.[15] The positive impact of electric vehicles will hinge on the type of electric vehicle, the source of energy generation, driving conditions, charging patterns, and availability of charging infrastructure, government policies, and the local climate in the region of use. Promotion of public transportation and slow mobility, such as walking and biking, should be at the heart of transition strategies in the transport and energy sectors.[16]

Between 1965 and 2015, the world's per capita energy consumption increased from 1.3 to 1.9 tons of oil equivalent but individual average consumption is three to four times higher in developed countries, where progress in energy efficiency has been able to limit only the rate of growth of demand.[17] Demand for energy is expected to increase by 25% in 2040, and the increase could be twice as large without continued improvements in energy efficiency.[18] According to the International Energy Agency, if annual investment in renewables does not at least double, fossil fuels will retain a predominant role in supplying up to 78% of total energy in 2030, and a similar share even in 2050.[19] The direct consequence will be the persistence of health-damaging pollution from fossil fuel burning and increasing greenhouse gas emissions that will also make it impossible to reach the Paris Agreement objective of holding the increase in the global average temperature to well below 2°C above pre-industrial levels.[20]

---

12 *Id*. at 95.
13 *Id*. at 3.
14 *Id*. at 85.
15 International Transport Forum (ITF), *ITF Transport Outlook 2019* 128 a). 19)G7, ansport Forum,6.6rgy, Woldemiological od, Law Professorater coservation, and its Lawests, combat desertificati(2019) www.oecd-ilibrary.org/transport/itf-transport-outlook-2019_transp_outlook-en-2019-en.
16 Tracking SDG7, *supra* note 6 at 128.
17 Hannah Ritchie & Max Roser, *Energy*, Our World in Data, https://ourworldindata.org/energy#citation (2015).
18 IEA, *World Energy Outlook 2019*, (2019) www.iea.org/reports/world-energy-outlook-2019 [hereinafter "World Energy Outlook 2019"].
19 *Id*.
20 Paris Agreement to the United Nations Framework Convention on Climate Change, Dec. 12, 2015, T.I.A.S. No. 16–1104, art. 2.

The share of electricity in global energy consumption is approaching 20% and is set to rise further.[21] A doubling of electricity demand in developing economies puts cleaner, universally available, and affordable electricity at the center of strategies for economic sustainable development and greenhouse gas emissions reduction provided that the electricity is not provided by fossil fuels. In that case, electrification brings benefits—both by reducing local pollution and climate change causation—and requires additional measures to decarbonize power supply if it is to unlock its full potential as a way to meet climate goals.[22]

All the above statistics are temporarily distorted by the consequences of worldwide economic collapses due to the COVID-19 pandemic, with current fossil fuel demand dramatically decreased as a result. When the virus is finally resolved, and as economic recovery begins, the potential for progress is clear, but its realization is dependent on political will that is unfortunately unclear. The convergence of cheaper renewable energy technologies, digital applications, and the rising role of electricity are crucial vectors for change. Solutions need to be context specific with energy mixes, including decentralized renewable energies, emerging from the disruptive changes in energy production and consumption.

Implementing SDG 7 on the Ground: Case Studies

Expanding Access to Electricity and Clean Cooking Solutions—The Case of Viet Nam

Viet Nam witnessed a significant breakthrough in electricity access over the past decades. Between 2000 and 2016, access to electricity in Viet Nam increased from around 76% to an impressive 99% and the country is on a good track to ensuring that most rural households have access to electricity by 2020.[23] Also, Viet Nam is 4th among the 20 countries with the fastest growing rates of access to clean cooking fuels.[24] According to an International Energy Agency (IEA) report, Viet Nam's cooking fuel access rate has reached 73% in 2018 compared with 14% in 2000.[25]

Viet Nam's progress in national electrification benefited from a variety of factors, such as extensive natural hydropower resources that allowed for the development of complementary off-grid hydropower systems at mini and pica scales; the important role of infrastructure in national development; and multiple funding sources, including those from overseas.[26] On top of that, rapid expansion of rural electrification was achieved, largely because it has been clearly stated as a national priority by the Government, responding to the unmet high demand for electricity. Viet Nam provides an example of how a government prioritized rural electrification and the substantive steps that were taken to make this priority a reality.[27]

---

21 *Id.* at. 129, 131.
22 *See id.* at. 107, 120.
23 Dep. of Sci., Educ., Natural Resources and Env't, *Viet Nam's Voluntary National Review on the Implementation of the Sustainable Development Goals 2018*, Viet Nam Ministry of Planning and Investment (June 4, 2018) https://sustainabledevelopment.un.org/content/documents/19967VNR_of_Viet_Nam.pdf.
24 Tracking SDG7, *supra* note 6, at 60.
25 World Energy Outlook 2019, *supra* note 18, at (need pg #).
26 Romilly Greenhill &Andrew Scott, *Turning the Lights on Sustainable Energy and Development in Viet Nam*, ODI (Sept. 2014), https://www.odi.org/publications/8798-turning-lights-sustainable-energy-development-viet-nam.
27 *Id.*

To achieve the goal of ensuring access to sustainable energy for all, Viet Nam has issued and enforced many important policies to meet the people's and the nation's socioeconomic development needs. A specific target for rural electrification was first introduced in 1996, aiming at achieving 100% electrification of districts, 80% of communes, and 60% of rural households by the year 2000.[28] This was successfully achieved and later revised upward in successive Power Development Master Plans. Further, the latest Electricity Plan VII is aimed at "ensuring that most rural households have access to electricity by 2020," which is aligned with the United Nations 2030 Agenda for Sustainable Development.[29] These high-level policy commitments helped to drive progress in the energy sector, with the policy on rural electrification appearing to have been strongly connected to other development strategies, including a national poverty reduction program. This is a practical approach for many developing countries to tackle energy poverty and its interlinkages with other development issues, such as health care and education.

The government policies and regulations were also flexible to tackling and adapting to changing challenges over time, fully considering its country's conditions—focusing first on maximizing access to electricity and then on inclusion and quality.[30] The establishment of Viet Nam's strong national policy on rural electrification is coupled with an empowered national institution to head the electrification drive, which allowed Viet Nam to take advantage of its natural hydropower resources and develop the infrastructure that allowed this source of electricity to expand, first to its base of agriculture and industry, and then into every community and household.[31]

Viet Nam's achievement of exceptionally rapid rural electrification also demonstrates what can be done through the mobilization of local resources. Rural electrification in Viet Nam has been financed largely by local stakeholders. Investment in rural electrification totaled an estimated $10.3 billion over the period of 1990 to 2012, including approximately 50% from all levels of government.[32] Some argue that Viet Nam's policies for equitable access to electricity were partly a response to the experience of relying on local resources for electrification, which does not necessarily lead to a focus on providing access for the poorest. However, utilizing local resources may have been the most efficient way for a region where access to electricity was very low. Local institutions for the development and operation of rural electricity services could quickly respond to the local demand for energy, mobilize funds from both the government and private sector, and rapidly replicate the success stories to extend access of electricity and clean cooking solutions to large numbers of people, including those living in remote countryside areas. Driven by the need for technical standardization to improve efficiency of the electricity network and to lower the operating cost and improve the management of qualified service, the government could gradually step in to drive the transition from unplanned and unregulated local electricity services.

While Viet Nam has made progress on expanding access to electricity and clean cooking solutions, there remain challenges to future progress, such as fully achieving universal access to modern energy as the poorest households are still lagging behind; expanding access

---

28 *Ibid.*
29 *Ibid.*
30 Asian Development Bank, Viet Nam's Success in Increasing Access to Energy through Rural Electrification (2011) [hereinafter "Asian Development Bank"].
31 *Id.*
32 *Id.*

to clean cooking, as around 26 million people still rely on traditional use of biomass and inefficient cook stoves; ensuring a reliable energy supply in remote areas; and reforming electricity subsidies while protecting access for the poorest.[33] To meet SDG7.1 targets, the Viet Nam Government is committed to further improve its institutional and policy system toward more sustainable energy production and use, in addition to continued investments in energy infrastructure with prioritized renewable energy development. Some portions of the Vietnamese experience with rural electrification are specific to the social, political, and cultural context of the country, but the majority of them are replicable. Sustained national commitment to electrification, coupled with dedicated rural electrification policy and institutions, are the keys to drive change. Viet Nam provides valuable lessons in balancing economic growth and poverty reduction with growing demand for energy and its sustainability.

Promoting Access with Renewable Electricity—The Case of Kenya

Renewable energy has contributed to Kenya's electrification since 1980.[34] According to Kenya's 2017 energy report, about 70% of the nation's electricity-installed capacity comes from renewable energy sources,[35] which is three times more than the global average.[36] Kenya has made remarkable progress in satisfying its domestic goals to reach 100% renewable energy by 2020,[37] and to achieve universal access to electricity for all Kenyans by 2022,[38] thereby setting an example to other developing countries of what can be done.

In Kenya, hydro has been the crucial source for generating electricity with a long history. However, water stress caused by droughts has limited its ability to provide consistent electricity. Developers have already begun to tap into new energy opportunities, with geothermal leading the way. In December 2014, for the first time, power generation from geothermal sources in Kenya accounted for more than half of Kenya's electricity output.[39] Furthermore, the government has attempted to diversify the sources of renewable energy, including by developing wind, biomass, and solar.[40]

---

33 *Ibid.*
34 *See Kenya Electricity Installed Capacity 1980–2012*, KENYA NATIONAL BUREAU OF STATISTICS—KENYA DATA PORTAL, https://kenya.opendataforafrica.org/ykswtxb/kenya-electricity-installed-capacity-1980-2012 (last visited Nov. 22, 2020).
35 *See National Energy Policy*, REPUBLIC OF KENYA at 47 (Oct. 2018), https://kplc.co.ke/img/full/BL4PdOqKtxFT_National%20Energy%20Policy%20October%20%202018.pdf.
36 *See* Leonard Owino Onyango, *Kenya Tops Africa, Ninth Globally in Geothermal Rankings*, DAILY NATION (June 5, 2018), www.nation.co.ke/business/Kenya-tops-Africa--ninth-globally-in-geothermal-rankings/996-4597034-o5iddy/index.html.
37 *See* Office of the President Kenya, *Kenya on Track to Achieve Full Transition to Renewable Energy By 2020, President Kenyatta* (Dec. 4, 2018), www.president.go.ke/2018/12/04/kenya-on-track-to-achieve-full-transition-to-renewable-energy-by-2020-president-kenyatta/.
38 *Kenya Launches Ambitious Plan to Provide Electricity to All Citizens by 2022*, WORLD BANK (Dec. 6, 2018), www.worldbank.org/en/news/press-release/2018/12/06/kenya-launches-ambitious-plan-to-provide-electricity-to-all-citizens-by-2022.
39 *Africa 2030: Roadmap for a Renewable Energy Future*, IRENA at 22 (2015), www.irena.org/-/media/Files/IRENA/Agency/Publication/2015/IRENA_Africa_2030_REmap_2015_low-res.pdf.
40 For wind power's development, see Abdi Latif Dahir, *Africa's Largest Wind Power Project Is Now Open in Kenya*, QUARTZ AFRICA (Jul. 22, 2019), https://qz.com/africa/1671484/kenya-opens-africas-largest-wind-power-project-in-turkana/. For biomass and solar development, *see Kenya Primary Energy Demand and GDP in the Stated Policies Scenario, 2010–2040*, IEA (last updated Jan. 27, 2020), www.iea.org/

Currently, the renewable energy supply in Kenya can be divided into two broad categories: On-grid renewable energy projects and off-grid projects. On-grid renewable energy projects are products for utility-scale and customer-scale applications where the power generated is sold to a variety of customers, including the utility.[41] Off-grid renewable energy projects are usually implemented with mini-grids in rural areas that are difficult to connect to the national grid, including for individual households, communities, and institutions in rural areas.[42] According to the Kenyan government, as of 2017, 73.5% of the population is connected to electricity compared to only 15% in 2004.[43] This case study aims to summarize the factors and lessons that accounted for Kenya's experience of promoting renewable energy electrification.

Overall Renewable Energy Developments

Reform of the power sector, which commenced in the early 1990s, has progressed to promote its efficiency and renewable energy resources. The Electric Power Act in 1997 and the Energy Act in 2006 accelerated the reform by creating an autonomous regulatory body and unbundling electricity utilities to promote the development and use of renewable energy technologies.[44] The latest energy legislation, the Energy Act of 2019, has paved the way for the energy sector to take further steps to help reduce greenhouse gas emissions and Kenya's reliance on non-renewable energy sources.[45]

This goal was further specified in *Kenya Vision 2030*, a long-term development blueprint for the country. In the first term (2008–2012) of Kenyan Vision 2030, the government successfully added 505 MW of electricity to meet the growing demand for electricity via a Least Cost Power Development Plan (LCPDP).[46] In the second term (2013–2017), renewable energy project development was the core of the plan, including increasing generation capacity of energy from solar, wind, biogas, and development of bio-energy, including bio-ethanol and biodiesel value chains.[47] Furthermore, renewable energy development and promotion are also highlighted as one of Kenya's national strategies in the context of climate change. As indicated in *The National Climate Change Response Strategy*, the Kenyan government aims to achieve a green economy by 2020 through a series of strategies, including sustainable infrastructure development, increased investment in renewable energy resources, and

---

data-and-statistics/charts/kenya-primary-energy-demand-and-gdp-in-the-stated-policies-scenario-2010-2040 (last visited Nov. 28, 2020).

41 *See* Richard Boampong and Michelle Andrea Phillips, *Renewable Energy Incentives in Kenya: Feed-in-Tariffs and Rural Expansion*, NAT'L. SCI. FOUNDATION'S SUSTAINABLE ENERGY PATHWAYS INITIATIVE at 8 (Jun. 12, 2016), https://bear.warrington.ufl.edu/centers/purc/docs/papers/1610_Boampong_Renewable%20energy%20incentives%20in%20Kenya.pdf.

42 *Id.*

43 *See* Republic of Kenya, *supra* note 35, at 46.

44 *See* Government of Kenya, *Energy Act 2006*, at 100–01, https://renewableenergy.go.ke/asset_uplds/files/The%20%20Energy%20%20Act.2006.pdf (last visited Nov. 28, 2020).

45 *See The Energy Act, 2019*, ENERGY & PETROLEUM REGULATORY AUTHORITY (Dec. 23, 2019), www.epra.go.ke/download/the-energy-act-2019/.

46 *See First Medium Term Plan (2008–2012)*, KENYA VISION 2030, http://vision2030.go.ke/2008-2012/#58 (last visited Nov. 28, 2020).

47 *See Second Medium Term Plan (2013–2017)*, KENYA VISION 2030, http://vision2030.go.ke/2013-2017/#58 (last visited Nov. 28, 2020).

promoting renewable energy access in remote areas.[48] From the above, the country has put the goal of renewable energy development on the national agenda and detailed the goal in national development at different stages.

After goal setting, the primary needs were infrastructure investment that could facilitate renewable energy construction, transmission, and distribution. To boost investment for building the infrastructures required for renewable energy, Kenya introduced a Feed-in Tariff (FIT) Policy for electricity from wind, biomass, and small hydropower in 2008, and revised the policy in 2010 and 2012 to accommodate more diverse energy sources and specific pricing for smaller project sizes.[49] For the last ten years, Kenya has been using the feed-in-tariff model where investors interested in wind power, geothermal, solar, hydropower, and biomass energy sources are offered a power purchase agreement to construct the power plant and sell the electricity to the Kenya utility.[50] However, this model has been criticized based on the following disadvantages of FIT applications: (1) they can lead to upward pressure on prices in the near-term; (2) they do not adequately address the high up-front costs of renewable energy technologies; (3) payment levels are often independent of market signals; (4) they do not encourage direct price competition between project developers; and (5) they make it difficult to allocate costs across ratepayer classes.[51] Therefore, the government now plans to scrap FIT, substituting an auction system where tenders are given for the company offering the lowest rates, thus demonstrating a very helpful flexibility.[52]

International support was essential to renewable energy development in Kenya. The country has received financial and technical help from international organizations, such as the World Bank, to develop renewable energy projects since 1997.[53] In February 2011, Kenya was also one of the first six pilot countries selected to receive funding through the Scaling Up Renewable Energy Program (SREP) Investment Plan.[54] The SREP has empowered Kenya to develop some major geothermal and solar energy projects, and an electricity modernization project.[55] Furthermore, Kenya has a vibrant donor community with multilateral and bilateral

---

48 *See National Climate Change Response Strategy*, GOVERNMENT OF KENYA at 15–16 (April 2010), www.environment.go.ke/wp-content/documents/complete%20nccrs%20executive%20brief.pdf; this target is reconfirmed in the *Kenya Green Economy Strategy and Implementation Plan (GESIP)*, at 14–15 (May 2015), www.oneplanetnetwork.org/sites/default/files/kenya-green-economy-strategy-and-implementation-plan-gesip-2015.pdf.

49 The Scaling Up Renewable Energy Program in Low Income Countries (SREP) is empowering transformation in the world's poorest countries by demonstrating the economic, social, and environmental viability of renewable energy. *See* FEED-IN TARIFFS POLICY FOR WIND, BIOMASS, SMALL HYDROS, GEORTHERMAL, BIOGAS AND SOLAR, 2012, MINISTRY OF ENERGY 2nd Ed., (Kenya 2012).

50 *Id*.

51 *See* Boampong & Phillips, *supra* note 41, at 9.

52 The transition is part of the recommendations contained in the Updated Least Cost Power Development Plan for the study period 2017–2037 ("Plan"). *See* Penninah Munyaka & Mbatia Mwasaria, *Looming Introduction of an Energy Auction System to Kenya*, RÖDL & PARTNER (Feb. 13, 2020),www.roedl.com/insights/renewable-energy/2020-02/looming-introduction-of-an-energy-auction-system-to-kenya.

53 *See Maximizing Financing for Development in Action: The Kenya Energy Sector Experience*, WORLD BANK (Apr. 18, 2019), www.worldbank.org/en/results/2019/04/18/maximizing-financing-for-development-in-action-the-kenya-energy-sector-experience.

54 *See Scaling-Up Renewable Energy Program (SREP) Joint Development Partner Scoping Mission*, CLIMATE INVESTMENT FUNDS (Feb. 7–11, 2011), www.climateinvestmentfunds.org/sites/cif_enc/files/Kenya_post_mission_report_March_10_2011.pdf.

55 *See Projects in Kenya*, CLIMATE INVESTMENT FUNDS, www.climateinvestmentfunds.org/country/kenya (last visited Nov. 28, 2020).

financiers who have contributed consistently to the evolving thinking across the sector value chain: On generation, transmission, distribution, and electrification.[56]

The Kenyan government has done a good job of promoting its energy reform programs. Since the country has prioritized the development of renewable energy, the public in Kenya has a strong perception of the reasons for adopting renewable energy. In a recent large-scale survey, about 96% of the rural respondents and 76% of the urban respondents preferred to have all their power supplies from renewable energy sources.[57] The consumers' acceptance of renewable technology also makes Kenya an appealing destination for investment.

Rural Electrification with Renewable Energy

Even though urban areas' grid development is growing dramatically, most Kenyans who live far from the grid in rural towns and villages cannot tap into the benefits of on-grid energy. The Rural Electrification Authority (REA) was established under the Energy Act 2006 with a special purpose to accelerate the pace of rural electrification through fund allocation and the promotion of renewable energy sources.[58] The REA has two strategies to promote the application of renewable energy, grid extension to connect to existing renewable energy supply and installation of renewable energy for off-grid supply.

As an important tool that can be used on- and off-grid, mini-grids are being adopted in Kenya to protect against grid failures for those who are already connected to the grid, as well as to provide dependable electricity for those who live in the off-grid areas. Mini-grids have a long history in Kenya, with the first installations dating back to the early 1980s.[59] Kenya has three different ownership/operating models for its mini-grids: Public mini-grids, community-owned mini-grids, and privately owned mini-grids.[60]

REA's work to advance mini-grid development in Kenya includes planning mini-grids in remote areas, which are locations where the Rural Electrification Master Plan (REMP) does not plan to extend the grid soon. After the REA's promotion of mini-grids, Kenya Power and Lighting Company (KPLC) takes over construction and ownership, and it sells the power to the consumers.[61] Since 2011, public-owned diesel-based mini-grid stations also have been transformed into hybrid diesel-solar and/or wind generators systems.[62]

---

56 *See* WORLD BANK, *supra* note 53.
57 In a recent survey, about 96% of the rural respondents and 76% of the urban respondents preferred to have all their power supplies from renewable energy sources. *See* Eliud Kiprop et al., *The Role of Household Consumers in Adopting Renewable Energy Technologies in Kenya*, MDPI ENV'TS 6, 95 (Aug. 13, 2019).
58 Following the enactment of the Energy Act 2019, the Rural Electrification Authority (REA) has now changed its name to Rural Electrification and Renewable Energy Corporation (REREC). REREC has an expanded mandate for spearheading Kenya's green energy drive, in addition to implementing rural electrification projects. *See Main Page*, REREC, www.rerec.co.ke/ (last visited on Nov. 28, 2020)
59 *See* Thomas Day & Marie-Jeanne Kurdziel, *The Role of Renewable Energy Mini-Grids in Kenya's Electricity Sector*, NEW CLIMATE INST. at 4 (Nov. 2019), https://ambitiontoaction.net/wp-content/uploads/2019/11/A2A-Kenya_Mini-grids-study_201911.pdf.
60 *See Mini Grids in Kenya: A Case Study of a Market at a Turning Point*, WORLD BANK, CLIMATE INVESTMENTS FUNDS & ENERGY SECTOR MGMT. ASSIST. PROGRAM at 24 (Nov. 2017), https://openknowledge.worldbank.org/bitstream/handle/10986/29022/ESM-cKenyaMiniGridsCaseStudyConfEd-PUBLIC.pdf?sequence=1&isAllowed=y.
61 *See id.* at 11.
62 *See* Day & Kurdziel, *supra* note 59, at 25.

The community and private-owned mini-grid models are crucial tools to allow the underserved areas in Kenya access to clean energy. Communities, generally through county governments, operate and maintain the whole system, from generation to distribution to payment collection, with their management committees.[63] Private mini-grid projects have emerged in recent years. Based on a 2017 World Bank Report, more than 21 private mini-grids serve between 1,000 and 2,500 customer households, with an aggregate capacity of approximately 500 kW.[64] However, the price of the electricity generated from private mini-grids is very high when compared to those connected to the national grid, which is heavily subsidized. This situation leads to low demand for electricity for low-income households in the off-grid areas covered by private mini-grids, which does not help the purpose of rural electrification.[65]

Despite the significant potential role that mini-grids could play in Kenya's electricity sector, the 2018 Kenya National Electrification Strategy (KNES) lacks a clear energy planning strategy for the deployment of mini-grids and grid extension projects. That being said, with the support of the government of Germany, Kenya prepared a draft of the Kenya Energy (Mini-Grid) Regulations in 2017, to fill a significant gap in the policy framework for mini-grid installation, operation, and interaction with the centralized grid.[66]

Combining renewable energy with cooking stoves is another unique way for Kenya to apply renewable energy.[67] The majority of Kenyan households relied primarily on solid fuels (wood and charcoal) for their cooking needs, which causes exposure to health-damaging environmental pollution through open fires and inefficient fuels.[68] The Kenyan government now promotes improved cooking stoves through market mechanisms, including reducing the import duty on solid biomass stoves, creating VAT exemptions for clean and efficient cook stoves and their related components, and increasing the tax on the sale of kerosene to de-incentivize its use.[69] Plus, the Kenyan government has been using the opportunities offered under the clean development mechanism (CDM) to promote use of improved cooking stoves. For example, as of 2016, 27 Gold Standard cleaning cooking stove-carbon credit projects have been established in Kenya, with a total savings of 786,821 metric tons of carbon emissions reduced annually.[70]

Under the Energy Act 2006, the Kenyan government introduced programs which focus on the demand side for existing fossil-fueled energy, including (a) mandatory energy audits of large commercial and industrial consumers;[71] (b) subsidies and other tax incentives to promote and sustain wider adoption of energy efficient electric installations, such as solar

---

63 *See id.*
64 *See Mini Grids, supra* note 60, at 24.
65 *See* AbuBakr Bahaj et al., *The Impact of an Electrical Mini-Grid on the Development of a Rural Community in Kenya*, 12(5) ENERGIES 778 (Feb. 26, 2019).
66 *See* Day & Kurdziel, *supra* note 59, at 11.
67 *See Second Medium Term Plan, supra* note 47.
68 *See Kenya*, Clean Cooking Alliance, www.cleancookingalliance.org/country-profiles/focus-countries/4-kenya.html (last visited on Nov. 28, 2020).
69 *See id.*
70 *See Gold Standard Improved Cookstove Activities Guidebook (2004–2016)*, GOLD STANDARD at 18, www.goldstandard.org/sites/default/files/documents/gs_ics_report.pdf (last visited Nov. 28, 2020).
71 The Kenya Association of Manufacturers (KAM)—through an agreement with the Ministry of Energy, since 2006 has hosted the national Center for Energy Efficiency and Conservation (CEEC) and is involved in program administration on behalf of the Ministry of Energy, notably its program of energy auditing for industrial sites and commercial buildings, as well as training and certification services. KAM

water heaters and compact fluorescent light bulbs;[72] (c) improvements to energy efficiency of buildings;[73] and (d) developing energy efficiency and conservation awareness campaigns across the country.[74]

However, the lack of clarity of the respective responsibilities of the central government agencies and local governments weakened the effectiveness of these energy efficiency programs. The newly released Energy Act 2019 seeks to resolve this problem.

Boosting Demand for Off-Grid Renewable Energy

As an additional measure, the Kenyan government also promotes solar lighting products, such as solar lanterns and solar home systems to increasingly provide Kenyans with decentralized clean energy. However, these products can be so expensive that customers often cannot purchase these solar home systems or solar lanterns up-front with cash.[75]

The introduction of a Pay-as-you-go (PayGo) model in 2011 has enabled Kenyans who live in off-grid areas to afford such renewable energy products. The PayGo model allows customers to make small payments to providers for their solar lighting product over a period of months or years, eventually paying off the purchase price for full ownership of the product. Since 2011, the private sector market for off-grid solar lighting products has expanded rapidly. Between 2009 and 2017, the number of solar home systems in Kenya has more than doubled, from 320,000 to 700,000.[76] According to the World Bank, Kenya is one of the two strongest markets for the PayGo model after examining 71 factors across demand, supply, and enabling environment.[77] It is worth mentioning that Kenya scores high, particularly when it comes to users' "willingness to pay." While Kenya also does well

---

has also greatly subsidized the cost of energy audits to ensure many facilities can afford to pay for quality energy audit services.

72 As of April 2017, it is estimated that Kenya's estimated capacity for installation of solar water heating was 64,739 systems. *See Study of the Solar Water Heating Industry in Kenya*, EED ADVISORY at 13, (Aug. 2017), www.solarthermalworld.org/sites/default/files/news/file/2018-10-31/study_of_the_swh_industry_-_kenya_high_res_final.pdf (noting that the government retrofitted 1.25 million Compact Fluorescent Lamps (CLFs) in exchange for existing incandescent bulbs through its Residential Efficient Lighting Program); *see also* John Hutia & Esther Wang'ombe, Kenya Presentation-Energy Efficiency Program: Presentation (Jul. 2012), www.usea.org/sites/default/files/event-presentations/WangombeIhuthiaPPT.pdf.

73 The Kenya Building Code specifies that new housing developments should have solar hot water for bathroom use, and should consider PV and wind. Further energy and sustainability measures for residential housing and promotion of green buildings to industry are scheduled for introduction through a Built Environment Bill (2017) and a Housing Bill (2017). *See Energy Efficiency in Buildings-Kenya*, GOV. OF KENYA, COPENHAGEN CENTRE ON ENERGY EFFICIENCY & BUILDING EFFICIENCY ACCELERATOR (Nov. 2018), https://c2e2.unepdtu.org/wp-content/uploads/sites/3/2018/11/2018-10-ee-in-buildings-kenya-web.pdf.

74 The Energy Efficiency Campaigns were conducted through road shows, fliers/posters/booklets, barazas, trade fairs, radio/television, and billboards. *See* Margaret Kanini, "Energy Efficiency from Kenya Power Perspective: A Presentation," Kenya Power (Apr. 2013).

75 *See* Savannah Carr-Wilson & Sandeep Pai, *Pay-As-You-Go: How a Business Model Is Helping Light Millions of Rural Kenyan Homes with Solar*, CASE STUD. IN THE ENV'T (Nov. 2018).

76 *See id.*

77 *See* World Bank et al., *Pay-As-You-Go Market Attractiveness Index 2019*, INT'L FINANCE CORP. (2019), www.lightingglobal.org/wp-content/uploads/2019/06/PAYGo-MAI-2019-Report.pdf.

on the supply side, driven by the availability of finance to support the sector, it also scores well on both legal/regulatory aspects of trade and commerce.[78]

Since 2015, solar loans, where a financial institution and a solar solution provider decide to partner, have been another tool that the Kenyan government has used to make renewable energy power affordable in rural Kenya.[79] Solar loans have been "rolling out" throughout Kenya's network of rural branches, and have diversified the offer of solar solutions (from solar lanterns to larger solar home systems, from domestic to productive use of energy). Even though solar loans help improve lighting and living conditions and other social benefits in Kenya, many users also mention the low quality of some solar products.[80]

Kenya has achieved exemplary progress in providing clean electricity to its population through careful long-term planning, establishment of ambitious goals, strong and lasting leadership and support of its government, involvement of its public and business community, adoption of innovative means of delivering electricity through mini-grids to its hard-to-serve rural population, and adoption of clever pay-as-you-save financing methods to make innovations more affordable. It made good use of energy efficiency and a wide variety of renewable energy resources, even extending its efforts to promote clean cooking stoves and incandescent light bulbs.

Boosting financing—The Case of Canada

As the world makes the transition to a lower-carbon future, Canada faces several key challenges, including meeting increasing energy demands while reducing greenhouse gas emissions, and facilitating the supply of alternative sources of energy to support a smooth transition. To realize these goals, the Government of Canada is making generational investments in energy efficiency, clean electricity, and cleaner fuels and is on track to meet its commitment to double investments in clean energy research and development from $387 million in 2014–2015 to $775 million in 2019–2020.[81] For example, through a Clean Growth Program with a $155 million planned investment, the Canadian government continuously provides co-funding of clean technology research, development and deployment projects with provinces and territories in Canada's energy, mining, and forestry sectors.[82]

Moreover, Canada committed $2.65 billion to help developing countries to tackle climate change, including through important investments in renewable energy.[83] For example, Canada is providing $150 million to the African Renewable Energy Initiative to reduce emissions and improve access to energy by leveraging private sector investment, and $20 million to promote the use of clean energy and access to efficient cook stoves in Haiti, particularly for women and girls.[84]

---

78 *See id.*
79 *See* Marion Allet, *Solar Loans through a Partnership Approach: Lessons from Africa*, 15 J. OF FIELD ACTIONS: FIELD ACTIONS SCI. REP. 128–37 (2016), https://journals.openedition.org/factsreports/4206.
80 *See id.*
81 *See* CANADA'S VOLUNTARY NATIONAL REVIEW ON THE IMPLEMENTATION OF THE SUSTAINABLE DEVELOPMENT GOALS 2018, GOV. OF CANADA (2018), https://sustainabledevelopment.un.org/content/documents/20312Canada_ENGLISH_18122_Canadas_Voluntary_National_ReviewENv7.pdf.
82 *See id.*
83 *See Canada's Clean Growth Program*, GOV. OF CANADA (last modified Nov. 2, 2020), www.nrcan.gc.ca/climate-change/canadas-green-future/clean-growth-programs/20254 (last visited Nov. 28, 2020).
84 *See id.*

Accelerating the Energy Transformation 269

Such kinds of investments have demonstrated the Government's leadership and efforts to ensure sufficient financing for SDG 7 and its related Sustainable Development Goals, such as SDG 8 on job creation and SDG 5 on gender equity. Increased national public spending is important, but it will not suffice alone to generate enough funding toward the Sustainable Development Goals. Given the scale of the investment needs, and the potential for energy investments to generate revenue and savings, a key characteristic of Canada's financing for SDG 7 is the central role of private finance and the role of public capital providers as enablers of private finance.

In June 2017, the Canada Infrastructure Bank (CIB) was established in response to a market gap between government-funded and privately funded infrastructure projects. CIB uses federal support to attract private sector and institutional investments to new revenue-generating infrastructure projects that are in the public interest. By leveraging the capital and expertise of the private sector, the Bank helps public dollars go further and keeps the grant dollars for those projects that are more appropriate for traditional grant funding mechanisms. Supported by the federal government, CIB will invest $5 billion alongside the private sector for green infrastructure projects, including those on renewable energy and energy efficiency.[85]

At the same time, Canada is working with the private sector in developing countries to increase and diversify the range of financing mechanisms available to support sustainable development. For example, Canada's newly established Development Finance Institute (FinDev Canada) supports sustainable development by providing financial services to the private sector in developing countries to reduce poverty through job creation (SDG 8), advance women's economic empowerment (SDG 5), ensure clean and affordable energy (SDG 7), and act on climate change (SDG 13).[86] With an initial capitalization of $300 million, FinDev Canada focuses on three high-impact sectors: Green growth, agri-business, and financial services for small and medium-sized enterprises.[87] During 2018, the first year of its operation, FinDev Canada has committed to and announced two transactions on energy projects. The first $10 million investment was awarded to M-KOPA—a "pay-as-you-go" energy provider to off-grid homes in East-Central Africa.[88] The second transaction came in December 2018 with a $20 million investment for Climate Investor One—an innovative blended finance platform aimed at bringing renewable energy solutions to developing countries.[89] To mainstream women's economic empowerment across its economic development and climate mandate, FinDev Canada partnered with other G7 development finance institutions to announce the 2X Challenge, which aims to mobilize $3 billion by 2020 to support investments in business activities that benefit women in developing countries, including those related to energy projects.[90]

Private finance is vital in achieving SDG 7 within Canada, particularly in helping to build thriving economies that generate jobs and invest in infrastructure. However, it will be key to

---

85 *Id*.
86 *See* DFI FILES: FINDEV CANADA'S MISSION POSSIBLE – NEW JOBS, EMPOWERED WOMEN AND FIGHTING CLIMATE CHANGE ACROSS THE PLANET, DEV. AID (Dec. 12, 2019), www.developmentaid.org/#!/news-stream/post/55921/dfi-files-findev-canadas-mission-possible-new-jobs-empowered-women-and-fighting-climate-change-across-the-planet.
87 *See id*.
88 *Id*.
89 *Ibid*.
90 *Ibid*.

make sure that such type of finance is suited to the targets and generate maximum impact. In this respect, government plays a critical role, as it can help to mobilize and channel investments from the private sector to the most needed areas, prioritize those at risk of being left behind, such as clean cooking solutions, and strengthen monitoring processes. This requires long-term planning and well-designed policies by both national governments and the private sector. Canada's practice illustrates how to turn needs into investment opportunities by utilizing creative financing tools.

Effects of the Coronavirus

The COVID-19 pandemic is the biggest global crisis in decades. Governments have launched an unprecedented level of economic recovery packages worth over $9 trillion.[91] Energy shall play a central role in these recovery efforts. Achievement of SDG 7 is central to the 2030 Agenda and the Paris Agreement. The crisis offers a unique opportunity to accelerate the investment into a 21st-century energy system that paves the way toward a more resilient, sustainable, and equitable world.

The foremost priority for all countries is to rebuild their economies utilizing energy efficient and renewable energy measures that are less expensive than fossil fuels. Savings from the phasing out of fossil fuel subsidies would provide substantial initial funding to develop green and resilient infrastructure.

The use of distributed energy resources and off-grid community-based renewable energy would be particularly advantageous in bringing electricity to unserved rural areas—avoiding the need to provide expensive and environmentally damaging roads and facilities to extend the grid to these areas—and use of on-bill financing of projects, both of which have been demonstrated to be successful in Kenya.

Climate change mitigation and related actions to protect the integrity of the world's forests and to alleviate the pollution caused by the burning of fossil fuels for energy are important to achieving the SDG 7 goals and to reducing the threat of future pandemics and the damages they cause. Restoring energy impact statements as well as air pollution and chemical regulations in the United States are also important.

To provide funds to finance reconstruction of the economies of developing countries so severely damaged by the virus, the International Monetary Fund (IMF) has a major role to play. While the Fund is financed by its members, composed of a majority of all countries, and its assistance generally reflects each member's contributions, it still has substantial funding available for low-income countries. It presently has a $1 trillion lending capacity to support member countries in dealing with the destabilizing effects of the virus on global currency stability.[92] It has several programs devoted particularly to assisting low-income countries including an emergency financial assistance program and a debt relief program, already having been approved for debt relief for 25 of IMF's poorest members.[93]

---

91 Bryn Battersby et al, *Tracking the $9 Trillion Global Fiscal Support to Fight COVID-19*, IMFBLOG (May 20, 2020), https://blogs.imf.org/2020/05/20/tracking-the-9-trillion-global-fiscal-support-to-fight-covid-19/.
92 *See The IMF's Response to COVID-19*, IMF (last updated Oct. 28, 2020), www.imf.org/en/About/FAQ/imf-response-to-covid-19 (last visited Nov. 28, 2020).
93 *See id.*

In addition, the IMF has a program of Special Drawing Rights (SDR) from funds paid by member countries, granting withdrawal rights to supplement member countries' financial reserves in the event of economic disruptions. While the allocation of presently available SDRs to low-income countries falls far short of their needs, there is $245.89 billion in SDR funds available, of which $14.06 billion is allocated to lower-income countries and $11.67 billion for lower-middle-income countries as an immediate resource.[94]

Recognizing the terrible financial predicament caused globally to world economies from COVID-19, with particular hardship for low-income countries, the IMF is considering substantially augmenting funding for its programs. The World Bank and regional international banks are preparing to make major additional resources available, having pledged $200 billion in additional assistance.[95]

Recommendations for Policymakers[96]

The world is making encouraging progress toward achieving SDG 7, but if it stays on the current trajectory, it will fall far short of meeting the targets by 2030. Closing the energy access gap should be priority number one to serve the unserved and leave no one behind. Yet it is a task that remains particularly challenging, especially in rural areas. Strong political commitment, long-term energy planning, improved private financing, and adequate policy and fiscal incentives are keys to success, as showcased by the case studies of Viet Nam and Kenya in this chapter. Achieving universal access to electricity and clean fuels and technologies is not necessarily in conflict with achieving climate objectives, but higher energy demand to support additional productive uses of electricity for economic development in underserved areas can lead to corresponding increases in emissions if that demand is not met exclusively by energy efficiency measures and use of renewable energy. As the Kenya case study shows, promoting off-grid electricity access solutions (including solar lighting, solar home systems, and mini-grids) are vital to close the access gap.

Significant challenges remain for closing the clean cooking gap, particularly in sub-Saharan Africa and developing Asia. Much more rapid progress will require particular attention to behavioral patterns, cultural norms, and regional variations, as there is no one-size-fits-all solution when it comes to clean cooking. This is because cooking practices are heavily dependent upon culture, cuisine, household dynamics, and gender roles, as well as the availability of socially acceptable and affordable fuels and technologies. Increased funding is absolutely vital and the World Bank's Clean Cooking Fund is an important step in this respect.

Mobilizing financing is crucial, as evidenced by the case study of Canada. Current financing levels are significantly below what is required. About $1.3 to $1.4 trillion per year

---

94 *Id.*
95 *See Transcript of IMG Managing Director Kristalina Georgieva's Opening Press Conference 2020 Spring Meetings*, IMF (Apr. 15, 2020), www.imf.org/en/News/Articles/2020/04/15/tr041520-transcript-of-imf-md-kristalina-georgieva-opening-press-conference-2020-spring-meetings.
96 *See* Bo Fu et al., *Key Messages for Policymakers, in Accelerating SDG 7 Achievement: SDG 7 Policy Briefs in Support of The High-Level Political Forum 2019*, at 16, UN DESA (May 2019) (noting that this section was written by the authors of this chapter) (further noting that the statistics were updated based on the 2020 Tracking SDG7—The Energy Progress Report published by the SDG 7 custodian agencies. The International Renewable Energy Agency (IRENA) (2020 chair), International Energy Agency (IEA), the World Bank (WB), World Health Organization (WHO), United Nations Statistics Division (UNSD)).

is required to meet SDG7, more than twice the current level.[97] Investment is not currently spread equally and is leaving out many developing countries, in particular least-developed countries, landlocked developing countries, and small island developing states. Enabling environments, integrating policies, de-risking instruments, and incorporating direct financial incentives and digital finance solutions are critical in all sectors.

Over 230 million children go to primary schools without any electricity, compromising educational and development outcomes under SDG 4.[98] Electrification at primary schools stands at only 69%.[99] Enabling policies are needed to incentivize and facilitate a more coordinated approach, along with investments in sustainable and clean energy, and education infrastructure and services, in order to close the electricity access gap in education, and also drastically improve girl-to-boy ratios in schools.[100]

Energy efficiency and renewable energy investments continue to act as robust socioeconomic drivers, including through net employment gains (SDG 8). Employment in the renewable energy sector stood at 10.3 million in 2017 and could potentially reach about 24 million by 2030.[101] However, assurance is needed that the global energy transformation is accompanied by policies enabling a just transition that will take into account fossil fuel sector jobs loss to ensure that no one is left behind. There are also significant opportunities for achieving a greater gender balance in the global energy transformation. Gender considerations must be mainstreamed into job creation efforts, including through building enabling environments for women entrepreneurs.

Ensuring access to affordable, reliable, sustainable, and modern energy for all is a key condition for reducing inequalities, achieving the principle of "leaving no one behind," and ensuring a just and inclusive energy transition (SDG 10). Policy makers should address the interlinkages between energy, climate change, poverty, and inequality by promoting productive uses of energy, while enhancing gender equality and health equity, acknowledging the special vulnerability of women, addressing conditions of fuel poverty, and also supporting renewable energy and energy efficiency investments by low-income households.

Updated Nationally Determined Contributions (NDCs) now due in 2021,[102] should fully reflect countries' ambitious goals for renewable energy and energy efficiency (SDG 13). Decarbonization of the world's energy systems and attainment of the targets of SDG 7, including ensuring universal access to modern energy, are mutually reinforcing and must be advanced at the same time. A unified approach, including on finance, is required to achieve SDG 7 and the Paris Agreement simultaneously. The rapid deployment of renewables, coupled with energy efficiency, can achieve most of the emission reductions and decarbonization in the energy sector needed by 2050, while at the same time advancing economic growth and development. Special emphasis should be placed on mainstreaming gender considerations into all SDG energy-related actions, including responses to climate change. Renewable energy targets at the country level should also be linked to their adaptation strategies.

---

97 *See generally id.*
98 *Id.* at 17.
99 *Id.*
100 *Ibid.*
101 *Ibid.*
102 *See* UN Climate Press Release, *COP Bureau Reschedules UNFCCC Subsidiary Body Meetings to 2021*, UNFCCC (Jun. 23, 2020), https://unfccc.int/news/cop-bureau-reschedules-unfccc-subsidiary-body-meetings-to-2021.

The potential benefits from the global energy transition will contribute to greater peace and security by fostering more inclusive, climate-resilient, and sustainable societies (SDG 16). The global energy transformation will have new and far-reaching geopolitical implications, which will need to be carefully managed. Developing effective, accountable, and transparent institutions at all levels can help achieve the potential benefits of this transformation.

Strengthening cooperation at the regional and sub-regional levels is critical to effectively address the different areas' unique challenges, and to promote innovation, investment, enhanced cross-border connectivity, capacity building, south-south cooperation, and synergetic actions to advance energy, climate change, environment, and other SDGs simultaneously.

Catalytic actions and partnerships for SDG 7 are needed in vulnerable countries. These are particularly important in African countries, Least Developed Countries, landlocked developing countries, and small island developing states, and should be promoted in the context of the Mid-Term Review of the Small Island Developing States Accelerated Modalities of Action (SAMOA) Pathway and the High-Level Mid-Term Review on the implementation of the Vienna Programme of Action for Landlocked Developing Countries in 2019.[103]

Digitalization has the potential to fundamentally transform the global energy system by breaking down sectoral boundaries, increasing flexibility, and enabling integration across systems. Well-designed policies are crucial to unlocking the full benefits of digitalization in achieving SDG 7, while managing potential risks around security, privacy, and rebound effects.

Summary Recommendations

- Work together to ensure universal access to affordable, reliable, and modern energy services through accelerating the cost-efficient provision of clean electricity;
- Make clean cooking solutions a top priority;
- Harness the potential of centralized and decentralized modern renewable energy solutions and introduce carbon pricing;
- Phase out fossil fuel subsidies and coal usage as a matter of urgency; and
- Collaborate to reshape the global energy system to transition to a net-zero-CO_2-emitting global energy system by 2050 that is central to meeting the goals of the Paris Agreement on Climate Change.

---

[103] *See generally* VIENNA PROGRAMME OF ACTION FOR LANDLOCKED DEVELOPING COUNTRIES FOR THE DECADE 2014–2024, UN-OHRLLS (2019), https://unohrlls.org/custom-content/uploads/2015/03/Vienna-Programme-of-Action.pdf.

18 Toward Sustainable Consumption and Production

Anna Shostya and Narinder Kakar

Introduction

When the United Nations (UN) adopted the 2030 Agenda for Sustainable Development in September 2015, it launched a new phase for multilateralism and the global community's commitment to improve human lives and protect the environment. The 17 Sustainable Development Goals (SDGs) that are at the heart of the 2030 Agenda address multifaceted challenges of global peace, security, inequality, and economic growth and development. These goals are much more compelling, interrelated, and universal than their predecessors, the Millennium Development Goals (MDGs) which were introduced by the UN in 2000. The 2030 Agenda is revolutionary because it calls for the entire world's commitment to secure a sustainable future, so that the environmental impacts of the ever-increasing demand for resources, as well as its effects on people and the economy, are minimized. This commitment to a sustainable future necessitates ensuring transformative changes in sustainable consumption and production (SCP) patterns, the main focus of SDG 12. Being an urgent call to action for a responsible management of the Earth's limited resources, SDG 12 is *the* most central goal of the 2030 Agenda.

This chapter assesses the progress that has been made toward SDG 12 thus far. We start with important definitions of SCP and resource efficiency and explain how the concept of SCP has evolved and become part of the 2030 Agenda. We then explain the fundamental principles and targets of SDG 12. This is followed by the assessment of the global, regional, and income-based progress toward the goal, with several case studies (*Moving toward SDG 12* boxes) that highlight progress (or lack thereof) in individual countries and regions. We argue that, with some exceptions, few advances have been made toward targets prescribed by the 2030 Agenda and that most countries have been struggling to make improvements in resource management and waste reduction. We conclude that urgent actions have to be taken, especially in the area of data collection and data sharing. We also emphasize the importance of national efforts toward SCP that have to be taken collectively, so no country is left behind.

Consumption and Production as a Sustainable Development Goal

Basic Definitions

What is SCP and why has it been so central to our future development and survival? The SCP is commonly defined as

> the use of services and related products which respond to basic needs and bring a better quality of life while minimizing the use of natural resources and toxic materials as well

as the emission of waste and pollutants over the life cycle of the service or product so as not to jeopardize the needs of future generations.[1]

The sustainable use of resources includes the way we extract, process, use, and dispose of resources at all the stages of the production and consumption chain. The main concept that SCP is based on is resource efficiency, which "refers to using less resource inputs to achieve the same or improved output. Resource efficiency can be achieved by increasing resource productivity or reducing resource intensity (resource use/value-added)."[2] Resource efficiency makes business sense because it cuts waste and therefore reduces the cost of production and increases competitiveness. It makes sense for consumers, too, because it reduces consumers' expenditures and thus leaves the consumers financially better off. It increases the chances of survival for those who struggle to make ends meet for their basic needs. It also can cut back resource depletion, reduce land-use degradation, and minimize climate change effects. In short, resource efficiency can benefit both the present and future generations. Yet, resource-use efficiency has been unchanged at the global level and, therefore, a bold and urgent political action is required to reduce further degradation of the environment. Why?

Several interconnected dynamic forces can explain the current SPC trends and sluggish progress toward improvements in resource efficiency and waste reduction. First are the demographic trends. The world population doubled to 6 billion between 1960 and 2000, and it is expected to reach 8.6 billion in 2030 and 9.8 billion in 2050, according to the UN estimates.[3] Larger population leads to a higher demand for resources, especially food and water. The second factor, which is also an underlying cause of the first one, is a marked improvement in the standard of living of millions of people. Global poverty decreased from 36% in 1990 to less than 10% in 2018, while the number of people in extreme poverty has fallen from almost 2 billion in 1990 to about 650 million in 2018.[4] This was possible because of the third factor—phenomenal economic growth and development that has reached more and more regions of the world. In fact, most of this economic growth has occurred in countries such as India, Indonesia, and China, where not so long ago, more than half of the population lived in extreme poverty.

This impressive economic and social progress has been associated with an ever-increasing use of resources. The rate of natural resource extraction has accelerated since 2000, and if this growth is not slowed down, it is projected to grow to 190 billion metric tons by 2060, doubling today's number.[5] The result of such a trend will be depletion of resources (especially non-renewable energy resources), deforestation, land degradation, increased

---

1 *Oslo Roundtable on Sustainable Production and Consumption*, §1.2 DEFINING SUSTAINABLE CONSUMPTION (1994), www.iisd.ca/ consume/ oslo004.html#top (last visited Dec. 6, 2020) (Sustainable Consumption).
2 *See generally* SUSTAINABLE CONSUMPTION AND PRODUCTION GLOBAL EDITION—A HANDBOOK FOR POLICYMAKERS, UNEP (2015), https://sustainabledevelopment.un.org/index.php?page=view&type=400&nr=1951&menu=35.
3 Population Division, *World Population Prospects 2019*, UNITED NATIONS, https://population.un.org/wpp/ (last visited Dec. 6, 2020).
4 *Piecing Together the Poverty Puzzle—Poverty and Shared Prosperity 2018*, International Bank for Reconstruction and Development & World Bank Group (2018), https://openknowledge.worldbank.org/bitstream/handle/10986/30418/9781464813306.pdf.
5 *The Sustainable Development Goals Report* 2019, DEP. OF ECON. & SOC. AFFAIRS (DESA) (2019), https://unstats.un.org/sdgs/report/2019/The-Sustainable-Development-Goals-Report-2019.pdf (SDG Report 2019).

levels of greenhouse gas emissions, and other types of environmental degradation.[6] De-coupling or de-linking economic growth from environmental degradation and reducing our "Material Footprint" (MF) (the total amount of raw materials extracted to meet final needs), is therefore essential if we care about our future and our planet.

Much of the thinking about SCP was inspired by the concept of sustainable development, defined by the 1987 'Brundtland Commission' of the UN as "development that meets the needs of the present without compromising the ability of future generations to meet their own needs."[7] The concept of SCP was further clarified at the UN Conference on Environment and Development in Rio de Janeiro in 1992 and the Oslo Symposium in 1994.[8] Chapter Four in Section One of Agenda 21 of the 1992 conference focused on unsustainable patterns of production and consumption and stressed the interrelationship between environmental degradation and development issues, such as poverty, economic growth, and demographic dynamics. It recognized the different issues in the consumption patterns between richer parts of the world (that overconsume) and poorer ones (that struggle to meet basic needs). It also stressed the importance of international efforts to protect the environment and ensure global patterns of SCP.[9] Perhaps its most important conclusion was that "changing consumption patterns will require a multipronged strategy, focusing on demand, meeting the basic needs of the poor, and reducing waste and the use of finite resources in the production process."[10] Agenda 21, however, fell short in identifying the means of implementing these objectives. It neither specified how the changes in SCP patterns could be financed, nor how to develop public awareness of SCP, nor how to build or enhance institutional capacity and collaboration to promote research and environmentally friendly practices.

Yet, Agenda 21 was a defining moment as it set the stage for developing a global understanding of the need for changing the world's patterns of consumption and production. As such, it became a preamble for the UN's 2030 Agenda that further advanced the concept of the SCP and emphasized the interrelations between SCP and other SDGs. In addition, the 2030 Agenda focused on the means of implementation and called for the development of national policies and strategies to encourage changes in SCP patterns. These policies should develop effective ways to reduce all kinds of waste, encourage recycling, and foster the use of renewable energy sources. They should aim at changes in the SCP patterns throughout the entire life cycle of the products and foster ideas of sustainability among all actors (governments, international organizations, industries, households, and the public).[11]

---

6 *Id.*
7 *Report of the World Commission on Environment and Development: Our Common Future*, at 43 (1987), https://sustainabledevelopment.un.org/content/documents/5987our-common-future.pdf (Brundtland Report).
8 Sustainable Consumption, *supra* note 1.
9 *Conference on Environment and Development (Agenda 21)*, UN SUSTAINABLE DEVELOPMENT, (Jun. 3–14, 1992), https://sustainabledevelopment.un.org/content/documents/Agenda21.pdf.
10 *Id.*
11 Livia Bizikova et al., *Sustainable Consumption and Production Indicators for the Future SDGs*, UNEP Discussion Paper DTI/1895/PA (Mar. 2015).

Centrality and Universality of SDG 12 Targets

The framework for SDG 12 consists of 11 *Targets* and 13 *Indicators*. Targets specify the goals and Indicators represent the metrics that can be assessed and tracked. The Targets focus on "promoting resource and energy efficiency, sustainable infrastructure, and providing access to basic services, green and decent jobs and a better quality of life for all."[12] This "doing more with less" concept makes SCP a central theme within the 2030 Agenda, and thus connects SDG 12 Targets with almost all other SDGs (for a detailed matrix of interlinkages between SDG 12 Targets and other goals, see Table 18.1). Making SCP a key dimension that is incorporated in other goals was done by design.[13] In fact, the High-Level Political Forum (HLPF) called the SCP "one of the most cost-efficient and effective ways to achieve economic development, reduce impacts on the environment and advance human well-being."[14] SCP brings together most of the other human aspirations, and it is explicitly connected to SDGs 1, 2, 6, 7, 8, 9, 11, 13, 14, and 15. It is indirectly related to a number of other goals. Progress in SCP will, therefore, ensure further progress in all the SDGs.

SCP is also a universal goal, which means it is relevant to all countries regardless of their level of development. In developed countries, it implies shifting toward more resource-efficient production that relies more on renewable sources of energy and is less polluting. It also implies adopting sustainable lifestyles and reducing unnecessary consumption that leads to over-use of resources. In developing countries, SCP means finding the least-cost ways of production that foster environmentally sound and competitive practices. People in all countries also have to understand what SCP is and be aware of how their lifestyles affect the environment and the future of their children.

Take, for example, food loss and waste (FLW) reduction, one of the targets of SDG 12. In predominantly agricultural economies, most food losses occur at the beginning of the supply chain—near the farm.[15] Some of these losses are due to inadequate rural infrastructure, machinery, or storage facilities (related to SDG 9), others because of labor shortages (related to SDG 8), or because of the poor health of farmers (related to SDG 3). These losses directly affect farmers' incomes (SDG 1) and their ability to feed their families (SDG 2). In other places, including Europe and North America, most of the food is wasted near the end of the supply chain—when supermarkets and consumers order/buy more than they can sell/consume. It is a waste of scarce resources (related to SDGs 6, 7, 14, and 15) and it leads to significant economic losses (related to SDG 8). Reducing FLW is associated with poverty reduction, eradication of hunger and malnutrition, and improvement in health. It can increase employment and stimulate economic growth. FLW, in turn, depends on the quality of infrastructure and availability of storage facilities, energy, and machinery.

---

12 *Goal 12: Ensure Sustainable Consumption and Production Patterns*, SUSTAINABLE DEVELOPMENT GOALS, www.un.org/sustainabledevelopment/sustainable-consumption-production/ (last visited Dec. 6, 2020).
13 David Le Blanc, *Towards Integration at Last? The Sustainable Development Goals as a Network of Targets*, DESA Working Paper No 141, ST/ ESA/ 2015/ DWP/ 141 (2015).
14 *2018 HLPF Review of SDGs implementation: SDG 12—Ensure Sustainable Consumption and Production Patterns*, United Nations, https://sustainabledevelopment.un.org/content/documents/196532018backgroundnotesSDG12.pdf (last visited Dec. 6, 2020).
15 Jocelyn Marie Boiteau, *Food Loss and Waste in the United States and Worldwide*, WORLD HUNGER NEWS (Jun. 13, 2018), www.worldhunger.org/food-loss-and-waste-in-the-united-states-and-worldwide/.

Table 18.1 Interlinkages between SDG12 and other SDGs.

GOALS	12.1 National plans	12.2 Use of resources	12.3 Food loss and waste	12.4 Hazardous waste	12.5 Recycling	12.6 Information	12.7 Public procurement	12.8 Education	12.a Capacity building help	12.b Tools to monitor tourism	12.c Fossil fuel subsidies
Goal 1: Poverty			1.5								1.3
Goal 2: Hunger	2.4		2.4	2.4							
Goal 3: Health				3.9							3.9
Goal 4: Education	4.7							4.7			
Goal 5: Gender Equality											
Goal 6: Water				6.3							
Goal 7: Energy		7.1					7.2				7.2/7.3
Goal 8: Growth	8.4/8.9	8.4	8.4		8.4	8.5	8.4	8.4	8.4	8.9	
Goal 9: Industry, Innovation	9.a			9.4					9.4/9.5		9.4
Goal 10: Inequality											
Goal 11: Cities	11.c				11.2 11.6						
Goal 12: SCP	12.3/12.7 12.8/ 12.a, 12.b	12.5		12.5/12.6	12.2/12.3	12.8	12.2	12.1			
Goal 13: Climate		13.1						13.3	13.1		
Goal 14: Oceans	14.7									14.7	
Goal 15: Life on land		15.1/15.2						15.a	15.1/15.a	15.1/15.2	
Goal 16: Inclusion											
Goal 17: Global Partnership	17.16 17.19								17.7/17.8		

Source: The authors; Charles Arden-Clarke, UN Environment, SDG Knowledge Platform (Jan. 2018), https://sustainabledevelopment.un.org/content/documents/26646ArdenClarke_10YFP_EMG_SCP_interlinkages_SDGs_240118f.pdf; Bizikova et al., *supra* note 11.

Assessment of Progress

SCP brings together key issues and thus needs to be recognized by all stakeholders as the most central SDG of the 2030 Agenda. There is, therefore, a need for evidence-based insights to evaluate the progress toward this goal and to share lessons learned so that we can design more effective national policies that are supported by effective international cooperation.[16] There are two important points related to the progress evaluation that are worth mentioning. First, in accordance with the Fundamental Principles of Official UN Statistics, SDG indicators "should be disaggregated, where relevant, by income, sex, age, race, ethnicity, migratory status, disability and geographic location, or other characteristics."[17] This is because the policy calibrations toward the achievement of the SDG are done on both national and international levels and thus there is a need to know where there is a need for a greater effort.[18]

Second, indicators and data are very limited for SDG 12. For example, the target level of sustainable MF is not defined and data on MFs is outdated and unavailable for the years after 2010. The target level of sustainable Material Consumption (MC) is not defined either. In addition, the definitions are often misleading. For example, Domestic Material Consumption (DMC) is a production-side measure, which does not account for supply chain inputs or exports. This means a country could have a lower DMC value if it outsources a large proportion of its materials. Thus, it is not possible to measure overall progress against many SDG Targets until common definitions are adopted and base-year levels have been quantified.

Below, we use available data (to our knowledge) to present the global achievements toward SDG 12, followed by the progress disaggregated by regions and income, with case studies that illustrate country-specific achievements in transforming SCP patterns.

Global Achievements

By 2018, 71 countries adopted an SCP national plan (12.1.1): 21 countries in Europe and North America, 14 countries in Latin America and the Caribbean, 14 in sub-Saharan Africa, 9 in Northern Africa and Western Asia, 8 in Eastern and South-Eastern Asia, and 5 in Central and Southern Asia.[19] By July 2019, 141 countries presented voluntary national reviews of implementation efforts at the High-Level Political Forum. All countries participated in the Montreal Protocol, 71% of them participated in the Rotterdam Convention, and more than half participated in the Basel Convention (57.45%) and the Stockholm Convention (51.14%) (12.4.1).[20]

---

16 SDG Report 2019, *supra* note 5.
17 G.A. Res. 68/261, 68th Sess. (Mar. 3, 2014).
18 There are no gender specific indicators for SDG 12. There is a belief that the UN 10-Year Framework of Programs on Sustainable Consumption and Production Patterns is also "largely gender-blind." *See* *10YFP—10 Year Framework of Programmes on Sustainable Consumption and Production Patterns*, UNEP, www.unenvironment.org/explore-topics/resource-efficiency/what-we-do/one-planet-network/10yfp-10-year-framework-programmes (last visited Dec. 7, 2020).
19 SDG Report 2019, *supra* note 16 at 47.
20 U.N. Secretary General, *Special Edition: Progress towards the Sustainable Development Goals*, Econ. & Soc. Council, E/2019/68, Agenda items 5(a) & 6 (Jul. 26, 2018–Jul. 24, 2019); Sustainable Development Goal 12: *Ensure Sustainable Consumption and Production Patterns*, SDG TRACKER, https://sdg-tracker.org/sustainable-consumption-production (last visited Dec. 7, 2020).

In 2017, worldwide MC reached 92.1 billion tons, a 5.9% increase from 2015 and a 254% increase from 1970 (27 billion).[21] MF per capita (12.2.1) increased to 12.18 tons in 2017, up from 11.84 tons in 2015 and 8.76 in 1990.[22] MF per Gross Domestic Product (GDP) (12.2.1) was at the same level in 2017 as it was in 2015 (1.16kg/$).[23] Limited data are available on waste generation globally. Data on the quantity of recycled municipal waste for the Organization for Economic Co-operation and Development (OECD) countries are only available till 2014–2015, with Germany, Slovenia, and Australia leading the pack (with more than 40% recycling rate).[24] Data for fossil fuel subsidies are available only for 2013–2015. No data are available for Targets 12.6–12.8, 12.A, 12.b, and Indicator 12.4.2.[25]

Regional Progress

Africa

Abundant with natural resources (about 30% of the world's mineral resources), the African continent relies heavily on primary export commodities.[26] Oil, gas, and minerals constituted more than 70% of African exports in 2017 and were responsible for almost half of African GDP.[27] There is a lot of empirical and theoretical evidence that such resource-dependent, non-value-added growth is unsustainable.[28] Coupled with a weak institutional framework and susceptibility to global fluctuations in commodity prices, such growth is more likely to lead to over-use and over-extraction of natural resources. In fact, Africa almost doubled its use of natural resources during the period of 2000–2007.[29] Hence the need to transform the economy from being a primary exports-driven one to a value-added one.

At the turn of the 21st century, the African Union[30] became concerned with the pressing issues of weak institutional governance, political instability and conflict, stagnant economic growth, poverty, and environmental degradation and recognizing the interlinkages between these issues. As a result, in 2013, it adopted the 2063 Agenda, a blueprint for the continent's economic, political, and social transformation. Together with the SDGs, this agenda is a long-term plan to improve Africans' standard of living, transform and restructure their economies, increase agricultural productivity, build capable institutions and leadership,

---

21 *SDG 12 in Numbers*, 24(6) UN DESA Voice (Jun. 3, 2019), www.un.org/development/desa/undesavoice/more-from-undesa/2019/06/45212.html.
22 SDG Tracker, *supra* note 20 at SDG 12.2.1 Material footprint.
23 A word of caution: MF per capita and MF per unit of GDP are fractions, so an increase in the world's population and an increase in the global GDP will impose a downward pressure on both indicators, respectively.
24 *Id*. at SDG Indicator 12.5.1 Recycling rates.
25 *Id*.
26 *Natural Resource Governance and Domestic Revenue Mobilization for Structural Transformation*, African Governance Report V at 8, U.N. ECONOMIC COMMISSION FOR AFRICA (2018), www.uneca.org/sites/default/files/PublicationFiles/agr-v_en.pdf.
27 *Id*.
28 *See for example*, Gobind T. Nankani, *Development Problems of Nonfuel Mineral Exporting Countries*, FINANCE AND DEVELOPMENT 17 (Jan. 1980); David Wheeler, *Sources of Stagnation in Sub-Saharan Africa*, WORLD DEVELOPMENT 12 (1984); and more recently, Jeffrey A. Frankel, *The Natural Resource Curse: A Survey*, No. w15836. NATIONAL BUREAU OF ECONOMIC RESEARCH (2010).
29 African Governance Report, *supra* note 26.
30 The African Union is a continental body that was formed in 2002 and that consists of 55 countries.

while retaining and enhancing cultural values and fostering environmental sustainability and climate resilience.[31]

Yet, there is not much progress that has been achieved. Plagued with environmental degradation, poverty, political instability and violence, financial vacuums, lack of strong and committed governments and institutions, and a lack of a legal framework that would protect ownership rights, most of the African countries (except for North Africa) have been struggling to move in the direction needed. Africa is home to more than 1.33 billion people and even though the material footprint per capita remains low (except for North Africa)—about 2.5 tons per capita during the period of 2000–2007, it accounts for most of the recent increase in global DMC.[32] Food waste, especially due to post-harvest losses, solid waste management, and recycling that are SCP targets have also been part of the Agenda 2063, but there is little evidence of the necessary progress.[33]

Two major problems that encumber the progress assessment of the SDGs in Africa are persistent data gaps and data quality.[34] Even though there have been several bold initiatives to harmonize statistics and ensure their quality, the progress has been rather marginal in this area. In fact, in 2017, less than 40% of SDG indicators had data on African countries.[35] At the 2016 conference in Addis Ababa, Ethiopia, African Ministers of Finance, Planning, and Economic Development agreed to adopt a single monitoring, evaluation, and reporting framework aligned with both Agenda 2030 and Agenda 2063. The framework's key document, a single periodic performance report, will supposedly be the most important milestone to the implementation of Agenda 2063 and the SDGs.[36]

The Arab Region

In December 2017, the 5th Arab Roundtable Meeting on SCP in the Arab region worked on aligning the Arab Strategy of SCP with the goals and targets of the 2030 Agenda. The Roundtable highlighted the experience of the 7 Arab countries (Algeria, Egypt, Jordan, Lebanon, Morocco, Palestine, and Tunisia) and requested the Technical Secretariat of the Roundtable to evaluate and monitor the implementation of SDG 12. It was a step forward in recognizing the importance of the 12.1.1 indicator.[37] By 2019, 15 countries submitted

---

31 *2017 Africa Sustainable Development Report: Tracking Progress on Agenda 2063 and the Sustainable Development Goals*, U.N. ECONOMIC COMMISSION FOR AFRICA (2017), www.uneca.org/sites/default/files/PublicationFiles/en_agenda2063_sdg-web.pdf.
32 *2018 Africa Sustainable Development Report: Toward a Transformed and resilient continent*, U.N. Economic Commission for Africa (2018), www.uneca.org/sites/default/files/PublicationFiles/asdr_2018_en_web.pdf.
33 According to the World Food Programme, food losses in Africa (except North Africa) were about 30% of total crop in 2014. *See* S.J. Costa, *Reducing Food Losses in Sub Saharan Africa: Improving Post-Harvest Management and Storage Technologies of Smallholder Farmers: An "Action Research" Evaluation Trial from Uganda and Burkina Faso*, WORLD FOOD PROGRAMME (2014), http://documents.wfp.org/stellent/groups/public/documents/special_initiatives/ WFP265205.pdf.
34 Megan Cassidy, *Assessing Gaps in Indicator Availability and Coverage*, SUSTAINABLE DEVELOPMENT SOLUTIONS NETWORK (2014).
35 *SDG Indicators: Revised List of Global Sustainable Development Goal Indicators*, U.N. STATISTICS DIV. (2017), https://unstats.un.org/sdgs/indicators/indicators-list/.
36 *African Ministers Call for Integrated Monitoring of SDGs-Agenda 2063*, IISD (2016) http://sdg.iisd.org/news/african-ministers-call-for-integrated-monitoring-of-sdgs-agenda-2063/.
37 *From action plans to implementation: Cairo Hosts Roundtable on Sustainable Consumption and Production*, EU NEIGHBOURS (Jan. 12, 2018), www.euneighbours.eu/en/south/stay-informed/news/action-plans-implementation-cairo-hosts-roundtable-sustainable-consumption.

Voluntary National Reviews (VNR) offering their visions within the national context.[38] In October 2019, the Center for Environment and Development for the Arab Region and Europe, in cooperation with the UN, held the 6th Arab Roundtable on SCP, the main theme of which was "From action plans to implementation."

Even though there are still numerous data gaps for the Arab region, the statistics that are available do exhibit some favorable trends. The proportion of the population serviced by municipal waste collection showed a 6% increase between 2002 and 2014.[39] The SDGs include a specific target (12.3) of halving per capita global food waste by 2030. Based on recent progress in the region, this target seems to be achievable if efforts in this area are continued.[40] However, the region suffers from conflict, political and social instability, and climate change effects that exacerbate the existing problems and slow down the progress toward SDG 12.

The Asia-Pacific Region

The Asia-Pacific region made substantial progress in the areas of poverty, education, and affordable and clean energy, yet, it has gone backward on the SCP goal.[41] In fact, resource use and CO_2 emissions grew at a faster rate than GDP did since 2000 and DMC more than doubled during this period, the largest increase among regions.[42] The increase that accounts for about two-thirds of the increase at the global level[43] is not solely due to the surge in the total quantity of goods produced and consumed. Rather, the inefficiencies imbedded in production are also factors. Data show that each dollar of GDP in the Asia-Pacific region requires twice the quantity of material resources as inputs compared with the rest of the world.[44] The net change in the MF during the period of 2000–2017 was 124%, compared to 29% for the rest of the world.[45]

Areas that need greater attention are governments' subsidies of fossil fuels, manufacturing production emissions, and consumers' material-intensive and high-carbon lifestyles. Consumers and producers also lack knowledge about over-consumption, sustainability, and the 2030 Agenda. Much of the increase (91%) in MF can be attributed to the increase in affluence, which led to a greater MC.[46] Resource-intensive growth, combined with a drastic increase in material production and high dependency on fossil fuels has led to a concomitant rise in greenhouse gas emissions and pollution. Fossil fuel subsidies of $242 billion exacerbate the problem.[47] Governments support the coal industry because it provides employment, tax revenues, and profits for state-owned mining enterprises in countries like China

---

38 *See 2019 Voluntary National Reviews Synthesis Report*, High-Level Political Forum on Sustainable Development, Dep. of Econ. & Soc. Affairs (2019), https://sustainabledevelopment.un.org/content/documents/252302019_VNR_Synthesis_Report_DESA.pdf.
39 Cameron Allen, *Progress on Sustainable Consumption and Production in The Arab Region*, Economic and Social Commission for Western Asia (2017).
40 *Id.*
41 *Special Edition: Progress towards the SDGS, supra* note 20.
42 *Economic and Social Survey of Asia and the Pacific: Towards Sustainable economies.* ESCAP, United Nations (2020).
43 SDG Report 2019, *supra* note 5, at 47.
44 *Id.*
45 *Economic and Social Survey, supra* note 42.
46 *Id.*
47 *Id.*

and India. The region is now home to 97 of the 100 most air-polluted cities in the world and 5 of the 10 countries most vulnerable to climate change.[48] According to Greenpeace, India alone is home to 22 of the world's 30 most polluted cities, and most of China's cities have been included in the 64% of cities around the world that exceed the World Health Organization (WHO) guidelines for ambient air quality.[49]

Latin America and the Caribbean

Recently, the governments of Latin American countries and the Caribbean (LAC) have shown a strong commitment and have developed regional and country-level institutional frameworks to ensure progress toward the SDGs. In 2016, the Economic Commission for Latin America and the Caribbean established a regional mechanism to monitor the implementation of the 2030 Agenda. By 2018, 16 countries (more than 50% of LAC) agreed to submit VNRs.[50] The region also had a dedicated action plan for regional cooperation on chemicals and waste management for 2019–2020.[51]

The need for such commitment has been substantiated by a multiplicity of economic, social, and environmental issues that have been impeding the sustainable development of the region. One of the major issues is that economic growth, especially in South America, depends on extractive activities and primary product exports, which contribute to the growing material footprint. Total domestic extraction (the sum of inputs extracted from the natural environment, except air and water) has increased from 5.46 gigatons in 2000 to 7.45 gigatons in 2010, while the material intensity of GDP has declined slightly.[52] In 2014, 83.4% of total export value in South America was the export of commodities, and this trend has been continuing as the global demand for commodities has been rising.[53] Growth that is not decoupled from resource use leads to resource depletion and environmental degradation and, in the case of the LAC region, comes at the cost of the forest ecosystem and soil quality.

Another area of improvement that desperately needs bold action is waste and recycling. The amount of waste per capita per day is still slightly lower than the global average (typical of developing and underdeveloped countries), but it is increasing faster than in most other

---

48 *Latest Air Pollution Data Ranks World's Cities Worst to Best*, IQAir (Mar. 5, 2019), www.iqair.com/us/blog/press-releases/IQAir-AirVisual-2018-World-Air-Quality-Report-Reveals-Worlds-Most-Polluted-Cities; David Eckstein et al., *Global Climate Risk Index 2019*, Germanwatch (2019), https://germanwatch.org/sites/germanwatch.org/files/Global%20Climate%20Risk%20Index%202019_2.pdf.
49 Nick Van Mead, *22 of World's 30 Most Polluted Cities Are in India, Greenpeace Says*, The Guardian (2019), www.theguardian.com/cities/2019/mar/05/india-home-to-22-of-worlds-30-most-polluted-cities-greenpeace-says.
50 See *Synthesis of Voluntary National Reviews 2019*, Div. for Sustainable Development, Dep. of Econ & Soc. Affairs (2016), https://sustainabledevelopment.un.org/content/documents/127761701030E_2016_VNR_Synthesis_Report_ver3.pdf.
51 *Annual Report on Regional Progress and Challenges in Relation to the 2030 Agenda for Sustainable Development in Latin America and the Caribbean*, ECLAC LC/L.4268(FDS.1/3)Rev.1 (Jun. 2017), www.cepal.org/en/publications/41189-annual-report-regional-progress-and-challenges-relation-2030-agenda-sustainable.
52 *Id.*
53 *The Economics of Climate Change in Latin America and the Caribbean: Paradoxes and Challenges of Sustainable Development*, ECLAC LC/G.2624 (Feb. 2015), www.cepal.org/en/publications/37311-economics-climate-change-latin-america-and-caribbean-paradoxes-and-challenges.

geographic regions. The recycling rate is relatively low at about 34% in 2013.[54] Carbon intensity (emission per unit of energy) has been, however, decreasing slowly since 2000, and there is more stable energy intensity (energy consumed per unit of output). This means greater penetration of clean energy. In fact, the LAC countries have a long history of hydropower and biofuels. More than half of their electricity production comes from renewable energy sources, which is more than double the global average.[55]

Moving toward SDG 12: Chile

Among the LAC region, Chile is a forerunner of institutional leadership and government commitment to the 2030 Agenda. It set up the National Council with the advisory function to the President of the country, on implementation of the SDGs. The Council also serves a coordinating function—through committees and working groups, it mobilizes international and domestic institutions and organizations to engage all stakeholders.[56] It gets technical advice and statistics from the National Institute of Statistics, which is under the purview of sectoral agencies. Chile's administrative network for implementation of the SDGs is highly decentralized, with representatives from 23 ministries, each gathering and processing information on policies and collaborating with other government bodies. The Ministry of Environment, for example, is responsible for environmental satellite accounts. To deal with such decentralized institutional structures, Chile has developed a number of institutional innovations, which include the adoption of a statistical framework, through the approval of the National Environmental Accounts Plan and the creation of an interinstitutional committee on environmental information that is responsible for environmental statistics and information.[57] Perhaps the most valuable outcome of Chile's bold actions is the state-sponsored strategy to ensure citizens' participation at the regional and local level. The country is also internationally known for its aggressive use of renewable energy, such as wind and photovoltaic solar energy.[58]

Eastern Europe, Caucasus, and Central Asia

Progress on the SCP, as on many other SDGs, has been rather slow in the region that went through a drastic economic, political, and social transformation in the 1990s. The countries that used to be part of the Soviet bloc for about half a century, and especially the countries that came out of the former Soviet Union, had struggled with the legacy of the state-run, highly rigid, and inefficient system that relied on extensive use of resources.[59] In addition, many countries inherited weak and corrupt institutions and a virtually non-existent legal

---

54 *Second Annual Report on Regional Progress and Challenges in Relation to the 2030 Agenda for Sustainable Development in Latin America and the Caribbean*, ECLAC LC/FDS.2/3/Rev.1 (Jun. 2018), www.cepal.org/en/publications/43439-second-annual-report-regional-progress-and-challenges-relation-2030-agenda.
55 *Id.*
56 ECLAC 2017, *supra* note 51.
57 Statistics Sweden, *Monitoring the Shift to Sustainable Consumption and Production Patterns in the Context of the SDGs*, SUSTAINABLE DEVELOPMENT GOALS KNOWLEDGE PLATFORM (Feb. 23, 2016), https://sustainabledevelopment.un.org/index.php?page=view&type=400&nr=2298&menu=1515.
58 ECLAC 2018, *supra* note 54.
59 Anna Shostya, *The Global Financial Crisis in Transition Economies: The Role of Initial Conditions*, 47(1) ATLANTIC ECONOMIC JOURNAL 37–51 (2019).

framework. The length of socialist regimes affected the functionality of institutions, and the longer the country was under the system of planned socialism, the weaker its institutional framework would be and the more cumbersome the decision-making process to design whatever policies would be.[60]

The closing of outdated plants and factories, the collapse of the soft-budget rule and severe disruption in supply and production chains due to political upheaval resulted in a transformational recession and a sharp decline in material use from 1990 to 2000.[61] Since then, the region's economies have rebounded, resulting in growing resource use. Today, per capita material use is around 15 tons, 5 tons up from the year 2000.[62] Most of this growth, however, is based heavily on raw material extraction and has little value-added. Material productivity and energy productivity have been similarly low.[63]

Income Inequalities

Traditionally, most high-income, high-development countries have been experiencing pressing challenges in the area of SCP. Their MFs are typically very high, despite their governments' commitment and high recycling rates.[64] In 2017, high-income countries had the highest MF per capita (around 27 metric tons per person), which is 60% higher than the upper-middle-income countries (17 metric tons per person) and more than 13 times the level of low-income countries (2 metric tons per person).[65] Their MF is greater than their DMC, indicating that consumption in those countries relies on materials exported from other countries. In fact, high-income countries rely on 9.8 metric tons per capita of primary materials extracted elsewhere in the world.[66] High-income regions also outsource the production-related environmental impacts to middle- and low-income countries. Over-consumption, too much waste, and fossil-fuel reliance hinder the progress toward SDG 12. The MF for fossil fuels is more than four times higher for developed than developing countries and signs of de-coupling of economic growth from the use of fossil energy in high-income countries are yet to be seen.[67]

Since the 1970s, different dynamics have affected the SCP patterns around the globe. First, newly industrializing countries have been building new infrastructure, and higher-income countries have been outsourcing the more material- and energy-intensive stages of production to emerging economies in the upper and lower-middle-income groups. Second, an increase in international trade and liberalization of financial markets opened up profitable opportunities to middle-income and lower-middle-income countries and led to the formation of a middle class. As the middle classes have grown globally, the MF has

---

60 *Id.*
61 *Sustainable Consumption and Production: A Guidebook for Policy Makers*, Global Edition 2015, UNEP (2015), https://sustainabledevelopment.un.org/content/documents/1951Sustainable%20Consumption.pdf.
62 *Id.*
63 *Id.*
64 The Nordic countries still lag behind European leaders (such as Belgium, the Netherlands, and Austria) in recycling rates. Belgium, for example, reports a recycling rate for all waste of 78% compared to the best-performing Nordic country at 59%. *See* Bjørn Bauer et al., *Sustainable Consumption and Production: An Analysis of Nordic Progress towards SDG12, and the Way Ahead*, Nordic Council of Ministers (2018).
65 SDG Report 2019, *supra* note 5.
66 *Id.*
67 *2018 HLPF Review of SDGs Implementation*, *supra* note 14.

increased because the middle-class rise has been associated with an increase in affluence and demand for material goods.[68] Data show that from 1970 to 2017, the share of DMC for high-income countries dropped from 52% to 22%, while upper-middle-income countries increased their global share of DMC from 33% to 56%. Per capita levels of DMC of this group surpassed those of the high-income group in 2012. The DMC for lower-middle-income groups increased by only 7% in that time, while low-income groups remained at about 3%.[69]

One of the reasons why meeting SDG 12 is a challenge for the middle-income and low-income regions is that despite relatively strong recent economic growth, poverty has been prevalent. In many middle-income countries, high and pervasive levels of poverty and inequality, vulnerability to shocks and the prospect of a "middle-income trap" pose formidable development challenges," according to the UN.[70] In low-income regions, these challenges are often exacerbated by political instability, ineffective or non-existent social safety net, and reliance on commodity exports that contributes to price level volatility.

Moving toward SDG 12: Canada and the United States (US)

The North American region, which includes Canada and the US, holds about 5% of the world's population and enjoys a high-income status.[71] In 2018, GDP per capita in Purchasing Power Parity (PPP) was about $51,500 in Canada and about $54,500 in the US.[72] The region accounts for 17% of the global ecological footprint, which has been on the rise since the 1960s,[73] with the US ecological footprint being slightly higher than that of Canada. Both the US and Canada scored poorly in the recent SDGs evaluation report published by the Bertelsmann Stiftung and Sustainable Development Solutions Network.[74]

Overall, material use in the US grew from 5.5 billion tons in 1970 to over 8 billion tons in 2010.[75] Since the 1980s, the country has been a net importer of materials, and net imports have been rising fast. Shockingly, 80% of US energy comes from fossil fuels and only 11.4% from renewable sources (8.4% from nuclear).[76] Wind is the fastest growing renewable

---

68 Joseph Morreale et al., *China's Rising Middle Class: A Case Study of Shanghai* COLLEGE STUDENTS, 11(2) J. OF INT'L STUD. (2018).
69 *Global Resources Outlook 2019: Natural Resources for the Future We Want*, UNEP (2019), https://wedocs.unep.org/handle/20.500.11822/27518.
70 Report of UNGA President to the High Level Meeting on the Middle Income Countries, 4 December 2018.
71 *North America Population*, WORLD POPULATION REVIEW, https://worldpopulationreview.com/continents/north-america-population (last visited Dec. 10, 2020).
72 *GDP Per Capita (Constant 2010 US$)—Canada, United States*, THE WORLD BANK DATA (2019), https://data.worldbank.org/indicator/NY.GDP.PCAP.KD?locations=CA-US&name_desc=false.
73 The Ecological Footprint uses yields of primary products (from cropland, forest, grazing land, and fisheries) to calculate the area necessary to support a given activity, *See* GLOBAL FOOTPRINT NETWORK, www.footprintnetwork.org/our-work/countries/ (last visited Dec. 7, 2020).
74 J. Sachs et al., *Sustainable Development Report 2019*, Bertelsmann Stiftung and Sustainable Development Solutions Network (SDSN) (2019), www.sdgindex.org/reports/sustainable-development-report-2019/.
75 Guidebook for Policy Makers, *supra* note 61, at 22.
76 U.S. Renewable Energy Factsheet, Center for Sustainable Systems, University of Michigan (2020), http://css.umich.edu/factsheets/us-renewable-energy-factsheet.

source, but it contributes only 2.4% of the total energy used in the country.[77] Extensive use of fossil fuels is heavily subsidized by the federal government.[78]

Total energy consumption in the US is disproportionally high. In 2018, it was about 101 quadrillion British Thermal Units (BTUs) out of the total world consumption of 598 quadrillion BTUs.[79] This is over 17% of the world consumption in a country that is home to only 4.25% of the Earth's population.[80] Two factors that have contributed to the steady rise in US energy consumption over the last several decades are robust economic growth and a swelling population (in 2019, there were more than 128 million households in the US, compared to about 53 million in 1960).[81] Together, they stimulated the growth in commercial and residential sectors, which boosted the demand for energy. In fact, it is estimated that electricity consumption by these sectors has increased from about one-third of the total energy consumption in 1980[82] to about 40% (about 40 quadrillion BTUs) of the total in 2018.[83]

At 14.8 tCO2 per capita, Canada's energy-related CO2 emissions are only slightly below that in the United States which stand at 15.5 tCO2 per capita.[84] However, Canada's production-based SO2 emissions at 55.9 kg per capita are higher than 34.9 kg per capita in the United States.[85] The country has a very low population density, which contributes to relatively higher energy and transportation costs. Canada's national strategy that aligns with SDG 12, therefore, includes a target that is supposed to decrease greenhouse gases. The goal is for zero-emission vehicles to represent 10% of new light-duty vehicle sales by 2025, 30% by 2030, and 100% by 2040.[86]

One of the biggest challenges that North America faces in implementing SDG 12 is the low level of awareness about the SCP and 2030 Agenda. Both countries have introduced several initiatives to increase awareness among businesses, nonprofit foundations, and government leaders and engage more stakeholders to ensure progress toward SDG 12. However, more has to be done in order to decrease excessive energy consumption, reduce fossil fuel use, and carbon emissions, and thus, minimize the environmental footprint in this high-income region.

Moving toward SDG 12: The European Union (EU) and the Nordic Region[87]

Despite an ambitious call to action that includes measures to completely de-carbonize energy by 2050 and transform land use and food systems in line with the Paris Agreement,

---

77 Id.
78 Id.
79 *Frequently Asked Questions*, ENERGY INFORMATION ADMINISTRATION (EIA) (December 15, 2020).
80 Ibid.
81 Erin Duffin, *U.S.: Number of Households 1960–2019*, STATISTA (2019), www.statista.com/statistics/18 3635/number-of-households-in-the-us/.
82 *Energy Efficiency Trends in Residential and Commercial Buildings*, U.S. DEP. OF ENERGY: ENERGY EFFICIENCY & RENEWABLE ENERGY (Oct. 2008), www1.eere.energy.gov/buildings/publications/pdfs/corporate/b t_stateindustry.pdf.
83 Monthly Energy Review, Energy Information Administration (August 2019), *supra* note 76.
84 J. Sachs et al., *supra* note 74.
85 Id.
86 *Towards Canada's 2030 Agenda National Strategy*, GOVERNMENT OF CANADA, www.canada.ca/en/emp loyment-social-development/programs/agenda-2030/national-strategy.html (last visited Dec. 7, 2020).
87 The Nordic region includes Denmark, Finland, Iceland, Norway, Sweden, Greenland, the Faroe Islands, and Aland, of which only Denmark, Sweden, Finland, and Aland belong to the EU.

the region-wide progress toward SDG 12 has been rather slow.[88] For example, in 2017 the Nordic region adopted Generation 2030, a program to monitor and foster the implementation of the 2030 Agenda, and established dedicated SCP policies. Since then, the region has made little progress in the area of efficient use of natural resources (12.2) and reducing inefficient fossil-fuel subsidies (12.c). It has shown moderate progress in the area of waste reduction (12.5) and developing sustainable tourism (12.B).[89] The progress reporting has also been complicated by data issues. DMC, DMC per capita, and DMC per GDP have been relatively low, not because of the efficient use of natural resources, but rather because of the outsourcing of both service and manufacturing production. This shifts the burden of MF onto developing and low-income countries.

This is not to say that the EU has not introduced important initiatives and policy transformations. For example, the EU has been a leader in quantifying their FLW. Using a common definition of food waste and uniform methodology, Member States will be required to monitor their food waste levels at each stage of the food supply chain (in line with SDG 12.3) from 2020 onward, with the first results expected by mid-2022. A few EU Member States are already taking steps to fulfill these new obligations (e.g. the Netherlands and Finland).[90]

In the Nordic region, Finland was one of the first countries to initiate the movement toward sustainability. As early as 2009, it introduced a policy requiring the inclusion of sustainability criteria in all state procurement by 2015.[91] In 2014, it adopted a material efficiency program designed to implement the 2030 Agenda and the EU's SCP Action Plan. Perhaps one of the most important achievements of Finland is raising awareness of SCP among its young generations. This is because sustainable development has been part of the core curriculum for basic education since 2006, with gradually increasing weight up to the present day.

Evaluating the Effect of the COVID-19 Pandemic

The progress to the SDGs can be jeopardized as a result of political, economic, geological, or meteorological shocks. Armed conflict, intercommunal violence, extreme weather, geological catastrophes, and economic downturns have all been reported as setbacks that slowed down the progress toward poverty reduction, eradication of hunger, improvement in health, food security, income growth, and other SDGs.[92] None of these shocks, however, has the scale of the novel coronavirus (COVID-19) pandemic. Although the actual economic and social impact of the ongoing pandemic has yet to be fully estimated, it is clear that it will hinder the progress toward all 2030 Agenda goals, especially in the most vulnerable regions that have limited capacity to moderate the economic downturn of such scale.

---

88 J. Sachs et al., *supra* note 74.
89 Bjørn Bauer et al., *supra* note 64.
90 *Directive of the European Parliament and of the Council of 30 May 2018 Amending Directive 2008/98/ EC on Waste*, The European Parliament and Council (May 30, 2018), https://eur-lex.europa.eu/legal-content/EN/ ALL/?uri=CELEX%3A32018L0851.
91 About KEINO, www.hankintakeino.fi/en/about-keino (last visited Dec. 7, 2020).
92 *Global Report on Food Crises: Joint Analysis for Better Decisions*, Food Security Information Network (FSIN) (2020), www.ifpri.org/publication/2020-global-report-food-crises-joint-analysis-better-decisions.

We can anticipate the short-term and long-term effects of COVID-19 on SCP. In the near-term, countries' own measures to contain the spread of the disease, such as quarantines, border closures, and suspension of productive activities, will be disruptive for their own consumption and production patterns. These measures will also disrupt the cross-border supply chains. One of the most affected areas will be the global food system. Food loss has already become a serious issue as movement restrictions and illnesses have reduced labor supply and have disrupted harvesting, transportation, processing, and deliveries.[93] Economies that rely mostly on agricultural production will suffer the most. The World Bank forecasts that in sub-Saharan Africa, agricultural output and food imports may decrease by 3–7% and 13–25%, respectively, depending on the extent and duration of the pandemic.[94] The processing industry in Africa has already been severely damaged because many firms lost a large portion of their workers.[95] At the same time, there is enormous food waste at the end of the supply chain. Panic-buying forced people to buy in bulk, more than they could consume. Additionally, traditional bulk buyers, like restaurants, hotels, and universities, have either reduced their food orders drastically or stopped ordering altogether. Even though people now buy more groceries because they cook at home, that will not make up for the loss in demand for food products.

The oil industry is also in trouble. On the one hand, there is a drastic decrease in the use of fossil energy as urban centers locked down or cut their public transportation and air travel. The recent photos of Earth from space show a remarkable change from just a few months ago—clear air and blue oceans have been visibly positive signs of changes in SCP due to COVID-19. Yet, there is a downside, too. The glut of oil pushed the world prices down and created a storage bottleneck. The oil storage tankers have reached their capacity, and a waste of a scarce energy resource is imminent.

In the long term, we can anticipate a sweeping reversal of benefits created by globalization and trade. Goods that previously were produced in less developed and developing nations because of abundant and inexpensive labor supply may now be considered to be items of national security. Production of face masks, sanitary wipes, gowns, disinfectants, and rubber gloves that were previously heavily concentrated in labor-intensive developing countries may, in the long run, be shifted to each individual country, despite the fact that many of these countries do not have a comparative advantage in producing these items. There might also be an increase in waste due to a reversal in supply chain design. The 1980s and 1990s embraced Lean manufacturing, whereby companies stockpiled fewer necessary components and relied on just-in-time deliveries. COVID-19 may reverse this trend and force companies to redesign their supply chains to ensure that they have bigger inventories.[96] This will lead to greater inefficiency and will severely impact progress toward SDG 12.

The pandemic, however, may improve SCP patterns in some ways. First, it can accelerate "trends in business organization that were already on the way."[97] Companies have

---

93 *Id.*
94 Simeon Ehui, *Protecting Food Security in Africa during COVID-19*, WORLD BANK BLOGS (Jun. 5, 2020), https://blogs.worldbank.org/nasikiliza/protecting-food-security-africa-during-covid-19.
95 *The Race to Feed Africa during a Pandemic*, THE ECONOMIST (Apr. 23, 2020), www.economist.com/middle-east-and-africa/2020/04/23/the-race-to-feed-africa-during-a-pandemic.
96 Schumpeter, *Covid-19 is Foisting Changes on Business That Could Be Beneficial*, THE ECONOMIST (Mar. 7, 2020), www.economist.com/business/2020/03/05/covid-19-is-foisting-changes-on-business-that-could-be-beneficial.
97 *Id.*

uncovered lots of inefficiencies in terms of space-utilization and thus may accelerate the provision of online services, including banking, education, and food deliveries. This may lead to the reinvention of office space and a lower demand for land. In addition, business travel may be reduced as companies now learn about the benefits of telecommuting and videoconferencing. This is likely to reduce the demand for fossil fuel energy. Consumers in high-income developed countries may change their behavior too, learning that, after all, they do not need as many material goods. This may reduce DMC in the countries that have been lagging behind this important SDG 12 goal. For low-income countries, the creation of food banks may become a priority. This could solve the problem of surplus disposal in developed countries and food shortages in LDCs, reducing FLW.

Policy Recommendations and Actions Needed

Overall, the data on current SCP patterns show that bolder actions are needed if we are to achieve SDG 12 by 2030. Country-specific evidence suggests that it is possible to make some significant changes, but these require determined leadership, aggressive policy-making behavior, international cooperation, and more active involvement of all stakeholders. Based on empirical evidence, we summarize the most pressing challenges and provide some specific suggestions that we believe can stimulate more SCP patterns. It is important to remember that participation in Agenda 2030 is voluntary; therefore, their recommendations preserve the original UN's language of "encouragement."

Challenge 1

Limited data on SPC, especially in some regions (Africa, the Pacific, the Middle East) and lack of harmonized statistical reporting on SPC progress.

Actions Needed

- Work toward creating a better statistical system to evaluate and report progress, especially in the regions that currently have been experiencing severe data limitations. Encourage more active help to developing nations to solve the problem of inadequate funding for sustainable statistical development. Strengthen national statistical systems and harmonize statistical reporting to help track the progress of all SDGs.
- Encourage more countries and regional blocks, like the Asia-Pacific Economic Cooperation, to provide systematic quantifications and reporting of their FLW. All countries must report data for the Food Loss Index, which has been approved as an official indicator for monitoring SDG 12.3.
- Incentivize more businesses to make a commitment to SCP and increase public reporting of their SCP actions. Incentivize structures to encourage governments to commit to SCP by setting up such structures as tax reductions, for example.

Challenge 2

Lack of quantifiable indicators that can be used to monitor progress toward the SCP goal; misleading definitions of some targets.

Actions Needed

- Introduce quantifiable indicators for *all* targets and ensure that some targets have gender-specific and age-specific benchmarks.
- Replace some of the indicators that are misleading in terms of interpretation. In particular, replace DMC (12.2.2) with Raw Material Consumption (RMC).
- Reconsider targets that are specified in terms of per capita.

Challenge 3

Very modest public awareness of the 2030 Agenda and the Sustainable Development Goals; lack of wide-spread knowledge of what SCP entails; lack of sustainable and institutional and financial resources to raise this awareness.

Actions Needed

- Foster sustainable and long-term awareness and attitudinal change with younger generations by making the concept of SCP and sustainability, in general, a mandatory component of education curricula, from primary through tertiary levels.
- Ensure that the education curricula that the SCP concepts and its interlinkages with other SDG are embedded in all subjects, especially social sciences, physical sciences, and natural sciences. Ensure that the younger generations' increased awareness leads to the next step—putting their knowledge into action.
- Encourage international organizations and governments to allocate more resources to increase public awareness and promote the SCP goal in everyday life.
- In high-income developed countries, public awareness campaigns should target the reduction of excessive energy consumption.

Challenge 4

Insufficient capacity building and difficulties of incorporating budgeting for the SCP initiatives into national financial frameworks.

Actions Needed

- Prioritize development of SCP funding through special financial instruments issued by corporations, financial consortiums, governments, and multilateral institutions.
- Strengthen capacity building in developing and least developed countries through developing national SCP strategies.
- Encourage more countries to submit their VNRs and build capacity to progress toward SCP; encourage developing an institutional framework in each country to monitor the progress toward SCP targets.

Challenge 5

The majority of global carbon emissions have been underpriced because polluters ignore negative spillover effects of their emissions. In fact, only 20% of them are currently under some pricing scheme or soon to become so, and the prices are below what they should be in order to curb the emissions.[98]

Actions Needed

- Promote carbon-pricing schemes (either tax or "cap-and-trade") on national levels and encourage their inclusion in national plans.
- Encourage more carbon-trading programs on regional and international levels so that countries can move toward a truly international carbon market.[99] These countries should design their systems using lessons from the California-Quebec and Australia-EU links to ensure compatibility and to move toward a truly international system.

Conclusions

This chapter evaluates the progress toward one of the most integral goals of the UN's 2030 Agenda, SDG 12, that centers on increasing resource efficiency and stimulating more SCP patterns. SCP plays an essential role in de-linking economic development and economic growth from environmental degradation, and thus, ensuring that we can operate within the limits of the planet's ecosystems. The chapter uses targets and indicators specified by the UN to evaluate current global SCP trends, as well as regional and income disparities. It provides specific examples and suggests specific steps that could be pursued in order to ensure the achievement of SDG 12 by 2030. Among other findings, we found that progress toward this goal is difficult to assess because of the lack of clear targets and insufficient and/or inadequate data.

SCP is a central goal of the Agenda 2030 and it is deeply interconnected with other SDGs. Improvement in SCP associated with resource efficiency, food loss, and waste reduction, and the use of renewable energy sources can enhance the quality of life, reduce poverty, improve air quality, reduce climate change impact, and ensure that hunger is non-existent. Yet, empirical evidence, disaggregated by region and income, shows that not much progress has been achieved toward meeting the SDG 12 targets. This is because most countries rely mainly on soft measures, such as partnerships and voluntary agreements to meet targets rather than harder economic or regulatory measures. It is also because countries have not yet achieved the level of cooperation that is necessary to produce country-based, high quality, homogeneous data that could be used to assess progress and calibrate the policies accordingly.

SCP is a universal goal yet, many developed and underdeveloped regions struggle to design game-changing policies. It is important to understand that there is no universal solution as the policies toward SDG 12 may be different depending on geographic characteristics, political systems, pressing existing issues both related to their SCP patterns, and other SDGs and country-specific features. In developing countries and LDCs, where there is a high rate of self-employment and home-based jobs, a large dependence on raw materials extraction and agriculture, and limited research and development, it is important to promote home-grown solutions to economic challenges that incorporate the principles of

---

98 *Taxing Carbon: The Contentious and Correct Option*, The Economist (May 23, 2020).
99 A good example of such a system is an Australia-EU cooperation. *See* Center for Climate and Energy Solutions, www.c2es.org/2012/12/linking-emissions-trading-programs-can-advance-climate-policy/.

SCP. In developed nations, it is important to transform consumers' and producers' attitudes toward SCP and ensure that all stakeholders actively participate in meeting the targets of SDG 12. Experiences of certain countries (as in our case studies) show that it is possible to make significant advances toward SCP. Doing so requires a radical revision of the values, incentive structures, and systems that shape current consumption and production patterns. It requires the transformation in both public and private sectors and drastic changes in governance structures and business models. It requires a commitment on behalf of all actors and all countries. In short, it requires everyone's willingness and ability to reduce the MF and ensure that the Earth is capable of housing, not only our children and grandchildren, but the many generations that will come after them.

19 Missing Climate Action
Gaps in the Implementation of the Paris Agreement on Climate Change

Vesselin Popovski

Two Hundred Years of Climate Science

Climate change skeptics say that global warming is a recent "hoax,"[1] a creation of some left-wing conspirators who want to intervene and control the markets.[2] Well, they miss 200 years of climate science: As early as 1822, the French mathematician Joseph Fourier, writing his "Analytical Theory of Heat," asked what makes the temperature on Earth's surface so pleasantly warm, and predicted that some gases help trap the sunlight infrared radiation, reflected from the Earth back to the atmosphere.[3] In 1938, the physicist Claude Pouillet, having no technology yet to measure gases in the atmosphere, guessed that water vapor and carbon dioxide (CO_2) might be these "greenhouse" gases that absorb the infrared radiation, keeping the planet's surface warm and making life possible.[4] What Fourier and Pouillet only predicted, in 1859 John Tyndall, a natural philosopher at London's Royal Institution, already having the necessary technology proved that while oxygen, nitrogen, and hydrogen were transparent to infrared radiation, water vapor, CO_2, and methane absorbed such radiation.[5] In 1896, with more technology available for experimentation, the Swedish scientist Svante Arrhenius calculated global warming of between 5 and 6°C, if the greenhouse gases in the atmosphere increase by 50%, and *vice versa*, the temperature could drop 5 or 6°C, if 50% of the greenhouse gases are removed from the atmosphere.[6] As the Industrial Revolution was rapidly developing at the time massively producing coal-burning steam engines, rail locomotives, ships, etc., Aarhenius warned that burning coal will emit vast quantities of CO_2 making the planet warmer.[7] Nobody paid much attention to this for another century, until

---

1 Mike McLeod, *Letter to the Editor: Don't Mess with Mother Earth. Climate Change is a Hoax*, BRADENTON HERALD, Nov. 18, 2019, www.bradenton.com/latest-news/article237480339.html.
2 Helier Cheung, *What Does Donald Trump Believe on Climate Change*, BRITISH BROADCASTING CORPORATION (BBC), Jan. 23, 2020, www.bbc.com/news/world-us-canada-51213003.
3 Dirk Jan Struik & *Joseph Fourier, French Mathematician*, BRITANNICA, www.britannica.com/topic/The-Analytical-Theory-of-Heat.
4 CLAUDE POUILLET, MEMOIR ON THE SOLAR HEAT, ON THE RADIATING AND ABSORBING POWERS OF THE ATMOSPHERIC AIR, AND ON THE TEMPERATURE OF SPACE (1846), *reprinted in* SCIENTIFIC MEMOIRS SELECTED FROM THE TRANSACTIONS OF FOREIGN ACADEMIES OF SCIENCE AND LEARNED SOCIETIES, AND FROM FOREIGN JOURNALS VOL. IV, 44–90 (Richard Taylor, ed., 1846).
5 Ruth Barton & *John Tyndall, Irish Physicist*, BRITANNICA, www.britannica.com/biography/John-Tyndall.
6 Svante Arrhenius, *On the Influence of Carbonic Acid in Air Upon the Temperature of the Ground*, 41 PHIL. MAG. AND J. SCI. 5, 37–276 (April 1896).
7 *Id.*

1992 when the United Nations Framework Convention on Climate Change (UNFCCC) was adopted.[8]

In 2020, the human-induced greenhouse gas emissions are at their highest levels in history and continue to rise, warming the Earth's surface rapidly, and producing huge negative effects: Rising sea levels and flooding, massive land degradation, extreme weather events, fires, and deforestation leading to significant human suffering, displacement, and disruption of economies.[9] The rising acidity in oceans has already destroyed half of the marine corals; hundreds of unique animal species have become extinct already and thousands more will disappear.[10] Climate change is affecting every community in every country on every continent. Although the threat is common, the economic disparities make the responsibilities of States different. Accordingly, the principle "Common but Differentiated Responsibilities" (CBDR) was adopted in the UNFCCC:[11] The Parties agreed that industrialized countries, by releasing more CO_2 emissions, should have greater responsibility, referring to the "polluter-pays" principle.[12] Historical contribution to climate change and respective ability become measures of responsibility. Developing countries often refer to their CO_2 emissions as "survival" emissions, claiming that for the industrialized countries these are "luxury" emissions.[13] In 1997, the Kyoto Protocol of the UNFCCC was adopted, and based on CBDR and polluter-pays principles, it imposed commitments only on industrialized countries.[14]

The adoption of the Paris Agreement on Climate Change in December 2015,[15] followed the Sustainable Development Goals (SDGs) in September 2015, with Goal 13 "Climate Action"[16] among them, and extended climate change obligations to all countries. SDG 13 does not simply advance human development and equality, as all other goals, but is instrumental for the entire survival of humanity. It has three parts: (a) mitigation, keeping global temperature rise below 2°C; (b) adaptation to consequences of climate change; and (c) strengthening governance institutions and mechanisms to address climate change.[17] The specific targets and indicators of SDG 13 are actionable and measurable: Target 13.1 calls to strengthen resilience and adaptive capacity to hazards and natural disasters and reduce direct casualties from these, and is measurable by the number of victims from natural disasters,

---

8 *See* UNITED NATIONS FRAMEWORK CONVENTION ON CLIMATE CHANGE (UNFCCC), https://unfccc.int (last visited Nov. 23, 2020).

9 *See* NATIONAL AERONAUTICS AND SPACE ADMINISTRATION (NASA), https://climate.nasa.gov/evidence/ (last visited Nov. 23, 2020). *See also* INTERNATIONAL PANEL ON CLIMATE CHANGE (IPCC), www.ipcc.ch/documentation/ (last visited Nov. 23, 2020).

10 *See* Intergovernmental Science-Policy Platform on Biodiversity and Ecosystem Services (IPBES) www.ipbes.net/ (last visited Nov. 23, 2020).

11 United Nations Framework Convention on Climate Change, 1992, A/AC.237/18 (Part II)/Add.1; 31 ILM 849, Art. 4.1 [hereinafter "UNFCCC"].

12 *Id*. at Art. 3.1.

13 Lavanya Rajamani, *The Principle of Common but Differentiated Responsibility and the Balance of Commitments under the Climate Regime*, 9 REV. EUR. COMMUNITY & INT'L ENVTL. L. 120, 128–29 (2012).

14 *See What is the Kyoto Protocol*, UNFCCC, https://unfccc.int/kyoto_protocol (last visited Nov. 23, 2020) ["hereinafter UNFCCC—Kyoto Protocol"].

15 Paris Agreement to the United Nations Framework Convention on Climate Change, Dec. 12, 2015, T.I.A.S. No. 16-1104, Art. 15 [hereinafter "Paris Agreement"].

16 *Goal 13, Take Urgent Action to Combat Climate Change and its Impacts*, UNITED NATIONS DEPARTMENT OF ECONOMIC AND SOCIAL AFFAIRS, https://sdgs.un.org/goals/goal13 (last visited Nov. 23, 2020) [hereinafter "SDG 13"].

17 *Id*.

the number of countries developing national disaster risk reduction strategies, and the proportion of local governments that adopt and implement local disaster risk reduction strategies.[18] Target 13.2 integrates climate change measures into national policies and planning. It requests States to communicate the establishment and operationalization of an integrated strategy, increase the ability to adapt to the adverse impacts, foster resilience, and lower greenhouse gas emissions in a manner that does not threaten food production and other indicators.[19] The third target 13.3 aims to improve education and raise awareness and institutional capacity on climate change mitigation, adaptation, impact reduction, and early warning, and is measurable by the number of countries that integrate these into their primary, secondary, and tertiary education; by countries that communicate the strengthening of institutional, systemic, and individual capacity building to implement adaptation, mitigation, and technology transfer, and development actions.[20]

SDG 13 set an ambitious target to mobilize $100 billion from both public and private sectors annually by the year 2020 in a Green Climate Fund (GCF) to address the needs and channel finance to developing countries.[21] The GCF, created in 2010, launched its initial resource mobilization in 2014, but so far only three countries in the world committed significantly per capita to the GCF in 2018—Sweden ($59.31), Luxembourg ($58.63), and Norway ($50.56), with Finland and the United Kingdom (UK) coming fourth and fifth just below the $20 per capita threshold.[22] Alarmingly, there is very low commitment from some G-7 countries: the United States (US) ($9.41), Canada ($7.79), and Italy ($4.51),[23] and these per capita are really worrisome. The GCF is aligned with the priorities of developing countries through the principles of local ownership and direct access modality, so that national and sub-national organizations can receive funds directly, without international intermediaries. The GCF is oriented especially on the least developed countries ("LDC") and small island developing states ("SIDS"), by promoting mechanisms for raising capacity, including focus on women, youth, and local and marginalized communities. The indicators to measure are the number of LDC and SIDS receiving specialized support, including finance, technology, and capacity building; and the number of capacity-building mechanisms for effective planning and management. The SIDS have played a leading role in raising awareness and advocating for strong climate action, notably through the Alliance of Small Island States (AOSIS). Despite their heterogeneity, they succeeded in building a common diplomatic discourse, influencing strategy, and mobilizing political leaders as well as talented negotiators and advisors. They succeeded to codify their special circumstances as vulnerable countries, demonstrated leadership in raising ambition to secure an ambitious long-term temperature goal, and advanced the complex debate on loss and damage.

---

18 *Id.*
19 *Id.*
20 *Id.*
21 *Id.*
22 *Green Climate Fund (GCF) Pledges per Capita, 2018*, OUR WORLD IN DATA, https://ourworldindata.org/grapher/green-climate-fund-pledges-per-capita?tab=chart&time=earliest..latest (last visited Nov. 18, 2020).
23 *Id.*

The Paris Agreement on Climate Change

The Paris Agreement on Climate Change demonstrates a novel approach to international law. In a previous book, the author of this chapter argued for a fundamental rethinking of State-centrism, and the adoption of an "eco v. ego" approach in the implementation of the Paris Agreement, describing it as a hybrid (between "hard" and "soft" law) agreement that allows States to decide on voluntary nationally determined commitments (NDCs), but once these commitments are made, they become legally binding.[24] Anne-Marie Slaughter described this as the "Paris Approach to Global Governance,"[25] whereas Richard Falk more skeptically wrote about "Voluntary International Law,"[26] that points to the deficiencies and lack of sanctioning measures for non-compliance. International law has been traditionally developed top-down through codifying norms and rules and imposing sanctions on States that fail to live up to these rules. The Paris Agreement is a departure from this tradition—instead of "Sanctions Committee" it proposes a much friendlier "Facilitation Committee"[27] expecting a synergy of "hard" obligations toward long-term goals made in a voluntary manner, with opportunity to re-adjust initial commitments over time, ensuring transparency, accountability, technology transfer, and finance. Such an approach to global governance is more conducive to a long-term normative agenda: It allows States a great deal of individual agency to interpret and enact targets within a clearly articulated long-term collective agenda. It demands constant interaction, communication, and information sharing, facilitating the implementation of the targets. The SDGs and the Paris Agreement follow the path of previous international environmental agreements—for example the 1987 Montreal Protocol that prohibits substances depleting the ozone layer—that does not envisage sanctioning measures to punish States for non-compliance, rather inviting States to comply based on ethical and reputational competition. More than a century ago, a Japanese philosopher Tsunesaburo Makiguchi, in his book *Geography of Human Life*, after surveying traditional forms of competition—military, political, and economic—concluded that these competitions exhaust human energy and do not bring peace and happiness.[28] He called for a new type of "humanitarian competition" synergizing humanitarian concerns and competitive energies.[29] This is a radical transformation from a winner-takes-all style of competition, to one that is conducted within a consciously acknowledged win-win mode. The humanitarian competition effectively reconciles cooperation and competition, sets aside egoistical motives, and protects not only our own life and wealth, but also the life and wealth of all other people.

---

24 Vesselin Popovski, *"Hard" and "Soft" Law on Climate Change: Comparing the 1997 Kyoto Protocol with the 2015 Paris Agreement, in* THE IMPLEMENTATION OF THE PARIS AGREEMENT ON CLIMATE, Ch. 2, (Vesselin Popovski, ed., 2018).
25 Anne-Marie Slaughter, *The Paris Approach to Global Governance*, PROJECT SYNDICATE, Dec. 28, 2015, www.project-syndicate.org/commentary/paris-agreement-model-for-global-governance-by-anne-marie-slaughter-2015-12?barrier=accesspaylog.
26 Richard Falk, *Voluntary International Law and the Paris Agreement*, GLOBAL JUSTICE IN THE 21ST CENTURY, Jan. 16, 2016, https://richardfalk.wordpress.com/2016/01/16/voluntary-international-law-and-the-paris-agreement/.
27 Paris Agreement, *supra* note 15 at Art. 15.
28 TSUNESABURO MAKIGUCHI, *Geography of Human Life, in* COMPLETE WORKS OF TSUNESABURO MAKIGUCHI Vol. 2, 23 (1903).
29 *Id*. at Vol. 1, 399.

The Paris approach to global governance attempts to address the 21st-century global challenges in a world of very diverse State and non-State actors, where top-down obligations most often would not work. The Paris Agreement shifts to bottom-up NDCs, which require governments and corporations to come together and determine what they can reasonably achieve. Instead of blaming or sanctioning one another for failure to comply with the targets, countries are expected to cooperate and address a shared problem. The transparency mechanism in the Paris Agreement supports this shift to bottom-up commitments, allowing citizens, climate experts, non-governmental organizations (NGOs), and businesses to publicize successes and failures, solicit help and advice, and offer support.

Comparing SDG 13 with the Paris Agreement

The Paris Agreement is complex in terms of legal characterization: It is written in a broad language to express the expected behavior of States, which varies from clear legal obligations to recommendations and general statements. It contains "hard" law, "soft" law and non-law. The agreement does not prescribe obligations quantifiable at individual level. States themselves must individually or collectively quantify their actions and create legal expectations and due diligence obligations to be fulfilled. This voluntarism would be unimaginable in domestic legal systems; however, in international law such an approach is not uncommon. International legal theories do not establish a minimal level of specificity, accountability, justiciability, and enforceability to clearly separate what is law, from what is not law. The Paris Agreement, although un-specific, still creates legal expectations. It constrains State behavior; therefore, in this author's opinion, it qualifies as international law.

The specificity of the SDGs is of a different nature, they are very specific and clearly time-bound—for example, SDG 1 is to eradicate extreme poverty (living on less than $1.25 a day) for all people everywhere by 2030.[30] However, such specific targets do not always translate into individualized normative expectations. On the contrary, the SDGs do not contain obligations to produce anything comparable to the regularly submitted NDCs, as under the Paris Agreement. Under the SDGs they only have to encourage ambitious national responses and issue progress reports. Both the SDGs and the Paris Agreement are grounded in normative context and express shared ambitions that contribute to the recognition of international society as a collective supra-State entity. With such goal-setting agreements, international law moves beyond interstate law and becomes what can be defined as global law of humankind. States need simultaneously to safeguard their national interests in a State-centered legal system, and at the same time to increasingly acknowledge overarching interests and ambitions at supranational level, defined as global law.

The drafters of the SDGs set specific clear-cut ambitions, expressed in binding and non-binding commitments. They referred to human rights and environmental goals in which rights and obligations are less specific. Many human rights, such as the right to housing, health, or education, and even all economic, social, and cultural rights, do not contain specific targets or time-limits. Equally, environmental treaties—for example management of transboundary water systems—do not contain much detail about the level of ambition for

---

30 United Nations G.A. Res. A/RES/70/1, *Transforming Our World: The 2030 Agenda for Sustainable Development*, at 15 (Sept. 25, 2015).

joint governance.[31] The SDGs, in contrast, put concrete timeframes inducing stakeholders to set agendas, express concrete ambitions and strategies, and show their substantial progress by 2030. The Paris Agreement has no specific timetable as to when States undertake what exactly type of action, rather the timetable is determined with models for various pathways to ensure mitigation. If more action is taken in the next 5 years, less will be needed in the following 5 years; and if less action is taken now, more and more costly action will be needed later. The Paris Agreement leaves the decision on concrete commitments to individual parties, but this does not necessarily disqualify it from being a legal document. It does contain specific timetables for procedural issues, such as periodical submission of performance data to the Conference of Parties (COP), the renewal of NDCs, etc.[32] From 2023, global stocktakes will take place every five years to assess whether the aggregate implementations of the NDCs is sufficient to meet the targets.[33]

The mechanisms for implementation of the SDGs are predominantly political. The review of implementation is left to the High Level Political Forum (HLPF), which meets under the auspices of the United Nations Economic and Social Council (ECOSOC) annually. Every four years the level is raised to Heads of State and Government for Comprehensive Policy Review under the auspices of the United Nations General Assembly. The SDGs have political and aspirational character and this is reflected in the absence of accountability mechanisms, save for the intention to ensure follow-up and review through voluntary state-led HLPF. To assess the SDGs implementation, global, regional, and national indicators are developed. Usefully, a SDG tracker is established to constantly monitor the implementation of all targets.[34]

The Paris Agreement has provisions on implementation at several levels. The annual COPs are responsible for reviewing the implementation now, and the global stocktake will serve as an essential mechanism from 2023. States can submit reports to the UNFCCC Secretariat at any time to be reviewed by technical experts, and an innovative mechanism to facilitate implementation and promote compliance is planned under Art. 15 of the Paris Agreement. Contrary to the Kyoto Protocol, the Paris Agreement has no penalties for non-compliance, and is entirely facilitative and non-adversarial. If the Kyoto Protocol was binding for 41 developed countries which were required to reduce emissions by at least 5% over 1990 levels in the period 2008–2012,[35] the Paris Agreement is binding only with respect to submitting NDCs every five years. At the time of writing, 187 States have submitted their first NDCs and two States only—Suriname and Marshall Islands—have submitted their second NDCs.[36]

Both SDGs and the Paris Agreement were adopted in high-level global meetings of Heads of States, underlying the importance of authority and legitimacy, essential to create a compliance pull. Highly legitimate commitments would normally lead to better

---

31 Sabine Brels, David Coates, & Flavia Loures, *CBD Technical Series No. 40: Transboundary Water Resources Management: The Role of International Watercourse Agreements in Implementation of the CBD*, SECRETARIAT OF THE CONVENTION ON BIOLOGICAL DIVERSITY (2008).
32 *See* United Nations Framework Convention on Climate Change (UNFCCC), Decision 1/CP.21 (Dec. 2015) [hereinafter "COP 21 Decision"].
33 Paris Agreement, *supra* note 15, at Art. 14.2.
34 *See SDG 13 Taking Urgent Action to Combat Climate Change and Its Impacts*, SDG TRACKER, https://sdg-tracker.org/climate-change.
35 UNFCCC—Kyoto Protocol, *supra* note 14.
36 *See* NDC Registry (interim), UNFCCC, www4.unfccc.int/sites/NDCStaging/Pages/All.aspx (last visited Nov. 23, 2020).

implementation than those with low legitimacy.[37] Whether legitimacy is static or evolving over time is debatable. When the SDGs were adopted, there was a strong momentum for carrying Agenda 2030 forward, but skepticism increased soon after as to whether the implementation may be jeopardized by national and international bureaucracies. With the Paris Agreement the situation was the opposite: Before the meeting in Paris there was a lot of skepticism about its achievability, but once it was adopted, most States quickly ratified it, even if later they fail to commit to sufficient climate action.

The justiciability of the SDGs is weak and it is unlikely that they will be directly invoked before courts and tribunals. However, some legal effect may emerge, if references to the goals are made to clarify State obligations in environmental or human rights instruments. It is also unlikely that States will seek SDGs enforcement through sanctions, as there are no supranational mechanisms to do this. The enforcement of the Paris Agreement is similarly weak, but not absent because States may use legal or other mechanisms to address non-compliant behavior of other States. The stronger element in the Paris Agreement is the emphasis on accountability: States realize that a regime, in which substantial obligations are formulated in an open manner as an obligation of conduct, rather than of final result, needs relatively strong procedures to monitor, supervise, and, if necessary, to correct the conduct of parties. The Paris Agreement's complex layered approach—where States have reporting obligations, these reports go through expert-based assessment, the COP plays a supervisory role, and the system can address specific non-compliant behavior—is still weaker than the Kyoto Protocol's very specific, quantifiable targets, including the option of issuing penalties in the case of serious non-compliance.

The Paris Agreement establishes a bottom-up system for submitting individual obligations every five years. The parties are encouraged, but not obliged, to submit increasingly stringent revisions of their NDCs based on their own judgment.[38] The idea of compliance, as a stamp of legality, is abandoned, which can be seen as a radical departure from the historic task of lawyers and tribunals to determine whether or not a signatory to an agreement is complying with its obligations. The Paris Agreement essentially substitutes transparency for compliance. It creates an enhanced transparency framework (Art. 13) to build mutual trust and promote effective implementation.[39] The subsequent Art. 14 creates a compliance mechanism of expert-based assessment, where the teams include climate scientists and policy experts, in addition to lawyers. It is a facilitative, non-punitive mechanism, functioning in a transparent, non-adversarial manner.[40] It looks more as a support group, not as a disciplinary committee. By traditional international legal standards, the Paris Agreement is essentially a statement of good intentions, setting forth aspirational goals. The drafters thought—correctly—that it would be unthinkable to include rigid binding commitments, into an Agreement, tackling problems so complex, uncertain, and fast-moving as climate change,

A comparison in specificity of the normative content between the SDGs and the Paris Agreement shows that there is less room for interpretation and discretion in application, the more specific and precise a provision is. One may think that a more precise provision would be preferable, as there is less doubt about the expected behavior of actors. A specific percentage of CO_2 emission reduction as an obligation might seem like a clear legal solution,

---

37 THOMAS FRANCK, THE POWER OF LEGITIMACY AMONG NATIONS (1990).
38 Paris Agreement, *supra* note 15, at Art. 3.
39 *Id.* at Art. 14.
40 *Id.* at Art. 15.

but it actually addresses only a small part of the problem. More openly formulated targets and rules of conduct allow for continuous discussion and adaptation to what is perceived to become necessary over time, without having to make formal changes in the Agreement. A broad approach creates a normative process that hinges on binding due diligence obligations. Whether this is effective depends on the inclusiveness and legitimacy of the process and the willingness of parties to engage in a genuine effort to reach commonly determined goals. When making choices to serve common interests, States can face various dilemmas: To make inclusive versus exclusive; broad versus specific; legal versus political; content versus process; or interstate versus supranational commitments. Achieving the collective interests with only half of the world participating will be difficult, if not impossible; however, trying to keep everybody aboard will need compromises, which may reduce the level of ambition and end up in ambiguous agreements. Both the SDGs and the Paris Agreement were designed to serve commonality rather than individuality in international society and both struggled with the above dilemmas and ambiguity.

A similar reasoning applies to the expectations from concrete targets—should these be formulated broadly, or more specifically? Adopting strict specific language may lead to fewer participants. More abstract language may create space for ambivalence and self-interpretation in the lack of supranational authority. For example, when a political form is chosen, such as a General Assembly Resolution, it will be easier to reach consensus as States can avoid political difficulties at home, because these resolutions do not require ratification, although this does not mean that States do not intend to lay down legally relevant normative expectations. When a legal form is chosen, this can signify a higher level of ambition and commitment and can be used both internationally to put pressure on other States to comply and domestically by urging legally bound implementation and action. Another consideration and choice to make is between an agreement, focusing on substantive commitments and clear results, and an agreement focusing on process of cooperation with less certain results. The UNFCCC is an example of the latter: It did not create substantive obligations for its parties but was fundamental to start the process of developing a climate governance model. The Paris Agreement is part of that process, which in itself creates some substantive expectations and, more importantly, contributes to further strengthening of the governance model. A further dilemma is whether States are willing to engage in a more supranational global governance model or prefer to stay within the old confines of interstate governance. Will they give up prerogatives by becoming subjected to the scrutiny of independent expert committees, or of binding third-party dispute settlement procedures? Depending on the issue, the sense of urgency, the general political climate, and other factors, hard choices need to be made and compromises found when facing these dilemmas.

A binary approach to international law might not help solve the pressing global challenges of climate change, pandemics, or sustainable development. The determination of what is legally binding is not binary, as there could be degrees, ranging from non-binding in form and content at one end, to fully legally binding in form and content at the other. A formal treaty with high legitimacy and authority may be lacking in substantive content and meaningful compliance mechanisms—effectively a "hard" law, but with "soft" content, or a "soft hard" law. In contrast, there could be texts without any formal legal force, for example proceedings from international conferences, but these may have a very precise content, a high degree of authority and legitimacy—a "hard soft" law. Both may lack justiciability and enforceability, but still be categorized as international legal agreements.

The choice between pragmatic and principled approaches has been predominantly a matter of theoretical perspectives on the nature of the international legal order and clarifying these may help the implementation of global law in situations where the legal rules and obligations are not straightforward in content and status. International law has evolved from entirely serving the interests of States in anarchical society into increasingly representing the common interests of the entire humankind. The SDGs and the Paris Agreement manifest how interstate law evolved into global law, how "soft" law became a pragmatic choice, when solutions creating elaborate sharp binding commitments were not possible. For the challenges of climate change, a framework treaty—UNFCCC—was chosen and further developed with the Kyoto Protocol and the Paris Agreement. For the developmental challenges, the Millennium Development Goals and SDGs were found as more realistic forms. Although different in format, all of them were "soft" instruments, reflecting the willingness of States to accept behavior-constraining measures without imposing sanctions and punishment for non-compliance.

Hybridity and Orchestration

The Paris Agreement and the SDGs are hybrid agreements, involving both State actors and non-State actors, but in a different manner. The Paris Agreement was negotiated by and creates obligations exclusively for States. It does not list an explicit role for non-State actors, despite the fact that such actors were very active in developing policies and coalitions to respond to climate change. In contrast, the SDGs were drafted after intensive public consultation with various stakeholders and accordingly, they became inclusive, creating a global partnership of State and non-State actors for implementation. The role of such partnerships is crucial especially for SDG 13, where networks of business corporations, civil society organizations, cities, research institutes, popular movements, youth, etc. committed to combat climate change is very important.

The Paris Agreement deepens and sophisticates the connections between State and non-State actors, creating an architecture of hybrid multi-stakeholder governance with two channels: (1) the State-led actions defined and stipulated by the parties through their NDCs and (2) the efforts by the UNFCCC to orchestrate transnational climate efforts. In both channels non-State actors are formally and informally woven, performing a range of increasingly important functions. Civil society has been recognized with its huge mobilizing potential, intended to gain influence through media attention, rallies, including disrupting the "politics as usual." The non-State actors exercised multiple roles, in the lead-up to the Paris Agreement, they acted as contributors within the formal multilateral negotiations; conductors and players in different orchestration efforts; partners in transnational networks; private governors; as well as supporters or protesters in a more conventional manner. They need to continue these multiple roles, as watchdogs of NDCs enhancing transparency, facilitating the stocktake, and pressuring for ratcheting up of NDCs, and as contributors and governing partners through orchestration. The Paris Agreement urged them to scale up their climate actions and register those actions on the Non-State Actor Zone for Climate Action platform.[41] This process is further coalesced under the SDG 13 Agenda.

The hybrid climate governance complicates—perhaps even renders superfluous—traditional categorizations of "top-down" and "bottom-up" initiatives which are common in the usual policy practices. The implications of this complex hybrid architecture are still to emerge by evaluating how non-State actors will contribute to the justice, the legitimacy, and

---

41 COP 21 Decision, *supra* note 35, at ¶117.

the effectiveness of the Paris Agreement. These three key parameters of hybrid State-non-State interaction have each generated significant academic debate. Three dimensions within each of the three parameters can be highlighted: For the parameter of justice, it would be curious to see how non-State actors generate *agency*, gain *access*, and alter *allocations*. For the legitimacy, the focus should be on how non-State actors promote *participation*, strengthen *representation*, and foster *accountability*. For the effectiveness of the Paris Agreement, it would be crucial to see how non-State actors can contribute to enhancing *transparency*, augmenting *compliance*, and affecting *outcomes*. The hybrid governance model unpacks how non-State actors' participation is structured, facilitated, and hampered to secure the broad goals of the Paris Agreement.

The presence and prominence of non-State actors within the Paris Agreement reflect a broader shift across the climate governance landscape in which business groups, think tanks, trade unions, cities, private governance arrangements, transnational networks, and sub-State authorities assume active roles. The hybrid governance is already bewilderingly complex and over-populated and what is needed is to put climate change on the top of the agenda of international and national actors, not simply in terms of discussion, but also in terms of operationalization and orchestration.

To implement soft law agreements, such as the SDG 13 and Paris Agreement, the modes of climate governance need to shift from regulation to orchestration, using soft power. The utility of the concept of orchestration was proven when the first HLPF on Sustainable Development in 2012 discussed the orchestration.[42]

The non-State actors have been centrally and crucially involved in climate governance in the form of transnational networks, epistemic communities, public–private and multi-stakeholder partnerships. The number of networks involved in the UNFCCC activities continue to rise. Private governance arrangements took the form of certification schemes and global standard-setting. The empirical uptick in private governance is evident in the sub-fields of forest or marine sustainability with the creation of the Forest Stewardship Council and the Marine Stewardship Council. Private rules are adopted across the climate regime as private actors seek to fill governance gaps. Big cities are increasingly brought within orchestration efforts by the UNFCCC and the World Bank. An increase of non-State actors and think tanks involvement is needed not only alongside the sessions of the General Assembly and the COPs, but also at all other possible environmental summits, including the Convention on Biological Diversity, the Renewable Energy and Energy Efficiency Partnership, the Asia-Pacific Partnership on Clean Development and Climate, etc. The role of non-State and private actors is crucial particularly where governments remain reluctant and ignorant.

Lack of Progress in Fulfilling SDG 13

Having in mind the huge planetary challenge and the global consensus behind the Paris Agreement and the SDGs, the lack of progress in implementation over the last five years is highly alarming. The HLPF in July 2019 reported that the failure on SDG 13 not only threatens the implementation of all other SDGs but may even reverse gains—poverty reduction, widespread immunization, decreasing child mortality, more access to

---

42 Kenneth W. Abbott & Steven Bernstein, *The High-Level Political Forum on Sustainable Development: Orchestration by Default and Design*, 6 GLOB. POL'Y 3, 222–33 (2015).

electricity—already achieved on other goals.[43] The response on SDG 13 has not been ambitious enough, increasing inequality among and within countries and leaving the most vulnerable people and countries to suffer the most. The Report pointed out that Year 2018 was the fourth warmest year on record; that CO2 level continued to increase; ocean acidity became 26% higher than in pre-industrial times and is projected to increase 100%–150% by 2100 at the current rate of CO_2 emissions.[44] In some regions the temperature change has been much more extreme. At very high latitudes—especially near the Poles—warming has been upwards of 3°C, and in some cases exceeding 5°C.[45] These are, unfortunately, often the regions which experience the largest impacts such as sea ice, permafrost, and glacial melt. The lack of progress is particularly apparent on climate action and biodiversity. Impacts of environmental deterioration are taking a toll on human lives. Extreme weather conditions, frequent and severe natural disasters, and the collapse of ecosystems lead to increased food insecurity, worsen people's safety and health, force many to suffer from poverty, displacement, and widening inequality. Despite the lack of action, the Report reminded that valuable opportunities exist to accelerate progress by leveraging the interlinkages across the SDGs.[46] Reducing greenhouse gas emissions, for instance, goes hand-in-hand with creating jobs, building more livable cities, improving health and prosperity for all.[47]

The UN Climate Action Summit in New York in September 2019 and the COP 25 in December 2019 continued to appeal for urgent action, expressed concerns with many gaps—such as insufficient funding and technology transfer, non-commitment of large emitters, lack of capacity in LDCs, political instability, etc. One challenge arising from these gaps is that Parties, willing to submit ambitious NDCs, cannot be certain how they will sustain and implement these NDCs. Another challenge is how to satisfy the growing energy needs in developing countries by introducing renewable energy at strategic levels. While the fossil fuels model worked well for two centuries in developed countries, it has drawbacks that penalize developing countries that today are yet to provide electricity to a large part of their population. With the cost-reduction of renewable energy technologies and more energy-efficient end-use appliances, an increasingly viable option is the decentralized power generation and distribution. Some estimates show that by 2030, 70% of rural areas will be connected either to mini-grid (65%) or stand-alone off-grid solutions (35%).[48]

COVID-19 hit humanity and presented us with five tests: A test of leadership, a test of international cooperation, a test of medical capacity, a test of human–human relationship, and a test of human relationship with nature[49]—the fifth one is the most crucial for our survival. The pandemic demonstrated how CO_2 emissions can be reduced only after weeks of industrial lockdown. As Victoria Crawford noted "neither the surge in cycling and expansion

---

43 External Press Release, UNFCCC Secretariat, *Climate Change Threatens Progress Across Sustainable Development, Warns New UN Report* (Jul. 9, 2019), https://unfccc.int/news/climate-change-threatens-progress-across-sustainable-development-warns-new-un-report [hereinafter "UNFCCC Press Release"].
44 *Id. See also The Sustainable Development Goals Report 2019*, at 48–49 (2019), https://unstats.un.org/sdgs/report/2019/The-Sustainable-Development-Goals-Report-2019.pdf.
45 *Id.*
46 *Id.* at 3.
47 *Id.*
48 *Energy Poverty—How to Make Modern Energy Access Universal?*, INTERNATIONAL ENERGY AGENCY, at 16, www.se4all.org/wp-content/uploads/2013/09/Special_Excerpt_of_WEO_2010.pdf (2010).
49 Vesselin Popovski, *COVID-19 and Environmental Sustainability*, 234 JAPAN SPOTLIGHT J. 47, 47 (2020), www.jef.or.jp/journal/pdf/234th_Special_Article_04.pdf.

of bike lanes in Bogota as citizens avoid public transport, nor the coronavirus work-from-home experiment, have required any new technology, but instead have relied on new thinking."[50]

The Sustainable Development Report 2020 published by Cambridge University Press in June 2020 predicted short-term reduction of carbon emissions, pressure to reduce environmental safeguards, lack of clarity on environmental investments, and slowdown in economic growth leading to reduction in energy price and oil, which may increase access to energy, but reduce incentives for renewables.[51]

The HLPF in July 2020 produced a SDG Progress Chart which re-confirmed the lack of sufficient climate action on SDG 13, described it as "far from target,"[52] despite the fact the carbon emissions are expected to drop because of the COVID-19 pandemic. The 2020 UN Sustainable Development Goals Report (SDGR) predicted a drop of 6% in CO_2 emissions, but pointed that to reach the 1.5°C temperature target, emissions reductions of 7.6% are needed every single year, starting from 2020.[53] The situation is indeed critical, when we cannot reduce greenhouse gas emissions at the necessary level to survive even after the worst pandemic and recession in modern history, costing millions of human lives and massive unemployment. COVID-19 will not do the work for us—a research based on Google/Apple mobility data on near-real-time travel and work patterns demonstrated that the long-term impact of COVID-19 on climate will be insignificant: Merely 0.01°C by 2030.[54] If some leaders, and those who continue to re-elect them, do not realize how crucial SDG 13 is compared to other goals, little hope remains. The failure on climate action would literally mean an inhabitable planet and the end of the human race, not just poverty, hunger, bad health, discrimination, insufficient education, and inequality, as with the other goals.

Performance of Major Countries

The Climate Action Tracker (CAT) in 2020 published updated assessments for 12 of the 36 countries it assesses, and included projections of the effect of the COVID-19 pandemic on 2020 emissions.[55] It reported that the economic downturn temporarily reduced emissions, and the real long-term difference can come from post-pandemic economic recovery packages and how they integrate low-carbon futures.[56] It's too early to predict their effect, but there

---

50 Victoria Crawford, *How COVID-19 Can Help Us Win the Fight Against Climate Change*, WORLD ECONOMIC FORUM, Mar. 31, 2020, www.weforum.org/agenda/2020/03/covid-19-climate-change/.
51 Jeffrey Sachs, et al., *The Sustainable Development Goals and COVID-19, Sustainable Development Report 2020*, CAMBRIDGE UNIVERSITY PRESS, https://s3.amazonaws.com/sustainabledevelopment.report/2020/2020_sustainable_development_report.pdf (June 2020).
52 *Sustainable Development Goals Progress Chart 2020*, UNITED NATIONS DEPARTMENT OF ECONOMIC AND SOCIAL AFFAIRS, https://sustainabledevelopment.un.org/content/documents/26727SDG_Chart_2020.pdf (June 2020).
53 *The Sustainable Development Goals Report 2020*, at 18 (2020), https://unstats.un.org/sdgs/report/2020/The-Sustainable-Development-Goals-Report-2020.pdf [hereinafter "SDG Report 2020"].
54 Zhu Liu, et al., *Near-real-time Monitoring of CO_2 Emissions Reveals the Effects of COVID-19*, 11 NAT. COMM. 5172 (2020).
55 *COVID-19 Pandemic Adds Uncertainty on Future Emissions—Jury Still Out on Whether They'll Rise or Fall*, CLIMATE ACTION TRACKER, July 30, 2020, https://climateactiontracker.org/press/covid-19-pandemic-adds-uncertainty-on-future-emissions-jury-still-out-if-theyll-rise-or-fall/.
56 *Id.*

does appear to be a worrying trend that many countries are protecting their fossil fuel industries.

The US Administration continues to systematically walk back on climate, using the pandemic as an excuse. If the law, rolling back Obama-era vehicle emissions standards, withstands legal challenges, a 12% share of electric vehicle sales in 2025, projected by the previous CAT assessment, will drop to 7%.[57] The $2 trillion recovery package, as promised, does not include climate policy. CAT's US emissions projections for 2030 are 5%–10% lower compared to the projections in 2019, mainly due to COVID-19 and the greening of the electricity sector due to market forces.[58] The only good news is that renewables continue to dominate investments.

China's post-COVID-19 recovery shows signs of improvement compared to previous recovery packages, with hints of commitment to accelerate renewables and electric vehicles. However, China's commitment to coal remains concerning and at odds with the global decline in coal capacity. The recent phase-out of subsidies for renewables and electric vehicles leads to uncertainty on the future of these sectors.[59]

The European Union (EU) continues to lead the way on climate policy but is still behind the Paris targets and stronger NDCs are discussed. The EU made climate mitigation one of three main priorities in its economic recovery, the European Council agreed to spend at least 30% of the multiannual budget and recovery for climate action.[60] It can revise most of its climate legislation and its 2030 target,[61] putting the health of the planet first and announcing a €750-billion Green New Deal (GND)[62] to recover jobs, boost green growth, and modernize and secure resilience.

India has not built new coal-fired power stations in 2020; however, the government is encouraging more coal mining and production. India can accelerate the expansion of renewable energy and electric vehicles, reduce emissions, and capitalize on sustainable development benefits, if it adopts a green economic recovery plan.[63]

Chile was one of the first countries to officially submit an updated second more ambitious NDC to the UNFCCC and its rating in CAT has been upgraded from "Highly Insufficient" to "Insufficient."[64] The CAT grades government's Paris Agreement 2030 targets with one of five possible ratings, based on its "fair share" methodology: 1.5°C Paris Agreement compatible, 2°C compatible, Insufficient, Highly Insufficient, and Critically Insufficient.[65]

Indonesia is one of a handful of countries to start a new coal plant construction in 2020 and has the fourth largest coal pipeline (30GW), globally. Its economic recovery plan also bailed out coal-heavy utilities, which contradicts the urgent need to phase out coal by 2040.[66]

---

57 *USA*, CLIMATE ACTION TRACKER, July 30, 2020, https://climateactiontracker.org/countries/usa/.
58 *Id*.
59 *China*, CLIMATE ACTION TRACKER, Sept. 21, 2020, https://climateactiontracker.org/countries/china.
60 *EU*, CLIMATE ACTION TRACKER, Sept. 22, 2020, https://climateactiontracker.org/countries/eu/.
61 *Id*.
62 *See A Green New Deal for Europe, Towards Green Modernization in the Face of Crisis*, GREEN EUROPEAN FOUNDATION, https://gef.eu/wp-content/uploads/2020/03/GEF_GND_for_Europe_publication_web.pdf (Oct. 2009).
63 *India*, CLIMATE ACTION TRACKER, Sept. 22, 2020, https://climateactiontracker.org/countries/india/.
64 *Chile*, CLIMATE ACTION TRACKER, Jul. 30, 2020, https://climateactiontracker.org/countries/chile/.
65 *Id*.
66 *Indonesia*, CLIMATE ACTION TRACKER, Sept. 22, 2020, https://climateactiontracker.org/countries/indonesia/.

Japan is shifting toward renewable energy and is planning to phase out inefficient coal-fired power plants and restrict overseas financing of coal power. Despite potential loopholes and limitations, these plans, together with a recently announced plan to boost offshore wind (10GW by 2030), may signal a shift in Japan's climate policy positions.[67]

Mexico used the pandemic to pass bills effectively halting private investment in renewables, favoring fossil fuel power generation. Even with the 2020 dip in emissions, Mexico needs to adopt ambitious policies to meet its target and use the NDC update process currently underway as an opportunity to strengthen its target.[68]

The UK government has yet to match its "build back green" rhetoric with stronger action. It has strengthened policies since legislating its 2050 net zero target but remains off track to meet it.[69] As upcoming COP 26 President, the UK needs to lead by example and submit a 2030 NDC in line with its 2050 net zero goal.

The 2020 CAT assessment covered 32 countries and concluded that only six countries (Bhutan, Costa Rica, Ethiopia, India, Kenya, and the Philippines) have made sufficient commitments and efforts to hold global warming well below 2°C, and only two countries (Morocco and The Gambia) are on track to hold warming below 1.5°C.[70] The strategies and policy actions in Argentina, Russian Federation, Saudi Arabia, Turkey, Ukraine, the US, and Vietnam are "critically insufficient," the worst label possible.[71]

COVID-19 made policy trackers even more relevant, demonstrating the long-term impacts of recovery strategies, for example the CAT roadmap for addressing the climate impact of COVID-19 and emerging recovery strategies, or the sustainability tests to assess recovery plans offered by "Think Sustainable Europe," etc.[72] To mitigate the threat of runaway climate change, we need a rapid fall of CO_2 emissions with 45% from 2010 levels by 2030, and to continue to drop off steeply to achieve net zero emissions by 2050.[73] The world is way off track to meet this target at the current level of NDCs. Global emissions of developed countries and economies in transition have declined by 6.5% over the period 2000–2018.[74] Meanwhile, the emissions of developing countries are up by 43.2% from 2000 to 2013.[75] The rise is largely attributable to increased industrialization and enhanced economic gross domestic product (GDP) output.

The COVID-19 pandemic, which has disrupted economic activity worldwide, offers an opportunity to reassess priorities, to rebuild economies to be greener and more resilient to climate change. The crucial time we live in has been brilliantly exemplified by Christiana Figueres and Tom Rivett-Carnac in their book *The Future We Choose: Surviving the Climate Crisis*, where the authors took a hard look at the frightening realities, but concluded that humanity still holds the pen and can write the history of the next hundred years, suggesting

---

67 *Japan*, CLIMATE ACTION TRACKER, Sept. 22, 2020, https://climateactiontracker.org/countries/japan/.
68 *Mexico*, CLIMATE ACTION TRACKER, Sept. 22, 2020, https://climateactiontracker.org/countries/mexico/.
69 *United Kingdom*, CLIMATE ACTION TRACKER, Sept. 22, 2020, https://climateactiontracker.org/countries/uk/.
70 *Countries*, CLIMATE ACTION TRACKER, https://climateactiontracker.org/countries/ (last visited Nov. 23, 2020).
71 *Id.*
72 Think Sustainable Europe, *Europe's Recovery Plan Must Pass Five Sustainability Plans*, EURACTIV MEDIA NETWORK, Apr. 23, 2020, www.euractiv.com/section/energy-environment/opinion/europes-recovery-plans-must-pass-five-sustainability-tests/.
73 SDG Report 2020, *supra* note 53, at 50.
74 *Id.*
75 *Id.*

ten concrete actions that each individual can take to create a better future for all, such as Be Citizen, not Consumer; Reforest The Earth; Invest In Clean Economy; Use Technology Responsibly; Build Gender Equality; Engage In Politics, etc.[76]

Climate Finance

The financing for climate action has increased, but it continues to be surpassed by investments in fossil fuels. The global climate-related financial flows saw a 17% rise from 2013–2014 to 2015–2016, or from $584 billion to $681 billion, largely due to high levels of new private investment in renewable energy—the largest segment in the total climate-related flow.[77] However, investments in climate activities across sectors continued to be surpassed by those related to fossil fuels in the energy sector, which totaled $781 billion in 2016.[78] To achieve a low-carbon, climate-resilient transition, a much greater scale of annual investment is required. Climate-related financing provided by developed countries to developing countries increased by 14% in 2016, reaching nearly $38 billion.[79] Climate change mitigation remained the predominant focus, at $24.3 billion, followed by climate change adaptation ($5.6 billion) and cross-cutting issues ($5.1 billion).[80]

The challenges to implementation are not only financial. Even when there is sufficient awareness and commitment, governments may lack the capacity to ensure that the public sector will create an enabling environment for investments. Both knowledge and political clout might be missing to create and enact appropriate regulations and tariffs, allowing bottom-up initiatives to unfold and grow. Potential entrepreneurs might be discouraged by bureaucratic processes or lack of resources to provide a timely public administration. Public utilities might be heavily indebted or suffer from mismanagement and corruption.

Recommendations

The author of this chapter recently proposed the idea of multiple Security Councils[81] and one of these new organs can be a "Climate Security Council," that can collectively tackle climate disasters, as well as the security implications from other urgent environmental concerns such as loss of biodiversity, land degradation, deforestation, oceans level rise resulting in salinization of arable land, air pollution, etc. The Climate Security Council can work together with the UNFCCC Secretariat in Bonn, the International Panel on Climate Change, the United Nations Environment Programme and other agencies, institutes, and networks. Instead of simply being a State-based organ, the Climate Security Council could involve actors from the business community, city mayors, indigenous groups, and philanthropists, among others.

---

76 Christiana Figueres and Tom Rivett-Carnac, The Future we Choose: Surviving the Climate Crisis (2020).
77 SDG Report 2020, *supra* note 53, at 50.
78 *Id.*
79 *Id.*
80 *Id.*
81 Vesselin Popovski, *Towards Multiple Security Councils, UN75 Global Governance Innovation Perspectives*, Stimson Center, www.stimson.org/wp-content/uploads/2020/06/GloCo-Issue-Brief-0520-Multiple-Security-Councils-R3-WEB-1.pdf (2020).

Also deserving attention is the "Climate Club" idea, proposed by the Nobel Peace Economist William Nordhaus, a measure to eliminate the free-riding problem with the implementation of the Kyoto Protocol and the Paris Agreement.[82] The members of the Climate Club receive proportionate privileges depending on their climate contributions. They agree to undertake emission reductions aimed to meet the Paris Agreement target and fix an international target carbon price. For example, they agree that they will implement policies that produce a minimum domestic carbon price of $50 per metric ton of CO_2 and that target price might rise over time. On the opposite side, reluctant States that are not part of the Club will be penalized, for example by uniform tariffs on imports from Club members. With such tariffs on non-participants, Nordhaus argues, the Climate Club would create a situation in which countries acting in self-interest would choose to enter the Club and undertake ambitious emission reductions because of the structure of the payoffs.[83]

Conclusion

It is important to have a long-term direction for a green economy, to guide investment plans and support companies and industries to build on positive short-term prospects due to plummeting industrial output at the time of COVID-19 and further the roll out of digital services and e-commerce to accelerate the transition to climate neutrality. It is essential to keep enforcing environmental laws despite lockdown and economic turmoil. A major challenge will be to direct the attention of senior policymakers to the climate crisis, and the scientific community should be vocal to provide the connection between COVID-19 recovery and investment in clean energy.

If the world does not act efficiently, sustainably, and forcefully, the catastrophic effects of climate change will be far greater than the COVID-19 pandemic, the World Wars, or any previous disasters. Governments and businesses should use the lessons learned and opportunities arising from this crisis to accelerate the transitions needed to fulfill SDG 13 and achieve the targets of the Paris Agreement. We need to redefine our relationship with the environment, make systemic shifts, and transformational changes to become low-carbon and climate-resilient economies and societies.

As the United Nations Report on the SDGs in July 2019 alarmingly put it, missing climate action may jeopardize not only SDG 13, but all other goals too.[84] In 2020, compared with 2019, the carbon emissions will drop between 6%[85] and 8%[86] because of COVID-19. What is curious however, is not how much the emissions drop, but how little—even with massive lockdowns, interruption of air travel, and global recession, if we still emit 94% or 92% of the greenhouse gases released in 2019, these are huge and dangerous amounts. COVID-19 hit the world severely, but also presented a chance to reduce environmental degradation. The human behavior radically changed during the pandemic, shifting to online meetings, stopping business travel, recycling and reusing materials, etc. These behavioral changes, however, need to be followed by structural changes. The post-pandemic recoveries

---

82 William Nordhaus, *Climate Clubs: Overcoming Free-Riding in International Climate Policy*, 105 AM. ECON. REV. 4, 1339–70 (April 2015).
83 William Nordhaus, *The Climate Club*, 99 FOREIGN AFF. 3 (May/June 2020).
84 UNFCCC Press Release, *supra* note 43.
85 SDG Report 2020, *supra* note 53, at 18.
86 *Global Energy Review 2020*, INTERNATIONAL ENERGY AGENCY, www.iea.org/reports/global-energy-review-2020/global-energy-and-co2-emissions-in-2020 (April 2020).

cannot be achieved with old methods and reliance on fossil fuels, not only because of climate implications, but also because of the economy itself facing negative cash flow and stranded assets. The lessons from COVID-19 for climate change are sharp and alarming: (1) delay is costly; (2) inequality can be exacerbated; (3) policy must overcome biases to human judgment; (4) climate change requires multi-faceted global cooperation; and (5) the transparency of normative positions navigates value judgments at the science-policy interface.[87] Learning from COVID-19 should enhance ambitions to reduce emissions and build resilience. The stimulus packages should combine socio-economic recovery with climate action into coherent unified responses to tackle the pandemic, improve public health, advance renewable energy, and achieve SDG 13.

Doctors say it is better "to make two surgeries with one anesthetic." Instead of focusing on the pandemic first, and delay steps toward carbon-zero economy for later, we better introduce immediately synergetic policies to build back green. It is high time to set bold and ambitious targets to drive change. Coming out of the COVID-19 crisis, there are excellent opportunities to combine economy and environment, public health with sustainable recovery.

---

87 David Klenert et al., *Five Lessons from COVID-19 for Advancing Climate Change Mitigation*, 76 ENVT'L & RES. ECON. 751, 752 (2020).

20 Climate Change and Small Islands

Tessel van der Putte

Introduction

Small Island Developing States (SIDS) comprise a special group of 38 United Nations (UN) Member States and 20 Non-UN Members (or Associate Members of regional commissions), spread over the Caribbean, Pacific, and the Atlantic, Indian Ocean, and South China Sea.[1] These nations face unique environmental, economic, and social vulnerabilities, leading to similar development challenges across the Sustainable Development Goals (SDGs). One theme in particular is their climate change adaptation and mitigation agenda that SIDS cope with under limited financial, administrative, and technical resources—concurrently with global climate action efforts, or a lack thereof.[2] The difficulties that all countries face with climate change are exacerbated in SIDS due to their small geographical area, exposure, and isolation.[3] As such, their vulnerability to climate change in particular, is also acknowledged widely in research.[4] Yet, some of their contextual realities concerning indigenous culture, future displacement, and possible loss of statehood due to climate change pose novel and unfamiliar dilemmas.

Hence, in light of SDG 13 on climate action and its related targets, this chapter will focus on the big challenges that SIDS face. The research will discuss sustainable development challenges such as sea-level rise and storms and cyclones threatening the reversal of development progress made[5] as well as more in-depth and context-sensitive challenges regarding social dynamics and political sovereignty. There will also be a section focusing on health and the current COVID-19 pandemic which could stagnate sustainable development.

The author of this research also conducted a case study on the Pacific SIDS, which is referred to and interwoven throughout the chapter, to illustrate the complexity and intersectional nature of the impacts of climate change—as well as the consequences of inadequate climate action. Both the research and the case study aim to contribute to a more

---

1 For a list of SIDS, *see Small Island Developing States*, UNITED NATIONS (UN), https://sustainabledevelopment.un.org/topics/sids/list.
2 Michelle Scobie, *Sustainable Development and Climate Change Adaptation: Goal Interlinkages and the Case of SIDS*, *in* DEALING WITH CLIMATE CHANGE ON SMALL ISLANDS: TOWARDS EFFECTIVE AND SUSTAINABLE ADAPTATION? 101–22 (Carola Klöck & Michael Fink, eds., 2019).
3 *See Responding to Climate Change in Small Island Developing States*, UN DEVELOPMENT PROGRAMME, https://sustainabledevelopment.un.org/content/documents/960SIDS_Flyer_SEPT_27_09[1].pdf (Sept. 2010).
4 Leonard Nurse et al., *Small Islands*, in CLIMATE CHANGE 2014: IMPACTS, ADAPTION AND VULNERABILITY. PART B: REGIONAL ASPECTS. CONTRIBUTION OF WORKING GROUP II TO THE FIFTH ASSESSMENT REPORT OF THE INTERGOVERNMENTAL PANEL ON CLIMATE CHANGE 1613–54 (V.R. Barros et al., eds., 2014).
5 *Id*.

in-depth and inclusive understanding of the diversity in climate change narratives that we need to consider and emphasize in the global urgency for climate action. In the final section, the chapter will discuss the main targets of SDG 13 with regard to SIDS and the progress and necessary actions that need to be further developed. The research will conclude by stating that we need both a focus on multilateralism to reach the targets set forth by SDG 13—as well as focus on local dimensions of inequality and the inclusion of un-explored knowledge and value systems.

Climate Change

Climate change generally refers to global warming due to greenhouse gas (GHG) emissions from anthropogenic sources (primarily fossil fuels).[6] The excessive carbon dioxide (CO_2) emissions caused by increased consumption of fossil fuels since the Industrial Revolution, is vastly disrupting the Earth's carbon cycle.[7] In the 2018 Intergovernmental Panel on Climate Change (IPCC) Special Report, it states that human activity is estimated to have caused approximately 1.0°C of global warming above pre-industrial levels and that global warming is likely to reach 1.5°C between 2030 and 2052[8]—if not sooner. Many researchers fear the world will go over this pre-industrial barrier to 2°C, which will result in heavy precipitation associated with tropical cyclones, droughts, floods, sea-level rising, and hazards (projected to be much higher compared to a 1.5°C global warming or below).[9] Hence, this benchmark is a vital issue of SDG 13 and the main lens of this chapter.

Climate Change and SIDS

When discussing climate action regarding SIDS, we have to understand the impacts of climate change in SIDS. A major consequence of climate change that has become steadily evident is the rising of sea levels.[10] The global mean sea level is currently expected to rise between a staggering 0.43 and 0.84 meters by 2100 due to global warming processes.[11] In addition to that, the Special Report by the IPCC in 2019 expects that sea levels will continue

---

6 Beyond the burning of fossil, also power generation, transportation, buildings, and industry; the generation of heat and electricity and land-use such as deforestation contribute to global warming. *See* N. H. STERN, THE ECONOMICS OF CLIMATE CHANGE: THE STERN REVIEW (2006); George Pring, Alexandra Haas, and Benton Drinkwine, *The Impact on Health, Environment, and Sustainable Development*, in BEYOND THE CARBON ECONOMY: ENERGY LAW IN TRANSITION (Zillmanet et al., eds., 2008); INTERNATIONAL ENERGY AGENCY, WORLD ENERGY OUTLOOK 2010.
7 See Hannah Ritchie & Max Roser, *CO_2 and Greenhouse Gas Emissions*, OUR WORLD IN DATA, https://ourworldindata.org/co2-and-other-greenhouse-gas-emissions (last visited Dec. 2, 2020).
8 Intergovernmental Panel on Climate Change (IPCC), *Global warming of 1.5°C. An IPCC Special Report on the impacts of global warming of 1.5°C above pre-industrial levels and related global greenhouse gas emission pathways, in the context of strengthening the global response to the threat of climate change, sustainable development, and efforts to eradicate poverty (Summary for Policymakers)*, at 32 (V. Masson-Delmotte et al. eds., 2018) available at www.ipcc.ch/sr15/chapter/spm/.
9 *Id.*
10 John Campbell & Olivia Warrick, *Climate Change and Migration Issues in the Pacific*, UNITED NATIONS ECONOMIC AND SOCIAL COMMISSION FOR ASIA AND THE PACIFIC, www.ilo.org/dyn/migpractice/docs/261/Pacific.pdf (August, 2014).
11 M. Oppenheime et al., *Sea Level Rise and Implications for Low-Lying Islands, Coasts and Communities*, in IPCC SPECIAL REPORT ON THE OCEAN AND CRYOSPHERE IN A CHANGING CLIMATE (H. Pörtner et al., eds., 2019).

to rise at an increasing rate even after 2100, while extreme sea-level events are projected to occur more frequently (at least once per year, by 2050).[12] Communities that live in close proximity to coastal environments, such as SIDS, are particularly vulnerable to this.[13]

This is mainly because SIDS are low-lying countries and often have development, infrastructure, and communities centered along coastal areas.[14] Their economic sectors also largely depend on natural resources and are climate-sensitive—such as fisheries, agriculture, and tourism.[15] Moreover, SIDS do not only battle with an up-marching sea-level line, eroding shores, and flooding of homes, but they are also in the front lines of increasingly heavy storms and cyclones due to increasing temperatures.[16] These changes lead to extreme floods and more frequent and longer droughts that are interchanged with more intense rainfall and changing rainfall patterns.[17] This also compromises water security and sanitation and leads to an increased risk of water-, vector-, and food-borne infectious diseases.[18] These hazards can translate into "increased mortality and morbidity from extreme weather events and climate-sensitive diseases (including mental health issues)"—threatening the very existence of SIDS and their social and cultural fabric.[19] All of the above, heightened by a limited adaptive capacity to respond, leads to the consideration that SIDS, such as in the regions of the Pacific, are "on the frontline of climate change."[20]

---

12 Nerilie Abram et al., *Special Report on the Ocean and Cryosphere in a Changing Climate (Summary for Policymakers)*, IPCC (2019).
13 *Id., See also Summary for Policymakers*; Luijendijk, et al., *The State of the World's Beaches*, SCIENTIFIC REPORTS 6641 (2018). Also, we see that in fact coastal zones world-wide constitute one of the most heavily populated and developed land zones and that 31% of the world's "ice-free shorelines" are sandy (which makes them extra vulnerable to these processes). Scientists have analyzed satellite-derived shoreline data, that shows us that 24% of the world's sandy beaches are eroding at rates "exceeding 0.5 meters a year" already.
14 *Climate Change & Small Island Developing States, 49th Session of United Nations Statistical Commission*, STATISTICAL INSTITUTE OF JAMAICA, https://unstats.un.org/unsd/statcom/49th-session/side-events/documents/20180307-1M-Jamaica-Climate-Change-&-SIDS-1March2018.pdf (Mar. 7, 2018) [hereinafter "Stat. Inst. of Jamaica"]. This presentation also mentions, that while most SIDS rely on fossil fuels (though they are also exploring renewable sources of energy), emissions from SIDS are very low compared to developed and industrialized countries.
15 *Id.*
16 *Id. See also Special Initiative: Climate Change and Health in Small Island Developing States*, WORLD HEALTH ORGANIZATION (WHO), at 2, www.who.int/globalchange/sids-initiative/180612_global_initiative_sids_clean_v2.pdf?ua=1 (2017) [hereinafter "WHO Special Initiative"] *and* Faisal Ahmed & Vinaytosh Mishra, *Estimating Relative Immediacy of Water-Related Challenges in Small Island Developing States (SIDS) of the Pacific Ocean Using AHP Modeling*, 6 MODEL EARTH SYS. & ENV'T. 201, 201–14 (2020). In which the research findings revealed that the most immediate challenge to SIDS under climate change, in terms of their relative immediacy weightage, were rising sea levels, followed by low water quality and its availability; and "spread of water-borne and vector-borne diseases."
17 WHO Special Initiative, *Id.*
18 *Id.*
19 *Id.* at 2.
20 Robert Oakes, *Culture, Climate Change and Mobility Decisions in Pacific Small Island Developing States*, 40(4) POPULATION & ENV'T. 480, 480–503 (2019).

The COVID-19 Pandemic

The ongoing coronavirus pandemic highlights the fact that SIDS are also particularly susceptible to the effects of global health crises.[21] As the UN Resolution 74/270 states, the pandemic has unprecedented effects on societies and livelihoods of people, disrupting economies, global travel, and commerce.[22] The document recognizes that the poorest and most vulnerable are hit the hardest by the coronavirus pandemic and that the impact of the crisis will reverse any hard-worn development gains, hampering progress toward achieving the SDGs in such areas.[23]

SIDS are largely reliant on income from tourism and trade,[24] making up around 60% of their gross domestic product (GDP) on average[25] and making them some of the most vulnerable nations to sudden changes in the travel and tourism industry. What is more concerning is that any shock of such magnitude is difficult to manage for small economies[26] and could hamper progress of SDG 1 to end poverty, relating to target 1.5 in particular;[27] SDG 8 on sustainable economic growth and employment;[28] and SDG 10 on inequality within and among countries. This also builds on top of other already existing natural and social vulnerabilities as discussed in this chapter, which are exacerbated by the pandemic (directly affecting SDG 3 to ensure health and well-being;[29] stagnating progress of SDG 5 on gender inequalities—but also endangering food security and climate resilience for instance). As Sheldon Yett, Pacific Representative for the United Nations Children's Fund stated, "[i]t is hard to imagine a more difficult situation, the catastrophe of COVID-19 and the disaster of a category five cyclone all wrapped into one."[30]

Moreover, "simple handlings" and solutions to contain the spread of the virus, such as keeping distance or washing hands, are not always as achievable for communities living in developing nations. In SIDS that are dealing with water and sanitation problems, their

---

21 *See* G.A. Res. A/RES/74/270, *Global Solidarity to Fight the Coronavirus Disease 2019 (COVID-19)* (April 3, 2020).
22 *Id.*
23 *Id.*
24 *World's Most Vulnerable Countries Lack the Capacity to Respond to a Global Pandemic*, UN OFFICE OF THE HIGH REPRESENTATIVE FOR THE LEAST DEVELOPED COUNTRIES, LANDLOCKED DEVELOPING COUNTRIES, AND THE SMALL ISLAND DEVELOPING STATES (OHRLLS) (April 28, 2020), http://unohrlls.org/covid-19/.
25 This share is over 50% for the Maldives, Seychelles, St. Kitts and Nevis and Grenada, when it comes to just tourism. Jodie Keane, *Covid-19 and Trade: Challenges Ahead for Least Developed Countries and Small Island Developing States*, OVERSEAS DEVELOPMENT INSTITUTE (April 1, 2020), www.odi.org/blogs/16804-covid-19-trade-challenges-ahead-least-developed-countries-small-island-developing-states.
26 Pamela Coke-Hamilton, *Impact of COVID-19 on Tourism in Small Island Developing States*, UN CONFERENCE ON TRADE AND DEVELOPMENT (April 24, 2020), https://unctad.org/en/pages/newsdetails.aspx?OriginalVersionID=2341.
27 G.A. A/RES/70/1, *Transforming our world: The 2030 Agenda for Sustainable Development SDG* (Oct. 21, 2015). SDG target 1.5: "By 2030, build the resilience of the poor and those in vulnerable situations and reduce their exposure and vulnerability to climate-related extreme events and other economic, social and environmental shocks and disasters."
28 *Id*. In particular also SDG target 8.10: "Strengthen the capacity of domestic financial institutions to encourage and expand access to banking, insurance and financial services for all."
29 *Id*. In addition, also SDG target 3.d: "Strengthen the capacity of all countries, in particular developing countries, for early warning, risk reduction and management of national and global health risks."
30 *COVID-19 Shocks Too Big to Handle for Small Island Nations, UN Warns*, THE UNITED NATIONS DEPARTMENT OF GLOBAL COMMUNICATIONS, www.un.org/en/un-coronavirus-communications-team/covid-19-shocks-too-big-handle-small-island-nations-un-warns (last visited May 20, 2020).

response to COVID-19 is more challenging (illustrating the importance of SDG 6 on sustainable management of water and sanitation). On top of that, lack of data monitoring makes it difficult to analyze the situation on the ground and act upon that accordingly (affecting effective leadership and policy making, for SDGs such as SDG 9 and 11 to build resilient and sustainable infrastructures, or SDG target 13.1 in building resilience and adaptive capacity to climate-related hazards and natural disasters).[31]

Some might say that due to lockdowns and with less global travel, there are also less GHG emissions, indirectly advancing the interests of SIDS with regard to the global warming discussion. However, such views fail to recognize that these GHG emissions are merely one part of a much larger system in which we will jointly need to change many components, mindsets, and habits (such as the deforestation processes, the agricultural sector, manufacturing industries, construction, and electricity sectors).[32] More than that, the travel and trade industries are very important for SIDS to access supplies and are crucial for their food reliance and tourism-dependent economies. In the end, such restrictions may in fact turn out to be more harmful for SIDS, outweighing the benefits of a temporary halt on global travel emissions.

Case Study: The Pacific SIDS

The Pacific Island region consists of 14 independent countries and eight territories, counting about 200 high islands and about 2,500 low islands and atolls.[33] Pacific SIDS are some of the most vulnerable nations in the world to the effects of climate change and natural disasters. According to the World Risk Index 2018, there are five Pacific Island states ranked among the top 20 most at-risk countries in the world, with Vanuatu and Tonga ranked first and second.[34] A sea-level rise of 0.43 to 0.84 meters by 2100 will have significant impacts on coastal ecosystems—especially on atolls and other small sand and low-lying islands[35]—and on infrastructure of urban areas near coastal zones, aquaculture, and ecosystems.[36]

---

31 Nina L. Hall et al., *Health and the Sustainable Development Goals: Challenges for Four Pacific Countries*, 34(1) INT'L. J. HEALTH PLAN. & MGMT. 845 (2019).
32 Mengpin Ge & Johannes Friedrich, *4 Charts Explain Greenhouse Gas Emissions by Countries and Sectors*, WORLD RESOURCES INSTITUTE (Feb. 06, 2020), www.wri.org/blog/2020/02/greenhouse-gas-emissions-by-country-sector; *See also* J.G.J. Olivier & J.A.H.W. Peters, *Trends in Global CO2 and Total Greenhouse Gas Emissions: 2019 Report*, PBL NETHERLANDS ENVIRONMENTAL ASSESSMENT AGENCY, www.pbl.nl/sites/default/files/downloads/pbl-2020-trends-in-global-co2-and-total-greenhouse-gas-emissions-2019-report_4068.pdf (2019).
33 Robert Gillett & Mele Ikatonga Tauati, *Fisheries of the Pacific Islands: Regional and National Information*, at iv, FOOD AND AGRICULTURE ORGANIZATION (2018).
34 *The World Bank In Pacific Islands*, THE WORLD BANK, www.worldbank.org/en/country/pacificislands/overview (Oct. 6, 2020).
35 POSITION ANALYSIS: CLIMATE CHANGE, SEA-LEVEL RISE AND EXTREME EVENTS: IMPACTS AND ADAPTATION ISSUES, ANTARCTIC CLIMATE & ECOSYSTEMS COOPERATIVE RESEARCH CENTRE 6 (2008) [hereinafter "Position Analysis"].
36 P. Bruun, *Sea-Level Rise as a Cause of Shore Erosion*, 88(1) J. WATERWAYS & HARBORS DIVISION *117*, 117–32 (1962). *See also* Orrin H. Pilkey, J. Andrew, & G. Cooper, *Society and Sea-level Rise*, 303(5665) SCIENCE 1781, 1781–82 (2004). This severity of shoreline recession goes "at a rate in the order of 100 times the amount of sea-level rise," according to the Bruun rule, which would implicate around 20 meters erosion landward, with every 0.2 meter sea level rise.

Take for example the atoll states Kiribati, Tuvalu,[37] and the Marshall Islands. Given their low elevation (one to two meters above sea level)[38] and the fact that they cover small areas of land, communities have little to no opportunity to retreat in the case of receding shorelines or inland flooding.[39] Global warming in this region will also contribute to the acidification and warming of ocean waters (thermic expansion), salinization, desertification, soil erosion, reef-bleaching, and more frequent and intense weather patterns (including tropical storms such as cyclones) as mentioned earlier.[40] This is especially distressing, as a high percentage of people in the Pacific SIDS live near the coast itself (many of which are located in low-lying areas). This means that they will increasingly be affected by inland flooding in the upcoming decades, even if the island in question has areas of higher elevation.[41]

Moreover, constant inland flooding and salinization are likely to affect freshwater reserves and the fertility of the soil,[42] resulting in the intrusion of coastal aquifers by saltwater. This makes communities increasingly more dependent on rainwater, which also poses an issue due to changing "precipitation patterns and prolonged drought conditions."[43]

Primary food sources will also be heavily affected, such as agricultural crops, potentially leading to more poverty and other inequalities.[44] In this, also the fisheries would be subjected to change—if not being subjected to it already.[45] With water currents and temperatures changing, marine species will gradually move away from the equator to colder waters resulting not only in a change of food resources, but also in a loss of traditional fisheries and jobs thereby creating instability for local economies.[46] Such challenges in the fishing industry could in fact completely disrupt local economies (that, while some of Pacific SIDS are also on the list of the least developed countries (LDC) in the world).[47]

SIDS' exposure to global warming processes are therefore "greatly heightened by the challenge of adapting to extreme weather events, and the serial 'stop-and-start' economic cycles that are associated with adjusting to the severe losses and damages caused by these

---

37 "Tuvalu, one of the least developed SIDS, is already seeing the devastating effects of climate change on its communities every day—from worsening extreme weather events, to increased spread of infectious diseases, to occupational health risks." *Health & Climate Change Country Profile 2020: Small Island Developing States Initiative*, WHO AND THE UNITED NATIONS FRAMEWORK CONVENTION ON CLIMATE CHANGE (UNFCCC) https://apps.who.int/iris/bitstream/handle/10665/330009/WHO-CED-PHE-EPE-19.3.3-eng.pdf (2020).
38 Jon Barnett & W. Neil Adger, *Climate Dangers and Atoll Countries*, 61(3) CLIMATIC CHANGE 321, 321–37 (2003).
39 Position Analysis, *supra* note 35 at 6.
40 *Id. See also* Campbell & Warrick *supra* note 10 *and* Rebecca Lindsey, *Climate Change: Global Sea-level*, CLIMATE.GOV (Nov.19, 2019), at 6, www.climate.gov/news-features/understanding-climate/climate-change-global-sea-level.
41 *Small Island Developing States in Numbers, Climate Change Edition 2015*, UN-OHRLLS, at 33, https://sustainabledevelopment.un.org/content/documents/2189SIDS-IN-NUMBERS-CLIMATE-CHANGE-EDITION_2015.pdf (2015) [hereinafter "UN-OHRLLS SIDS in Numbers"].
42 *Id.* at 7.
43 *Id.*
44 *Id. See* Position Analysis, *supra* note 35 at 15 (which could be a source of conflict thereupon as well); *See also* Piers K. Dunstan et al., *How Can Climate Predictions Improve Sustainability of Coastal Fisheries in Pacific Small-Island Developing States?* 88 MARINE POL'Y 295, 295–302 (2018) and Statistical Institute of Jamaica, *supra* note 14.
45 *Id.*
46 UN-OHRLLS SIDS in Numbers, *supra* note 41. *See also* William Cheung, Reg Watson, & Daniel Pauly, *Signature of Ocean Warming in Global Fisheries Catch*, 497 NATURE 365 (2013).
47 UN-OHRLLS, *Id.*

events."[48] Increasing flooding and extreme weather events as storms and cyclones harm the resilience of communities significantly and can cause or worsen serious social displacement challenges (including Kiribati and the Marshall Islands, but also the Solomon Islands and the Federated States of Micronesia, for example).[49] For these reasons, a major social implication is the possibility of displacement and migration.[50]

In the context of displacement of Pacific Islanders, migration may be a way to escape risks and find more secure livelihoods. Yet, Pacific political and community leaders have stressed that "mobility can be a threat to sovereignty and culture and should only be considered as a last resort."[51] There are significant information gaps relating to the costs and adaptive challenges of such climate-induced migration[52] that pose legal conundrums.

Political Consequences of Climate Change

The latter item brings us to another implication of climate change, the 1.5°C barrier and SIDS: Political (in)stability and potential loss of statehood.[53] As the future will likely see various kinds of human displacement due to climate change, one aspect of this may be complete "state extinctions" as Vaha brings forward in "Small Island States and the Right to Exist."[54] According to the IPCC, rising sea levels linked to global warming pose an alarming threat to "the very existence of some atoll nations"[55] as it dismantles their territory and livability. Displacement of entire populations and their governments could lead to statelessness. This is a completely novel phenomenon.[56]

Processes such as increased flooding of low-lying islands and coastal regions, soil erosion, and disruption of water systems may (partly) wash away the ground under the feet of SIDS inhabitants over time.[57] With no adequate tools to protect SIDS against such events, the lack of economic capacity to re-build and strengthen resilience, and without international collaboration realizing SDG 13 firmly and urgently, rising tides threaten to drown entire islands in these parts of the world. The latter makes climate change a discussion of sovereignty and statehood too.

Statehood, in brief, requires four main elements: A defined territory, a permanent population, an effective government, and the capacity to enter into relations with other

---

48 Manuel F. Montes, *The Right to Development, Small Island Developing States and the SAMOA Pathway*, SOUTH CENTRE, at 2, www.southcentre.int/wp-content/uploads/2016/05/PB25_Right-to-development-and-SAMOA-pathway_EN.pdf (May 2016).
49 *Id.*
50 Oakes, *supra* note 20.
51 *Id.*
52 Campbell & Warrick, *supra* note 10 at 2. It is estimated that the global number of migrants moving due to climate change, will range between 25 million and 1 billion people by 2050, as cited by the International Organization for Migration.
53 *See* Position Analysis, *supra* note 35 *and* Lindsey, *supra* note 40.
54 Milla Emilia Vaha, *Drowning under: Small Island States and the Right to Exist*, 11(2) J. INT'L. POL. THEORY 207 (June 1, 2015).
55 Nurse et al., *supra* note 4 at 1618.
56 Susin Park, *Climate Change and the Risk of Statelessness: The Situation of Low-Lying Island States*, Legal and Protection Policy Research Series, UN HIGH COMMISSIONER FOR REFUGEES, at 3 (May 10, 2011)
57 Frank Dietrich & Joachim Wündisch, *Territory Lost—Climate Change and the Violation of Self-determination Rights*, 2(1) MORAL PHILOSOPHY AND POLITICS 83, 83 (2015).

States.[58] Though "all four criteria would seemingly need to be present for a State to come into existence, the lack of all four may not mean the end of a State."[59] However, according to Park, a "submersion of the entire territory through rising sea-levels" with no other territory being ceded, would make it difficult to argue "that the constitutive elements of statehood continue to exist, even with the lower threshold and presumption of continuity applicable for States already in existence."[60] While the existence of air space and sea territory would physically continue to exist, "these are generally considered appurtenances to the land territory" and, so are presumed to disappear together with the land territory.[61]

What is important to mention here as well, is that we should not focus on the loss of territory alone as the main indicator of a State's disappearance due to climate change: SIDS may actually become uninhabitable long before they physically disappear.[62] For example, insufficient freshwater could be the most apparent trigger for rendering low-lying islands uninhabitable. Tuvalu and Kiribati are starting to exhibit this issue.[63] This would mean that while some part of the territory could continue to exist, the (lack of) presence of a permanent population would essentially be the most determining factor in this unfamiliar and uncomfortable debate. In short, although rising tides that drown entire island states speak strongly to the imagination (and I invite you to let it), both low and high elevated SIDS will be heavily affected by the processes of sea-level rise and global warming in general, in due time.

Whatever the outcome of this unusual discourse would be however, it is thought that the response of the international community and the SIDS themselves will be substantially defining on many levels.[64] For example, in light of maintaining statehood and with an eye on the future, Kiribati's president Anote Tong finalized the purchase of a 20 square kilometer island from Fiji in 2015.[65] Despite the fact that most people in Kiribati are still opposed to the idea of seeking refuge in another country, Kiribati would not have the financial resources alone to protect its land from the rising tides, making the purchase a "dire necessity" considering its Least Developed Country status.[66] Among SIDs, Kiribati has arguably done most to anticipate the future needs of its population to launch this "migration with dignity" policy in an attempt to avoid a humanitarian evacuation in the future.[67]

The discussion on nationhood and climate change dynamics unravels the necessity of SDG 13 and the urgency to protect the rights of people that would come to find themselves

---

58 Jane McAdam, *Disappearing States, Statelessness and the Boundaries of International Law*, 2 UNIVERSITY OF NEW SOUTH WALES LAW RESEARCH PAPER 5 (2010).
59 *Id.*
60 Park, *supra* note 56 at 14.
61 *See* JAMES CRAWFORD AND IAN BROWNLIE, BROWNLIE'S PRINCIPLES OF PUBLIC INTERNATIONAL LAW, 6TH ED. 105, 117–18 (2003).
62 Park, *supra* note 56 at 1–2.
63 *See* Nobuo Mimura et al., *Small Islands*, *in* CLIMATE CHANGE 2007: IMPACTS, ADAPTATION AND VULNERABILITY: CONTRIBUTION OF WORKING GROUP II TO THE FOURTH ASSESSMENT REPORT OF THE INTERGOVERNMENTAL PANEL ON CLIMATE CHANGE (ML Parry et al., eds., 2007).
64 Park, *supra* note 56 at 14.
65 Inge van Schooneveld, *Rising Tides Force Kiribati To Acquire Land Elsewhere*, SINCHI FOUNDATION, https://sinchi-foundation.com/news/climate-change-pacific-kiribati-fiji/ (2018).
66 *Id.*
67 Nic Maclellan, *Kiribati's Policy for "Migration with Dignity,"* DEVPOLICY BLOG, https://devpolicy.org/kiribati_migration_climate_change20120112/ (Jan. 12, 2012).

in "limbo" as disappearance of the state would imply no statehood, no state responsibility, and no protection toward their citizens.[68]

Case Study: The Pacific and Nuclear Waste

A regional-specific issue that cannot be lacking from this chapter, is the presence of nuclear waste in the Pacific region due to the nuclear testing by France[69] and the United States (US) in the past. During the Cold War, the US detonated 67 nuclear weapons over the Bikini and Enewetak atolls in the Marshall Islands.[70] The nuclear waste material was "pumped" into a crater that had been left by an atomic bomb explosion[71] and then covered with a thin shell of cement less than 18 inches thick.[72] Now, a huge "kind of coffin" (in the words of UN Secretary General António Guterres) houses the deadly radioactive debris from the 1980s.[73] Currently sitting "unmarked and unguarded in a small island" vulnerable to rising tides,[74] radiation from the Marshall Islands has already been detected in the South China Sea[75]—as well as in the sediments around the lagoon outside the dome.[76] With an increased sea-level rise and risk of being torn apart by storms and cyclones, the consequences of this nuclear coffin to the region could potentially be disastrous.

Case Study: The Pacific and the Importance of Cultural Context

It is also of paramount importance to discuss the cultural context when discussing climate action in SIDS. Pacific SIDS are the homes and traditional lands of many Indigenous Peoples. In fact, SIDS have some of the highest percentages of indigenous communities in relation to national population in the entire world.[77] For example, in independent Pacific Island nations

---

68 "Nationality is a practical prerequisite for accessing political and juridical processes and for obtaining economic, social and cultural rights," David Weissbrodt & Clay Collins, *The Human Rights of Stateless Persons*, 28(1) HUM. RTS. Q. 265 (2006). *See also*, PAUL WEIS, NATIONALITY AND STATELESSNESS IN INTERNATIONAL LAW 136 (2nd ed., 1979). In International law we observe that when a State ceases to exist, likely so does the nationality of that State.
69 *See* Angelique Chrisafis, *French Nuclear Tests Showered Vast Area of Polynesia with Radioactivity*, THE GUARDIAN, www.theguardian.com/world/2013/jul/03/french-nuclear-tests-polynesia-declassified (2013).
70 Michael B. Gerrard, *America's Forgotten Nuclear Waste Dump in the Pacific*, 35(1) SAIS REV. INT'L AFF. 87, 87–97 (2015).
71 DEFENSE NUCLEAR AGENCY, THE RADIOLOGICAL CLEANUP OF ENEWETAK ATOLL 428–31 (1981).
72 Gerrard, *supra* note 70. *See also* NATIONAL RESEARCH COUNCIL, COMMITTEE ON EVALUATION OF ENEWETAK RADIOACTIVITY CONTAINMENT, EVALUATION OF ENEWETAK RADIOACTIVITY CONTAINMENT 29 (1982).
73 Kyle Swenson, *The U.S. Put Nuclear Waste under a Dome on a Pacific Island. Now It's Cracking Open*, THE WASHINGTON POST, www.washingtonpost.com/nation/2019/05/20/us-put-nuclear-waste-under-dome-pacific-island-now-its-cracking-open/ (May 20, 2019).
74 Gerrard, *supra* note 70 at 92. "Although the dome was designed to withstand severe storm wave and typhoon activity, the typhoons in this part of the world are so severe that a series of these conceivably could cause breachment of the dome structure."
75 *Id.;*
76 *Id.;* Terry Hamilton, *A Visual Description of the Concrete Exterior of the Cactus Crater Containment Structure*, LAWRENCE LIVERMORE LABORATORY, at 1 (2013); Victor E. Noshkin & William L. Robison, *Assessment of a Radioactive Waste Disposal Site at Enewetak Atoll*, 73(1) HEALTH PHYSICS 234, 246 (July 1997).
77 *Cultural Landscapes of The Pacific Islands—UNESCO World Heritage*, INTERNATIONAL COUNCIL ON MONUMENTS AND SITES (ICOMOS), at 18, https://whc.unesco.org/document/10061 (2007); Anita Smith & Kevin L. Jones, *Cultural Landscapes of the Pacific Islands*, ICOMOS, at 18 (2007).

we find that around 90% of the land continues to be held in traditional ownership, the highest proportion in any geo-cultural region in the world.[78] It indicates a continuation of traditional and indigenous systems of authority, alongside Western governance as established during and after colonization periods.[79]

These traditional land tenure systems across much of the region are a testament of the inseparable relationship between Pacific Island people, land, and seascapes.[80] As many of the Pacific Islanders carry a unique social, political, economic, and even spiritual connection to their (wet)lands, there are some scholars that have argued that "the Pacific Island landscapes are essentially complete cultural landscapes."[81]

For Indigenous Peoples, in SIDS and globally, the recognition of their rights to traditional (wet)lands and natural resources, as well as the "possession" and access of it,[82] is "crucial to achieving equal opportunities in society and self-determination as indigenous peoples."[83] As ancestral lands are not merely an economic asset for indigenous cultures, but a defining element for their (cultural) identity, political status, and relationship to their ancestors and future generations, "there is a need for recognition of indigenous land tenure systems as well as of the situation of Indigenous nomadic and semi-nomadic communities" to the extent that this recognition will effectively bridge global sustainability efforts too.[84]

Yet, in contrast to this holistic approach, we often see that indigenous peoples "in multiple geographical contexts have been pushed into marginalized territories that are more sensitive to climate impacts, in turn limiting their access to food, cultural resources, traditional livelihoods, and place-based knowledge ... [and therefore undermining] aspects of social-cultural resilience."[85] While traditional settlements on high islands in the Pacific were often located inland, the move to coastal locations was in fact historically encouraged

---

78 Smith, *Id*. at 9: "Cultural landscapes have been identified in a number of forums and workshops in the Pacific as being a highly appropriate way to recognizing the unique heritage of the region, because they reflect the ways in which Pacific Island communities have interacted with the Oceanic environment through time."
79 *Id*. at 27.
80 *Id*.at 9.
81 *Id*.at 30; Also, on the relationships of people with their environment, their cultural and social practices with regard to the landscape of intangible and tangible heritage, Gosden writes, "The term 'social landscape' is often used to describe traditional Pacific Island landscapes in recognition that they are the result of actions planned, organized and carried out by local communities." CHRISTOPHER GOSDEN, SOCIAL BEING AND TIME (1994).
82 On an equitable basis taking into account the needs of all inhabitants.
83 Meredith Gibbs, *The Right to Development and Indigenous Peoples: Lessons from New Zealand*, 33(8) WORLD DEV. 1367 (2005).
84 *Briefing Note: Indigenous Peoples' Rights and the 2030 Agenda*, OFFICE OF THE HIGH COMMISSION FOR HUMAN RIGHTS (OHCHR) AND THE UN DEPARTMENT OF ECONOMIC AND SOCIAL AFFAIRS (UN-DESA), at 4, www.un.org/development/desa/indigenouspeoples/wp-content/uploads/sites/19/2016/10/Briefing-Paper-on-Indigenous-Peoples-Rights-and-the-2030-Agenda.pdf (2007) [hereinafter "IP Rights and the 2030 Agenda"].
85 James Ford et al., *Including Indigenous Knowledge and Experience in IPCC Assessment Reports*, 6(4) NAT. CLIMATE CHANGE 349, 350 (2016). Also, Indigenous People are entitled to the right of self-determination, right to their culture and cultural practices, including their traditional and native home lands, *see* G.A. Res. 61/295, Declaration on the Rights of Indigenous Peoples (Oct. 2, 2007) and Convention No. 169 Concerning Indigenous and Tribal People in Independent Countries, 1650 U.N.T.S. 383, 27 June 1989 (entered into force 5 September 5 1991).

by colonial and religious authorities—and more recently, by the development of tourism.[86] These dynamics can play a critical role in explaining the emergence of the vulnerability of people in SIDS—especially those of Indigenous Peoples.[87]

In the context of atolls, the growing pressure on freshwater resources together with the loss of local knowledge (such as how to collect water from certain plants or trees), results in communities being increasingly exposed to "brackish, polluted groundwater, inducing water insecurity, and health problems."[88] Thus, global warming amplifies the exposure and vulnerability of peoples on SIDS, intersecting with already existing social dynamics of inequality and vulnerabilities, such as those of indigenous communities and their (cultural) rights.

Furthermore, on the matter of migration or displacement due to rising tides and all the other processes of nature, we are in fact embarking on much more intricate discussions on cultural rights and identity for the Pacific region as well. In the words of Kiribati climate activist Maria Tiimon Chi-Fang, though some may think "climate change is just about moving people to a safer place"—it is much more a matter of "equity, identity, and human rights."[89] McAdam voices similar concerns too, stating that "[f]or many Tuvaluans and i-Kiribati, the issues of key importance to them are the retention of 'home'—land, community, and identity— rather than preserving the political entity of the State itself."[90]

Other Intersectional Consequences of Climate Change on SIDS

Paramount characteristics of the 2030 Agenda are its universality, transformability, and inclusivity. Where the Millennium Development Goals are applied to developing countries, the SDGs is a universal framework applicable to *all countries*. As an agenda for "people, planet, prosperity, peace, and partnership"—its transformative goals and targets offer "a paradigm shift from the traditional model of development" and provide "a transformative

---

86 Valerie Ballu et al., *Comparing the Role of Absolute Sea Level Rise and Vertical Tectonic Motions in Coastal Flooding, Torres Islands (Vanuatu)*, 108(32) PROC. NAT'L. ACAD. SCI. USA 13019, 13019–22 (Aug. 9, 2011); Nurse et al., *supra* note 4 at 1623. *See also* Virginie Duvat et al., *Trajectories of Exposure and Vulnerability of Small Islands to Climate Change*, 8(6) WILEY INTERDISC. REV.: CLIMATE CHANGE 1, 1–14 (2017).

87 Donovan Storey & Shawn Hunter, *Kiribati: An Environmental "Perfect Storm,"* 41(2) AUSTL. GEOGRAPHER 167, 167–181 (2010); *See also* Heather Lazrus, *Risk Perception and Climate Adaptation in Tuvalu: A Combined Cultural Theory and Traditional Knowledge Approach*, 74(1) HUM. ORG. 52, 52–61 (2015).

88 *Id.*

89 Maria Tiimon Chi-Fang, cited in Carol Farbotko & Heather Lazrus, *The First Climate Refugees? Contesting Global Narratives of Climate Change in Tuvalu*, 22(2) GLOBAL ENVTL. CHANGE 382, 383 (2012). *See also* John Campbell, *Climate-Induced Community Relocation in the Pacific: The Meaning and Importance of Land*, in CLIMATE CHANGE AND DISPLACEMENT: MULTIDISCIPLINARY PERSPECTIVES, at 19 (Jane McAdam, ed., 2010).

> "Cultural misunderstandings about the importance of land and cultural identity remain at the heart of discussions today about relocating entire Pacific communities in response to climate impacts. While some suggestions to relocate entire communities are no doubt well-intentioned, there are significant implications of doing so with a top-down approach. As Campbell notes, the effects of dislocation from home can last for generations, and can have significant ramifications for the maintenance and enjoyment of cultural and social rights by resettled communities."

90 JANE MCADAM, CLIMATE CHANGE, FORCED MIGRATION, AND INTERNATIONAL LAW (2012)—*Author's Interview with Government Official, Ministry of Foreign Affairs in Kiribati (12 May 2009)*.

vision for people and planet-centered, human rights-based, and gender-sensitive sustainable development that goes far beyond the narrow vision of the MDGs."[91] Adding to that, the framework carries out the phrase "leave no one behind" and stresses the importance of respect for equality and non-discrimination, between and within countries (reaffirming the responsibilities of all States to "respect, protect and promote human rights, without distinction of any kind as to race, color, sex, language, religion, political or other opinions, national and social origin, property, birth, disability, or other status").[92]

In this regard, it is essential to mention other intersectional contexts and realities of SIDS, when it comes to climate change impacts, climate action, and policy making. Whether we are talking about Indigenous or non-Indigenous Peoples' contexts, the gender-lens cannot be lacking. As gender inequalities persist around the world, climate change impacts are also experienced differently by women and men. Women commonly face higher risks and greater burdens from the impacts of climate change and are likely to be more vulnerable compared to their male counterparts in practice.[93] As has been established in works that go far beyond the scope of this chapter, climate change can aggravate pre-existing gender inequalities and in this, place a special burden on girls and women in two evident ways: Firstly, women are more likely to live in poverty and are thus more vulnerable, and secondly, women are often the main care-providers of the family, and responsible for getting water, fuel for heating, and preparing food—all of which are affected by climate change.[94] Yet, women also more often work in agriculture, and are therefore more likely to be affected by climate change in the first place.[95]

Furthermore, in (natural) crises, women tend to be more vulnerable because their specific needs are often overlooked (such as menstrual hygiene, anti-conception, or pregnancy), and because they are subjected to (sexual) violence as well.[96] Studies have shown that natural resource scarcity and natural disasters tend to increase sexual and gender-based violence against women.[97]

Where on one side, there is still a lack of female leadership and participation in political and decision-making levels, women seem to be "disproportionately vulnerable to the effects of climate change" on the other side - which consecutively can aggravate existing gender disparities even further.[98] This same narrative draws similarities with other people with a disadvantaged place in society, such as internally displaced peoples, refugees, disabled peoples,

---

91 *Human Rights and the 2030 Agenda for Sustainable Development*, OHCHR, www.ohchr.org/EN/Issues/SDGS/Pages/The2030Agenda.aspx (last visited May 20, 2020).
92 *Id.*
93 Seema Arora-Jonsson, *Virtue and Vulnerability: Discourses on Women, Gender and Climate Change*, 21(2) GLOBAL ENVTL. CHANGE 744, 744–51 (2011). *See also Introduction to Gender and Climate Change*, UNFCCC, https://unfccc.int/gender (last visited Dec. 2, 2020).
94 Stat. Inst. of Jamaica, *supra* note 14; Eric Neumayer and Thomas Plümper, *The Gendered Nature of Natural Disasters: The Impact of Catastrophic Events on the Gender Gap in Life Expectancy, 1981–2002*, 97(3) ANNALS ASS'N A. GEOGRAPHERS 551, 551–66 (2007).
95 *Id.*
96 CAROLINE CRIADO PEREZ, INVISIBLE WOMEN: EXPOSING DATA BIAS IN A WORLD DESIGNED FOR MEN (2019).
97 Itza Camey et al., *Gender-based violence and environment linkages: The violence of inequality*, at 272, International Union for the Conservation of Nature (IUCN) (2020).
98 *See* Global Gender and Climate Alliance, *Overview of Linkages between Gender and Climate Change*, UN DEVELOPMENT PROGRAMME, www.undp.org/content/dam/undp/library/gender/Gender%20and%20Environment/PB1_Africa_Overview-Gender-Climate-Change.pdf (2012).

people suffering in extreme poverty,[99] or children. Hence, like SIDS who contribute less than 1% to the world's GHG emissions, suffering *disproportionately* from the damaging impacts of climate change,[100] so do Indigenous Peoples, women, and girls in societies all over the world (as well as many more marginalized or minority groups) suffer disproportionally from something they do not have an equal proportion and say in.

There are numerous direct and indirect ways through which climate change can exacerbate poverty, "particularly in less developed countries and regions"—thus requiring policy-makers to make linkages between climate change and the multifaceted, complex, and context-specific group or region at attention. [101]

Sustainable Development Goal 13: Climate Action

So, let us link all of the above back to the following SDG 13 targets:[102]

(13.1) "Strengthen resilience and adaptive capacity to climate-related hazards and natural disasters in all countries."[103] As we have seen, this is a major challenge and an increasingly difficult-to-reach objective for SIDS, due to the very nature of the problems they are facing. The impacts of climate change create a vicious cycle in which resilience and capacity for sustainable development are weakened and hard-worn progress that may have been achieved is reversed.

(13.2) "Integrate climate change measures into national policies, strategies and planning."[104] As the chapter highlights, it is of vital importance to cut down GHG emissions nationally and globally (as the SDGs are universal), to remain below the global 1.5°C barrier. However, SIDS are not the main contributors to climate change or GHG emissions in the world,[105] although they are battling the consequences of a lack of climate action of the global plane as a whole. While dealing with the consequences of a global lack of climate action, their resources and capacity for sustainable development are spread thinly—making such measures at the national level challenging, especially without external assistance or funding.

A major effort in strengthening the targets of the 2030 Agenda as a whole, and in particular the latter two targets of SDG 13, was the adoption of the SIDS Accelerated Modalities of Action (SAMOA Pathway).[106] Led by a Member States-driven Steering Committee, this

---

99 Stat. Inst. of Jamaica, *supra* note 14. The impacts of climate change will be greater on the poor, due to their "socioeconomic status, living conditions, lack of access to potable water and proper health care infrastructure."
100 CO_2 *Emissions by Country Population*, WORLD POPULATION REVIEW, http://worldpopulationreview.com/countries/co2-emissions-by-country/ (Sept. 12, 2019). Mainly industrialized and developed countries have the highest contributions of CO2 emissions.
101 Robin Leichenko & Julie A. Silva, *Climate Change and Poverty: Vulnerability, Impacts, and Alleviation Strategies*, 5(4) WILEY INTERDISC. REV.: CLIMATE CHANGE 539, 539–56 (2014). *See also* Stephane Hallegatte & Julie Rozenberg, *Climate Change through a Poverty Lens*, 7 NAT. CLIMATE CHANGE 250, 250–256 (2017); IPCC, *Climate Change 2014: Impacts, Adaptation, and Vulnerability (Summary for Policymakers)* (C. Field et al., ed., 2014); Clionadh Raleigh, Lisa Jordan, & Idean Salehyan, *Assessing the Impact of Climate Change on Migration and Conflict*, at 5–6, THE WORLD BANK (2008).
102 *See Sustainable Development Goals*, UN, https://sustainabledevelopment.un.org/topics/sustainabledevelopmentgoals.
103 *Id.*
104 *Id.*
105 *Id.*, *SIDS in General, Produce a Low Percentage of Greenhouse Gas Emissions That Cause Climate Change*.
106 The document founded "a unique intergovernmental SIDS Partnership Framework, designed to monitor progress of existing, and stimulate the launch of new, genuine and durable partnerships for the

framework has, since 2014, been keeping the importance of partnerships for SIDS a focus point on the UN's agenda, "providing a multi-stakeholder platform for reviewing progress made by SIDS partnerships, and for sharing of good practices and lessons learned among all stakeholders, on an annual basis."[107]

SIDS have also pledged to become carbon neutral through the use of renewable energy by 2030.[108] Several countries have made similar pledges to become carbon neutral.[109] So, while many SIDS have made advances in achieving sustainable development and are vocal about it, their inherent vulnerabilities, narrow resource base, and current capacity, imply that progress toward such goals as set out in the 2030 Agenda will be rather challenging (and this is likely to become even more difficult as the region of the Pacific will be affected increasingly by adverse impacts of climate change).[110] Becoming carbon neutral will require strong, consistent, and sustainable financing and technology transfer actions on the part of the global community, led by developed countries

(13.3) "Improve education, awareness-raising and human and institutional capacity on climate change mitigation, adaptation, impact reduction and early warning."[111] When it comes to the latter concepts, this chapter has highlighted that the voice and role of SIDS could in fact be exemplary and educational to the rest of the world. It is not only their climate change diplomacy that raises awareness on climate change mitigation, it is also by the very example of their realities. The experience of SIDS alarms us about what is to come if we do not pay more attention to SDG 13 and invest in adaptation, impact reduction, and early warning.[112]

Following from this, 13.a urges us to adhere to the commitments made by developed-country parties to the United Nations Framework Convention on Climate Change to mobilise $100 billion annually by 2020, to address the needs of developing countries and fully operationalize the Green Climate Fund as soon as possible.[113] As of 2020, the Green Climate Fund has raised USD 10.3 billion equivalent in pledges from 49 countries, regions, and cities,[114] and there is still a long way to go.[115] Where SDG 13 will not be attainable for

---

    sustainable development of SIDS." *UNGA to Conduct a High-Level Review of the SAMOA Pathway in 2019*, UN-DESA, https://sustainabledevelopment.un.org/sids/samoareview (2019).

107 *Id*. In recognition of the adverse impacts of climate change and sea-level rise on SIDS, it re-emphasizes the challenge climate change poses for SIDS' sustainable development and survival.

108 Montes, *supra* note 48 at 4.

109 Elena Kosolapova, *77 Countries, 100+ Cities Commit to Net Zero Carbon Emissions by 2050 at Climate Summit*, INTERNATIONAL INSTITUTE FOR SUSTAINABLE DEVELOPMENT, https://sdg.iisd.org/news/77-countries-100-cities-commit-to-net-zero-carbon-emissions-by-2050-at-climate-summit/ (Sept. 2019).

110 UN-OHRLLS, SIDS in Numbers, *supra* note 41 at 5.

111 Sustainable Development Goals, *supra* note 102.

112 Especially since it is not uncommon to find major developed cities with significant (global) economic value that are located in coastal regions in the world (cities like Hong Kong, Melbourne, Tokyo, and Rotterdam to mention a few). Robert Muggah, *The World's Coastal Cities Are Going Under. Here's How Some Are Fighting Back*, WORLD ECONOMIC FORUM, www.weforum.org/agenda/2019/01/the-world-s-coastal-cities-are-going-under-here-is-how-some-are-fighting-back/ (2019).

113 Sustainable Development Goals, *supra* note 102.

114 *See Resource Mobilization Overview*, GREEN CLIMATE FUND, www.greenclimate.fund/about/resource-mobilisation/irm.

115 Adequate climate action and sustainability will likely require significant economic transformations. Especially, as development linked to climate change tends to be viewed under "development finance" in which the allocation of financial resources committed by the developed countries to assist developing countries in the adaptation and mitigation strategies, measures, planning and management, is a

SIDS without the help of developed and industrialized nations, financial aid alone will not be sustainable. Aid will also have to take form in climate action and affirmative efforts to remain below the global 1.5°C level.

Finally, 13.b opts to "[p]romote mechanisms for raising capacity for effective climate change-related planning and management in least developed countries and small island developing States, including focusing on women, youth and local and marginalized communities."[116] Climate change forces us to come to terms with existing issues of inequality and inequity, not only between nations but also within them. Therefore, the action section of this chapter specifically includes the importance of indigenous voices and local knowledge, as well as the role of girls and women in climate action.

Hence, when it comes to getting a grip on human-induced global warming, can we already talk about progress or are we merely slowing down a disastrous race? It is a start—although more than pledges and funds, SDG 13 will require firm action to remain below the 1.5°C barrier. We see how SDG 13 is transboundary to all 2030 goals and targets[117]—and that it influences most, if not all, human rights. It is a vicious cycle, as the impacts of climate change seem to lower the capacity to use and create efficient and sustainable means of energy production and sustainable development (not *just* in SIDS).

And although the topics of global cooperation, making concessions, and cuts in GHG emissions are complex as well as sensitive and controversial at times (as they challenge and require us to transform entire economies), they also have the potential to foster friendly relations between states, create international solidarity and cooperation.

Secretary General Antonio Guterres reinforced this thought of opportunity and the urge for international cooperation in an interview with TIME magazine, where he was recorded while standing knee-height in the coastal waters of Tuvalu (in suit and all), to raise awareness on the impacts of climate change. He stated that climate change is "a problem for us all" but that it also offers "an opportunity for multilateralism to prove its value"—while referring to the 2020 Paris Agreements.[118] The preamble of the Paris Agreement highlights that it is important that nations come together in the acknowledgment that climate change is a common concern of humankind and that "[p]arties should, when taking action to address climate change, respect, promote and consider their respective obligations on

---

central and controversial point of discussion. *See* Paris Agreement to the UNFCCC, Dec. 12, 2015, T.I.A.S. No. 16–1104, Article 9; UNFCCC, at 53–57, FCCC/CP/2015/L.9/Rev.1 (Dec. 12, 2015); A/RES/70/1, *supra* note 27 at SDG 13; *See also* Priscilla Schwartz, *Climate Change, the Right to Development and the 2030 Agenda for Sustainable Development*, OHCHR, UNIVERSITY OF PEACE, AND UNITED NATIONS UNIVERSITY, www.ohchr.org/Documents/Issues/Development/SR/AddisAbaba/ClimateChange_2030AgendaSustainable.pdf (2018); HENRY SHUE, CLIMATE CHANGE JUSTICE: VULNERABILITY AND PROTECTION (2014); MIHIR KANADE, THE MULTILATERAL TRADING SYSTEM AND HUMAN RIGHTS: A GOVERNANCE SPACE THEORY ON LINKAGES (2017).

116 *See Goal 13 Targets*, UN DEVELOPMENT PROGRAMME, www.undp.org/content/undp/en/home/sustainable-development-goals/goal-13-climate-action/targets.html.

117 A/RES/70/1, *supra* note 27. See for example SDG1: No Poverty; SDG2: Zero hunger; SDG3: Good health and well-being; SDG5: Gender equality or SDG10: Reduced inequalities; SDG6: Clean water and sanitation; SDG7: affordable and clean energy; SDG8: Decent work and economic growth; SDG11: sustainable cities and communities; SDG14: life below water; SDG15: life on land; SDG16: on the topic of peace, justice.

118 Justin Worland, *U.N. Head: Climate Change Can Prove the Value of Collective Action*, TIME (2019).

human rights" (stating this includes the rights of Indigenous Peoples and the Right to Development, too).[119]

Actions Needed

There are a myriad of actions necessary to advance the implementation of SDG 13. In relation to the themes discussed in this chapter. However, the author of this chapter wishes to draw attention to the following points in particular:

Empowerment through inclusivity and leadership is in line with 13.b.

(1) Especially in the context of Pacific SIDS, it is important to carefully listen to local and indigenous communities and the inter-generational knowledge they have of their lands and waters. Similarly, indigenous land rights may play a significant role in safeguarding more sustainable practices and bio-diversity. There is a link of paramount importance when it comes to sustainable practices and Indigenous culture that requires a more consolidated attention,[120] especially as such practices would strengthen sustainability efforts as well as align with human rights standards (granting peoples the access and control over the ancestral lands they are entitled to).
(2) Furthermore, there is a need for more engagement with communities to recognize and validate their knowledge and position on climate change in general (which is also particularly relevant in the migration issue of Pacific SIDS), in order to facilitate and implement effective and well-informed policies and projects.[121] In this, the role of women is especially instrumental. It is "through their experiences and traditional knowledge as stewards of many natural resources" that women offer invaluable insights into "better managing scarce resources and mitigating climate risks."[122] Women ought to be equally included in policy making (on local, national, and international levels) and given leadership roles in projects on such levels as well.[123]

More research is necessary to monitor changes and collect data on the exact impacts of climate change on SIDS, in the Pacific, and worldwide. In line with the Paris Agreement, it is important to set out clear guidance for parties to develop, share, manage, and deliver climate change knowledge (Article 7.7), of which information and data is an essential means to strengthening cooperation and climate change adaptation.[124]

---

119 Montes, *supra* note 48 at 1–2.
120 IP Rights and the 2030 Agenda, *supra* note 84 at 4. "We need recognition of Indigenous land tenure systems as well as of the situation of Indigenous nomadic and semi-nomadic communities."
121 Oakes, *supra* note 20.
122 *See SDG 13: Take Urgent Action to Combat Climate Change and Its Impacts*, UN WOMEN, www.unwomen.org/en/news/in-focus/women-and-the-sdgs/sdg-13-climate-action (last visited May 20, 2020).
123 "It's really important to emphasize that women aren't merely helpless victims when it comes to climate change.... Their participation and leadership can have transformative effects in their countries and communities." As stated by Mayesha Alam, an expert in climate, women's rights, and conflict at Yale University. Joe McCarthy, *Why Climate Change Disproportionately Affects Women*, GLOBAL CITIZEN, www.globalcitizen.org/en/content/how-climate-change-affects-women/ (Mar. 5, 2020).
124 Samuel Mackay et al., *Overcoming Barriers to Climate Change Information Management in Small Island Developing States: Lessons from Pacific SIDS*, 19(1) CLIMATE POL'Y 125, 125–38 (2019).

Last, but not least: concerning global warming, it is vital for this planet to remain below the 1.5°C barrier. National policies worldwide should prepare for carbon-neutrality, even if they cannot manage this on their own. As SIDS will need financial aid to back up similar efforts, the Green Climate Fund needs enough contributions each year to facilitate this process. Decarbonization of economies can include replacing fossil fuels with renewables and setting fuel efficiency standards but should especially include the conservation of forests and wetlands—or "re-establishing" those. The latter is equally important in building climate change resilience.

Despite the intricacy that is wrapped around climate action, "[t]he magnitude and complexity of the challenges posed by climate change demand immediate action" nevertheless.[125] A failure to achieve SDG 13 in a timely manner will directly affect human livelihoods and people's rights worldwide, ranging from "increased diseases and mortality" to "food insecurity, water scarcity, and threats to the survival of communities and future generations."[126] Thus far, governments have largely been unable to adequately respond to the challenges of climate change.[127] However, rooted in the philosophy that our multilateral system was once built on, there lies a moral duty to keep searching for more adequate ways to respond.

The preamble of the UN Charter reaffirms the dignity and fundamental human rights of the individual, but also equality of nations, large and small. It asks all nations to establish conditions under which justice and respect for the obligations arising from treaties and other sources of international law can be maintained, while promoting social progress and "better standards of life in larger freedom.[128] The UN Charter furthermore states that for these ends, it is required to "practice tolerance and live together in peace with one another as good neighbors, and to unite our strength to maintain international peace and security."[129] In many ways, this text is vital and still relevant to the phenomena we are witnessing in this 21st century.

Conclusion

Our global climate efforts today are guided by, and also rooted in SDG 13 of the 2030 Agenda for Sustainable Development. This recognizes the adverse impacts of climate change on all nations and the need to "take urgent action" to combat climate change and its impacts.[130] In doing so, the goals also prescribe practical ways in which nations can work toward addressing climate change threats, by using an international cooperative framework.[131] In fact, the document calls for the widest possible international cooperation in order to reduce GHG emissions and to address climate change adaptation and mitigation.[132]

---

125 *See* Thomas Greiber, Melinda Janki, & Marcos A. Orellana, *A Rights-Based Approach to Climate Change Mitigation*, in CONSERVATION WITH JUSTICE: A RIGHTS-BASED APPROACH, No. 71, at 37, (IUCN, 2009).
126 *Id.*
127 Marcos Orellana, *Climate Change and the Right to Development: International Cooperation, Financial Arrangements, and the Clean Development Mechanism*, at 12, HUMAN RIGHTS COUNCIL (2010).
128 U.N. Charter, Preamble.
129 *Id.* at
130 A/RES/70/1, *supra* note 27 at SDG 13.
131 *Id.*
132 A/RES/70/1, *supra* note 27 at ¶14 and ¶31.

In this, we not only need a focus on increased international responsibility and cooperation to reach the targets set forth by SDG 13, we also need to include people at local levels and emphasize the importance of participation. Hence, the consideration of contexts such as those of SIDS, Indigenous Peoples, women and girls, and other minority or marginalized groups in society, should form a part of the discussion and of the policies created upon those. Especially as, without proper implementation of SDG 13 and reduction of GHG emissions, they will carry a distressing weight of climate change on their shoulders. For SIDS, this will show in the deterioration of their lands, livelihoods, and well-being, but also in their security and chances of (sustainable) development, their cultural fabric, and even their sovereignty.

Finally, what states and people need perhaps the most is international solidarity that matches our growingly interconnected and globalized world. We are dependent on each other, as we are experiencing now with the global COVID-19 pandemic. We need multilateralism in its most ethical form, matching the needs of today's modern world, inclusivity when it comes to the different realities of climate change, and a global consciousness that is acted upon, mirrored by SDG 13—so that truly, "no one is left behind."

21 Achieving SDG 14

Time for a Global Ocean Approach

Kristina M. Gjerde and Marjo Vierros

Introduction

The adoption of Sustainable Development Goal 14 (SDG 14) (*Conserve and sustainably use the oceans, seas and marine resources*) as a standalone goal for the ocean represented a historic achievement that elevated the prominence of ocean issues on the international level and set the stage for governments to consider ocean governance as a part of their sustainable development plans and policies. Largely neglected in the context of the Millennium Development Goals, the SDGs demonstrate a growing understanding of the role of the ocean in supporting human lives and livelihoods, and in the achievement of other SDGs including those relating to hunger, health, innovation, and climate change. Rather than being seen as purely an environmental issue to be dealt with in isolation, the ocean has become central to realizing all other SDGs.

SDG 14's 10 targets cover a broad range of ocean pressures and drivers. The fact that many of these expired in 2020 underscores the urgency for action. In summary, the SDG 14 targets are 14.1 prevent and significantly reduce marine pollution (2025), 14.2 sustainably manage and protect marine and coastal ecosystems (2020), 14.3 minimize ocean acidification (2030), 14.4 improve marine fisheries management and end illegal fishing (2020), 14.5 conserve at least 10% of coastal and marine areas (2020), 14.6 prohibit harmful fisheries subsidies (2020), and 14.7 increase economic benefits to Small Island Developing States and Least Developed Countries (2030).[1] Cross-cutting targets for 2030 are 14.A increase scientific knowledge, research capacity, and technology; 14.B enhance access for small-scale artisanal fisheries; and 14.C implement international law as reflected in the United Nations Convention on the Law of the Sea (UNCLOS) to improve ocean conservation and sustainable use.[2]

The importance of the ocean and international law was further emphasized by the 2017 resolution of the UN General Assembly to initiate negotiations for a new international legally binding instrument under UNCLOS. As a result, a landmark treaty for marine areas beyond national jurisdiction could be adopted as early as 2020, affording improved management, protection, and governance to the 64% of the ocean that is international waters. Taken together, these developments highlight a growing consensus that improved ocean governance is essential for building human and ecosystem resilience in a changing world, and that resilience, in turn, is vital for supporting societies and economies.

---

[1] United Nations G.A. Res. A/RES/70/1, *Transforming Our World: The 2030 Agenda for Sustainable Development*, (Sept. 25, 2015) [hereinafter "2030 Agenda"].
[2] *Id.*

This chapter assesses progress overall toward achieving SDG 14, with a focus on the broadest of the targets, SDG 14.2.[3] A case study on the Costa Rica Dome, a highly dynamic and productive ecosystem that shifts and straddles five countries and international waters, illustrates how progress toward achieving SDG14.2 in the global ocean could be accelerated through the emerging UNCLOS implementing agreement on marine biodiversity beyond national jurisdiction (BBNJ agreement). This chapter concludes with policy recommendations to help drive implementation of SDG 14 through key elements of the BBNJ agreement as well as stepped up scientific capacity development and technology initiatives, including in light of the COVID-19 pandemic. Combining these elements will be essential to strengthen global ocean health and build resilience across multiple spatial and temporal scales.[4]

Assessment of Progress

Despite a growing global understanding about the importance of the ocean for sustainable development, the biodiversity in the ocean continues to decline. According to reporting by the UN[5] and other sources, the indicators for SDG 14 targets on fisheries and ocean acidification show a generally declining trend. While marine pollution remains a widespread problem, some countries have made progress through improved waste and wastewater management. Progress has also been made in the establishment of marine protected areas, although gaps remain, particularly in areas beyond national jurisdiction, as well as regarding management effectiveness.[6]

Like all SDGs, SDG 14 is implemented on multiple levels from global to local. Primary responsibility lies with national governments; however, the implementation of SDG 14 can only be achieved through persistent, supportive, and inclusive international cooperation and collaboration.[7] The progress that has been made toward achieving SDG 14 was kick-started by the United Nations Ocean Conference, held in June 2017, and led by Sweden's and Fiji's governments. With approximately 6,000 people in attendance, the conference aimed to "be the game changer that will reverse the decline in the health of our ocean for people, planet and prosperity."[8] A second UN Ocean Conference, now postponed due to COVID-19, was scheduled to take place on June 2–6, 2020, in Lisbon, Portugal.[9]

As part of the outcomes of the 1st Conference, stakeholders registered voluntary commitments for implementation of SDG 14. The registration of these commitments

---

3 *See* SDG 14.2 (By 2020, sustainably manage and protect marine and coastal ecosystems to avoid significant adverse impacts, including by strengthening their resilience, and take action for their restoration in order to achieve healthy and productive oceans).
4 Guillermo Ortuño Crespo et al., *Beyond Static Spatial Management: Scientific and Legal Considerations for Dynamic Management in the High Seas*, MARINE POLICY (July 2020) 1, 10 https://doi.org/10.1016/j.marpol.2020.104102.
5 UN Statistics Division, *Reporting on SDG 14*: https://unstats.un.org/sdgs/report/2019/goal-14/.
6 *Marine Protected Areas*, PROTECTED PLANET, www.protectedplanet.net/marine.
7 Ronán Long, Mariamalia Rodriguez Chaves, *Bridging the Ocean, Water and Climate Action Goals under the 2030 Agenda on Sustainable Development*, *in* THE MARINE ENVIRONMENT AND UNITED NATIONS SUSTAINABLE DEVELOPMENT GOAL 14: LIFE BELOW WATER 83, 110 (Myron H. Nordquist, John Norton Moore, Roman Long eds., 2019).
8 *See* UN SDG MEDIA WEBSITE: www.un.org/sdgmediazone/ocean_conference-2017.shtml.
9 *See* UN OCEAN CONFERENCE WEBSITE: www.un.org/en/conferences/ocean2020. "https://www.un.org/en/conferences/ocean2020" https://www.un.org/en/conferences/ocean2020

continues, and to date 1,643[10] commitments have been registered by entities including governments, the United Nations (UN) system, other intergovernmental organizations, international and regional financial institutions, non-governmental organizations, civil society organizations, academic and research institutions, the scientific community, the private sector, and philanthropic organizations and other actors, either individually or in partnership. Collectively, the commitments cover all ocean basins and SDG 14 targets, with most commitments relating to more than one target.[11] Many commitment-makers continue to work together on priority SDG 14-related topics through "Communities of Ocean Action." The UN Secretary-General appointed a Special Envoy for the Ocean, Peter Thomson, to foster progress.[12]

The SDG 14 commitments range widely in focus, scope, and ambition.[13] Some topics are of emerging focus such as marine plastics, blue economy development and ocean acidification, and climate adaptation and mitigation. Other topics are older, but still priorities, including:

- Ecosystem-based management, marine spatial planning (MSP), and marine protected area (MPA) establishment;
- Improved fisheries management, ending illegal, unreported, and unregulated (IUU) fishing (including through the Port State Measures Agreement), support to RFMOs, and industry initiatives;
- Sustainable shipping—industry initiatives for low carbon fuels;
- Increasing scientific knowledge—ocean observation, monitoring, scientific research, and capacity building;
- Empowering small-scale and artisanal fishers.

While these voluntary commitments come with a considerable monetary commitment of approximately $25.5 billion,[14] large questions remain as to whether these voluntary commitments can collectively help deliver the SDG 14 targets. Financial data remains patchy and incomplete. Monitoring and reporting remain a major challenge in assessing progress. Many commitments do not undertake formal monitoring, making it difficult to determine both individual and collective impact. Only approximately 24% of the voluntary commitments have provided updates, although the number will likely increase prior to the second UN Ocean Conference.[15]

The High-Level Political Forum (HLPF) has had a slightly better reporting rate on SDG implementation by governments. In the years between 2016 and 2019, 142 countries in

---

10 *Note* this number is current as of August 10, 2020.
11 Marjo Vierros & Roberto Buonomo, *In-Depth Analysis of Ocean Conference Voluntary Commitments to Support and Monitor Their Implementation*, 1, 74 UN-DESA (2017), https://sustainabledevelopment.un.org/content/documents/17193OCVC_in_depth_analysis.pdf.
12 *Mr. Peter Thomson of Fiji—Special Envoy for the Ocean*, UN (Sept. 12, 2017), www.un.org/sg/en/content/sg/personnel-appointments/2017-09-12/mr-peter-thomson-fiji-special-envoy-ocean.
13 *The Registry of Voluntary Commitments*, UN OCEAN CONFERENCE, https://oceanconference.un.org/commitments/ [hereinafter "Registry"].
14 *See* Vierros, *supra* note 11.
15 This figure was calculated based on the Voluntary Commitment Registry, *see supra* note 13. Out of the 1,614 commitments, 387 have reported on their progress. Thirty are less than a year old and are not yet due for a report. Note that this figure is correct as of August 10, 2020, but the reporting percentage has remained consistent since the first calculations were made in early 2020.

total have submitted voluntary national reviews (VNRs).[16] However, not all of the VNRs include information on SDG 14 implementation, and the quantity and quality of information provided was variable, focusing in general on national regulations, policies and management actions, as well as challenges faced. The Inter-Agency Expert Group on SDG Indicators reported that it lacks sufficient data to assess progress toward most of the ocean targets.[17] As discussed in the section below on the Central Role of SDG 14.2, some of the indicators themselves may be insufficient to truly measure progress. It had been hoped that the June 2020 2nd UN Ocean Conference could help to accelerate progress, but the Conference has been postponed due to COVID-19 until at least 2021.[18]

However, it is unlikely that this action, including the galvanization the UN Ocean Conference could have provided, had it occurred, would match the scale of the cumulative stressors facing the global ocean, including increasing impacts from climate change.[19] As noted in the recent report from the UN Secretary-General on implementation of SDG 14,[20] progress varies between countries and regions, and "depends on various factors such as the availability of science and innovation, capacity-building and financing, as well as the level of intersectoral and interdisciplinary cooperation at the national, regional and global levels."[21] Further challenges include the integration of the conservation and sustainable management of marine and coastal ecosystems into national development plans; mainstreaming the consideration of biodiversity into sectors such as fisheries and aquaculture; embracing gender equality and women's empowerment; lack of consistent, accessible data; insufficient data sharing; limited coordination and insufficient resources; increases in risks to critical coastal transportation infrastructure; and inadequate cooperation and synergies in implementing biodiversity-related conventions.[22]

Going forward, the conservation and management of the ocean will be impacted in a variety of ways by COVID-19.[23] Early indications are that the demand for seafood has declined, resulting in reduced income and health risks for fishers and fishworkers, along with economic and social insecurity. While reduced enforcement and suspension of fisheries observer programs may lead to an increase in IUU fishing, the reduction in fishing effort may conversely also provide an opportunity for certain vulnerable stocks to recover.[24] Conservation and ocean science may suffer from social distancing measures, as well as

---

16 *Voluntary National Reviews Database*, SUSTAINABLE DEVELOPMENT KNOWLEDGE PLATFORM, https://sustainabledevelopment.un.org/vnrs/.
17 *Measuring Progress: Towards Achieving the Environmental Dimension of the SDGs*, UN ENVIRONMENT 2019, https://wedocs.unep.org/bitstream/handle/20.500.11822/27627/MeaProg2019.pdf?sequence=1&isAllowed=y.
18 G.A. Decision 74/548—*Decision to Postpone the Conference to a Later Date*, www.un.org/pga/74/2020/04/07/un-ocean-conference-3/ (accessed Nov. 5, 2020).
19 *Special Report on the Ocean and the Cryosphere in a Changing Climate*, IPCC, Summary for Policymakers (2019), www.ipcc.ch/srocc/.
20 Rep. of S-G, U.N. Doc. A/74/360 (Dec. 24, 2019), https://undocs.org/en/a/74/630.
21 *Id*. Further details on the implementation of each target is available in the SDG 14 progress report for 2019: https://sustainabledevelopment.un.org/sdg14.
22 *Id*.
23 UN General Assembly, *Global Solidarity to Fight the Coronavirus Disease 2019 (COVID-19)*, A/RES/74/270 (Apr. 3, 2020), https://undocs.org/en/A/RES/74/270.
24 *How is COVID-19 Affecting the Fisheries and Aquaculture Food Systems*, FOOD AND AGRICULTURE ORGANIZATION OF THE UNITED NATIONS (Apr. 10, 2020), www.fao.org/3/ca8637en/CA8637EN.pdf; Nathan J. Bennett et al., *The COVID-19 Pandemic, Small-Scale Fisheries and Coastal Fishing Communities*, 48 COASTAL MANAGEMENT (May 22, 2020), https://doi.org/10.1080/08920753.2020.1766937.

reduced funding as governments deal with an economic slowdown or recession. Many oceanographic cruises have already been put on hold.[25] Reduced tourism will also impact marine conservation, given that many marine protected areas are funded through visitor fees, and may need to lay off staff and reduce management, monitoring, and enforcement measures.[26] Internationally, several important ocean-relevant meetings, such as the 2020 United Nations Ocean Conference and the 4th Intergovernmental Conference[27] have been put on hold.

At the same time, COVID 19 has brought to focus the importance of the rich marine biodiversity in the ocean for human health. Drugs from marine sources are being investigated for their potential to help in the fight against the pandemic, and Remdesivir, an experimental antiviral derived from sea sponges is being explored for use in the treatment of patients with COVID-19.[28] In addition, the Woods Hole Oceanographic Institute recently reported that an enzyme isolated from a hydrothermal vent bacteria discovered by their scientists years ago is now being used in the test to diagnose the novel coronavirus.[29] These developments highlight the importance of marine biodiversity, including genetic diversity, for future solutions for humankind's pressing problems.

The following sections look more specifically at SDG 14.2, using as a case study the Costa Rica Dome, an area spanning both national waters and areas beyond national jurisdiction.

The Central Role of SDG 14.2 for Ocean Sustainability and Resiliency

Key priority actions for implementing SDG 14 are outlined in target 14.2, which aims to, "by 2020, sustainably manage and protect marine and coastal ecosystems to avoid significant adverse impacts, including by strengthening their resilience, and take action for their restoration in order to achieve healthy and productive oceans."[30] SDG 14.2 thus requires a science-based and ecosystem-based approach to its implementation. Broken down into component parts, this means (a) current uses are ecologically sustainable; (b) all marine and coastal ecosystems are effectively managed and/or protected; and (c) current and any future activities are managed to avoid significant adverse impacts, including with respect to cumulative effects. It also means that management and decision-making are guided by the need to strengthen the resilience of ecosystems and human communities and restore ocean ecosystems and species.

Because of the multiple actions included in SDG 14.2, it is also the target that received the most voluntary commitments, which currently total 828.[31] The measures pledged

---

25 *IOC Responses to the COVID-19 Crisis: Information* (Apr. 27, 2020), https://en.unesco.org/news/ioc-responses-covid-19-crisis-information-meeting; Robert Monroe, *Research in the Time of COVID* (Apr. 9, 2020), Scripps Institution of Oceanography, https://scripps.ucsd.edu/news/research-time-covid-19.
26 *COVID-19 and Marine World Heritage: A Pathway for a Resilient Ocean* (May 20, 2020), whc.unesco.org/en/news/2118.
27 *Note*: Meetings aimed to negotiate a new international legally binding instrument under UNCLOS.
28 Torsten Thiele, *A Healthy Ocean Can Help Fight Pandemics*, CHINA DIALOGUE OCEAN (May 4, 2020), https://chinadialogueocean.net/13619-healthy-ocean-help-fight-pandemics/; Daniel O'Day, *An Open Letter from our Chairman & CEO*, Stories @ Gilead (Apr. 29, 2020), GILEAD news release at www.gilead.com/stories/articles/an-open-letter-from-our-chairman-and-ceo-april-29.
29 Elisa Hugus, *Finding Answers in the Ocean*, WHOI (Mar. 19, 2020), www.whoi.edu/news-insights/content/finding-answers-in-the-ocean/.
30 2030 Agenda, *supra* note 1.
31 *Registry*, supra note 13.

toward this target generally include aspects of ecosystem-based management, including integrated coastal management, MSP, and MPAs. The Large Marine Ecosystem (LME) Approach was an important measure in these commitments, as were community-based marine areas and climate adaptation measures.[32] There is a large degree of overlap between measures addressing this target and target 14.5 on conserving 10% of coastal and marine areas, given that area-based measures can provide for sustainable management, conservation of specific areas, and climate resilience. Target 14.4 on sustainable fisheries is closely related to the present target because many of the measures to implement it (particularly the LME approach and marine managed areas) also address fisheries management.[33]

Measuring progress toward SDG 14.2 is made more difficult because the relevant indicator focuses solely on areas within national jurisdiction ("*Proportion of national exclusive economic zones managed using ecosystem-based approaches* (Indicator 14.2.1)).[34] Yet the ocean is inherently interconnected. It is thus vital to coordinate research and management action from coastal areas to national Exclusive Economic Zones (EEZs) and into areas beyond national jurisdiction. Actions undertaken in isolation are unlikely to be as effective as they could be when coordinated across ocean spaces. Other indicators for SDG 14 do not make a distinction between marine life within or beyond national jurisdiction, and indeed most could not be achieved without global cooperation.[35] Actions undertaken to implement SDG 14.2 should similarly reflect the reality of the interconnected ocean by aiming to improve the status of biodiversity beyond national jurisdiction including through the application of ecosystem-based approaches.[36] Such efforts would be accelerated by the four primary elements of the BBNJ agreement: (a) area-based management tools, including marine protected areas, (b) environmental impact assessments (EIAs) and strategic environmental assessments, (c) capacity building and technology transfer, as well as (d) mechanisms for sharing benefits related to marine genetic resources.[37]

Similarly, the indicator for the cross-cutting target 14.C relates to the number of countries making progress in ratifying, accepting, and implementing through ocean-related frameworks and instruments that implement international law, as reflected in UNCLOS for the conservation and sustainable use of the oceans and their resources. It should more specifically refer to progress in developing, ratifying, and implementing a key tool for making this happen: the emerging BBNJ agreement on marine biodiversity beyond national jurisdiction. Thus, further attention to elaborating additional indicators is required to comprehensively track the implementation of SDG 14.

Addressing marine degradation beyond national jurisdiction through the BBNJ agreement is essential for ensuring environmental security for all States. However, for the BBNJ

---

32 *See* Vierros, *supra* note 11.
33 *Id.*
34 UN General Assembly, *Work of the Statistical Commission Pertaining to the 2030 Agenda for Sustainable Development*, A/RES/71/313 (Jul. 10, 2017), https://undocs.org/A/RES/71/313.
35 *Sustainable Development Goals Knowledge Platform: SDG 14 Targets & Indicators*. https://sustainabledevelopment.un.org/sdg14.
36 Kristina Gjerde & Glen Wright, *Towards Ecosystem-Based Management of the Global Ocean: Strengthening Regional Cooperation through a New Agreement for the Conservation and Sustainable Use of Marine Biodiversity in Areas Beyond National Jurisdiction*, IDDRI (Dec. 2019), www.iddri.org/en/publications-and-events/report/towards-ecosystem-based-management-global-ocean.
37 Glen Wright et al., *The Long and Winding Road: Negotiating a Treaty for the Conservation and Sustainable Use of Marine Biodiversity in Areas Beyond National Jurisdiction*, IDDRI, 1, 82 (Aug. 2018), www.iddri.org/en/publications-and-events/study/long-and-winding-road-negotiating-high-seas-treaty.

agreement to become a priority for developing countries, it will need to provide clear national benefits for biodiversity and people through reducing hunger and poverty, and by improving economic development through sustainable blue economies. Thus, those negotiating the new international agreement on BBNJ will need to consider/include overlaps with SDG 14 and those tasked with implementing SDG 14 need to ensure that they consider activities across the entire ocean.

This is not happening at the present time since the focus of a majority of the commitments is on national EEZs and coastal areas, and there has, to date, been little focus on biodiversity beyond national jurisdiction. A closer look at the voluntary commitments covering actions of relevance to ocean protection and management reveals that only 27 of the 1,586 commitments explicitly reference "areas beyond national jurisdiction," "high seas," and/ or "international waters."[38] Out of these, six relate to commitments that primarily address marine areas beyond national jurisdiction, while the rest pertain to both areas within and beyond national jurisdiction.[39] The six commitments address improving collaboration between regional fisheries and biodiversity management organizations; improving scientific knowledge of the deep sea; creating a database of managed areas in the high seas; strengthening capacity for international cooperation in ecosystem-based management of the Antarctic Large Marine Ecosystem; developing new tools to support conservation and sustainable management of marine biodiversity; and improving scientific knowledge of fish stocks in the Central Arctic Ocean.[40] It is likely that the registry of voluntary commitments contains other activities that are of direct relevance to Areas Beyond National Jurisdiction (ABNJ) even if this relevance is not specifically articulated, and thus the numbers as reflected here may be a slight underestimate.

While the above measures are important for realizing target 14.2, they do not represent the full range of important actions that should be deployed in the context of this target. Particularly in the context of national EEZs, as well as the emerging BBNJ agreement, SDG 14.2 could further incorporate EIAs and strategic environmental assessments (SEAs) accompanied by requirements to manage activities to "avoid significant adverse impacts," or not to authorize the activity to proceed. The broader application of SEAs based on integrated ecological assessments of relevant eco-regions, in particular, would provide for improved implementation of an ecosystem approach, while also taking into account impacts of climate change in future management measures. It would also provide for closer linkages between SDG 14 and a new BBNJ agreement. This topic is discussed in more detail in the Case Study and Policy Recommendations sections.

Case Study on Costa Rica Dome

The value of combined implementation of SDG 14, and in particular 14.2, with the major components of a new international agreement on BBNJ can be demonstrated through a case study involving the Costa Rica Dome. The Costa Rica Dome is a biodiversity hotspot in the Eastern Tropical Pacific. It is an oceanographic feature straddling areas within and beyond national jurisdiction, and its high productivity is due to the upwelling of deep nutrient-rich water, which supports an entire food chain from plankton to whales. Multiple species

---

38 *Registry*, supra note 11.
39 *Id.*
40 *Id.*

benefit from this habitat, including yellowfin tunas, blue whales, dolphins, sailfish, silky sharks, and leatherback turtles.[41] Due to its high productivity and importance as a habitat for marine species, the Costa Rica Dome has been recognized by the Convention on Biological Diversity as an Ecologically or Biologically Significant Area (EBSA).[42]

The species inhabiting the Dome bring economic benefits to countries in the region. For example, in 2009 the fishing industry in Central America generated approximately $750 million for economies within the region, thus benefiting close to 450,000 people.[43] Tourism related to sea turtle nesting generated approximately $2,113,176 in 2004 for tour operators and related businesses close to Las Baulas Marine National Park in Costa Rica,[44] while whale and dolphin watching is a growing industry in the region that produces important economic income for coastal communities.[45] These and many other species utilizing the Costa Rica Dome are highly migratory, connecting the Dome habitat to coastal areas of Central America, Mexico, North America, and, in the case of the leatherback turtle, the Pacific Islands.[46]

Marine species spending parts of their life cycles at the Costa Rica Dome face threats such as incidental bycatch in fisheries (dolphins, leatherback turtles, silky sharks), collision with ships and noise from shipping (leatherback turtles, blue whales), alteration of coastal and nesting beach habitat and unsustainable egg harvest (leatherback turtles), and other less well-understood threats such as climate change.[47] The blue whale is considered endangered due to past indiscriminate fishing, which caused a drastic decline in its population. Even though it has been protected internationally since 1986, its population remains reduced.[48] The biomass of silky sharks has been reduced by more than 90% in the region,[49] while leatherback turtles are considered critically endangered in the Pacific Ocean, having experienced severe population declines.[50]

Response measures that need to be undertaken to protect the Dome and the species that utilize it include (a) a region-wide environmental assessment to identify priorities for protection and management on an ecosystem-basis (while acting on a precautionary basis using the best available knowledge to reduce ongoing impacts); (b) EIAs prior to new

---

41 *The Costa Rica Thermic Dome*, MARVIVA, http://crdome.marviva.net/?page_id=2677&lang=en.
42 CBD COP Decision XII/22 (Oct. 2014) Marine and coastal biodiversity: ecologically or biologically significant marine areas (EBSAs) welcoming the EBSA workshop reports including on the Eastern Tropical and Temperate Pacific (Galapagos, Ecuador, August 28–31, 2012); *See* UNEP/CBD/RW/EBSA/ETTP/1/4 for the workshop report, and the CBD EBSA website for an interactive map and links to further information: www.cbd.int/ebsa/.
43 *Pacific Ocean Synthesis: Scientific Literature Review of Coastal and Ocean Threats, Impacts, and Solution*, CENTER FOR OCEAN SOLUTIONS, at 42 (2009), www.pacificclimatechange.net/document/pacific-ocean-synthesis-scientific-literature-review-coastal-and-ocean-threats-impacts-and.
44 Sebastian Troëng & Carlos Drews, *Money Talks: Economic Aspects of Marine Turtle Use and Conservation*, WWF (Jan. 7, 2009), wwf.panda.org/wwf_news/?153802/wwwpandaorglacmarineturtlespublications.
45 MarViva, *supra* note 41.
46 George L Shillinger et al., *Persistent Leatherback Turtle Migrations Present Opportunities for Conservation*, 6 PLOS BIOLOGY 1408, 1416 (Jul. 15, 2008), https://doi.org/10.1371/journal.pbio.0060171.
47 Jorge A, Jiménez, *The Thermal Dome of Costa Rica: An Oasis of Productivity at the Pacific Coast of Central America*, FUNDACIÓN MARVIVA (2017), https://marviva.net/sites/default/files/documentos/el_domo_termico_de_cr_ingles_web_.pdf.
48 *Id.*
49 *IUCN Red List of Threatened Species*, IUCN, www.iucnredlist.org.
50 *Id.*; Scott R. Benson et al., *Leatherback Turtle Populations in the Pacific Ocean*, in THE LEATHERBACK TURTLE: BIOLOGY AND CONSERVATION, 110–22 (James R. Spotila & Pilar Santidrián Tomillo, eds., 2015).

activities being approved or existing activities expanded; (c) area-based management tools to protect, maintain, or rebuild resilience in accordance with SDG 14 targets 2 and 5, including one or more highly protected MPAs, potential shipping routing measures, dynamic area-based management; and (d) fisheries by-catch measures consistent with SDG 14 targets 2 and 4. Collaboration among regional countries and the global community have already advanced scientific knowledge about the Dome, with likely further work on the way, and have catalyzed regional attention toward governance solutions.

However, the Costa Rica Dome presents a particular challenge because its diameter and position changes as part of an annual cycle as well as from year to year. Depending on its annual cycle, its position can include parts of the Exclusive Economic Zones of Costa Rica, Nicaragua, El Salvador, Guatemala, and Mexico, as well as areas beyond national jurisdiction. There is currently no legal mechanism that would allow countries in the region to undertake comprehensive science-based multisectoral area-based management of the Dome, particularly in areas beyond national jurisdiction, undertake EIAs or SEAs, nor access information and data to enable near-real time dynamic ocean management to protect mobile species and their habitat.[51] Thus, without an international BBNJ agreement that would provide for such management measures, it will be difficult for countries in the region to realize SDG 14 for the Costa Rica Dome, and by extension the coastal areas that are ecologically interconnected with it. This case study demonstrates how the implementation of SDG 14 is dependent on the legal framework of a new BBNJ agreement.

Policy Recommendations for Jointly Implementing SDG 14 and the BBNJ Agreement

As noted above, implementation of SDG 14.2 entails a comprehensive, science-based, and multijurisdictional ecosystem approach guided by effective governance and management institutions with shared objectives of ecological sustainability; protecting and managing marine and coastal ecosystems to avoid significant adverse impacts; and strengthening the resilience of ecosystems and human communities to safeguard and restore ocean ecosystems and species.

As evidenced by the Costa Rica Dome case study, achieving SDG 14 requires ambitious action on the scale of the global ocean, as coastal areas are interconnected with the high seas, and migratory species and ocean currents connect countries and continents. An important enabling condition for ambitious action is coherence between policy processes, which include SDG 14 and the BBNJ agreement, as well as other global, regional, and national ocean-relevant processes. Creating such policy coherence would align global and regional goals, obligations, standards, and principles for integrated ocean management. Viewed through an ecosystem approach perspective, actions to implement SDG 14 would need to be taken across the ocean in its entirety, be holistic and cross-sectoral, and engage the coordinated efforts of all ocean users and stakeholders.

For this to happen, key requirements for advancing ecosystem-based management in the global ocean, as adapted from Gjerde and Wright (2020)[52] include the following:

---

51 Crespo et al., *supra* note 4; *See also* Maxwell et al., *Mobile Protected Areas for Biodiversity on the High Seas*, 367 SCIENCE 252–54 (Jan 17, 2020), DOI. 10.1126/science.aaz9327.
52 *The Science We Need for the Ocean We* Want, United Nations Decade of Ocean Science for Sustainable Development, Preparatory Phase 2018–2020, www.oceandecade.org/.

- **Improving scientific understanding of ocean ecosystems**, their functioning, and the impacts of multiple stressors on their capacity to provide goods and services, including for human health. Increasing capacity for scientific research and associated technology through international cooperation, as well as by publishing and openly sharing data and information, are key for achieving both SDG 14.A and the BBNJ agreement. Initiatives such as the UN Decade on Ocean Science have the potential to improve scientific capacity worldwide and to improve the scientific basis upon which governance decisions are based.
- **Advancing the ecosystem approach**, through management action applying available and tested tools and approaches, including MPAs, MSP, and other area-based management tools, including dynamic area-based management tools, based on eco-regional SEAs. To reduce ongoing impacts and build resilience to future impacts, ecosystem-based action would need to be undertaken on a precautionary basis, using the best available knowledge, including science and traditional knowledge.
- **Avoiding significant adverse impacts**. SEAs, EIA processes, management, and decision-making should reflect the need to manage activities to avoid significant adverse impacts as called for in SDG 14.2.
- **Ensuring consistent and long-term monitoring**. Monitoring tools need to address global, regional, and local impacts on marine ecosystems and species, to underpin adaptive management to adjust activities as required. In addition, the current indicators selected to measure SDG 14.2 and 14.C need to be refined so that progress is measured across the entire ocean.
- **National strategies and action plans** should (a) address marine biodiversity within and beyond national jurisdiction, linking these measures to national sustainable development and climate adaptation strategies through inter-agency collaboration; (b) consider how these measures contribute, on a regional scale and through collaboration with regional agencies, to management measures undertaken in ABNJ; and (c) ensure that activities under the jurisdiction and control of the State do not negatively affect marine biodiversity in ABNJ.
- **An enabling institutional environment** should include (a) sufficient and sustainable financing, capacity, staff, and technology (see Box 21.1) to create strong national and regional institutions; (b) mechanisms for national and regional cross-sectoral dialog to ensure policy coherence in implementation of all ocean-relevant obligations, and in linking SDG 14 to other SDGs; and (c) for ABNJ, key institutional elements to accompany the overarching environmental obligations and principles, including: a robust global body such as a Conference of Parties capable of taking decisions and adopting recommendations; strengthened regional mechanisms for integrated policy development and coordination; robust science-policy advisory mechanisms; and regular compliance and implementation review.
- **Sustainable financing, capacity development, and technology transfer** to ensure that all countries are able to implement both the BBNJ agreement and SDG 14, and to benefit from the development of sustainable and inclusive blue economies. In particular, it is important to increase the capacity and opportunities available for young scientists in developing countries, including young women.

In the short term, it is important that governments view post-COVID recovery as an opportunity to put in place the actions and policies that are needed for a more sustainable ocean, and that help build more equitable blue economies that promote the well-being of all people, including the marginalized. While COVID-19 recovery plans should provide immediate relief measures for the most vulnerable, they should also prioritize measures that support conservation and restoration of ocean life, and that fund activities by ocean sectors that are both economically and socially sustainable, as agreed upon in SDG 14.

> **Box 21.1 New 'Omics Tools as an Example of How Capacity Development and Technology Transfer with Respect to Marine Genetic Resources under the BBNJ Agreement Could Provide Multiple Benefits for Sustainability**
>
> Given the sustainable development focus of SDG 14, its implementation could also further innovate on new tools that bring together economic development with social and environmental sustainability, such as new genomics tools. 'Omics (e.g., genomics, proteomics, metabolomics) show promise across fisheries management, aquaculture development, food and water safety, species and habitat conservation, seafood consumer protection, and natural products discovery. 'Omics also provides a case study of some of the relationships that connect SDG 14 to other SDGs.
>
> 'Omics tools can jointly advance SDGs 14 and 3 (good health and well-being) through their ability to detect and monitor harmful algal blooms, toxins, pathogens, and invasive species, thus protecting human health and coastal economies. They can advance SDG 14.4 and SDGs 2 and 8 (zero hunger and decent work and economic growth) by improving fisheries management and consumer protection through genetic analysis to identify fraudulent and illegally sourced seafood products. Fisheries management (SDG 14.4) will benefit from the ability of 'omics to increase the understanding of fisheries population structure, distribution, and food webs. Human health and national economies, including in Small Island Developing States (SIDS) and Least Developed Countries (SDG 14.7 and SDGs 3 and 8) can benefit from advancing the discovery of natural products that may have medical or other commercial value, and such economic development can also advance gender equality through providing skilled jobs, including for women (SDG 5 on gender equality). Better access to 'omics tools could also help both developing and developed countries in transitioning to sustainable blue economies, and promote sustainable resource use both within and beyond national jurisdiction. They can also help implement the marine genetic resources and benefit-sharing provisions of the BBNJ agreement. Overall, such tools foster innovation, which jointly supports the attainment of SDGs 14 and 9 (industry, innovation, and infrastructure), and the BBNJ agreement.

Conclusions

Most of the priority actions discussed in the previous section contribute to several SDG 14 targets, as well as to other SDGs, and represent priorities for governments wishing to maximize co-benefits and win-win scenarios. For example, area-based management, including through MPAs, builds ecosystem resilience to the impacts of climate change linking it to SDG 13, enhances the recovery and overall health of fisheries and human communities depending on seafood (SDG 2 and 3), provides economic opportunities through marine tourism (SDG 8), and builds more sustainable communities (SDG 11). At the same time, the success of these priority actions, and the overall achievement of SDG 14, depends on many other SDGs, including SDG 12 on responsible consumption and production (including for achieving responsible fishing and reduction of marine plastics and wastewater), SDG 13 on climate change (including for controlling ocean warming, acidification, and de-oxygenation), SDG 15 on peace, justice, and strong institutions (including for putting in place good governance and strong institutions), and SDG 15 on terrestrial ecosystems (including for controlling land-based sources of marine pollution). These are but a few examples of the many interlinkages that need to be taken into account in implementing SDG 14. Thus, collaboration and cooperation between agencies and organizations implementing various SDGs is key for realizing co-benefits and win-win situations.

In summary, SDG 14 has been successful in increasing focus on the ocean in the context of sustainable development. It has also been successful in providing for inclusive participation from stakeholders. Communities for Ocean Action and a UN Envoy for the Ocean are new tools for implementation. SDG 14 has provided focus on emerging issues, like ocean plastics and the blue economy. There has been less success however in producing accountability (e.g., reporting on measures taken, particularly for voluntary commitments), making it difficult to measure the collective impact of the actions taken on the ocean and its biodiversity. On top of this, the actions taken may not be on a scale sufficient to respond to global problems such as ocean degradation due to climate change. And unless the issues of high seas degradation and transboundary cooperation are addressed, progress will be stymied.

In short, achievement of SDG-14 depends on four concrete actions accompanied by improved SDG 14 indicators to assess progress:

(1) Mechanisms to enhance inter-sectoral cooperation between ocean-related agreements, including pursuant to a robust and rapidly finalized BBNJ agreement, and within agencies globally, regionally, and nationally to implement coordinated ecosystem-based action across the entire ocean;
(2) Shared obligations and objectives to promote in-situ conservation of ecosystems and natural habitats and to mainstream biodiversity commitments including SDG 14 into all decision-making bodies and processes;
(3) The strengthening of regional cooperation by supporting and upgrading existing institutions, establishing new ones where necessary, such as cross-sectoral platforms for cooperation; and
(4) A large-scale commitment to mandatory funding, capacity building, and technology transfer to ensure that ocean action is equitably and sustainably resourced in the long term, and that no country or community is left behind.

22 Legal Tools in Combating Marine Pollution and Mitigating the Effects of Acidification

Annick de Marffy-Mantuano

After almost three decades, too little progress has been achieved in protecting, preserving, and promoting the sustainable use of the ocean and its resources for the benefit of mankind. Many efforts, however, have been deployed within conferences, summits, and meetings with highly competent experts, such as scientists, diplomats, and international lawyers covering a wide range of fields. After all these years, the state of the marine environment is not improving as fast as it should be. The question to ask is why has so little progress been achieved? The answer belongs once more to the international community, as well as to national policymakers. They should take more forceful actions in implementing the Sustainable Development Goals (SDGs) contained in the 2030 Agenda.[1]

The tools exist to achieve the SDGs, and particularly SDG 14 in combating marine pollution. However, national governments lack the political will to implement decisions at the international level. Policymakers have been the first in line for implementing commitments made at the international level since 1972 when the first summit took place in Stockholm to protect our planet.[2] Many treaties and agreements have been adopted to comply with such commitments.

The long political process that led to the adoption of the SDGs, and among them SDG 14 dealing with oceans, has been very rich, bringing a wealth of information and coherent proposals. These decisions have contributed to the adoption of relevant regulations and measures aimed at improving the health of the oceans at both the state and international level. These instruments are either compulsory, like treaties or agreements, or voluntary, such as programs, recommendations, or resolutions (soft law), that States and international organizations should endeavor to apply.

The section "Instruments, Compulsory or Voluntary, to Combat all Kinds of Pollution and to Mitigate the Effects of Acidification" of this chapter will explore the international instruments that could

> [by 2025] prevent and significantly reduce marine pollution of all kinds, in particular from land-based activities, including marine debris and nutrient pollution;"[3] "minimize

---

1 *See* U.N. Secretary General, *Implementation of Agenda 21, the Programme for the Further Implementation of Agenda 21 and the outcomes of the World Summit on Sustainable Development and of the United Nations Conference on Sustainable Development*, U.N. Doc. A/71/212 (Jul. 26, 2016).
2 *See* Stockholm, United Nations Conference on the Human Environment, A.Conf.48/14/Rev. (Jun. 15–16, 1972).
3 G.A. Res. 70/1, *Transforming our world: the 2030 Agenda for Sustainable Development*, Goal 14.1 at 23 (Sept. 25, 2015) [hereinafter "2030 Agenda"].

and address the impacts of ocean acidification including through enhanced scientific cooperation at all levels[4]

and

enhance the conservation and sustainable use of oceans and their resources by implementing international law as reflected *in* UNCLOS, which provides the legal framework for the conservation and sustainable use of oceans and their resources, as recalled in paragraph 158 of The Future We Want.[5]

The section "An Assessment on the Degree of Implementation of Legal Instruments" will discuss the essential elements in determining the efficiency of legal instruments. Multiple levels of analysis could be conducted to determine the efficacy of existing instruments that could curb marine pollution. One such analysis is determining whether States consented to become parties to treaties and monitoring actions taken by international organizations to implement programs, such as adopting new rules and regulations. This chapter concludes by recommending that States efficiently implement existing rules and notes that there must be sufficient knowledge and understanding of applicable international instruments, particularly those that enhance coordinated approaches between States to avoid duplicative efforts.

Instruments, Compulsory or Voluntary, to Combat all Kinds of Pollution and to Mitigate the Effects of Acidification

The UN Convention on the Law of the Sea (UNCLOS) is recognized by Goal 14 as reflecting the international rules which could, if effectively implemented, enhance the conservation and sustainable use of oceans and their resources.[6] Articles 192 and 194 contain general obligations to protect and preserve the marine environment and request States to take measures to prevent, reduce, and control pollution of the marine environment.[7] States shall adopt laws and regulations to deal with specific sources of pollution of the marine environment, such as from land-based activities, from seabed sources subject to national jurisdiction, from activities in the area, by dumping, from vessels, and from and through the atmosphere (Articles 207 to 212).[8] Another set of rules established by the Convention requires States to adopt enforcement measures to comply with the laws and regulations to combat all kinds of pollution (Articles 213 to 222).[9]

Part XII of the Convention recognizes and mandates regional approaches (Article 197).[10] The provisions regulating the marine environment are also found outside Part XII, which

---

4 *Id*. at Goal 14.3 at 23.
5 *Id*. at Goal 14.c at 24.
6 U.N. Convention on the Law of the Sea, art. 1(4), Dec. 10, 1982, 1833 U.N.T.S. 397 (UNCLOS). The term pollution is defined in article 1 (4). It reads as follows: "pollution of the marine environment means the introduction by man, directly or indirectly, of substances or energy into the marine environment, including estuaries, which results or is likely to result in such deleterious effects as harm to living resources and marine life, hazards to human health, hindrance to marine activities, including fishing and other legitimate uses of the sea, impairment of quality for use of sea water and reduction of amenities."
7 *Id*. at art. 192, 194.
8 *Id*. at art. 207–12.
9 *Id*. at art. 213–22.
10 *Id*. at art. 197.

reflects the close relationship between the different parts of UNCLOS. The Convention has struck an important balance between the protection of the marine environment and the uses of the oceans and their resources.[11]

UNCLOS has three important features, which have contributed to shaping the development of marine environmental law. First, the Convention calls for international rules, standards, and recommended practices and procedures to be further developed at the global and regional levels, as long as the specific obligations assumed by States under special conventions are carried out in a manner consistent with the general principles and objectives of UNCLOS (Article 237).[12] Second, the Convention, as a dynamic instrument, requires that rules established through competent international organizations or diplomatic conferences be re-examined from time to time as necessary.[13] Finally, the Convention has called for the development of non-binding instruments (soft law), such as recommended practices, guidelines, and criteria, which establish benchmarks for the development of national laws and policies.

In addition to UNCLOS, other conventions, agreements, programs, and guidelines have called for the protection of the environment. Agenda 21 requests States to combat pollution originating from land-based sources, from ships, and by dumping, which legal instruments have been adopted to combat.[14]

Instruments to Combat Land-Based Sources of Pollution

Land-based sources contribute to 80% of marine pollution.[15] Many of the polluting substances are particularly concerning due to their toxicity, persistence, and bioaccumulation of harmful toxins in the food chain of the marine environment. There are no general binding instruments addressing this issue at the global level except for those aimed at combating specific pollutants. At the regional level, binding conventions have been adopted to combat pollution from land-based activities.

At the Global Level

UNCLOS sets out specific provisions for the prevention, control, and reduction of pollution from land-based sources. The Convention gives States a degree of discretion with respect to implementing international rules, in deference to the sovereignty that a State exercises over the territory where such land-based pollution may arise.

Under Article 207 of UNCLOS, States shall adopt laws and regulations to prevent, reduce, and control pollution from land-based sources, taking into account internationally agreed rules, standards, and recommended practices and procedures, and shall *endeavor* to

---

11 *See* U.N. Secretary General, *Protection and preservation of the marine environment*, U.N. Doc. A/44/461 (Sept. 18, 1989).
12 UNCLOS, *supra* note 6, at art. 237.
13 *Id*. at art. 207 §4, 208 §5, 209 §1, 210 §4, and 211 §1.
14 *See Protection of the Oceans, All Kinds of Seas, Including Enclosed and Semi-Enclosed Seas, and Coastal Areas and the Protection, Rational Use and Development of Their Living Resources*, *in* Report of the United Nations Conference Environment and Development ¶ 17.21, A/CONF.151/26 (June 3–14, 1992) (Agenda 21).
15 *Land-Based Pollution*, UNEP, www.unenvironment.org/explore-topics/oceans-seas/what-we-do/working-regional-seas/land-based-pollution (last visited Nov. 19, 2020).

establish such rules, standards, and recommended practices and procedures at the global and regional levels, acting especially through competent international organizations and diplomatic conferences.[16] In Article 213, States shall enforce their laws and regulations adopted in accordance with Article 207.[17] At the time of the adoption of UNCLOS, only regional rules were in existence, such as the Convention for the Protection of the Marine Environment of the North-East Atlantic (OSPAR Convention).[18]

The Governing Council of the United Nations Environmental Programme (UNEP) identified the question of land-based sources of pollution as one of the three priorities for the development of marine environmental law. In 1985, the Montreal Guidelines for the Protection of the Marine Environment from Land-based Sources were adopted.[19] The Guidelines have set the stage for a more comprehensive and global approach to address the causes of marine and coastal degradation.

Additionally, Chapter 17 of Agenda 21, on the basis of the Montreal Guidelines, made a major contribution in advancing the issue of land-based sources of pollution with an emphasis placed on an integrated approach.[20] The UNEP Governing Council recommended to "consider updating, strengthening and extending the Montreal Guidelines."[21] In an effort to implement the recommendations of the United Nations Conference on Environment and Development (UNCED), two major international documents were adopted in November 1995: (1) the Washington Declaration on the Protection of the Marine Environment from Land-based Activities and (2) the Global Program of Action for the Protection of the Marine Environment from Land-based Activities (GPA).[22] The UN General Assembly, at its Fifty-First Session, adopted the institutional arrangements for the implementation of the GPA and designated UNEP as the lead agency in implementing the GPA.

The GPA addresses the impacts of land-based activities on the marine and coastal environment, including contaminants, physical alteration, point and non-point sources of pollution, and such areas of concern as critical habitats, habitats of endangered species, and the protection of ecosystem components, such as breeding and feeding grounds.[23] The GPA was designed to be a source of conceptual and practical guidance to assist States in addressing land-based sources of pollution.[24] From a strictly legal perspective, both the Washington Declaration and the GPA have no binding force and are considered to be "soft law." They

---

16 UNCLOS, *supra* note 6, at art. 207, ¶¶1,4.
17 *Id.* at art. 213.
18 The Paris Convention on Land Based Sources adopted in 1974 is now the Convention for the Protection of the Marine Environment of the North-East Atlantic, adopted in 1992 (OSPAR). *See About OSPAR*, OSPAR COMMISSION, www.ospar.org/about (last visited Nov. 19, 2020).
19 *See Montreal Guidelines for the Protection of the Marine Environment against Pollution from Land-Based Sources*, Decision 13/18/II of the Governing Council of UNEP, UNEP (092)/ES (May 24, 1985).
20 *See* U.N. Conference on Environment and Development, *Chapter 17: Protection of the Oceans, All Kinds of Seas, Including Enclosed and Semi-Enclosed Seas, And Coastal Areas and The Protection, Rational Use and Development of Their Living Resources*, U.N. Doc. A/CONF.151/26 (Vol. II), (Aug. 13, 1992).
21 *Id.* at ¶ 17.25(a).
22 *See* U.N. GAOR, 51st Sess., U.N. Doc. A/51/116 (Apr. 16, 1996) (adoption of the Washington Declaration and of the Global Program of Action) (GPA).
23 *Id.*
24 *See* G.A. Res. 55/274, *Report on the Work of the United Nations Open-Ended Informal Consultative Process on Oceans and the Law of the Sea at Its first meeting*, ¶ 84 (Jul. 28, 2000).

have obtained, however, an enormous amount of support from States, intergovernmental and non-governmental organizations.[25]

The GPA is viewed as an essential instrument for combating marine environmental degradation from land-based activities. Such an endorsement was reinforced when the Informal Consultative Process (ICP), the body established by the United Nations General Assembly (UNGA),[26] chose the question of land-based activities and the GPA as one of the main issues in need of further review and implementation. The General Assembly incorporated recommendations on this subject emanating from the ICP in its annual resolution.[27] A conference took place in 2001 to review the GPA and involve efforts with the UNEP regional seas program, which provides the most comprehensive institutional framework to effectively implement the GPA.[28]

The Manila Declaration is also celebrated as a "giant leap" in the sustainable development of the coastal and marine environment.[29] It aims to further implement the GPA and encourages States to develop policies to reduce and control wastewater, marine litter, and pollution from fertilizers and to identify approaches to address current and emerging issues for the period 2012–2016.[30]

New actions and strategies were adopted in Bali in 2018 to accelerate the GPA's implementation. They are contained in *The Global Program of Action for the Protection of the Marine Environment from Land-Based activities: A 20 years Perspective on a Unique Program to Advance the Ocean Agenda*.[31] Governments reiterate their commitments on enhancing capacity building, knowledge sharing, and mainstreaming coastal and marine ecosystem protection, especially from threats caused by increased nutrients, wastewater, marine litter, and microplastics.[32] These developments relate to improving the GPA's implementation and give new tools to policymakers.

In addition to the GPA, binding conventions at the global level aim to protect the environment, specifically the marine environment, from harmful pollutants. These conventions are:

---

25 *See generally* UNGA, Report of 1st ICP Meeting, A/55/274 (Jul. 31, 2000).
26 *See* G.A. Res. 54/33, *Results by the Review of the Commission on Sustainable Development of the Sectoral Theme of "Oceans and Seas": International Coordination and Cooperation* (Nov. 24, 1999) (note that this resolution is consistent with the legal framework provided by UNCLOS and the goals of Chapter 17 of Agenda 21, according to the recommendations of the CSD 7).
27 *See* G.A. Res. 55/7, ¶ 27–29 (Feb. 27, 2001).
28 *Report of the First Intergovernmental Review Meeting on the Implementation of the Global Programme of Action for the Protection of the Marine Environment from Land-Based Activities*, UNEP, UNEP/GPA/IGR.1/9 (Dec. 22, 2001).
29 Emmanuel Roucounas, *Manila Declaration on the Peaceful Settlement of International Disputes*, AUDIOVISUAL LIBRARY OF INT'L LAW (Nov. 15, 1982), https://legal.un.org/avl/ha/mdpsid/mdpsid.html.
30 *See* Manila Declaration on Furthering the Implementation of the Global Programme of Action for the Protection of the Marine Environment from Land-based Activities, Jan. 26, 2012, UNEP/GPA/IGR.3/CRP.1/Rev.1 (Manila Declaration).
31 *See* UNEP, *Future Direction of the Global Programme of Action for the Protection of the Marine Environment from Land-Based Activities*, UNEP/GPA/IGR.4/INF/3 (Sept. 1, 2017).
32 *See* Bali Declaration on the Protection of the Marine Environment from Land-Based Activities, Mar. 6, 2019, UNEP/GPA/IGR.4/6 (Bali Declaration).

- The *Basel Convention on the Control of Transboundary Movements of Hazardous Wastes and Their Disposal*, 1989,[33] was adopted to reduce the movements of hazardous wastes between countries and specifically from developed to less developed countries.
- The *Rotterdam Convention on the Prior Informed Consent Procedures for Certain Hazardous Chemical and Pesticides in International Trade*, 1998, promotes shared responsibility and cooperative efforts among parties in the international trade of certain hazardous chemicals.[34]
- The *Stockholm Convention on Persistent Organic Pollutants (POPs)*, 2001,[35] aims to eliminate or restrict the production and use of persistent organic pollutants which are chemical substances that persist in the environment, bio-accumulate in fatty tissues, bio-magnify through the food chain, and adversely affect human health and the environment. The Convention represents a major achievement in the control of the ten most dangerous chemical substances released in the marine environment.
- The *Minamata Convention on Mercury* was adopted in 2013 and aims to protect from the adverse effects of mercury, a particularly harmful pollutant.[36]

In all, these four treaties can contribute to limiting pollutants from land-based sources.

At the Regional Level

It is certainly more effective to combat land-based sources of pollution at the regional level. It ensures a better way to control implementation, although all regions are not at the same level of development. Several regional conventions were adopted in the 1970s under the Regional Seas Program of UNEP.[37] This program addresses the degradation of oceans and coastal areas, and is seen as one of the most comprehensive institutional frameworks for regional cooperation in the oceans.

Currently, five Regional Seas Conventions have protocols that deal with land-based sources of pollution.

1. The *Protocol for the Protection of the Mediterranean Sea against Pollution from Land-Based Sources and Activities*, 1980, amended in 1996. The concepts, such as the precautionary principle and the polluter pays principle, were incorporated in the preamble of the Protocol.[38]

---

33 Basel Convention on the Control of Transboundary Movements of Hazardous Wastes and Their Disposal, Mar. 22, 1989, 28 I.L.M. 657 (1989); 1673 U.N.T.S. 125.
34 Rotterdam Convention on the Prior Informed Consent Procedure for Certain Hazardous Chemicals and Pesticides in International Trade, Sept. 10, 1998, 2244 U.N.T.S. 337.
35 *See* Convention on Persistent Organic Pollutants, May 8, 2009, UNEP/POPS/CONF/4 (Stockholm Convention) (note that this Convention entered into force in 2012) (POPS).
36 *See generally Minamata Convention on Mercury*, UNEP (Oct. 2013), www.mercuryconvention.org (noting that the Convention entered into force in 2017).
37 For the list of conventions and protocols, *see* U.N. Secretary General, *Oceans and the Law of the Sea*, U.N. Doc. A/56/58 (Mar. 9, 2001); for the texts of those conventions and protocols, *see Working with Regional Seas*, UNEP, www.unep.org/explore-topics/oceans-seas/what-we-do/working-regional-seas (last visited Nov. 19, 2020).
38 See Protocol for the Protection of the Mediterranean Sea against Pollution from Land-Based Sources and Activities, Conference of Plenipotentiaries of the Coastal States of the Mediterranean Region, UNEP(OCA)/MED IG.7/4 (Mar. 7, 1996).

2. The *Protocol for the Protection of the South-East Pacific against Pollution from Land-Based Sources*, 1983.[39]
3. The *Protocol on Protection of the Black Sea Marine Environment against Pollution from Land-Based Sources*, 1992.[40]
4. The *Protocol Concerning Marine Pollution from Land-Based Sources and Activities (Wider Caribbean)*, 1999. This Protocol provides for the adoption by the Parties of guidelines concerning environmental impact assessments and reviews where a planned land-based activity on a territory is likely to cause substantial pollution of, or significant and harmful changes to, the convention area.[41]
5. The *Protocol for the Protection of the Marine Environment against Pollution from Land-Based Sources*, 1990 (Kuwait Region). This Protocol also provides for environmental impact assessments (EIAs) and also uses an annex system that sets up guidelines, regulations, and permits for the release of wastes.[42]

Two other regional conventions, which fall outside of the UNEP Regional Seas Program umbrella, contain provisions aimed at combating land-based sources of pollution.[43] Unfortunately, not all areas of the oceans have been covered by instruments dealing with land-based sources of pollution.

Instruments to Combat Pollution from Ships

States are required under Article 211 of UNCLOS to establish international rules and standards to prevent, reduce, and control the pollution of the marine environment from vessels.[44] A flag State must adopt rules for vessels flying its flag in accordance with Article 217.[45] Enforcement rules are established to be applied by port States (Article 218) and coastal States (Article 220).[46] Article 94, which sets out the duties of the flag State, is also relevant in this context.[47]

The International Maritime Organization (IMO) is the main "competent international organization" in the UN system responsible for developing the global rules and standards relating to maritime safety, prevention of marine pollution from vessels and by dumping.[48]

---

39 *See* Protocol for the Protection of the South-East Pacific Against Pollution from Land-Based Sources, UNEP, UNEP (092)/M352 (July 23, 1983).
40 *Protocol for the Protection of the Black Sea Marine Environment Against Pollution from Land-Based Sources, in* Bucharest Convention, Black Sea Commission (1992).
41 *See* Protocol concerning Marine Pollution from Land-Based Sources and Activities (Wider Caribbean), Cartagena Convention, Conference of Plenipotentiaries Oct. 6, 1999, https://wedocs.unep.org/bitstream/handle/20.500.11822/27861/UNEP1999-en.pdf?sequence=1&isAllowed=y.
42 *See generally* Protocol for the Protection of the Marine Environment against Pollution from Land-Based Sources, Feb. 21, 1990, UNEP/GPA/IGR.1/3.
43 Convention for the Protection of the Marine Environment of the North-East Atlantic, Sept. 22, 1992, 2354 U.N.T.S. 67; Convention on the Protection and Use of Transboundary Watercourses and International Lakes, Mar. 17, 1992, 1936 U.N.T.S. 269 (HELCOM or Helsinki Convention) (noting that this Convention covers the whole of the Baltic Sea).
44 UNCLOS, *supra* note 6, art. 211.
45 *Id.* at art. 217.
46 *Id.* at art. 218, 220.
47 *Id.* at art. 94.
48 *See* International Convention for the Prevention of Pollution from Ships, 1978 Protocol, International Maritime Organization, U.N. GA Res. A/RES/57/141, www.un.org/Depts/los/general_assembly/contributions_texts/imo.pdf (MARPOL 73/78).

The major IMO instrument regulating pollution from ships is the International Convention for the Prevention of Pollution from Ships, 1973, as modified by the Protocol of 1978 relating thereto (The International Convention for the Prevention of Pollution from Ships (MARPOL) 73/78). Together with six annexes,[49] it contains most of the international rules and standards on the prevention, reduction, and control of pollution from ships.

Due to an increase in maritime traffic, it is necessary to strengthen rules to combat greenhouse gas (GHGs) emissions. The Regulations for the Prevention of Air Pollution from Ships took form in the new Annex VI to MARPOL 73/78, which was adopted in 1997 and amended in 2011 by adding a new chapter 4 entitled "Regulations on energy efficiency for ships."[50] The parties agreed to establish the first-ever mandatory global GHG reduction regime for an international industry sector. The mandatory regime, in force since 2013, is aimed at limiting or reducing GHGs from ships and includes the adoption of both technical and operational measures.[51] These are designed to provide best practices for maximum efficiency: The Energy Efficiency Design Index (EED) for new ships and the Ship Energy Efficiency Plan (SEEMP) for both new and existing ships.[52]

In 2018, the IMO adopted an initial strategy for reducing GHG emissions from ships.[53] The strategy contains a "pathway of CO2 emissions reduction consistent with the Paris Agreement temperature goals."[54] In May 2019, the Marine Environment Protection Committee (MEPC) adopted a resolution inviting Member States to encourage voluntary cooperation between the port and shipping sector in order to facilitate reduction of GHGs from ships (for example, Onshore power supply, Safe on efficient bunkering of alternative low carbon and zero carbon fuel).[55] On the basis of Rule 14.1.3 of Annex VI of MARPOL 73/78, the IMO mandated that the world limit on sulfur in marine fuel be at 0.50% as of January 1, 2020.[56]

Some other conventions dealing with specific aspects of the management of ships and damaging pollution may also prove to be significant. First, the International Convention on the Control of Harmful Anti-Fouling Systems on Ships prohibits the use of organotin compounds, which act as biocides in anti-fouling systems on ships' hulls.[57] The presence

---

49 Annex I addresses pollution by oil; Annex II deals with noxious liquid substances such as chemicals carried in bulk; Annex III regulates harmful substances carried in package form; Annex IV deals with sewage discharges; Annex V addresses disposal at sea of ship-generated garbage; and Annex VI deals with pollution from the atmosphere by ships.
50 IMO, *supra* note 46.
51 *Id.*
52 See *Reduction of GHG Emissions from Ships: Third IMO GHG Study 2014*, IMO, 67th Sess, MEPC 67/6 (Jul 1. 2014); *see also* U.N. Secretary General, *Oceans and the law of the sea*, U.N. Doc. A/69/71/Add.1 ¶ 105 (Sept. 1, 2014).
53 See *Reduction of GHG Emissions from Ships: Report of the Working Group on Reduction of GHG Emissions from Ships*, 72nd Sess., MEPC 72/WP.7 (Apr. 12, 2018).
54 The Paris Agreement, the successor of the Kyoto Protocol, aims to strengthen the global efforts to reduce greenhouse gas emissions, including CO_2, was adopted on 12 December 2015 at COP 21 to the United Nations Framework Convention on Climate Change. It was signed by 195 States and entered into force on 4 November 2016.
55 MEPC Res. 323/74, *Invitation to Member States to Encourage Voluntary Cooperation between the Port and Shipping Sectors to Continue to Reduce GHG Emissions from Ships* (May. 17, 2019).
56 *Supra* note 51, at Annex VI ¶ 14.1.3.
57 See International Convention on the Control of Harmful Anti-Fouling Systems on Ships, Oct. 18, 2001, AFS/CONF/26.

of such compounds on ships' hulls, external parts, or surfaces has been banned.[58] Second, the International Convention for the Control and Management of Ships' Ballast Water and Sediment (BWM Convention) requires ships to implement a ballast water management plan. The code of approval of ballast water management systems was adopted in 2018 and has been in force since October 2019.[59]

Instruments to Combat Pollution by Dumping

States are required by Articles 210 and 216 of UNCLOS to adopt and enforce national laws, regulations, and measures, which must be at least as effective as the global rules and standards enacted through competent international organizations or diplomatic conferences.[60]

The global rules and standards referred to in the Convention are contained in the 1972 Convention on the Prevention of Marine Pollution by Dumping of Wastes and Other Matter[61] and the 1996 Protocol to the 1972 Dumping Convention,[62] both of which set up the legal regime to regulate the dumping of wastes and other matter into the oceans. In both instruments, dumping is similarly defined as "any deliberate disposal into the seas of wastes or other matter from vessels, aircrafts, platforms or other man-made structures at sea."[63] They conform with the definition given in Article 1 of UNCLOS.[64]

The Protocol represents a major change of the approach to dumping from the 1972 Convention. It enhances the application of the precautionary approach and the polluter pays principles.[65] The Protocol also prohibits the dumping of any waste except those types listed in the treaty.[66] This is a reversal of the system used by the parent Convention, which forbids the dumping of some substances but allows dumping of any other substances subject to certain conditions.[67]

Under the 1972 Convention and the 1996 Protocol, progress had been made in regulating the capture and sequestration of CO_2 waste streams in sub-seabed geological formations, to permanently isolate CO_2. Carbon capture in sub-seabed geological formations stabilizes CO_2 atmospheric emissions that contribute to climate change.[68] These formations are located worldwide and can store amounts of CO_2 that otherwise have entered the atmosphere and the oceans, thus contributing to global warming.[69]

---

58 *See id.*
59 *See* International Convention for the Control and Management of Ships' Ballast Water and Sediments, Feb. 16, 2004, BWM/CONF/36.
60 UNCLOS, *supra* note 6, at art. 210, 216.
61 The Convention was adopted on December 29, 1972 and entered into force on August 30, 1975.
62 The Protocol to the Convention of Marine Pollution by Dumping of Wastes and Other Matter was adopted on November 7, 1996, and entered into force on March 24, 2006. It supersedes the Convention as between contracting parties to the Protocol which are also parties to the Convention (Article 23).
63 *See* Convention on the Prevention of Marine Pollution by Dumping of Wastes and Other Matter, Dec. 29, 1972, 1046 U.N.T.S. 120; *see also* Protocol to the Convention of Marine Pollution by Dumping of Wastes and Other Matter, 110th Congress, 1st Sess., Treaty Doc. 110–15 (Mar. 21, 1998) (Marine Pollution).
64 UNCLOS, *supra* note 6, at art. 1.
65 Marine Pollution, *supra* note 61.
66 *Id.*
67 *Id.*
68 *Ocean Acidification*, Nat'l Oceanic and Atmospheric Admin., www.noaa.gov/education/resource-collections/ocean-coasts/ocean-acidification (last visited Nov. 23, 2020).
69 *Id.*

In 2012, the meeting of Contracting Parties adopted a revised version of the specific guidelines for the assessment of carbon dioxide streams for disposal into sub-seabed geological formations to take into account the transboundary migration of carbon dioxide wastes.[70] A 2013 amendment to the 1996 Protocol has been adopted to regulate marine engineering, including ocean fertilization.[71]

Instruments to Minimize the Impact of Ocean Acidification

Changes in the marine environment are due to ocean acidification, a phenomenon caused by a decrease in the pH of the sea water as a result of the absorption of emitted CO_2 in the atmosphere.[72] Ocean acidification has significant impacts on marine ecosystems, particularly on the shell populations, like crustaceans and corals reefs, which play an important role in the food chain.[73] The consequences on the livelihood of millions of people who depend on fisheries for their living are very substantial. It impacts coastal protection, transportation, and tourism. The disruptions to marine ecosystem services caused by ocean acidification and climate change will seriously affect the economy of coastal communities, resulting in increased food insecurity and poverty.

There are no international instruments which specifically address ocean acidification or its impacts on the marine environment. The international instruments aiming at combating different sources of pollution which affect the marine environment, as discussed above, could be of relevance in addressing ways to prevent the increase of acidification of the ocean and to mitigate its effects. In this context, the Paris Agreement under the United Nations Framework Convention on Climate Change (UNFCCC) could also play an important role in reducing CO_2 emissions.[74]

A number of instruments of a voluntary nature may also help mitigate ocean acidification. First, resolutions on UNCLOS are adopted every year, which deal with all issues of marine affairs in an integrated approach (omnibus resolution). These resolutions have become more and more substantial and contain specific recommendations. For instance, the question of ocean acidification was first introduced in Resolution A/RES/62/215, adopted in 2007.[75] Hence, each year, the General Assembly continued to deal with this troubling phenomenon in order to make States more aware of ocean acidification and its dangerous consequences to the marine environment.[76] After Rio + 20 and the recommendations contained in *The Future We Want*, UN resolutions devoted more paragraphs and requested more action, effort, and initiatives to conduct further studies to enhance international cooperation to minimize the effects of acidification.[77] Second, the Informal Consultative Process devoted

---

70 *Id.*
71 *See* U.N. Secretary General *Oceans and the Law of the Sea*, *supra* note 50, ¶ 108.
72 *See supra* note 68.
73 *Id.*
74 Paris Agreement to the United Nations Framework Convention on Climate Change, Dec. 12, 2015, T.I.A.S. No. 16-1104.
75 GA Res. 62/215, *Oceans and the Law of the Sea* (Dec. 22, 2007).
76 *See as examples*, GA Res. 63/111, *Oceans and the Law of the Sea*, ¶ 99 (Dec. 5, 2008); GA Res. 64/71, *Oceans the Law of the Sea*, ¶ 113 (Dec. 4, 2009); GA Res. 65/73, *Oceans and the Law of the Sea*, ¶ 129 (Dec. 7, 2010); GA Res. 66/231, *Oceans and the Law of the Sea*, ¶ 134 (Dec. 24, 2011); and GA Res. 74/19, *Oceans and the Law of the Sea*, ¶ 209-14 (Dec. 10, 2019).
77 *Id.* at §209-14.

its fourteenth meeting to "The impacts of ocean acidification on the marine environment." It emphasized the need to better understand ocean acidification and its link with climate change on marine ecosystems.[78]

Additionally, the Secretary General prepared a special report for the ICP meeting held in June 2013.[79] The report contains all the different aspects to understand acidification from a scientific point of view, as well as solutions to mitigate its impacts, particularly on ecosystems. Among all the issues and ideas raised during the meeting, two of them were particularly important: (1) the need for additional research on the impact of ocean acidification on marine ecosystems, including the assessment of their economic and social consequences, as well as the assistance of the development of mitigation and adaptation policies and (2) the importance of adaptation measures.[80] In this context, several delegations highlighted the need to also reduce the impacts of other stresses on the marine environment, including pollution, coastal erosion, destructive fishing practices, and overfishing, in order to enhance the resiliency of marine ecosystems to ocean acidification.[81] This issue clearly links the increase of acidification to pollution from land-based activities.[82]

For now, as requested by many forums, States should pursue further marine scientific research and monitoring of ocean acidification through enhanced cooperation and also in the dissemination of information and data sharing, especially in supporting the establishment of a global ocean acidification observing network. If legal instruments are ignored by political deciders when they are voluntary or are not implemented by States through ratification, accession, or adhesion when they are compulsory, the marine environment will not be protected. Environmental degradation will increase, as well as biodiversity loss. It is therefore necessary to assess the degree in which these legal instruments are followed.

An Assessment on the Degree of Implementation of Legal Instruments

The 2019 UN Report on the SDGs provides an overview of the world's implementation efforts toward achieving the 2030 Agenda. It highlights areas of progress and areas where more action needs to be taken at the national level,[83] focusing on strategies and policy implementation and not as much on international law. SDGs vary in nature, ranging from political, legal, economic, and social elements, requiring a vast array of competencies. Regarding Goal 14, the Secretary General (SG) mentions that the number of marine protected areas has doubled since 2010.[84] As of December 2018, 17% of water under national jurisdiction were covered by protected areas, a significant increase from 12% in 2015.[85] The Secretary General further acknowledges that there is a better concerted effort to fight against illegal,

---

78 See Summary of the 14th Meeting of the United Nations Open-Ended Informal Consultative Process on Oceans and the Law of the Sea, 25(89) EARTH NEGOTIATIONS BULLETIN 1, INT'L INST. FOR SUSTAINABLE DEV. (June 23, 2013).
79 See U.N. Secretary General, Oceans and the Law of the Sea, A/68/71 (Apr. 8, 2013).
80 See, id.
81 Id.
82 See Report on the Work of the United Nations Open-Ended Informal Consultative Process on Oceans and the Law of the Sea at Its Fourteenth Meeting, 68th Sess., A/68/159 ¶ 13, 16 (Jul. 17, 2013).
83 See The Sustainable Development Goals Report, 2019 at 64 (UNITED NATIONS 2019), https://unstats.un.org/sdgs/report/2019/The-Sustainable-Development-Goals-Report-2019.pdf (SDG REPORT 2019).
84 Id. at 17.
85 Ibid.

unreported, and unregulated (IUU) fishing, but he deplores once more the deterioration of the marine environment indicating that sea levels are rising and ocean acidification is accelerating.[86] The core of the report deals mainly with the sustainable use of ocean resources, the necessity to combat overfishing, ocean acidification, and coastal eutrophication.[87] All issues contained in Goal 14, however, have not been assessed. One such issue which remains to be assessed is the call to prevent and reduce marine pollution of all kinds as well as the call to implement international law as reflected in UNCLOS.

It is certainly a difficult task to evaluate how targets in Goal 14 have been implemented so far. The assessment presented in the SG report is done in very general terms, very often showing negative results. For example, the report cites a 26% increase in ocean acidity (the UN resolution adopted in December 2019 mentions 30%);[88] a 90% (1974) to 67% (2015) decline of fish stocks within biologically sustainable levels; and marine protected areas cover only 17% of water under national jurisdiction.[89] Positive results based on actions taken relate only to coastal water. The report indicates that 104 out of 220 coastal regions improved their water quality.[90] As far as legal aspects are concerned, the Port State Agreement is the only reference made to a treaty adopted to fight illegal fishing.[91] Legal evaluation is absent from the report.

Each goal contains themes which are very different in nature; some are political while others are legal, economic, and social, requiring a vast array of competencies. The attempt to offer some evaluation with regard to targets 14.1, 14.3, and 14.c, selected in this study will focus specifically on how legal tools could contribute to combating all kinds of pollution to the marine environment and minimizing the impacts of ocean acidification.

Multiple levels of analysis could be conducted to determine the efficacy of the relevant legal tools to combat marine pollution. The first level, which is relatively easy to assess, consists of determining the number of States that have agreed to be bound by the relevant treaties. Such information is one indication of the world's commitment to the recommendations contained in the SDG 14 targets. The second level of assessment consists of analyzing national laws and regulations which have been enacted in compliance with the applicable treaties, then to evaluate how such law and regulations are applied at all levels, in particular, at the local level. The third level involves an assessment of programs and initiatives (including actions taken by international organizations to fill legal gaps) that complement legal and regulatory action. The fourth level, the most complex, requires an assessment of how the laws and regulations of various sectors are complementing (or not) the progress toward curbing marine pollution. Such assessment could include a review of data from other relevant SDGs, such as SDGs 12 and 13.

Only the first level will be examined below following the same structure as shown above. Some relevant actions taken by international organizations to fill legal gaps in compliance with the targets' recommendations will also be described.

---

86 U.N. Secretary General, *Progress towards the Sustainable Development Goals*, U.N. Doc. E/2019/68 (May 8, 2019).
87 SDG Report 2019, *supra* note 80.
88 GA Res. 74/19, *supra* note 76, at §209.
89 *Id*. at 17.
90 *Ibid*.
91 Agreement on Port States Measures to Prevent, Deter and Eliminate Illegal, Unreported and Unregulated Fishing, 112th Congress, 1st Sess., Treaty Doc. 112–14 (Nov. 22, 2009) (noting that as of today 66 States are parties to it).

With Regard to Land-Based Sources of Pollution

The instruments dealing with land-based pollution are different in nature depending on whether their scope of application is at the global or at the regional level. At the global level, only those dealing with specific pollutants are binding. At the regional level, most of the agreements are compulsory.

At the Global Level

The 2019 SDG report underlines land-based pollutants including sewage and nutrient runoff leading to coastal eutrophication and impairment of coastal marine ecosystems, giving a diagnostic of the cause but not offering the remedies used by coastal States to reduce the flow of pollutants into coastal waters.[92] As Agenda 21 states "A precautionary and anticipatory rather than a reactive approach is necessary to prevent the degradation of the marine environment."[93] There has been some progress in dealing with dangerous pollutants.

Besides UNCLOS, which has received quasi-universal acceptance[94] and contains rules of a general nature, several conventions have been adopted and are aimed at restricting the use of dangerous chemicals or controlling their transportation. They have received a wide interest. The number of country parties to them have taken important action in expanding the list of substances to be banned or in enhancing their efficiency in looking for synergy between them. Progress has been achieved in dealing with those hazardous chemicals such as pesticides, industrials chemicals, and plastics causing adverse effects on human health and causing grave damage to the marine environment.

The relevant conventions include:

- *Basel Convention on the Transboundary Movement of Hazardous Waste and Their Disposal*, adopted on 22 March 1989, entered into force 5 May 1992, (187 parties).[95]
- *The Rotterdam Convention on the Prior Informed Consent Procedures for Certain Hazardous Chemicals and Pesticides in International Trade*, adopted on 10 September 1998, entered into force 24 February 2004, (161 parties).[96]
- *The Stockholm Convention on Persistent Organic Pollutants*, adopted on 22 May 2001, entered into force 17 May 2004, (184 parties).[97]
- *The Minamata Convention on Mercury*, adopted on 10 October 2013, entered into force on 16 August 2017, (116 parties).[98]

It is encouraging to observe that a large number of States have agreed to be bound by these conventions with the common objective of protecting human health and the environment from hazardous chemicals and wastes.

In 2019, several achievements were made. First, a major step was taken to enhance a higher degree of efficiency in the implementation of those treaties when the Basel, Rotterdam,

---

92 *See* SDG Report 2019, *supra* note 80 at 50.
93 *See* Agenda 21, *supra* note 1.
94 *See* UNCLOS, *supra* note 6.
95 Basel Convention, *supra* note 33.
96 Rotterdam Convention, *supra* note 34.
97 POPS, *supra* note 35.
98 Minamata Convention, *supra* note 36.

and Stockholm Conventions (known as the BRS block), held joint Conferences of the Parties (COPs) meeting in May 2019.[99] The Secretariat of the Minamata Convention was also asked to join.[100] Second, several important decisions were adopted. The parties to the Basel Convention took major steps forward in adding plastic waste to the list of hazardous waste.[101] Exporter States have to obtain consent from receiving countries before shipping contaminated mixed or unrecyclable plastic.[102] Under the Stockholm Convention, parties adopted a decision for a global ban on PFOA (perfluorooctane sulfonic acid) used worldwide as an industrial surfactant in chemical processes and as a material feedstock, a suspected carcinogen and endocrine disrupter.[103] It is known to have contaminated drinking water.[104] Finally, after fifteen years of discussion, the Rotterdam Convention has finally established a compliance mechanism to the Convention that would facilitate the implementation of the parties' obligations.[105]

At the Regional Level

Most of the regional Conventions dealing with the marine environment, compulsory for the States bound by them, have added Protocols dealing with land-based sources of pollution. First, the Protocol for the Protection of the Mediterranean Sea against Pollution from Land-Based Sources (1980) has 22 parties.[106] It was amended in 1996 by the Protocol for the Protection of the Mediterranean Sea against Pollution from Land-Based Sources and Activities which entered into force in 2008. It counts 17 State parties.[107]

Second, the Protocol for the Protection of the South-East Pacific against Pollution from Land-Based Sources adopted in 1983, entered into force on January 31, 1984. Five States are parties to it: Chile, Peru, Ecuador, Colombia, and Panama.[108] Third, the Protocol on the Protection of the Black Sea Marine Environment against Pollution from Land-Based Sources and Activities adopted on April 21, 1992, entered into force on January 15, 1994.[109] Six States are parties to it: Bulgaria, Georgia, Romania, Russian Federation, Turkey, and Ukraine.[110] Finally, the Protocol concerning Pollution from Land-Based Sources and Activities to the Convention for the Protection and Development of the Marine Environment of the Wider Caribbean region was adopted on October 6, 1999, and entered into force on August 13, 2010. It has 12 parties as of April 2016.[111]

---

99 *See 2019 Meetings of the COPS to the Basel, Rotterdam, and Stockholm Conventions,* (BC COP-14, RC COP-9, SC COP-9), THE GEF (April 29–May 10, 2019), www.thegef.org/events/2019-meetings-cops-basel-rotterdam-and-stockholm-conventions.
100 For the joint COP meeting (Geneva April 29–May 10, 2019), COP14 to the Basel Convention, COP9 to the Rotterdam Convention, and COP9 to the Stockholm Convention, *see 2019 Meetings of the Conferences of the Parties to the Basel, Rotterdam and Stockholm Conventions,* IISD, https://enb.iisd.org/chemical/cops/2019/ (last visited Nov. 23, 2020).
101 *Id.*
102 *Id.*
103 *Ibid.*
104 *Ibid.*
105 *Ibid.*
106 See, Mediterranean sea, *supra* note 38.
107 *Ibid.*
108 *See* South-East Pacific, *supra* note 39.
109 *See,* Black Sea, *supra* note 40.
110 *Id.*
111 *See,* Wider Caribbean, *supra* note 41.

All these protocols constitute very important tools to combat land-based sources. The scope of their application being limited to specific geographical areas gives better opportunities to have the necessary means to be effective. The seas regions have geographical, biodiversity, and ecosystem similarities.

With Regard to Pollution from Ships

MARPOL and its six annexes[112] contain most of the international rules and standards on the prevention, reduction, and control of pollution from ships. Under Annex VI to MARPOL 73/78 and its chapter 4 entitled "*Regulations on energy efficiency for ships,*" three new steps have been taken that will reduce pollution from ships.

First, the IMO adopted an initial strategy which contains a "pathway of CO2 emissions reduction consistent with the Paris Agreement temperature goals" in 2018.[113] Second, in May 2019, the MEPC adopted a resolution inviting Member States to encourage voluntary cooperation between the port and shipping sector to contribute to reducing GHGs emissions from ships (for example, onshore power supply, safe on efficient bunkering of alternative low carbon and zero carbon fuel).[114] Third, on January 2020 the global limit for sulfur in fuel oil entered into effect. This was a major step forward as it will significantly reduce the amount of sulfur oxide emanating from ships, having major benefits for the population living closer to ports and coasts.

With Regard to Pollution by Dumping

The 2006 Protocol to the London Dumping Convention[115] has helped deal with the dumping of wastes. A reverse list approach was adopted which implies that all dumping is prohibited unless explicitly permitted.[116] For example, incineration at sea is prohibited. Under the protocol, substances that can be dumped must be authorized. In 2012, the meeting of Contracting Parties adopted a revised version of the specific guidelines for assessing CO_2 streams and disposal into sub-seabed geological formations to account for the transboundary migration of CO_2 wastes.[117] A 2013 amendment to the 1996 Protocol has been adopted to regulate marine engineering, including ocean fertilization.

With Regard to Acidification

The 2019 SDG report also gives a grim picture as there is a 26% increase in ocean acidification since pre-industrial times.[118] If no specific agreement exists to deal with acidification, the agreements described above to combat pollution from land-based activities or pollution from ships could play an important role in preventing any aggravation of the phenomenon and mitigating its effects. Scientific research and cooperation between States will also help mitigate ocean acidification.

---

112 MARPOL 73/78, *supra* note 48.
113 *Id.*
114 MEPC 74, *supra* note 53.
115 Marine Pollution, *supra* note 61.
116 *Id.*
117 *Ibid.*
118 *See*, SDG Report 2019, *supra* note 80, at 17.

Conclusion

The existing legal instruments, if efficiently implemented by States, could assist in combating all kinds of pollution and in reducing the impact of acidification. It will be counterproductive to negotiate new instruments, as the marine environment has already seen a hypertrophy of recommendations and programs, as well as rules and regulations. It will be far more efficient to ensure that States (1) have sufficient knowledge and understanding of the overwhelming number of existing instruments and the synergies that exist between them and (2) are in a position, according to their capabilities, to adopt, at the national level, the necessary measures to conform and implement all these policies, declarations, and legal texts.

The issue of capacity building is of paramount importance to assist States, particularly developing States, to implement the applicable international instruments and to facilitate their task to comply with measures and recommended practices. Very few States are able to navigate through the maze of environmental agreements. The need to provide for integrated planning and management of ocean-related affairs at the national level is of major importance. The implementation of international rules remains the challenge that needs to be addressed forcefully.

The issue of cooperation between States, a fundamental obligation under UNCLOS, is also an area in need of serious attention. Relevant institutions, whether global, regional, or national, are requested to enhance collaboration with each other, taking into account their respective mandates, with a view to providing coordinated approaches, avoiding duplication of effort, enhancing effective functioning of existing organizations, and ensuring better access to and broadening the dissemination of information.[119] Cooperation and an integrated approach will ensure good governance in protecting and preserving the marine environment for the conservation and sustainable use of oceans and their resources. It is also necessary to take into account all aspects of legal, economic, political, and environmental factors. States have no excuse but to act, since the targets contained in Goal 14 are "action-oriented, concise and easy to communicate."

---

119 *See* Commission on Sustainable Development, 7th Sess., 7/1 §37 (1998–1999).

23 Marine Pollution
Maximizing Synergies for Transformative Changes

Hiroko Muraki Gottlieb

Introduction

Humankind's survival depends on the ocean. The largest ecosystem of the Earth provides essential resources, such as oxygen and food. It provides ecosystem services, such as mitigating climate change impacts.[1] The ocean is also an important economic,[2] social, and cultural source. However, there has been insufficient progress to foster the protection, conservation, and sustainable use of the ocean.[3] From a scientific perspective, the ocean is one, since it is interconnected[4] as recognized in the United Nations Convention on the Law of the Sea (UNCLOS), which states in the preamble, "the problems of ocean space are closely interrelated and need to be considered as a whole." Indeed, many challenges, including marine pollution, cannot be solved by one country but require a coherent and collective effort because of the transboundary effects.

In the case of marine pollution, work to reverse the tide continues at the global, regional, national, and sub-national levels, including through legal instruments and voluntary initiatives. Multi-stakeholder engagement is also accelerating, covering a wide range of disciplines.[5] Yet, the ocean is degrading at an unprecedented rate and marine pollution is certainly a key element of cumulative impacts suffered by the ocean. The question to ask is, why has there been so little progress? The answer to this question is complex since the challenges are multifaceted and multidimensional.[6] This chapter aims to provide a

---

1 *See generally* A. Alegría et al., *Chapter 5: Changing Ocean, Marine Ecosystems, and Dependent Communities*, IPCC SPECIAL REPORT ON THE OCEAN AND CRYOSPHERE IN A CHANGING CLIMATE (2019) [hereinafter "IPCC SPECIAL REPORT 2019"].
2 *See* Ove Hoegh-Guldberg et al., *Reviving The Ocean Economy: The Case for Action—2015*, 60, WORLD WILDLIFE FUND INT'L, (NCP SA, Switzerland, April 2015) (noting that the so called "Blue Economy" grosses about $2.5 trillion USD a year); *see generally* Anna-Sophie Liebender et al., *The Ocean Economy in 2030*, OECD (Paris, Apr. 27, 2016) http://dx.doi.org/ (noting that the Blue Economy sector is projected to double by the year 2030).
3 SPECIAL IPCC REPORT 2019, *supra* note 1; *see generally also* J. Agard et al., *Global Assessment Report on Biodiversity and Ecosystem Services of the Intergovernmental Science-Policy Platform on Biodiversity and Ecosystem Services*, IPBES SECRETARIAT (2019).
4 *See Summary of the First Global Integrated Marine Assess.*, ¶ 10, U.N. GAOR Doc. A/70/112. A/70/112 (Jul. 21, 2015); U.N. Convention of the Law of the Sea, Preamble, Nov. 16, 1994, 1833 U.N.T.S. 397.
5 For example, *see* FRIENDS OF OCEAN ACTION, www.weforum.org/friends-of-ocean-action (last visited Nov. 16, 2020).
6 Various sources of ocean pollution come from land and the ocean (i.e. municipal sources, land-based agricultural activities, ocean-based aquaculture, industrial sector, and maritime pollution). Cumulative impacts of various pollutants create synergistic effects, creating greater negative outcomes than the sum

perspective to this question by reflecting on the challenges associated with marine pollution, and a possible multifaceted way toward accelerating the slow progress to curb this global challenge.

The first section, "Marine pollution and SDGs: pre and post COVID-19 pandemic and interlinkages between SDG 14 and other SDGs," provides a summary of the achievements thus far on the relevant targets and indicators of Sustainable Development Goal (SDG) 14 on marine pollution based on the Sustainable Development Report 2020—The Sustainable Development Goals and COVID-19 (2020 SDGs Report) and the Report of the Secretary-General, Progress towards the SDGs[7] (Secretary-General's 2020 SDGs Report), and where relevant, from the previous year's reports. It is noteworthy that the two 2020 SDGs reports were issued during the COVID-19 pandemic.[8] The global pandemic continues to have unprecedented health, economic, and social impacts around the world and pushed back the global progress toward achieving Agenda 2030. This section will, therefore, provide some reflections on the impacts of the COVID-19 pandemic on curbing marine pollution. Further, this section explores possible interlinkages between SDG 14 and other SDGs, which could be incorporated into legal and policy considerations for the purposes of prioritizing, building positive synergies, and avoiding unintended consequences in addressing marine pollution.

The section "Case Study: Combating Marine Plastic Pollution—an Urgent Global Multidimensional Challenge," explores marine plastic pollution as a case study on the challenges and opportunities associated with fostering the progress of attaining the SDGs on marine pollution. Marine plastic pollution, a multidimensional challenge, will be used to explore ways to improve ocean governance by breaking down siloes and maximizing positive synergies through cooperation and collaboration among a wide range of stakeholders. A focus will be on a possible global binding legal instrument on marine plastic pollution, a move toward a multilateral approach to fill the identified legal and institutional gaps to improve the governance of marine plastic pollution in a holistic and an integrated manner.

The section "Recommendations for Action on Combating Marine Pollution," provides the key recommendations to accelerate the States' progress on meeting the SDGs on marine pollution. Two complementary sets of recommendations are provided: 1. legal instruments, policies, and institutional frameworks, and 2. supporting elements to accelerate the attainment of the SDGs on marine pollution.

---

of their individual impacts. Further, marine pollution causes multidimensional negative impacts on ecosystems, marine biodiversity, human health, and economies. Finally, there are human dimensions to this challenge. For detailed discussion on the multi-faceted and multi-dimensional aspect of marine pollution, *see* Brajesh Dubey et al., *Leveraging Multi-Target Strategies to Address Plastic Pollution in the Context of an Already Stressed* Ocean, WORLD RESOURCES INSTITUTE (May 27, 2020) (Noting that pages 5–17 cover various sources of marine pollution, pages 21–28 cover the impacts of ocean pollution on ecosystems, marine life, human health, and economies, and pages 39–40 cover human decisions and behaviors).

7 U.N. Secretary General, *Progress towards the Sustainable Development Goals*, U.N. Doc. E/2020/57 (Apr. 28, 2020) [hereinafter "SECRETARY-GENERAL'S 2020 SDGS REPORT"]; U.N. Statistics Division, *The Sustainable Development Goals Report 2020*, U.N. DEP. OF ECON. & SOC. AFFAIRS (2020) [hereinafter "2020 SDGS REPORT"].

8 For information on COVID-19, *see Coronarvirus Disease*, WORLD HEALTH ORGANIZATION, www.who.int/emergencies/diseases/novel-coronavirus-2019 (last visited Nov. 16, 2020); *see also Coronavirus Resource Center*, JOHNS HOPKINS UNIVERSITY OF MEDICINE, https://coronavirus.jhu.edu/ (last visited Nov. 16, 2020).

This chapter concludes with a call for those with resources to provide adequate, predictable, and sustained capacity building and technology transfer to ensure an enabling environment for all to address marine pollution. The call for urgent action also encourages the policy makers to use the precautionary principle, ecosystem-based approaches, and the best available science to make informed decisions, with a strong commitment to cooperation and collaboration toward achieving a healthy ocean for the current and future generations.

Marine Pollution and SDGs: Pre- and Post-COVID-19 Pandemic and Interlinkages Between SDG 14 and Other SDGs

Sustainable Development Goals Reports: Pre- and Post-COVID-19 Pandemic

The 2020 SDGs Report and the Secretary-General's 2020 SDGs Report (2020 SDGs Reports) provide an overview of the States' efforts toward achieving Agenda 2030 by highlighting certain SDG targets, focusing on progress as well as challenges. SDGs vary in nature, ranging from political, legal, economic, and social elements, requiring a vast array of competencies. Due to the lack of adequate resources and insufficient data, not all SDG targets and indicators are included in the 2020 SDGs Reports, which is no different than in previous years' reports. The year 2020's reports are unique, however, in the sense that the world is suffering from a global pandemic that has significantly pushed back progress toward Agenda 2030.[9] Indeed, the 2020 SDGs Reports include some reflections on the impacts of COVID-19 for each SDG. For SDG 14, the reports make a hopeful statement that applies to all of the SDG 14 targets and indicators: "[t]he drastic reduction in human activity brought about by COVID-19 may be a chance for oceans to recuperate."[10]

The Report of the Secretary-General on SDG Progress 2019 Special Edition (2019 Secretary-General's SDGs Report) emphasizes that a paradigm shift is necessary for any government to effectively mainstream the SDGs into their national plans, policies, and budgets.[11] To that end, one of the key challenges associated with the review of the progress on SDGs is the lack of data. In the 2019 SDGs Report, the United Nations (UN) Under-Secretary-General states:

> This report also highlights the importance of investing in data for the full implementation of the 2030 Agenda. Most countries do not regularly collect data for more than half of the global indicators. The lack of accurate and timely data on many marginalized groups and individuals makes them "invisible" and exacerbates their vulnerability. While considerable effort has been made to address these data gaps over the past four years, progress has been limited.[12]

The COVID-19 pandemic is exacerbating deficits in the collection and production of data, where even the routine operations throughout the global statistical and data systems are

---

9 U.N. G.A. Res. A/RES/70/1, *Transforming Our World: The 2030 Agenda for Sustainable Development*, 1 (Sept. 25, 2015) [hereinafter "2030 Agenda"].
10 2020 SDGs Report, *supra* note 7, at 19.
11 U.N. Secretary General, *Progress towards the Sustainable Development Goals*, 32–34, U.N. Doc. E/2019/68 (May 8, 2019) [hereinafter "Secreatry-General's 2019 SDGs Report"].
12 *See generally*, U.N. Statistics Division, *The Sustainable Development Goals Report 2019*, U.N. Dep. Of Econ. & Soc. Affairs (2019) [hereinafter "2019 SDGs Report"].

disrupted, especially in the resource-scarce States.[13] The need has never been greater for investments in innovative data and statistics systems that can provide adequate coverage of all population groups as well as a system that can foster "internal consistency, comparability and overall quality of data produced."[14]

SDG 14, with a Focus on Marine Pollution: Pre- and Post-COVID-19 Pandemic

SDG 14 is no exception in terms of the limited data that are available to analyze the progress on SDGs.[15] For curbing marine pollution, the following targets are covered in the 2020 SDGs Report:[16]

- Use of ecosystem-based approaches to manage marine areas within national jurisdiction (SDG target 14.2);
- Acidification (SDG target 14.3);
- Marine protected areas (SDG target 14.5); and
- Sustainable use of marine resources by Small Island Developing States (SIDS) and Least Developed Countries and all countries (SDG target 14.7).

Most of the relevant SDG 14 targets on marine pollution are not on a positive trajectory. On SDG 14.2, the 2020 SDGs Report states that "the global Ocean Health Index appears to have been static over the last eight years. Some regions have low scores on ocean health that are likely worsening," resulting in the global failure to meet the 2020 deadline for that target.[17] On SDG 14.3, ocean acidification increased 10 to 30% between 2015 and 2019 and the report projects that by the end of this century, there will be a 100 to 150% rise in acidity.[18] While the 2019 SDGs Report covered SDG 14.1

---

13 2020 SDGs Report, *supra* note 7, at 4.
14 *Id.* at 5.
15 The article by the United Nations Educational, Scientific and Cultural Organization-Intergovernmental Oceanographic Commission (UNESCO-IOC) provides information on some of the negative impacts of the COVID-19 pandemic on the collection of marine data: Emma Heslop, *COVID-19 Disruptions in Ocean Observations Could Threaten Weather Forecast and Climate Change Predictions*, UNESCO (June 23, 2020), https://en.unesco.org/news/covid-19-disruptions-ocean-observations-could-threaten-weather-forecast-and-climate-change (last visited Nov. 16, 2020); *see also* U.N. Statistics Division, *The Tier Classifications for Global SDG Indicators*, Inter-agency and Expert Group on SDG Indicators, 51st session, E/CN.3/2020/2 (Apr. 17, 2020) (noting that there has been significant improvement). Tier III represents, "[n]o internationally established methodology or standards are yet available for the indicator, but methodology/standards are being (or will be) developed or tested." The following indicators are still in Tier II (i.e. [i]ndicator is conceptually clear, has an internationally established methodology and standards are available, but data are not regularly produced by countries.): SDG 14.1.1(a); 14.1.1(b); 14.2.1; 14.3.1; 14.a.1; and 14.c.1. The following SDG 14 indicators are in Tier I (i.e. [i]ndicator is conceptually clear, has an internationally established methodology and standards are available, and data are regularly produced by countries for at least 50% of countries and of the population in every region where the indicator is relevant): 14.4.1; 14.5.1; 14.6.1; 14.7.1; and 14.b.1. Except for the indicator on protected areas (SDG 14.5.1), the other SDGs that are relevant to marine pollution are in the Tier II category.
16 2020 SDGs Report, *supra* note 7, at 19, 52–53; *see also* Secretary-General's 2020 SDGs Report, *supra* note 7, at 15–16.
17 *Id.* at 60.
18 *Id.* at 52 ; *see also* Secretary-General's 2020 SDGs Report, *supra* note 7, at 15.

for land-based pollution, marine debris, and the water quality of the coastal regions (i.e., 104 out of 220 improved but water quality challenges are prevalent),[19] the SDGs Report in 2020 is silent on this SDG target.

There are two brighter spots in the SDG 14 targets and indicators in the 2020 SDGs Report that are relevant for marine pollution. The first is on marine protected areas. As of December 2019, more than 24 million km² or 17% of marine areas under national jurisdiction became protected, exceeding the 2020 deadline to achieve SDG 14.5 and 15.5.1.[20] The second is on SDG 14.7.1, where contributions of sustainable marine-capture fisheries to gross domestic product (GDP) is greater than 10 times higher in SIDS in Oceania and in the Least Developed Countries (LDCs)[21] compared to the global percentage (1.55% and 1.11%, respectively for 2011–2017 versus 0.1% per year globally).

On the other hand, two key SDG 14 targets would benefit from additional resources to be allocated by the States. On SDG 14.a (i.e., increased scientific knowledge, develop research capacity and transfer marine technology), the 2020 SDGs Reports did not include any information on this target. To measure progress, SDG indicator 14.a.1 uses the "proportion of total research budget allocated to research in the field of marine technology."[22] To leave no one behind, especially the SIDS and the LDCs, which is the ultimate goal of Agenda 2030 and its 17 SDGs, it is imperative that future SDG Reports focus on SDG 14.a since capacity building and transfer of marine technology are key elements to achieving conservation and sustainable use of the ocean.[23] On legal instruments (SDG 14.c.1), there is very limited information, where only the data on the Agreement on Port State Measures on illegal, unreported, and unregulated fishing is included in the 2020 SDGs Reports.[24] Greater transparency on SDG 14.c will help policy makers understand the degree to which the States are embracing international legal instruments that contribute to improving ocean governance.

Overall, as the 2020 SDGs Reports show, significant additional efforts by governments, supported by adequate resources, are urgently needed to collect and report data on the relevant SDG 14 targets and indicators to understand the level of global progress on tackling marine pollution. Robust monitoring and reporting based on standardized measures are

---

19 2019 SDGs REPORT, *supra* note 12, at 12 (stating that "[a]nalysis of the clean water indicator, a measurement of the degree of ocean pollution, shows that water quality challenges are widespread, but are most acute in some equatorial zones, especially in parts of Asia, Africa and Central America").
20 SG's 2020 SDGs REPORT, *supra* note 7, at 15 (noting that most of the marine protected areas are in Oceania, Latin America, and the Caribbean); for information on the 2020 deadline, *see* 2020 SDGs REPORT, *supra* note 7, at 60.
21 2020 SDGs REPORT, *supra* note 7, at 53 (emphasizing that the percentages are significant because the fishing activities are vital for local communities and Indigenous Peoples).
22 *See generally* U.N. Statistics Division, *Sustainable Development Goals: SDG Indicators*, DEP. OF ECON. & SOC. AFFAIRS, (Sept. 2020), https://unstats.un.org/sdgs/metadata/ (last visited Nov. 16, 2020).
23 On the state of ocean science around the world, *see* Luis Valdez et al., *Global ocean science report: the current status of ocean science around the world*, IOC-UNESCO (2017).
24 Indian Ocean Tuna Commission (IOTC), *Agreement on Port State Measures to Prevent, Deter and Eliminate Illegal, Unreported and Unregulated Fishing*, Res. 10/11, 30/04/2010 FAO (June 5, 2016); 2020 SDGs REPORT, *supra* note 7, at 16, 19 (noting that 97 countries have signed the agreement and nearly 70% of countries reported scoring high on the implementation). For more information, *see Agreement on Port State Measures*, FAO, www.fao.org/port-state-measures/background/parties-psma/en/ (last visited Nov. 16, 2020).

critical components for determining the efficacy of policies.[25] To that end, the recent update to SDG 14.1.1[26] coupled with robust capacity building to achieve uniform application of the relevant guidance and the methodology[27] will provide additional information that the policy makers and stakeholders can use to make better informed decisions on specific, albeit partial, aspects of marine pollution.

Interlinkages among SDGs on Marine Pollution

While individual SDG targets and indicators provide valuable insights on a specific topic, understanding the nexus between and among the relevant data can be a basis for a more comprehensive understanding of an issue, particularly if the challenge is multidimensional and involves a wide range of stakeholders. As stated by the Under-Secretary-General in the 2019 SDGs Report, "solutions ... and other global challenges are also interlinked. Valuable opportunities exist to accelerate progress by examining interlinkages across Goals."[28] For addressing marine pollution, while SDG14 is the Goal that is specific to the ocean, other SDGs are relevant.[29] For example, as discussed in the 2019 SDGs Report, on SDG 14.1, "improvements require policy commitments at the country level to expand access to wastewater treatment and to reduce chemical and nutrient runoff from agricultural sources, along with global commitments to reduce plastic debris."[30] Indeed, there are potential synergistic links between the relevant SDG 14 targets and other SDGs to curb marine pollution.

Box 23.1 provides select SDG targets that may interlink with SDG 14 targets on marine pollution, which may lead to positive or negative synergies.[31]

---

25 P.J. Kershaw et al., *Guidelines for the Monitoring and Assessment of Plastic Litter and Microplastics in the Ocean*, GESAMP JOINT GROUP OF EXPERTS ON THE SCI. ASPECTS OF MARINE ENVTL. PROTECTION, 130, 99 REP. AND STUD (2019).

26 G.A. Res. 71/313, *Work of the Statistical Commission Pertaining to the 2030 Agenda for Sustainable Development*, (Jul. 6, 2017) ; U.N. Econ. & Soc. Council, *Report of the Inter-Agency and Expert Group on Sustainable Development Goal Indicators*, 49th Sess., Annex II, E/CN.3/2018/2 (Dec. 19, 2017); U.N. Econ. & Soc. Council, *Report of the Inter-Agency and Expert Group on Sustainable Development Goal Indicators*, 51st Sess., Annex II & III, E/CN.3/2020/2 (December 20, 2019) [hereinafter "Global Indicator Framework"].

27 Elisabetta Bonotto et al., GLOBAL MANUAL ON OCEAN STATISTICS: TOWARDS A DEFINITION OF INDICATOR METHODOLOGIES, U.N. Env't, 46 (2018); *see generally also* U.N. Statistics Division, *SDG Indicators: Metadata Repository*, DEP. OF ECON. & SOC. AFFAIRS (2020), https://unstats.un.org/sdgs/metadata/ (last visited Nov. 16, 2020); Agreement on Port State Measures, *supra* note 24.

28 2019 SDGs REPORT, *supra* note 12, "Introduction."

29 For an analysis of some of the co-benefits between SDG 14 and the other 16 SDGs, *see* William Cheung et al., *Oceans and the Sustainable Development Goals: Co-Benefits, Climate Change & Social Equity*, NIPPON FOUNDATION - NEREUS PROGRAM, 28 (2017).

30 2019 SDGs REPORT, *supra* note 12, at 52.

31 The above list provides some of the relevant SDGs targets. The description in parenthesis is a shorthand of the targets for ease of reference. For the full description of the targets and indicators, *see* Global Indicator Framework, *supra* note 26.

BOX 23.1 Select SDG Targets That May Interlink with SDG 14 Targets on Marine Pollution

- **SDG 1.2** (proportion of men, women, and children of all ages living in poverty in all its dimensions)
- **SDG 2.4** (sustainable food production systems that help maintain ecosystems)
- **SDG 3.9** (number of deaths and illnesses from hazardous chemicals)
- **SDG 4.7** (mainstream sustainable development in education)
- **SDG 5.5** (women's full and effective participation and equal opportunities for leadership)
- **SDG 6, all targets** (availability and sustainable management of water and sanitation for all)
- **SDG 7, all targets** (affordable, reliable, and sustainable and modern energy for all)
- **SDG 8.4** (global resource efficiency in consumption and production, decouple economic growth from environmental degradation)
- **SDG 9, all targets** (resilient infrastructure, promote inclusive and sustainable industrialization, and foster innovation)
- **SDG 10.b** (official development assistance and financial flows to States where the need is greatest)
- **SDG 11.6** (environmental impacts of cities)
- **SDG 12.4** (environmentally sound management of chemicals and wastes throughout their life cycle), **SDG 12.5** (substantial reduction in waste generation), **12.6** (sustainable practices and integration of sustainability information into the company's reporting), **12.7** (sustainable public procurement practices), **12.8** (access to information to live in harmony with nature), **12.a** (support for developing countries), **12.b** (sustainable development impacts on sustainable tourism), **12.c** (inefficient fossil-fuel subsidies that encourage wasteful consumption)
- **SDG 13, all targets** (combat climate change impacts)
- **SDG 15.1** (conservation, restoration, and sustainable use of terrestrial and inland freshwater ecosystems), **15.2** (sustainable management of all types of forests), **15.3** (restoration of degraded land), **15.4** (conservation of mountain ecosystems), **15.9** (integration of ecosystem and biodiversity values into national and local planning), **15.a** (financial resources to conserve and sustainably use biodiversity and ecosystems) and **15.b** (finance sustainable forest management)
- **SDG 16.2** (trafficking and all forms of violence of children), **16.3** (rule of law at the national and international levels), **16.5** (corruption and bribery), **16.6** (effective, accountable, and transparent institutions at all levels), **16.7** (representative decision-making at all levels), **16.8** (participation of developing countries in global governance), **16.10** (public access to information and protection of fundamental freedom), and **16.a** (relevant national institutions for building capacity at all levels)
- **SDG 17, all targets** (global partnerships for sustainable development)

The select SDG targets in Box 23.1 relate to the lives of the global population and the means to address the multidimensional and cumulative impacts of the stressors that contribute to marine pollution.[32] The listed SDG targets also take into consideration the needs of the resource-scarce States on capacity building, technology transfer, and funding.

Toward Positive Synergies: Maximizing the Strengths of Collective Contributions

While outside of the scope of this chapter, consideration of the relevant SDGs in an integrated and a coherent manner would be an imperative assessment to identify trade-offs, positive synergies, and unintended negative consequences. Such assessment to provide options for a way forward could provide useful insights that could be incorporated into legal and policy considerations for prioritizing, building positive synergies, and avoiding unintended negative consequences in addressing marine pollution. Also, the generated knowledge could contribute to improving the work associated with the SDG indicators,[33] leading to a better understanding of where the world stands on achieving the SDG targets and the indicators. Further, identification of linkages and a holistic analysis thereof can be the basis of an integrated approach to addressing marine pollution, as the world looks to rebuild during and after the COVID-19 pandemic:

> "Building back better and greener" needs to be at the center of the COVID-19 response, and mainstreaming nature into our decision making will be critical to support people's lives and livelihoods; manage risks and build resilience; addresses climate change, biodiversity loss and pollution; and ensure that human rights are upheld and no one is left behind.[34]

Marine pollution governance based on the ecosystem-based approaches[35] utilizing the best available science is needed to effectively tackle the cumulative impacts of human activities on biodiversity. In fact, a more holistic approach[36] can generate great benefits. For example, a study on four ocean-based sectors found that investments in sustainable ocean solutions

---

32 For examples of the cumulative human impacts on marine pollution, *see* IPCC SPECIAL REPORT 2019, *supra* note 1; IPBES Global Assess., *supra* note 3; First Global Integrated Marine Assess., *supra* note 4; WORLD RESOURCES INSTITUTE, *supra* note 6.

33 For the current status and the future work on the indicators, *see Report of the Inter-Agency and Expert Group on Sustainable Development Goal Indicators—Note by the Secretary-General*, U.N. ECON & SOC. COUNCIL, 51st Sess., Annex A (Timeline), E/CN.3/2020/2 (December 20, 2019)

34 High-Level Political Forum on Sustainable Development, *Protecting the Planet and Building Resilience*, 2020 Sess., 1 ¶ 3, (Jul. 8, 2020).

35 *See* U.N. Secretary General, *Oceans and the Law of the Sea—Report of the Secretary-General*, 38 ¶ 136, U.N. Doc. A/61/63 (March 9, 2006). (The unique aspect of the ecosystem approach is that "it is integrated and holistic, taking account of all the components of an ecosystem, both physical and biological, of their interaction and of all activities that could effect them." Consideration of human activities is a crucial part of the approach.)

36 For a discussion on integrated ocean management, *see* Ines Aguiar Branco et al., *Integrated Ocean and Management: 5 Success Stories of Ocean Health and Wealth*, WORLD RESOURCES INSTITUTE (May 19, 2020), www.wri.org/ (last visisted Nov. 16, 2020).

have a high rate of return.[37] Indeed, robust multi-stakeholder partnerships, which include the private sector, can lead to innovative transformative changes.[38]

The COVID-19 pandemic also raises important questions in the context of marine pollution, specifically, governance measures in a time of a crisis. As the world suffers from loss of lives and livelihoods, some governments have made decisions to relax important regulatory or economic measures designed to counter marine pollution.[39] In drafting instruments or policies and in the governance thereof, it will be important to consider what, if any, emergency measures may need to be adopted. To that end, policymakers would benefit from scrutinizing what is meant by an emergency in a given law or policy and minimize suspension or change(s) in the measures (e.g., duration, scope, mitigation measures, etc.) so that short-term gains would not significantly outweigh the mid- to long-term benefits that the governance measures were intended to achieve. To that end, application of the ecosystem-based approaches and the precautionary principle[40] are imperative to ensure that policy decisions do not lead to unintended negative consequences.

If the roles, responsibilities, and moreover, the existing and possible contributions of various stakeholders can be identified and understood, pathways could be created to maximize resources (i.e., within governments and among various governments, intergovernmental organizations, non-governmental organizations, the private sector, etc.). Boosting partnerships, cooperation, and collaboration can lead to creating positive synergies, so that issues can be streamlined and resources can be pooled in a systematic manner to avoid disagreements on what needs to be prioritized. Therefore, investing in the work to identify and assess possible interlinkages among various issues to de-silo fragmented initiatives with an eye toward a transition to a holistic approach can lead to greater gains by all.

---

37 *See* Helen Ding & Manaswita Konar, *A Sustainable Ocean Economy for 2050: Approximating Its Benefits and Costs*, WORLD RESOURCES INSTITUTE (Jul. 20, 2020), www.investableoceans.com/ (last visited Nov. 16, 2020). (The analysis focused on four sustainable ocean-based investments (i.e. conserving and restoring mangrove habitats; scaling up offshore wind production; decarbonizing the international shipping sector; and increasing the production of sustainably sourced ocean-based proteins to ensure a healthy, balanced human diet by 2050).)

38 IOC-UNESCO, *Advancing Science for Sustainable Ocean Business: an opportunity for the private sector*, UNESCO, IOC/INF-1389, 24 (2020).

39 For a list of mask mandates, *see* Andy Markowitz, *State-by-State Guide to Face Mask Requirements*, AARP (Nov. 17, 2020), www.aarp.org/health/ (last visited Nov. 16, 2020). (The use of face masks and gloves, in certain circumstances) are widely encouraged (and mandated in certain geographic areas) to stop the spread of COVID-19. Such need has caused a surge in the use of disposable masks and gloves); *see also* Joana C. Prata et al., *COVID-19 Pandemic Repercussions on the Use and Management of Plastics*, ENVIRON. SCI. TECH., 54, 13, 7760–65 (June 12, 2020.) (The study estimates the global use of 129 billion face masks and 65 billion gloves per month); *see also* U.N. NEWS, *COVID-19 Environmental Roll Bank "Irrational and Irresponsible": Rights Expert*, (Apr. 15, 2020), https://news.un.org/ (last visited Nov. 16, 2020); (Plea by David Boyd, U.N. Special Rapporteur on human rights and the environment); Laura Tenenbaum, *The Amount of Plastic Waste Is Surging Because of The Coronavirus Pandemic*, FORBES, (Apr. 26, 2020, 1:58pm EDT), www.forbes.com/ (last visited Nov. 16, 2020) (article discussing the movement to relax measures countering plastic pollution).

40 On a discussion on the origin, legal status, content, and context of application, *see generally* Gerd Winter, *International Principles of Marine Environmental Protection, in* HANDBOOK ON MARINE ENV'T PROTECTION, 595–98 (Til Markus & Markus Salomon eds., 2018).

Case Study: Combating Marine Plastic Pollution—An Urgent Global Multidimensional Challenge

Marine Plastic Pollution: Multidimensional Issue Involving a Wide Range of Stakeholders

Among the myriad of threats to ocean health, marine plastic pollution (i.e., plastic litter and microplastics)[41] presents a challenge that is truly multidimensional where an assessment of interlinkages of the relevant SDGs are of critical importance. Since Leo Baekeland in 1907 invented the first fully synthetic plastic as "the material of a thousand uses,"[42] our lives have progressively become intricately entwined with the material. While offering wide-ranging benefits to consumers,[43] the negative societal, economic, and ecological costs have become significant and the severe impacts continue to accelerate.[44] In addition, microplastics are pervasive and not only impact biodiversity, but also have potential human health implications.[45]

Marine plastic pollution damages impact on a wide range of sectors (e.g., shipping, tourism, fisheries, etc.), and biodiversity as well as posing potential threats to human health. The damages can be "direct" (i.e., the increased costs to conduct business) and "indirect" (i.e., negative impacts on biodiversity, human health, and productivity in various marine sectors).[46] The cost to address the impacts are high; for example, one study estimates that damages to the environment (exclusive of the costs on environmental function damages) are at least $8 billion per year at the global level.[47] Another study estimates that there is an annual loss of $500–$2500 billion in the value of benefits derived from marine ecosystem services.[48] A comprehensive study that provides a reliable data on the costs estimates of direct and indirect damages and a clear identification of the industries involved (e.g., producers, waste/wastewater treatment, shipping, fisheries, aquaculture sectors, etc.), as well as the relationship with the final impacts of the pollutants are not available.[49] However, what is clear is that a vast number of stakeholders are involved and that the problems are severe, long-term, and global, in need of an urgent and sustained action.

There are numerous SDG targets that are relevant to marine plastic pollution. In addition to the specific SDG 14 indicator on marine plastic pollution (SDG 14.1.1(*b*)), many of the other SDGs identified in Box 23.1 as well as other SDG 14 targets and indicators[50]

---

41 U.N.E.P. Res. 11, 2nd Sess., at ¶ 1, U.N. Doc. UNEP/EA.2/Res.11 (Aug. 4, 2016). (Defining microplastics as "[p]lastic particles less than 5 millimetres in diameter, including nano-sized particles").
42 On the history of synthetic plastic, *see History and Future of Plastics*, SCIENCE HISTORY INSTITUTE, www.sciencehistory.org/ (last visited Nov. 16, 2020).
43 For information on some of the benefits of the use of plastic in products, *see* Jennifer Killinger & Allyson Wilson, *Plastics: Consumer Benefits*, AMERICAN CHEMISTRY COUNCIL, https://plastics.americanchemistry.com/ (last visited Nov. 16, 2020).
44 *See generally* U.N.E.P., *Marine Plastic Debris and Microplastics—Global Lessons and Research to Inspire Action and Guide Policy Change*, U.N. ENVIRONMENT PROGRAMME (2016), https://wedocs.unep.org/ (last visited Nov. 17, 2020); *see also* U.N. Environment Programme, 3rd Sess., at 19, UNEP/EA.3/INF/5 (Oct. 5, 2017) [hereinafter "UN Environment 2017"].
45 *Id.* at 81; *see also* U.N.E.P. Res. 11, *supra* note 41.
46 *Id.* at 19.
47 *Id.* at 82–83.
48 *See* Nicola J. Beaumont et al., *Global Ecological, Social and Economic Impacts of Marine Plastic*, 142 MARINE PLASTIC BULLETIN, 189–95 (May 2019) (this study acknowledges that there is a need for a more comprehensive assessment to understand the multidimensional damages associated with marine plastic pollution).
49 UN Environment 2017, *supra* note 44, at 84–85.
50 The other relevant SDG 14 targets and indicators on marine plastic pollution are SDG 14.2, 14.2.1, 14.5, 14.5.1, 14.7, 14.7.1, 14.a, 14.a.1,14.c, and 14.c.1.

are relevant. Therefore, the multidimensional aspects of marine plastic pollution provide "a unique opportunity to consolidate all the principles of Sustainable Development" by implementing "long-term and robust strategies to achieve a considerable reduction of marine litter, including by partnering with stakeholders at relevant levels to address their production, marketing and use"[51] and on other elements, such as the product end of life processes, protection of biodiversity, human health, and food security. A comprehensive framework is consistent with Agenda 2030 because "[s]ustainable development requires coherent policy that aims for environmental, social, and economic outcomes. Effects on biodiversity, human health, and food security would be important considerations in achieving sustainable practices, as well as the right to a healthy environment."[52]

Existing Governance Measures and Institutional Framework Plus an Outlook for the Future

In terms of governance measures, international legal instruments and institutional frameworks play important roles in combating marine pollution. Indeed, numerous agreements and various institutional arrangements exist.[53] However, some subject matters (e.g., governance of marine biodiversity areas beyond national jurisdiction)[54] may benefit from a new global, integrated, and coordinated action because of the multidimensional nature of the challenges, as well as the gaps in legal and institutional arrangements where sectoral and fragmented governance measures are ineffective. Marine plastic pollution arguably falls into such a category. For example, while nearly 30 international policies have been agreed to on reducing land-based sources of plastic pollution since the beginning of the year 2000, none offer global, binding, specific, and measurable targets.[55] Also, other elements of marine plastic pollution need to be considered, which the existing laws and institutional arrangements do not comprehensively address.

At the third meeting of the United Nations Environment Assembly (UNEA)[56] in 2017, significant gaps in existing legal and policy framework at the international, regional, and sub-regional levels were identified. The assessment concluded that a fragmented approach to governance is insufficient to tackle the global marine plastic pollution problem.[57] Based on the extensive analysis, the UN Assessment suggests that one of the three options,[58] "a new

---

51 UN Environment 2017, *supra* note 44, at 85.
52 *Id*. at 89.
53 *See* Annick de Marffy-Mantuano, *Legal Tools in Combatting Marine Pollution and Mitigating the Effects of Acidification*, *in* FULFILLING THE SUSTAINABLE DEVELOPMENT GOAL (Kakar, Popovski, & Robinson eds., 2020).
54 *See* Kristina Gjerde & Marjo Vierros, *Achieving SDG 14: Time for a Global Ocean Approach*, *in* FULFILLING THE SUSTAINABLE DEVELOPMENT GOAL (Kakar, Popovski, & Robinson eds., 2020).
55 Rachel Karasik et al., *20 Years of Government Responses to the Global Plastic Pollution Problem: The Plastics Policy Inventory*, 114, NICHOLAS INSTITUTE FOR ENVTL. POL'Y SOLUTIONS, DUKE U. (2020) [hereinafter "The Plastics Policy Inventory"].
56 The U.N. Environment Assembly is the highest level decision-making body on the environment in the world.
57 *See generally* UN Environment 2017, *supra* note 44; *see also* Ad hoc open-ended expert group on marine litter and microplastics, 1st mtg, *Combating marine plastic litter and microplastics: an assessment of the effectiveness of relevant international, regional and subregional governance strategies and approaches*, U.N. Doc. UNEP/AHEG/2018/1/INF/3 (May 8, 2018).
58 *See id*. at 86 (The other two options are (1) Maintain the status quo and continue current efforts and (2) Review and revise existing frameworks to address marine plastic litter and microplastics and add a component to coordinate industry. For a summary chart of the three options with additional information, *see id*. at 87–88).

global architecture with a multilayered governance approach, combining legally binding and voluntary measures" can be a platform to facilitate the following:

- An international body (i.e., existing or a new body) that coordinates and strengthens governance measures under various instruments;
- An integrated approach to governance by incorporating principles from various SDGs, including "goals for sustainable cities and communities, chemicals management, reductions in production of waste and pollution, as well as protection of the marine environment;" and
- A comprehensive global strategy that takes into consideration industry innovation, best available science, and a platform for multi-stakeholder collaboration.[59]

It is important to note that the above option is a hybrid (i.e., binding and voluntary) multi-layered approach which would allow for regional differences. Such flexibility may promote engagement by States and industry sectors in private–public partnerships and industry-led initiatives.

Numerous experts support the idea of an international binding agreement[60] and discussions at the UNEA continue on the fate of an integrated global approach.[61] In addition, momentum continues to grow among various regional groups and Member States toward this global architecture.[62] Such partnerships and collaborative work may galvanize the necessary political will to move forward toward a new global binding treaty.

While a global governance approach has potential, it is not without challenges. In fact, some experts caution that development of a binding global treaty could take decades due to various factors[63] (i.e., wide range of stakeholders and the binding nature of

---

59 *Id.* at 150.
60 The Plastics Policy Inventory, *supra* note 55, at 114; *see also Report of the Fourth Meeting of the Ad Hoc Open-Ended Expert Group on Marine Litter and Microplastics,* 4th mtg, U.N. Doc. UNEP/AHEG/4/7 (18 November 2020).
61 *See generally Schedule,* U.N. ENVIRONMENT ASSEMBLY, https://environmentassembly.unenvironment.org / (last visited Nov. 16, 2020).
62 IUCN resolution on marine plastic pollution, WCC-2020-Res-019-EN Stopping the global plastic pollution crisis in marine environments by 2030 https://portals.iucn.org/library/sites/library/files/ resrecfiles/WCC_2020_RES_019_EN.pdf was approved. The results are available at: https://iucn.s3.eu-west-3.amazonaws.com/results_4_november_final_022.pdf Through 2024, IUCN will take the lead in implementing this resolution with all the stakeholders. Governments of Ecuador, Germany, Ghana and Vietnam are jointly organizing a Ministerial Conference in September 2021 to build momentum and political will to advance a coherent global strategy to end marine litter and plastic pollution. https:// www.bmu.de/en/pressrelease/upcoming-international-ministerial-conference-to-build-a-global-vision-to-tackle-marine-litter-and-p-1/ Julien Rochette et al., *Combating Marine Plastic Litter: State of Play and Perspectives,* 9, IDDRI, (Jun. 8, 2020); *see also,* Our Ocean 2019, *Commitment 238,* NORWEGIAN MINISTRY OF FOREIGN AFFAIRS, https://ourocean2019.no/ (last visited Nov. 16, 2020) ("Norway will work for a global agreement on marine plastic litter and microplastics by 2023"); *Group of Friends to Combat Marine Plastic Pollution,* NORWEGIAN MINISTRY OF FOREIGN AFFAIRS, https://www.norway.no/ (last visited Nov. 16, 2020) (On June 8, 2020, Group of Friends to Compact Marine Plastic Pollution was launched as an initiative that focuses on the diplomatic community at the UN Headquarters in New York, which is intended to complement the on-going discussions at UNEA. There are 44 founding Member States plus the European Union).
63 The Plastics Policy Inventory, *supra* note 55, at 115 (noting, however, that UN Environment 2017 provides a scenario where an international binding instrument could be completed within a shorter period of time); UN Environment 2017, *supra* note 44, at 120.

such an agreement,[64] complexity of the issues, and the consensus-based negotiations). The effectiveness of a global marine plastic treaty will also depend on the design and the level of stakeholder engagement in the negotiation process.[65] Further, as with any other global agreements, a critical mass of States' participation, as well as robust implementation, enforcement, monitoring, reporting, and review at the national and sub-national levels will dictate the level of success of the treaty. Finally, a review at the global level on the progress (or not) on the measures implemented could determine if and what refinements would be required to maximize the positive impacts of the new global architecture.

To address the possible long duration in negotiating and adopting a global binding treaty, UN Environment 2017's hybrid approach prioritizes an urgent undertaking of voluntary measures and in parallel, development of a treaty.[66] Indeed, immediate to short-term measures[67] need not wait for a global treaty and could complement an international effort. For example, increasing investments in research, education, and partnerships is a critical bridge between now and when (if) there is a global treaty on marine plastics governance. To that end, a platform, such as the Intergovernmental Oceanographic Commission's Decade of Ocean Science, could contribute as an enabler to quickly bring multi-stakeholders in a multidisciplinary way to accelerate transformative changes.[68]

Recommendations for Action on Combating Marine Pollution

Below are three key recommendations for countries to consider in accelerating the attainment of the relevant targets and indicators of SDG 14[69] on marine pollution, with a focus on legal instruments, policies, and institutional frameworks:

- Identify and ratify international agreements that combat marine pollution[70] and ensure that the agreed-upon commitments at the global level are effectively implemented at

---

64 *See id.* at 77–78, 150; *see also* GLOBAL PLASTIC ACTION PARTNERSHIP, https://globalplasticaction.org (last visited Nov. 16, 2020).
65 *Id.* at 99–120 (provides three options (i.e. maintain the status quo; review and revise existing frameworks; and a new global binding agreement)). *See generally also* Philippe Le Billon & Ina Tessnow-von Wysocki, *Plastics at Sea: Treaty Design for a Global Solution to Marine Plastic Pollution*, 100 ENVTL. SCI. & POL'Y, 94–104 (2019) (in the paper, Tessnow-von Wysocki and Le Billon identify seven treaty elements that are likely to contribute to a successful plastics regime: (a) the inclusion of the principle of common but differentiated responsibilities; (b) a scope addressing sea-based and land-based sources, as well as chemical additives and all stages of the lifecycle of plastics; (c) issue-linkage to international plastics trade; (d) a financial mechanism to support necessary implementation measures; (e) effective monitoring, reporting, and review procedures; (f) flexibility to adapt to local contexts and new scientific findings; and (g) enforcement through incentivizing compliance and deterring non-compliance).
66 *Id.* at 85–127.
67 *Id.* at 87–88, 104–127 (on various plastic pollution governance measure recommendations and the timeline thereof); *see also* Brajesh Dubey et al., *Leveraging Multi-Target Strategies to Address Plastic Pollution in the Context of an Already Stressed Ocean*, 41–50, WORLD RESOURCES INSTITUTE (May 27, 2020); *see also* The Plastic Policy Inventory, *supra* note 55, at 92–103.
68 *See* OCEAN DECADE: THE SCIENCE WE NEED FOR THE OCEAN WE WANT, IOC-UNESCO, IOC/BRO/2018/7 REV (2019), www.oceandecade.org (last visited Nov. 17, 2020).
69 The relevant SDG 14 targets and indicators are SDG 14.1, 14.1.1(*a*), 14.1.1(*b*), 14.2, 14.2.1, 14.3, 14.3.1, 14.5, 14.5.1, 14.7, 14.7.1, 14.a, 14.a.1, 14.c, and 14.c.1.
70 *See* Marffy-Mantuano, *supra* note 53 (for further discussions on the various international agreements on marine pollution).

the regional, national, and sub-national levels through legal, policy, and institutional frameworks;
- Identify legal, policy, and institutional framework gaps related to marine pollution at the international, regional, national, and sub-national levels, and address such gaps through legal instruments or voluntary measures; and
- Identify combating marine pollution as a priority for the diplomatic mission and actively engage in the work of intergovernmental and international organizations (e.g., UN General Assembly, UNEA, etc.), including the on-going negotiations on the high seas treaty[71] and the discussions on a global binding marine plastic pollution treaty[72].

In addition, below are some of the supporting elements to accelerate the attainment of SDGs associated with marine pollution:

- Conduct needs assessment to strengthen the State's ability to meet the relevant SDGs targets on marine pollution and fill the gaps with adequate resources (e.g., human, technology, infrastructure, etc.) supported by sustained, predictable, and adequate funding;
- Foster science and incorporate it into making informed decisions[73] based on the precautionary principle, ecosystem approach, and the best available science;
- Increase standardized data outputs on SDGs that are relevant to marine pollution to contribute to a holistic understanding of marine pollution at the global, regional, national, and sub-national levels, supported by enhanced investments in innovative data systems that can promote internal consistency, comparability, and overall quality of data;
- Breakdown the siloes within the government by identifying relevant SDG targets and indicators to find positive synergies to maximize available resources and transition to a holistic approach with an unwavering commitment to cooperation and collaboration;[74] and
- Actively identify and engage in partnerships with various stakeholders (including other States, intergovernmental organizations, non-governmental organizations, the private sector, etc.) toward finding and implementing an innovative fit for purpose solutions. Consider ways to provide incentives to boost partnerships that will lead to innovative initiatives.

---

71 *See* Gjerde, *supra* note 54.
72 For a discussion on some of the insights that can be gained from the high seas treaty negotiations, see, H. Muraki Gottlieb, *Filling the Gaps in the Global Governance of Marine Plastic Pollution*, Natural Resources & Environment, The American Bar Association, Section of Environment, Energy, and Resources, Vol. 35, No.4, Spring 2021.
73 In this context, "science" refers to natural and social sciences as well as Indigenous Knowledge. *See* Oran R. Young, et al., *Governing Arctic Seas: Regional Lessons from the Bering Strait and Barents Sea*, INFORMED DECISION MAKING Volume 1, Preface (2020).
74 *Enhancing NDCs by 2020: Resources for Strengthening National Climate Action*, 29, WORLD RESOURCES INSTITUTE (Dec. 5, 2019), www.ndcs.undp.org/ (last visited Nov. 17, 2020) (for example, "[r]esearch shows ocean-based actions to reduce or sequester greenhouse gas emissions could deliver emission reductions of up to 4 billion tonnes CO2e per annum by 2030 and 11 billion tonnes CO2e per annum by 2050"); *see generally also* Taryn Fransen et al., *Enhancing NDCs, A Guide to Strengthening National Climate Plans for 2020*, WORLD RESOURCES INSTITUTE, (Sept. 2019).

In addition, for the States with resources, fostering capacity building and technology transfer in resource-scarce countries will contribute toward global attainment of the SDGs. Such contributions can be made in the form of adequate, predictable, and sustained in-kind resources or funding.

Conclusion

The actions of humankind are destroying the ocean and the biodiversity that we need to survive. Marine pollution is certainly a key part of the puzzle that accelerates ocean degradation. To effectively address this issue, a coherent and enhanced collaboration is necessary. However, while various efforts are underway, progress has been too little and too slow, as indicated in various studies and reports, including the 2020 SDGs Reports. The unique feature of SDGs is that they are interlinked and indivisible.[75] There are numerous interlinkages between SDG 14 and other SDGs, and the nexus could be identified and assessed. Insights from such analysis can be incorporated into legal and policy considerations for the purposes of prioritizing, building positive synergies, and avoiding unintended negative consequences in addressing marine pollution.

An example of a governance area that may benefit from an integrated approach through a global binding instrument is marine plastic pollution. The concern for "yet another agreement" may be mitigated if the new legal instrument plays a role to fill the gaps in governance (i.e., complement various existing legal instruments and voluntary initiatives as well as institutional frameworks) and for an international body to play a coordinating role by facilitating collaboration at the global, regional, and national levels. Any new legal instrument will benefit from inclusion of robust measures to foster science, provide needed capacity building and technology transfer, as well as a funding mechanism to create an enabling environment for acutely resource-constrained States. Such resources are particularly important for SIDS since they largely depend on marine resources for their economies and disproportionately suffer from marine plastic pollution.[76] Finally, strong engagement of a wide spectrum of stakeholders will be critical for the new global architecture's success.

As science advances and our biodiversity changes, we will need flexibility to adapt to ensure that governance measures continue to be effective, using the precautionary principle, ecosystem based-approaches, and the best available science as the basis of informed decision-making.[77] While we have much to gain from further research, we have sufficient knowledge,

---

75 The Preamble of the Agenda 2030 states, "[t]he 17 Sustainable Development Goals and 169 targets which we are announcing today demonstrate the scale and ambition of this new universal Agenda. They seek to build on the Millennium Development Goals and complete what these did not achieve. They seek to realize the human rights of all and to achieve gender equality and the empowerment of all women and girls. They are integrated and indivisible and balance the three dimensions of sustainable development: the economic, social and environmental." *See* 2030 Agenda, *supra* note 9.

76 Florina Lachmann et al., *Marine Plastic Litter on Small Island Developing States (SIDS): Impacts and Measures*, SWEDISH INSTITUTE FOR THE MARINE ENV'T (2017), https://havsmiljoinstitutet.se/ (last visited Nov. 17, 2020).

77 For example, SDGs are currently silent on anthropogenic underwater noise and deoxygenation. There are increasing scientific studies and data to support that time may be ripe to consider incorporating certain aspects of the issues in the SDG indicators. For information on noise pollution, *see generally* U.N. Secretary General, *Oceans and the Law of the Sea—Report of the Secretary-General*, 73rd Sess., U.N. Open-ended Informal Consultative Process (ICP) (Mar. 13, 2018). For presentations from the ICP, see

resources, and the experience to act now, in solidarity, to combat marine pollution so that the ocean can continue to provide the bounties we depend on for our survival. As we celebrate the 75th anniversary of the UN, let us embrace the Decade of Action[78] and deliver on the SDGs through innovative fit-for-purpose solutions to build a world that is inclusive, equitable, and sustainable.

---

www.un.org/Depts/los/consultative_process/icp19_panellist.pdf. The following literature provides an extensive study on ocean deoxygenation: D. Laffoley & J.M. Baxter, *Ocean Deoxygenation: Everyone's Problem—Causes, Impacts, Consequences and Solutions* 1, 588 IUCN (2019), https://portals.iucn.org/library/sites/library/files/documents/2019-048-En.pdf (last visited Nov. 17, 2020).

78 *See* UN DECADE OF ACTION, www.un.org/ (last visited Nov. 17, 2020).

24 Using Terrestrial Ecosystems Sustainably and Halting Biodiversity Loss

John G. Robinson and Federica Pesce

Introduction

Nature is the foundation of our societies, our economies, and the existence and well-being of all people. Nearly half of the world's population directly depends on natural resources for their livelihoods and more than half of the world's total gross domestic product (GDP)— $44 trillion—is dependent on nature and its services.[1]

Sustainable Development Goal (SDG) 15 focuses on the conservation and sustainable use of terrestrial ecosystems and biodiversity, including halting desertification and land degradation and combating illegal trade of endangered species. Given the importance of the integrity of nature for the human endeavor, SDG 15 is a foundational goal for the other SDGs. This chapter assesses the progress, or lack of it, toward meeting specific SDG 15 targets designed to create action to protect and restore "Life on Land." It will reflect on the importance of SDG 15 for the achievement of other SDGs and the 2030 Agenda for Sustainable Development (Agenda 2030) and consider policy pathways that will advance their implementation.

Agenda 2030 builds on previous multilateral environmental agreements (MEAs) and treaties. A number of targets for SDG 15 were derived from the Aichi[2] Biodiversity Targets (Aichi Targets) and have a 2020 end date. This chapter is timely, therefore, as the international community considers its global commitments, and takes stock of the progress achieved.

The COVID-19 outbreak has underlined the importance of understanding the social, economic, and ecological conditions that enable the emergence of zoonoses. The chapter includes a case study that examines how the lack of progress on achieving SDG 15 targets is linked to the possible emergence of future zoonoses.

---

1 *Nature Risk Rising: Why the Crisis Engulfing Nature Matters for Business and the Economy*, WORLD ECONOMIC FORUM (Jan. 19, 2020), www.weforum.org/reports/nature-risk-rising-why-the-crisis-engulfing-nature-matters-for-business-and-the-economy.
2 Aichi is the Prefecture in Japan which hosted the Conference of the Parties of the Convention on Biological Diversity (CBD) in 2010. *See* Convention on Biological Diversity, Jun. 5, 1992, 1760 U.N.T.S. 69 (CBD); *Summary of the Tenth Conference of the Parties to the Convention on Biological Diversity*, IISD REPORTING SERVICES: EARTH NEGOTIATIONS BULLETIN (Oct. 18–29, 2010), https://enb.iisd.org/vol09/enb09544e.html.

Progress toward Selected SDG 15 Targets

SDG 15 builds on the Aichi Targets, which define the United Nations (UN) strategy for biodiversity conservation and have been influential in structuring national responses to conserving biodiversity and ecosystem services. Table 24.1 summarizes the linkages between SDG 15 targets and the Aichi Targets.

Of the 20 Aichi Targets, some are generally focused on the pressures on biodiversity (Targets 5–10), some on the status of biodiversity (Targets 11–13), and others on the responses of government and society to the challenge of the loss of biodiversity and ecosystem services (Targets 1–4, 14–20). SDG 15 also focused on addressing pressures (Targets

Table 24.1 Summary of linkages between SDG 15 targets and Aichi Biodiversity Targets (based on CBD, 2016).

Sustainable Development Goal 15 Targets		Relevant Aichi Biodiversity Targets
15.1	Conservation, restoration, and sustainable use of terrestrial and inland freshwater ecosystems and their services (by 2020)	4—Sustainable production and consumption 5—Habitat loss halved or reduced 7—Sustainable agriculture, aquaculture, and forestry 11—Protected areas 14—Ecosystem services 15—Ecosystem restoration and resilience
15.2	Halt deforestation, sustainably manage and restore forests, increase afforestation and reforestation (by 2020)	4—Sustainable production and consumption 5—Habitat loss halved or reduced 7—Sustainable agriculture, aquaculture, and forestry 14—Ecosystem services 15—Ecosystem restoration and resilience
15.3	Combat desertification, restore degraded land and soil (by 2030)	4—Sustainable production and consumption 5—Habitat loss halved or reduced 15—Ecosystem restoration and resilience
15.4	Conservation of mountain ecosystems (by 2030)	11—Protected areas 14—Ecosystem services 15—Ecosystem restoration and resilience
15.5	Reduce natural habitats degradation, halt biodiversity loss (by 2030), protect and prevent the extinction of threatened species (by 2020)	5—Habitat loss halved or reduced 12—Reducing risk of extinction
15.6	Promote fair and equitable sharing of the benefits arising from the utilization of genetic resources	16—Access to and sharing benefits from genetic resources
15.7	End poaching and trafficking of protected species	12—Reducing risk of extinction
15.8	Prevent the introduction, reduce the impact of, and control invasive alien species (by 2020)	9—Invasive alien species prevented and controlled
15.9	Integrate biodiversity values into planning, development, strategies, and accounts (by 2020)	2—Biodiversity values integrated

Source: *Biodiversity and the 2030 Agenda for Sustainable Development Technical Note*, CBD (2016), www.cbd.int/development/doc/biodiversity-2030-agenda-technical-note-en.pdf.

15.2, 15.3, 15.5, 15.7, 15.8), improving states (15.1, 15.4), and identifying responses (15.6, 15.9, 15.a, 15.b, 15.c). Please see Table 24.1.

The State of Natural Ecosystems

SDG 15 covers forests, wetlands, mountains and drylands, and their conservation (15.1, 15.3, 15.4). Aichi Target 5 covers "all natural habitats, including forests." One measure of the trend in natural habitats is the loss of "wilderness", defined as habitats that have not been significantly modified by human activities.[3] Today, only 23% of the land surface meets this definition, and of this, an estimated 3.3 million km² of wilderness have been lost since 1990, with most loss occurring in South America (29.6%) and Africa (14%).[4] Using a somewhat different definition of natural habitat, the 2019 Intergovernmental Science-Policy Platform on Biodiversity and Ecosystem Services (IPBES) examined its global extent, and concluded that there had been a significant decline in the percentage since 2010.[5]

Forests

Forests are critical ecosystems for the world's biodiversity. According to The State of the World's Forests Report, forest area as a proportion of total land area (as per SDG indicator 15.1.1) decreased from 32.5% to 30.8% between 1990 and 2020, with a slowing in the average rate of forest cover loss of approximately 40% since 1990.[6] However, these figures aggregate natural forest and plantations. If one focuses just on natural forests, the rate of forest loss has *increased* by 43% since the New York Declaration of Forests in 2014.[7] Loss rates vary with forest type: Boreal forest loss is estimated at 0.18%/year, temperate broadleaf at 0.35%, temperate coniferous forest at 0.28%, tropical moist forest at 0.45%, and tropical dry forest at 0.58%.[8]

The pattern of loss is also evident in the continued loss of primary forests, which are disproportionately important for biodiversity.[9] Primary forests have declined by 2.5% globally and by 10% in the tropics over the period 1990–2015.[10] Over a similar time frame between 1993 and 2009, Watson et al. estimated a 35% decline in intact forests, which

---

3 James E. Watson et al., *The Exceptional Value of Intact Forest Ecosystems*, 2 NATURE ECOLOGY AND EVOLUTION 599–601(2018); James E. Watson et al., *Protect the Last of the Wild*, NATURE (Oct. 31, 2018).
4 James E. Watson, *Catastrophic Declines in Wilderness Areas Undermine Global Environment Targets*, 26(21) CURRENT BIOLOGY 2929–34 (Nov. 2016).
5 E. S. Brondizio et al. (eds.), *Global Assessment Report on Biodiversity and Ecosystem Services of the Intergovernmental Science-Policy Platform on Biodiversity and Ecosystem Services*, IPBES SECRETARIAT (2019), https://ipbes.net/global-assessment.
6 *See generally The State of the World's Forests 2020: Forests, Biodiversity and People* FAO & UNEP (2020), https://doi.org/10.4060/ca8642en.
7 Ingrid Schulte et al., *Protecting and Restoring Forests: A story of Large Commitments yet Limited Progress*, New York Declaration on Forests Five-Year Assessment Report, NYDF Assessment Partners, Climate Focus, (Sept. 2019).
8 Allie Goldstein et al., *Protecting Irrecoverable Carbon in Earth's Ecosystems*, 10 NATURE CLIMATE CHANGE 287–95 (Mar. 31, 2020).
9 Toby A. Gardner et al., *Prospects for Tropical Forest Biodiversity in a Human-Modified World*, 12(6) ECOLOGY LETTER 561–82 (Jun. 2009).
10 David Morales-Hidalgo et al., *Status and Trends in Global Primary Forest, Protected Areas, and Areas Designated for Conservation of Biodiversity from the Global Forest Resources Assessment 2015*, 352 FOREST ECOLOGY AND MGMT. 68–77 (Sept. 7, 2015).

include primary forests and are defined as largely free of human degradation.[11] Potapov et al. reported that intact forests worldwide had decreased by 7.2% between 2000 and 2013, driven largely by a tripling of the rate of loss when 2011–2013 is compared to ten years earlier.[12]

The world is not on track to meet global targets such as the UN Strategic Plan for Forests Goal 1 to increase forest area by 3% worldwide by 2030[13] and the New York Declaration on Forests Goal 1 to halve the rate of loss of natural forests globally by 2020.[14]

Wetlands

Wetlands, as part of SDG 15, comprise non-forested peatlands, marshes, and swamps. Data shows that we are not on track to meet global targets to halt wetland habitat loss. Estimates show that approximately 35% of the world's wetlands were lost between 1970 and 2015, and the loss rate has increased annually since 2000.[15] Human-made wetlands, however, increased by 233% from 1970 to 2014.[16] Goldstein et al. report that the recent annual loss rate of the area of marshes is 0.25%—while the loss rate of boreal and temperate peatlands was 0.0%, and the loss of tropical peatlands was 0.60%/year.[17]

Mountains

Mountain ecosystems, be they forests, grasslands, or wetlands, are threatened by agricultural expansion, unsustainable logging, climate change, and invasive species,[18] but there is little data on the trends in mountain ecosystems *per se* since the inception of the SDGs. The Food and Agriculture Organization's (FAO) Mountain Green Cover Index provides a preliminary baseline as of 2017, by measuring the percentage of land area covered by "green vegetation," including forests, shrubs, grasslands, and cropland.[19] Globally, 76% of mountain areas are covered with green vegetation. Mountain green cover was lowest in Western Asia and North Africa (60%), and highest in Oceania (96%).[20] Overall, there is a positive correlation

---

11 Watson et al., *supra* note 3.
12 Peter Potapov et al., *The Last Frontiers of Wilderness: Tracking Loss of Intact Forest Landscapes from 2000 to 2013*, 3(1) SCI. ADV. (Jan. 13, 2017).
13 G.A. Res. 71/285, *United Nations Strategic Plan for Forests 2017–2030*, 21st Sess. (Apr. 27, 2017).
14 NYDF Assessment Report, *supra* note 8.
15 C. Max Finlayson & Nick C. Davidson, *Global Wetland Outlook: Technical Note on Status and Trends*, SECRETARIAT OF THE RAMSAR CONVENTION ON WETLANDS (2018), https://static1.squarespace.com/static/5b256c78e17ba335ea89fe1f/t/5bcaeb0624a694d6076938eb/1540025105566/TN+-+Status+final+051018.pdf.
16 Sarah Darrah et al., *Improvements to the Wetland Extent Trends (WET) Index as a Tool for Monitoring Natural and Human-Made Wetlands*, 99 ECOLOGICAL INDICATORS 294–98 (Jan. 2019); *Wetland Extent Trends Index*, BIODIVERSITY INDICATORS PARTNERSHIP, www.bipindicators.net/indicators/wetland-extent-trends-index (last visited Dec. 3, 2020).
17 Goldstein et al., *supra* note 8.
18 Eva M. Spehn et al., *Mountain Biodiversity and Global Change*, Global Mountain Biodiversity Assessment of DIVERSITAS, Institute of Botany, U. of Basel (2010).
19 *Indicator 15.4.2—Mountain Green Cover Index*, FOOD & AGRI. ORG. (FAO) (2017), www.fao.org/sustainable-development-goals/indicators/1542/en/.
20 *Tracking Progress on Food and Agriculture—Related SDG indicators 2020*, FAO, (2019), www.fao.org/sdg-progress-report/en/.

between the health of mountain ecosystems (including their capacity of providing services) and the extent of green cover in mountain areas.

Drylands

SDG 15.1 focuses on the conservation of drylands, and 15.3 aims to combat desertification. Drylands, which cover something over 40% of the global land area, are probably most at risk from desertification. Approximately, 44% of the worlds' cultivated systems occur in these regions and they support the livelihoods of 1.5 billion people[21] and 50% of the world's livestock.[22] Estimates of the extent and severity of desertification are not consistent with one another, though perhaps 10–20% of drylands are degraded, with an additional 12 million ha degraded every year.[23] On top of that, Goldstein et al. report that the actual loss every year of tropical grasslands is 0.14% (equivalent to 1 million ha), and that of temperate grasslands is 0.14% (equivalent to 0.7 million ha).[24]

Aichi 5.1 targeted a decrease in the rate of loss of all natural habitats, including forests, and SDG 15.1 called for the conservation of terrestrial ecosystems. However, the state of terrestrial natural ecosystems continues to deteriorate.

The State of Ecosystem Services

SDG 15.1 also called for the conservation of ecosystem services, as does Aichi 14. Shepherd et al. assessed 13 indicators of ecosystem services (e.g. production of forest services) and 21 indicators of the state of nature (e.g. forest extent), and found that, while 60% of the services were increasing (people were receiving more services from nature), ultimately 86% of the state indicators were declining.[25] In other words, people are continuing to harvest services from nature and the use of those services is increasing, but at a cost to nature.

The State of Wild Species

SDG 15.5 strongly calls for halting "the loss of biodiversity and, by 2020, protect and prevent the extinction of threatened species," and Aichi 12 seeks to prevent extinction and improve the conservation status of species.

One measure of the state of wild species is the Living Planet Index, which aggregates trends in the population numbers of vertebrate species. According to the 2020 Living Planet Report, between 1970 and 2016 there has been an average 68% fall in monitored populations of mammals, birds, amphibians, reptiles, and fish.[26] This declining trend

---

21 Eshetu Yirdaw et al., *Rehabilitation of Degraded Dryland Ecosystems—Review*, 51(1B) SILVA FENNICA 1673 (2017).
22 *First Thematic Report—Biodiversity: Status and Trends of Species in Mediterranean Wetlands*, MEDITERRANEAN WETLANDS INITIATIVE MWO—OZHM (2016), https://medwet.org/publications/first-thematic-report-biodiversity-status-and-trends-of-species-in-mediterranean-wetlands/.
23 *Id.*
24 Goldstein et al., *supra* note 8.
25 Ellen Shepherd et al., *Status and Trends in Global Ecosystem Services and Natural Capital: Assessing Progress toward Aichi Biodiversity Target 14*, 9(6) CONSERVATION LETTERS 429 37 (2016).
26 *Living Planet Report 2020—Bending the Curve of Biodiversity Loss*, WWF (2020), https://livingplanet.panda.org/ (last visited Dec. 3, 2020).

continues. The International Union for Conservation of Nature (IUCN) Red List provides the best measure of the status of wild species, and while the status of some 120,000 species has been evaluated, this probably accounts for less than 5% of all species.[27] The Red List trends are discouraging, with the extinction risk of most taxonomic groups increasing, and some (like corals and cycads) increasing dramatically. The latest estimate of the percentage of threatened species with well-studied taxonomic groups include: Cycads (63%), amphibians (41%), selected dicot plants (36%), conifers (34%), reef-forming corals (33%), mammals (25%), and birds (14%).[28]

There has been little progress on stopping the loss of biodiversity and our planet is set to lose up to one million species, unless pressures on nature are drastically reduced. Some land use models indicate that it is possible to halt and reverse terrestrial biodiversity loss while also providing food for a growing human population.[29] This will require additional conservation and restoration actions, as well as efforts to increase the sustainability of global food systems.

The State of Genetic Diversity

The loss of natural ecosystems and wild species undoubtedly has concomitant losses in overall genetic diversity, but this is difficult to measure in its entirety. Aichi 13 focuses on the more measurable genetic diversity of cultivated plants, domesticated animals, and their wild relatives. IPBES 2019 reports that there has been a significant increase in plant genetic resources secured in conservation facilities (Aichi 13.1).[30] In contrast, the situation with animals is less sanguine. There has been a significant increase in at-risk terrestrial domesticated animal breeds (Aichi 13.2), and a significant increase in the Red Listing of wild relatives of farmed and domestic species (Aichi 13.3).[31]

Pressures on Nature

When considering the pressures on natural systems, it is useful to distinguish between direct drivers of loss (e.g. habitat loss, overexploitation, invasive species, climate change), indirect drivers (e.g. agriculture, fishing and forestry, water use, infrastructure), and root causes (e.g., unsustainable production and consumption patterns, demographic dynamics).[32] Rapid economic growth is often associated with higher levels of consumption per capita, which are accelerated by demographic dynamics leading to increased pressures on natural capital and resources. Global movement of goods and people is triggering increased levels of pollution and of the presence of invasive alien species. Resource extraction and rapid urban and infrastructure development are sources of air and soil pollution, causing adverse effects on ecosystems while heavily impacting human health. These trends are exacerbated by raising

---

27 *IUCN Red List of Threatened Species, Summary Statistics*, IUCN (2020), www.iucnredlist.org/about/summary-statistics (last visited Dec. 3, 2020).
28 *Id.*
29 David Leclère et al., *Bending the Curve of Terrestrial Biodiversity Needs an Integrated Strategy*, 585 NATURE 551–56 (Sept. 10, 2020).
30 IPBES (2019), *supra* note 5.
31 Red List, *supra* note 27.
32 IPBES (2019), *supra* note 5.

inequalities as the poorest fragments of societies are more dependent on nature and exposed to environmental changes.[33]

Direct Pressures on Natural Ecosystems

In forested landscapes, habitat loss is driven largely by industrial logging, agricultural expansion, transport infrastructure, and subsequent disturbance from these drivers.[34] Of these, conversion of forest for agriculture, because of the extent of the transformation, has the most significant impact on natural systems and biodiversity. Large-scale, industrialized agriculture accounts for most of this.[35] Over one-third of the world's land surface and nearly three-quarters of available freshwater resources are allocated to crop or livestock production, generating approximately 25% of global greenhouse gas emissions, 75% of which come from animal-based food production.[36] Commercial agriculture is estimated to account for about 80% of deforestation worldwide,[37] though subsistence agriculture conversion is important in developing countries. Conversion for agriculture and livestock, both historically and recently, has also been the greatest driver of the loss of natural grasslands.[38]

There are many other pressures on natural ecosystems. In forested areas, logging, mining, and other forms of resource extraction, and concomitant infrastructure development are additional pressures. Between 1990 and 2015, logging accounted for a total reduction of 290 million hectares in native forest cover, while illegal timber harvests and trade represent around 10–15% of global forestry.[39] In grasslands as well, much of the conversion is for agriculture and livestock, and these are often associated with infrastructure development, changes in fire regimes, and desertification and degradation.

Climate change interacts with other drivers, and specifically targets certain ecosystems. For instance, models predict sea-level rise of about 1 meter resulting from climate change would result in significant impacts on coastal ecosystems as well as force the displacement of around 40 million people.[40]

Direct Pressures on Wild Species

SDG 15.1 through 15.4 establish targets for conserving natural habitats, and the decline in those habitats will have direct impacts on many wild species. SDG 15.7 addresses the poaching and trafficking of species, and SDG 15.8 and Aichi 9 recognize the impact of invasive species on biodiversity.

---

33 *Human Development Report 2019: Beyond Income, Beyond Averages, Beyond Today—Inequalities in Human Development in the 21st Century*, UNDP (2019), http://hdr.undp.org/sites/default/files/hdr_2019_overview_-_english.pdf.
34 Potapov et al., *supra* note 12.
35 R. Eisner et al., *Are Changes in the Global Oil Production Influencing the Rate of Deforestation and Biodiversity Loss*, 196 BIOLOGICAL CONSERVATION 147–55 (Apr. 2016).
36 IPBES (2019), *supra* note 5.
37 Gabrielle Kissinger et al., *Drivers of Deforestation and Forest Degradation: A Synthesis Report for REDD+ Policymakers*, LEXEME CONSULTING (2012).
38 Robin White et al., *Pilot Analysis of Global Ecosystems: Grassland Ecosystems*, WORLD RESOURCES INSTITUTE (Dec. 2000), www.wri.org/publication/pilot-analysis-global-ecosystems-grassland-ecosystems.
39 IPBES (2019), *supra* note 5.
40 *Id.*

Overexploitation or non-sustainable use of species, whether legal or illegal, is considered to be a major reason for species loss.[41] SDG 15.7 considers the illicit harvest and trade in wildlife. Information on the illegal harvesting and trade of specific species is available, and estimates of the extent and trends extrapolated from seizure data,[42] but precise measurements of wildlife trafficking, because of its illegality, are difficult to make.[43] Nevertheless, by most estimates, poaching and trafficking, both domestic and international, are increasing in scale and complexity.

With respect to invasive species, there is every indication that trends are going in the wrong direction. IPBES 2019 reports significant increases in the number of alien species introductions, and significant increases in the proportion of animals listed on the Red List affected by invasive species.[44]

Climate change has a direct effect on many species and interaction with other key drivers amplifies these impacts. Around 47% of the terrestrial mammals and 23% of birds, which are threatened with extinction, might have already been negatively impacted by climate change.[45]

Responses

Interventions that directly affect the conservation of biodiversity and ecosystem services include the establishment and management of protected areas (SDG 15.1), and the management of natural resources (SDG 15.2), and institutional changes, especially at the national level (SDG 15.6. 15.9, 15a, 15b, and 15c). According to the Global Biodiversity Outlook 5, five of the response-related targets will be partially achieved by 2020 (i.e. Aichi Targets 11, 16, 17, 19, 20).[46] However, this has not prevented the continuing loss of biodiversity globally.

Protected Areas

Aichi 11 specifies that by 2020, at least 17% of terrestrial and inland water areas … especially areas of particular importance for biodiversity and ecosystem services, are conserved through effectively and equitably managed, ecologically representative and well-connected systems of protected areas and other effective area-based conservation measures[47] and this is recognized to be the most direct way to deliver on SDG 15.1. According to the Protected Planet report, terrestrial coverage has slightly increased from 14.7% in 2016

---

41 T. Mazor et al., *Global Mismatch of Policy and Research on Drivers of Biodiversity Loss*, 2 NATURE ECOLOGY & EVOLUTION 1071–74 (2018).
42 *World Wildlife Crime Report: Trafficking in Protected Species*, UN OFFICE ON DRUGS & CRIME (2016), www.unodc.org/unodc/en/data-and-analysis/wildlife.html.
43 Michael 't Sas-Rolfes et al., *Illegal Wildlife Trade: Patterns, Processes, and Governance*, 44 ANNU. REV. ENV'T RESOURCES 201–28 (2019).
44 IPBES (2019), *supra* note 5.
45 *Id.*
46 *Global Biodiversity Outlook 5*, SECRETARIAT OF CBD (2020), www.cbd.int/gbo/gbo5/publication/gbo-5-en.pdf.
47 *Aichi Target 11*, CBD, www.cbd.int/aichi-targets/target/11 (last visited Dec. 3, 2020).

to 15.1% in 2020 (whereas marine coverage increased more dramatically from 10.2% to 17.2% in national waters).[48]

Area-based conservation, through the establishment and management of protected and conserved areas, has been the cornerstone of modern conservation. IPBES 2019 reports that there has been a significant increase in the area covered by protected areas (Aichi 11.3, SDG 15.1), and a significant increase in the area of Key Biodiversity Areas (KBAs) (Aichi 11.4, SDG 15.1)—sites not necessarily protected or managed, which contribute to the persistence of biodiversity. In addition, there was a significant increase in the protected area's coverage of bird, mammal, and amphibian distributions (Aichi 11.5), and a significant increase in the number of protected area management effectiveness assessments (SDG 15.1).[49]

If there has been such progress in establishing protected areas, why is the state of ecosystems and species continuing to decline? One answer is that protected areas are not located in places that afford adequate biodiversity protection. For example, Hanson et al. report that of 19,937 vertebrate species globally, existing protected areas inadequately protect the habitats of 4,836 (93.1%) amphibian, 8,653 (89.5%) bird, and 4,608 (90.9%) terrestrial mammal species.[50] IPBES 2019 reports that less than half of KBAs are covered by protected areas. The proportion that is completely covered is less than 20%.[51]

Another answer is that many protected areas that do exist are not effectively protecting biodiversity. Jones et al. calculate that about one-third of all protected land is under intense human pressure, with land being converted and wild resources being exploited.[52] Another measure examines the funding available for protected area management. Coad et al. estimate that less than a quarter of all protected areas are adequately resourced.[53]

Sustainable Natural Resource Management

SDG 15 calls for the sustainable use of terrestrial ecosystems, SDG 15.2 seeks to promote the sustainable management of forests, and Aichi Target 7 seeks to increase the forest area under sustainable management. Based on data from the Forest Stewardship Council and the Programme for the Endorsement of Forest Certification, Martinez et al. report that between 2000 and 2012, the area of certified forest has increased from 53 million ha to 407 million ha.[54] IPBES reports a significant 37% increase in the area of certified logging between 2010 and 2016.[55] These results are encouraging. However, the link between certification and forest management is not absolute, for many well-managed forests are not certified, and many

---

48 *Protected Planet Digital Report 2020*, UNEP-WCMC, IUCN & NGS (Oct. 2020), https://livereport.protectedplanet.net/.
49 IPBES (2019), *supra* note 5.
50 Jeffrey O. Hanson et al., *Global Conservation of Species' Niches*, 580 NATURE 232–24 (2020).
51 C. Martinez et al., *Chapter 18: goal 15 Life on Land. Sustainably Manage Forests, Combat Desertification, Halt and Reverse Land Degradation, Halt Biodiversity Loss*, in INTERNATIONAL SOCIETY AND SUSTAINABLE DEVELOPMENT GOALS, Thomson Reuter Proview EBooks (P.D.Y. Lalaguna et al. eds., 2016).
52 Kendall R. Jones et al., *One-Third of Global Protected Land is under Intense Human Pressure*, 360 SCIENCE 788–91 (2018).
53 Lauren Coad et al., *Widespread Shortfalls in Protected Area Resourcing Undermine Efforts to Conserve Biodiversity*, 17(5) FRONTIERS IN ECOLOGY & THE ENV'T (May 6, 2019).
54 Martinez et al., *supra* note 51.
55 IPBES (2019), *supra* note 5.

certified forests are not sustainably managed, especially in the tropics.[56] This measure is only a weak reflection of the sustainability of forest management, as prevalence of certification at a national level does not reliably predict less tree cover loss.[57]

Tools for Implementation and Mainstreaming

Institutional changes necessary to increase awareness, mobilize knowledge, and create the processes and policies to protect biodiversity and ecosystem services are identified in both the Aichi targets (Aichi 1, 2, 4, 16–20) and the SDG 15 targets (15.6, 15.9, 15a, 15b, 15c). To date, 191 of 196 Parties to the CBD have developed at least one National Biodiversity Strategy and Action Plan, thus contributing to the partial achievement of Aichi target 17 and SDG 15.9. In addition, 126 countries have ratified the Nagoya Protocol on Access to Genetic Resources and the Fair and Equitable Sharing of Benefits Arising from their Utilization, as per Aichi target 16 and SDG 15.6. A significant increase in funding has been registered, with biodiversity aid flows reaching $8.7 billion annually.[58] However, current resource mobilization may not be sufficient to completely achieve Aichi target 17, thus increasing pressure on the implementation of SDG 15a and 15b by 2030.

Overall, there have been advancements in the implementation of policy responses and actions to conserve nature and ensure the sustainable use of its resources. However, progress has not been sufficient to bend the curve of nature degradation, thus increasing the likelihood of missing most of the Aichi Targets.[59] As 12 of the 21 SDG targets with an end date in 2020 stem from the Aichi Targets, limited progress could put the achievement of Agenda 2030 at risk.

SDG15 Contributions to Other SDGs

Biodiversity and healthy ecosystems are the bases on which the sustainable development of our societies depend. Fourteen of the 17 Sustainable Goals contain nature's elements that are critical to their delivery and success. Current negative trends, as underlined in the previous section, significantly undermine the achievement of 80% of the SDG targets related to poverty, hunger, health, water, cities, climate, oceans, and land.[60]

There is widespread recognition that human–nature interaction underpins Agenda 2030. The successful implementation of SDG 15 could, therefore, lead toward steady progress under various other SDGs targets. For instance, restoring wetland ecosystems (SDG 15.1) may increase access to clean water (SDG 6) and contribute to food production (SDG 2), hence potentially improving human health (SDG 3) while reducing greenhouse gas emissions (SDG 13).

---

56 Claudia Romero & Francis E. Putz, *Theory-of-Change Development for the Evaluation of Forest Stewardship Council Certification of Sustained Timber Yields from Natural Forests in Indonesia*, 9(9) FORESTS 547 (2018).
57 Allen Blackman et al., *Does Eco-Certification Stem Tropical Deforestation: Forest Stewardship Council Certification in Mexico*, 89(C) J. ENV. ECON. MANAG. 306–33 (2018); Pushpendra Rana & Erin O. Sills, *Does Certification Change the Trajectory of Tree Cover in Working Forests in the Tropics? An Application of the Synthetic Control Method of Impact Evaluation*, 9(3) FORESTS 98 (2018).
58 IPBES (2019), *supra* note 5.
59 *Id*.
60 *Id*.

Seven out of 15 SDGs are "indivisible" or "dependent" on biodiversity.[61] Other SDGs are largely "co-beneficial" or "independent" on biodiversity conservation. In particular, SDG 15.1 and 15.2 (conservation, restoration, and sustainable use of key ecosystems) directly affect achievement of 25% of all SDG targets, and produce co-benefits for an additional 24%.[62] However, interactions between SDGs are also characterized by a set of trade-offs. According to Pradhan et al., SDG 15 is associated with the highest number of trade-offs, as it presents negative correlations with 12 other Goals (SDGs 1–11, and 17).[63] Given the limited timeframe, Scharleman et al. argue that understanding human-environment linkages and acting upon them would be crucial to achieving the Agenda 2030.[64]

Because of the underpinning value of biodiversity for sustainable development, IPBES introduced the concept of "nature's contribution to people" to underline all contributions of organisms, ecosystems, and their associated ecological and evolutionary processes to the good quality of human life.[65] These contributions can be both beneficial (such as food provision or flood control) and detrimental. Of the 18 categories of nature's contributions to people analyzed by IPBES 2019, 14 show a decline in the capacity of nature to sustain contributions to good quality of life from 1970 to the present—a result consistent with the IPBES 2019 conclusion that, even as indicators of the state of nature decline, people are increasingly dependent on ecosystem services.[66]

Some of nature's declining contributions might be replaced by human-made solutions, though the latter frequently do not provide the full range of benefits. For example, water treatment facilities can be installed to obtain high-quality drinking water. Yet, coastal mangroves would achieve the same result while regenerating fish habitats, preventing erosion, and shielding from extreme weather conditions.[67] For these reasons, biodiversity loss has been increasingly recognized by businesses and the economic sector as a major material risk.[68]

More than half the world's GDP is moderately or highly dependent on nature[69] and the global value of ecosystem services is estimated to average between $125–$145 trillion annually, an order of magnitude similar to the global economy.[70] Yet investment in sustaining biodiversity lags. Recent estimates of actual global investment are around $52 billion per

---

61 UNDP, *The Indivisible Nature of Sustainable Development*, A discussion paper exploring the relevancy of biodiversity to SDG targets and indicators, (2019).
62 *Id.*
63 Prajal Pradhan et al., *A Systematic Study of Sustainable Development Goal (SDG) Interactions*, 5(11) EARTH'S FUTURE 1169–79 (2017).
64 Jorn P. W. Scharlemann et al., *Towards Understanding Interactions between Sustainable Development Goals: The Role of Environment–Human Linkages*, 15 SUSTAINABILITY SCI. 1573–84 (Apr. 1, 2020).
65 Unai Pascual et al., *Valuing Nature's Contributions to People: the IPBES Approach*, 27–27 CURRENT OPINION IN ENVTL. SUSTAINABILITY 7–16 (Jun. 2017).
66 IPBES (2019), *supra* note 5.
67 IPBES (2019), *supra* note 5.
68 *Global Risk Report 2020*, WORLD ECONOMIC FORUM (Jan. 15, 2020), www.weforum.org/reports/the-global-risks-report-2020.
69 Amanda Russo, *Half of World's GDP Moderately or Highly Dependent on Nature, Says New Report*, WORLD ECONOMIC FORUM (Jan. 19, 2020), www.weforum.org/press/2020/01/half-of-world-s-gdp-moderately-or-highly-dependent-on-nature-says-new-report/.
70 Robert Costanza et al., *Changes in the Global Value of Ecosystem Services*, 26 GLOBAL ENVTL. CHANGE 152–168 (2014).

year,[71] while estimates of the amount needed to sustain nature and its contribution to our societies and economies are between $150 and $440 billion per year.[72]

Experts called for socioeconomic systems to operate within "planetary boundaries," defined as the safe-space within which humanity can thrive.[73] Nine such boundaries have been identified, beyond which the Earth's state is put at risk. Four of the nine boundaries (climate change, loss of biosphere integrity, land-system change, and altered biogeochemical cycles) were already found to be crossed, two of which (climate change and loss of biosphere integrity) are considered as "core boundaries" with the potential of destabilizing the state of the Earth system.[74]

A recent review entitled the "Economics of Biodiversity"[75] argues that the total demand on the goods and services that nature provides should not exceed its ability to supply those goods and services on a sustainable basis, and therefore to regenerate. Acknowledging that our economies are embedded within—not external to—nature would help us recognize its limits.

Achieving SDG 15 Would Help Prevent New Zoonotic Diseases

When people and animals come into direct contact, there is a chance for the transmission of zoonotic diseases that spread between animals (typically vertebrates) and humans. While, for every specific interaction, the probabilities of spillover are very low, Jones et al. tracked 335 new diseases that emerged between 1940 and 2004, and reported that 60% of these were zoonoses, and 72% originated in wildlife (as opposed to domestic animals).[76]

The emergence of COVID-19 in early 2020 has underlined the importance of understanding the social, economic, and ecological conditions that enable the emergence of zoonoses. There is abundant evidence that the loss and degradation of natural ecosystems and the trade in and consumption of wild meat increase the prevalence of viral zoonoses in humans. Progress toward SDG 15 targets would reduce the emergence of zoonoses in the future.

Halting the Loss and Degradation of Natural Ecosystems

The loss and degradation of natural ecosystems, and thus habitat for wildlife species, directly influence probabilities of emerging diseases (SDG 15.1 recognizes the importance of maintaining the integrity of natural ecosystems and SDG 15.3 recognizes the danger of ecosystem degradation). While the complete loss of natural ecosystems is actually less likely to result in new zoonoses than ecosystem degradation because human–wildlife interactions decrease in

---

71 C. Parker et al., THE LITTLE BIODIVERSITY FINANCE BOOK, 3rd ed. (Global Canopy Program 2012).
72 *The BIOFIN Workbook 2018: Finance for Nature*, The Biodiversity Finance Initiative, UNDP (2018), https://biodiversityfinance.net/sites/default/files/content/publications/BIOFIN%20Workbook%202018_0.pdf.
73 Johan Rockström et al., *A Safe Operating Space for Humanity*, 461 NATURE 472–75 (2009).
74 Will Steffen et al., *Planetary Boundaries: Guiding Human Development on a Changing Planet*, 347(6223) SCIENCE 736 (2015).
75 Dasgupta et al. *Independent Review on the Economics of Biodiversity*, Interim Report, United Kingdom (Apr. 2020), https://assets.publishing.service.gov.uk/government/uploads/system/uploads/attachment_data/file/882222/The_Economics_of_Biodiversity_The_Dasgupta_Review_Interim_Report.pdf.
76 Jones et al., *supra* note 52.

time and space,[77] one example is provided by studies of flying fox foraging incursions into farmland in Queensland, Australia, where eucalyptus forest clearing increases the probability of Hendra virus spillover.[78] The mechanism for doing so might be quite complex. Plowright et al. suggested that habitat loss decreased migratory behavior of flying foxes, which in turn reduced viral transmission leading to decreased "herd immunity" in the bats and increased intensity of Hendra virus outbreaks when they occurred.[79] Another example is provided by the loss of caves to tourism and extractive industries, which has been linked to the emergence of the Nipah virus. These provide roosting habitats for many species of bats, which as a group exhibit a higher likelihood of viral sharing.[80]

Large-scale conversion and transformation of natural ecosystems is widely recognized to be associated with the transmission of disease to humans (e.g. Chagas, yellow fever, leishmaniasis, Lyme disease, malaria) from wild species.[81] Deforestation and habitat fragmentation create "edges" where humans and wildlife interact, with concomitant spread of vectors for disease (e.g. mosquitoes, ticks) and direct transmission of diseases from wildlife to humans.[82] The presence of roads and resource extraction, like mining, amplifies the interface between humans and wildlife, as well as facilitating the spread of disease directly.[83]

The case of Ebola is a well-studied example of land use change and viral transmission. Rulli et al. found a strong association between hotspots of forest fragmentation and viral outbreaks in West and Central Africa.[84] The link to fragmented forests is also described in Bangladesh, where the roosts of flying foxes, which are associated with Nipah virus spillovers, were more likely to be found in such forests.[85] In general, forest incursions and fragmentation and the building of infrastructure, such as logging roads, are expected to affect the risk of zoonotic infection to humans.[86]

Ecosystem degradation also results in the disruption of animal communities, the breakdown of trophic levels, and, of interest for this question, the amplification of populations of certain wildlife species. An illustrative example of a link to the emergence of viruses is the increases in rodent populations, triggered by an El Niño event, which were associated with

---

77 Nathan D. Wolfe et al., *Bushmeat Hunting, Deforestation and Prediction of Zoonoses Disease*, 11(12) EMERG. INFECT. DIS. 1822–27 (2005).
78 John R. Giles et al., *Environmental Drivers of Spatiotemporal Foraging Intensity in Fruit Bats and Implications for Hendra Virus Ecology*, 8(9555) SCI. REP. (2018).
79 Raina K. Plowright et al., *Urban Habituation, Ecological Connectivity and Epidemic Dampening: The Emergence of Hendra Virus from Flying Foxes (Pteropus spp.)*, 278(1725) PROC. R. SOC. 3703–12 (2011).
80 Anna R. Willoughby et al., *A Comparative Analysis of Viral Richness and Viral Sharing in Cave-Roosting Bats*, 9(3) DIVERSITY 35 (2017).
81 Jonathan A. Patz et al., *Unhealthy Landscapes: Policy Recommendations on Land Use Change and Infectious Disease Emergence*, 112(1) ENVIRON. HEALTH PERSPECT, 1092–98 (2004); William B. Karesh et al., *Ecology of Zoonoses: Natural and Unnatural Histories*, 380 ZOONOSES 1936–45 (2012).
82 *Id.*
83 T. Vilela et al., *A Better Amazon Road Network for People and the Environment*, 117 PNAS 7095–102 (2020).
84 Maria Cristina Rulli et al., *The Nexus between Forest Fragmentation in Africa and Ebola Virus Disease Outbreaks*, 7 SCI. REP. 41613 (Feb. 14, 2017).
85 Micah B. Hahn et al., *Roosting Behaviour and Habitat Selection of Pteropus giganteus Reveals Potential Links to Nipah Virus Epidemiology*, 51(2) J. APPL. ECOL. 376–87 (2014).
86 Wolfe et al., *supra* note 77.

hantavirus outbreaks in the United States.[87] This example also illustrates the potential effects of climate change on viral outbreaks.

In addition, protected areas serve to maintain the integrity of natural ecosystems, and there is some evidence that the presence of protected areas has public health benefits. Using data at a municipal level, Bauch et al. found that the prevalence of malaria, diarrhea, and acute respiratory infection in the Brazilian Amazon varied inversely with the extent of area under protection.[88]

Because of the clear link between deforestation and virus emergence, halting deforestation is a cost-effective and large-scale measure to reduce probabilities of zoonotic emergence.[89] Financial mechanisms, such as payments for ecosystem services and carbon markets, may be used to drop deforestation rates, increase revenues for ecosystems restoration, and help forest frontier communities to prosper.[90] A recent study has shown that if another 12 countries were to adopt tropical carbon taxes, such as the ones established by Colombia and Costa Rica, $1.8 billion could be raised each year and reinvested in natural habitats that benefit local communities and the climate.[91]

Controlling the Trade in Wildlife Species for Human Consumption

Meat from wild species is a major source of protein and income to millions of people. Nielsen et al. estimate that 154 million households across Central and South America, sub-Saharan Africa, China, Southeast Asia, and Indochina rely to some extent on wild meat.[92] Rural consumption of wild meat in Africa and Latin America is an important part of household food security, but the trade is also a source of rural income.[93] In the Congo basin, while rural peoples rely on wild meat for animal protein, a high proportion is sold at urban markets, where it is a luxury commodity, and consumed in towns and cities. In Latin America, while it is on the rise,[94] urban consumption is less important.[95] In Asia, wild meat is mostly for urban consumption. There is a high demand for wild meat in China and Southeast Asia from the emerging middle class and urban elites. Live animals and meat from wild species are typically sold in markets along with domestic animals and seafood.[96]

---

87 B. Hjelle & G.E. Glass, *Outbreak of Hantavirus Infection in the Four Corners Region of the United States in the Wake of the 1997–1998 El Niño Southern Oscillation*, 181(5) J. INFECT. DIS. 1569–73 (2000).
88 Simone C. Bauch et al., *Public Health Impacts of Ecosystem Change in the Brazilian Amazon*, 112(24) PNAS 7414–49 (2015).
89 Andrew P. Dobson et al., *Ecology and Economics for Pandemic Prevention*, 369(6502) SCIENCE 379–81 (2020).
90 World's Forests 2020, *supra* note 6.
91 Edward Barbier et. al. *Adopt a Carbon Tax to Protect Tropical Forests*, 578(7794) NATURE 213–16 (2020).
92 M.R. Nielsen et al., *The Importance of Wild Meat in the Global South*, 146 ECOL. ECON. 696–705 (2018).
93 Lauren Coad et al., *Towards a Sustainable, Participatory and Inclusive Wild Meat Sector*, CENTER FOR INT'L FORESTRY RES. (2019), www.cifor.org/publications/pdf_files/Books/BCoad1901.pdf.
94 *Id.*
95 J.E. Fa & Carlos A. Peres, *Game Vertebrate Extraction in African and Neotropical Forests: An Intercontinental Comparison, in* CONSERVATION OF EXPLOITED SPECIES 203–241 (John D. Reynolds et al. (eds.), Cambridge University Press 2001).
96 Eleanor J. Milner-Gulland et al., *Wild Meat: The Bigger Picture*, 18(7) TRENDS IN ECOL. & EVOL. 351–57 (Jul. 2003).

The butchering and sale of meat from wild species in markets has been widely implicated in the emergence of viral zoonotic diseases.[97] Wolfe et al. provide a summary of zoonotic pathogens that have emerged from the Cameroon-Congo basin associated with bushmeat hunting.[98] These include Ebola, monkeypox, HIV-1 and HIV-2, Anthrax, and Simian foamy viruses. The 2002 SARS pandemic emerged from a live animal market in China.[99] COVID-19 was a spillover in the Wuhan seafood market, where live and freshly killed wildlife was for sale,[100] though an argument has been made that the jump to humans might have happened earlier in the wildlife trade chain.[101]

COVID-19 is a coronavirus, a class of viruses that was also implicated in the SARS pandemic. Bats have long been recognized as a reservoir for coronaviruses, and samples from a live animal market in China indicated that SARS likely emerged in the human population via masked palm civets, which served as an intermediate host.[102] Middle East respiratory syndrome (MERS) also has a link to coronaviruses in bats, though the jump to humans most likely was through camels as the intermediary host.[103] With COVID-19, there is also a link to coronaviruses in bats.[104] Teams sampling bats in China report finding many novel coronaviruses.[105]

SDG target 15.7 seeks to reduce the illegal wildlife trade (not the harvesting and consumption per se), both illegal hunting and trafficking. In the consideration of what is legal and what is not, it is useful to distinguish three social and economic contexts for the consumption of meat from wildlife species:[106] (1) Rural forest communities, where domestic meat is less available, hunting is more of an important livelihoods strategy, and consumption is important for subsistence; (2) newly urbanizing populations, where livestock supply is still limited, and wild meat is supplied from more rural areas; and (3) populations in cities and other metropolitan areas (and also international consumers), where wild meat is a desirable cultural and gustatory luxury by rich elites.[107]

While there is considerable variation in their specific laws, many countries distinguish legally between hunting and trade in these three contexts. In Africa, outside of protected areas, in season, and not involving legally protected species, typically rural people can hunt

---

97 Kristine M. Smith et al., *Zoonotic Viruses Associated with Illegally Imported Wildlife Products*, 7(1) PLoS One e29505 (2012); Jennifer Caroline Cantlay et al., *A Review of Zoonotic Infection Risks Associated with the Wild Meat Trade in Malaysia*, 14 ECOHEALTH 361–88 (Mar. 22, 2017).
98 Wolfe et al., *supra* note 77.
99 L.F. Wang & B.T. Eaton, *Bats, Civets and the Emergence of SARS*, 315 CURR TOP MICROBIOL. IMMUNOL. 325–44 (2007).
100 Qun Li et al., *Early Transmission Dynamics in Wuhan, China, of Novel Coronavirus–Infected Pneumonia*, 382(13) N. ENGL. J. MED. 1199–207 (2020).
101 IDSA Contributor, *UPDATE Wuhan coronavirus – 2019-nCoV Q&A #6: An Evidence-Based Hypothesis*, SCIENCE SPEAKS: GLOBAL ID NEWS (Jan. 25, 2020), https://sciencespeaksblog.org/2020/01/25/wuhan-coronavirus-2019-ncov-qa-6-an-evidence-based-hypothesis/.
102 Wang et al., *supra* note 99.
103 Ali M. Zaki et al., *Isolation of a Novel Coronavirus from a Man with Pneumonia in Saudi Arabia*, 367 N ENGL. J. MED. 1814–20 (Nov. 8, 2012).
104 Peng Zhou et al., *A Pneumonia Outbreak Associated with a New Coronavirus of Probably Bat Origin*, 579 NATURE 270–73 (2020).
105 Jon Cohen, *Mining Coronavirus Genomes for Clues to the Outbreak's Origins*, SCIENCE (Jan. 31, 2020), www.sciencemag.org/news/2020/01/mining-coronavirus-genomes-clues-outbreak-s-origins.
106 Coad et al., *supra* note 93.
107 *Id.*; Gabriele Volpato et al., *Baby Pangolins on My Plate: Possible Lessons to Learn from the COVID-19 Pandemic*, 16(19) J. OF ETHNOBIOLOGY & ETHNOMEDICINE (Apr. 21, 2020).

using traditional methods (not guns and snares), but sale is illegal.[108] The Republic of Congo is one exception, which allows urban market sales with special permits. In much of Latin America, typically rural people can hunt and consume wild meat, but the commercial sale and consumption of wildlife in urban areas is illegal.[109] In Asia, outside of protected areas, hunting of non-protected species is legal (sometimes requiring a license), except in India where all hunting is illegal. Commercial sale of wild species for human consumption is more tightly controlled. In India, Cambodia, and Myanmar, all sales are illegal, and in China and Lao PDR, only the sale of captive bred wild species for human consumption is permitted.[110] In all parts of the world, enforcement of national laws is highly variable. Significant progress toward SDG 15.7 target would be achieved by controlling or modulating the sale of wild species for human consumption, especially in urban markets. Every indication is that stopping the illegal trade would directly reduce the emergence of new zoonoses.

There is an increasing recognition of the need for an integrated "One Health" approach[111] involving holistic interventions on human, animal, and environmental health[112] as pathogens originated in animals are transmitted to humans because of degradation of natural ecosystems and wildlife trade. The latest International Livestock Research Institute (ILRI) and United Nations Environmental Program (UNEP) report on zoonotic diseases recommends improving health governance worldwide.[113] This would include increased research and information sharing among medic, ecologic, and veterinary sectors, monitoring animal reservoirs, early detection of emerging diseases, and prevention of pandemics.[114] Dobson et al. argue that such approaches are highly cost-effective, especially given the economic consequences of global pandemics like COVID-19.[115]

Achieving SDG 15

Despite the considerable efforts in terms of sustainable forest management, protected areas coverage, and legislation to protect biodiversity and ecosystems, overall progress has not been sufficient and much more needs to be done to meet SDG 15. Direct and indirect pressures on nature, such as unsustainable production and consumption, rapid demographic growth, unsustainable trade and technological development, bad governance, conflicts, and epidemics result in resource depletion and ecosystem degradation. If SDG 15 is to be achieved by 2030, transformative changes toward sustainability and nature conservation are needed.

---

108 Katharine Anne Abernethy, *Bushmeat in Gabon*, Ministry of Water & Forests, Government of Gabon (Dec. 2010), www.researchgate.net/publication/306286911_Bushmeat_in_Gabon.
109 Andre Pinassia Antunes et al., *A Conspiracy of Silence: Subsistence Hunting Rights in the Brazilian Amazon*, 84 LAND USE POL'Y 1–11 (May 2019).
110 E.L. Bennett & L. Li, *A Review of Wildlife Trade in China*, Wildlife Conservation Society, Beijing, China (2009) (Unpublished report).
111 Kim Gruetzmacher et al., *The Berlin Principles on One Health—Bridging Global Health and Conservation*, in SCIENCE OF THE TOTAL ENVIRONMENT (Oct. 12, 2020), https://doi.org/10.1016/j.scitotenv.2020.142919.
112 Nicholas A. Robinson, *The Next Pandemic Is Here*, THE ENVTL. FORUM, 30–35 (Pace Law School Nov./Dec., 2020).
113 *Preventing the Next Pandemic: Zoonotic Diseases and How to Break the Chain of Transmission*, UN Environment Programme & Int'l Livestock Research Institute (UNEP & ILRI) (2020), www.ilri.org/publications/preventing-next-pandemic-zoonotic-diseases-and-how-break-chain-transmission.
114 Delia Grace, *The Business Case for One Health*, 81(2) ONDERSTEPOORT J. OF VETERINARY RES. A725 (2014).
115 Dobson et al., *supra* note 89.

Such an ambition, while necessary for long-term survival, might seem out of reach in myopic focus on economic growth. If there is a silver lining in the COVID-19 pandemic, it has emphasized that if we ignore our impact on the natural world, we do so at our peril. The emergence of zoonotic diseases is a direct result of failure to make progress toward SDG 15. This pandemic might be a harbinger of the challenges that we face as natural systems are degraded, ecosystem services are lost, and climate change escalates.

There are positive policy pathways for necessary change that would tackle the drivers of biodiversity loss and help to conserve and restore nature, and an array of opportunities for countries to reset their relationship with nature and its services, and to build back better. Nature-sensitive recovery policies will be key to accelerate transformative pathways, while avoiding perpetuating unsustainable practices.

These upcoming events may provide a timely opportunity toward living in harmony with nature:

- The Conference of the Parties of the CBD in Kunming (China) had, even before the coronavirus pandemic, been touted as the make-or-break meeting for the global commitment on biodiversity conservation. The emerging framework already provides some elements of guidance on goals, measurable targets, indicators, baselines, and monitoring mechanisms aimed at tackling the drivers of biodiversity loss and achieve transformational change.[116] Countries' commitment to ambitious goals and targets will be key to address the drivers of biodiversity loss and catalyzing restoration actions to become a basis of progress toward the SDGs by 2030.
- The upcoming Conference of Parties to the United Nations Framework Convention on Climate Change (UNFCCC) in Glasgow (United Kingdom) is a good opportunity for further aligning the climate change and biodiversity agendas through the use of Nature-based Solutions (NbS)—cost-effective alternatives to sequester and store carbon while preserving ecosystems. In the review process of Nationally Determined Contributions (NDCs), signatories of the Paris Agreement are encouraged to take into consideration NbS as a key tool to achieve both climate and biodiversity objectives.[117] Ultimately, conserving biodiversity and the services provided by natural ecosystems will depend on addressing the challenge of climate change.
- Already embraced by 124 countries, the Land Degradation Neutrality (LDN) initiative in the framework of the UN Convention to Combat Desertification is designed to avoid degradation, restore ecological integrity, and promote economic, social, and ecological sustainability.

Additionally, countries will need to strengthen national **conservation and restoration efforts** so as to bend the curve of biodiversity loss. Increasing the proportion of land under effective conservation to 40%, combined with restoring around 100 million hectares of degraded land and other sustainable practices, could reduce biodiversity loss by 2050.[118] Promoting the effective management of protected and conserved areas would not only pro-

---

116 *Report of the Open-Ended Working Group on the Post-2020 Global Biodiversity Framework on its Second Meeting*, 2nd mtg., CBD/WG2020/2/4 (Feb. 24–29, 2020).
117 Nathalie Seddon et al., *Global Recognition of the Importance of Nature Based Solutions to the Impacts of Climate Change, in* GLOBAL SUSTAINABILITY 3, e15, 1–12 (Cambidge U. Press May 12, 2020),
118 Leclère et al., *supra* note 29.

vide direct ecological benefits, but also support local communities, who live in and around these areas and are strongly dependent on them. Including indigenous people, local communities, women, and youth in early planning and decision-making will enhance their life quality, which depends heavily on biodiversity and ecosystem services, while improving nature safeguards by incorporating traditional knowledge.[119]

Addressing negative and perverse financial subsidies and incentives must also be a priority. These are recognized to incentivize unsustainable practices that degrade life-support systems. A major driver supporting this conversion of forests and natural grasslands are some $700 billion/year in agricultural subsidies worldwide, of which $530 billion is paid directly to farmers.[120] The Food and Land Use Coalition (2019) global consultation reports that from an environmental perspective, these negative and perverse incentives often support more input-intensive forms of agriculture. Of the $700 billion/year, some $220 billion/year goes into supporting the production of emission-intensive goods, such as livestock, soy, and palm oils, which in turn support natural land conversion and only about 15% are aimed at public goods, supporting services, including ecological services, that create the enabling conditions for the agricultural sector.[121] Not all of this conversion for agriculture and livestock is directly influenced by financial subsidies. However, addressing financial subsidies in general is critical if we are to attain sustainability in our future.

Recommendations

If the targets of SDG 15 are to be achieved, the following actions are necessary. Three relate to the **policy pathways**, whose urgency has been further underlined by the outbreak of the COVID-19 pandemic:

1 The Parties to the CBD should establish a set of goals and measurable targets whose implementation would prevent the loss of natural ecosystems, ensure the sustainable use of the biodiversity associated with them, and maintain the ecological integrity of natural areas. Only the highest level of ambition can achieve the vision of living in harmony with nature by 2050.[122]
2 The Parties to the UNFCCC should incorporate NbS into NDCs to address climate action. This would allow accounting for the storage and sequestration of carbon through both the conservation of intact ecosystems, and through ecological restoration, so as to achieve both biodiversity conservation targets and address the challenges of climate change.
3 The UN Decade on Ecosystem Restoration 2021–2030 will be a key moment to join forces behind a common goal: Preventing, halting, and reversing the degradation of ecosystems worldwide. A whole-society approach—including governments, private sector, and civil society—is needed to enhance our collective wealth and well-being in harmony with nature.

119 *Id.*
120 Abdullah Mamum et al., *Reforming Agricultural Subsidies for Improved Environmental Outcomes*, International Food Policy Research Institute (IFPRI) (2019), www.ifpri.org/publication/reforming-agricultural-subsidies-improved-environmental-outcomes.
121 *Id.*
122 Sandra Díaz et al., *Set Ambitious Goals for Biodiversity and Sustainability*, 370(6515) SCIENCE 411–13 (2020).

In response to COVID-19, **fiscal recovery packages** have the potential to support sustainable fiscal reform to deliver on economic, climate, and biodiversity goals.[123] This would include phasing out unequal and harmful fossil fuels and agricultural subsidies, and the potential shift of the latter toward sustainable agroecological farming practices. Investment in climate-resilient infrastructure and green technology would also provide development benefits while minimizing environmental impacts. Ecological restoration and green infrastructure development could increasingly become a source of job creation and investing in education, training, and reskilling would be fundamental to ensure just and sustainable transitions.

4 Provide financial support for the management of protected and conserved areas, and to communities living in and around these areas.[124]
5 Shift financial subsidies from environmentally harmful ones, such as agricultural subsidies that support the conversion of forests and natural grasslands, to those that promote environmental resilience, such as sustainable agro-ecological farming practices.[125]
6 Invest in jobs in ecological restoration and green infrastructure development, which create employment in a cost-effective way, and provide direct ecological benefits.[126] Government-supported work programs should target communities of color and youth, both groups hit hard by the pandemic.
7 Support businesses and financial mechanisms that promote nature-positive actions and catalyze private investments in nature-based solutions.[127] Further financial disclosure should also be incentivized in order to ensure full participation of the private sector to create an inclusive and sustainable recovery.
8 Ensure that investments in infrastructure, which are a focus of many emerging stimulus packages, both provide development benefits that will minimize environmental impacts and invest in climate-resilient, green infrastructure where and when appropriate.[128]

---

123 Cameron Hepburn et al., *Will COVID-19 Fiscal Recovery Packages Accelerate or Retard Progress on Climate Change?*, OXFORD SMITH SCHOOL OF ENTERPRISE & THE ENV'T Working Paper 20-02 (May 4, 2020).
124 Marc Hockings et al., *Covid-19 and Protected and Conserved Areas*, 26(1) PARKS 7–24 (May 1, 2020).
125 Edward Barbier & Joanne Burgess, *Sustainability and Development after COVID-19*, 15 WORLD DEV. 135 (Jul. 10, 2020).
126 Pamela McElwee et al., *Ensuring a Post-COVID Economic Agenda Tackles Global Biodiversity Loss*, 3(4) ONE EARTH 448–61 (2020).
127 Siddarth Shrikanth, *Investors Line up for the Post-Pandemic Green Recovery*, FINANCIAL TIMES (Jul. 20, 2020), www.ft.com/content/860c2c82-183a-4d65-978e-454bf3ce8c0d.
128 Michael Drescher & Lucas Mollame, *How Investing in Green Infrastructure Can Jump-Start the Post-Coronavirus Economy*, THE CONVERSATION (Jun. 17, 2020), https://theconversation.com/how-investing-in-green-infrastructure-can-jump-start-the-post-coronavirus-economy-139376.

25 Restoration of Ecosystems and Land Degradation Neutrality

Ben Boer and Ian Hannam

Introduction

Land, and its primary constituent element, the soil,[1] is fundamental for the generation, maintenance, and continuation of life on Earth, including human life. As Montgomery states, "unless more immediate disasters do us in, how we address the twin problems of soil degradation and accelerated erosion will eventually determine the fate of modern civilization."[2] Until recently, soil law and policy have taken a back seat to international and national laws concerning higher-profile environmental and natural resources issues, such as the effects of rapid climate change and the vast losses of biodiversity.[3] Now it is more widely recognized that the health of soils is closely related to climate change and biodiversity loss; indeed, the process of biological sequestration of carbon from the atmosphere via forests and other plant matter into soils and sediments underlines their vital functions.[4]

The increasing awareness of the importance of soil to global biodiversity as well as to the production of food through agriculture and grazing has stimulated the development of the concept of land degradation neutrality (LDN). This chapter provides a brief analysis of the problems of land degradation worldwide, and the various ways in which LDN can be promoted through international legal mechanisms as well as at the national level. It also makes the point that LDN, as a part of Sustainable Development Goal (SDG) 15 and in conjunction with other SDGs, can play a role in COVID-19 recovery by contributing to healthier and more productive agricultural soil systems, leading to greater food security. The chapter concludes with a set of recommended steps that might be followed in order to incorporate LDN into national-level legislation.

---

1 Land and soil are differentiated as follows: "while soil constitutes one of the most essential natural elements of our planet, the land comprises a multifunctional ecological system, whose natural capital, soil and biodiversity, interacting with water and atmosphere, generate the flow of ecosystems services that support human well-being by securing the life and livelihood of individuals and communities." *See* United Nations Convention to Combat Desertification [UNCCD], *Land Degradation Neutrality: Resilience at Local, National and Regional Levels*, at 22, (2015) www.unccd.int/Lists/SiteDocumentLibrary/Publications/Land_Degrad_Neutrality_E_Web.pdf.
2 David R. Montgomery, Dirt: the erosion of Civilizations, at 2, (2007).
3 *See* Ben Boer, *Land Degradation as a Common Concern of Humankind*, International Law for Common Goods: Normative Perspectives on Human Rights, Culture and Nature 289–307 (Federico Lenzerini and Ana Filipa Vrdoljak, eds., 2014).
4 Ian Hannam, *Aspects of a Legislative and Policy Framework to Manage Soil Carbon Sequestration*, International Yearbook of Soil Law and Policy 2020 (Harald Ginzky et al., eds., 2020); *see also* Ronald Vargas-Rojas et al., *Unlocking the Potential of Soil Organic Carbon: A Feasible Way Forward*, International Yearbook of Soil Law and Policy 373–95, (Harald Ginzky et al., eds., 2016).

SDG 15—Life on Land

The 2030 UN Agenda for Sustainable Development (Agenda 2030) places strong emphasis on integrated approaches that can harness synergies and minimize potential trade-offs in achieving the SDGs and their associated Targets. This was specifically recognized in relation to desertification and land degradation by the 2017 Ordos Declaration: "Emphasizing the important role of combating desertification/land degradation and drought in achieving other related SDGs (such as those related to poverty, food security, environmental protection and sustainable use of natural resources) and for reducing risks and vulnerabilities to natural hazards."[5]

While a number of the SDGs are important in achieving sustainable land management, the general aim of SDG 15 is to "conserve and restore the use of terrestrial ecosystems such as forests, wetlands, drylands and mountains by 2020." The *Global Land Outlook* observes that "SDG 15 … puts a strong emphasis on the need to scale up transformative management practices" with the goal to "Protect, restore and promote sustainable use of terrestrial ecosystems, sustainably manage forests, combat desertification, halt and reverse land degradation, and halt biodiversity loss."[6] The concept of LDN was introduced as "a new paradigm in environmental politics for SDG 15 for avoiding, reducing and reversing land degradation."[7] It is linked to the idea of zero net land degradation, known as ZNLD. As explained in a 2012 United Nations Convention to Combat Desertification (UNCCD) report:

> Zero Net Land Degradation means the achievement of a state of land degradation neutrality. Achieving it involves a combination of reducing the rate of further degradation of land and offsetting newly occurring degradation by restoring the productivity and other ecosystem services of currently degraded lands. The ZNLD is best achieved by the introduction and promotion of SLM practices on a global basis. In effect, this means reducing land degradation globally to negligible levels while also restoring the quality and productivity of degraded lands.[8]

LDN was further defined by the Twelfth Session of the Conference of the Parties to the UNCCD in 2015 as "A state whereby the amount and quality of land resources, necessary to support ecosystem functions and services and enhance food security, remains stable or increases within specified temporal and spatial scales and ecosystems."[9]

---

5 *Thirteenth Session of Conference of the Parties to the UNCCD*, UNCCD, www.unccd.int/conventionconference-parties-cop/unccd-cop13-ordos-china (last visited July 14, 2020).
6 This document is an outcome of the United Nations Convention to Combat Desertification in Countries Experiencing Serious Drought and/or Desertification, Particularly in Africa [UNCCD] (June 17, 1994) 33 ILM 1328 (entered into force Dec. 26, 1996). See *Global Land Outlook*, UNCCD, https://knowledge.unccd.int/glo/GLO_first_edition.
7 G. Metternich and A. Cowie, *Kill Not the Goose That Lays the Golden Egg: Striving of Land Degradation Neutrality*, INTERNATIONAL INSTITUTE FOR SUSTAINABLE DEVELOPMENT, SDG KNOWLEDGE HUB (23 November 2017), http://sdg.iisd.org/commentary/guest-articles/kill-not-the-goose-that-lays-the-golden-egg-striving-for-land-degradation-neutrality/.
8 Rattan Lal, Uriel Safriel, & Ben Boer, *Zero Net Land Degradation: A New Sustainable Development Goal for Rio+ 20*, UNCCD, at 14, https://catalogue.unccd.int/991_Zero_Net_Land_Degradation_Report_UNCCD_May_2012.pdf (2012).
9 UNCCD, at 2, ICCD/COP(12)/20/Add.1 (Jan. 21, 2016).

Globally, 2.6 billion people depend directly on agriculture, but 52% of the land used for agriculture is moderately or severely affected by soil degradation, while 74% of the poor are directly affected by land degradation globally.[10] However, the economic impact of COVID-19 could increase global poverty for the first time in three decades, pushing more than half a billion people, or 8% of humanity, into poverty, thus putting more pressure on land resources.[11] The UNCCD Secretariat has also focused on the effects of COVID-19; It states:

> Beyond the devastating public health crisis, the COVID-19 pandemic has evolved into a complex emergency with significant humanitarian, socio-economic, political and security dimensions. It has laid bare the vulnerability of both our human and natural systems, which were already threatened by climate change.[12]

The Need for a Land Degradation-Neutral Target

The urgent need to set a global target for LDN was underlined by the Global Land Outlook, which indicated that

> [F]rom 1998 to 2013, approximately 20 per cent of the Earth's vegetated land surface showed persistent declining trends in productivity, apparent in 20 per cent of cropland, 16 per cent of forest land, 19 per cent of grassland, and 27 per cent of rangeland. These trends are especially alarming in the face of the increased demand for land-intensive crops and livestock.[13]

Over the past few decades, around 33% of the world's arable lands have been lost because of various forms of soil erosion and pollution.[14] The UN Sustainable Development Goals Report 2019 states:

> Twenty per cent of the Earth's total land area was degraded between 2000 and 2015, resulting in a significant loss of services essential to human well-being. That estimate is relatively conservative given the underlying sub-indicators, which only represent three variables: changes in land cover, land productivity and organic carbon in soil. In all regions, except Europe and Northern America and Northern Africa and Western Asia,

---

10 Life on Land, *Sustainable Development Goals*, www.un.org/sustainabledevelopment/biodiversity/.
11 Press Release, UN Office for the Coordination of Humanitarian Affairs, COVID-19 Fallout Could Push Half a Billion People into Poverty in Developing Countries (Apr. 8, 2020) https://reliefweb.int/report/world/estimates-impact-covid-19-global-poverty.
12 *Supporting the Global Response to the COVID-19 Pandemic: Land-Based Solutions for Healthy People and a Healthy Planet,* UNCCD, at 3, www.unccd.int/sites/default/files/documents/2020-06/1498_UNCCD_%20Covid_%20layout-low%20res-1.pdf (2020).
13 *Global Land Outlook*, UNCCD, at 11, https://knowledge.unccd.int/sites/default/files/2018-06/GLO%20EnglishFullReportrev1.pdf (2017).
14 *See* Duncan Cameron et al., *A Sustainable Model for Intensive Agriculture,* GRANTHAM CENTRE, 2, http://grantham.sheffield.ac.uk/wp-content/uploads/A4-sustainable-model-intensive-agriculture-spread.pdf (Dec. 2015).

the extent of degradation covered 22.4 per cent to 35.5 per cent of land area, directly impacting the lives of over one billion people.[15]

While the SDGs are not legally binding, governments are expected to take ownership and establish national frameworks to achieve its Goals and associated Targets. One suggestion is the introduction of a Paris-style agreement for soils, which would incorporate nationally determined targets for LDN.[16] In our view, with respect to the achievement of LDN, such frameworks should desirably be incorporated into legislation at a national level.

Global Policy Platform for LDN

This chapter canvasses legal and policy materials that may support the implementation of LDN. These include global challenges related to poverty, inequality, climate change, environmental degradation, peace, and justice. These are common elements of many of the 17 SDGs, which underlines the fact that they are all interconnected and to be achieved by 2030, at the latest.[17] Specifically, SDG 15: Life on Land and its Target 15.3 on LDN encourage countries to "combat desertification, restore degraded land and soil, including land affected by desertification, drought and floods, and strive to achieve a land degradation-neutral world by 2030."[18]

The initial policy platform for LDN stemmed from the 2012 UN Conference on Sustainable Development (Rio+20),[19] with a commitment to "strive to achieve a land degradation-neutral world."[20] This aim was subsequently adopted by the UN General Assembly as part of SDG 15 of Agenda 2030.[21] Immediately after the UN adopted the SDGs, the UNCCD took on the challenge of SDG Target 15.3 and the objective of LDN to drive implementation of the Convention. Improved management of land is central to the overall Agenda 2030, as recognized in a United Nations General Assembly (UNGA) resolution, which stated that it:

> Welcomes Target 15.3 of the Sustainable Development Goals, to combat desertification, restore degraded land and soil, including land affected by desertification, drought and floods, and strive to achieve a land degradation-neutral world, takes note with appreciation of the voluntary land degradation neutrality target setting programme

---

15 UN Department of Economic and Social Affairs, *UN Sustainable Development Goals Report 2019*, at 52, www.un.am/up/library/SDG_Report_2019.pdf (2019).
16 *See* Rob Fowler & Ian Hannam, *Critique of the Report Improving International Land Governance: Analysis and Recommendations*, INTERNATIONAL YEARBOOK OF SOIL LAW AND POLICY 2020 (Harald Ginzky et al., eds., forthcoming 2021).
17 United Nations G.A. Res. A/RES/70/1, *Transforming our world: the 2030 Agenda for Sustainable Development*, (Sept. 25, 2015) [hereinafter "2030 Agenda"].
18 *SDG 15: Protect, Restore and Promote Sustainable Use of Terrestrial Ecosystems, Sustainably Manage Forests, Combat Desertification, and Halt and Reverse Land Degradation and Halt Biodiversity Loss*, UN DEPARTMENT OF ECONOMIC AND SOCIAL AFFAIRS, https://unstats.un.org/sdgs/report/2019/goal-15/ (last visited Nov. 3, 2020).
19 The 2012 conference was known as Rio+20 as it took place two decades after the 1992 "Earth Summit" in Rio de Janeiro that launched the Rio Conventions and placed sustainable development on the global policy agenda.
20 United Nations G.A. Res. A/RES/66/288, *The Future We Want*, at 206 (Sept. 11, 2012).
21 2030 Agenda, *supra* note 17.

under the Convention and the work of the secretariat of the Convention and partners to assist States in carrying out voluntary target setting activities, and in this respect invites States that have not yet subscribed to the programme to do so.[22]

The General Assembly also stated that it "reiterates that degraded land, if recovered, would, inter alia, contribute to restoring natural resources, thus potentially improving food security and nutrition in the affected countries, and in the process could, inter alia, contribute to the absorption of carbon emissions."[23]

Assessment of Progress in Implementing LDN

Since Agenda 2030 was adopted in 2015, over 120 countries have committed to setting LDN targets[24] and considerable progress has been made. Most states do not have specific legislation to address the broad range of processes involved in land degradation. However, a number of global initiatives have been important in establishing international rules which, when transposed to the national level, can be directed toward the control and prevention of land degradation. It is obvious that the phenomenon of land degradation is a cross-cutting issue that intersects with the conservation of biodiversity, the causes and effects of climate change, the transport and disposal of hazardous wastes, and the incidence of contaminated lands. It is also becoming increasingly clear that it affects the capacity of countries and regions to sustain their human populations and to guarantee food and water security. Each of these has obvious human rights implications.[25] In addition to the UNCCD, we argue that the 1992 United Nations Convention on Biological Diversity and the 1995 United Nations Framework Convention on Climate Change also have a role to play in the protection of land, as they include provisions that could be used to promote sustainable land use, even though those provisions are generally tangential to the particular needs of soil.[26]

Scientific Conceptual Framework for LDN

In implementing the concept of LDN, the UNCCD has introduced a scientific framework (SCF), technical guidance, and practical tools to help countries to assess the current state of their land and the drivers of degradation. The framework is designed to "focus particularly on laying the foundation to achieve LDN by (i) establishing enabling policies and (ii) applying integrated land-use planning, informed by preparatory assessments, as described in the LDN-SCF."[27] The guide helps to better understand the key attributes of the framework,

---

22 United Nations G.A. Res. A/RES/72/220, *The Future We Want*, at 13 (Jan. 30, 2018).
23 United Nations G.A. Res. A/RES/71/229, *Implementation of the UNCCD*, at 11 (Feb. 7, 2017).
24 *The LDN Target Setting Programme*, UNCCD, www.unccd.int/actions/ldn-target-setting-programme last visited Nov. 3, 2020 [hereinafter "LDN Target Setting Programme"], *see also Countries Setting Voluntary LDN Targets*, UNCCD, https://knowledge.unccd.int/home/country-information/countries-with-voluntary-ldn-targets last visited Nov. 3, 2020 [hereinafter "Voluntary LDN Targets"].
25 "Recalling that in striving to achieve SDG Target 15.3, it is also important to address wider elements of the 2030 Agenda" in UNCCD, at 8, ICCD/COP(12)/20/Add.1., Decision 3/COP.12 (Jan. 21, 2016).
26 Ben Boer and Ian Hannam, *Land Degradation*, Oxford Handbook of Comparative Environmental Law Lees, 444 (Emma Lees and Jorge Viñuales, eds., 2019).
27 Annette Cowie, *Guidelines for Land Degradation Neutrality: A Report Prepared for the Scientific and Technical Advisory Panel of the Global Environment Facility*, at 5, https://catalogue.unccd.int/1474_LDN_Technical_Report_web_version.pdf (2020).

and is a reference point for knowledge on LDN to support implementation among countries pursuing LDN targets.[28] The three components of the guide show how LDN can be used as a policy tool to improve land management and land use planning at the national level.[29] These are the main policy drivers that were established in the LDN Target Setting Programme and the Global Mechanism. The UNCCD secretariat, in collaboration with 18 international partners, has assisted countries to set their LDN targets and associated measures, and to move toward LDN through policy integration and investments in transformative projects and programs.[30]

LDN Principles

An important part of the SDG 15.3 policy platform is the set of 19 LDN principles that govern the LDN implementation process.[31] They are designed to ensure that LDN achieves positive outcomes, while avoiding or minimizing unintended and negative outcomes. The principles are viewed as the foundations of the scientific conceptual framework for LDN and the necessary minimum requirements for successful implementation and attainment of LDN.[32] The three basic principles are: maintain or enhance land-based natural capital; protect human rights and enhance human well-being; and respect national sovereignty.[33]

Land restoration programs that are designed to achieve multiple benefits simultaneously should not only help to ensure that LDN is maintained or exceeded, but also contribute to meeting the targets of a range of other SDGs. Target 15.3 has the potential to become a strong vehicle for driving UNCCD implementation as well as contribute to the achievement of multiple SDGs, including those related to climate change mitigation and adaptation, biodiversity conservation, food and water security, disaster risk reduction, and poverty reduction. It also has the potential to promote the various human rights associated with these issues. The LDN targets address SDG 15.3 and many other SDGs in a synergistic manner and are intended to be implemented in accordance with national priorities of individual countries. These targets also strengthen the implementation of UNCCD National Action

---

28 UNCCD, *Land Degradation Neutrality Target Setting Programme Land Degradation Neutrality Target Setting—A Technical Guide*, https://knowledge.unccd.int/publication/ldn-target-setting-technical-guide (May 2016).
29 *Guide to the Scientific Conceptual Framework for Land Degradation Neutrality*, UNCCD, https://knowledge.unccd.int/knowledge-products-and-pillars/guide-scientific-conceptual-framework-land-degradation-neutrality (last visited July 20, 2020).
30 *See* Voluntary LDN Targets, *supra* note 24.
31 Conference of the Parties called upon "Parties pursuing LDN to consider the guidance provided by the scientific conceptual framework for land degradation neutrality and observe the LDN principles, taking into account national circumstances" *in* UNCCD, at 2, ICCD/COP(12)/20/Add.1, Decision 18/COP.13 (Oct. 23, 2017).
32 Each of the principles is connected to a module of the scientific conceptual framework for LDN, which presents the LDN concept and provides guidance on the application of the principles, *see The Principles for Land Degradation Neutrality Implementation*, UNCCD, https://knowledge.unccd.int/knowledge-products-and-pillars/guide-scientific-conceptual-framework-ldn/principles land, last accessed July 11, 2020.
33 *Id.*

Programs.³⁴ Cowie urges that, at a minimum, safeguards must be applied in planning and implementing LDN projects with respect to land governance.³⁵

UNCCD Actions—LDN Target Setting Programme

Through the LDN Target Setting Programme, the Global Mechanism, and the Secretariat of the UNCCD, and in collaboration with multiple international partners, support is given to countries with their national LDN target-setting processes, including setting national baselines, targets, and associated measures to achieve LDN.³⁶ To date, of the 123 countries that have committed to setting LDN targets, more than 80 have already completed that task.³⁷

An important contribution of LDN is the idea that better management of land is central to Agenda 2030. Avoiding, reducing, and reversing land degradation is essential for reaching many of the SDGs, including poverty reduction, food and water security, and gender equality, as well as biodiversity conservation.³⁸ A recent expert assessment found that land degradation was relevant to the targets of all 17 Goals, and that synergies were available in every case. The scientists recognized that there are many measures associated with LDN, including sustainable land and forest management, ecosystem conservation, and land restoration, which contribute to climate change adaptation and mitigation.³⁹ Land degradation neutrality is seen as one such contributor.⁴⁰

Progress on LDN

At the Twelfth Session of the Conference of Parties of the UNCCD in 2015, States reached a "breakthrough" agreement to endorse the vision of LDN and to link the implementation of the UNCCD to the SDGs generally, and to Target 15.3 in particular.⁴¹ Agenda 2030 puts a strong emphasis on an integrated approach to achieving the SDGs that can harness synergies and minimize potential trade-offs. Land plays an important part in accelerating the achievement of many of the SDGs. In 2016, it was stated that "operationalizing LDN

---

34 LDN Target Setting Programme, *supra* note 24, *see also* UNCCD, *Achieving Land Degradation Neutrality at the Country Level, Building Blocks for LDN Target Setting*, at 4, www.unccd.int/publications/achieving-land-degradation-neutrality-country-level-building-blocks-ldn-target-setting (2016) [hereinafter "Achieving LDN at the Country Level"].
35 Annette Cowie, *supra* note 27, at 8.
36 LDN Target Setting Programme, *supra* note 24.
37 *Id*.
38 Achieving LDN at the Country Level, *supra* note 34, at 5.
39 Stephen Graham, *Technical Report: Land Degradation Neutrality for Biodiversity Conservation*, UNCCD, https://catalogue.unccd.int/1340_LDN_BiodiversityGM_Report.pdf (2019).
40 *See* graphic, *Id*. at 16.
41 "The 2015 Conference of the Parties in Ankara was responding to a key target for 2030, which is to combat desertification, and restore degraded land and soil, including land affected by desertification, drought and floods, and strive to achieve a land-degradation neutral world" in *UNCCD COP 12: Ankara Turkey*, UNCCD, www.unccd.int/convention/conference-parties-cop/unccd-cop12-ankara-turkey (last visited July 22, 2020).

requires establishing a scientifically robust and consistent baseline against which to measure future changes in the rates of land degradation."[42]

In 2016, the UNCCD stated that the SDG agenda is global, but that practical solutions will be needed at both the local and landscape scale where sustainable land management, rehabilitation, and restoration can provide immediate and cost-effective benefits.[43] Target 15.3 has therefore become a strong vehicle for driving implementation of the UNCCD, while at the same time contributing to the achievement of multiple SDGs. The UNCCD argues that:

> Transformative LDN projects and programmes employ the concept of transformational change. They have the potential to fundamentally change the lives of poor people, are ambitious in scope, involve multiple instruments, develop over longer periods of time and have a lasting effect.[44]

Further, under the LDN policy and the Strategic Framework, a series of notable changes can be seen to the principles and approach of the UNCCD. Jones cogently argues that as a result "the UNCCD now operates within expanded geographical and ideological contexts." He further argues that this "compromises its ability to respond to the ecological and socioeconomic needs particular to desertification-afflicted communities."[45] While there clearly have been notable changes, we would assert that it is too early to assess whether those changes inhibit the UNCCD's ability to respond to those specific needs.

The LDN Target Setting Programme addressed SDG Target 15.3 in a synergistic and cost-effective manner and in accordance with countries' specific national contexts and development priorities. These targets also strengthen the implementation of the countries' UNCCD National Action Programmes. The assumption, yet to be demonstrated, is that achieving LDN can become an accelerator of achieving SDGs across the board.

Legal Mechanisms for Implementation of LDN

The UNCCD states that LDN encourages countries to adopt a broad range of measures to avoid, reduce, and reverse land degradation. These measures include appropriate planning, regulation, and sustainable land management practices, "combined with localized action to reverse past degradation, through land restoration and rehabilitation, to achieve a state of no net loss of healthy and productive land."[46] The question in the present context is what appropriate regulatory mechanisms are required. At the international level, the UNCCD is

---

42 Sara Minelli, Alexander Erlewein, & Victor Castillo, *Land Degradation Neutrality and the UNCCD: From Political Vision to Measurable Targets*, INTERNATIONAL YEARBOOK OF SOIL LAW AND POLICY 101, (Harald Ginzky et al., eds., 2016).

43 UNCCD, *A Natural Fix, Sustainable Development Goals, A Joined-Up Approach to Delivering the Global Goals for Sustainable Development*, at 9, www.unccd.int/sites/default/files/documents/22042016_A%20Natural%20Fix_ENG.pdf (2016).

44 UNCCD, *Land Degradation Neutrality: Transformative Action, Tapping Opportunities*, at 14, www.unccd.int/sites/default/files/documents/2017-10/171006_LDN_TP_web.pdf (2017).

45 Maximus Jones, *How Land Degradation Neutrality Compromises the Interests of Developing Countries*, 18 UNSW L. J. STUDENT SERIES 5, 12 (2018).

46 UNCCD, *Land Degradation Neutrality for Biodiversity Conservation: How Healthy Land Safeguards Nature, Global Mechanism of the UNCCD*, at 5, https://www.unccd.int/publications/land-degradation-neutrality-biodiversity-conservation-how-healthy-land-safeguards (2019).

the only binding global instrument that addresses land degradation, albeit that it is relatively narrowly focused on the world's drylands. Nevertheless, as drylands make up some 40% of the terrestrial globe, a significant difference could be made by developing a specific set of mechanisms for drylands to promote LDN. Those mechanisms could be incorporated into each of the six current annexes to the Convention, or by adding a separate specific protocol to the UNCCD for the implementation of LDN. Alternatively, an extra annex on LDN to the UNCCD, which would be applicable to all relevant regions and national jurisdictions covered by the Convention, could be added. We would argue that such a technical annex, focused on setting targets for the achievement of zero net land degradation, would most readily introduce an LDN mechanism within the confines of the Convention.[47] Such an annex could encourage countries to promote LDN through national legislation and relevant policies. However, it could not apply to lands other than those classified as drylands under the Convention. For this reason, a global regime for the protection and conservation of soil has also been promoted by the current authors.[48]

National Implementation of LDN

In October 2015, UNCCD Member States determined that SDG Target 15.3 would be a strong vehicle for driving the implementation of the Convention and requested the UNCCD Secretariat and various UNCCD bodies "to take the initiative and invite other relevant agencies and stakeholders … to seek cooperation to achieve SDG target 15.3."[49] The following five elements were identified as part of this process:[50]

1. LDN targets: Setting targets and establishing the level of ambition;
2. Leverage and impact: Catalyzing the multiple benefits that LDN provides from climate change mitigation and adaptation to poverty reduction;
3. Partnerships and resource mobilization: Rationalizing engagement with partners, overcoming fragmentation, and systematically tapping into increasing finance opportunities, including climate finance;
4. Transformative action: Designing and implementing bold LDN transformative projects that deliver multiple benefits; and
5. Monitoring and reporting: Tracking progress toward achieving the LDN targets.

The Food and Agriculture Organization's Global Soil Partnership has recently established a global database called "SoiLEX" to gather and classify national legislation on soil protection, conservation, and restoration, with the intention of providing "access to information on the existing legal instruments in force and bridge the gap between the various soil

---

47 *See* UNCCD, *supra* note 6 at Art. 31, provides for addition of technical annexes.
48 Ben Boer and Ian Hannam, *Developing a Global Soil Regime*, 1 INTL. J. OF RURAL L. & POL'Y 1,1 (2015).
49 UNCCD, at 9, ICCD/COP(12)/20/ Add.1, Decision 3/COP.12 (Jan. 21, 2016).
50 UNCCD, *Country Profile of Burkina Faso, Investing in Land Degradation Neutrality: Making the Case*, at 12, https://www.unccd.int/sites/default/files/inline-files/Burkina%20Faso_1.pdf (2018) [hereinafter "Country Profile of Burkina Faso"].

stakeholders."[51] In due course, as states implement LDN through legislation, SoiLEX could become a source for measuring the rate of legally backed uptake of LDN. [52]

The LDN Target Setting Program country reports[53] referred to above and/or country commitments to achieve LDN are listed under Annexures I–V of the UNCCD Knowledge Hub.[54]

Example: Burkina Faso's National Voluntary LDN Targets and Measures

Burkina Faso is among the countries that have set a national voluntary LDN target, established the LDN baseline, and formulated associated measures.[55] The LDN targets are seen as providing Burkina Faso with a strong vehicle to develop new policies and actions by aligning the national LDN targets with measures from the Nationally Determined Contributions of the Paris Agreement and other national commitments.[56] Investing in LDN is also seen as accelerating the advancement of other SDGs due to the close linkages between land and other goals and targets, such as Goal 1 (No poverty), Goal 2 (Zero hunger), Goal 5 (Promote gender equality), Goal 6 (Clean water and sanitation), Goal 8 (Decent work and economic growth), and Goal 13 (Climate action).[57]

In order to arrest land degradation in Burkina Faso, the country has committed to achieving LDN by 2030 by restoring some five million hectares of degraded lands and by preventing degradation of non-degraded lands. More specifically, Burkino Faso has committed itself to:

> Put an end to deforestation by 2030; improve the productivity of savannas and cultivated lands that show productivity decline, that is, 2.5 million hectares; improve carbon stocks in 800,000 ha to reach a minimum of 1 per cent of organic matter (bring 5T of organic matter (OM) per hectare every 2 years; and retrieve 300,000 ha of bare land from a total of 600,000 ha.[58]

The specificity of these sub-targets is an important facet of the overall LDN restoration target.

---

51 *Global Soil Partnership*, Food and Agriculture Organization of the United Nations, www.fao.org/global-soil-partnership/resources/highlights/detail/en/c/1274929/ accessed July 17, 2020.
52 *Id*. The legislation is categorized according to 14 keywords, most of which are specific soil degradation processes as well as soil quality and soil monitoring.
53 LDN Target Setting Program, *supra* note 24.
54 Voluntary LDN Targets, *supra* note 24. These Annexures cover Africa, Asia, Latin America and the Caribbean, and Central and Eastern Europe. The example of Burkina Faso is representative of a number of such country reports that have published their national voluntary targets and measures.
55 Country Profile of Burkina Faso, *supra* note 50.
56 Paris Agreement to the United Nations Framework Convention on Climate Change (Paris Agreement), Dec. 12, 2015, T.I.A.S. No. 16-1104, Art. 4. The Paris Agreement, Article 4, paragraph 2, requires each Party to prepare, communicate, and maintain successive nationally determined contributions (NDCs) that it intends to achieve, *see Nationally Determined Contributions*, United Nations Framework Convention on Climate Change (UNFCCC) https://unfccc.int/process-and-meetings/the-paris-agreement/the-paris-agreement/nationally-determined-contributions-ndcs (last visited July 22, 2020).
57 Country Profile of Burkina Faso, *supra* note 50.
58 *Id*. at 13.

COVID-19 and Land Degradation

The COVID-19 pandemic has been described as an "unprecedented wake-up call, laying bare deep inequalities and exposing precisely the failures that are addressed in the 2030 Agenda for Sustainable Development and the Paris Agreement on climate change."[59] The UNCCD recognizes that "land use change is the primary transmission pathway for emerging infectious diseases, and the rate of land conversion is accelerating." Moreover, the UNCCD also states that, "the foundation for building back better in the face of climate change and the wake of the COVID-19 pandemic will be centered upon future land-use decisions."[60] It appears likely that particular SDGs could play their part in ameliorating the effects of the COVID-19 pandemic, especially Goal 2 on Hunger, Goal 6 on Clean Water and Sanitation, and Goal 15 on Life on Land.

The SDGs are regarded as "vital for a recovery that leads to greener, more inclusive economies, and stronger, more resilient societies."[61] Three human rights are seen as being at the frontline of the pandemic: right to life, the right to health and access to health care, and the important issue of freedom of movement.[62] Of relevance to Target 15.3 is the issue of food security: "[T]he COVID-19 crisis has brought to light the stark inequities that leave tens of millions in persistent hunger and poverty in the U.S. and almost a billion worldwide" and

> [T]he right to food is both a call to action and a global legal framework for coordinated reform in food and agriculture. As the pandemic reshapes public life around the globe, it also offers an opportunity to organize and protect everyone's basic human right to food in the U.S.[63]

With increasing pressure on land for the production of food during the COVID-19 pandemic, the achievement of LDN has become more important by the day.

Outline Framework for National Level Law for LDN

The drive to achieve LDN globally involves a complex set of legal issues that must be confronted. One study that analyzed the implementation of LDN at the national level was reported in 2017.[64] It presented an important analysis as to the kind of legal elements that

---

59 *The Sustainable Development Goals: Our Framework for COVID-19 Recovery*, UNITED NATIONS, www.un.org/sustainabledevelopment/sdgs-framework-for-covid-19-recovery/ (last visited Nov. 3, 2020) [hereinafter, "COVID-19 Framework"].
60 *Role of Land in COVID-19 Response*, UNCCD, www.unccd.int/news-events/role-land-covid-19-response (last visited July 22, 2020), *see also* UNCCD, *Supporting the Global Response to the COVID-19 Pandemic: Land-based Solutions for Healthy People and a Healthy Planet*, www.unccd.int/sites/default/files/documents/2020-06/1498_UNCCD_%20Covid_%20layout-low%20res-1.pdf (2020).
61 COVID-19 Framework, *supra* note 59.
62 United Nations, *COVID-19 and Human Rights We Are All in This Together 2020*, at 4, www.un.org/sites/un2.un.org/files/un_policy_brief_on_human_rights_and_covid_23_april_2020.pdf (April 2020).
63 Denisse Córdova Montes et al., *Violations of the Human Right to Food During COVID-19 in the United States, Submission to the United Nations Special Rapporteur on the Right to Food*, at 2, www.ohchr.org/Documents/HRBodies/SP/COVID/Academics/UiniversityofMiamiSchoolofLawHumanRightsClinic.pdf (2019).
64 Stephanie Wunder et al., *Implementing Land Degradation Neutrality (SDG 15.3) at National Level: General Approach, Indicator Selection and Experiences from Germany*, INTERNATIONAL YEARBOOK OF SOIL

could be considered in a national law to provide for LDN.[65] The authors cautioned that, as with the other SDGs, each government should set their own targets and indicators. They set out seven key strategic steps and guiding questions for the implementation of LDN on a national level. These are: define and tailor LDN in the national context; define suitable indicators; define a baseline and set targets; specify the spatial dimension; determine compensation mechanisms; set up and maintain monitoring systems; and improve the enabling environment.[66]

The identification of these physical issues is a good starting point to approach the drafting of legislation to implement LDN to more effectively deal with land degradation.

Conclusion

A 2019 report, The Future is Now—Science for Achieving Sustainable Development argues: "[T]he 2030 Agenda represents a new mode of governance, one ultimately defined not through legally binding international agreements, but through Goals."[67] While we agree that the emphasis should continue to be on the attainment of the goals for the SDGs as a whole, we contend that robust national-level legal frameworks would add strength to the achievement of LDN. As Cowie argues, "Successful implementation of LDN interventions requires an enabling environment—a combination of institutional capacity, financial resources, policy and regulatory mechanisms, and science-policy interaction."[68]

To this end, the Soil, Sustainable Agriculture and Desertification Specialist Group of the International Union for Conservation of Nature (IUCN) World Commission on Environmental Law advocates the negotiation of an international instrument on the conservation and protection of soils that would add to and go beyond the UNCCD.[69] In the past two years the debate regarding such an instrument has become more focused, with a suggestion that the Paris Agreement could provide a model for a soil agreement that would include specific nationally determined targets for the achievement of LDN, with specified reporting and transparency requirements.[70]

The challenge would be to convert Target 15.3 into implementable national, and where relevant, sub-national legislation and policies to deliver LDN. The five modules of the Scientific Conceptual Framework for Land Degradation Neutrality are a good basis on which to formulate legal elements to be accommodated with a legislative framework for LDN.[71]

LAW AND POLICY 191–219, (Harald Ginzky et al., eds., 2017), *see also* Ralph Brodie, *Implementing Land Degradation Neutrality at National Level: Legal Instruments in Germany*, INTERNATIONAL YEARBOOK OF SOIL LAW AND POLICY 287–307, (Harald Ginzky et al., eds., 2017).

65 Stephanie Wunder, *Id.* at 198–206.
66 *Id.* at 198.
67 Independent Group of Scientists 2019, *Global Sustainable Development Report 2019: The Future is Now—Science for Achieving Sustainable Development*, UN DEPARTMENT OF ECONOMIC AND SOCIAL AFFAIRS, at 29, https://sdgs.un.org/publications/future-now-science-achieving-sustainable-development-gsdr-2019-24576 (2019).
68 Annette Cowie, *supra* note 27, at 27.
69 Ben Boer & Ian Hannam, *supra* note 48.
70 A draft resolution has been formulated along these lines for the IUCN World Conservation Congress in 2021.
71 The five modules of the LDN-SCF are set are in Annette Cowie, *supra* note 27, at 13, *see* Figure 2.

Summary Recommendations

The following points summarize the basic legal steps to achieve LDN:

- At the international level, a Paris-style agreement should be drafted that requires States to set their own nationally determined targets for achieving LDN.
- At the national level, LDN legislation should include goals and objectives that establish the mandate to control and manage land degradation.
- LDN goals and objectives should be embodied within an ecologically sustainable land management approach.
- Principles and elements of the legislation should be adapted from, inter alia, the procedural material of the UNCCD, the Paris Agreement 2015 relating to climate change, and other relevant international treaties, strategies, and policies concerning the conservation of nature, biodiversity, and sustainable land management.
- Country-specific indicators, taking into account the physical threats and drivers of land degradation, should be identified as a basis for developing strategies for the achievement of LDN.
- Legislative provisions should enable participation of all stakeholders in the development of policies, guidelines, and ecological standards for LDN and to enable governments, landowners and land managers, and the community to share responsibility for land degradation management. These would include procedures for policy implementation, development of special codes of practice, land management indicators, and the physical and ecological limits of land use.[72]

---

72 Cowie, *Id*. at 7, specifies that "LDN will only be achieved through concerted and coordinated efforts to integrate LDN objectives with land-use planning and land management, underpinned by sound understanding of the human-environment system and effective governance mechanisms. The[se] guidelines [for LDN] focus particularly on laying the foundation to achieve LDN by establishing enabling policies and applying integrated land-use planning, informed by preparatory assessments, as described in the Scientific Conceptual Framework for LDN."

D
Peace

26 Peaceful Societies and Leaving No One Behind

Fatima Akilu

Introduction

On the premise that sustainable development cannot be achieved without peace, security, and stability, the 2030 Agenda for Sustainable Development Sustainable Development Goals (SDGs) was adopted in 2015 and sets out a comprehensive and complex global agenda that paints an aspirational picture of what the world could look like in 2030. The SGDs established a new round of development targets for the world, following on from the Millennium Development Goals (MDGs),[1] which were in place from 2000 to 2015. For its part, Goal 16 aims to promote peaceful and inclusive societies for sustainable development, provide access to justice for all, and build effective, accountable, and inclusive institutions at all levels.

In assessing the impact of the goals, what is clear is that democratic governance, peace, and security, and the rule of law, which encompasses the protection of human rights for all groups, are essential to sustainable development. Yet efforts to achieve these remain uneven today. For example, corruption, organized crime, and illicit financial flows continue to erode sustainable development outcomes and undermine the rule of law.[2] Democratic recession influenced by authoritarian governments in emerging countries and the politics of nationalism in developed countries[3] only serve to compound the problem and diminish the immense potential for global coordination and leadership in achieving SDG 16, with implications for social equality and economic stability. Issues of accountability, transparency, and over-sight of public institutions, which drive inclusion, participation, and representation remains a challenge owing to the lack of capacity and/or independence of such institutions to promote the rule of law and access to justice and protect the human rights of marginalized or disadvantaged groups.

In recent years, while various regions have experienced increased and sustained peace and security, violent conflict has surged in several countries, leaving a trail of human suffering, displacement, and protracted humanitarian crises. In 2016, the year after the adoption of SDG 16, more countries were involved in some form of violent conflict than at any other time in nearly 30 years.[4] In the same year, some 26,000 people were killed as a result of

---

1 *Transitioning from the MDGs to the SDGs*, World Bank Group, UNDP 1, 176 (2013).
2 *High Level Political Forum on Sustainable Development—Discussion on SDG 16, Peace, Justice and Strong Institutions*, UNITED NATIONS (Jul. 12, 2019), https://sustainabledevelopment.un.org/content/documents/23621BN_SDG16.pdf [hereinafter "HLPF SDG 16"].
3 Larry Diamond, *Facing up to the Democratic Recession*, 26 JOURNAL OF DEMOCRACY 144–155 (Jan. 2015), www.journalofdemocracy.org/wp-content/uploads/2015/01/Diamond-26-1_0.pdf.
4 *Pathways for Peace—Inclusive Approaches to Preventing Violent Conflict*, WORLD BANK GROUP EXECUTIVE SUMMARY (2018), https://olc.worldbank.org/system/files/Pathways%20for%20Peace%20Executive%20Summary.pdf.

terrorist attacks, while another 560,000 people lost their lives because of violence. Global displacement figures today are at their highest since the end of the Second World War.[5] At the end of 2018, approximately 70.8 million people globally were recognized as refugees, asylum seekers, or internally displaced. Of these numbers, 84% live in emerging countries that face their own economic and development challenges.[6] Furthermore, the rate of violence against women and children remains high, as well as the incidence of trafficking in persons and homicide, especially in developing countries.

The slow pace of progress notwithstanding, SDG 16 is central to achieving the 2030 Agenda. This is true whether the goal is related to education, health, economic growth, crime and justice, or climate change.[7] Without sustained peace, which goes beyond the absence of violence and includes respect for human rights and the rule of law, and without inclusion and access to justice for all, the inequalities that create poverty and threaten socio-economic development will steadily increase, and the global commitment to leaving no one behind will not be achieved.

Progress and Challenges in Achieving SDG 16: A Critical Analysis

Progress toward SDG 16 remains a challenge that requires action in both developing and developed countries, albeit in different ways. For developing countries, gaps in institutional capacity represent a significant barrier to meaningful SDG 16 implementation.[8] These capacity issues are often, though not exclusively, pronounced in countries that are in a post-conflict phase, transitioning out of conflict, fragile, or least developed.

Therefore, as with the rest of the 2030 Agenda, while governments must play a leading role, achieving SDG 16 will require a "whole-of-society" approach to deliver positive results.[9] Achieving this will require strengthening the role of development collaborators such as civil society organizations and human rights institutions to join efforts aimed at delivering the dividends of peace, justice, and inclusion as implementers and advocates for under-represented groups within national populations, such as women, youths, and other marginalized groups. For its part, the private sector can also make meaningful contribution to efforts toward the equitable distribution of economic opportunities, which advances inclusion, and promotes the rule of law by eliminating acts of environmental damage and corruption, as fundamentals to creating a physical and social environment conducive to development where business can thrive.[10]

Furthermore, the international community, supported by multilateral institutions such as the United Nations (UN), must do more to prevent and eradicate conflict. This is even as they support improving the lives of those living in fragile and conflict-affected regions,

---

5 *Conflict and Fragility—What We Know*, IDA WORLD BANK GROUP, http://ida.worldbank.org/theme/conflict-and-fragility (accessed on Apr. 2, 2020).
6 *Id.*
7 *Enabling the Implementation of the 2030 Agenda through SDG 16+: Anchoring Peace, Justice and Inclusion*, GLOBAL ALLIANCE REPORT (Jul. 2019), www.sdg16hub.org/system/files/2019-07/Global%20Alliance%2C%20SDG%2016%2B%20Global%20Report.pdf [hereinafter "Global Alliance SDG 16+ Report"].
8 HLPF SDG 16, *supra* note 2.
9 Asako Okai, *Opinion: SDG 16 Is an Accelerator for the Entire 2030 Agenda*, DEVEX (Jul. 15, 2019), www.devex.com/news/opinion-sdg-16-is-an-accelerator-for-the-entire-2030-agenda-95289.
10 BUSINESS AND SECURITY: PUBLIC-PRIVATE SECTOR RELATIONSHIPS IN A NEW SECURITY ENVIRONMENT (Alyson Bailes & Isabel Frommelt eds., Oxford University Press, 2004), www.sipri.org/sites/default/files/files/books/SIPRI04BaiFro/SIPRI04BaiFro.pdf.

by reducing the drivers of fragility and violent conflict, making progress on all other SDGs, and improving ways of reaching marginalized populations affected by violence or conflict.

Status and Trends: Breaking Down the Figures

While some progress has been made over the last four years in implementing SDG 16, the findings point to the need for sustained urgent action, as the goal of peaceful, just, and inclusive societies is still a long way off. Throughout the world, efforts to end violence, promote the rule of law, strengthen institutions, and increase access to justice remain uneven as millions of people still live in insecurity and continue to be deprived of their rights and opportunities.[11] Unsurprisingly, significant divergences exist across regions and in countries in very different situations. Regrettably, the most vulnerable countries are bearing the brunt of the current obstacles to the implementation of SDG 16.[12]

In 2018, the number of people fleeing war, persecution, and conflict exceeded 70 million, the highest level recorded by the United Nations High Commissioner for Refugees in almost 70 years.[13] All are particularly vulnerable to various forms of abuse, including trafficking, violence, and non-inclusive decision-making. Ensuring that they receive adequate protection is paramount to achieving the goal of inclusive societies and sustainable development.[14]

To understand the level of progress and challenges encountered by countries and regions, developed and developing, in achieving the various targets that make up SDG 16, it is vital to first look at existing trends in the implementation of SDG 16. Crucially, however, it must be observed that the common impediment to tracking the SDGs 16's implementation is the significant gap in reliable data, which makes it difficult to measure true progress in meeting the goal's targets. Critics of the SDGs have long questioned whether the SDGs can be measured and monitored.[15] Fragile and conflict-affected states often have incomplete, imperfect, or a total lack of data, while all countries of the world vary hugely in their capacity to collect, monitor, and track SDG 16 targets. Besides, obstacles to achieving the goals of SDG 16 are increasingly encountered in urban areas.[16] Increases in city-dwelling populations are expected to rise to almost 70% by 2050,[17] and cities register higher rates of homicide, violence, and organized crime than rural areas.[18] The challenges found within "fragile cities"—characterized by rapid, unregulated urbanization, high levels of inequal-

---

11 HLPF SDG 16, *supra* note 2, at 3.
12 *Report of the Secretary General on SDG Progress 2019*: Special Edition, UNITED NATIONS, 1, ii, https://sustainabledevelopment.un.org/content/documents/24978Report_of_the_SG_on_SDG_Progress_2019.pdf (accessed April 3, 2020) [hereinafter "SG Progress Report 2019"].
13 *Worldwide Displacement Tops 70 million, UN Refugee Chair Urges Greater Solidarity in Response*, UNHCR: UN Refugee Agency (Jun. 19, 2019, www.unhcr.org/news/press/2019/6/5d03b22b4/worldwide-displacement-tops-70-million-un-refugee-chief-urges-greater-solidarity.html.
14 *Sustainable Development Goals Report*, UN STATS (2019), https://unstats.un.org/sdgs/report/2019/The-Sustainable-Development-Goals-Report-2019.pdf (accessed Apr. 2, 2020).
15 Ranjula Bali Swain, *A Critical Analysis of the Sustainable Development Goals*, HANDBOOK OF SUSTAINABILITY SCIENCE AND RESEARCH, 341–55 (Oct. 2017), DOI: 10.1007/978-3-319-63007-6_20.
16 David M. Malone, *On SDG 16: Peace, Justice and Strong Institutions*, UNITED NATIONS UNIVERSITY (May 14, 2018), ourworld.unu.edu/en/sdg-16-peace-justice-and-strong-institutions.
17 *68% of the World Population Projected to Live in Urban Areas by 2050*, UNITED NATIONS NEWS, Department of Economic and Social Affairs (May 2018), www.un.org/development/desa/en/news/population/2018-revision-of-world-urbanization-prospects.html.
18 Swain, *supra* note 15.

ity, unemployment, and violence; poor access to key services; and exposure to climate threats—mean that realizing SDG 16 will require action not only at the national level, but also at the subnational level.[19]

Globally, the number of intentional homicides per 100,000 population ticked up from 6.0 in 2015 to 6.1 in 2017, largely because of an increase in the rate of homicides in Latin America,[20] the Caribbean, and some countries in sub-Saharan Africa.[21] On trafficking and exploitation of persons, the data available indicates an overall increase in the detection of victims of human trafficking.[22] Such progress points to a positive trend, attributable to successful global media campaigns such as CNN's Freedom Project or Nigeria's "Not for Sale" Project. Alternatively, however, increased detection could either also point to the enhanced efforts of law enforcement authorities in trafficking-affected countries to identify and rescue victims or refer to a larger trafficking problem.[23]

Furthermore, the rise of populist, nationalist governments over the past five years has led to an increase in hate speech, racism, and xenophobic rhetoric around the world. From Hungary to the United States, political actors are increasingly resorting to race, gender, ethnicity, anti-refugee, or anti-immigrant stances that promote fear and distrust, and encourage violence against vulnerable minority groups.[24] Available evidence points to the use of discriminatory policies and practices by governments to exclude minority, disadvantaged, or marginalized groups from accessing public services, public threats, and use of violence, as well as the selective enforcement of laws, including harassment and assault by law enforcement authorities—particularly the police.[25]

SDG 16.3—Promoting the Rule of Law at the National and International Levels and Ensure Equal Access to Justice for All

The global picture looks promising as many countries recorded gains on key aspects of the target.[26] For example, while judicial independence remained particularly poor in Africa, 35% of Africans however benefited from the progress made in providing increased access to justice.[27] For people detained in prison without recourse to a trial, the ratio remained high albeit largely constant at the rate of 30%, when compared against the overall prison population.[28] This is a major concern, especially for countries in Africa, such as the Central African Republic and Sierra Leone, and Central America where citizens can be unlawfully

---

19 *Id.*
20 *Note*: Homicide rate in major Latin American countries: Brazil (27 per 100,000 population); Columbia (27 per 100,000 population); Honduras (60 per 100,000 population); El Salvador (60 per 100,000 population); Mexico (25 per 100,000 population).
21 Global Alliance SDG 16+ Report, *supra* note 7, at 27.
22 HLPF SDG 16, *supra* note 2, at 3.
23 SG Progress Report 2019, *supra* note 12, at 27.
24 Sarah Deardorff Miller, *Xenophobia Towards Refugees and Other Forced Migrants*, WORLD REFUGEE COUNCIL RESEARCH PAPER, (Sep. 2018), https://reliefweb.int/sites/reliefweb.int/files/resources/WRC%20Research%20Paper%20no.5.pdf (accessed May 14, 2020).
25 *Id.*
26 *Tracking Progress on Sustainable Development Goal 16 with Global State of Democracy Indices*, The Global State of Democracy: In Focus 1, 9 (Sep. 2019), www.idea.int/sites/default/files/publications/tracking-progress-sdg16-with-gsod-indices.pdf [hereinafter "Tracking progress SDG 16"].
27 *Id.*
28 Global Alliance SDG 16+ Report, *supra* note 7, at 105.

arrested and detained in prisons for long periods of time without trial.[29] By contrast, in Europe, approximately 18% of the overall population had experienced a decline in options for access to justice, while in a context of democratic backsliding in Central and Eastern Europe, challenges to judicial independence have emerged, with recorded instances of intrusions in the work of the Judiciary.[30]

On the need to substantially reduce corruption and bribery in all its forms (SGD 16.5), available data indicates that while 43% of countries in the world continue to experience high levels of corruption, progress made since 2013 demonstrates an increasingly positive trend in relation to this target.[31] This is very important because SDG 16.5 has serious implications for the achievement of the entire 2030 Agenda, and the absence of corruption is highly correlated with human development. For example, with the shrinking democratic space in many countries today, the independence of national institutions responsible for safeguarding the rights of disadvantaged groups and upholding the rule of law has become very important. As an example, in countries where politicians interfere with the appointment of judges, evidence suggests that the perception of corruption is high among local populations, and this is likely to lead to a breakdown in social order and respect for the rule of law.[32] For Africa and the Middle East, which have the highest incidence of corruption globally, despite the challenges, in 2019, around 30% of countries in Africa recorded a fall in the level of corruption over a four year period.[33]

Continuing on a positive trend, Africa recorded the most progress in implementing SDG 16 targets in 2019, while the Middle East remained the lowest scoring region in the world on all targets linked to SDG 16. For Africa, however, that is where the good news ends. The region continues to lag behind on many areas of SDG 16.6.

SDG 16.6—*Effective, Accountable, and Transparent Institutions at All Levels*

The areas of lag include the lack of effective, accountable, and transparent institutions such as an independent judiciary; the low level of democratic development compared to the rest of the world; and the existing pockets of conflict in the region, with populations in the Lake Chad Basin the worst affected.[34]

Moreover, in 2018, only 39% of all countries had in place a National Human Rights Institution (NHRI),[35] compliant with internationally agreed standards (the Paris Principles). NHRIs are essential to hold governments accountable to their human rights obligations, strengthen national protection legislation and mechanisms for marginalized groups, support cross-cutting collaboration with civil society and other development partners, and ensure that policies fit the needs and aspirations of populations that they are intended for.[36]

---

29 *Id.*
30 Sean Leo Hanley, *Rethinking Democratic Backsliding in Central and Eastern Europe—Looking Beyond Hungary and Poland* (2018) JOURNAL OF EASTERN EUROPEAN POLITICS 34 (3): 243–56
31 Tracking Progress SDG 16, *supra* note 26, at 9.
32 Global Alliance SDG 16+ Report, *supra* note 7, at 41.
33 *Id.*
34 Tracking Progress SDG 16, *supra* note 26, at 3.
35 Global Alliance SDG 16+ Report, *supra* note 7, at 103 (note: NHRIs refers to Human Rights Commissions within countries with such a national agency).
36 *Id.* at 61.

SGD 16.10—Public Access to Information and Protect[ion] of Fundamental Freedoms in Accordance with National Legislation and International Agreements

Therefore, accelerating the establishment of such a key institution in non-compliant countries must be a priority of their governments as well as multilateral institutions such as the United Nations.

SGD 16.10—Public Access to Information and Protect[ion] of Fundamental Freedoms in Accordance with National Legislation and International Agreements

Although 125 countries have adopted laws and policies providing citizens with a right to access information held by public institutions, over half of the population in Latin America and the Caribbean are not able to exercise these rights, while 39% and 28% of populations in Asia Pacific and Europe, respectively have witnessed similar declines in relation to this target.[37] Of the 123 countries that supplied data, citizens from 40 countries still do not have an established right to appeal to an independent administrative body for public access to information, which is considered essential to the achievement of the target.[38]

SDG 16.1—Significantly Reduce All Forms of Violence and Related Death Rates Everywhere

The killings of human rights activists, journalists, advocates, and trade unionists, contrary to SDG 16.1 and 16.10 are on the rise.– Between 2017 and 2018, the UN recorded and verified 431 killings across 41 countries, with 99 journalists and bloggers among the victims.[39] The spate of killings saw an increase in the murder of frontline activists working to build a more inclusive and equal society from one victim a day, observed from 2015 to 2017, to at least 8 murders every week by 2018.[40]

In many countries, while measuring the progress on SDG 16 is considered to be politically, technically, and financially possible, institutional mechanisms at the national and local levels to gather data and monitor policy efforts and impact are weak. Thus, partnerships between national statistical agencies and regional and local governments, civil society organizations, think tanks, and academia, as well as the private sector and international organizations can enhance the capacity of countries to gather, analyze, and use data on SDG 16 targets and indicators.[41] Nevertheless, the findings show that the number of countries reporting on SDG 16 is increasing, although more needs to be done to ensure that SDG 16 is also included as part of development planning, prioritization, and budgeting in many countries around the world.[42]

The COVID-19 Pandemic: Implications for Forward Progress on SDG 16

The COVID-19 virus pandemic represents a significant public health crisis which is hard to overstate. Already, the number of cases confirmed in fragile parts of the Middle East

---

37 Tracking Progress SDG 16, *supra* note 26, at 1.
38 Global Alliance SDG 16+ Report, *supra* note 7, at 117.
39 SDG Progress Report 2019, *supra* note 12, at 27.
40 *Id*.
41 Global Alliance SDG 16+ Report, *supra* note 7, at 31.
42 Okai, *supra* note 9.

and Africa are on the rise, albeit not at the same pace as experienced in Europe. For countries where the global health challenge intersects with conflicts or conditions—such as weak institutions, communal tensions, or the lack of trust in leaders—that could give rise to new crises or exacerbate existing ones. Besides, the dramatic global economic slowdown caused by the pandemic will disrupt trade flows and create economic inequalities, characterized by high unemployment among poor and marginalized populations, which could reinforce the same dynamics that create instability and conflict in the first place.[43] Moreover, if the disease spreads in fragile countries with densely populated urban centers and poor access to health and sanitation services, the consequences would be devastating.

In almost all cases, countries experiencing or emerging from fragility or conflict, with social challenges compounded by mismanagement, corruption, or foreign sanctions, will have national health systems that are profoundly ill-prepared to deal with COVID-19.[44] In Libya, for example, the health system has collapsed due to an exodus of health professionals during the war.[45] In Iran, the impact of sanctions by the United States, compounded by the slow response of the Iranian government to the pandemic, has devastated its health system and led to the deaths of thousands.[46] In Palestine, where the health system has been weakened by years of blockade by Israel, the Health Ministry is struggling to obtain the necessary supplies and health staff needed to serve its high-density population and respond to the COVID-19 pandemic.[47]

In Nigeria, decades of mismanagement and corruption in the public health system has left the country with wholly inadequate emergency care facilities, poor medical supply networks, insufficient numbers of well-trained health professionals, and poor disease detection (but strong community surveillance)[48] to manage a crisis of the scale possible with the disease outbreak. This has in turn created mass public distrust in the government's ability to manage the pandemic.

For internally displaced people, asylum seekers, and refugees with limited or no access to healthcare, and fleeing conflict, the risk of exposure to outbreaks of COVID-19 is particularly high. Furthermore, practicing social distancing will be impossible for such vulnerable groups because they often sleep in crowded and cramped living spaces, and typically lack basic resources, such as running water or soap, to maintain basic hygiene. In these cases, where displaced populations, refugees, and asylum seekers face large-scale outbreaks and attempt to flee to safety, local populations or authorities may react forcefully to contain them, which creates the potential for escalating violence. Additionally, nations attempting to stop the spread of the disease are likely to view new refugee flows fearfully, and close their borders, creating significant human suffering and a humanitarian crisis.[49]

---

43 *COVID-19 and Conflict: Seven Trends to Watch*, INTERNATIONAL CRISIS GROUP, 2 (Mar. 24, 2020) https://d2071andvip0wj.cloudfront.net/B004-covid-19-seven-trends_0.pdf [hereinafter "COVID Seven Trends"].
44 *Id.*
45 Sara Creta, *Libyan Doctors Battle on Two Dangerous Fronts: COVID-19 and War*, THE NEW HUMANITARIAN (Jun. 10, 2020), www.thenewhumanitarian.org/news-feature/2020/06/10/Libya-war-coronavirus-hospital-doctors.
46 COVID Seven Trends, *supra* note 43, at 3.
47 *Id.*
48 *Nigeria's Polio Infrastructure Bolster COVID-19 Response*, WORLD HEALTH ORGANISATION: NIGERIA (Apr. 4, 2020), www.afro.who.int/news/nigerias-polio-infrastructure-bolster-covid-19-response.
49 COVID Seven Trends, *supra* note 43, at 5.

Travel restrictions have begun to weigh on international mediation, as well as multinational peace-keeping and security assistance efforts. For instance, UN envoys in the Middle East have experienced difficulty traveling to and within the region due to airport closures.[50] A Security Council decision to set up a new political mission to support Sudan's transition to civilian rule has been postponed as part of the virus containment measures.[51] More broadly, the main adverse effect of the COVID-19 pandemic on global peace and security efforts is that world leaders, focused on the domestic issues arising as a result of the pandemic, have little or no time to devote to conflicts or peace processes.[52]

At variance with the responsibility to ensure transparency, accountability, and representative decision-making, some authoritarian governments have taken steps to limit public access to information as it relates to the pandemic. In Egypt, for example, media reporters are censored by the government from reporting on the COVID-19 pandemic, at a time when media reporting on the pandemic is considered critical to maintaining public health and safety.[53]

On the whole, while the COVID-19 pandemic poses a potentially significant threat to peace, security, and stability, and will likely slow down the pace of progress on SDG 16 over the short term, there have been positive outcomes. The outbreak has created opportunities for humanitarian gestures between rivals. The United Arab Emirates (UAE) has, for example, airlifted over 30 tons of humanitarian aid to Iran to deal with the disease, while the government of the Philippines recently announced a one-month unilateral ceasefire with communist rebels to enable government forces to focus on dealing with the pandemic.[54] Modest as these outcomes may appear, the pandemic creates an opportunity to push governments and opposing parties to find common ground and cease hostilities as a condition for receiving future international assistance to address the economic devastation that will inevitably be caused by the pandemic.

Conclusion

To date, while there are 162 countries and territories working toward the 2030 Agenda, and 131 UN country teams supporting efforts to implement the SDGs' strategic priorities,[55] achieving SDG 16 by 2030 will be challenging. Visionary and committed country-level leadership is essential to accelerate progress on SDG 16 and transform societies to prevent conflict, tackle inequalities, reduce injustices, be more inclusive, and ensure that no one is left behind.[56]

Conflicts and instability in many parts of the world have intensified, causing untold human suffering, undermining the realization of the SDG 16 and even reversing the progress already made. In addition, economic, social, and environmental trends, such as demographic shifts, growing inequalities, forced displacement, rapid urbanization, and discrimination

---

50 *Id.* at 6.
51 *Id.*
52 *Id.*
53 *Reporting on the Coronavirus: Egypt Muzzles Critical Journalists*, DEUTSCHE WELLE (Apr. 3, 2020), www.dw.com/en/reporting-on-the-coronavirus-egypt-muzzles-critical-journalists/a-53009293.
54 Global Alliance SDG 16+ Report, *supra* note 7, at 12–13.
55 *Our Impact in Coordination*, UN SUSTAINABLE DEVELOPMENT GROUP, https://unsdg.un.org/ (accessed Apr. 5, 2020).
56 Global Alliance SDG 16+ Report, *supra* note 7, at 31.

against marginalized groups are reshaping the governance landscape at all levels. Therefore, building strong institutions that support the attainment of all SDGs in the context of rising public expectations poses major challenges and opportunities.[57]

Bold public sector reform and transformation for peaceful, just, and inclusive societies will be essential, along with serious efforts to combat corruption which affects public confidence in government and the rule of law, and significantly limits the beneficial impact institutions can have on the everyday life of individuals. Ensuring participation and inclusiveness in decision-making adds a significant dimension to the principle of "leaving no one behind," by ensuring that for those already left behind, they have a voice in government decisions that affect them.[58]

Achieving these goals will require partnerships, integrated solutions, and for countries to take charge and lead in reshaping the institutional and social landscape, preparing grounds for important reforms that help build sustainable peace.[59] A key part of the envisaged partnership must include the collaboration between national statistical agencies, local governments, civil society organizations, think tanks, and academia, as well as the private sector and international organizations to enhance the capacity of countries to gather, analyze, and use data on SDG 16 targets and indicators to track progress, target resource investment, and achieve meaningful outcomes.

This is particularly significant considering that four years into the ambitious agenda, one of the critical challenges to implementing and tracking the progress of SDG 16 is the major gap in the official SDG 16 indicators. These gaps are created by inconsistent methodologies and indicators employed by different countries in collecting data on SDG indicators, limited resources, and the weak capacity of national statistics agencies, especially in, but not exclusive to, developing countries to define clear national (statistical or otherwise) targets for all SDG 16 indicators.[60] What is however clear is that in view of the expected impact of the COVID-19 pandemic on peace, security, and development, and the slow progress on the implementation of SDG 16 so far, world governments must now decide whether to support more cooperative approaches to handling crises, not only in relation to the global public health crisis, but also in challenges to peace, stability, and, ultimately, development.

Realizing these goals would require an inclusive and participatory approach to development to tackle the impact of marginalization and exclusion of certain groups in societies, amidst the continued rise and risks posed by populism, nationalism, and xenophobia across the world. Accountable and inclusive institutions must be alive to their responsibility to ensure participatory decision-making and responsive public policies that leave no one behind. This includes promoting and ensuring unfettered access to justice for all citizens and the rule of law, without which there can be no sustainable development. Ultimately, what must never be forgotten is that SDG 16 cannot be achieved by governments alone. It requires a whole-of-society response and important multi-stakeholder partnerships involving actors from all facets of national life.

---

57 *Transitioning from the MDGs to the SDGs, supra* note 1, at 7.
58 *Id.*
59 Malone, *supra* note 16.
60 *The Sustainable Development Goals Report* (2019), https://unstats.un.org/sdgs/report/2019/The-Sustainable-Development-Goals-Report-2019.pdf.

Recommendations for Stakeholders

Coordinating a global effort such as the SGD 16 targets can be immensely challenging, even at the best of times. Therefore, the recommended steps that key stakeholders with a role to play in delivering the SDGs must consider to realign their efforts and get back on track are as follows:

Indicators and Uniform Reporting

A major challenge with tracking the true state of SDGs 16's implementation is the significant gap in reliable data and the divergent indicators used by different countries. This brings about difficulty in measuring the progress of countries on specific indicators that relate to disadvantaged or marginalized groups for example. Thus, it is important to consider the introduction of sets of indicators agreeable to all nations, depending on their level of development and context, to make it possible to track progress, promote uniform reporting, and ensure institutional reforms that are sustainable in the long run.

Collaboration and Partnership

Learning from the missed opportunity to work together in an effort to find a global solution to the COVID-19 pandemic, world governments must do more to support fragile and developing countries to strengthen their institutional responses, adequately plan the use of resources, share resources where possible, and build capacities to achieve the SDG 16 targets. More so, national governments must also ensure that their national frameworks and action plans for implementing the SDGs take a whole-of-society approach and include very clear roles and responsibilities for civil society organizations, the private sector, multilateral organizations, and communities to contribute to the success.

Capacity Building

National governments, especially those in fragile or developing nations, currently lack the institutional mechanisms and capacity at the national and local levels to monitor and implement policy efforts and measure impact. Thus, it is important for national institutions, through partnerships with multilateral institutions, civil society organizations, think tanks, and academia, as well as the private sector to enhance their capacity to achieve SDG 16 targets. This includes building the capacity of government policy makers and officials to take into account SDG 16 targets into their development planning, prioritization, and budgeting.

Improving Accountability for Action

For national governments that fail to report data or take tangible action on the implementation of measures to achieve the SDG targets, multilateral institutions such as the United Nations should develop a system of accountability that considers naming and shaming errant governments for taking actions inconsistent with the SGD targets.

27 Nigeria's Alternative Pathway to Peace

Fatima Akilu

Introduction

The world today stands at a critical junction, juxtaposed by the need to support human progress and advancement without losing sight of the need to address significant challenges that threaten the sustainability of such development. These challenges range from climate change to rising global inequality and poverty, volatile financial markets, reversed development gains, increasing rates of hunger, gender inequality, threats to peace and security, as well as increased conflicts. The 2030 Agenda for Sustainable Development, known as the Global Goals, adopted by all United Nations Member States in 2015, provides a shared blueprint for peace and prosperity for all people and the planet, now and into the future. In Nigeria, the Boko Haram crisis continues to threaten the implementation of the Sustainable Development Goals (SDGs). Despite multiple approaches taken by Nigeria and her neighbors in pursuit of peace and stability, the ruthless terrorist group has continued to pose a significant security and development challenge. The growth and rise of groups such as Boko Haram has been linked to several social, economic, environmental, and political factors such as poverty, access to education, inequality, marginalization, and the drying up of Lake Chad—leading to lost economic opportunities.

Violence and Religious Extremism in Nigeria

Nigeria is one of the world's most diverse and complex nations. Expectedly, with its rich diversity comes the challenges of integration and cohesion among its many ethnic nationalities. This rich diversity not managed properly, alongside structural challenges such as corruption, impunity, poverty, and inequality has exacerbated existing ethno-religious fault lines and led to national disunity that emerged shortly after the country attained its independence in 1960. Nigeria's fight against violent extremism is often traced back to 2009. According to Council on Foreign Relations (CFR) Nigeria Security Tracker (NST), insurgency has since claimed 37,530 lives among which 50% were Boko Haram militants, 45% were civilians, and 5% were state actors.[1] Boko Haram is not the first radical Islamist organization to have emerged. While several groups have emerged and sought to realize their ideological goals by undermining the stability of the country, the most infamous revolt in Nigeria, prior to Boko Haram, dates back to the 1980s.

---

1 John Campbell & Asch Harwood, *Boko Haram's Deadly Impact*, COUNCIL ON FOREIGN RELATIONS (Aug. 20, 2018), www.cfr.org/article/boko-harams-deadly-impact.

Time and experience have shown that ideologies cannot be fought with guns alone. In the intervening years and since Boko Haram, many other radical groups holding religious, political, and economic ideologies have sprung up across Nigeria. Having identified the conditions that increase vulnerability to radicalization especially in Nigeria's North East, the Federal Government of Nigeria in 2012 broadened its counter-terrorism approach to include new laws, strategies, frameworks, partnerships, and institutions.

Nigeria's Alternative Pathway to Peace

The nature and scope of the Boko Haram insurgency forced Nigeria to innovate rapidly as it responded to the insurgency. Terrorism provided Nigeria an unexpected opportunity to reform her criminal justice system, broaden legal frameworks, and create a counter-terrorism strategy. Nigeria had to adopt an unconventional and multi-disciplinary approach that was holistic, long-term, and robust to address the main causes of the insurgency. Broadly led by government and supported by civil society organizations and multilateral organizations, this approach complemented the kinetic military action. Laws that sought to check illegal activities related to terrorism were enhanced. State Governments from Borno to Kaduna and Katsina instituted Islamic preaching boards, with a view to curbing the spread of incendiary rhetoric and ideology through the regulation of sermons and granting of preaching licenses. As a long-term response to terrorism, government took steps to prioritize poverty alleviation and job creation in the country, especially in the North East where infrastructural and development deficit was most acutely felt. In line with this, a regional economic revitalization plan was developed. Previously known as the Presidential Initiative for the North East (PINE), it has since morphed into the Presidential Committee on the North East Initiative (PCNI) and has now been established by way of legislation—the North East Development Commission Act.[2] Furthermore, the intense nature of the conflict led to the development and refinement of national strategies. A Counter Terrorism Center (CTC) domiciled in the Office of the National Security Adviser (ONSA) was created and in 2014, Nigeria's National Counter-Terrorism Strategy (NACTEST) was launched.[3] Accompanying a revision to the National Security Strategy was the development of a National Policy Framework and Action Plan on Preventing and Countering Violent Extremism (P/CVE).

Nigeria also adopted a civil-military strategy or a soft approach to counterterrorism. This approach known as Nigeria's Countering Violent Extremism Programme was coordinated by the Directorate of Behavioral Analysis and Strategic Communication within ONSA.[4] The CVE Programme represents the nation's first attempt at a truly multidimensional response to combating terrorism. To achieve these goals, three streams of the CVE Programme were identified, with different layers of both state and non-state actors. The streams included the following:

- **Counter-Radicalization**: Designed to engage vulnerable populations through education and economic intervention projects aimed at preventing radicalization and

---

2 *North East Development Commission: Explanatory Memorandum*, 1–17 (2017), https://placng.org/i/wp-content/uploads/2019/12/North-East-Development-Commission-Act-2017n.pdf.
3 *Nigerian National Security Strategy 2014*, OFFICE OF THE NATIONAL SECURITY ADVISER: COUNTER TERRORISM CENTRE (Mar. 8, 2020), http://ctc.gov.ng/nigerian-national-security-strategy-2014/.
4 *Id.*

recruitment. It was also designed to work across all levels and tiers of government on the one hand and civil society, faith-based organizations, and other non-state actors on the other—to create awareness of the threat of violent extremism. It sought to identify and strengthen credible voices in communities, collate data on religious figures, sects, and places of worship and capture the kind of teachings or preaching in schools and worship centers.

- **De-radicalization**: Designed to be a prison-based initiative driven by the Ministry of Interior and the Nigerian Prisons Service (NPS), the goal of the program was beyond disengagement from violence to ideological disengagement, therefore highlighting the need for acquisition of vast resources. Under the de-radicalization program also are specific responses, which were tailored to address the needs of certain demographics such as women and girls in battle, victims, and failed suicide bombers. The de-radicalization curriculum has since been institutionalized and is taught in prison training schools across the country.
- **Strategic Communications**: Designed to produce a counter-narrative messaging system which presents subtle ideological/religious views as a way of countering the radicalized proposition of extremists. Built around promoting core national values and principles, it coordinated a national messaging system that is a necessary tool in activating attitudinal and behavioral change among the citizenry, which instantly and consciously dispels contrary messaging by terrorists. The government's strategic communication approach to tackling the nation's security challenges were hinged on certain key principles that enhanced tolerance, the dissemination of Islamic knowledge, and dispelling the misconstruction that the fight against terror is a persecution of Islam among others.[5]

Today, the conflict is gradually waning. Military gains saw improved security in parts of North East Nigeria allowing a window of opportunity to focus on early recovery and conflict stabilization measures; this has enabled the partial strengthening of local conflict prevention systems, restoration of local governance and basic services, the fostering of social cohesion and ensuring the reintegration of former combatants and their families. As the conflict has evolved, so also has the approach and actors involved. Today, there is a de-radicalization, rehabilitation, and reintegration (DRR) program established as the vehicle to receive repentant insurgents. Known as Operation Safe Corridor, the program is a major component of Nigeria's P/CVE efforts warranting a section on its own.[6] Operation Safe Corridor, which has its facility in Gombe State, provides a range of rehabilitation services including psychotherapy, religious counseling, addiction counseling, and recreational activities such as sports, education, and vocational training.[7]

In the search for lasting peace, government efforts have also been complemented by civil society organizations and multinational cooperation. Parallel to setting up a Multinational Joint Task Force (MNJTF) under the auspices of the Lake Chad Basin Commission, the first Lake Chad Basin Governors' Forum for regional cooperation on stabilization was hosted in

---

5 Dr. Fatima Akilu, Paper presented at Nigerian Army Resource Center, Abuja. Monthly Lecture Series—*Countering Violent Extremism in Nigeria: Rehabilitation and Reintegration*, (Mar 2019).
6 *Id.*
7 *Id.*

May 2018.[8] While the MNJTF has been instrumental in ensuring the safety of citizens and property, the impact of the Governor's Forum is yet to be felt. With the legitimacy of the Nigerian state threatened across many communities in the North East, many civil society organizations have leveraged on innovation to foster peace outside the framework of a functional state. Civil society organizations (CSOs) have been known to fill service gaps.

Nigeria and the Sustainable Development Goals

In tandem with Nigeria's commitment to addressing her security problems, the country has shown a commitment to the Sustainable Development Goals through leadership and ownership of the implementation process by setting up of the office of the Special Adviser to the President on the SDGs (OSSAP-SDGs) and an increased buy in on the side of other relevant government agencies.[9] The OSSAP-SDGs is charged with the responsibility for inter-governmental coordination, planning, multi-stakeholders' partnership, resource mobilization, as well as ensuring seamless and robust strategic communications and advocacy around the SDGs agenda.[10] These efforts have led to a strong national SDGs ownership in the country. While these efforts at creating an alternative pathway to peace, since the rise of Boko Haram have been commendable, Nigeria as a country still remains behind target to achieve SDG 16. In practice, the OSSAP-SDGs have been unable to significantly advance Goal 16 in the context of the Boko Haram conflict. Widespread allegations of corruption and ineffective coordination have also hampered the humanitarian and civilian response to the crisis. While there has been a glaring need for a comprehensive strategic DDR framework as the conflict moves to a post-conflict stage, the country remains without one. Despite several calls for a coordinated regional response to the crisis, the region does not have an effective political infrastructure, and cooperation has been primarily externally driven.[11] In addition to this, the conflict has led to the pervasive spread of trauma induced by the long years of the insurgency.

To achieve SDG 16, more commitment is required in strengthening collective ownership and deepening continuous sensitization and awareness on SDGs with more engagement of the CSOs and the private sector. Ensuring the availability of timely data and the adoption of appropriate technological and capacity strengthening is needful for advancing the implementation of the SDGs.

Lessons Learned and Policy Recommendations

The Nigerian response to radicalization and violent extremism, though initially hesitant and slow, has attempted to match the ambitions and imagination of the terrorists. Increasingly, this has meant understanding that any counter-insurgency effort must include a whole of

---

8 *Lake Chad Basin Governors' Forum: Peacebuilding, Prevention, Stabilization and Regional Cooperation*, UNDEP (Jul 10, 2018), www.ng.undp.org/content/nigeria/en/home/library/democratic_governance/lake-chad-basin-governors-forum-documents-.html.
9 *Implementation of the SDGs A National Voluntary Review*, SDGs Nigeria (Jun. 2017), https://sustainabledevelopment.un.org/content/documents/16029Nigeria.pdf.
10 *Id.*
11 Saskia Brechenmacher, *Stabilizing Northeast Nigeria After Boko Haram*, CARNIE ENDOWMENT FOR INTERNATIONAL PEACE (May 3, 2019), https://carnegieendowment.org/2019/05/03/stabilizing-northeast-nigeria-after-boko-haram-pub-79042.

government approach, which includes all of society, to reclaim the ground that a decade-long terrorist campaign had staked. In light of the challenges and lessons learned, policymakers must consider that addressing violent extremism and implementing the SDGs will require a focus that puts into context a multi-faceted approach.

Investments in Human Capital

It has become ever more crucial for State Governments to invest in the well-being and development of their population, with key investments in improving access to education, healthcare, social infrastructure, and security. Notwithstanding the challenge of inadequate funding to make necessary investments, state governments must devise clear and consistent policies for investing in social welfare, with a credible system for checking against waste and the misuse of public funds.

Addressing Environmental Issues

Evidence shows that communities in the Lake Chad region have suffered slow economic growth, exacerbated by the shirking of Lake Chad. Understanding that climate change is critical to achieving the SDGs and has disproportionate effects on the poor, countries in the Lake Chad Basin must work closely with the Basin Commission as a matter of urgency to implement measures that reverse the effects of desertification and that recharge the Lake Chad region. This is critical to preventing food insecurity (due to drought, malnutrition, etc.) and conflict over land, which often give rise to tensions that spill over into full scale violence.

Strengthening Expertise

While the government and civil society have worked to develop the expertise required to prevent violent extremism, the need to scale rehabilitation and reintegration interventions that provide pathways for survivors of conflict and perpetrators alike remains significant. It is therefore recommended that the government should collaborate with the private sector and civil society to continue to develop a cadre of practitioners in rehabilitation and reintegration. This should include psychologists, peacemakers, educators, social workers, humanitarian-development workers, as well as researchers.

Addressing Human Rights Violations

In its quest to repel Boko Haram's attacks, the Nigerian military has sometimes detained innocent individuals during raids on territories occupied by the insurgents and taken other unlawful action against terror suspects. For successful reintegration, it is worth drawing on peacebuilding models from other countries such as Rwanda and Sierra Leone to design effective conflict resolution techniques as all efforts to reverse the tide of violence would prove futile without forgiveness and reconciliation.

Improving Coordination

Currently, no agency or arm of government can account for the total number of suspects held by different agencies. More worrying, while it is well understood that a significant proportion of fighters that exit the conflict return straight back into their communities, there is no system or process of identifying, tracking, and assessing the level of threat they pose to their communities on return or whether they continue to support the conflict by providing resources taken from their communities. To consolidate the gains made in the fight against violent extremism, efforts must be nationally coordinated and driven. While non-governmental organizations (NGOs) have done creditably well in filling the gaps, the government must take responsibility for implementing large reintegration programs underpinned through its various agencies.

Ultimately, the success of Nigeria's counter-insurgency initiatives is hinged on strengthening civil–government relations, building strong inclusive institutions, and implementing large-scale responses. With these steps, tensions and grievances can be mitigated and violent extremism completely prevented. Only by doing so can Nigeria promote peaceful and inclusive societies for sustainable development and provide access to justice for all.

E
Partnership

28 Partnering for a Better World
Shift from Sustainable Finance to Financing Sustainable Development

Joe E. Colombano, Marco Nicoli, and Aniket Shah

Introduction

When the agreement on the 2030 Agenda for Sustainable Development and its Sustainable Development Goals (SDGs) was reached in September 2015, many heralded the dawning of a new era, the beginning of a braver, more equal, and sustainable world. The Agenda is imbued with the sense of our shared humanity in the face of universal challenges and strengthening a Global Partnership among all actors in society is considered critical to turn that vision into reality. In that spirit, businesses also welcomed the new agenda, having worked hard on its preparation alongside all other stakeholders in the years prior. Many corporate leaders from all sectors engaged directly in what was to be the broadest set of consultations ever undertaken by the United Nations (UN). Sustainability has since become a central tenet of corporate activity, no longer confined to the ancillary role of corporate social responsibility, but ever closer to corporate business models and their Environmental, Social, and Corporate Governance (ESG) focus. This rising wave of sustainability soon also reached the shores of the financial sector, whose actors, traditionally more aloof when it comes to UN initiatives, this time were quick to embrace the SDGs as a reference point for their activities. As a result, a large number of financial instruments have been labeled "sustainable," "green," or "responsible," and made available to the market in order to tap into a growing pool of increasingly sophisticated consumers and investors hungry for sustainable products.

Five years after the 2015 agreement, how far have we come? What is the status of the Global Partnership? What are the prospects for the so-called "sustainable finance" to become mainstream and revolutionize the way in which financial capital is allocated? How has the COVID-19 pandemic changed the trajectory of sustainable development and affected the Global Partnership required to implement it? While the paradigm shift envisioned in 2015 is yet to come, the Global Partnership has progressed substantially, including in the financial sector. However, progress is now at risk in view of the geopolitical impact of both national dynamics, such as the emergence of populism, and external shocks, such as that brought about by the pandemic. Our conclusion is that there is a clear opportunity to capitalize on the new and widespread attention to the issues of sustainability and purpose, provided the right steps are taken, starting with investing in the resilience of our economy and our society overall.

A Brave New Business World? The Promise of the SDGs

More than any other UN initiative before, the 2030 Agenda and its 17 SDGs— the world's agenda for its people, planet, and prosperity agreed by all 193 members of the United

Nations in 2015—have resonated with enterprises around the world. Businesses took a great interest in the process established to define the SDGs, contributed largely to their final shape, and remain key players in their implementation. This is because business "gets" the SDGs. Corporates have long realized that consumer preferences and shareholders' values have shifted. It is no longer just about making products available to the largest number of customers at the lowest costs. It is about brand values, and how they align with those of customers and investors. This is not only about corporate social responsibility. It is about core business, competitiveness, and profit. Ultimately, it is about having a sense of purpose. As a result, across industries and sectors, businesses are establishing sustainability divisions, to adapt to the changing demands of an increasingly aware and sophisticated clientele and public opinion.

In truth, enterprises have understood the relevance of the SDGs to their bottom line long before the SDGs were even conceived. The SDGs, and their predecessors the UN Millennium Development Goals, built on decades of evolving sensitivities around environmental and social issues in the corporate world. However, the claim of the SDGs is to offer a coherent and comprehensive framework to bring Corporate Social Responsibility (CSR) and Environmental, Governance, and Social (EGS) to the core of corporate activities and turn them from cost centers into profit centers. This is because the business opportunity of the SDGs has become clearer. A 2017 report by the Business and Sustainable Development Commissions estimates that the SDGs opened up around US$30 trillion of market opportunity.[1] To seize it, corporates are reviewing their business models to integrate the goals across their operations, through their supply networks, production lines, and distribution and retail channels.

The biggest challenge, however, remains implementation. While it is true that one of the greatest *atouts* of the SDGs is their comprehensiveness—"no one left behind"—this also makes for a high level of complexity when it comes to integrating the SDGs into corporate business models. The SDGs are a framework of 17 interlinked goals, 169 targets, and 232 indicators,[2] which are intended as an indivisible agenda rather than a pick-and-choose menu. They cover all aspects of social and economic development including poverty, hunger, health, education, gender equality, water, sanitation, energy, employment, growth, industry, infrastructure, inequalities, urbanization, environment, and social justice. The framework, to be achieved by 2030, is further complicated by the nuances of the diplomatic language used in the official UN document, left at times intentionally opaque and open to interpretation, a negotiation expedient to facilitate an agreement, but often a cause of confusion when it comes to implementation.

Such complexity leads to a variety of approaches to integrate the goals into corporate business models. The UN Global Compact alone, the main interface of the UN with the business world, has developed over 200 resources—ranging from sets of guidance to good practices—that cover a large range of sustainability topics.[3] Several of the largest international management-consulting firms are contributing to such efforts and developing their own

---

1 *Better Business Better World: The Report of the Business & Sustainable Development Commission*, BUSINESS & SUSTAINABLE DEVELOPMENT COMMISSION (Jan. 2017), https://sustainabledevelopment.un.org/content/documents/2399BetterBusinessBetterWorld.pdf.
2 *Final List of Proposed Sustainable Development Indicators*, REPORT OF THE INTER-AGENCY AND EXPERT GROUP ON SUSTAINABLE DEVELOPMENT GOAL INDICATORS (E/CN.3/2016/2/Rev.1), https://sustainabledevelopment.un.org/content/documents/11803Official-List-of-Proposed-SDG-Indicators.pdf.
3 *Marking Global Goals Local Business*, UN GLOBAL COMPACT, www.unglobalcompact.org/sdgs.

matrixes and policies, as are many business federations, industry associations, and individual corporate entities around the world.[4] While these are all commendable efforts heading in the right direction, the risk is that the diversity of corporate approaches in implementing the SDGs produces fragmented and at times discording models. As a result, the market gets swamped with products and services presented as "sustainable," while the final consumer has little understanding, let alone guarantee, of what this means and what they buy.

In addition, the complexity of the SDGs framework, when combined with the growing popularity of the sustainability movement, may give rise to episodes of free riding behavior. With the "sustainability wave" on the continuous rise, it has become difficult to distinguish genuine efforts to reform from those of actors that are simply updating their marketing strategies to exploit the latest corporate fad, without really changing how their business operates. Bundling a couple of green bonds in an otherwise traditional portfolio does not make for SDG-compliant sustainable finance. A growing number of serious players complain of the lack of a level playing field. While investing efforts and resources in changing their business model to integrate the SDGs, they find themselves in competition with others whose commitment to the SDGs is limited to marketing campaigns and official websites. Increasingly, there have been calls for a formal process to be established, to reward those players that are effectively adopting the SDGs, and to incentivize others to do the same.

Finally, the complexity of the framework also makes its communication difficult. While everybody seems to be riding the sustainability waive, knowledge of the SDGs is limited to the Heads of State and Government that agreed them, high-level advocates, a few illuminated business leaders, and development experts and practitioners in general. Much remains to be done for the SDGs to be popularized and brought to the layman and woman around the world. Most importantly, only few understand the innovation span by the SDGs and the paradigm shift this requires. Typically, sustainability is understood as environmental policy, with little, if any, attention to the important social and economic dimensions of the framework. The SDGs themselves, partly because they are the product of a UN initiative, are taken to be pertaining to the developing world alone, with no relevance to the advanced economies. Rather, it is their universality to make the SDGs such a radical departure from earlier efforts, and one with the potential to induce a drastic change in corporate behavior. Without a full understanding of such elements, the opportunity of the SDGs would be missed.

Partnering for Sustainability: SDG 17

A corollary of the universality and complexity of the SDGs is realizing they will require everyone. The Heads of State and Government that signed up to the agreement in 2015 did so in representation not just of their cabinets and constituencies, but also on behalf of all parts of society, including business, civil society, the academic and scientific community, youth associations, faith organizations, and beyond. Member States made it clear that this is an agenda "of the people, by the people and for the people."

---

4 *See Sustainable Development Goals Industry Matrix*, KPMG, https://home.kpmg/xx/en/home/about/our-role-in-the-world/citizenship/sdgindustrymatrix.html; *See Navigating the SGS: A Business Guide to Engaging with the UN Global Goals*, PwC, www.pwc.com/gx/en/sustainability/publications/PwC-sdg-guide.pdf; *See How We Create Value*, UNILEVER VALUE CHAIN, www.unilever.com/Images/2495-how-we-create-value-100418_tcm244-521463_en.pdf.

A whole of society approach is indeed required given the investment needs associated with implementing the 2030 Agenda. The UN estimated that the cost of achieving the SDGs approximates $5–7 trillion, i.e. close to 7–10% of the world economy.[5] This makes it immediately clear that development budgets alone are not sufficient. At about $150 billion in 2018, Official Development Assistance is such a small fraction of the total amount that the international community is collaborating to bring in private and public, national and international sources into a new partnership, with a new mindset, approach, and accountability. This is the spirit of SDG 17, *to strengthen the means of implementation and revitalize the Global Partnership for Sustainable Development*.

The collaborative approach achieved through partnerships enhances open discussions, research, knowledge sharing, co-generation of innovative solutions, competition, and teamwork, cutting across all the 5 "Ps" of the 2030 agenda: People, planet, prosperity, peace, and, of course, partnership. Achieving a fairer and more sustainable world will require a joint effort through a broad partnership among all stakeholders, including public and private players, each with its own distinct set of roles, rules, and responsibilities.

Business is critical to the success of the global partnership envisioned by SDG17 as part of the global efforts to realize the 2030 Agenda. Because of the richness of their resources—both financial and human; the nimbleness of their ways of working; and the extent of their reach— in both advanced economies and developing countries, business is an indispensable partner to governments in the implementation of the SDGs. In so doing, business can rely on a long and successful experience of collaborative initiatives undertaken in the pursuit of public goods, as done, for example, in the fight against corruption by way of collective actions, integrity pacts, and codes of conduct (see Box 28.1).

Box 28.1 Business-Driven Initiatives to Fight Corruption

Collective actions enable corruption to be fought collectively, with various interest groups, working together and building an alliance against corruption so that the problem can be approached and resolved from multiple angles.

Integrity Pacts ensure that the award of orders in the case of public sector contracts is free from corruption. They were developed by Transparency International, the non-governmental organization dedicated to fighting corruption, and are intended to guarantee transparency in the order-awarding process and to rule out bribery in the awarding of public sector contracts. Following an invitation to tender from a public sector customer, the bidding companies sign legally binding contracts, and commit themselves to behave with integrity from the start of the tender process until the end of the project. If the contract is breached, sanctions are imposed which can be as severe as the exclusion of the company from further invitations to tender. An independent monitor supervises the contract-awarding process and observance of the Integrity Pact. The Integrity Pact ensures that the bidder is selected on the basis of fair criteria and serves all the stakeholders as a means of protecting the integrity of the project.

---

5 *Financing for SDGs—Breaking the Bottlenecks of Investment, from Policy to Impact*, Concept Note 1 (Jun. 11, 2018), www.un.org/pga/72/wp-content/uploads/sites/51/2018/05/Financing-for-SDGs-29-May.pdf.

> **Sector-wide codes of conduct** take various forms, ranging from principles-based provisions to legally binding agreements. In the latter case, companies that violate the anti-corruption code are penalized with sanctions. However, the principles-based codes also have a high degree of effectiveness, as the public commitment to anti-corruption and transparency exerts increased pressure on the participating companies not to breach the agreement. This type of collective action is particularly suitable in oligopolistic markets. The uncompromising support of senior management within the companies concerned is critical to the success of the initiative. In order to avoid breaches of anti-trust law, it is vital to enlist the services of an external, independent monitor.

In the achievement of the SDGs more specifically, business can be a driver for innovation, as it responds to consumer demand, and a catalyst for public sector action on the SDGs.[6] Business also compensates for slow action on the part of the public sector, as it is happening in the field of ESG investing, where private actors are stepping in to agree common definitions and rules whenever public regulators and authorities lag behind. Finally, business also acts as a first adopter and drives the evolution of standards, as seen for example in the prompt adoption of the SDGs as the most favored metrics for sustainable finance for both public and private sector actors at national and international levels.

While business has a critical role to play in the global partnership envisioned by SDG17 to deliver the 2030 Agenda, it cannot replace the public sector in the fundamental role to accompany society along its quest toward sustainability. This entails a political commitment to implementing the 2030 Agenda, and the provision of the institutional underpinning required for it. Specifically, the public sector has the duty of providing an enabling legal, regulatory, and administrative environment, as well as an efficient and fair judicial system, and sustainable policies and practices at every level of government. Finally, the public sector has the responsibility to mobilize national resources through efficient and progressive tax policy. None of this can be provided by any actor other than the government authority of each sovereign country.

In recent years, the kind of partnership envisioned by SDG17 has resulted in many initiatives with a focus on sustainability under the aegis of different actors, including international organizations, business, academia, foundations, and more.[7] The proliferation of such partnerships comes, in part, from the regulatory role of public policies at international, regional, and national level, and also from market evolutions on both the demand and the supply side. This includes, for example, a genuine attitude of some enterprises toward a more equitable and sustainable way of doing business on the supply side, and, on the demand side, the growing number of responsible consumers looking for sustainable products and services.

International organizations have played an important part in bringing together private and public actors in partnerships for sustainability. The system of universal, regional, and sub-regional international organizations—their institutional flaws and weaknesses notwithstanding—has been undoubtedly instrumental in convening, promoting, and

---

6 *Note*: Market-driven change extends also to State-owned enterprises and the public sector at large, including public procurement.
7 *See* a non-exhaustive list is included in Annex 28.1.

supporting partnerships that have achieved progresses in almost all aspects of our society. Such institutions have been the engine for the identification, negotiation, and agreement of a shared and ambitious agenda for sustainable development. They have been the catalyst and the fora for the dialog and collaboration among public entities; the convener, facilitator, and coordinator of the private sector' engagement; and the guarantor of the active participation of civil society organizations. Recently, however, the surge of nationalist movements around the world is affecting the viability of the multilateral system and posing significant risks to the SDGs.

The negative effects of the current political environment are showing in the results from the latest Sustainable Development Goals Report 2019, which highlights a weakening of the Global Partnership for Development, as indicated by declining official development assistance (ODA) and ongoing trade tensions, with some governments retreating from multilateral action. This results in adverse effects on consumers and producers worldwide, with a negative impact on business and financial markets. Those tensions also cast doubt on the future of a sound multilateral trading system under the World Trade Organization.[8] Given the inauspicious public sector environment, many turn to the private sector, and the financial sector especially, as a way to ensure that countries have the means to achieve the SDGs.

From "Sustainable Finance" to "Financing Sustainable Development"

Sustainable finance is part and parcel of the collaborative approach promoted by SDG17. Its proper functioning requires serious and committed financial players, competent and efficient regulators (to establish effective rules, standards, indicators, certifications, ratings, and a coherent system of fiscal incentives and disincentives linked to sustainability performance indicators), responsible citizens (in their roles as investors, consumers, and labor force), and a historic paradigm shift to achieve the overall goal of channeling existing financial flows toward bankable sustainable development projects. This process requires matching demand and supply of "sustainable finance" based on clear definitions, rules, and transparency.

In this section, we take a deep dive into the role of the financial sector in achieving the SDGs and we reflect on the progress made since 2015. In doing so, we offer two main contributions. First, we observe that despite a growing agreement of the need for several trillions of dollars of incremental investment per annum globally for the SDGs, there is no universal definition of what "sustainable finance" means. We note that different aspects of the financial industry are using this term for different outcomes and reasons, leading to significant confusion. We provide an overview of some of the main approaches from different public and private financial providers with regard to sustainability and sustainable finance. Second, we observe that there have been examples of constructive projects and initiatives around financing sustainable development, and we highlight a few of these examples. Some practical suggestions of how to move the financial services industry forward in playing a more constructive role in global efforts around sustainable development are presented in the conclusion following this section.

---

8 *The Sustainable Development Goals Report 2019*, UNITED NATIONS (2019), https://unstats.un.org/sdgs/report/2019/.

Definitions of Sustainable Finance

Our first observation is that there is no single answer to what the financial industry means by this term. The challenge of defining "sustainable finance" is inherent in the complexity around two words that make up the phrase—"sustainable" and "finance." With regards to the term "sustainable," there are multiple definitions and approaches to the concept. For some, the term "sustainable" is linked to the *conceptual and aspirational framework* laid out by Gro Brundtland's Our Common Future report in 1987, which defines sustainable development as, "development that meets the needs of the present without compromising the ability of future generations to meet their own needs."[9] This approach toward "sustainable finance" allows for a more conceptual and directional approach toward sustainable finance.

For others, the term "sustainable" is a *scientific and quantitative* target of investments, based on global and national policies such as the SDGs and the Paris Agreement. With regards to the term "finance," it is important to note here that the global financial system is comprised of several sub-sectors (i.e. banking, investment management, insurance) and parts of the economy (i.e. public, private, mixed).

Bringing the two concepts together, "sustainable finance" can be meant in either an aspirational sense or a scientific and quantitative sense. In the aspirational sense, sustainable finance means a general orientation of public and private financial capital toward sectors and areas considered in line with the sustainable development agenda—renewable energy, agriculture, low-carbon transportation, energy efficiency, and other related sectors. In this approach, the focus would be on the intention and general orientation of the financial flow. In the scientific sense, a definition of sustainable finance would follow a much more top-down set of definitions that directly link the financial flow with science-based targets around specific SDGs and the Paris Agreement. This approach would require linking the financial flow directly with how that capital—either public or private—is supporting the efforts of sustainable development.

Given the inherent complexities of the term "sustainable finance," we note that different participants in the financial industry have been using the term in significantly different ways. For the private sector participants, sustainable finance is most often related to two broad areas: Commitments to "sustainable finance" from large financial institutions and as ESG and impact investing. For the public sector, sustainable finance has been mostly focused on public sector investments in sustainable development-related sectors, both within countries and between countries.

In terms of "commitments to green finance," we note that there has been significant activity from the largest financial institutions in the world in making commitments to sustainable finance. As of June 2019, according to a World Resources Institute analysis, twenty-three out of the fifty largest banks in the world had made commitments to sustainable finance, for a total of $2.6 trillion.[10] Despite this being a significant number, we note three challenges. First, there is no common standard to what the individual banks meant by activities that contribute to "sustainable finance." It is not clear, for example, whether these sustainable finance activities are incremental to their business-as-usual plans or whether these commitments are simply categorizing investments that would otherwise have been made.

---

9 OUR COMMON FUTURE, World Commission on Environment and Development, Oxford University Press (1087).
10 *Green Targets: A Tool to Compare Private Sector Banks' Sustainable Finance Commitments (as of July 2019)*, WORLD RESOURCES INSTITUTE, www.wri.org/finance/banks-sustainable-finance-commitments/.

In some instances, including for major global banks such as JP Morgan Chase and Bank of America, there is no accounting methodology provided to the public regarding what will be considered part of this broader commitment. [11]

Second, from a climate perspective, most financial institutions are still investing considerably more in fossil fuels than they are in their sustainable finance activities. Third, we note that in terms of total quantum of financing, the commitments made by twenty-three of the world's largest financial institutions pale in comparison to the needs of private sector investments in low-carbon energy and transportation, just two of the various sectors of sustainable development. According to the International Energy Agency (IEA), renewable energy spending—just one part of the broader sustainable development agenda—would need to be over $700 billion per annum through 2035 to be on a path of below 2.0°C. [12]

In terms of ESG and impact investing, there has been a significant uptake within the investment management industry around these concepts. This fact is best evidenced by the rise of the Principles for Responsible Investing (PRI). As of 2019, there are over 2,300 signatories to the PRI, which is a set of six aspirational principles around integrating environmental, social, and governance considerations into investment processes and engagement with companies and issuers. These 2,300 signatories manage collectively over $90 trillion in global investable assets, which is approximately 40% of total investment assets. [13] Related to the rise of ESG investing is the concept of impact investing, which broadly refers to investments that have both a financial and non-financial outcome in mind. According to the Global Impact Investing Network, the total size of the impact investment universe is $502 billion, with over 1,300 impact investment managers. [14]

On the other hand, sustainable finance for the public sector has focused mostly on both government-outlays in health, education, transportation, agriculture, and energy and on the public policies (both fiscal and monetary) that are related to public sector investments in these key sustainable development sectors. Unfortunately, there remains no global analysis done—including by the major development agencies—that seeks to harmonize national level investments by sector, making it very difficult to understand the size and scope of the change of public sector sustainable finance at the aggregate level.

As noted above, the term sustainable finance has a broad set of meanings, ranging from the considerations with which pension fund managers invest in publicly listed securities (i.e. "ESG investing") ranging to the direct outlays of national governments to specific sectors in their economies. In order to reconcile these various different uses of sustainable finance, the most coherent approach to the question of what is "sustainable finance" lies in a change in the term; instead of sustainable finance, a more constructive and useful approach is "financing sustainable development."

By using a "financing sustainable development" approach, the global financial industry will benefit in two main ways. First, this approach allows for a shared understanding of what the end goal is, which is achieving a sustainable development path as outlined by the sustainable development goals. This shared understanding of the goal of these efforts is a

---

11 *See Id.*
12 *IEA: The Marginal Cost of Two Degrees*, CARBON BRIEF: CLEAR ON CLIMATE (Jun. 3, 2014), www.carbonbrief.org/iea-the-marginal-cost-of-two-degrees.
13 *About the PRI*, PRI: Principles for Responsible Investment, www.unpri.org/pri.
14 Abhilash Mudaliar & Hannah Dithrich, *Sizing the Impact Investing Market*, GIIN (Apr. 1, 2019), thegiin.org/research/publication/impinv-market-size.

useful conceptual breakthrough for the sustainable finance space. Second, this approach allows for a conceptualization around the investment needs to achieve the SDGs. We note various excellent costing exercises, including by the International Monetary Fund[15] and the UN Sustainable Development Solutions Network,[16] on public and private sector investment needs to achieve the major targets within the SDG framework.

Case Studies: Green Bonds and Local Development Institutions

Our second observation is that there have been positive examples of financial institutions—both public and private—taking the broader sustainable development agenda forward.

In the private financial world, since 2007, there a new asset class within the global bond markets, known as "green bonds" have developed. A green bond is a fixed-income instrument that is specifically earmarked to raise money for climate and environmental projects. The green bond market is a strong example of positive private sector contribution to the sustainable development agenda because it has done, in our view, more than anything else in socializing the concept of "green investment" in the private sector financial industry and has proven to investors that positive environmental outcomes can be achieved without giving up financial returns. In 2019 alone, there were over $250 billion in green bond issuances, from 496 issuers in 51 jurisdictions.[17] In the period of 2015–2019, the annual green bond issuance increased by a factor of six.[18]

In the public financial world, one area of significant positive momentum around public finance and sustainable development is the growing emphasis on regional and national development finance institutions. Their importance is evidenced both in the policy and practice of financing sustainable development.

From a policy perspective, the importance of development banking for this agenda is clearly articulated in the Addis Ababa Action Agenda, which serves as the broader financing framework for the Agenda 2030. The outcome document of the conference includes thirty-three references to development banks for financing development, and explicitly states: "We note the role that well-functioning national and regional development banks can play in financing sustainable development, particularly in credit market segments in which commercial banks are not fully engaged and where large financing gaps exist."[19] It is clear in the

---

15 Vitor Gaspar et al., *Fiscal Policy and Development: Human, Social, and Physical Investments for the SDGs*, IMF Staff Discussion Note 1, 45 (Jan. 23, 2019), www.imf.org/en/Publications/Staff-Discussion-Notes/Issues/2019/01/18/Fiscal-Policy-and-Development-Human-Social-and-Physical-Investments-for-the-SDGs-46444.

16 Vanessa Fajans-Turner & Taylor Smith, *SDG Costing & Financing for Low-Income Developing Countries (LIDCs)*, SUSTAINABLE DEVELOPMENT SOLUTIONS NETWORK (Sept. 24, 2019), www.unsdsn.org/new-report-estimates-sdg-financing-needs-for-59-of-the-worlds-lowest-income-countries.

17 Leena Fatin, *Green Bond Highlights 2019: Behind the Headline Numbers: Climate Bonds Market Analysis of a record year*, CLIMATE BONDS INITIATIVE (Feb. 6, 2020) www.climatebonds.net/2020/02/green-bond-highlights-2019-behind-headline-numbers-climate-bonds-market-analysis-record-year.

18 Leena Fatin, *Record 2019 GB Issuance $255bn! EU largest market: US, China, France Lead Top 20 National Rankings: Sovereign GBs & Certified Bonds Gain Momentum*, CLIMATE BONDS INITIATIVE (Jan. 16, 2020), www.climatebonds.net/2020/01/record-2019-gb-issuance-255bn-eu-largest-market-us-china-france-lead-top-20-national.

19 *Sustainable Development Goals*, UN, https://sustainabledevelopment.un.org/index.php?page=view&type=400&nr=2051&menu=35.

foundational documents of the sustainable development era that development banks should play an important role in mobilizing public and private capital.

In practice, there has already been considerable progress in expanding the global development banking presence for efforts around sustainable development. This is both true in terms of the number and scale of operations of development banks. We note with optimism the creation and launch of development banks and green banks at various spatial scales, ranging from the Asian Infrastructure Investment Bank (AIIB) and New Development Bank in 2014 and 2015, respectively to the New York and Connecticut Green Banks in the United States. We also note, with optimism, that existing development banks have increased their lending capacity. The African Development Bank, for example, increased their capital base by $115 billion in 2019, its largest capital increase since its formation, increasing the lending capacity and resilience of the institution for its important role in providing capital for development across the African continent.

Conclusions: COVID-19 and the Opportunity to "Build Back Better" by Financing Sustainable Development

At the time of the drafting of this chapter, the world is in the grips of the novel coronavirus COVID-19 pandemic. In an unprecedented effort to suppress contagions, more than half of the world population is currently in lockdown. What started as a crisis of our public health systems has now grown into an economic crisis with global consequences, and a major test for society as a whole. The real impact of the crisis on the SDGs is yet to be seen, but the first signs are worrying. In its March 2020 report on the response to the socio-economic impacts of the pandemic, the UN warns of the profound and negative effect on sustainable development efforts, with the most vulnerable, including women, children, the elderly, and informal workers, hit the hardest. Moreover, it is clear that the virus poses a risk to social cohesion within countries, and reports have emerged of episodes of stigmatization and violence against groups wrongly considered "responsible" for the diffusion of the virus.[20]

From the perspective of SDG 17, perhaps the gravest concern is the lack of a real and coordinated global response to the pandemic, in the spirit of the Global Partnership for sustainable development heralded by the 2030 Agenda. At least in the advanced economies, this has been noticeably missing, as governments were largely caught by surprise by the magnitude and speed of the crisis, and resorted to measures such as closing their borders, banning travel, and in some instances even introducing protectionist policies, including for medical supplies and equipment. While some of these measures are certainly warranted in some cases, especially when they are part of a temporary emergency response, the lack of political leadership is regrettable, as is the absence of a realistic prospect for a Global Partnership to address the impact of the pandemic at the global level.

In sharp contrast with the response of the public sector, the private sector has stepped up to the challenge. While the pandemic rages on, businesses around the world are taking measures to protect their employees, repair their supply chains, and introduce experimental measures to soften the blow, cope, and ensure some form of continuity of their operations. Often, such experimental measures display remarkable ingenuity, are focused on the

---

20 United Nations, *Shared Responsibility, Global Solidarity: Responding to The Socio-Economic Impacts Of Covid-19* (Mar. 2020), UN, New York, https://unsdg.un.org/sites/default/files/2020-03/SG-Report-Socio-Economic-Impact-of-Covid19.pdf.

opportunity to solve problems rather than selling products, and are inspired not just by the need to survive, but also by a deep sense of solidarity and sacrifice in the face of an unprecedented challenge. Recent updates of the Edelman Trust Barometer,[21] the annual survey of public trust in non-governmental organizations, business, government, and media, confirm that in the first months of the pandemic, businesses are the institutions that people trust the most, well above governments.

In spite of the tragedy and destruction brought about by the spread of the virus and the measures to contain it, it is possible to find a silver lining. The global reset imposed by the crisis can be seen as an opportunity for a new start, to rebound forward toward realizing a sustainable world as per the 2030 Agenda, rather than backward to the original system with its flaws, as we did, for example, after the 2008 financial crisis. COVID-19 can accelerate the dynamic of stakeholder capitalism and its focus beyond short-term results toward longer-term social objectives and responsibilities. It is vital that in the response to the COVID-19 pandemic, countries keep the sustainable development goals and climate commitments in focus to hold on to past gains, and in the recovery, to make investments that propel us toward a more inclusive, sustainable, and resilient future.

Financing sustainable development has an increasingly important role in the efforts to "build back better" once the COVID-19 pandemic is behind us. Financing sustainable development is of critical importance now, as we set out to build COVID-ready economies and help us achieve a sustainable future. In this sense, financing sustainable development means investing in resilience, to allow our society to face shocks and persistent structural changes without losing its ability to deliver well-being for its community in a sustainable way. In order for this to happen, the global financial industry should work toward taking some very simple and practical next steps to move the financing sustainable development agenda forward. We highlight here what we see as four main areas of priority.

First, the international policy community should agree on a set of investment needs for achieving the SDGs. As we note above, the right approach for sustainable finance is indeed financing sustainable development, and an important aspect of this will be for there to be broad agreement on what the needs are. We note that the International Monetary Fund (IMF)'s work in this space for low-income countries has been significant and needs to be expanded for all countries around the world.

Second, the international financial community should come to agreement on a set of institutional and public policy changes that are most needed for sustainable development. One of the key aspects of financing sustainable development is getting the "rules of the game" right in terms of key fiscal and monetary issues related to sustainable development, namely tax (specifically, increased domestic resource mobilization and carbon pricing) and risk weighting adjustments for high-carbon versus low-carbon assets on bank balance sheets. Efforts for financing sustainable development would be greatly benefited by more emphasis on the institutional underpinnings of the real economy and the financial sector that operates within it.

Third, the private investment world would benefit from one set of standards around ESG and impact investing. Although we applaud the rise of ESG investing, we remain concerned regarding the lack of standard definitions of what ESG investing means in practice. The most important next step for the private investment community will be to constructively develop

---

21 *See 2020 Edelman Trust Barometer* (Jan. 19., 2020), www.edelman.com/trustbarometer.

clear, outcome-oriented guidelines and pathways for private investment and sustainable development that have the support of national financial regulators and accounting boards.

Fourth, the public finance world should take the lead in building and expanding public financial institutions at the global, regional, national, and local levels. The positive momentum of the past ten years in growing the capital base of various large development banks and creating new ones like the Asian Infrastructure Investment Bank and New Development Bank should be expanded upon.

These four practical steps will go a long way toward shifting the current approach of the global financial industry from talking about sustainable finance toward financing sustainable development. This in turn will contribute to building societies that are resilient to external shocks such as the current COVID-19 pandemic. Ultimately, financing sustainable development will prove a formidable instrument to achieve the Global Partnership envisioned by SDG17 and realize the future promised by the 2030 Agenda.

Annex 28.1. Examples of Partnerships for Sustainability

A—Led by International Organizations

1. United Nations Global Compact, www.unglobalcompact.org.
2. Platform for Collaboration on Tax, www.oecd.org/tax/beps/platform-for-collaboration-on-tax.htm.
3. OECD Social Impact Investment Initiative, www.oecd.org/dac/financing-sustainable-development/development-finance-topics/social-impact-investment-initiative.htm.
4. Global Reporting Initiative (GRI), www.globalreporting.org/information/about-gri/Pages/default.aspx.

B—Led by Business

1. Sustainable Stock Exchanges (SSE) Initiative, www.sseinitiative.org/about/.
2. US SIF Forum for Sustainable and Responsible Investment, www.ussif.org/.
3. GIIN Initiative for Institutional Impact Investment, https://thegiin.org.

C—Led by Academia

1. MIT Impact Investing Initiative (Mi3), *See* https://mi3.mit.edu/.
2. Impact Investing and Next Gens, https://iri.hks.harvard.edu/impact-investing-and-next-gens.
3. Columbia Impact Investing Initiative (CI3), https://sipa.columbia.edu/faculty-research/libraries-resources/columbia-impact-investing-initiative-ci3.

D—Led by Foundations and Others

1. The World Resource Institute (WRI) Sustainable Investing Initiative, /www.wri.org/our-work/project/greening-private-finance/sustainable-investing-initiative.
2. Zero Gap Fund, /www.rockefellerfoundation.org/initiative/zero-gap-fund/.
3. World Benchmarking Alliance (WBA), www.worldbenchmarkingalliance.org.

29 Private Corporations and Environmental Social Governance

An Uneven Response

Mark E. Meaney

Introduction

The Global Compact and Corporate Social Responsibility (CSR)

In 1999, Secretary-General Kofi Annan issued a clarion call to private sector corporations around the world to voluntarily align their strategies and operations with a set of principles in support of human rights, labor standards, environmental sustainability, and anti-corruption.[1] At the World Economic Forum in Davos, Switzerland, Secretary-General Annan spoke to hundreds of business executives: "I propose that you, the business leaders ... and we the United Nations initiate a Global Compact of shared values and principles, which will give a human face to the global market."[2] With these words, Secretary-General Annan substantially contributed to the evolution of the Corporate Social Responsibility movement through the creation of the United Nations Global Compact (UNGC). His call echoed around the world. Numerous business leaders, such as Sir Mark Moody Stuart, stepped forward and dedicated their lives to translate Annan's vision of the Global Compact into the world's largest CSR initiative. Over the course of subsequent years, business leaders from Lebanon to China, from South Africa to Iceland, and from Argentina to Canada created the UNGC Local Networks informed by universal principles to change business practices. Starting with a few hundred corporations, the UNGC has grown to a membership of over 12,000 organizations based in 170 countries.[3]

Since Secretary-General Annan's pronouncement, the issue of CSR and sustainability has continued to gain considerable attention. The Ten Principles (Principles) of the Global Compact establishes a framework that combines the four categories of human rights, labor standards, environmental standards, and anti-corruption.[4] The components of the framework have, in turn, influenced the development of multiple models and tools for CSR and sustainability programs. For example, over 5,000 corporations worldwide use the Global Reporting Initiative (GRI) Sustainability Reporting Guidelines (Guidelines) for their impact

---

1 Press Release, *Secretary-General Proposes Global Compact on Human Rights, Labour, Environment, in Address to World Economic Forum in Davos*, UN PRESS RELEASE (Feb. 1, 1999), www.un.org/press/en/1999/19990201.sgsm6881.html.
2 *Id.* at 1.
3 *Explore Our Participants*, UNITED NATIONS GLOBAL COMPACT, www.unglobalcompact.org/interactive.
4 *Id., The Ten Principles of the UN Global Compact*, UNITED NATIONS GLOBAL COMPACT, www.unglobalcompact.org/what-is-gc/mission/principles.

reporting, considered the gold standard of CSR and sustainability reporting.[5] Launched in conjunction with the founding of the UNGC, the Guidelines were the first standards for CSR and sustainability reporting and continue to represent best practices for impact reporting on a wide range of governance, environmental, and social indicators.

The Origin of Environmental, Social, and Governance (ESG) Standards

Secretary-General Annan not only facilitated in the creation of the UNGC, but he also played a pivotal role in the evolution of the modern social impact-investing movement. Annan invited CEOs of some of the world's largest asset owners and managers to the launch of the UN-backed Principles for Responsible Investment (UN PRI) at the New York Stock Exchange in April 2006.[6] There are now over 7,000 of the world's leading asset owners and managers in 135 countries as signatories to the Principles for Responsible Investment framework.[7] They have thereby made a commitment to integrate the Six Principles of responsible investment into their evaluation of the organizational structure of corporations based on environmental, social, and governance indicators.[8]

Finally, the Sustainability Accounting Standards Board (SASB) is an independent standards board that has developed a set of sustainability accounting standards juxtaposed to financial reporting accounting standards.[9] SASB has developed a complete set of standards for 77 different industries that are intended to help businesses identify, manage, and report out on financially material ESG metrics for prospective investors.[10] The standards help investors evaluate the organizational structure of corporations with a focus on their ESG performance.[11] All of these different models and tools have encouraged companies to take an active role in integrating internal CSR and external ESG performance metrics into corporate strategy, culture, and day-to-day operations.

An Uneven Response

A 2018 KPMG survey concludes that business interest in the Sustainable Development Goals (SDGs) has grown rapidly since their launch in September 2015.[12] However, recent studies indicate there has been an uneven response on the part of private sector corporations

---

5 *GRI: The Gold Standard in CSR/ ESG/ SDG/ Sustainability Reporting*, FBRH CONSULTANTS, https://fbrh.co.uk/en/80-percent-of-the-world%E2%80%99s-250-largest-companies-report-according-to-gri.

6 Press Release, *Secretary-General Launches "Principles for Responsible Investment" Backed by World's Largest Investors*, UN PRESS RELEASE (April 6, 2006), www.un.org/press/en/2006/sg2111.doc.htm.

7 *About the PRI*, PRINCIPLES FOR RESPONSIBLE INVESTMENT (Nov. 8, 2020), https://bit.ly/38my83Q.

8 Brian Edmondson, *What Is Corporate Social Responsibility?: Definition and Examples of Corporate Social Responsibility*, THE BALANCE (Jul. 7, 2020), www.thebalance.com/corporate-social-responsibility-csr-4772443.

9 *Governance Mission*, Sustainability Accounting Standards Board (SASB) Foundation, www.sasb.org/governance/.

10 *Standards Overview*, Sustainability Accounting Standards Board (SASB) Foundation, www.sasb.org/standards-overview/.

11 *Integrating ESG Holistically in Private Equity: A Strategic Approach,* Sustainability Accounting Standards Board, (Oct. 2020), www.sasb.org/wp-content/uploads/2020/10/IntegratingESGPrivateEquity-101420.pdf

12 *How to Report on the SDGs*, KPMG, https://home.kpmg/xx/en/home/insights/2018/02/how-to-report-on-the-sdgs.html.

in implementing CSR and ESG performance metrics toward the achievement of the SDGs. Three new studies show that corporations must do more to meet key impact performance indicators (KIPIs) to achieve relevant SDGs by 2030.[13] With ten years to go, it is clear that corporations are not on track. In fact, the GreenBiz Group's Report (GreenBiz) shows that corporations may have actually taken significant steps backward in substantive CSR activities and ESG performance metrics.

In this chapter, I will first review the findings of three studies in a consideration of corporate engagement in specific areas of CSR implementation and ESG performance. The reasons why private sector corporations are falling short of expectations in relation to ending poverty (SDG 1), gender equality (SDG 5), water management (SDG 6), decent work and economic growth (SDG 8), widening social inequalities (SDG 10), and climate action (SDG 13) will be assessed.[14] I then highlight recommendations on steps corporations must take to enhance SDG engagement. Based on the recommendations, Nike will be used as a case study to assess the implementation of appropriate impact targets in the achievement of relevant SDGs by 2030. I evaluate execution progress by using the interaction between Nike executives and undergraduate students from the Leeds School of Business at the University of Colorado, Boulder, to illustrate how corporations and business schools can work together to leverage their efforts in addressing the SDGs. I will also use Nike to draw attention to the fact that corporations ought to assist governments in ending poverty (SDG 1) and gender discrimination (SDG 5) by offering women economic opportunities in helping to close the economic gender gap.[15] I argue Nike and other private sector corporations can do much more to assist governments with the achievement of SDGs 1, 5, 8, and 10. I conclude the chapter with an observation on how corporations can leverage their efforts to address the COVID-19 pandemic to advance SDGs 1, 5, and 8.

Uneven Progress

The "E" in ESG: Global Goals 6 and 13

Every year in a "State of Green Business" report, GreenBiz estimates the costs associated with the impact on the environment of the top publicly traded companies in the United States and the world in assessing their environmental sustainability.[16] Eighty-five percent of the S&P 500 publish CSR and Sustainability Impact Reports.[17] GreenBiz uses impact reports as the primary means of measuring these costs. In assessing corporate environmental performance, GreenBiz gives an overview of key trends beginning with "natural capital costs" that measures corporate externalities. Companies consume natural resources and generate pollution as a result of their business activities. "Natural capital" is the limited stock

---

13 *UN Global Compact Report 2019*, UNITED NATIONS GLOBAL COMPACT (2019), www.unglobalcompact.org/library/5716#:~:text=Provides%20an%20assessment%20of%20how,on%20the%20Sustainable%20Development%20Goals.&text=The%20report%20also%20takes%20a,of%20climate%20and%20gender%20equality; *See also The Decade to Deliver—A Call to Business Action: UN Global Compact-Accenture Strategy CEO Study on Sustainability 2019*, www.unglobalcompact.org/library/5715.
14 United Nations G.A. Res. A/RES/70/1, *Transforming our world: the 2030 Agenda for Sustainable Development*, 1 (Sept. 25, 2015) [hereinafter "Agenda 2030"].
15 *Id.*
16 *The 2019 State of Green Business Report*, GREENBIZ GROUP (2019), www.greenbiz.com/report/2019-state-green-business-report [hereinafter "GreenBiz Report"].
17 *Id.* at 57.

of the Earth's natural resources on which business and society depend for prosperity, security, and well-being.[18] It includes things such as clean air and water, land, soil, biodiversity, and geological resources. According to the GreenBiz Report, natural capital is declining at an alarming and unsustainable rate.[19] The total value of natural capital to society globally has been estimated to be up to $72 trillion per year according to the UN Environment Program.[20] If companies had to internalize all of the natural capital costs associated with their business, their profit would dramatically decline. The natural capital cost generated by the largest 1,200 companies in the world is more than twice their net income.[21]

GreenBiz concludes that the cost of natural capital impacts—the dollar value of resources extracted and pollution emitted—by companies increased for the first time since 2013 year over year in 2016 and in 2017.[22] Among all types of corporate environmental impacts, greenhouse gas emissions (GHG) is the largest (53%).[23] Corporate efforts in this regard fall far short of the commitments to the GHG reductions required using science-based or context-based target setting approaches in alignment with SDG 13.[24] Top global and US companies account for a substantial share of global GHG emissions. The GreenBiz Report estimates that the proportional reductions these companies need to achieve by 2050 and 2100 to achieve the 2°C target specified in the Paris Agreement are 3.8 and 6.2 gigatons of carbon dioxide equivalent ($GtCO_2$ e) for global companies, and 1.3 and 2.2 $GtCO_2$ e for US companies.[25] The GHG reduction targets set by top global and US companies in 2016 (1.0 and 0.4 $GtCO_2e$) account for only 26% and 27% of their share of reduction needed by 2050.[26] The gap between existing reduction targets and those needed to meet 2°C aligned targets by 2100 is even wider, currently at 16% of the necessary reductions by both US and global companies.[27] Yet, only 35% of CEOs say they have or plan to set a science-based target (SBT) within the next year, down from 43% in 2015.[28]

Among types of environmental impacts, water consumption accounts for 16%, heavy metal pollution for 12%, and fertilizer-related organic pollutants and nutrients for 6% of natural capital costs.[29] Water consumption and nutrient and organic pollutants accounted for the greatest type of impact in 2016 and in 2017 (SDG 6).[30] The total natural capital cost of water pollution increased by over 2% year over year in 2017.[31] Water use by companies saw an increase of 7% year on year.[32] These four main types of environmental impact jointly account for nearly 90% of the total natural capital cost of the 1,200 companies assessed.[33] It is important to note that GreenBiz reports that on average 78% of a company's environmental

---

18 *Id.* at 60.
19 *Id.* at 46.
20 *Id.* at 60.
21 *Id.* at 59.
22 GreenBiz Report, *supra* note 16, at 59.
23 *Id.* at 61.
24 *Id.* at 46.
25 *Id.* at 65.
26 *Id.*
27 *Id.* at 57.
28 GreenBiz Report, *supra* note 16, at 71.
29 *Id.* 61.
30 *Id.* at 70.
31 *Id.* at 64.
32 *Id.*
33 *Id.* at 61.

impact is embedded in its supply chain and does not come from its own operations.[34] For example, water consumption and nutrient and organic pollutants account for the greatest type of environmental impact because of production increases within agricultural supply chains.

The 2019 UN Global Compact Progress Report and the 2019 UN Global Compact-Accenture Strategy CEO Study echo the GreenBiz Report findings on environmental impact, especially in relation to SDGs 6 and 13. According to these UNGC Reports, global carbon emissions reached the highest level in human history in 2018.[35] GHG emissions are 50% higher than 1990 levels, and emissions continue to increase far beyond the limits aimed for in the 2015 Paris Agreement on climate change.[36] While 94% of companies have implemented corporate policies related to environmental impact, only 36% of companies report on their GHG emissions (up slightly from 32% in 2009) in alignment with SDG 13.[37] Less than 25% have reported incorporating climate change policy into their overall corporate strategy.[38] The UNGC Reports cite the Intergovernmental Panel on Climate Change (IPCC) and highlight the fact that global temperatures will increase by more than 1.5°C by 2030 at the current rates of GHG emissions, which the world's preeminent climate scientists identify as the "safe" upper limit for global temperature rise.[39]

The UNGC Reports also bolster the findings of the GreenBiz Report in relation to water consumption.[40] The agricultural sector, for example, uses over two-thirds (69%) of all water globally.[41] More than 80% of wastewater is discharged into water bodies without any treatment, resulting in nearly 1,000 child deaths each day due to preventable water and sanitation-related diarrheal diseases.[42] As of 2018, only 59% of wastewater is collected and treated, while the remaining entreated water poses environmental and public health risks.[43] Increased private investment in wastewater management is critical to achieving SDG 6. Given these circumstances, only one-third (30%) of companies report having activities in support of SDG 6.[44] Less than 25% of the companies surveyed reported having water management fully integrated into their corporate strategy and business operations, and less than 50% have set minimum water reduction targets.[45]

The "S" in ESG: SDG 5.5

Target 5.5 of the SDG Gender Equality seeks to ensure women's full and effective participation and equal opportunities for leadership at all levels of decision-making in political, economic, and public life.[46] The indicator 5.5.2 further specifies that corporations

---

34 *Id.* at 59.
35 UN Global Compact Progress Report 2019, *supra* note 13, at 21.
36 *Id.* at 28.
37 GreenBiz Report, *supra* note 16, at 66.
38 *Id.*
39 UN Global Compact Progress Report 2019, *supra* note 13, at 28.
40 *Id.* at 49.
41 *Id.*
42 *Id.*
43 *Id.*
44 *Id.*
45 *Id.*
46 *Achieve Gender Equality and Empower All Women and Girls: Targets and Indicators*, UNITED NATIONS DEPARTMENT OF ECONOMIC AND SOCIAL AFFAIRS, https://sdgs.un.org/goals/goal5.

must measure and report on the proportion of women who hold managerial positions.[47] By any measure, the pace of change among private sector corporations to achieve SDG 5.5 is alarmingly slow. In fact, according to the World Economic Forum's 2020 Global Gender Gap Report (WEF Report), it will take two centuries to close the economic gender gap.[48] This represents ten generations of women!

Private sector corporations are not only stalling, but they have actually moved backward in terms of women's participation in the labor force.[49] For example, among corporations in India, women's participation in the labor force dropped from 30.4% in 1990 to 23.4% in 2019.[50] While the percentage of women in business leadership roles has increased, the increase of women in managerial positions is occurring at a snail's pace.[51] Moreover, only 27% of managers and leaders are women (ranging from 11% in the Arab States to 39% in the Americas), a figure that has changed very little over the past 30 years.[52] While women may lead more Fortune 500 companies than ever before, corporations have only managed to move the needle to a mere 6.6%.[53] Globally, men occupy approximately 80% of board seats and over 18.6% of companies have an all-male board.[54] Furthermore, while 68% of companies report that they have a leadership commitment to gender equality and 41% of companies publicly advocate for gender equality, only 28% of companies include time-bound, measurable goals and targets in their gender equality strategy as required by SDG 5.5.2.[55] This is at the root of why commitments by private sector corporations have yet to translate into real impact in the achievement of gender equality. Yet corporations can make significant progress through the implementation of programs that simultaneously have a dramatic impact on SDG 1, Ending Poverty.

Best Practice Partnerships

Case Study: Nike, the Global Compact, and the Global Reporting Initiative

We can also glean recommendations from the three studies on how corporations ought to respond to their notable deficits. In order to make meaningful progress, the three studies all agree that private sector corporations need to (1) build CSR and sustainability performance metrics into their overall corporate strategy and business operations; (2) set time-bound, measurable targets based on CSR and sustainability metrics; and (3) work with

---

47 *Id.*
48 *Global Gender Gap Report 2020*, at 16 WORLD ECONOMIC FORUM (2020), www3.weforum.org/docs/WEF_GGGR_2020.pdf.
49 *Labor Force Participation Rate, Female*, THE WORLD BANK, https://data.worldbank.org/indicator/sl.tlf.cact.fe.zs
50 *Id.*; *See also Labor Force Participation Rate, Female—India*, THE WORLD BANK, https://data.worldbank.org/indicator/SL.TLF.CACT.FE.ZS?locations=IN.
51 Global Gender Gap Report 2020, *supra* note 48, at 16.
52 *A Quantum Leap for Gender Equality: For a Better Future of Work for All*, at 28 INTERNATIONAL LABOUR ORGANIZATION (2019), www.ilo.org/global/publications/books/WCMS_674831/lang--en/index.htm.
53 *Historical List of Women CEOs of the Fortune Lists: 1972–2020*, at 2, FORTUNE MAGAZINE (May 28, 2020), www.catalyst.org/research/historical-list-of-women-ceos-of-the-fortune-lists-1972-2020/.
54 *Women on Boards 2019 Progress Report*, at 4, MSCI, www.msci.com/www/research-paper/women-on-boards-2019-progress/01667826614.
55 *Women's Empowerment and Business: 2020 Trends and Opportunities*, at 5 UN Global Compact, BSR (2020), www.bsr.org/reports/WEP-AnnualReport2020.pdf [hereinafter "Women's Empowerment"].

their suppliers in the value chain to integrate CSR and sustainability performance.[56] Nike is used as a case study to illustrate how private sector corporations ought to implement such recommendations to address deficiencies in CSR and sustainability targets for the achievement of relevant SDGs by 2030. The Nike case study also emphasizes that corporations ought to do more to assist governments in ending poverty and gender discrimination by offering economic opportunities to close the economic gender gap.[57] I argue Nike and other private sector corporations can do much more to assist governments with the achievement of SDGs 1, 5, 8, and 10.

In the 1990s, Nike was a company on a sharp growth trajectory when Oxfam discovered the company used sweatshops and employed child labor in its supply chain.[58] Nike executives were forced to confront the truth that its governance structure and value chain needed to be completely re-designed with CSR impact at the center.[59] To this end, Nike became a Global Compact signatory. Nike executives made the commitment to integrate the Ten Principles into strategic planning and corporate operations.[60] They recognized that the company could remedy its ethical shortcomings, broaden risk and opportunities portfolios, and thereby increase the company's long-term value by operationalizing commitments to human rights, decent work practices, a reduction of environmental impact, and zero tolerance of corruption within its operations and spheres of influence.[61]

Nike looked to the UNGC for guidance to begin efforts at cultural transformation to embrace CSR and sustainability. The UNGC provided guidance through its UNGC Management Model (the Model).[62] The Model walks companies through an iterative six-step process of organizational transformation in embracing CSR and sustainability. By becoming a UNGC signatory and adopting the Model, Nike formally committed to assessing, defining, implementing, measuring, and communicating a CSR strategy.[63] Nike thereby committed to demonstrating for all its stakeholders the extent to which the company was meeting key impact performance indicators (KIPIs) and reporting out on targets through the lens of CSR and sustainability performance.

At the core of the Model, the UNGC recommends that corporations commit to the Global Reporting Initiative.[64] The GRI supplies companies with tools that guide them in conducting a CSR and sustainability risk assessment process.[65] Based on the company's risk assessment and the impact of its operations on a range of ESG performance indicators,

---

56 *See also* Gina Roos, *Ten Best Practices for Writing a Great CSR Report*, ENVIRONMENT + ENERGY LEADER (Jan. 28, 2010), www.environmentalleader.com/2010/01/ten-best-practices-for-writing-a-great-csr-r eport/.
57 *See also* Myriam Robin, *Why Businesses Fail on Corporate Social Responsibility*, SMART COMPANY (Feb. 14, 2013), www.smartcompany.com.au/people-human-resources/leadership/why-businesses-fail-on-corp orate-social-responsibility/.
58 David Doorey, *The Transparent Supply Chain: From Resistance to Implementation at Nike and Levi-Strauss*, 103 J BUS. ETHICS 587–603 (2011).
59 *Id*. at 592.
60 *What Is the Mandate?*, CEO WATER MANDATE, https://ceowatermandate.org/about/what-is-the-mand ate/.
61 *Id*. at 2.
62 *UN Global Compact Management Model*, at 8, UNITED NATIONS GLOBAL COMPACT, Deloitte (2010), www .unglobalcompact.org/library/231.
63 CEO Water Mandate, *supra* note 60, at 3.
64 UN Global Compact Management Model, *supra* note 62, at 15.
65 *Id*. at 13.

the company then develops and refines goals and metrics specific to its operating context and creates a roadmap to carry out its corporate sustainability program. The Guidelines assist corporations in setting goals to address its risks, reduce and mitigate negative impacts, and enhance positive impacts in relation to the UNGC Ten Principles. The Guidelines also provide companies with a format to report out to its stakeholders on progress in the implementation of KIPIs for their CSR and sustainability activities.

For example, Nike has used the GRI Sustainability Reporting Guidelines to develop and publish its Sustainability Impact Reports on an annual basis together with a GRI Index to demonstrate progress on the operationalization of the company's commitment to a corporate sustainability program.[66] Nike's Impact Reports document the environmental, social, and economic impacts caused by its everyday activities. Nike used the Guidelines to identify a reduction of the company's carbon footprint as a high priority. Through the risk assessment process, Nike identified five elements that are the greatest sources of GHG emissions essential to its manufacturing process: Polyester, the plastic ethylene vinyl acetate (EVA), rubber, leather, and cotton.[67] Given these materials, Nike calculated the average carbon footprint for each of its products. Footwear carbon footprint is measured in kg CO_2e per pair from highest to lowest footprint: Air Force 1, Zoom Vaporfly, Air Max 95, Air Zoom Pegasus, Air Max 90, Air Vapormax Flyknit, Free Flyknit, and Tanjun.[68] Based on these calculations, Nike committed to a 10% reduction in the average environmental footprint in each pair by FY2020.[69] It proposes to do this by using the best sustainable materials, improving pattern efficiency, and cutting waste.[70]

Nike recognizes that the strategic goal of reduced environmental impact requires sustained and integrated work across its entire value chain. To this end, Nike has committed to the procurement of renewable energy for all of its owned or operated facilities.[71] Nike also made a commitment to work with its suppliers in its supply chain to increase energy efficiency and move toward renewable energy in their facilities.[72] In an initiative called Move to Zero, Nike aims to achieve a zero-carbon footprint by FY25.[73] Nike's Sustainability Impact Reports document the company's progress to this end. The company adopted the GRI Reporting Standard on "Emissions" under the GRI Guideline on the environment to measure its upstream and downstream GHG emissions in its owned or operated facilities on an annual basis.[74] In addition, under the category of "Renewable Energy Owned or Operated," Nike reports on the percentage of renewable energy in its owned or operated facilities year over year.[75] By 2019, Nike reports that it has contracted for nearly 600,000 megawatt hours of renewable energy per year, which is more than 75% of the company's global electricity load.[76] In alignment with the third recommendation of the three studies, this is an example

---

66 *Purpose Moves Us,* at 79 FY19 NIKE, Inc. Impact Report, https://purpose-cms-preprod01.s3.amazonaws.com/wp-content/uploads/2020/02/11230637/FY19-Nike-Inc.-Impact-Report.pdf.
67 *Id.* at 42
68 *Id.* at 36.
69 *Id.* at 6.
70 *Id.*
71 *Id.*
72 *Id.*
73 *Note*: Nike's commitment to a reduction in carbon emissions and greenhouse gases will become the company's commitment to SDGs 12 and 13.
74 Nike Impact Report, *supra* note 66, at 6.
75 *Id.* at 42.
76 *Id.*

of how a corporation ought to use the Guidelines to work with suppliers in its value chain to integrate ESG performance.

As a consequence of the company's original commitment to the Global Compact's Ten Principles, Nike used the Model to promote organizational transformation by creating an infrastructure to operationalize its CSR programing. Additionally, Nike committed to use the GRI Sustainable Reporting Guidelines to produce Sustainability Impact Reports that communicate the company's progress toward making a positive impact on society and the environment to its stakeholders on an annual basis.[77] Finally, Nike adopted best practices by using the audit firm of PriceWaterhouseCoopers to audit its Sustainability Impact Reports to verify its numbers.[78]

This infrastructure that operationalizes Nike's commitments to the Global Compact and its Ten Principles will serve as a framework for the company's seamless integration of the SDGs into its business practices and operations. Nike will already have undergone an organizational transformation through the application of the Model. Moreover, the company will have refined its business practices and operations by adopting a commitment to the GRI Sustainability Reporting Guidelines. Finally, Nike will have developed an institutional habit of reporting on its everyday activities through the lens of the CSR and sustainability performance metrics.

Nike, the Leeds School of Business, and the SDG Compass

The United Nations Principles for Responsible Management Education (UN PRME) is an initiative supported by the United Nations through the UNGC. The UNGC and PRME were linked by Secretary Ban-Ki Moon with the launch of PRME to serve as an interface between the UN, the UN Global Compact, and business schools.[79] By becoming PRME signatories, business schools educate students about the importance of the Ten Principles of the Global Compact. In learning about the importance of the Ten Principles as performance indicators, students become encouraged to become the next generation of socially conscious, values-driven business leaders. The two initiatives are not only linked at the international level but are also linked at the local level through the relationship between UNGC Local Networks and PRME Chapters. Through the Local Networks and Chapters, corporations and business schools are encouraged to engage in partnerships and open dialog to their mutual benefit.

For example, Nike executives agreed to partner with business students from a UN PRME signatory, the Leeds School of Business at the University of Colorado, Boulder, on a project to identify the specific SDGs that align with Nike's business practices and operations. In a three-phased project, the Leeds Team planned to (1) perform an audit of three of Nike's prior Sustainability Impact Reports to determine how the company's business practices and operations align with the SDGs; (2) conduct a competitive analysis in determining best practices by comparing Nike's current practices to the practices of competitors in the analysis of key impact performance indicators of progress toward the achievement of specific targets of relevant SDGs; and (3) complete a final report with recommendations on changes to Nike's business practices and operations given the requirements of the relevant SDGs.

---

77 *Id.* at 74
78 *Id.* at 68.
79 *What Is PRME?*, UNITED NATIONS PRINCIPLES OF RESPONSIBLE MANAGEMENT EDUCATION, www.unprme.org/about.

The Leeds Team used the targets and indicators of the SDG Compass to perform its audit.[80] The SDG Compass is a tool developed in a partnership between the Global Compact and the GRI.[81] The SDG Compass translates the GRI Sustainability Reporting Guidelines into 1,500 indicators relative to the SDGs.[82] A company can use the SDG Compass to map its value chains and then assess the current and future positive or negative impacts of its operations on specific SDGs. For example, the Leeds Team used the SDG Compass to translate Nike's efforts to promote gender equality into the language of SDG 5. The Team then drilled down in identifying specific targets and indicators. In SDG 5.5, the SDG Compass recommends that companies ensure women's full and effective participation and equal opportunities for leadership at all levels of decision-making.[83] In the indicator 5.5.2, the SDG Compass further clarifies that companies should implement time-bound metrics and then report out on the proportion of women versus men in managerial positions.[84] To meet the requirements of this indicator, the Team recommended that Nike report on its efforts to promote gender equality by using the more granular category of "management positions held by men vs. women," as well as by establishing time-bound, measurable goals to promote more women into managerial positions.

Conclusion

Narrowing the Economic Gender Gap

The UN Global Compact and UN PRME have been effective in engaging corporations and institutions of higher learning in the integration of the SDGs into practices and operations through cultural transformation. However, recent studies indicate an uneven response to the SDGs among private sector corporations. Results from these studies show just how far corporations must progress if the SDGs are to be achieved by 2030, especially to achieve SDG 5.[85] Moreover, the slow pace of change represents a missed opportunity to address additional SDGs, such as SDG 1, Ending Poverty, and SDG 8, Decent Work and Economic Growth.[86] Corporations can contribute to helping governments end poverty by simultaneously addressing the issue of gender equality. Corporations can do much more in partnership with governments to achieve SDGs 1, 5, 8, and 17.

The economic gender gap arises from unequal access to economic opportunity. Discriminatory norms keep women in certain occupations in working for wages less than those of men. Through a commitment to SDGs 1, 5, and 8, government leaders have pledged to ensure that women have equal rights to economic opportunities by developing policy frameworks based on gender-sensitive strategies.[87] Corporations ought to partner with governments in closing the economic gender gap by offering women the kinds of economic opportunities that governments simply cannot (SDG 17).[88] To close the economic

---

80 *SDG Compass: A Guide Business Action on the SDGs*, GRI, UN Global Compact, wbcsd (2015), https://sdgcompass.org/.
81 *Id.* at 4.
82 *Id.* at 4.
83 *Inventory of Business Indicators*, 5.5, SDG COMPASS, https://sdgcompass.org/business-indicators/.
84 *Id.*
85 *See* Agenda 2030, *supra* note 14, at 14.
86 *Id.*
87 *Id.*
88 *Id.*

gender gap, the three studies cite the need for corporations to address the gap between commitment and action. While 68% of companies committed to gender equality and 40% of companies publicly advocate for gender equality, more than 70% of companies fail to include time-bound, measurable goals and targets in their strategy.[89] According to the three studies, this is at the root of why efforts by corporations have yet to translate into real impact in closing the economic gender gap.

A Gender-Based Response to the COVID-19 Pandemic

To help drive responsible corporate action toward the achievement of SDGs 1, 5, and 8, the Global Compact has partnered with UN Women to launch an initiative in response to the COVID-19 pandemic called Target Gender Equality (TGE).[90] The initiative poses a challenge to thousands of companies to raise their level of ambition in the context of the pandemic to meet the needs of women by fully integrating SDG 5 into business strategy and operations. The COVID-19 pandemic is magnifying all forms of discrimination faced by women, posing a serious threat to women's employment and livelihoods. As a consequence, business leaders have a responsibility to ensure their companies take action to combat COVID-19 in a way that responds to the unique and unequal economic impacts on women. If the private sector is to be part of the solution, corporations must place women at the very center of their efforts both during and after this crisis. The TGE principles provide corporations with guidance on how to advance gender equality in the workplace in recognizing and responding to the gender-specific impacts of COVID-19. By setting ambitious and time-bound, measurable targets for women's participation in managerial positions, corporations can move the needle forward for change in both responding to the pandemic and in closing the economic gender gap.

For example, the TGE principle of ensuring women's representation and inclusion at all levels of planning and decision-making requires specific actions that companies must take to advance SDG 5. Corporations can apply this principle in the constitution of crisis task forces and response teams to ensure that women are represented in COVID-related processes. Corporations should thus work to ensure that women participate in COVID-19 leadership decisions to embed gender expertise and gender concerns within response plans. The goal of TGE is a minimum of 40% representation of women on response teams.[91] The implementation of the principles of TGE could thereby ensure that women's perspectives and voices are adequately represented in corporate decision-making and transform corporate governance and leadership to better deliver on SDG 5.5 and close the economic gender gap in addressing SDGs 1 and 8.

The COVID-19 pandemic is also dramatically disrupting global supply chains. Women play a key role at every level of the supply chain as workers, entrepreneurs, buyers, service providers, corporate managers, etc. The TGE principle of the implementation of enterprise development, supply chain, and marketing practices that empower women requires the support of women across the value chain in the communities where corporations operate. To

---

89 Women's Empowerment, *supra* note 55, at 5.
90 *Target Gender Equality*, UN GLOBAL COMPACT (Mar. 25, 2020), www.unglobalcompact.org/take-action/target-gender-equality.
91 Lisa Klingo, *Gender Equality at a Snail's Pace*, GREENBIZ (Mar. 6, 2020), www.greenbiz.com/article/gender-equality-snails-pace.

address SDGs 1 and 5, the Global Compact and UN Women call on corporations to make payments on existing orders to help keep suppliers that rely heavily on female labor afloat and paying their workers. The principle might also include providing leniency to women entrepreneurs, offering financial products and services to save them from bankruptcy, and deliberately looking to build relationships with women-owned businesses as part of recovery efforts in closing the economic gender gap.

The TGE principle to promote equality through community initiatives and advocacy requires corporations to partner with government and other sectors to tackle COVID-19 in supporting recovery efforts (SDG 17).[92] The responsibility of corporations to respect and support women's rights does not end at the company's walls, but rather, obliges corporations to engage in multi-stakeholder partnerships. Corporations should work together with government to build a network of peers, UN partners, and experts to support their gender equality strategies and work collectively to tackle persistent barriers to the economic opportunity of women. Corporations should publicly acknowledge the relevance of gender equality and women's economic empowerment during the response to the COVID-19 pandemic.

The UNGC and UN Women also seek to help private sector corporations learn valuable lessons from their responses to the COVID-19 pandemic that can provide guidance in closing the economic gender gap by simultaneously addressing SDGs 1, 5, 8, and 17. A silver lining of the pandemic is the possibility that more corporations will adopt more gender-inclusive workplace policies and practices. Using this experience to accelerate progress toward a gender-equitable future will be key to bringing private sector corporations together with government, civil society, and other actors to scale ambition and commitment to address key barriers to women's economic inclusion.

Recommended Action Steps

- According to a recent study, the single most important independent variable for corporate engagement with the SDGs is participation in the UN Global Compact.[93]
- Corporations must also build CSR and ESG performance metrics into their overall corporate strategy and business operations.
- Corporations must set time-bound, measurable targets to address such issues as poverty, gender equality, climate change, water remediation, and decent work and economic growth.
- Corporations must work with their suppliers in the value chain to integrate impact performance metrics into their operations.
- Corporations must partner with governments to end poverty by simultaneously addressing the issue of the economic gender gap (SDG 17).
- Following upon their response to the COVID-19 pandemic, corporations must adopt gender-inclusive workplace policies and practices.

---

92 *See* Agenda 2030, *supra* note 14.
93 Johannes W.H. van der Waal & Thomas Thijssens, *Corporate Involvement in Sustainable Development Goals: Exploring the Territory*, 252 J. OF CLEANER PRODUCTION (Apr. 10, 2020), https://doi.org/10.1016/j.jclepro.2019.119625.

30 From Means of Implementation to Implementation of Means
Realizing the Sustainable Development Goals as If They Matter

Mihir Kanade

The first five years of implementation of the Sustainable Development Goals (SDGs), despite the enormous expectations evoked by their adoption in 2015,[1] have unfortunately been disappointing. By the end of 2019, progress on many targets had in fact decelerated compared with previous years.[2] This downward spiral has only been exacerbated in 2020 with the world brought to its knees by the COVID-19 pandemic.[3] This chapter contends that this alarming result—prior to, during, and most likely after COVID-19—is the inevitable consequence of the lack of a normative framework around which the implementation of the 2030 Agenda can converge. Implementation of the SDGs has been underpinned by a "business as usual" approach of development viewed through the lens of charity, privilege, or generosity. This is especially true of the "means of implementation" (MOI) of the SDGs incorporated in the 2030 Agenda. This chapter contends that the only way in which the 2030 Agenda can be successful is if its realization is based on the normative framework of development viewed as a human right of all persons and peoples with corresponding duties on States with respect to the MOI, including most importantly, the duty of international cooperation. This chapter demonstrates that such an essential normative framework is encapsulated in the right to development (RtD), and that its operationalization can not only lead to a better realization of the 2030 Agenda, but the same is indispensable for any prospects of success.

The Means of Implementation of the SDGs: Case Study on Financing for Development through International Aid and Assistance

A specific structural improvement in the 2030 Agenda over its predecessor, the Millennium Development Goals (MDGs), is that it "crucially, defines means of implementation" of the development goals.[4] Under a heading by that name, the agenda acknowledges that its scale and ambition "requires a revitalized Global Partnership to ensure its implementation" and records the commitment of States to do so.[5] It envisages such partnership to "work in a spirit

---

1 G.A. Res. A/RES/70/1, *Transforming Our World: The 2030 Agenda for Sustainable Development* (Sept. 25, 2015) [hereinafter "2030 Agenda"].
2 *See The Sustainable Development Goals Report (2019)*, https://unstats.un.org/sdgs/report/2019/The-Sustainable-Development-Goals-Report-2019.pdf [hereinafter "2019 SDG Report"].
3 *Id.*
4 2030 Agenda, *supra* note 1 at ¶17.
5 *Id.* at ¶ 39.

of global solidarity, in particular solidarity with the poorest and with people in vulnerable situations."[6] It further notes that this partnership will be multi-stakeholder, "bringing together Governments, the private sector, civil society, the United Nations (UN) system and other actors," and will mobilize all available resources to "facilitate an intensive global engagement in support of implementation of all the Goals and targets."[7]

The Agenda incorporates MOI under two separate streams. The first stream is captured through several targets under SDG 17 entitled "Strengthen the means of implementation and revitalize the global partnership for sustainable development." The targets thereunder are divided under the five heads of finance, technology, capacity-building, trade, and systemic-issues, the last of which is further divided into three sub-heads of policy and institutional coherence, multi-stakeholder partnerships, and data, monitoring and accountability. Each of these heads and sub-heads contains several targets, in total numbering 19; it is these 19 targets identified under SDG 17 that constitute the overarching MOI for all the preceding 16 SDGs.

The second stream of MOI is comprised of targets that are specific to each of the first 16 SDGs. These are listed under each SDG separately in alphabetical order (for instance, Targets 1.a and 1.b under SDG 1) below the targets mentioned in numerical order (for instance Target 1.1, 1.2, 1.3, etc. under SDG 1). These "a, b, c targets" constitute the specific MOI for the "1, 2, 3 targets" under each of the initial 16 SDGs. Together, SDGs 1 to 16 contain 43 MOI targets, bringing the total of such targets under the 2030 Agenda to 52.

The Agenda recognizes that these 52 MOI targets are "key to realizing" it.[8] While it recognizes that "each country has primary responsibility for its own economic and social development," it also sets out a framework for "a revitalized global partnership for sustainable development" through these MOI.[9] Progress on all SDGs is therefore directly proportional to progress on these MOI. It is in this context that this chapter seeks to analyze progress on one of the most important MOI, viz. financing for development through international aid and assistance.

The 2030 Agenda and Financing for Development through International Aid and Assistance

The 2030 Agenda rightly places significant importance on "financing for development" through global partnership as an indispensable MOI.[10] This term encompasses many forms of financial flows, both domestic and international, as well as public and private. These include foreign direct investment, remittances, domestic revenue sources like taxation, government borrowing, and external debt, as well as development aid and assistance. The case study in this chapter will focus on development aid and assistance as MOI.

---

6 *Id.*
7 *Id.*
8 *Id.* at ¶ 40.
9 *Id.* at ¶ 41.
10 *Id.* at ¶ 40, ¶ 41, ¶ 43, and ¶ 86, and SDG 17.

In July 2015, as a lead-up to Agenda 2030, States adopted the Addis Ababa Action Agenda (AAAA) at the Third International Conference on Financing for Development.[11] The AAAA records the commitment of all States to "respect each country's policy space and leadership to implement policies for poverty eradication and sustainable development, while remaining consistent with relevant international rules and commitments."[12] This is an important acknowledgment in light of persistent criticism, as shall be discussed presently, that development aid limits policy space of recipient countries through conditionalities. Having done so, it acknowledges that "at the same time, national development efforts need to be supported by an enabling international economic environment, including coherent and mutually supporting world trade, monetary and financial systems, and strengthened and enhanced global economic governance."[13] For these reasons, the AAAA records the commitment of States "to pursuing policy coherence and an enabling environment for sustainable development at all levels and by all actors, and to reinvigorating the global partnership for sustainable development."[14]

Specifically, with respect to financing through international assistance and aid, the AAAA notes "international public finance plays an important role in complementing the efforts of countries to mobilize public resources domestically, especially in the poorest and most vulnerable countries with limited domestic resources."[15] It further records the reaffirmation by Official Development Assistance (ODA) providers regarding their respective ODA commitments, including the commitment by many developed countries to achieve the target of 0.7% of gross national income for ODA (ODA/GNI) and 0.15 to 0.20% of ODA/GNI to Least Developed Countries (LDCs).[16] However, it also expresses concern that many of these donor countries were falling short of their ODA commitments and reiterates that "the fulfilment of all ODA commitments remains crucial."[17]

The AAAA was incorporated as "an integral part" of the 2030 Agenda,[18] which recognizes that "the full implementation" of the AAAA is "critical for the realization of the SDGs and targets."[19] As such, financing for development as an MOI for the 2030 Agenda is governed by the principles and framework of the AAAA.

In the 2030 Agenda, financing for development in general is covered under SDG 17 through targets 17.1 to 17.5. There are three targets within these that relate to development aid and assistance through international cooperation. See Box 30.1.

---

11 See G.A. A/RES/69/313, *Addis Ababa Action Agenda of the Third International Conference on Financing for Development (Addis Ababa Action Agenda)* (Aug. 17, 2015) [hereinafter "AAAA"].
12 *Id.* at ¶ 9.
13 *Id.*
14 *Id.*
15 *Id.* at ¶ 50.
16 *Id.* at ¶ 51.
17 *Id.*
18 2030 Agenda, *supra* note 1 at ¶ 40 and ¶ 62.
19 *Id.* at ¶ 40.

> **Box 30.1 Development Aid and Assistance Targets under SDG 17**
>
> 17.1 Strengthen domestic resource mobilization, including through international support to developing countries, to improve domestic capacity for tax and other revenue collection
>
> 17.2 Developed countries to implement fully their official development assistance commitments, including the commitment by many developed countries to achieve the target of 0.7 per cent of ODA/GNI to developing countries and 0.15 to 0.20 per cent of ODA/GNI to least developed countries; ODA providers are encouraged to consider setting a target to provide at least 0.20 per cent of ODA/GNI to least developed countries
>
> 17.4 Assist developing countries in attaining long-term debt sustainability through coordinated policies aimed at fostering debt financing, debt relief, and debt restructuring, as appropriate, and address the external debt of highly indebted poor countries to reduce debt distress

Financing for development in the form of aid and assistance is also envisaged in Targets 1.a, 1.b, 2.a, 3.c, 7.a, 8.a, 9.a, 10.b, 11.c, 15.a, and 15.b as MOI for the specific SDG they fall under. In particular, under SDG 10 on reducing inequality within and among countries, target 10.b aims to

> encourage official development assistance and financial flows, including foreign direct investment, to States where the need is greatest, in particular least developed countries, African countries, small island developing States and landlocked developing countries, in accordance with their national plans and programmes.[20]

Effectiveness of International Development Aid and Assistance as MOI

The importance of financing for development through international aid and assistance, as MOI for the entire 2030 Agenda, cannot be overemphasized. While its volume is certainly crucial, its effectiveness is also the key to the realization of all SDGs. Serious concerns regarding effectiveness of development aid have been persistently raised for years,[21] especially with respect to one of its most important forms viz. official development assistance provided by members of the Development Assistance Committee (DAC) of the Organization of Economic Cooperation and Development (OECD).[22] ODA has since 1969 constituted the standard means through which international aid and assistance has been provided by DAC

---

20 *Id*. at SDG 10.
21 *See* WILLIAM EASTERLY, WHITE MAN'S BURDEN: WHY THE WEST'S EFFORTS TO AID THE REST HAVE DONE SO MUCH ILL AND SO LITTLE GOOD (2006); DAMBISA MOYO, DEAD AID: WHY AID IS NOT WORKING AND THERE IS A BETTER WAY FOR AFRICA (2010); MIHIR KANADE, THE MULTILATERAL TRADING SYSTEM AND HUMAN RIGHTS: A GOVERNANCE SPACE THEORY ON LINKAGES 169–94 (2018).
22 The OECD's DAC comprizes the following 30 members: Australia, Austria, Belgium, Canada, Czech Republic, Denmark, European Union, Finland, France, Germany, Greece, Hungary, Iceland, Ireland, Italy, Japan, Korea, Luxembourg, The Netherlands, New Zealand, Norway, Poland, Portugal, Slovak Republic, Slovenia, Spain, Sweden, Switzerland, United Kingdom, United States (US). *See Development*

countries.²³ To qualify as ODA, such aid and assistance must first be provided by official agencies, including state and local governments, or by their executive agencies, must secondly be concessional (i.e. grants and soft loans) and must thirdly be administered with the promotion of the economic development and welfare of developing countries as the main objective.²⁴

Amidst persistent criticism over aid effectiveness, several guiding principles on the policy and practice of development aid emerged since 2005 and were agreed upon by donor countries and institutions, including multilateral financial institutions. In particular, these included the Paris Declaration on Aid Effectiveness (2005),²⁵ the International Health Partnership Plus (2007),²⁶ the Accra Agenda for Action (2008),²⁷ the Busan Partnership for Effective Cooperation (2011),²⁸ and the Global Partnership for Effective Development Cooperation (GPEDC) (2011).²⁹ Collectively, these documents enumerate six principles for aid to be effective viz. country ownership over programs; alignment between donor funding and country priorities; harmonization of donor activities to prevent or mitigate fragmentation and duplication of efforts; ensuring transparency and accountability; provision of predictable and long-term funding; and engagement of civil society.³⁰ These documents are not legally binding instruments and hence outline only guiding principles that remain largely discretionary without accountability in case of breach. In any case, their successful implementation prior to the adoption of the 2030 Agenda remained extremely doubtful.³¹

Neither the AAAA nor the 2030 Agenda specifically refer to them. The AAAA, however, "welcome[s] continued efforts to improve the quality, impact and effectiveness of development cooperation and other international efforts in public finance, including adherence to agreed development cooperation effectiveness principles."³² Unfortunately, recent empirical data on development aid and assistance as MOI for the SDGs demonstrates that not only have donor countries miserably failed to abide by their commitments, but also that the agreed principles of effectiveness have been rampantly trampled upon or ignored.

Assistance Committee, ORGANISATION FOR ECONOMIC COOPERATION AND DEVELOPMENT (OECD), www.oecd.org/dac/development-assistance-committee/ (last visited Dec. 2, 2020).
23 *Id.*
24 *Id.*
25 *See The Paris Declaration on Aid Effectiveness and the Accra Agenda for Action* (2005), OECD, www.oecd.org/dac/effectiveness/34428351.pdf.
26 *See* INTERNATIONAL HEALTH PARTNERSHIP PLUS, www.uhc2030.org/ (last visited Dec. 2, 2020).
27 *See supra* note 25.
28 *See The Busan Partnership for Effective Development Cooperation*, OECD, www.oecd.org/dac/effectiveness/busanpartnership.htm (2011).
29 *See* Global Partnership for Effective Development Cooperation, http://effectivecooperation.org/ (last visited Dec. 2, 2020).
30 For in-depth analyses, *see* Deepthi Wickremasinghe et.al., *It's About the Idea Hitting the Bull's Eye": How Aid Effectiveness Can Catalyse the Scale-up of Health Innovations*, 7(8) INT'L. J. HEALTH POL'Y & MGMT. 718, 718–27 (2018).
31 Catherine Blampied, *Where Next for Development Effectiveness? Building a Renewed Consensus* (2016), OVERSEAS DEVELOPMENT INSTITUTE, www.odi.org/sites/odi.org.uk/files/events-documents/10936.pdf.
32 AAAA, *supra* note 11 at ¶ 58.

Data on International Development Aid and Assistance as MOI

This section relies on the following four reports to cull out the most updated available data: The Sustainable Development Goals Report 2019, prepared by the UN Secretariat (hereinafter, the "SDG 2019 report");[33] the Financing for Sustainable Development Reports of 2019 and 2020 prepared by the UN's Inter-agency Task Force on Financing for Development to monitor implementation of the AAAA (hereinafter, "FSDR 2019" and "FSDR 2020," respectively);[34] and the report of the OECD entitled "DAC Untying Recommendations" (hereinafter, the "OECD 2018 Report").[35] Additionally, preliminary data for 2019 in the Sustainable Development Goals Report 2020 has been considered.[36] These reports collectively reveal the following information:

Global Situation

As per FSDR 2019, the world economic growth had likely peaked at 3% in 2018.[37] More than half a trillion dollars' worth of goods were subject to trade restrictions, seven times more than in 2018.[38] At the same time, debt risks were rising. Around 30 LDCs and other vulnerable countries were either in or at high risk of debt distress, putting dents in their ability to invest in the realization of the SDGs.[39] ODA is the largest source of external financing for LDCs.[40] LDCs faced large financing gaps and "their annual spending on education alone would need to more than triple in order to achieve universal pre-primary, primary and secondary education."[41] Clearly, this situation has worsened dramatically in 2020 due to the COVID-19 pandemic and the related global economic and commodity price shocks. FSDR 2020 points out that in this scenario, 44% of LDCs and other low-income developing countries are currently at high risk or in debt distress, and this figure is likely to rise.[42] This represents a doubling of debt risk in less than five years from 22% in 2015 when the 2030 Agenda was adopted.[43]

---

33 2019 SDG Report, *supra* note 2.
34 *Financing for Sustainable Development Report 2019*, UN INTER-AGENCY TASK FORCE ON FINANCING FOR DEVELOPMENT, https://developmentfinance.un.org/sites/developmentfinance.un.org/files/FSDR2019.pdf (2019) [hereinafter "FSDR 2019"]. *See also Financing for Sustainable Development Report 2020*, UN INTER-AGENCY TASK FORCE ON FINANCING FOR DEVELOPMENT, https://developmentfinance.un.org/sites/developmentfinance.un.org/files/FSDR_2020.pdf (2020) [hereinafter "FSDR 2020"].
35 *Report on the DAC Untying Recommendation 2018*, OECD, www.oecd.org/dac/financing-sustainable-development/development-finance-standards/DCD-DAC(2018)12-REV2.en.pdf (2018) [hereinafter, "OECD 2018 Report"].
36 *The Sustainable Development Goals Report* (2020), https://unstats.un.org/sdgs/report/2020 [hereinafter, "SDG Report 2020"].
37 FSDR 2019, *supra* note 34 at iii.
38 *Id*. at xvii.
39 *Id*.
40 SDG 2019 Report, *supra* note 2 at 56.
41 FSDR 2019, *supra* note 34 at iii.
42 *Id*. at 7 and 129.
43 *Id*. at xvii.

Volume of Development Aid and Assistance

As per FSDR 2019, DAC countries contributed USD147.2 billion as ODA in 2017, representing a decline of 0.1% in real terms over 2016.[44] However, measuring ODA contributions over time in real terms is misleading. In 2017, none of the DAC members, except five, met the target of contributing 0.7% of ODA/GNI to developing countries and 0.15% to 0.20% to LDCs.[45] On aggregate, DAC donors provided only 0.31% of GNI as ODA.[46] In other words, while the committed amount was USD332.4 billion, the shortfall ended up being a massive USD185.2 billion. Overall, ODA to LDCs amounted to only 0.09% of DAC members' GNI in 2017 (including imputed multilateral flows).[47] Total ODA flows to Small Island Developing States (SIDS) dropped to USD2.7 billion in 2017 from USD4.6 billion in 2016.[48] With respect to Target 17.1, ODA dedicated to domestic revenue mobilization in recipient countries fell significantly from USD329 million in 2016 to USD193 million in 2017, accounting for 0.18% of ODA.[49]

The situation worsened further in 2018. According to the SDGs Report 2019 which was based on preliminary figures, net ODA totaled USD149 billion in 2018, down by 2.7% in real terms from 2017.[50] Humanitarian aid fell by 8% in real terms.[51] In 2018, bilateral ODA to LDCs fell by 3% in real terms from 2017, and aid to Africa fell by 4%.[52] FSDR 2020 provides updated statistics using a new methodology for calculation. According to this report, ODA in fact fell by 4.3% in 2018.[53] ODA by DAC countries in 2018 was equivalent to 0.31% of the combined GNI, that is, more than 50% below the 0.7% commitment in the AAAA and Target 17.2.[54] Similar to 2017, all but five DAC countries failed to meet these commitments.[55] Specifically with relation to LDCs, ODA fell by 2.1% and accounted for only 0.09% of DAC members' GNI, well below the 0.15–0.20% LDC target.[56] ODA to Africa, landlocked developing countries, and SIDS dropped by 1.8, 8.9, and 2.1%, respectively.[57] Worryingly, preliminary figures for 2019 show that ODA reduced even further to USD147.4 billion.[58]

Country Ownership over Programs and Alignment between Donor Funding and Country Priorities

In addition to a serious drop in the volume of ODA, reports also demonstrate that existing practices continued to violate the agreed principles of aid effectiveness. A good measure of

---

44 *Id.* at 78.
45 The only five countries that reached the target were Denmark, Luxembourg, Norway, Sweden, and the United Kingdom. *See Id.*
46 *Id.*
47 *Id.*
48 *Id.*
49 *Id.* at 46.
50 SDG 2019 Report, *supra* note 2 at 56.
51 *Id.*
52 *Id.*
53 FSDR 2020, *supra* note 34 at 81.
54 *Id.* at 82.
55 *Id.* As in 2017, these five were Denmark, Luxembourg, Norway, Sweden, and the United Kingdom (UK).
56 *Id.*
57 *Id.*
58 SDG 2019 Report, *supra* note 2 at 58.

whether ODA is adequate to ensure the availability of funds for financing national priorities expressed in national sustainable development strategies is the share and sector allocation of country programmable aid (CPA), which excludes items such as humanitarian aid, debt relief, in-donor refugee costs, and administrative costs.[59] FSDR 2019 records that while CPA increased from 46.9% in 2016 to 48.3% in 2017, partially reversing a longer-term declining trend, it was still 6.6% points below the share of CPA in 2010.[60] A similar trend is reported in FSDR 2020. CPA overall increased marginally by 0.3%, but fell by 1.1%, 7.2%, and 0.1%, respectively for LDCs, Landlocked Developing Countries (LLDCs), and African countries.[61]

More importantly, sector allocations reported in FSDR 2019 tell a story of their own. Social spending fell as a percentage of total ODA, from 40% in 2010 to 35% in 2017; the largest decline is attributed to the share of spending on education, which fell from 8.8% of total ODA in 2010 to 7.1%.[62] The report notes that this decreasing share of assistance for social sectors, "after growing rapidly in the first decade of the millennium during the era of the MDGs, reflects a shift in donors' focus to economic aid and support for production sectors."[63] It is telling that ODA for the social sector decreased for LDCs between 2010–2013 and 2016–2017, while aid for economic infrastructure and services and production sectors increased in real terms over the same period.[64] This trend is consistent with critiques that donors' choices of sectors for allocation of ODA tend to be based on commercial interests rather than for social welfare.

FSDR 2020 further laments the need for the allocation of ODA to align with country priorities and plans and frameworks. It highlights that "despite considerable strengthening in developing countries' planning processes, development partners' alignment to country priorities and country-owned results frameworks is declining."[65] It notes that in 2018, while 83% of new projects had objectives aligned to country priorities, only 59% of results indicators were drawn from country-owned results frameworks, and only 50% aligned with their statistics and monitoring systems.[66] Finally, the report notes that medium-term predictability was declining, with limited provision of forward expenditure and implementation plans by development partners.[67]

Loans or Grants

FSDR 2019 notes that since 2010, "the concessionality of bilateral ODA has declined, owing to an increased reliance on concessional loans and a decline in grants."[68] Loans increased from constituting 12.4% of ODA in 2010–2012, to 15.2% in 2016–2017.[69] LDCs bore a bigger brunt with the share of loans rising from 2.8% to 8.3%.[70] The report also notes

---

59 See also *Country Programmable Aid*, OECD, www.oecd.org/dac/financing-sustainable-development/development-finance-standards/cpa.htm (last visited Dec. 2, 2020).
60 FSDR 2019, *supra* note 34 at 79.
61 FSDR 2020, *supra* note 34 at 82.
62 FSDR 2019, *supra* note 34 at 79.
63 *Id.*
64 *Id.*
65 FSDR 2020, *supra* note 34 at 99.
66 *Id.*
67 *Id.*
68 FSDR 2019, *supra* note 34 at 80.
69 *Id.*
70 *Id.*

that more than 60% of ODA financing for the economic infrastructure and services sector has been through loans, mainly in the transport and energy sectors. Importantly, the report notes that "the increase in loans also raises questions of whether ODA may be contributing to the build-up of debt in developing countries."[71] Several scholars have for long critiqued the practice of development aid in the form of loans due to their inherent debt-augmenting nature.

Tied or Untied Aid

In 2018, the OECD produced a report on "the DAC Untying Recommendation." This report is progressive and makes several recommendations to DAC countries on moving toward untying aid based on empirical evidence.[72] It focuses significantly on the fact that "a large part of aid contracts continue to be awarded to companies from the donor country awarding the contract."[73] Clearly, this is not in alignment with recipient interests because open competitive bidding might lead to more competitive contractors from non-donor countries. It notes that 65% of contracts in 2015 and 2016 were awarded to in-donor companies.[74] In terms of the underlying value of contracts, in-donor share increased from 46% in 2014 to 51% in 2016.[75] When only projects implemented in LDCs and non-LDC Heavily Indebted Poor Countries (HIPC) are taken into account, the in-donor share was at 84.4% in 2015 and 57.3% in 2016.[76]

FSDR 2019 looks more broadly at tied aid beyond the award of contracts. It notes that in 2016, the share of untied aid reported by DAC countries was high and accounted for 79.8% of total ODA.[77] However, it also notes that "DAC procurement statistics illustrate that 'informal tying' remains a major challenge."[78] These include the in-donor contracts. The report then highlights that against the backdrop of ongoing efforts to scale-up blended finance,[79] "development partners must take urgent action to remove barriers, to allow developing countries, including LDCs, to better tap into the important double dividend that local procurement can bring when economic conditions are right."[80] The promotion of blended finance in this environment poses a real risk of proliferation of tied or informally tied aid.[81] Similarly, FSDR 2020 notes that despite increase of untied ODA to 82% in 2018, these figures mask the informal tying of aid through in-donor contracts.[82]

---

71 *Id.*
72 OECD 2018 Report, *supra* note 34.
73 *Id.* at 3.
74 *Id.*
75 *Id.* at 8.
76 *Id.*
77 FSDR 2019, *supra* note 34 at 93.
78 *Id.* at 94.
79 Blended finance is described as "the strategic use of development finance for the mobilisation of additional finance towards sustainable development in developing countries." *See Blended Finance*, OECD, www.oecd.org/dac/financing-sustainable-development/blended-finance-principles/ (last visited Dec. 2, 2020).
80 FSDR 2019, *supra* note 34 at 94.
81 *Id.*
82 FSDR 2020, *supra* note 34 at 99.

Transparency and Accountability

Most worryingly, despite DAC countries reporting significant share of their aid as untied, the OECD 2018 report notes that "the adherence to transparency provisions, intended to address concerns that de jure untied aid might remain de facto tied, is mixed."[83] The DAC Untying Recommendation included transparency provisions that call for ex ante notification of untied aid offers to be posted on the Untied Aid public bulletin board of the OECD, as well as reporting of ex post statements on contract awards. The OECD 2018 report notes that the vast majority of DAC members do not report any ex ante notifications.[84] It further notes that "given limited compliance with the provision for *ex ante* notifications, transparency remains limited, and the provision cannot be expected to contribute to building confidence about *de facto* adherence to the Recommendation by the DAC Membership overall."[85] Finally, it records its helplessness that "repeated past calls for reporting have not resulted in improved reporting, and observance has had an overall declining trend over time."[86]

With respect to ex post contract awards, the report notes that there is "room for significant improvement" while a few members continue to not report any contract awards.[87] It then hastens to question the veracity of the reported cases as well, noting that "it remains difficult to reconcile the number and value of contracts awarded in a given year with the activities reported to the CRS in earlier years."[88] It points out that for some members in particular, "the amounts notified are persistently small in comparison to ODA volumes provided to countries covered by the Recommendation."[89]

The aforesaid analysis clearly demonstrates that financing for development through international aid and assistance as MOI has been entirely off-track in the first five years of implementation of the 2030 Agenda, and where it is practiced, it continues to be contrary to agreed principles of aid effectiveness. The next section contends that this failure is the direct result of lack of operationalization of the RtD in the implementation of this MOI, and that doing so is the only way the "business as usual" approach can be turned around.

The Right to Development and SDGs: MOI as Duty of International Cooperation

The Context and Content of the RtD

The birth of the RtD was a consequence of the disillusionment of newly decolonized countries in the 1960s and 1970s with the then-existing international economic regime. This regime was created by victors of the Second World War in the 1940s when most of what we today call the developing world did not even exist as independent countries.[90] The sense of

---

83 OECD 2018 Report, *supra* note 34 at 3.
84 *Id.* at 6, ¶ 14.
85 *Id.*
86 *Id.* at 6, ¶ 15.
87 *Id.* at 7, ¶ 19.
88 *Id.*
89 *Id.*
90 Daniel Whelan et al., *The Right to Development: Origins, History, and Institutional Development*, in OPERATIONALIZING THE RIGHT TO DEVELOPMENT FOR IMPLEMENTATION OF THE SUSTAINABLE DEVELOPMENT GOALS (Mihir Kanade & Shyami Puvimanasinghe, eds., 2019).

unfairness generated by being born into debt-creating prescriptions of the World Bank and International Monetary Fund and the experience of these new countries with the untimely opening of markets under the General Agreement on Tariffs and Trade (GATT) 1947, eventually culminated in recognition of the RtD as a human right, first in the 1981 African Charter on Human and People's Rights,[91] and then at the global level through the adoption of the Declaration on the Right to Development (DRTD) by the UN General Assembly in 1986.[92] The DRTD was adopted with an overwhelming majority of 146 countries voting in favor, eight countries abstaining, and only the US voting in opposition.[93] Since then, the RtD has been reiterated and reaffirmed unanimously by all States in numerous declarations, resolutions, and agendas, including most recently, in the 2030 Agenda.[94] Today, the divisions among North-South lines are mostly on the scope of the RtD and the appropriate means for operationalizing it.

Key features of the DRTD may be summarized as follows:[95]

a. The RtD is an inalienable self-standing human right.[96] Development, and as will be pointed out below, sustainable development, are thus not mere privileges enjoyed by human beings, nor are they just subjects of charity or generosity.
b. The RtD denotes the entitlement of the right-holders to three things viz. to participate in, contribute to, and enjoy economic, social, cultural, and political development.[97]
c. The RtD also implies the full realization of the right of peoples to self-determination.[98]
d. Operationalizing the RtD involves respecting, protecting, and fulfilling all other human rights—civil, political, economic, social, and cultural—along with generating the resources of growth such as gross domestic product (GDP), technology, etc.[99] This means that given the very nature of development as a human right, it cannot be realized when there are violations of other human rights.
e. The RtD requires focusing not only on outcomes which are sought to be achieved as a result of a development plan (the "what" question), but also on the process by which those outcomes are achieved (the "how" question). Both the processes and outcomes of development must be consistent with and based on all other human rights.[100]
f. Human beings are individually (all human persons) and collectively (all peoples) the right-holders of the RtD against their States as well as other States.[101] Every State is

---

91 African Charter on Human and Peoples' Rights, Art. 22, June 27, 1981, CAB/LEG67/3 rev.5.
92 G.A. Res. A/RES/41/128, *Declaration on the Right to Development* (Dec. 4, 1986) [hereinafter, "The Declaration"].
93 Countries that abstained were Denmark, Finland, Germany, Iceland, Israel, Japan, Sweden, and the UK.
94 *See* Zamir Akram (Special Rapporteur to the UN Working Group on the Right to Development), *Review of the progress made in the promotion and implementation of the right to development, Draft convention on the right to development*, at Preamble ¶14, A/HRC/WG.2/21/2 (Jan. 17, 2020).
95 Whelan et al., *supra* note 90 at Ch. 3.
96 The Declaration, *supra* note 92 at Art. 1(1).
97 *Id.*
98 *Id.* at Art. 1(2).
99 Arjun Sengupta (Independent Expert on the Right to Development), *Third Report of the Independent Expert on the Right to Development*, at ¶ 9–10, E/CN.4/2001/WG.18/2 (Jan. 2, 2001).
100 Arjun Sengupta (Independent Expert on the Right to Development), *Study on the Current State of Implementation of the Right to Development Submitted*, at ¶ 36, E/CN.4/1999/WG.18/2 (July 27, 1999).
101 The Declaration, *supra* note 92 at Article 1(1).

entitled, as an agent of all persons and peoples subject to its jurisdiction, to demand respect for their RtD by other States and international organizations.[102]

g. The DRTD entails duties on all States to respect, protect, and fulfil the RtD across the following three levels:[103]
   (i) States acting individually as they formulate national development policies and programs affecting persons within their jurisdiction; and
   (ii) States acting individually as they adopt and implement policies that affect persons not strictly within their jurisdiction; and
   (iii) States acting collectively in global and regional partnerships.

h. The RtD imposes an obligation on States, individually and collectively, to eliminate existing obstacles to its realization, refrain from making policies which are adverse to its realization, and to positively create conditions favorable to its realization.[104]

i. Most importantly, the RtD imposes a duty on States with respect to international cooperation to realize the RtD.[105] The duty to cooperate is of primary importance to the RtD and flows from the UN Charter.[106] The DRTD refers to it twice in the preamble and at least thrice in the substantive provisions.[107] The duty to cooperate applies to all facets of the RtD. Because its realization requires an enabling national *and* international environment, the duty to cooperate is indispensable.

The Symbiotic Relationship between the RtD and the SDGs

The DRTD contains no references to sustainable development, primarily because sustainable development as a concept and framework emerged on the global policy agenda only in 1987, one year after the DRTD was adopted.[108] The obvious symbiotic relationship between the RtD and sustainable development was specifically recognized for the first time in the 1992 Rio Declaration on Environment and Development, stipulating in its third principle that the "right to development must be fulfilled so as to equitably meet developmental and environmental needs of present and future generations."[109] This was reiterated in the Vienna Declaration of 1993.[110] The Millennium Declaration adopted unanimously in 2000, and from which the MDGs emanated as actionable and achievable goals, explicitly incorporated "making the right to development a reality for everyone" as one of its stated objectives.[111]

---

102 *Id.* at Art. 2. *See also* Anne Orford, *Globalization and the Right to Development, in* PEOPLE'S RIGHTS (Philip Alston, ed., 2001).
103 G.A. Res. A/HRC/15/WG.2/TF/2/Add.2, *Report of the High-Level Task Force on the Implementation of the Right to Development* (Mar. 8, 2010).
104 The Declaration, *supra* note 92 at Arts. 1(1), 2(3), 3(1) and (3), 4(1), 6(1) and (3) and 10.
105 *See* Mihir Kanade, *Commentaries to the Draft Convention on the Right to Development*, in Zamir Akram (Chair-Rapporteur to the UN Working Group on the Right to Development), *Draft Convention on the Right to Development, with commentaries*, A/HRC/WG.2/21/2/Add.1 (Jan. 20, 2020).
106 U.N. Charter Arts, 1(3), 55 and 56.
107 *See Id.* at articles 3(2), 3(3), and 4(2).
108 WORLD COMMISSION ON ENVIRONMENT AND DEVELOPMENT, OUR COMMON FUTURE (1987).
109 UN Conference on Environment and Development, *Rio Declaration on Environment and Development*, at Principle 3, A/CONF.151/26 (Vol. I) (Aug. 12, 1992).
110 World Conference on Human Rights, *Vienna Declaration and Programme of Action*, A/CONF.157/23 (July 12, 1993).
111 G.A. Res. A/RES/55/2, *Millenium Declaration* (Sep.18, 2000).

Finally, Agenda 2030 notes that it is "informed by" the DRTD.[112] It has been pointed out from the text of Agenda 2030, that it further reaffirms the RtD and acknowledges that the agenda is "grounded" in the RtD.[113]

The very adoption of Agenda 2030 by States could be seen as an implementation by them of their duty stipulated in the DRTD to "take steps, individually and collectively, to formulate international development policies with a view to facilitating the full realization of the right to development."[114] In this sense, the SDGs are a policy expression by States of their intention individually and collectively to realize their obligations under the DRTD and a plan of action for operationalizing the RtD.[115] On the other hand, operationalizing the RtD can in turn significantly bolster the realization of Agenda 2030 by providing its MOI with a normative framework effectively stipulating that the participation in, contribution to, and enjoyment of sustainable development by all human persons and peoples ought not to be seen as a charity, bestowed upon them by States, but as a human right with corresponding duties.[116] By insisting that development is a human right with clearly identified duty-bearers, the RtD hammers down the point that the only way development can be sustainable is if it is itself treated as a right and not as a charity, and if it encompasses all human rights as equally important and ensures that no human right is undermined.[117]

Operationalizing the RtD then entails infusing MOI with the normative framework of the RtD so that they are realized within the ambit of the duty of international cooperation.

To put the aforesaid in the context of our chapter, unfortunately, data discussed earlier on financing for development through international aid and assistance demonstrates that there has been a complete failure to operationalize the RtD. Aid and assistance practices are bereft of a normative framework of rights and duties resulting inevitably in failure to make progress as MOI. The continual reduction in volume in breach of commitments by DAC countries demonstrates that aid and assistance still operate very much within the framework of charity, is fungible, and under total control of donors with respect to processes and outcomes. While the commitments of 0.7% of GNI as ODA to developing countries and 0.15% to LDCs are not by themselves legally binding obligations and hence enforceable, continual failure to meet these commitments can be seen as failure to comply with the duty to cooperate inherent to the RtD. Data also demonstrates that current ODA practices continue to undermine the development priorities of the recipients in terms of sector allocations, alignments, and country ownership. They also actively infringe upon the RtD of the recipients through adverse conditionalities (in-donor contracts) and design (as loans) that promote the economic interests of the donors rather than the recipients. While principles for effectiveness of aid exist, they haven't translated into reality because they as well lack a normative framework. Indeed, it has been pointed out that since the adoption of Agenda 2030, the aid effectiveness agenda has practically stalled and commitments on effectiveness principles

---

112 2030 Agenda, *supra* note 1 at ¶ 10.
113 *Id*. at ¶ 11 and ¶ 12. *See also* Mihir Kanade, *The Right to Development and the 2030 Agenda for Sustainable Development*, at 4, www.ohchr.org/Documents/Issues/Development/SR/AddisAbaba/MihirKanade.pdf (Jan. 2018).
114 The Declaration, *supra* note 92 at Article 4(1).
115 Kanade, *supra* note 113 at 9.
116 *Id*.
117 *Id*.

by donor countries have dissipated.[118] The absence of operationalizing the RtD inevitably results in the realization of this MOI in a manner that is counterproductive and a recipe for the failure of Agenda 2030 itself.

Conclusions and Recommendations

The year 2020, unfortunately, has unleashed the COVID-19 pandemic unleashing disastrous consequences in its wake. It has plunged an already struggling global economy into the worst economic downturn since the Great Depression.[119] As the UN Secretary General (UNSG) has pointed out, "this is much more than a health crisis ... it is a human crisis ... the coronavirus disease (COVID-19) is attacking societies at their core."[120] Unsurprisingly, the most severe impacts are bound to be on the weakest and poorest countries.[121] The UNSG has raised the alarm that "the situation in developing countries, LDCs, LLDCs and SIDS in particular, is of special concern," where even before the crisis, debt accumulation has outpaced the growth of income.[122] As he has pointed out, 44% of LDCs and other low-income developing countries are at high risk or in debt distress.[123] Worryingly, middle-income countries are also highly vulnerable to a debt crisis, lost market access, and capital outflows.[124]

Resultantly, both the UNSG, and several special procedures of the UN,[125] have called for unprecedented debt relief and lifting of sanctions on countries as part of immediate measures to handle the crisis. More importantly, there is a clear recognition that meeting the ODA commitments and injecting significantly more financial aid and assistance into developing and vulnerable countries has never been more necessary. The UNSG has called for a "large-scale, coordinated and comprehensive multilateral response amounting to at least 10 per cent of global GDP."[126] In the wake of COVID-19, he has also highlighted the urgent need of "reversing the backsliding we are seeing in the commitments enshrined in the [AAAA], including the decline in [ODA], especially to [LDCs], and the growing debt distress of low-income and vulnerable countries."[127]

---

118 Osondu Ogbuoji & Gavin Yamey, *Aid Effectiveness in the Sustainable Development Goals Era*, 8(3) INT'L J. HEALTH POL'Y. MGMT. 184, 184–86 (2019).
119 *Debt and COVID-19: A Global Response in Solidarity*, UN, at 5, www.un.org/sites/un2.un.org/files/un_policy_brief_on_debt_relief_and_covid_april_2020.pdf (17 April 2020) [hereinafter "Debt and COVID-19"].
120 *Shared Responsibility, Global Solidarity: Responding to the Socio-Economic Impacts of COVID-19*, at 1, https://unsdg.un.org/sites/default/files/2020-03/SG-Report-Socio-Economic-Impact-of-Covid19.pdf (March 2020) [hereinafter "Shared Responsibility"].
121 *Id.*
122 *Id.* at 8.
123 *Id.* at 14.
124 Debt and COVID-19, *supra* note 119 at 4.
125 *UN Rights Expert Urges Governments to Save Lives by Lifting All Economic Sanctions Amid COVID-19 Pandemic*, OFFICE OF THE UNITED NATIONS HIGH COMMISSIONER FOR HUMAN RIGHTS (OHCHR), www.ohchr.org/en/NewsEvents/Pages/DisplayNews.aspx?NewsID=25769&LangID=E (April 3, 2020). *See also US Must Lift Its Cuba Embargo to Save Lives Amid COVID-19 Crisis, Say UN Experts*, OHCHR, www.ohchr.org/EN/NewsEvents/Pages/DisplayNews.aspx?NewsID=25848&LangID=E (April 30, 2020).
126 Shared Responsibility, *supra* note 120 at 1.
127 FSDR 2020, *supra* note 34 at iii.

There has never been a more urgent moment for international solidarity, the RtD, and the duty of international cooperation to be operationalized.[128] In the context of this chapter, this will require financing for development through aid and assistance as MOI to be ramped up at least to the ODA commitments made by DAC countries, and in the short term, much beyond. This must, however, happen not with the business-as-usual approach of charity or generosity, but through the normative lens of the duty to cooperate inherent in the RtD. The objective of financing for development through international aid and assistance must be realizing the RtD of the recipients and not the promotion of economic interests of the donors. Such aid and assistance, when given, must respect the right of recipients to participate in, contribute to, and enjoy development as defined by them. Respect for this troika means that donors must align their aid and assistance with development priorities, policies, and local systems of the right-holders, and ensure that aid is not tied with conditionalities that infringe on the RtD of the recipients. During and in the aftermath of COVID-19, such aid must certainly not be in the form of loans that are debt-augmenting for already fragile countries on the verge of unraveling. It is high time that mechanisms are adopted beyond the self-regulation-based evaluation of aid and assistance practices conducted by the OECD of its own DAC members. Current OECD mechanisms request recalcitrant countries for compliance because aid is seen as a charity; new mechanisms are needed that would admonish for non-compliance because aid carries duties. The zero draft of the proposed legally binding instrument on the RtD, negotiations on which are set to commence later in 2020, incorporates mechanisms conceived of on similar lines.[129] Ultimately, the only question before us is whether the SDGs should be realized as if they matter.

---

128 Obiora Okafor, *Solidarity Key to Post COVID-19 Response*, OPEN GLOBAL RIGHTS, www.openglobalrights.org/solidarity-key-to-post-covid-19-response/?lang=English (April 28, 2020).
129 Akram, *supra* note 94 at Arts. 24 and 26.

III
Integrating the SDGs

III

Integrating the SDGs

31 Interlinkages between Climate Change, Economic Inequality, and Human Migration

Joseph C. Morreale[1]

Introduction

Debates about climate change are as much about inequality, poverty, and distribution of power in a society as they are about whether scientists have enough evidence depicting the breadth and depth of climate change per se. This is because climate change effects are not equal and differ across nations. Poorer nations are more vulnerable than richer ones. Developing economies are more vulnerable than developed ones. Agricultural and manufacturing societies are more vulnerable than service-based ones. S. Nazrul Islam and J. Winkel in their paper, *Climate change and social inequality* state:

> Available evidence indicates that this relationship [climate change and social inequality] is characterized by a *vicious cycle*, whereby *initial* inequality causes the disadvantaged groups to suffer *disproportionately* from the adverse effects of climate change, resulting in greater *subsequent* inequality.[2]

Traditionally, scholars believed that underdeveloped and developing nations were responsible for much of the environmental impact. Yet today research shows that it is large economies, mostly the US and China, that are major CO_2 emitters and thus are key contributors to the "greenhouse effect" that is responsible for climate change. In fact, about 35% of the global carbon emissions originate in these two countries.[3] The Least Developed Countries (LDCs), on the other hand, are the ones that are most vulnerable to the environmental changes. A recent study by the Potsdam Institute for Climate Impact Research found strong evidence that global warming has increased global inequality due to the differential impact of global warming on annual economic growth. The authors asserted that over the course of decades, global warming has resulted in "substantial declines in economic output in hotter, poorer countries with simultaneous increases in many cooler, wealthier countries."[4] Global

---

1 The author wishes to acknowledge and thank his colleague, Dr. Anna Shostya, Associate Professor of Economics, Pace University, for her insightful and useful comments about and help in editing this chapter.
2 S. Nazrul Islam & John Winkel, *Climate Change and Social Inequality*, Dep. of Econ. and Soc. Affairs, DESA Working Paper No. 152 (Oct. 2017), www.un.org/esa/desa/papers/2017/wp152_2017.pdf.
3 T.A. Boden et al., *National CO2 Emissions from Fossil-Fuel Burning, Cement Manufacture, and Gas Flaring: 1751–2014*, Carbon Dioxide Information Analysis Center (2017), doi 10.3334/CDIAC/00001_V2017.
4 Noah S. Diffenbaugh & Marshall Burke, *Global Warming Has Increased Global Economic Inequality*, 116 pnas 9808–13 (May 14, 2019), https://doi.org/10.1073/pnas.1816020116.

climate change has decreased economic growth of countries in lower latitudes and has facilitated economic growth of countries in higher latitudes.

What is important to remember is that planetary environmental changes are not just about global warming. The term global warming is too narrow. Even climate change is too narrow. Intertwined with climate change are other significant alterations, such as ocean acidification, the redistribution of plant and animal species, ambient air pollution, and water contamination.[5] What forces contributed to these phenomena? Although there is a multitude of interrelated forces, the most fundamental ones have been economic growth and development. Over the course of the last 300 years, human activities have brought about an accelerated rate of environmental resource exploitation, urbanization, deforestation, industrial production, and consumption. Combined with a drastic increase in carbon emissions due to the burning of fossil fuels and increase in methane from livestock and manure, these changes have reshaped our planet and made weather less stable and less predictable.

Humans had to adapt to this unpredictability. Historically, this adaptation has taken many different forms and shapes, depending on the intensity and type of environmental impact, geographic location and terrain, financial constraints, and other factors. Flood defenses, early warning systems for hurricanes and cyclones, switching to alternative crops, and redesigning communication systems are some adaptation strategies. One of the most drastic solutions that humans have created is migration. Migration as a source and a result of economic growth has been explored in the scholarly literature extensively. Yet, environmental migration—moving from one's homeland to avoid the effects of climate change—has become the focus of the discussion among scholars only recently. This is exactly what this chapter focuses on—the interrelationships among inequality, human migration, and environmental changes.

Even though debates on the relationship between environmental change and migration and environmental change and inequality have intensified in the last decade, most discussions are uni-directional and oversimplified, focusing only on specific effects and failing to take into account a broader, more complex, picture. We will discuss a model that incorporates the interrelationships between these three global issues. We will do so by building on previous social science approaches and using case studies of specific countries that are vulnerable to environmental risks and economic instability. We will also assess the progress of four of the 17 Sustainable Development Goals (SDGs) of the United Nations' (UN) 2030 Agenda for Sustainable Development. In addition, the chapter discusses the role of government and policy choices dealing with these vulnerabilities, as well as with the new challenges associated with the ongoing COVID-19 pandemic. We offer some policy recommendations that suggest how to support implementation efforts and achieve the SDGs through both international and national strategies and the involvement of the public and private sectors of impacted countries.

Climate-Related Migration and Global Inequality

Although the term climate refugees is not legally accepted by the 1951 Refugee Convention or the UN, the UN recognizes climate change as a driver of migration.[6] According to the

---

5 Merrill Singer, Climate Change and Social Inequality: The Health and Social Costs of Global Warming 25 (Routledge: London & New York, 1st ed. 2018).
6 U.N. General Assembly, global compact for safe, orderly and regular migration, 9 (Dec. 10–11, 2018), www.un.org/pga/72/wp-content/uploads/sites/51/2018/07/180713_Agreed-Outcome_Global-Compact-for-Migration.pdf.

Internal Displacement Monitoring Centre (IDMC) worldwide data, over a period of eleven years (2008–2018), about 265.3 million people were displaced internally as a response to disasters.[7] In 2017, 68.5 million people were forcibly displaced, more than at any point in human history.[8] In 2018 alone, 17.2 million people in 144 countries and territories were newly displaced in the context of disasters within their own country.[9] According to some estimates, approximately one-third of these migrations were forced displacements caused by a sudden onset weather event, such as flooding, forest fires after droughts, and intensified storms.[10] While the remaining two-thirds of displacements are the result of other humanitarian crises, it is becoming obvious that climate change is also contributing to so-called slow-onset events such as desertification, sea level rise, ocean acidification, air pollution, rain pattern shifts, and loss of biodiversity.[11] This deterioration will exacerbate many humanitarian crises and may lead to more people being on the move. In 2018, the World Bank estimated that three regions (Latin America, sub-Saharan Africa, and Southeast Asia) will generate 143 million more climate migrants by 2050.[12]

While the majority of this mobility in the context of environmental disruption and climate change more generally (including disaster displacement), occurs within the borders of their countries, some people are forced to leave their homeland and move abroad.[13] Global data on cross-border movement in the context of disasters are, however, limited, with only a few notable cases being examined so far. In some cases, official sources on humanitarian visas by countries such as the United States, Brazil, and Argentina humanitarian visas for Haitians by countries can be used.[14,15] In 2018, the total new displacement of populations was 28.2 million, 17.2 of which were natural disasters caused primarily by extreme weather events, especially storms (9.3 million), and cyclones, hurricanes, and typhoons (7.9 million).[16] Particularly devastating were the southwest monsoons in India and Typhoon Mangkhut in China and the Philippines. Slow-onset processes such as droughts or sea level rise also increasingly affect people's mobility worldwide. Though specific data on migration due to these changes are not available, case studies do provide some insights.[17] These studies indicate that some of the relocation of communities in the context of environmental and climate change is also increasingly implemented by

---

7 INTERNAL DISPLACEMENT MONITORING CENTER (IDMC), *Global Report on Internal Displacement*, 2–3 (Geneva, Switzerland, 2019) www.internal displacement.org/global-report/grid2019 [hereinafter "IDMC"].
8 *Id.* at 6–11.
9 *Ibid.*
10 *Ibid.*
11 *Ibid.*
12 John Podesta, *The Climate Crisis, Migration, and Refugees*, BROOKINGS (Jul. 25, 2019) www.brookings.edu/research/the-climate-crisis-migration-and-refugees/ (last visited Nov. 18, 2020).
13 *See generally* DINA IONESCO ET AL., THE ATLAS OF ENVIRONMENTAL MIGRATION 2–20 (IOM 2017) [hereinafter "ATLAS"].
14 IDMC, *supra* note 7.
15 Humanitarian visas are granted by some countries to fulfill their international obligation to protect refugees from persecution. The Convention relating to the Status of Refugees (1951 Refugee Convention) is often used as the main criteria in assessing whether or not there is a legitimate claim for protection.
16 IDMC, *supra* note 7, at 2–3.
17 ATLAS, *supra* note 13; *see generally also* ETIENNE PIGUET & FRANK LACZKO (eds.), PEOPLE ON THE MOVE IN A CHANGING CLIMATE, 2nd Vol. (Springer Netherlands 2014).

governments.[18] Historically, tens of thousands of people have been relocated in Haiti[19] and in Vietnam;[20] hundreds of thousands in Ethiopia;[21] about a million in the Philippines;[22] and several million in China.[23]

The World Bank Report suggests that the most likely types of migration related to climate change will be the movement of impoverished people in developing countries from rural to urban areas and from coastal zones to inland areas.[24] The report uses the term vulnerability in stating that people living in areas where natural hazards are prevalent are most at risk to suffer forced migration. It asserts that environmental refugees are becoming a much larger factor in many developing countries and that the greatest risks with respect to forced migration will come from natural hazards and sea level rises. This is because of the many types of insecurities brought about by climate change.[25] These include

- Natural resource insecurity (risks associated with deforestation and land degradation);
- Food insecurity (due to the loss of productive land associated with desertification and drought);
- Water insecurity (this may be a result of more frequent and intense droughts, flash floods, and tsunamis);
- Energy insecurity (this is the result of unstable energy production and distribution infrastructure); and
- National insecurity (40% of all intrastate conflicts in the past 60 years are linked to the control and allocation of natural resources).[26]

Some types of human livelihood systems are inherently more impacted by particular climate stimuli than others. According to a recent study, between 1961 and 2010 rising temperatures have led to a 17–30% decline in per capita wealth in the poorest countries.[27] This yields a ratio between the top and bottom deciles that is 25% larger than in a world without global

---

18 For a summary of recent relocation programs, *see ibid.*; *see also* Grace Benton, *Planned Relocation: An Annotated Bibliography Update*, INSTITUTE FOR THE STUD. OF INT'L MIGRATION (Georgetown U. Walsh School of Foreign Service, May 2017), https://georgetown.app.box.com/s/v1496c75f0saouevj5yfump4k5am8shz.
19 *See generally* Hancy Pierre, *Defis, Enjeux et Politiques: Migrations, Environnment Et Changements Climatiques En Haiti*, 31–34 (IOM Oct. 2015) https://publications.iom.int/system/files/assessing_the_evidence_haiti.pdf.
20 *See generally* Han Entzinger & Peter Scholten, *Relocation as an Adaptation Strategy to Environmental Stress: Lessons from the Mekong River Delta in Viet Nam*, MIGRATION, ENV'T & CLIMATE CHANGE: POL'Y BRIEF SERIES Vol. 1 (6) (IOM Nov. 2015).
21 Foresight, *Migration and Global Environmental Change*, Final Project Report, 9–22, 177 ¶ 2 (The Gov't Office for Sci., London, UK 2011) [hereinafter "Foresight"].
22 Lloyd Ranque & Melissa Quetulio-Navarra, *"One Safe Future" in the Philippines*, FORCED MIGRATION REVIEW 49, at 51 May (2015), www.fmreview.org/climatechange-disasters/ranque-quetulionavarra.
23 *China*, IOM, www.iom.int/countries/china (last visited Nov. 18, 2020).
24 Kanta Kumari Rigaud et al., *Groundswell: Preparing for Internal Climate Migration*, THE WORLD BANK, at 18 (March 19, 2018), www.worldbank.org/en/news/infographic/2018/03/19/groundswell---preparing-for-internal-climate-migration.
25 *See generally* ROBERT MCLEMAN, CLIMATE AND HUMAN MIGRATION: PAST EXPERIENCES, FUTURE CHALLENGES (Cambridge University Press 2014).
26 *Groundswell, supra* note 24, at 18.
27 Marshall Burke & Noah Diffenbaugh, *Global Warming Has Increased Global Economic Inequality*, PNAS Vol. 116 (20) 9808–13, at 9809 (Potsdam Institute for Climate Impact Research, April 22, 2019).

warming. Populations in LDCs are especially vulnerable to climate change partly because of the disproportionate number of people participating in climate-sensitive livelihood systems (e.g. agriculture and fishing). Their survival depends on the productivity of land, access to fresh water, and forest resources. Therefore, land degradation, desertification, and forest depletion resulting from climate change often undermine, not just the security and development, but also the chances of survival of the people in LDCs. Recent statistics support this argument.[28] Small Island Developing States (SIDS)[29] have been disproportionately affected by natural hazards during the last decade. They are a group of small island countries that tend to share similar sustainable development challenges, including small but growing populations, limited resources, remoteness, susceptibility to natural disasters, vulnerability to external shocks, excessive dependence on international trade, and fragile environments.

Migration is a multi-causal and multidimensional phenomenon. In general, all scholars agree that for migration to take place, there must be some *push* factors that push people from their homeland and *pull* factors that pull people in specific new residence areas.[30] Perhaps one of the earliest models that combined all these factors together and delineated the role of environmental changes in migration decisions came from the 2011 London Government Office for Science report.[31] The report suggested that the decision to migrate is influenced by five broad categories of drivers: political economic, social, demographic, and environmental.[32] According to this model, climate change influences migration outcomes through affecting existing drivers of migration. Yet, it is really difficult to isolate and estimate its impact.

Environmental change is equally as likely to prevent migration as it is to cause migration. Migration decisions depend on a number of factors and personal and household characteristics. Substantial social, economic, and human capital may be required to enable people to migrate, especially internationally. Climate change may affect an environmental driver, such as agricultural productivity, and individuals who may not have adequate financial means will respond by migrating. Environmental change may also erode important assets and thus environmental change can make migration less likely. Therefore, climate change exacerbates global inequality as it increases poverty and deprivation in already impoverished regions.

---

28 *See Land and Human Security*, U.N. CONVENTION TO COMBAT DESERTIFICATION, www.unccd.int/issues/land-and-human-security (2019).

29 Currently, the United Nations Department of Economic and Social Affairs lists 57 small island developing states. These are broken down into three geographic regions: the Caribbean the Pacific; and Africa, Indian Ocean, Mediterranean and South China Sea (AIMS).

30 *See generally* George Borjas, *Economic Theory and International Migration*, INTERNATIONAL MIGRATION REVIEW 23 (3): 457–85 (1989); *see also* George Borjas, Immigration Economics (Harvard U. Press June 9, 2014).

31 Foresight, *supra* note 21.

32 More specifically, the included drivers are political: Discrimination/persecution, conflict/insecurity, and direct coercion; economic: Employment opportunities, income/wages/well-being, and cost of living; social: Seeking education and family/kin obligations; demographic: population size/density, population structure, and disease prevalence; and environmental: Exposure to hazard, ecosystem services, land productivity; habitability, and food/energy/water security.

Assessment of Progress toward Implementing the SDGs

Even though the international community has recognized potential risks associated with environmental degradation several decades ago, the specific interlinkages between environmental changes and sustainable development have become a center of attention only relatively recently. One of the most effective UN-initiated environmental treaties, the Montreal Protocol, enacted in 1987, has had more than 30 years of success in reducing the substances that deplete the ozone layer.[33] The Protocol now has 197 countries participating and resulted in the phasing-out of 99% of nearly 100 ozone-depleting chemicals.[34] Its success is attributed to effective leadership and innovative and highly flexible approaches that allowed for stricter controls over time.[35] The structure of the Protocol was built on five pillars. One was the trade provision, which called for limiting the signatories to trade only with the signatories.[36] Two, the requirements of countries were clearly articulated, so countries could plan to meet the requirement.[37] Three, it provided a stable framework that allowed the private sector to plan long-term research and innovation as companies adjusted to the new regulations.[38] Four, a Multilateral Fund provided funding for developing countries to help them meet their compliance targets.[39] And the fifth pillar dealt specifically with the problem of non-compliant countries.[40] This was the Protocol's compliance procedure to help the laggards to meet the requirements. It created a procedure set up by a UN agency to prepare an action plan to return them to compliance and gain funding resources from the Multilateral Fund for short-term projects.[41]

The success of the Montreal Protocol, however, is one sided and does not address the interconnection of environmental sustainability and other developmental issues. The UN targeted sustainability much more holistically when it introduced 17 SDGs in 2016. Given the focus of this chapter on the interconnections among climate change, inequality, and human migration, we assess the following four specific UN SDGs:

- **SDG 10 (especially Target 10.7)**: Reduce Inequality Within and Among Countries (see the list of all Targets in Appendix);
- **SDG 13**: Take Urgent Action to Combat Climate Change and Its Impacts (see the list of all Targets in Appendix);
- **SDG 14**: Conserve and Sustainably Use the Oceans, Sea, and Marine Resources for Sustainable Development;

---

33 Naomi Schalit, *Saving the Ozone Layer: Why the Montreal Protocol Worked*, THE CONVERSATION (Sep. 9, 2020), https://theconversation.com/saving-the-ozone-layer-why-the-montreal-protocol-worked-9249.
34 Id.
35 It should be pointed out that the Nagoya Protocol enabled the Montreal Protocol to mitigate climate change. *See* Nagoya Protocol on Access to Genetic Resources and the Fair and Equitable Sharing of Benefits Arising from their Utilization, 29 October 2010, 3008 U.N.T.S. 1 (entered into force 12 October 2014).
36 Schalit, *supra* note 33.
37 Id.
38 Id.
39 Ibid.
40 Ibid.
41 *Tribute to Dr. Mario Molina (1943–2020)*, MULTILATERAL FUND, www.multilateralfund.org/default.aspx.

- **SDG 15**: Protect, Restore, and Promote Sustainable Use of Terrestrial Ecosystems, Sustainably Manage Forests, Combat Desertification, and Halt and Reverse Land Degradation and Halt Biodiversity Loss.

In **SDG 10**, the 2030 Agenda directly calls for reducing income inequality, yet income inequality continues to rise in many parts of the world, particularly in LDCs. The UN measures inequality using the Kuznets ratio.[42] It finds that although the income of the poorest groups (the bottom 40%) were growing at a faster rate than the national average, they still received less than 25% of the overall national income.[43] The UN Development Program is one of the main Organizations with a specific focus on migration and displacement. It has four specific policy areas that address **SDG 10.7** (Facilitate orderly, safe, regular, and responsible migration):

- Addressing the root causes of displacement and mitigating the negative drivers of migration and factors compelling people to leave their homes;
- Supporting governments to integrate migration and displacement issues in national and local development plans;
- Supporting refugees, migrants, internally displaced persons (IDPs), and host communities to cope, recover, and sustain development gains in crisis and post-crisis situations;
- Supporting national and local authorities to achieve sustainable community based re/integration.[44]

The overall conclusion from the review of the progress toward the SDGs achievement is that it is being made but at a slower pace than the UN 2030 Agenda targets. Even though more than three-quarters of 105 countries that were surveyed developed policies to facilitate safe and orderly migration, only slightly more than half of them had policies on migrants' rights and their socioeconomic well-being. Another area where the world has fallen below the 2030 target is the transaction costs of migrant remittances. In 2018, none of the world regions had costs lower than 5.4%, with sub-Saharan Africa having almost double that. This is well below the Target (10.C) of less than 3% set by the UN. It is not likely that any remittance corridors with costs higher than 5% across all regions and countries will be eliminated by 2030, according to the UN's goal.[45]

In **SDG 13**, the 2030 Agenda directly focuses on the climate change problem. Unfortunately, the four-year review indicates that greenhouse gas (GHG) levels "continue to climb, climate change is occurring much faster than anticipated, and its effects are evident

---

42 *Note*: The Kuznets Ratio is a measurement of the ratio of income going to the highest-earning households (usually defined by the upper 20%) and the income going to the lowest-earning households, which is commonly measured by either the lowest 20% or lowest 40% of income. Its values go between 0 and 1. As the ratio rises, income inequality becomes less unequal and more equal.
43 *See* UN STATS: *SDG 10 Reduce Inequality within and among Countries*, UNstats.un.org/sdgs/report/2020/goal-10.
44 *Promoting Development Approaches to Migration and Displacement*, UNDP (Updated Feb. 2019), www.undp.org/content/undp/en/home/librarypage/crisis-prevention-and-recovery/development-approaches-to-migration-and-displacement_4_areas.html.
45 The Sustainable Development Goals Report, at 13, UNITED NATIONS (2019), https://unstats.un.org/sdgs/report/2019/The-Sustainable-Development-Goals-Report-2019.pdf.

worldwide."[46] In fact, in 2017, atmospheric CO_2 concentration was 146% of the preindustrial levels, which is well above the 2030 targets. According to SDG 13, in order to reduce the global warming effect, global carbon emissions have to be reduced to 55% of 2010 levels by 2030 and then need to continue the descending trend to zero by 2050.[47] Many developing countries have only launched processes to formulate and implement national adaptation plans (NAPs) to reduce their vulnerability and integrate the adaptation into national development planning. Of the 186 countries that signed the Paris Agreement in 2016, 91 (49%) have adopted NAPs and only 14 of these (15%) have developed implementation strategies. Moreover, climate-related financial sources have increased ($681 billion in 2016) but are small in comparison to the scale of the problem, and this amount is surpassed by the funding for fossil fuels ($781 billion in 2016).

SDG 14 focuses on the adverse effects of ocean acidification, climate change, and sea level rise, coastal erosion, overfishing, and the decline of future fishing stocks, the heating up of the ocean and its effect on hampering the ocean's role in moderating climate change, and land–based pollutants and marine debris that threaten coastal habitats. Some progress has been made in the areas of stabilizing the decline in fish stocks, increasing marine protected areas, and developing greater government roles in combating illegal, unreported, and unregulated fishing.[48] Yet, water acidity has been rising, which endangers marine life and less than half of the worlds' coastal regions improved their coastal water quality by 2018.[49]

SDG 15 deals with desertification, land degradation, loss of forest acreage, and continuing decline in biodiversity. Land degradation is affecting one-fifth of the Earth's land area and the lives of 1 billion people. The change in land degradation during the period 2000–2015 ranged from 22.4% to 35.5% in the various regions of the world. Those regions that were above 20% included Oceania, Central and South Asia, Latin America, Eastern and South-Eastern Asia, and sub-Saharan Africa. Moreover, during the same period, forest area as a percentage of total land area decreased from 31.1% to 30.7%.[50] This represents the loss of more than 58 million hectares of forests. Most of the loss occurred in the tropics with the most sizable declines found in Latin America and sub-Saharan Africa. The conversion of forest land for agricultural use, such as growing crops and raising livestock to meet growing population demand for food, is considered the key driver in the loss of forests acreage. As reported by the UN update on the progress of this goal, there has been some progress on **SDG 15** in protecting terrestrial ecosystems and biodiversity. Forest loss is slowing down and more financial assistance is going to biodiversity protection. However, the 2030 targets of sustainable development are "unlikely to be met" since degradation continues and biodiversity loss is occurring at an "accelerated rate."[51]

Having reviewed the assessment by the UN of the progress on the four important SDGs in this study, in the next two sections, we provide an analysis of implemented policies and case studies.

---

46 *Id.* at 48.
47 *Ibid.*
48 *Ibid.*
49 *Ibid.*
50 *Id.* at 18.
51 *Ibid.*

Policies to Curb Carbon Emissions in Developed Countries: Case Studies

The European Union

Many European countries have adopted national programs aimed at reducing emissions, with the European Union (EU) being a leader in setting the targets and specific measures and monitoring them. Having achieved its objectives under the Kyoto Protocol for the period from 2008 to 2012, the EU adopted the 20-20-20 target for 2020—a 20% reduction of greenhouse gas emissions compared with 1990, a 20% share of renewables in EU energy consumption, and 20% energy efficiency improvement. To achieve this target, a cap was set for the EU Emissions Trading System (ETS). For emissions in sectors not covered by the ETS, individual national targets were set under the Effort Sharing Decision.[52] At the same time, the EU has adopted legislation to increase the use of renewable energy, such as wind, solar, hydro, and biomass, and to improve the energy efficiency of a wide array of equipment and household appliances. The EU also aims to support the development of carbon capture and storage technologies to trap and store CO_2 emitted by power stations and other large installations.[53] As part of a framework of climate and energy policies, the EU has set a binding target to cut emissions in the EU territory by 2030 to levels at least 40% below those in 1990. An EU mechanism monitors Member State climate change mitigation policies and uses measures according to the United Nations Framework Convention on Climate Change (UNFCCC) and the Kyoto Protocol. It also evaluates and reports progress toward meeting the goals.

The United States (US)

In contrast to the EU's bold strategies and deterministic approach to curb carbon emissions and slow down the effects of climate change, the US has recently taken the position as a bystander. President Donald Trump announced on June 1, 2017, that the US would withdraw from the Paris Agreement.[54] He argued that the voluntary agreement was not necessary since the harmful effects of climate change "have not been proven" and that such an agreement would be detrimental to the national economic interests of the US[55] He also has been concerned that the Agreement

- Saddles the US with a $3 billion commitment to the UN to provide aid to developing countries;
- Intrudes on American sovereignty to set its own environmental standards;
- Biases US energy production choices in moving away from fossil fuel-produced energy from coal and oil to alternative low-carbon-using processes which are more expensive;

---

52 *Overall Progress towards the EU's 20-20-20 Climate and Energy Targets*, EUROPEAN ENVIRONMENT AGENCY (Aug. 3, 2018), www.eea.europa.eu/themes/climate/trends-and-projections-in-europe/trends-and-projections-in-europe-2017/overall-progress-towards-the-european.
53 *Climate Change Mitigation*, EUROPEAN ENVIRONMENTAL AGENCY, www.eea.europa.ed/themes/climate-change-mitigation-in-EU-countries.
54 Michael D. Shear, *Trump Will Withdraw the U.S. From the Paris Climate Agreement*, NEW YORK TIMES (Jun. 1, 2017), www.nytimes.com/2017/06/01/climate/trump-paris-climate-agreement.html.
55 *Id.*

- Reduces the employment of workers in the coal mining and oil production industries and forces a reduction in automobile production and usage; and
- Restricts future economic growth.[56]

On November 4, 2020, the US became the first nation in the world to formally withdraw from the Paris agreement. Trump's policy is a reversal of President Obama's Climate Change Policy that, as early as June of 2013 (before the Paris Agreement), offered a detailed action plan (including a shift from coal power to solar and natural gas production) to reduce CO_2 emissions by 17% by 2020. Obama pledged to bypass Congress to tackle climate change and agreed to a contribution of $3 billion to aid developing countries in dealing with the impacts of climate change.[57] In November of 2014, the US and China, the two largest polluters, signed a joint agreement to work together to lead the world in cutting carbon emissions.[58] According to this agreement, the US agreed to reduce CO_2 emissions by 26–28% from its 2005 level by 2025.[59]

The Trump decision clearly indicated one of the major weaknesses of the Paris Agreement in that it made participation, planning, and goal setting voluntary for the nations of the world. This voluntary nature of the agreement requires the UN to have more impactful policies to both maintain the involvement of the major polluting countries and to achieve the SDGs. It is fortunate that President Biden was elected in the November 2020 presidential election. He quickly reversed the decision of President Trump and reinstated the US's inclusion in the Paris Agreement.

China

China is moving ahead to make up for the US withdrawal and to take the lead in climate change policy. It has already invested heavily in green technologies such as electric cars, wind turbines, and solar panels.[60] In fact, President Xi Jinping agreed to stop increasing carbon emissions by 2030 and increase clean-energy sources to 20% of China's total energy production. China has taken a bold step to build the world's largest cap-and-trade policy program[61] through the use of carbon emissions permits.[62] One can only hope that these new initiatives can counter the potential negative impact that could come about due to the US decision. Given the Trump political position, a shift in diplomatic strategy has already begun. The EU worked to confirm both the EU's and China's commitment to the Paris Agreement. It also provided millions of dollars to aid Chinese emission control efforts.[63]

---

56 Lisa Friedman, *Trump Serves Notice to Quit Paris Climate Agreement*, NEW YORK TIMES (Nov. 4, 2019), www.nytimes.com/2019/11/04/climate/trump-paris-agreement-climate.html.
57 *Id*.
58 Mark Lander, *U.S. and China Reach Climate Accord After Months of Talks*, NEW YORK TIMES (Nov 11, 2014), www.nytimes.com/2014/11/15/us/politics/obama-climate-change-fund-3-billion-announcement.html.
59 *Id*.
60 Keith Bradsher & Lisa Friedman, *China Unveils an Ambitious Plan to Curb Climate Change Emissions*, NEW YORK TIMES (Dec. 19, 2017), www.nytimes.com/2017/12/19/climate/china-carbon-market-climate-change-emissions.html.
61 *Note*: Europe and California already use the cap-and-trade model. It sets a ceiling for greenhouse gas emissions and allows businesses to buy and sell emissions permits.
62 Chris Buckley, *Xi Jinping Is Set for a Big Gamble with China's Carbon Trading Market*, NEW YORK TIMES (June 23, 201), www.nytimes.com/2017/06/23/world/asia/china-cap-trade-carbon-greenhouse.html.
63 UN News, *China, EU Reaffirm Strong Commitment to Paris Agreement* (Jul. 17, 2018), https://unfccc.int/news/china-eu-reaffirm-strong-commitment-to-paris-agreement.

Mitigation and Adaptation Policies in Affected Less Developed Countries: Case Studies

While major emitters' policies focus on reducing carbon emissions, LDCs have been designing mitigation and adaptation policies that help them survive the effects of climate change. Some of these policies are short-term, as they address unpredictable cataclysmic events, such as hurricane Mathew that hit Haiti in 2016 or major floods that impacted Indonesia in January 2020. The environmental emigration policies in such cases often have been coordinated by the impacted countries and the countries that receive refugees. Affected countries also have introduced policies that deal with long-term effects of climate change, such as deforestation, desertification, and land degradation. The Spencer report focuses on four case studies of mitigation and adaptation policies.[64] These include a deforestation and forest degradation program in Indonesia, a mangrove restoration project ongoing in Guyana, a wastewater recycling and reuse program for productive use in Lima, Peru, and soil and water conservation management projects and policies in Burkina Faso and Niger.[65]

Due to a vast variety of country-specific policies, it is nearly impossible to generalize them. A case-study approach may offer a better way to describe mitigation and adaptation strategies that have been introduced by some countries in response to certain effects of climate change. In this chapter, we provide three case studies: Haiti, Darfur in Sudan, and Indonesia.

Haiti, Latin America

With a $1,656 Gross Domestic Product (GDP) per capita in Purchasing Power Parity (PPP) (in 2018)[66] and a number four ranking in terms of the Global Climate Risk Index,[67] Haiti is a classic example of an LDC that has been suffering from short-term and long-term climate change effects. In fact, during the 20-year period (1998–2017), Haiti lost on average around $420 million (PPP)[68] in GDP and about 280 people annually due to extreme weather events.[69] The short-term policies to deal with such events have been introduced in 2010 and focus on mitigation of human losses, infrastructure and housing destruction, and migration.[70] The United Nations Development Program (UNDP) reports

> Appropriate adaptation measures that are currently being given priority implementation are in the following project sectors: Coastal/Marine ecosystems, Water Resources,

---

64 For more details and more country-specific policies, *see* Benjamin Spencer et al., *Case Studies in Co-Benefits Approaches to Climate Change Mitigation and Adaptation*, 60 J. OF ENVTL. PLANNING AND MGMT. 647–67 (2016), http://dx.doi.org/10.1080/09640568.2016.1168287.
65 *Id.*
66 *See World Bank Group*, https://data.worldbank.org/indicator/Haiti.
67 The Global Climate Risk Index is calculated annually by GermanWatch and is based on the number of fatalities and losses in US$. The index is also reported for the period of 20 years—1998–2017; *See Global Climate Risk Index* 2020, GERMAN WATCH, germanwatch.org/en/17307.
68 One popular macroeconomic analysis metric to compare economic productivity and standards of living between countries is purchasing power parity (PPP). It is an economic theory that compares different countries' currencies through a "basket of goods" approach; *see* Mary Hall, *What Is Purchasing Power Parity (PPP)?*, INVESTOPEDIA (Aug. 19, 2020), www.investopedia.com/PPP.
69 *See Global Climate Risk Index* 2020, *supra* note 66.
70 *See Climate Change*, HAITI ADVOCACY WORKING GROUP, https//haitiadvocacy.org/climate-change.

Terrestrial ecosystems and Food security. Every two to three years, Haiti faces cyclones, storms or tropical depressions. These events constitute the most fatal natural disasters and are responsible for floods, landslides, tidal wave, epidemics, loss of cattle and cultures and destruction of infrastructures and habitats.[71]

The long-term adaptation policies in Haiti aim at restoration of the land (for example, protection of the land by constructing barriers and stabilizing sand dunes for wind protection), reforestation (planting new trees and restoring forests), developing sustainable agricultural practices, and investing more aid in rural development.[72] Some of the policy recommendations today include making the environment a national priority and part of economic development strategies.[73] Preparing for disasters is generally more cost-effective than responding with adaptation strategies after the fact. The fundamental problem is that countries in the Caribbean all too often underinvest in risk reduction and prevention.[74]

Sudan, North Africa

A very compelling example of the intertwining of warfare and conflict and climate change is seen in Sudan. In 2017, the combined effects of civil war and drought left nearly 5 million people (over 40% of the country's population) food-insecure.[75] Conflict is not a new phenomenon in Sudan and South Sudan—it has been ongoing for close to 40 years, causing millions of civilian deaths over that period. Long-running tensions in the era following British colonial occupation between the Arab–Islamic central government in Khartoum and the predominantly non-Arab south in Sudan led to one of the longest civil wars in African history. First from 1955 to 1972, and then again from 1983 to 2005, conflict between the North and South of the country has persisted, culminating in the Comprehensive Peace Agreement that led to South Sudan's independence vote in 2011.[76]

Darfur, an isolated western-most region of Sudan, where the war is still ongoing, has been labeled the "first climate change conflict" by many observers, given the convergence of environmental and political factors leading to conflict.[77] Sudan and the Darfur region are home to diverse ecological zones, ranging from arid deserts in the north to semi-tropical environments in the south. In the decades leading up to the 2003 outbreak of war, the Sahel region of northern Sudan had witnessed the Sahara Desert advance southward by almost a mile each year and a decrease in annual median rainfall of 15 to 30%.[78] These long-term climatic trends have had significant consequences for Sudan's two predominant, and sometimes competing, agricultural systems: Small farmers relying on rain-fed production and

---

71 See UNDP, *Climate Change Adaptation: Haiti*, www.adaptation-undp.org/explore/caribbean/haiti.
72 Vereda Johnson Williams, *A Case Study of Desertification in Haiti*, 4 JOURNAL OF SUSTAINABLE DEVELOPMENT, 20–31 (Jun. 3, 2011).
73 Id.
74 Inci Otker & Krishna Srinivasan, *Bracing for the Storm: For the Caribbean, Building Resilience Is a Matter of Survival*, 55 FINANCE & DEVELOPMENT 48–51 (Mar. 2018), www.imf.org/external/pubs/ft/fandd/2018/03/otker.htm.
75 Chase Sova, *The First Climate Change Conflict*, WORLD FOOD PROGRAM USA (Nov. 30, 2017), www.wfpusa.org/articles/the-first-climate-change-conflict/ (last visited Nov. 18, 2020).
76 Id.
77 Jeffrey Mazo, *Chapter Three: Darfur: The First Modern Climate-Change Conflict*, 49 THE ADELPHI PAPERS, 73–86, https://doi.org/10.1080/19445571003755538.
78 Id.

nomadic pastoralists. Fast-moving desertification and drought slowly eroded the availability of natural resources to support livelihoods and the peaceful coexistence of these two groups in the region. As the UN Secretary General Ban Ki-moon commented in 2007, "Amid the diverse social and political causes, the Darfur conflict began as an ecological crisis, arising at least in part from climate change."[79]

Indonesia, South-East Asia

Another example of an LDC that has been suffering from both short-term effects and long-term effects of climate change is Indonesia. From 1998 to 2017, Indonesia lost on average $1.8 billion in GDP (PPP) and 252 people per year due to extreme weather events.[80] Indonesia also faces the environmental impact of sea level rise, coastal erosion, and land subsidence. Combined with a high population density and concentration of economic activities in low elevation coastal zones, these climate change effects make Indonesia particularly vulnerable and result in displaced coastal villages and a great number of environmental refugees. Adding to this vulnerability is the fact that low-income urban coastal residents are highly dependent on their natural resources. Most households derive their income from fishing, fishponds, or agricultural activity. Rising ocean surface temperatures, ocean acidification and pollution, and unsustainable fishing practices impact the coastal population by damaging infrastructure, water supplies, and fish stock. Faced with a reduction in income, some coastal residents choose to migrate further inland or to an urban center. This exacerbates the inequality within the country.

Indonesia also has had long-term problems of forest fires and deforestation, mostly because of commercial activities. Small farmers in Indonesia have long practiced slash-and-burn agriculture, but in recent decades, large corporations have expanded and commercialized the practice. They dig drainage canals through peatlands (that provide a habitat for rare species) to float out logs and dry out the peat to plant dryland crops, especially oil palm and acacia trees for pulp and paper. They set fires that burn out of control and release vast quantities of greenhouse gases. In fact, Indonesian tropical peatlands, 36% of the world's total, hold an estimated 28.1gigatons of carbon, according to a 2017 study—more than all the country's upland forests.[81]

Indonesia has taken a number of counter measures to reduce environmental damage. In 2014, the government of Indonesia launched its National Action Plan that introduced a number of short-term and long-term policies to mitigate the effects of climate change. Some deal with improved climate and disaster resilient infrastructure. At the family level, these include elevating household home infrastructure and building water-resistant platforms to protect family valuables. At the village level, they include building wave breaks, developing natural barriers made from mud or mangrove reforestation, and creating draining and pumping systems to reduce flooding. More long-term human capital adaptation programs

---

79 Ibid.
80 See WORLD BANK OPEN DATA, https://data.world bank.org/indicator/Indonesia.
81 Dennis Nomile, *Indonesia's Fires Are Bad but New Measures Prevented Them from Becoming Worse*, SCIENCE (October 1, 2019), www.sciencemag.org/news/2019/10/indonesias-fires-are-bad-new-measures-prevented-them-becoming-worse (last visited Nov. 18, 2020).

include livelihood diversification through increased education, improvement of skill levels of the rural population, and the development of alternative sources of income.[82]

In January 2016, the government established the Peatland Restoration Agency (BRG)[83] in Jakarta, in an attempt to restore more than 2.6 million hectares of degraded peatlands by 2020. The agency blocks drainage canals and also replants degraded areas with native vegetation and encourages local communities to use the lands in a sustainable way for fishing and planting crops adapted to wetlands. By the end of 2018, the agency had initiated restoration projects in 366 villages in seven provinces.[84] The Indonesian government also made permanent a temporary moratorium on converting primary forests and peatlands to agricultural use and promised stricter enforcement of laws (including criminal prosecution) that make concession holders responsible for fires in their holdings.

There are many loopholes, however, that limit the effectiveness of both BRG's efforts and the ban on forest conversion. The maps defining where the permanent moratorium applies are incomplete and often revised. And enforcement is lax. Indonesian courts found a number of concession holders liable for damages from the 2015 fires, but the government has still not moved to collect payment.[85] Bolder and more aggressive actions are needed, including stricter enforcement of a ban on setting fires.

A New Ongoing Challenge of the COVID-19 Pandemic

Whether the world will achieve the 2030 Agenda goals depends not only on current trends but also on how these trends are affected by unexpected global events, like the ongoing COVID-19 pandemic. Shutting down tourism, restricting movement of people, close down of factories and small businesses, lockdowns, and quarantines, have reduced demand and supply for many goods and services and drastically reduced demand for fossil fuels. Between January and March of 2020, demand for coal dropped by 8% and oil by 5%, compared with the same period in 2019. By the end of the year, energy demand may be down 6% overall, according to the International Energy Agency.[86] What effect will this have on carbon emissions in the short run and long run?

Emissions in 2020 are expected to be 2–7% lower than in 2019, if the global lockdowns only continue until mid-June and around 3–13% if the lockdowns stay in place until the end of the year.[87] This, however, does not mean that the world is well on track to meet SDG 13 by 2030. Empirical evidence from the collapse of the Soviet Union in 1991, the Asian financial crisis of 1997, and the Great Recession of 2007–2009 suggests that emissions "stumble briefly before beginning to rise again."[88] Also, climate change is a cumulative phenomenon

---

82 Adriana Sierra Leal & Meylin Gonzales Huaman, *Migration, Environment and Climate Change in Coastal Cities in Indonesia, Migration, Environment and Climate Change: Policy Brief Series*, 5 IOM UN Migration 1–13 (Nov. 2019), https://publications.iom.int/system/files/pdf/policy_brief_series_vol5_issue2.pdf.

83 Humas, *President Jokowi Establishes Peat Land Restoration Agency (BRG)*, Cabinet Secretariat Of The Republic of Indonesia (Jan. 14, 2016), https://setkab.go.id/en/president-jokowi-establishes-peat-land-restoration-agency-brg/ (last visited Nov. 18, 2020).

84 Nomile, *supra* note 79.

85 Id.

86 *The Other Crisis: Can Covid Help Flatten the Climate Curve?*, The Economist (May 21, 2020), www.economist.com/briefing/2020/05/21/can-covid-help-flatten-the-climate-curve.

87 Id.

88 Ibid.

and one year drop, even the largest one we have seen, may only make a marginal difference or may not make any difference at all.

The COVID-19 pandemic may also slow down the progress toward SDG 10. This is because the pandemic is straining some countries' generous positions toward their many refugees and migrants and is exacerbating anti-immigrant feelings in those countries where sentiments toward immigrants were negative to begin with. Countries that employ migrant labor from neighboring states set up travel restrictions and shed many informal jobs due to the severe cuts in business activities. A strict lockdown in Colombia, for example, left many Venezuelan immigrants worse-off. At least 12,000 of them lost their jobs and had to return to Venezuela.[89] This means that the pandemic outbreak may have long-term effects of reducing migration flows between countries and thus increase inequality between and within countries.

Conclusions and Policy Recommendations

There is a new emphasis in disaster-prone nations, particularly developing nations, on the financial preparation and adaptation to environmental risks. Better preparation and preventive measures would greatly help the LDCs to face the costs of extreme weather events. Yet recent experience of these countries still sees underinvestment in these preventive measures. This is because obtaining funds to prepare for a disaster is limited and insurance coverage remains low given its high cost and high risk for insurers. Recognizing these issues, in June 2019, the IMF endorsed the investment in resilience building by disaster-prone nations to reduce expected losses, improve economic stability, and provide better continuity of public services.[90] The IMF has outlined a three-pronged approach. The first one deals with improvements in infrastructure, telecommunications, water supplies, and sanitation systems. The second is post-disaster and social resilience contingency planning and investments to ensure an efficient disaster response focusing on minimal disruption of public services, such as for sheltering people and providing immediate and medium-term direct relief. Finally, there is a special focus on creating financial resilience in advance of potential disasters. To implement all three parts of this approach, the International Monetary Fund (IMF) has put forth specific policies for 12 Caribbean countries that have suffered the largest damage costs in relation to their GDP since 1950.[91]

The World Bank has also been playing an increasing role in developing policies and strategies to help at-risk nations to deal with environmental and physical damages brought about by climate change. It has established the Caribbean Catastrophe Risk Insurance Facility (CCRIF) and the Catastrophe Draw Down Option to aid high-risk Caribbean nations. The former allows governments to limit the financial impact of natural disasters by providing quick liquidity when a major disaster strikes. However, the payouts by the CCRIF have been inadequate relative to actual costs. Catastrophe Bonds have been created to allow private markets to fund the risks and gain a return on their bonds through regular coupon

---

89 Bogota, *Colombia Cools on Venezuelan Refugees: The Welcome Mat Frays*, THE ECONOMIST (May 2, 2020).
90 Bob Simison, *Investing in Resilience: Disaster-Prone Countries Strengthening Their Ability to Withstand Climate Events*, 56 FINANCE & DEVELOPMENT 22–25 (Dec. 19, 2019).
91 *Id.*

payments. The second program provides immediate access to emergency funding through a credit line that can be accessed by middle-income nations suffering from natural disasters.[92]

There are also two other sources of funding established by the UN: Official Development Assistance (ODA) from Organization for Economic Co-operation and Development (OECD)/Development Assistance Committee (DAC)[93] countries and the Green Climate Fund.[94] The former is specifically referenced in SDG 17.2 with a recommended target of 0.70% of GNI to be devoted to ODA by developed countries.[95] However, the actual disbursement of $152.8 billion is only 0.30% making the implementation well short of the recommended target.[96] The Green Climate Fund was supposed to devote $103 billion per year to support developing countries in mitigation and adaptation work. We are well short of this target, as well.

Aside from funding sources to aid developing countries, the two main measures taken to reduce the effects of climate change are a carbon tax and cap-and-trade programs.[97] Ian Parry, a principal environmental fiscal policy expert in the IMF, has argued that the main rationale for carbon taxes "is that they are generally an effective tool for meeting domestic emission mitigation commitments."[98] Increases in taxes, however, are very hard to sell in democracies. Moreover, in using a carbon tax, it is difficult in practice to achieve specific levels of CO_2 emissions. The other approach is the use of a cap-and-trade program that specifies that maximum amount of carbon that could be emitted and permits would be restricted to meet the target. The EU has attempted this approach with some modest success, and China is now implementing this policy on a large scale. However, governments using the cap-and-

---

92 Otker, *supra* note 72; *see also* Francis Ghesquiere et al., *Caribbean Catastrophe Risk Insurance Facility: A Solution to the Short-Term Liquidity Needs of Small Island States in the Aftermath of Natural Disasters*, FINANCING FOR RELIEF AND DEV., www.wmo.int/pages/prog/drr/events/cat-insurance-wrm-markets-2007/documents/Session%204/Documents/CS%208%20-%20Mahul%20-%20WB%20Caribbean%20Facilty.pdf (last visited Nov. 18, 2020).

93 *See Official Development Assistance (ODA)*, OECD, www.oecd.org/dac/financing-sustainable-development/development-finance-standards/official-development-assistance.htm. Official development assistance flows are defined as those flows to countries and territories on the DAC List of ODA Recipients and to multilateral development institutions which are provided by official agencies, including state and local governments, or by their executive agencies; and each transaction of which is administred with the promotion of the economic development and welfare of developing countries as its main objective.

94 *Note* the Green Climate Fund (GCF) is the world's largest dedicated fund helping developing countries reduce their greenhouse gas emissions and enhance their ability to respond to climate change. It was set up by the United Nations Framework Convention on Climate Change (UNFCCC) in 2010. GCF has a crucial role in serving the Paris Agreement, supporting the goal of keeping average global temperature rise well below 2°C. It does this by channeling climate finance to developing countries, which have joined other nations in committing to climate action. *See* THE GREEN CLIMATE FUND, www.greenclimate.fund/.

95 UN SDG 17.2 Developed countries to implement fully their official development assistance commitments, including the commitment by many developed countries to achieve the target of 0.7% of ODA/Gross National Income (GNI) to developing countries and 0.15 to 0.20%of ODA/GNI to least developed countries; ODA providers are encouraged to consider setting a target to provide at least 0.20% of ODA/GNI to least developed countries.

96 ODA 2019 detailed summary, *Aid by DAC Members Increases in 2019 with More Aid to the Poorest Countries*, OECD (Apr. 16, 2020), www.oecd.org/dac/financing-sustainable-development/development-finance-data/ODA-2019-detailed-summary.pdf (last visited Nov. 18, 2020).

97 *Hot and Bothered: Special Report Climate Change*, THE ECONOMIST 13–14 (Nov. 28, 2016); *How to Design Carbon Taxes*, FINANCE & ECON. (Aug. 18, 2018), www.economist.com/finance-and-economics/2018/08/18/how-to-design-carbon-taxes.

98 Ian Parry, *Putting a Price on Pollution: Carbon Pricing Strategies Could Hold the Key to Meeting the World's Climate Stabilization Goals*, 16–19 FINANCE & DEV. (Dec. 2019).

trade policy have typically sold or handed out an oversupply of permits, thereby reducing the price of emissions and blunting the incentive to cut CO_2 emissions. Either approach requires many countries to adopt these policies; otherwise there is an incentive for countries to "free ride."

Thus, we offer some additional recommendations to address the issue of climate change and ensure the achievement of the four SDGs that are associated with it:

1 **Recommendation 1**: There is a great need to unite the global efforts to mitigate migration flows. Whether in terms of limited access to clean water, food scarcity, agricultural degradation, or violent conflict, climate change will intensify these challenges and be a significant push factor in human migration patterns. As a result, there will be a continuing rise in human migration of environmental refugees. The UN must insist upon acknowledgment and acceptance of the definition of "environmental refugees" to ensure universal support. It is also necessary to establish legal status for these increasing refugees and grant them the same protections as are granted to other classes of refugees.
2 **Recommendation 2**: Multilateral institutions, development agencies, and international law must do far more to thoroughly examine the challenges of climate change. Neither a multilateral strategy nor a legal framework exists to account for climate change as a driver of migration. This is sorely needed.
3 **Recommendation 3**: President Trump's withdrawal of the US from the Paris Agreement must be countered by the UN. The UN could emulate the past success of the Montreal Protocol treaty by bringing together all nations to develop a protocol for the development and implementation of policies that are designed to achieve SDG 13. A carbon tax would also be very helpful, but a targeted approach at high carbon using products for non-compliant countries would be more effective. A special fund like the Multilateral Fund could also be established particularly to help developing nations in creating national plans for ameliorating and mitigating environmental disasters especially in rural areas that would lead to environmental migration.
4 **Recommendation 4**: Subsidizing consumer purchases of either hybrid or electric cars would reduce black carbon emissions and so would developing cheap, clean stoves for the populations of poor developing countries. In addition, we recommend increasing the funding for new technologies that are cheaper and more dependable than present-day solar farms and wind turbines.
5 **Recommendation 5**: There is much that can be done to incentivize private companies to become more committed to achieving the UN's SDG 13 and thereby help to reduce the effect of climate change on environmental migration. In fact, companies around the world have already started getting involved in tackling air pollution, motivated by the opportunity to innovate in clean technologies, sustainable products, and clean-air solutions. In addition, they are incentivized by the changes in consumer behavior, as more consumers want brands that are environmentally friendly. One way to foster promotion of best practices and showcasing companies' successful efforts is through the UN Global Compact that was established in 2000. Being one of the most ambitious corporate initiatives to encourage sustainability by private companies and enjoying a voluntary membership of more than 10,000 organizations from 166 countries, allows signatories to retain their membership for one year without producing a report on

progress.[99] Many organizations that fail to show progress drop out, while using the membership as a marketing tool. Making a stricter entry requirement for the Global Compact membership (so the companies can show some progress in changing their practices) can induce companies around the world to show more commitment to sustainable production.

As it continues to affect internal and cross-border migration and exacerbate domestic and global inequality, climate change has become a serious concern not only for the affected (mostly poor and underdeveloped) countries but for the entire international community. The UN's 2030 Agenda for Sustainable Development and its SDGs is a giant leap forward in terms of addressing inequality, combating climate change, and promoting conservation and sustainable use of terrestrial ecosystems and natural resources (SDGs 10, 13, 14, and 15). Yet, there is still much to be done, both by the largest emitters (the US, the EU, and China) that have to curb their carbon and methane levels, and by the affected developing countries that have to improve their adaptation strategies. The international organizations, such as the IMF, the World Bank, and the UN, need to join their efforts to help the latter countries to become more resilient and financially secure. This will reduce environmental migration or, if such must take place, will ensure safety and economic well-being of environmental refugees. A globally coordinated, unwavering, and persistent response to climate change and its short-term and long-term effects is a necessary condition to achieve the UN's goals of sustainable development and make this planet a better and safer place for current and future generations.

Actions to Be Taken: The Road Ahead

- The UN could bring together all nations to develop a protocol for the development and implementation of policies that are designed to achieve SDG 13.
- The UN must insist upon acknowledgment and acceptance of the definition of "environmental refugees" to ensure universal support. It is also necessary to establish the legal status for these increasing refugees and grant them the same protections as are granted to other classes of refugees.
- A special fund like the Multilateral Fund could be established particularly to help developing nations in creating national plans for amelioration and mitigating environmental disasters.
- Governments in developed countries should increase the funding for new technologies that are cheaper and more dependable than present-day solar farms and wind turbines.
- Multilateral institutions, development agencies, and international law must do far more to thoroughly examine the challenges of climate change.
- The UN should make the entry requirement for the Global Compact membership stricter. Organizations that apply for the membership should exhibit the initiation efforts toward sustainable practices.

---

99 *See* UN GLOBAL COMPACT WEBPAGE, unglobalcompact.org.

32 Indigenous Peoples, the SDGs, and International Environmental Law

Anxhela Mile and Railla Puno

Introduction

While a significant wealth of academic writing and policies on Indigenous Peoples (IPs) have been developed since the end of the Second World War, the definition and scope of the term remain unclear.[1] The United Nations (UN) Human Rights Council however, has identified factors that are indicative of indigeneity which led to the development of a modern understanding of "indigenous." These non-exhaustive factors remain to be the most efficient identifier of IPs[2] and include strong links to territories, ties to surrounding natural resources, and the determination to maintain and reproduce distinct ancestral environments.[3]

These identifiers highlight the unique and intrinsic relationship between IPs and the environment. In fact, it is estimated that IPs occupy over 20% of the Earth's territory,[4] protecting 80% of the planet's biodiversity.[5] Unfortunately, legal protections afforded to IPs vary across the world. Only a few countries recognize indigenous land rights, and even in those countries, legal security is lacking due to implementation delays and corruption.[6] Despite the adoption of the UN Declaration on the Rights of Indigenous Peoples (UNDRIP), which confirmed IPs' rights to land and recognized the contribution of indigenous knowledge, cultures, and traditional practices in sustainable development and environmental management,[7] IPs are not well integrated into the Sustainable Development Goals (SDGs) and national laws.

---

1 Cher Weixia Chen, *Indigenous Rights in International Law*, in OXFORD RESEARCH ENCYCLOPEDIA OF INTERNATIONAL STUDIES (Renée Marlin-Bennett ed., 2017).
2 Chairperson-Rapporteur, Working Paper by the Chairperson-Rapporteur, Mrs. Erica-Irene A. Daes. On the concept of "indigenous people," U.N.Doc. E/CN.4/Sub.2/AC.4/1996/2 (Jun. 10, 1996).
3 *Fact Sheet 1: Indigenous Peoples and Identity*, U.N. Permanent Forum on Indigenous Issues, United Nations Department of Economic and Social Affairs: Indigenous People (UNPFII), www.un.org/esa/socdev/unpfii/documents/5session_factsheet1.pdf (last visited Nov. 3, 2020).
4 Jim Robbins, *Native Knowledge: What Ecologists Are Learning from Indigenous People*, YALE ENVIRONMENT 360 (Apr. 26, 2018), https://e360.yale.edu/features/native-knowledge-what-ecologists-are-learning-from-indigenous-people.
5 *Thematic Report for the High Level Political Forum of Agenda 2030*, Indigenous Peoples Major Groups for Sustainable Development (2020) [hereinafter "Thematic Report HLPF"], www.indigenouspeoples-sdg.org/index.php/english/all-resources/ipmg-position-papers-and-publications/ipmg-reports/global-reports/162-ipmg-thematic-report-for-hlpf-2020/file.
6 *Environment*, UNPFII, www.un.org/development/desa/indigenouspeoples/mandated-areas1/environment.html (last visited Nov. 2, 2020).
7 G.A. Res. 61/295, Declaration on the Rights of Indigenous Peoples (Oct. 2, 2007).

As natural resources dwindle and population growth rises, IPs are being forced out of their traditional lands and into poverty. IPs currently account for 15% of the world's poor,[8] further exacerbated by the rising impacts of climate change, land grabbing, and COVID-19. While Agenda 2030 aims to "leave no one behind," it overlooks IPs' need for protection from unsustainable development or even environmental conservation and has done the opposite. According to the IPs' Thematic Report for the High Level Political Forum (HLPF) of Agenda 2030, IPs have not only been left behind but are being "pushed further behind" through land grabbing, increased poverty and hunger, destruction of cultural heritage, forest degradation, loss of biodiversity,[9] and climate displacement. Agenda 2030 also disregards the great wealth of traditional knowledge (TK) that IPs can contribute toward sustainable development.

Fortunately, international environmental law (IEL) has increasingly recognized the need for greater inclusion and strengthened protections for IPs, both inside and outside the context of Agenda 2030. In this chapter, we focus on the use of TK, the implementation of IPs' rights in IEL, and ways in which the law is helping fulfill the purpose of the SDGs.

Indigenous Rights and the SDGs

Within Agenda 2030, IPs are referenced in the political declaration, in the section on follow-up and review, as well as in SDG 2.3 (Zero Hunger) and SDG 4.5 (Education):

SDG 2.3:

By 2030, double the agricultural productivity and incomes of small-scale food producers, in particular women, indigenous peoples, family farmers, pastoralists and fishers, including through secure and equal access to land, other productive resources and inputs, knowledge, financial services, markets and opportunities for value addition and non-farm employment.

SDG 4.5

By 2030, eliminate gender disparities in education and ensure equal access to all levels of education and vocational training for the vulnerable, including persons with disabilities, indigenous peoples and children in vulnerable situations.[10]

This is insufficient as it largely ignores the important role IPs can play in helping achieve targets including poverty (SDG 1); education (SDG 4); climate change (SDG 13); ocean conservation (SDG 14); biodiversity (SDG 15); and peace and justice (SDG 16), to name a few.

The SDGs also disregard the particular situations of IPs. For example, SDG 1 aims to "end poverty in all forms everywhere" but makes no reference to IPs and their relationship to the environment.[11] For IPs, land is not only an economic asset, but it is a reflection of

---

8 Thematic Report HLPF, *supra* note 5.
9 *Id.* at 2.
10 *See also* United Nations G.A. Res. A/RES/70/1, *Transforming Our World: The 2030 Agenda for Sustainable Development*, at 14–15, 17 (Sept. 25, 2015) [hereinafter "Agenda 2030"].
11 *Id.* at 15.

their identity, culture, and tradition.[12] Pertaining to SDG 1, the Major Group for IPs has stated:

> For Indigenous Peoples around the world, "leaving no one behind" means respecting subsistence economies and promoting nonmonetary measures of well-being. For instance, ... the financial measure of $1.25/day for extreme poverty is inappropriate for Indigenous Peoples, for whom security of rights to lands, territories and resources is essential for poverty eradication. From this perspective, the linear monetary measure of poverty can contribute to further impoverishing Indigenous Peoples under the guise of the theme "leaving no one behind."[13]

Furthermore, SDGs 1, 3, and 4 on social security, health, and education are silent as to IPs' own methods of ensuring language diversity, education in mother tongue, health practices, and traditional medicines.[14] SDG 5, which aims to achieve gender equality and empower all women and girls, should also have a more concrete focus on IPs and local communities. The 2019 SDG Status Report, which only mentioned indigenous communities once, shed light on defenders and activists, stating "one in two victims had been working with communities on issues involving land, the environment, poverty, the rights of minorities and indigenous peoples, or the impact of business activities. And, overall, every tenth victim was a woman."[15] IPs are also becoming victims of violence due to environmental and human rights activism in defending their territories. However, the SDGs do not address how economic development has adversely affected IPs and contributed to violence (SDG 16), further perpetuating gender inequality (SDG 5). SDG 16, in particular, could provide IPs better access to transitional justice, greater engagement in peace processes, and protection for human rights activists.[16]

The UN Permanent Forum on Indigenous Issues (UNPFII), a high-level advisory body that oversees work on indigenous issues, also advocates for better data disaggregation for IPs.[17] This need has been highlighted by the 2020 SDG Status Report which does not provide concrete updates on IPs. Instead, IPs are only mentioned twice: in the foreword and the sustainable fisheries section.[18] Involving SDGs 2 and 4, COVID-19 has affected food insecurity and education, the two SDGs that IPs are included within. For example,

---

12 Briefing Note, *Indigenous People's Rights and the 2030 Agenda*, Office of the High Commission for Human Rights (OHCHR) and the UN Department of Economic and Social Affairs (UN-DESA), at 4, www.un.org/development/desa/indigenouspeoples/wp-content/uploads/sites/19/2016/10/Briefing-Paper-on-Indigenous-Peoples-Rights-and-the-2030-Agenda.pdf (2017) [hereinafter "IPs Rights and Agenda 2030"].
13 Danielle DeLuca, *What Do the Sustainable Development Goals Mean for Indigenous Groups*, CULTURAL SURVIVAL (Dec. 2017), www.culturalsurvival.org/publications/cultural-survival-quarterly/what-do-sustainable-development-goals-mean-indigenous.
14 IPs Rights and Agenda 2030, *supra* note 12, at 5.
15 *The Sustainable Development Goals Report*, UNITED NATIONS, at 55 (2019) [hereinafter "2019 SDG Report"], https://unstats.un.org/sdgs/report/2019/The-Sustainable-Development-Goals-Report-2019.pdf.
16 IPs Rights and Agenda 2030, *supra* note 12, at 6.
17 *Indigenous Peoples and the 2030 Agenda*, UN-DESA, www.un.org/development/desa/indigenouspeoples/focus-areas/post-2015-agenda/the-sustainable-development-goals-sdgs-and-indigenous.html last visited Nov. 8, 2020.
18 See *The Sustainable Development Goals Report*, UNITED NATIONS, at 2, 53 (2020) [hereinafter "2020 SDG Report"], https://unstats.un.org/sdgs/report/2020/The-Sustainable-Development-Goals-Report-2020.pdf.

"an estimated 25.9 per cent of the global population—2 billion people—were affected by moderate or severe food insecurity in 2019, an increase from 22.4 per cent in 2014,"[19] and "about 90 per cent of all students (1.57 billion) were out of school" because of COVID-19.[20] However, the statistics do not specify the extent to which IPs are particularly affected.

International Environmental Law and Indigenous Rights

While SDGs 13, 14, 15, and 16 reflect IPs' priorities of protecting ecosystems and conserving biodiversity, the SDGs do not mention existing IPs' rights such as the principle of Free and Prior Informed Consent (FPIC).[21] Fortunately, the Convention on Biological Diversity (CBD), the Nagoya Protocol on Access to Genetic Resources, and the Fair and Equitable Sharing of Benefits Arising from their Utilization (Nagoya Protocol), the United Nations Framework Convention on Climate Change (UNFCCC), and environmental principles are more inclusive and have contributed to IPs' legal rights and protections. IEL has helped promote IPs' collective rights to their lands, their cultural heritage, and participation in decision-making related to protecting biodiversity and mitigating climate change.

The CBD and the Nagoya Protocol: Indigenous Communities and PIC

IPs' rights are incorporated in various IELs and treaties related to the conservation of biological diversity, in particular the CBD and the Nagoya Protocol. The CBD's objectives are to conserve the diversity of living organisms, as well as the "sustainable use of its components, and the fair and equitable sharing of the benefits arising out of the utilization of genetic resources."[22] Its resulting protocol on genetic resources, the Nagoya Protocol, aims to ensure the "fair and equitable sharing of benefits arising from the utilization of genetic resources."[23] This relates to SDG 15, protecting life on land as nearly "one million animal and plant species are threatened with extinction,"[24] as the planet enters the sixth mass extinction.[25]

Article 8(j) of the CBD

The CBD is lauded for recognizing the importance of TK and developing the intrinsic relationship between IEL and human rights concerning IPs' rights. Art. 8(j) states that Parties shall, as far as possible and as appropriate:

> Subject to national legislation, respect, preserve and maintain knowledge, innovations and practices of indigenous and local communities embodying traditional lifestyles

---

19 *Id.* at 26.
20 *Id.* at 32.
21 IPs Rights and Agenda 2030, *supra* note 12, at 5.
22 Convention on Biological Diversity, 5 June 1992, 1760 U.N.T.S. 79, www.cbd.int/convention/text/ [hereinafter "CBD"].
23 Nagoya Protocol on Access to Genetic Resources and the Fair and Equitable Sharing of Benefits Arising from their Utilization, 29 October 2010, 3008 U.N.T.S. 1 (entered into force 12 October 2014) [hereinafter "Nagoya Protocol"] at Art. 1.
24 Life on Land, *Sustainable Development Goals*, www.un.org/sustainabledevelopment/biodiversity/.
25 *See* ELIZABETH KOLBERT, THE SIXTH EXTINCTION: AN UNNATURAL HISTORY (Henry Holt & Co, 2014).

relevant for the conservation and sustainable use of biological diversity and promote their wider application with the approval and involvement of the holders of such knowledge, innovations and practices and encourage the equitable sharing of the benefits arising from the utilization of such knowledge innovations and practices.[26]

Through this, the CBD integrates issues on biological and cultural diversity to further its goal to conserve the world's biodiversity.[27] To implement the provision, a Working Group on Article 8(j) and a Programme of Work was established in 1998 and in 2000, respectively with five general principles:

> (1) full and effective participation of indigenous and local communities, and women especially, in all stages of the Programme of Work; (2) TK should be given the same respect and considered as useful and necessary as all other forms of knowledge; (3) holistic approach consistent with the spiritual and cultural values and customs of the IPs and their rights to have control over their TK, innovations and practices; (4) ecosystem strategy for the integrated management of land, water and living resources that promotes conservation and sustainable use of biological diversity in an equitable way; and (5) access to TK, innovations and practices of IPs should be subject to prior informed approval from the holders of such knowledge, innovations and practices.[28]

These principles were integrated by the Conference of Parties (COP) in 2019 within the post-2020 global biodiversity framework to ensure IPs' participation in ongoing and future work of the CBD and Agenda 2030.[29] While these principles have translated into policies—including voluntary guidelines for the conduct of assessments, guidelines for the repatriation of TK, and methodological guidance on the contributions of IPs[30]—Parties agree that much work remains to be done. For this new Programme of Work, Parties proposed focusing on implementing guidelines previously adopted by the CBD COP, supporting community and indigenous protected areas, encouraging food security for indigenous and local communities, and elaborating a safeguards framework.[31]

Art. 6 of the Nagoya Protocol: Principle of PIC

The Nagoya Protocol is also inclusive of indigenous rights and clarifies the role of indigenous communities in relation to benefits arising from the utilization of genetic resources. Under Art. 6, the Protocol requires Parties to have PIC of IPs.[32] The principle of PIC includes

---

26 CBD, *supra* note 22, at Art. 8(j).
27 ANNECOOS WIERSEMA, *Sharing Common Ground: A Cautionary Tale on the Rights of Indigenous Peoples and the Protection of Biological Diversity*, *in* LINKING HUMAN RIGHTS AND ENVIRONMENT, (Romina Picolotti & Jorge Daniel Taillant eds., 2003).
28 CBD, at 143, UNEP/CBD/COP/5/23 Decision V/16 Annex (May 2000).
29 Ad Hoc Open-Ended Inter-Sessional Working Group on Article 8(j) and Related Provisions of the CBD, *Indigenous Peoples and Local Communities and the Post-2020 Global Biodiversity Framework*, at ¶ 10, CBD/WG8J/11/4 (Oct. 12, 2019).
30 *Id.* at ¶ 13.
31 *Id.* at ¶ 14.
32 Nagoya Protocol, *supra* note 23, at Art. 6.

(1) a requirement that when one State plans to operate in another State, it must seek that State's prior informed consent and (2) a requirement emanating from indigenous rights that communities, particularly indigenous communities, have the right to give (or withhold) their free, prior informed consent to activities that affect them.[33]

Additionally, under Art. 12, the Protocol requires Parties to "take into consideration indigenous and local communities' customary laws, community protocols and procedures ... with respect to traditional knowledge associated with genetic resources."[34] Within Art. 12(3), the Protocol emphasizes women's rights, as parties must support "the development of indigenous and local communities, including women within these communities."[35] Art. 9 concerns capacity building to encourage users and indigenous people of the benefits of conserving biological diversity.[36]

The Nagoya Protocol helps IPs empower themselves through the principle of PIC, with an emphasis on TK associated with genetic resources. By incorporating indigenous rights, IPs have played an important role in securing biodiversity within the CBD.[37] The Protocol facilitates technology transfer, collaboration, and cooperation in research, thereby ensuring that policymakers take all stakeholders into account.[38]

The Protocol also protects indigenous communities from the effects of commercialization of natural resources through fair access and benefit sharing. Art. 5 mandates Parties to implement policies so "benefits arising from the use of genetic resources that are held by IPs ... are shared in a fair and equitable way with the communities concerned."[39] This is important since IPs' land is constantly at risk of biodiversity loss, deforestation, land grabbing, and environmental pollution.[40]

The promotion of IPs' rights under the Nagoya Protocol, while suffering from the lack of implementation at the national level, strengthens accountability for these environmental crimes and promotes working with, and not against, indigenous communities.[41] While the Nagoya Protocol does not entirely encompass IPs' rights, it is a step forward to ensuring IPs are not left behind.

The Nagoya Protocol's inclusion of IPs also highlights a missed opportunity within the SDGs. SDG 15 encompasses the protection of biodiversity and should have recognized and promoted the key role that IPs hold in the achievement of this goal.[42] Many IPs live "within ecosystem boundaries," engaging in "agroforestry, pastoralism ... and traditional

---

33 DAVID HUNTER ET AL., INTERNATIONAL ENVIRONMENTAL LAW AND POLICY, 493–94 (5th ed., 2015).
34 Nagoya Protocol, *supra* note 23, at Art. 12.
35 *Id.* at 12(3).
36 *Id.* at Art. 9.
37 *The central Roles of Indigenous Peoples and Local Communities in Achieving Global Commitments on Biodiversity: Technical Policy Brief for the HPLF on Sustainable Development Goal 15*, www.indigenouspeoples-sdg.org/index.php/english/all-resources/ipmg-position-papers-and-publications/ipmg-submission-interventions/95-the-central-roles-of-indigenous-peoples-and-local-communities-in-achieving-global-commitments-on-biodiversity/file [hereinafter "Policy Brief SDG 15"].
38 Maria Yolanda Teran, *The Nagoya Protocol and Indigenous Peoples*, INT. INDIG. POLICY J. 7(2) (Apr. 2016).
39 Nagoya Protocol, *supra* note 23, Art. 5.
40 Policy Brief SDG 15, *supra* note 37, at 9.
41 Teran, *supra* note 38.
42 *See also* Agenda 2030, *supra* note 10.

forest management,"[43] practices that do not deplete the land of its nutrients compared to industrialized agriculture.[44] While SDG 15 promotes sustainable ecosystem practices, it does not mention IPs' skills in managing biodiverse forests, such as their fire management practices or their use of swidden agriculture.[45] By promoting traditional systems and knowledge, the international community will help conserve more biodiversity and mitigate climate change.

Environmental Defenders and Land Grabbing

IPs are also increasingly becoming victims of violence for their efforts in protecting environmental land. According to one study "between 2002 and 2017, 1,558 people in 50 countries were killed for defending their environments and lands."[46] In 2019, "the UN tracked 357 killings (decreased from 476 in 2018) and 30 enforced disappearances of human rights defenders, journalists and trade unionists in 47 countries."[47] While the 2019 SDG Status Report included such statistics, the report did not state how 40% of those killed due to land and environment disputes are indigenous groups.[48] Statistics such as these need to be included in SDG status reports to demonstrate the plight of IPs.

Regulation of environmental criminal activity is highly lacking within the international community[49] and is largely absent from the SDGs, specifically SDG 16. According to a United Nations Environment Programme-The International Criminal Police Organization (UNEP-INTERPOL) report, the root causes of environmental crime include "poor governance, corruption, inadequate institutional support, and minimal benefits to local communities."[50] While SDG 16 notes "conflict and other forms of violence are an affront to sustainable development,"[51] the SDGs should have further emphasized the need to enforce

---

43 DRAWDOWN: THE MOST COMPREHENSIVE PLAN EVER PROPOSED TO REVERSE GLOBAL WARMING, *See section on* Land Use: Indigenous Peoples' Land Management, 125 (Paul Hawken ed. 2017) [hereinafter "Drawdown"].

44 Studies have shown that agroecological plots have had 40% more topsoil than conventional plots, lost 18% less arable land to landslides than conventional plots, and averaged 69% less gully erosion compared to conventional farms. *See* Eric Holt-Giménez, *Measuring Farmers' Agroecological Resistance after Hurricane Mitch in Nicaragua: A Case Study in Participatory, Sustainable Land Management Impact Monitoring*, 93 AGRIC. ECOSYSTEMS AND ENV'T. 87–105 (2002), www.panna.org/sites/default/files/HurricaneMitch-Agroeco.pdf.

45 Drawdown, *supra* note 43, at 125–26 (*note:* Swidden agriculture is also known as shifting cultivation); *See also* 2030 Agenda, *supra* note 10.

46 Nathalie Butt et al., *The Supply Chain of Violence*, 2 NATURE SUSTAINABILITY 742, 747 (Aug. 2019).

47 *Id.*; *See also* U.N. Economic and Social Council, *Progress towards the Sustainable Development Goals*, E/2020/xxx at 21 (Jul. 22–25, 2002), https://sustainabledevelopment.un.org/content/documents/26158Final_SG_SDG_Progress_Report_14052020.pdf [hereinafter "Progress towards SDGs"].

48 Patrick Greenfield & Jonathan Watts, *Record 212 Land and Environment Activists Killed Last Year*, THE GUARDIAN (Jul. 29, 2020), www.theguardian.com/environment/2020/jul/29/record-212-land-and-environment-activists-killed-last-year.

49 Christian Nellemann et al., *The Rise of Environmental Crime: A Growing Threat to Natural Resources, Peace, Development, and Security*, a UNEP-INTERPOL RAPID RESPONSE ASSESSMENT 1 (2016), https://wedocs.unep.org/bitstream/handle/20.500.11822/7662/-The_rise_of_environmental_crime_A_growing_threat_to_natural_resources_peace,_development_and_security-2016environmental_crimes.pdf.pdf?sequence=3&isAllowed=y.

50 *Id.* at 9.

51 2019 SDG Report, *supra* note 15, at 54.

laws and policies, especially laws protecting IPs' rights. For example, land grabbing[52] threatens IPs' traditional lands and leads to deforestation, biodiversity loss, water and air pollution, and human rights violations.[53] UN Human Rights experts explain rising poverty among IPs, particularly in Asia due to land grabbing.[54] Additionally, "90% of Africa's rural land is undocumented … making it highly vulnerable to land grabbing and expropriation."[55] The UNPFII has also promoted the need to incorporate IPs within SDG 16, having the theme of "Peace, justice and strong institutions: the role of indigenous peoples in implementing Sustainable Development Goal 16" for its 2020 Session (postponed due to COVID-19).[56]

IPs have advocated incorporating land rights within SDG 1. Gam Shimray, Secretary-General for the Asia Indigenous Peoples Pact (AIPP), has stated, "land is the only basis for continuity of identity and also of holistic development … if land is left out, we are already being left behind."[57] IPs have been fearful of losing their collective rights to land through the veil of "sustainable development" because governments implement policies that focus on individual rights compared to community rights. In the case of environmental defenders, SDGs 1 and 16 need to be more inclusive of IPs' rights and promote collective ownership, as well as require their PIC, and respect IPs' relationship to nature, their sustainable resource management, and TK.[58]

Indigenous Rights under the UNFCCC

Alongside biodiversity treaties, IPs' agenda has been progressing in the UNFCCC talks since 2015 when a best practices platform was established to "strengthen the knowledge, technologies, practices and efforts of local communities and IPs related to addressing and responding to climate change."[59] In the Paris Agreement, both the Preamble and Art. 7.5 recognize the need to respect and promote IPs' rights when undertaking climate action, with Article 7.5 specifying that TK and local knowledge systems should be considered when implementing adaptation measures.[60] This is progress from the UNFCCC text where IPs were largely overlooked.

Agenda 2030 was adopted a few months before the Paris Agreement, and SDG 13 is the only SDG with a qualification that acknowledges the primacy of the UNFCCC on climate issues as the principal international, intergovernmental forum for negotiating the global response to climate change.[61] Because of this, SDG 13 only details various elements of cli-

---

52 IWGIA: *Indigenous Peoples' Rights to Land: The Threat of Land Grabbing*, IWGIA, www.iwgia.org/images/publications//0693_fact_sheet_land_grabbing-pr.pdf ("Land grabbing is the large-scale acquisition of land for commercial or industrial purposes, such as agricultural and biofuel production, mining and logging concessions or tourism … with limited (if any) consultation of the local communities.").
53 *Id.* at 1–2.
54 UN News: *Land-Grabbing in Asia Displaces Indigenous Peoples and Destroys Environment, Says UN Rights Expert* (Sep. 8, 2020), www.ohchr.org/EN/NewsEvents/Pages/DisplayNews.aspx?NewsID=26213
55 Policy Brief SDG 15, *supra* note 37, at 6.
56 UN Economic and Social Council, at 3, E/C.19/2020/7 (Jan. 30, 2020).
57 DeLuca, *supra* note 13.
58 *Id.*; *See also* IWGIA, *supra* note 52, at 2.
59 United Nations Framework Convention on Climate Change (UNFCCC), at ¶ 135, Decision 1/CP.21 (Dec. 2015) [hereinafter "UNFCCC 1/CP.21"].
60 Paris Agreement to the UNFCCC, Dec. 12, 2015, T.I.A.S. No. 16-1104, Preamble ¶ 11 and Art. 7.5.
61 *SDG 13 Update: Joining UP NDC and SDG Planning*, INTERNATIONAL INSTITUTE FOR SUSTAINABLE DEVELOPMENT (Oct. 26, 2017), http://sdg.iisd.org/commentary/policy-briefs/policy-sdg-13-update-joining-up-ndc-and-sdg-planning/.

mate action. SDG 13.b on climate planning and management focuses on Least Developed Countries and Small Island Developing States, as well as women, youth, and local and marginalized communities, but it does not specifically refer to IPs' rights and specific needs.

UNFCCC Local Communities and IPs' Platform

In 2017, building on COP 21 mandates, the overall purpose and functions of the platform, officially named the UNFCCC Local Communities and Indigenous Peoples Platform (LCIPP) was decided by the Parties. The LCIPP's goal was to

> Strengthen the knowledge, technologies, practices, and efforts of local communities and indigenous peoples related to addressing and responding to climate change, to facilitate the exchange of experience and the sharing of best practices and lessons learned on mitigation and adaptation in a holistic and integrated manner, and to enhance the engagement of local communities and indigenous peoples in the UNFCCC process.[62]

The platform aims to facilitate the exchange of knowledge by "applying, strengthening, protecting, and preserving traditional knowledge, knowledge of indigenous peoples and local knowledge systems" with their FPIC.[63] The LCIPP also seeks to improve IPs' capacity to engage in climate discussions and provides assistance to allow Parties and stakeholders to engage with indigenous groups. Lastly, the platform seeks to mobilize the IPs' valuable contributions by integrating their knowledge into local plans and policies.[64] This is an important development from the SDGs given that Target 13.b only raises support for "local and marginalized communities" without taking note of IPs' contribution to climate change planning and management.[65]

Since 2017, the LCIPP has undertaken various activities to implement a workplan covering 2020–2021. These include regional consultations with indigenous groups, development of awareness and information materials on TK, in-session workshops, multi-stakeholder consultations, and mapping of existing policies on the participation of IPs in various climate-related fora.[66]

The IPs' Policy of the Green Climate Fund

IPs' rights are also recognized under the Green Climate Fund (GCF), an operating entity of the UNFCCC's financial mechanism established to enable significant and ambitious contributions to global efforts on climate change.[67] As of November 2020, the GCF has a total value of $23.2 billion and 159 projects in its portfolio, $1.4 billion of which

---

62 UNFCCC, at ¶ 5, Decision 2/CP.23 (Feb. 8, 2018).
63 *Id.* at ¶ 6.
64 *Id.*
65 Agenda 2030, *supra* note 10, at 23.
66 UNFCCC Subsidiary Body for Scientific and Technological Advice (SBSTA), *The 1st Meeting of the Facilitative Working Group of the Local Communities and Indigenous Peoples Platform: Annex*, FCCC/SBSTA/2019/4 (2019).
67 UNFCCC, at ¶ 4, FCCC/CP/2011/9/Add.1 Annex (Mar. 15, 2012).

have been disbursed,[68] far from the agreed upon $100 billion per year goal.[69] Given the potential for negative impacts from the implementation of grants, the GCF adopted interim environmental and social safeguards to avoid or mitigate negative impacts and ensure that projects do not result in harm to people or the environment.[70] The seventh performance standard is on IPs and the related objective is as follows:

> PS7: Indigenous peoples
> (a) Ensure full respect for indigenous peoples
>   (i) Human rights, dignity, aspirations;
>   (ii) Livelihoods;
>   (iii) Culture, knowledge, practices;
> (b) Avoid/minimize adverse impacts;
> (c) Sustainable and culturally appropriate development benefits and opportunities;
> (d) Free, prior, and informed consent in certain circumstances.[71]

In 2018, the GCF Board adopted the Indigenous Peoples Policy so indigenous populations benefit from GCF projects and do not suffer from their design and implementation. It gives due importance to TK and engages IPs in the planning process.[72] Additionally, the GCF has an Independent Redress Mechanism (IRM) that considers grievances related to the Fund's policies and procedures. IRM members work closely with the GCF's environmental and social safeguards team to prevent conflict and strengthen grievance mechanisms, which results in greater accountability.[73] For example, a routine press monitoring of the IRM in 2018 found IPs living within a wetlands project in Peru were not adequately considered and weak enforcement of the FPIC process. As a result, remedial measures were taken by the GCF Secretariat including guidance on FPIC requirements and risk categorization for IP projects.[74]

IPs and Climate Displacement

Unlike the UNFCCC, SDG 13 does not address how IPs are already affected by climate change and threatened by climate displacement.[75] Similarly, SDG 10.7 makes no reference to migration caused by climate change nor the particular vulnerabilities of IPs.[76]

---

68 *Portfolio Dashboard*, GREEN CLIMATE FUND (GCF), https://www.greenclimate.fund/projects/dashboard. (last accessed Nov. 18, 2020).
69 UNFCCC 1/CP.21, *supra* note 59, at ¶ 114.
70 *In Brief: Safeguards*, GCF, www.greenclimate.fund/sites/default/files/document/gcf-brief-safeguards_0.pdf (2018) [hereinafter "GCF Safeguards"].
71 GCF, at 35, GCF/B.07/02 Annex IV (May 7, 2014).
72 GCF Safeguards, *supra* note 70.
73 *Accountability in Action: Independent Redress Mechanism—2019 Annual Report*, GCF, https://irm.greenclimate.fund/documents/1061332/1197271/IRM+Annual+Report+2019/1ebf8082-6970-550e-9596-f82ab652eb6e (Feb. 2020).
74 *Summary of the Preliminary Inquiry Report, and Undertakings Provided by the GCF Secretariat*, GCF, https://irm.greenclimate.fund/documents/1061332/1198301/IRM_initiated_proceedings_C-0002_-_Peru.pdf/4e333fd6-22b5-4fbe-a28d-0513b57a3eb4 (May 8, 2019).
75 *Environment, Disasters, and Climate Change*, UNHCR, www.unhcr.org/en-us/environment-disasters-and-climate-change.html [hereinafter "UNHCR"].
76 Agenda 2030, *supra* note 10, at 21.

The UN High Commissioner for Refugees has cited "since 2009, an estimated one person every second has been displaced by climate or weather-related disaster since 2009 with an average of 22.5 million people displaced by climate or weather-related events since 2008."[77] Fortunately, there have been several COP decisions that recognize climate displacement, migration, and planned relocation. A Task Force on Displacement was created during COP 21 under the Executive Committee of the Warsaw International Mechanism for Loss and Damage Associated with Climate Change Impacts to develop recommendations for "integrated approaches to avert, minimize, and address displacement related to the adverse impacts of climate change."[78] While its 5-year rolling workplan recognizes that indigenous people and the ecosystems on which they depend are vulnerable,[79] there has not been a substantial status report on this issue.

Outside the auspices of the UNFCCC, many IPs and climate migrants who live in vulnerable areas are seeking protection through international litigation. For example, the Isle de Jean Charles Band of BiloxiChitimacha-Choctaw Indians and other indigenous groups filed a complaint to the UN against the United States (US), alleging "climate-forced displacement threatens the full enjoyment of a wide range of human rights."[80] Echoing the rights discussed in the Nagoya Protocol, the complaint notes the right of FPIC, the lack of FPIC regarding a resettlement plan, and the "tribe's right to preserve spiritual connection to land, water and homeland."[81]

Additionally, the Human Rights Committee, a body of experts that monitor the International Covenant on Civil and Political Rights, reviewed a case in which a Kiribati citizen, Teitiota, applied for refugee status in New Zealand claiming he should be protected as a refugee.[82] The Committee concluded that governments *should not return* migrants to countries where lives would be threatened by climate change.[83] While the Committee ultimately agreed that Teitota was not a refugee as defined by the Refugee Convention, the decision acknowledged the connections between climate change, migration, and human rights, emphasizing the need for countries to act to prevent and mitigate climate change.[84] Such language should have been incorporated within the SDGs.

---

77 UNHCR, *supra* note 75.
78 UNFCCC 1/CP.21, *supra* note 59, at ¶ 49.
79 UNFCCC SBSTA, *Report of the Executive Committee of the Warsaw International Mechanism for Loss and Damage associated with Climate Change Impacts: Annex*, FCCC/SB/2017/Add.1 (2017).
80 Complaint at 3, Rights of Indigenous People in Addressing Climate-Forced Displacement (Jan. 15, 2020), http://blogs2.law.columbia.edu/climate-change-litigation/wp-content/uploads/sites/16/non-us-case-documents/2020/20200116_NA_complaint-1.pdf.
81 *Id.* at 40–41.
82 *See also UN Landmark Case for People Displaced by Climate Change*, AMNESTY INTERNATIONAL (Jan. 20, 2020), www.amnesty.org/en/latest/news/2020/01/un-landmark-case-for-people-displaced-by-climate-change/.
83 Press Release, Human Rights Committee, Historic UN Human Rights Case Opens Door to Climate Change Asylum Claims (Jan. 21, 2020), www.ohchr.org/en/NewsEvents/Pages/DisplayNews.aspx?NewsID=25482&LangID=E; *See also* Mark Baker-Jones & Melanie Baker-Jones, *Teitiota v the Chief Executive of Ministry of Business, Innovation and Employment—A Person Displaced*, 15 QUT L. Rev. 102, 121, https://eprints.qut.edu.au/111864/1/111864.pdf.sEvents/Pages/DisplayNews.aspx?NewsID=25482&LangID=E.
84 *Id.*

International Principles

In addition to the CBD, the Nagoya Protocol, and the UNFCCC, principles under international law have contributed to fulfilling IPs' rights, reflecting political consensus on environmental issues and providing a framework for negotiating new mechanisms for environmental governance.[85] Most often, they translate into national law and become legally binding, benefiting IPs given their intrinsic relationship to nature. In particular, the principles that will be discussed are Environmental Impact Assessments (EIAs) and Rights to Mother Earth.

Environmental Impact Assessments and Standing Rock

The duty to complete an EIA is customary international law "when there is a risk that the proposed industrial activity may have a significant adverse impact."[86] In *Pulp Mills on the River Uruguay*, the International Court of Justice held:

> it may now be considered a requirement under general international law to undertake an [EIA] where there is a risk that the proposed industrial activity may have a significant adverse impact in a transboundary context, in particular, on a shared resource.[87]

The Rio Declaration also supports EIAs under Principle 17.[88]

Indigenous communities have recently experienced a victory when the court ordered the shut down of the Dakota pipeline[89] because of the failure to produce an EIA.[90] The lawsuit was brought by the Standing Rock Sioux Tribe, along with three other plaintiff Tribes, in opposition to the pipeline. The Court ruled that the US Army Corps of Engineers violated US law by not producing an EIA, which is required to "inform the public that [agencies have] considered environmental concerns in [their] decisionmaking process."[91]

While EIAs do have shortfalls, they are useful tools and have helped achieve the SDGs. EIAs are analytical tools designed to inform decision-making, encourage local scientific involvement, and promote science diplomacy by accumulating data for policymakers.[92] With environmental protection and sustainable development as the overarching objective of EIAs,

---

85 Hunter, *supra* note 33, at ¶ 433-438.
86 *Pulp Mills on the River Uruguay* (Argentina v. Uruguay), Judgment, 2010 I.C.J. ¶ 119 (April 20).
87 *Id.*; *See also* Alan Boyle, *Developments in International Law of EIA and Their Relation to the Espoo Convention* 1, 10 UNECE, www.unece.org/fileadmin/DAM/env/eia/documents/mop5/Seminar_Boyle.pdf.
88 NICHOLAS A. ROBINSON, *The Nature of Courts, in* COURTS AND THE ENVIRONMENT 1, 31 (Christina Voigt & Zen Makuch eds., 2018); Rio Declaration on Environment and Development, Jun. 13, 1992, 31 ILM 874 (1992).
89 The Dakota pipeline has been a source of much controversy in the US. Opponents, including the Standing Rock Sioux tribe, have argued that the people would disrupt sacred burial lands, contaminate drinking waters, and exacerbate climate change. *See* Justin Worland, *What to Know About the Dakota Access Pipeline Protests*, TIME (Oct. 28, 2016), https://time.com/4548566/dakota-access-pipeline-standing-rock-sioux/.
90 *See Standing Rock Sioux Tribe v. U.S. Army Co. of Eng'rs*, No. 16-1534 (JEB) (D.D.C. 2020) https://earthjustice.org/sites/default/files/files/standing_rock_sioux_tribe_v._army_corps_of_engineers.pdf.
91 *Id.* at 2 (citing *Weinberger v. Catholic Action of Haw.*, 454 U.S. 139, 143 (1981)).
92 Nicholas A. Robinson, *International Trends in Environmental Impact Assessment*, 19 B.C. ENVTL. AFF. L. REV. 591, 593-95 (1992), http://lawdigitalcommons.bc.edu/ealr/vol19/iss3/15.

expanding this procedure will help achieve SDGs by contributing to inclusive, participatory, and integrative action on social, environmental, and economic issues.[93] EIAs ensure that SDG 12 (sustainable consumption and production) and SDG 10 (reduced inequality) are linked with the other SDGs and can safeguard that development projects consider sustainable options.[94] In a Meetings of the Parties to the Espoo (EIA) Convention, delegates stressed the SDGs can be achieved by considering adverse environmental consequences when making economic decisions.[95]

TK can make an important contribution, as can scientific and engineering knowledge,[96] to further SDGs implementation. In Canada, the use of traditional ecological knowledge in EIAs is seen as a means of reinforcing the identity of IPs in their path toward development and improving Western science.[97] The Canadian Environmental Assessment Act takes into account cultural, environmental, economic, political, and spiritual inter-relationships to improve the assessment of historical knowledge, project design, and relationship between proponents of the project.[98] TK is also a key component of Norwegian legislation and has been included in several EIAs.[99]

The International Convention on the Elimination of All Forms of Racial Discrimination (CERD) Committee also recognizes how the duty to conduct EIAs can (1) help assess the impact of development on IPs' land; (2) "ensure the participation of [IPs] in decision-making concerning their land;" (3) ensure "compensation to [IPs'] impacted by natural resource exploitation;" and (4) ensure IPs' affected by natural resources "have effective access to judicial action."[100] The CERD emphasizes that "a failure to recognize [IPs'] rights to the land and its resources" with respect to various economic activities "constitutes a threat to their health and environment and serious violations of their rights."[101] Therefore, scientific assessment within EIAs is an existing tool that can help safeguard IPs' traditional land rights against land and natural resource exploitation.[102]

---

93 Taako George et al., *An Evaluation of the Environmental Impact Assessment Practice in Uganda: Challenges and Opportunities for Achieving Sustainable Development*, 6 HELIYON 9, 2 (Sep. 2020), www.ncbi.nlm.nih.gov/pmc/articles/PMC7505666/pdf/main.pdf.
94 *Id.*
95 *Environmental Assessments Key to Achieving SDGs*, Climate Goals, IISD: SDG Knowledge Hub (June 27, 2017), http://sdg.iisd.org/news/environmental-assessments-key-to-achieving-sdgs-climate-goals/.
96 Marc Stevenson, *Indigenous Knowledge in Environmental Assessment*, 49 ARCTIC 279, 2981 (1996), http://pubs.aina.ucalgary.ca/arctic/Arctic49-3-278.pdf.
97 BARRY SADLER, *Back to the Future: Traditional Ecological Knowledge and Modern Environmental Assessment, A Frame of Reference*, in TRADITIONAL KNOWLEDGE AND ENVIRONMENTAL IMPACT ASSESSMENT 1, 1 (Barry Sadler and Peter Boothroyd eds., 1994).
98 *Considering Aboriginal Traditional Knowledge in Environmental Assessments Conducted under the Canadian Environmental Assessment Act, 2012*, GOVERNMENT OF CANADA, (Mar. 2015), www.canada.ca/en/impact-assessment-agency/services/policy-guidance/considering-aboriginal-traditional-knowledge-environmental-assessments-conducted-under-canadian-environmental-assessment-act-2012.html.
99 Elinar Eythorsson & Alma Thestad, *Incorporating Traditional Knowledge in Environmental Impact Assessments—How Can It Be Done?* 6 ARCTIC REV. ON L. AND POL. 132, 145 (Nov. 15) www.researchgate.net/publication/283821080_Incorporating_Traditional_Knowledge_in_Environmental_Impact_Assessment-How_Can_It_Be_Done.
100 U.N. Office of the High Commissioner for Human Rights, Mapping Human Rights Obligations Relating to the Enjoyment of a Safe, Clean, Healthy and Sustainable Environment, Rep. No. 3 (Dec. 2013), at ¶ 21.
101 *Id.* at ¶ 43.
102 *Id.* at ¶ 47.

Rights of Mother Earth

The emerging principle of Mother Earth holds that nature has rights distinct from any benefit or claim that people have over it. This concept has roots in indigenous beliefs and their deep respect for the environment.[103] The international community has a great deal to learn from IPs' relationship to Mother Earth, which has helped provide more rights to protect biodiversity.

In 2008, Ecuador was the first nation to provide explicit constitutional recognition of the rights of nature, stating: "Nature or Pachamama, where life plays and performs, is entitled to full respect, existence, and the maintenance and regeneration of its vital cycles, structure, functions, and evolutionary processes."[104] In 2010, Bolivia organized the People's Conference on Climate Change and the Rights of Mother Earth attended by over 35,000 people from around the world.[105] In this Conference, the Universal Declaration on the Rights of Mother Earth, which states that "every human being is responsible for respecting and living in harmony with Mother Earth,"[106] and the People's Agreement, calling for the new world view that involves living in harmony with nature, were adopted.[107] In the same year, the Bolivian Law of Mother Earth was passed and nature was given the legal rights to life, regeneration, biodiversity, water, clean air, balance, and restoration, requiring an economic and societal reorientation.[108]

More recently, in New Zealand, the Whanganui River and a national park formerly known as Te Urewera were recognized by law as living beings and legal entities stemming from an indigenous struggle by Maori Tribes.[109] This follows the Millennium Ecosystem Assessment's key conclusion that ecosystems have an intrinsic value that is "something in and for itself, irrespective of its utility for someone else."[110] This also relates to the wishes of AIPP Secretary-General Shimray who advocated to include land rights within SDG 1 to respect IPs' unique relationship to nature.

Concluding Remarks

The integration of IPs into the SDGs, while currently limited to SDGs 2 and 4, is an acknowledgment that the world cannot achieve sustainable development without safeguarding TK and indigenous territories.[111] IEL has helped incorporate IPs' rights and

---

103 Pablo Solon, *The Rights of Mother Earth*, in CLIMATE CRISIS 107, 108–09 (Vishwas Satgar, ed., 2018).
104 David R. Boyd, *The Status of Constitutional Protection for the Environment in Other Nations*, DAVID SUZUKI FOUNDATION 1, 19, https://davidsuzuki.org/wp-content/uploads/2013/11/status-constitutional-protection-environment-other-nations.pdf
105 *People's Conference on Climate Change and the Rights of Mother Earth*, GLOBAL ALLIANCE FOR THE RIGHTS OF NATURE, https://therightsofnature.org/cochabama-rights/ [hereinafter "GARN"].
106 Universal Declaration of Rights of Mother Earth, Bolivia, Art 2(b)(c)(f), Art 3 (Apr. 22, 2010) https://therightsofnature.org/wp-content/uploads/FINAL-UNIVERSAL-DECLARATION-OF-THE-RIGHTS-OF-MOTHER-EARTH-APRIL-22-2010.pdf.
107 GARN, *supra* note 105.
108 Nick Buxton, *The Law of Mother Earth: Behind Bolivia's Historical Bill*, GLOBAL ALLIANCE FOR THE RIGHTS OF NATURE, https://therightsofnature.org/bolivia-law-of-mother-earth/.
109 Kennedy Warne, *A Voice for Nature*, NAT. GEO., www.nationalgeographic.com/culture/2019/04/maori-river-in-new-zealand-is-a-legal-person/.
110 Millennium Ecosystem Assessment, *Ecosystems and Human Well-Being: Synthesis* (Island Press, 2005).
111 Jeffrey Campbell, *No Sustainable Development Without Indigenous Peoples*, INTERNATIONAL INSTITUTE FOR SUSTAINABLE DEVELOPMENT (Aug. 8, 2019), https://sdg.iisd.org/commentary/guest-articles/no-sustainable-development-without-indigenous-peoples.

provided more protections than the SDGs through the CBD, the Nagoya Protocol, the UNFCCC, and international law principles. However, more work needs to be done.

As resources continue to dwindle and the impacts of climate change and biodiversity loss increase, the international community needs to double its efforts in ensuring full enforcement of IPs' rights. The loss of biodiversity has led to an increase in zoonotic diseases,[112] including COVID-19 that inordinately affect IPs who are at higher risk for infection.[113] Earthjustice attorney, Jan Hasselman, who represented the Standing Rock Sioux Tribe stated, "if the events of 2020 have taught us anything, it's that health and justice must be prioritized early on in any decision-making process if we want to avoid a crisis later on."[114]

Many living on tribal lands in the US have been hit hard by the COVID-19 pandemic,[115] but the full extent is difficult to account for since IPs are being excluded from certain data sets.[116] IPs' traditional ways of living are also threatened since many communities live in multigenerational housing.[117] As Anne Nuorgam, Chair of the UN Permanent Forum on Indigenous Issues said, the international community has to "include the specific needs and priorities of indigenous peoples in addressing the global outbreak of COVID 19."[118]

The unique skills and techniques that IPs have developed over years of managing their natural environment have proven to support healthy ecosystems.[119] Mechanisms for access and benefit sharing in the utilization of TK can help achieve multiple SDG targets, as the SDGs are interconnected and related to one another.

The UN is currently negotiating a new treaty on marine biodiversity of areas beyond national jurisdiction (BBNJ) and a number of countries have advocated for the inclusion of TK. The EU, in particular, recognizes TK as a source of information for area-based management tools.[120] Narau has also advocated that the legally binding instrument (LBJ) "include the role of traditional knowledge and indigenous peoples in the conservation and sustainable use of BBNJ."[121] By incorporating TK within the LBJ, the international community can

---

112 Felicia Keesing et al., *Impacts of Biodiversity on the Emergence and Transmission of Infectious Disease* 468 NATURE 647–52 (2010).
113 Jay C. Butler et al., *Emerging Infectious Diseases Among Indigenous Peoples.* EMERG INFECT DIS. 7(3 Suppl) 554–55 (2001).
114 *Judge Orders Dakota Access Pipeline to Shut Down*, EARTHJUSTICE PRESS (Jul. 6, 2020), https://earthjustice.org/news/press/2020/judge-orders-dakota-access-pipeline-to-shut-down.
115 Sarah Hatcher et al., *Morbidity and Mortality Weekly Report: COVID-19 Among American Indian and Alaska Native Persons*, CENTERS FOR DISEASE CONTROL AND PREVENTION (2020), www.cdc.gov/mmwr/volumes/69/wr/pdfs/mm6934e1-H.pdf.
116 Lizzie Wade, *COVID-19 Data on Native Americans Is "A National Disgrace'." This Scientist Is Fighting to Be Counted*, SCIENCE (2020), www.sciencemag.org/news/2020/09/covid-19-data-native-americans-national-disgrace-scientist-fighting-be-counted; *See also* IWGIA, *supra* note 52, at 2 ("States should develop databases … to ensure more transparency, and ultimately, more accountability.").
117 *COVID-19 and Indigenous People*, UNITED NATIONS www.un.org/development/desa/indigenouspeoples/covid-19.html (last accessed on Dec. 6, 2020).
118 *Id.*
119 *Traditional Knowledge, Innovation and Practices*, Secretariat of the CBD, UN Decade on Biodiversity, www.cbd.int/undb/media/factsheets/undb-factsheet-tk-en.pdf.
120 Kantai Tallash et. al., *Summary of the Second Session of the Intergovernmental Conference on an International Legally Binding Instrument under the UN Convention on the Law of the Sea on the Conservation and Sustainable Use of Marine Biodiversity of Areas Beyond National Jurisdiction*, 25 EARTH NEGOT. BULL. 195, 6 (2019).
121 Kantai Tallash et. al., *BBNJ IGC-2 Highlights: Monday, 25 March 2019*, 25 EARTH NEGOT. BULL. 186, 1 (2019).

meet targets within SDG 14, such as conserve fisheries (SDG 14.4), reduce marine pollution (SDG 14.1), and increase scientific knowledge (SDG 14.a).[122]

IPs have a wealth of knowledge to share that can help achieve targets within the SDGs. Moving forward, IPs' rights should be fully incorporated into EIAs to ensure that both scientific knowledge and TK are integrated when considering economic development. Clearer procedural mechanisms and guidelines can help countries incorporate TK into EIAs so IPs have a stake at the negotiating table. In all, the international community must heed the call to achieve progress on Agenda 2030, and it must be done in an inclusive manner, taking into account IPs' rights and unique circumstances.

Recommendations

Greater Inclusion of IPs' Rights into Agenda 2030

IPs play an integral role in sustainable development, protecting biodiversity, mitigating climate change, and promoting human rights. The international community should focus on ensuring that IPs' rights and TK are protected, recognized, and utilized responsibly within Agenda 2030 in the spirit of leaving no one behind.

Better Incorporation of IPs in Data Sets, Including the SDG Status Reports

IPs have been lacking in statistics, data, and monitoring, diminishing the extent to which the SDGs have affected IPs (SDGs 1, 2, 4, for example). Accountability is needed so no one is left behind and to create a better and more sustainable future for all.

Further Incorporation of IPs' Rights and TK into the Implementation of IEL

While some multilateral environmental agreements, including those involving climate change, biodiversity, and ocean conservation, have taken steps into doing so, opportunities for greater collaboration between IPs' rights and IEL must be developed and fully utilized. Respecting indigenous rights and the principle of Mother Earth helps improve our relationship to the planet.

Consideration of IPs' Unique Relationship to Nature within the SDGs

IPs' unique relationship to the land must be considered in a holistic manner when promoting the SDGs. IPs have a wealth of knowledge that can help achieve particular SDGs, including but not limited to SDGs 13, 14, and 15. When promoting economic growth, the SDGs should include IPs' collective rights to their land, potentially within SDG 1.

Stronger Enforcement of IPs' Policies

Law enforcement needs to be stronger to protect IPs' rights from abusive tactics like land grabbing. More data, monitoring, and accountability will help achieve the SDGs, particularly SDGs 1 and 16, and respect and uphold IPs' rights.

---

122 Agenda 2030, *supra* note 10, at 23–24.

33 Codification and Implementation of Customary International Law

Juan Carlos Sainz-Borgo

The international community established a reference framework for its actions within the 2030 Agenda of the Sustainable Development Goals (SDGs) and agreed upon by political consensus of the Member States of the United Nations General Assembly (UNGA) in 2015.[1] From a normative point of view, the creation of the SDGs and the 2030 Agenda was approved by the UNGA, under the mandate granted in the UN Charter. This approval from the UNGA represents a political, institutional, and normative evolution from the Millennium Development Goals (MDGs)[2] approved by the Member States as "The Millennium Declaration."[3]

The purpose of this chapter is to depart from the 2030 Agenda as a political consensus approved by the UNGA and to read it as part of the development of the juridical international legal discourse. The method is to present the SDGs, within the framework of the sources of international law and its institutional structure, using the advances and evolution in other areas of the international law as best practices to analyze, in particular, the importance of the customary law and the role of the international organization in the crystallization of it. The object is to present the SDGs from an institutional and legal perspective, as a normative framework and not only as a political improvement within the sustainable development discourse.

The 2030 Agenda as Part of the International Legal Discourse

This chapter frames Agenda 2030 as part of international legal discourse. International legal discourse refers to "any collection of verbal exchanges of legal proposition,"[4] leaving the binding effect of it aside. The binding effect will then be analyzed in light of the theory of sources of international law.

Sovereign states generally consider international treaties or conventions as the best way to establish international obligations, although, for many practitioners the terms of the treaty

---

1 *The 17 Goals*, UNITED NATIONS DEPARTMENT OF ECONOMIC AND SOCIAL AFFAIRS (UN-DESA), https://sustainabledevelopment.un.org/?menu=1300 (last visited Nov. 6, 2020).
2 *End Poverty—Millennium Development Goals and beyond 2015*, UNITED NATIONS (UN), /www.un.org/millenniumgoals/ (last visited 6 November 2020).
3 G.A. Res. A/RES/55/2, *The Millennium Declaration* (Sept. 18, 2000).
4 ULF LINDERGALK, UNDERSTANDING JUS COGENS IN INTERNATIONAL LAW AND INTERNATIONAL LEGAL DISCOURSE 1 (2020).

are assimilated with internal law, creating great confusion.[5] Nevertheless, in no case can we consider that treaties are the only normative expression of international law.

From an exegetical perspective, the Statute of the International Court of Justice (ICJ), in Article 38, makes a brief list of the sources of international law and catalogs five different categories: Treaties or conventions, international custom, general principles of law, jurisprudence, and doctrine. Furthermore, this list has been enriched with a normative category identified as "Soft Law" by Lord McNair to

> describe instruments with extra-legal normative effect."[6] Also "the term…is used in the legal literature to describe principles, rules or standards that govern international relations and which are not considered an integral part of the bases of the sources of international.[7]

The sources included in the Statute, but especially those not mentioned such as soft law, are explained by the definition of International Law provided by Rosalyn Higgins: "International Law is not rules. It is a normative system…. Normative systems make possible that degree of order if society is to maximize the common good."[8] The order could be developed from different perspectives: Political, legal, or even conjectural. The UN represents that privileged forum of coordination referred to as multilateralism by Rosalyn Higgins, where the horizontal coordination effort finds its best expression and the General Assembly is the most comprehensive of its forums. The functions of the UNGA are distributed in several articles of the UN Charter, from 10 to 17, providing the mandate "to discuss any questions or any matters within the scope of the present Charter."[9] Nonetheless, the analysis of the capacity of the UNGA is usually caught in the formalism of the Charter itself. The Security Council is the body with the treaty-making power and the UNGA just the political body.

From a more functionalist perspective, each of the 193 heads of mission at the General Assembly, each of the individuals with the rank of Ambassador or High Commissioner, is a public official who represents and commits their state to participate in that forum, political or not.[10] National vote within international organizations is a vital element within the nature of the sources of international law, especially in the case of customary law, to evaluate the category of state practice, but particularly *opinio juris*.[11] This national responsibility is of special relevance concerning the mechanisms of implementation of the SDG Agenda.

---

5 Eugenio Hernández Breton, *Los tratados no son leyes*, 62 Boletín de la Academia de Ciencias Políticas y Sociales 131 (1995).
6 Daniel Thürer, *Soft Law*, Max Planck Encyclopedia of Public International Law (2009).
7 *Id*.
8 Rosalyn Higgins, Problems and Process: International Law and How We Use It 14 (1994).
9 U.N. Charter art. 11.2, "The General Assembly may discuss any questions or any matters within the scope of the present Charter or relating to the powers and functions of any organs provided for in the present Charter, and, except as provided in Article 12, may make recommendations to the Members of the United Nations or to the Security Council or to both on any such questions or matters."
10 Hans Kelsen, The Law of the United Nations: A Critical Analysis and Its fundamental Problems 155 (2008).
11 "A practice does not become a rule of customary international law merely because it is widely followed. It must, in addition, be deemed by states to be obligatory as a matter of law. This test will not be satisfied if the practice is followed out of the courtesy or if the states believe that they are legally free to depart from it at any time. The practice must comply with the opinion juris." *See* Thomas Buerguental and Sean Murphy, Public International Law in a Nutshell 22 (1990).

However, many authors and governments represented in the UNGA maintain that the SDG Agenda is a mere political agenda with some recommendations in the framework of an ambitious proposal for global cooperation.[12] In this sense, much has been said about the non-binding nature of the resolutions of the General Assembly, given their character of recommendation, as is clear from the content of chapter 4 of the UN Charter. Furthermore, this vision is reinforced by the contrast with the competences of the UN Security Council clearly established in article 25 of the Charter, about the binding powers of its decisions.[13]

The debate about UNGA decisions has been wide and extensive. Tomuschat ratifies the mandate of the Charter as "non-mandatory;"[14] however, the article reiterates the provisions that jurisprudentially have been developed to ratify the diversity of decisions that can be taken by the UNGA and its various legal procedures. It makes clear that

> those decisions that are adopted by consensus (such as the 2030 Agenda) have more common legal basis than a cluster of scattered elements of legal practice, taken fundamentally from the diplomatic practice of the countries of the "First World", that in the past were taken for the factual elaboration of the norms of customary law.[15]

The UNGA has a mandate over the development of International Law that is included in article 13 of the UN Charter.[16] Pursuant to this specific task, the UNGA approved in 1947

---

12 Democracy Development Programme, *The Roles of Civil Society in Localising the Sustainable Development Goals*, AFRICAN CIVIL SOCIETY CIRCLE, at 3, www.gppi.net/media/KAS_CSO_2016_Localizing_SDGs.pdf (2016).
13 U.N. Charter art. 25, "The Members of the United Nations agree to accept and carry out the decisions of the Security Council in accordance with the present Charter."
14 Christian Tomuschat, *United Nations General Assembly*, MAX PLANCK ENCYCLOPEDIA OF PUBLIC INTERNATIONAL LAW (2011). "It has frequently been argued in recent times that resolutions adopted unanimously or by consensus should be considered as legally binding stricto sensu if they purport to set forth legal rules. This reasoning applies primarily to resolutions which are specifically identified as 'Declarations'. Two types of such 'Declarations' may be distinguished. On the one hand, a 'Declaration' may set out legal propositions that are conceived of as aims of legal policy. The most prominent case in point is the Universal Declaration of Human Rights (1948). Originally, therefore, the Universal Declaration did not constitute a set of binding legal rules, but some of its provisions have crystallized as customary international law in the more than 60 years since its adoption. On the other hand, a 'Declaration' may intend to codify existing rules of customary international law or particularize the provisions of an international treaty. This latter classification applies, in particular, to the Friendly Relations Declaration. In its judgment in the Military and Paramilitary Activities in and against Nicaragua Case (Nicaragua v United States of America), the Court acknowledged that the Friendly Relations Declaration stands as an act mostly embodying existing customary law (at paras 188–91). Reference to the Friendly Relations Declaration was also made in the Legality of the Threat or Use of Nuclear Weapons (Advisory Opinion) ([1996] ICJ Rep 226 para. 102). It is true that, in particular, a declaration adopted by consensus embodies much more common legal substance than the dispersed elements of legal practice, mostly taken from the diplomatic intercourse of countries of the 'First World', that in the past were taken as the factual basis of rules of customary law. Resolutions under which the GA simply takes note of a set of rules do not confer on those rules any authoritative legitimacy (see, eg, UNGA Res 56/83 'Responsibility of States for Internationally Wrongful Acts' [12 December 2001] [GAOR 56th Session Supp 49 vol 1, 499], which took note of the ILC Draft Articles on Responsibility of States for Internationally Wrongful Acts); however, the GA thereby acknowledges that the instrument concerned is a worthwhile piece of legal craftsmanship, which is likely to obtain the formal seal of approval in the near future."
15 *Id.*
16 U.N. Charter art. 13, "The General Assembly shall initiate studies and make recommendations for the purpose of: a. Promoting international co-operation in the political field and encouraging the progressive development of international law and its codification."

the creation of the International Law Commission (ILC) and divided its functions clearly: Codification and the Progressive Development of International Law.

According to Watts, the codification of customary law "arises from the need to strengthen the institution of international practice."[17] It also adds that the codification process involves two concepts: "codification and progressive development of international law, although in practice the concept includes both actions which contain different elements."

Determining the normative quality of UNGA resolutions is complex, due to the indefinite nature of the Charter itself. As explained by Simma, "UNGA declarations convey strong indications of elements of international *ordre public*. They are establishing certain rules of customary law. However, given their non-binding character, it is necessary to examine further whether declarations contained in resolution can acquire a binding legal status by way of customary international law.[18, 19]

In the case of the SDGs, the UNGA has vaguely marked its role as a codifier and at the same time promoter of new areas of international law.[20] The introduction of the 2030 Agenda grounded the concepts in the evolution of the international law, "guided by the purposes and principles of the Charter of the United Nations"[21] and articulating with the Millennium Declaration and the Declaration of the Right of Development.[22]

The SDG Agenda takes a cautious approach toward a straight reference to codification or development of international law. For example, paragraph 17 explains the following: "The framework we are announcing today goes far beyond the MDGs. Alongside continuing development priorities such as poverty eradication, health, education, and food security and nutrition."[23] The wording of the article referred to the role as a developer of international

---

17 Sir Arthur Watt, *Codification and Progressive Development of International Law*, MAX PLANCK ENCYCLOPEDIA OF PUBLIC INTERNATIONAL LAW (2009). "'Codification' is for convenience often used to cover both concepts—and will occasionally be so used in this contribution—but the two notions have distinct meanings: 'codification' connotes the more precise articulation of rules of international law in fields where there has already been extensive practice leading to the emergence of customary rules, while 'progressive development' connotes the development of rules on subjects not yet regulated by international law or where the law is insufficiently developed."
18 Simma Bruno et al., THE CHARTER OF THE UNITED NATIONS: A COMMENTARY 270 (2nd ed., 2002).
19 *Id*. at Page 271.
20 Juan Carlos Sainz Borgo, *El Derecho internacional consuetudinario, Una visita a partir del Estudio del Comité Internacional de la Cruz Roja* (CICR), *in* LA CRISIS DE LAS FUENTES DEL DERECHO EN LA GLOBALIZACIÓN (Joaquin González and Eloy García López, eds., 2011).
21 G.A. A/RES/70/1, *Transforming our world: The 2030 Agenda for Sustainable Development SDG*, at ¶10 (Oct. 21, 2015). "The new Agenda is guided by the purposes and principles of the Charter of the United Nations, including full respect for international law. It is grounded in the Universal Declaration of Human Rights, international human rights treaties, the Millennium Declaration and the 2005 World Summit Outcome Document. It is informed by other instruments such as the Declaration on the Right to Development."
22 *Id*. at ¶19. "We reaffirm the importance of the Universal Declaration of Human Rights, as well as other international instruments relating to human rights and international law. We emphasize the responsibilities of all States, in conformity with the Charter of the United Nations, to respect, protect and promote human rights and fundamental freedoms for all, without distinction of any kind as to race, colour, sex, language, religion, political or other opinion, national or social origin, property, birth, disability or other status."
23 *Id*. at ¶17. "In its scope, however, the framework we are announcing today goes far beyond the Millennium Development Goals. Alongside continuing development priorities such as poverty eradication, health, education and food security and nutrition, it sets out a wide range of economic, social and environmental objectives. It also promises more peaceful and inclusive societies. It also, crucially, defines

law rooted in the concept, noting the following: "Reflecting the integrated approach that we have decided on, there are deep interconnections and many cross-cutting elements across the new Goals and targets."[24]

In this way, the international community represented in the UNGA articulates the SDGs within the framework of the evolution of International Law, both from the general perspective, as the case of the UN Charter itself and the treaties in the field of Human Rights, but also more specifically, by making the MDGs a key precedent in evolution itself, as well as many other precedents for the rest of the SDGs.

I consider the process of building SDGs as much more complex and ambitious than just the natural evolution from MDGs to SDGs. The work that represents the continuation of one paradigm to the other denoted an arduous task of compiling all the information produced, including also the normative elements, which allowed states to assume these new commitments, especially the work of specialized UN agencies and programs that can be summarized in soft law. This process largely represented codifying work on the part of the UN General Secretariat and the drafting committee. The process of determining the practice of the states for the SDGs includes many other sources of international law, including human rights.

However, I would like to highlight here that SDGs do not constitute a simple political agreement, the product of consensus. The 2030 Agenda is political evolution, but above all, a normative work of the international community, expressed in a resolution from the UNGA, where the 2030 Agenda becomes an evolution with juridical relevance, close to a form of crystallization of the customary norm.

The arguments previously expressed demonstrate the normative nature of the SDG Agenda. The approval process, as a resolution of the UNGA, is overcome by the broad support of the international community, granting it a category in the area of international legal discourse; consequently, as part of the sources of international law. The way in which the 2030 Agenda is expressed strengthens the codifying role of the UNGA itself.

SDGs as a Source of International Law

The normative quality of the SDG Agenda has been presented in the previous section, whether we understand it as a normative resolution that codifies the existing practice or the role of the UNGA evidences the existence of another normative expression, such as it could be a sample of a soft law evolved from the perspective of contemporary international law. In this section, we will devote ourselves to assessing some possibilities.

The analysis that we propose is fundamentally exegetical and, as stated, uses the normative list by Article 38 of the Statute of the ICJ, that defined international custom, as "evidence of a practice generally accepted as law."[25] This characterization in itself has presented throughout the history of the Statute numerous criticisms for its lack of clarity. Alain Pellet

---

means of implementation. Reflecting the integrated approach that we have decided on, there are deep interconnections and many cross-cutting elements across the new Goals and targets."
24 Id.
25 Art. 38, I.C.J.

called it illogical since it refers to an upstream concept, which requires an accepted practice that later becomes law.[26]

One of the challenges that international customary law presents is the need for materialization as a norm, which can be presented in two ways: The crystallization of the custom or its systematization through works carried out under international, national, or academic governmental initiatives.

The first can be presented in several ways. Crystallization occurs through the implementation of the Statute of the ICJ. States can claim a certain practice as compulsory and once it appears reflected in the text of a sentence, it acquires all its force as customary law. Second, states can declare the existence of the custom bilaterally or multilaterally, either through political declarations, joint communiqués, votes, or resolutions in international organizations. This way of crystallizing custom is permanently verified in international law and its abuse can sometimes lead to the institution's weakening due to its almost permanent rhetorical use.[27]

This process of determining custom is not merely a mechanical process according to the ICJ. As Pellet points out, it is full of legal decisions and appreciations that can result in various kinds of custom, such as regional practice, and the density and consistency of that practice.[28] In the words of Judge Thomas Buergenthal, "every practice is subject to an examination."[29]

Secondly, the codification of international custom can have an official or informal character or an academic character, depending on the institution that carries it out. This process can also be called the systematization of international practice.

Some international organizations develop the process of codification. As mentioned, the most important one is the ILC. Other institutions have influence, like the International Committee of the Red Cross in the case of the International Humanitarian Law[30] or the International Law Association in other areas, like Helsinki Rules for the international water law.[31]

However, in the case of Agenda 2030, there is an additional challenge: Each SDG reflects a different topic and finds in its content diverse international practices or regulatory developments. In the absence of a clear process of codification, the international judge would have the last word in each case, in particular establishing the density of the customary norm to each particular SDG in a given case. Another possibility could be that the ILC, or other international organizations, governmental or not, continue the work done by the UNGA on this case, but acting as a codifier of the practice reflected on the SDG.

The methodology developed by the UNGA in the case of Agenda 2030 largely confirms how the universal system has been working in relation to international obligations in certain forums. Agenda 2030 creates a normative space that is entrenched in firmly pre-existing

---

26 Allain Pellet, *The Statue of the International Court of Justice, in* ENCYCLOPEDIA OF PUBLIC INTERNATIONAL LAW (Rudolf Bernhardt and Peter MacAlister-Smith, eds., 1992).

27 Andrew T. Guzman, *Saving Customary International Law*, 27 MICH. J. INTL. L. 115, 121 (2005).

28 Pellet, *supra* note 26.

29 Buergenthal and Murphy, *supra* note 11 at 22.

30 *See* JEAN-MARIE HENCKAERTS & LOUISE DOSWALD-BECK, CUSTOMARY INTERNATIONAL HUMANITARIAN LAW VOL. I RULES (2005).

31 *See Articles on Cross-Media Pollution Resulting from the Use of the Waters of an International Drainage Basin,* INTERNATIONAL LAW ASSOCIATION, /www.internationalwaterlaw.org/documents/intldocs/ILA/I LA-Articles_on_Cross-Media_Pollution-Helsinki1996.pdf (last visited Nov. 6, 2020).

obligations and based on these seeks advances in the consolidation of new objectives, which are largely the elaboration or improvement of initially planned goals.

There are two approaches for the States. First, the SDGs are consolidated in international practice. The evolution of the previous norms would advance with the support of a small group of countries, assuming it as obligations; later, relying on the "recommendations" or "non-mandatory norms" based on "soft law" could start to be implemented, either at the domestic level or as international commitment. Second, other countries could refer to the result as "just soft law," emphasizing the soft rather than the law element of the expression. It is just a politically driven legal explanation, leaving aside the normative value of the SDGs.

Nevertheless, it is possible to analyze the SDGs as a highly evolved and global form of soft law. This complex category of international law sources is a residual classification. As already mentioned, soft laws are "rules or standards that govern international relations and which are not considered an integral part of the bases of the sources of international law."[32] This is how many governments will regard the SDGs. This short shrift neither gives much in the way of a normative or practical solution, since it does not allow articulation of its importance within a hierarchical legal scheme, nor has an inclusive explanation of the legal diversity of the SDGs.

The permanent work within an international organization: Reiterating general obligations, ratifying certain interpretations, and accepting the advance of certain international rules is the way that customary law emerges today.

Koskenniemi points out in the Report on the Fragmentation of International Law, about the need for general codification:

> In an increasingly specialized legal environment, few institutions are left to speak the language of general international law, with the aim to regulate, at a universal level, relationships that cannot be reduced to the realization of special interests and that go further than technical coordination. The International Law Commission is one such institution. The work for codification and development it has carried out has been precisely about elucidating the content of "general international law" as an aspect of what can only be understood as a kind of an international public realm.[33]

Agenda 2030 could be interpreted as a taking back of the codification mandate from the ILC to the UNGA.

The emphasis we have placed on customary international law in this article should not be interpreted as an isolated event. However, as Mendelson wrote, it is important to remember that: "in the quite recent past, when to be interested in customary international law was to risk being labeled as old-fashioned, not to mention reactionary."[34] The prominence given to

---

32 Thürer, *supra* note 6.
33 G.A. A/CN.4/L.682, *Report of the Study Group of the International Law Commission Fragmentation of International Law: Difficulties arising from the diversification and expansion of International Law*, at 255 (April 13, 2006).
34 Maurice Mendelson, *The Formation of Customary International Law*, in Collected Courses of the Hague Academy of International Law Vol. 272 (1999). "There was a time, in the quite recent past, when to be interested in customary international law was to risk being labeled as old-fashioned, not to mention reactionary. Customary international law, communist states and their jurists told us, had been created by bourgeois, Western States in the exercise of their hegemony and for their own benefit. This found an echo in some quarters in the Third World. Treaties, we were told, were preferable, because

custom as a part of the sources of international law refers to the effectiveness of argument that lies in the way they can be used to oppose historically effective power to renounce an international commitment. As Koskenniemi explains, the "technique of legal sources intervenes precisely to protect professional arguments from the critique of being too political because dependent on unverifiable abstractions."[35]

The SDGs, in their development as a normative space, advance a process of densification of international norms that increases its relevance in the context of general international law and strengthens the way to achieving the objectives that states initially set out in the negotiation process and subscription to the international obligation. Agenda 2030 represents a process of codification where the UNGA systemizes the state practice on many of the objectives, following its mandate from the UN Charter. Consequently, SDGs in the format of custom norms are more relevant than just the political agreement within the UNGA.

SDG 17—An Opportunity for the Codification

Considering Agenda 2030 as a process of codification could initiate a different approach to the work carried out so far. The SDGs as a political consensus lack the capacity to be implemented. It has no efficacy on the ground. However, SDGs as a part of the principal sources of international law increase the effectivity of the consensus.

Koskenniemi elaborates about the importance of the consensus at the multilateral level in the following:

> If there is no formal treaty, then the only possibility seems to be to regard it as custom. But this destroys the normative distinction between custom and treaties: both arise now from consent. The sole distinction would seem to be the descriptive one: treaties describe consent in written while custom is consent in non-written form. But as non-formal agreements, too, tend to be written down in recommendations, resolutions, "Final Acts", etc.,[36]

As explained by Brownlie, "there is the principle that the general consent of States creates rules of general application. The definition of custom is essentially a statement of this principle."[37]

Agenda 2030 is a clear example of agreement, the *spirit de corp* to construct a consensus. This expression requires a process of materialization in practical terms. Agenda 2030 comprises objectives and targets. The objectives are the clear political mandates and the targets are the statistical way to measure. This mechanics is more or less correct in the majority of the objectives. As such, it is important to identify the areas where the consensus reaches the level of a customary norm in order to codify and promote it. As Taki explained, "Unlike

---

they respected sovereign equality: no State could be compelled to accept a treaty if it did not wish to do so. Of course, this was an oversimplification: although the treaty process respects sovereign equality in a formal sense, it is not immune from politics; and, in the politics of the real world, States are by no means completely equal."

35 Martti Koskenniemi, *Methodology of International Law*, MAX PLANCK ENCYCLOPEDIA OF PUBLIC INTERNATIONAL LAW (2007).
36 MARTTI KOSKENNIEMI, FROM APOLOGY TO UTOPIA THE STRUCTURE OF INTERNATIONAL LEGAL ARGUMENT 409 (2005).
37 IAN BROWNLIE, PRINCIPLES OF PUBLIC INTERNATIONAL LAW 6 (2003).

with municipal law, the international legal order has no central organ that is empowered to apply and enforce law, and such functions are entrusted to the States concerned."[38] The idea to promote obligation to comply within a customary norm framework is more likely for a government than just a political agreement at the multilateral level.

Agenda 2030, Paragraph 60, shows a consensus about the way to implement the SDG:

> We reaffirm our strong commitment to the full implementation of this new Agenda. We recognize that we will not be able to achieve our ambitious Goals and targets without a revitalized and enhanced Global Partnership and comparably ambitious means of implementation.[39]

This Global Partnership requires institutional leadership on the construction of the platform. On the successive Reports from the United Nations Secretary-General, the language of SDGs has seemed to lose this political driving force. The crisis of multilateralism provoked by COVID-19 has impacted the targets of the SDGs. As expressed by the Secretary-General on the opening ceremony of the 75th Session of the UNGA, "We are careening off track in achieving the Sustainable Development Goals."[40]

The SDG requires a two-level approach: (1) the monitoring and evaluation process to understand the factual advances and (2) a process of codification of the norms collected by the UNGA from Agenda 2030.

The SDGs planned monitoring and revision mechanisms will be important, but they will not be able to gather the necessary sponsorship to mobilize the support that can change the reality that motivates the effort of Agenda 2030. The normative discourse of the SDGs, convening the ILC or various organizations, could use the specific mandate of SDG 17 to build the needed synergies to codify the norms presented in the 2030 Agenda. The codification of the SDGs beyond the UNGA's resolution could form the mechanism that allows consolidating the necessary elements to strengthen compliance with its objectives.

The First Report by the Secretary-General explained well the objective of the SDG 17: "Achieving the ambitious targets of the 2030 Agenda requires a revitalized and enhanced global partnership that brings together Governments, civil society, the private sector, the United Nations system and other actors and mobilizes all available resources."[41] A wide and collective project of codification of the most pressing objectives of Agenda 2030 is a good starting point to construct a platform to promote effectiveness.

The International Committee of the Red Cross (ICRC) developed a methodology on its study of Customary International Humanitarian Law[42] articulating the obligations contracted

---

38 Hiroshi Taki, *Effectiveness*, MAX PLANCK ENCYCLOPEDIA OF PUBLIC INTERNATIONAL LAW (2013).
39 *Id*. "We reaffirm our strong commitment to the full implementation of this new Agenda. We recognize that we will not be able to achieve our ambitious Goals and targets without a revitalized and enhanced Global Partnership and comparably ambitious means of implementation. The revitalized Global Partnership will facilitate an intensive global engagement in support of implementation of all the Goals and targets, bringing together Governments, civil society, the private sector, the United Nations system and other actors and mobilizing all available resources."
40 U.N. Secretary General, *Address to the Opening of the General Debate of the 75th Session of the General Assembly*, www.un.org/sg/en/content/sg/speeches/2020-09-22/address-the-opening-of-the-general-debate-of-the-75th-session-of-the-general-assembly (Sept. 22, 2020).
41 U.N. Economic and Social Council E/2019/68, *Progress towards the Sustainable Development Goals*, at 32–34 (May 8, 2019).
42 Henckaerts & Doswald-Beck, *supra* note 30.

directly by the state and systematizing them, in order to promote the crystallization of international humanitarian law, in a higher mandatory degree[43] or connection than the so-called "soft law" empirical base on which a good part of contemporary multilateralism seems to be built particularly in the Agenda 2030. As a result, the ICRC's Report developed rules easily applied by judges, practitioners, and governments to implement the customary rules.

States should reaffirm the SDGs as part of the political declaration being discussed for the 50th anniversary of the 1972 Stockholm Conference and the 30th anniversary of the 1992 Rio Earth Summit in 2022. The work of the summit and global conventions represent an important political work particularly on the process of consolidating and crystalizing customary norms.

The UNGA should also ask the ILC to examine the codification of the SDGs among its study of general principles of international law, and the UNGA (6th committee) should address several ILC reports now pending before it, in order to promote the advance of the normative responses in the midst of increasingly unstable political multilateralism. Civil society should mobilize governments to reflect the SDGs in their national legislation as a confirmation of state practice, promoting the importance of the objectives of the plan within Agenda 2030 from a local perspective.

SDG 17 creates the institutional platform to work together on a multilevel process of crystallization of the customary norms into rules of legal value and easy application. Agenda 2030, as explained, represents a clear evolution of the consensus in many topics of international law and leads the way for the construction of a process of codification of customary international law. The objectives, targets, and successive reports demonstrate in many of the areas the possibility to draw elements that strengthen codification, following the recommendations from the ILC to prevent the fragmentation.

Conclusion

The construction of the SDGs represents a great effort of codification by the UNGA, which was accepted and assimilated by the community of states within the framework of the political agreements of the general assembly.

The SDGs are elements of international law, not just political agreements without normative value. In this sense, the value that the SDGs represent as a source of international law is significant for the international legal community, academics, and judges. The SDGs as part of the legal discourse can be used to oppose the conjunctural idea of Agenda 2030.

Agenda 2030's value as a codification of international law is undeniable. Most of the objectives and goals are articulated in previous international agreements and commitments, which have been assimilated by the States, with different levels of acceptance. Using the SDGs as a customary norm will articulate the political consensus with its need for compliance, at the municipal level as well as the international level, bringing a new institutional dimension to the process of achieving Agenda 2030. The recognition of the SDGs as customary law could strengthen the capability of civil society to work together with national governments on a global agenda.

The work carried out by the ICRC marked an important path to be evaluated by various international institutions, both within and outside the UN System. Institutions like the

---

43 *Ob. Cit.*

International Law Commission or the International Union for Conservation of Nature (IUCN) should evaluate the ICRC's working methodology to develop environmental standards that could serve as a model for the international legal community. The International Law Commission could select the most crystallized areas of the SDGs to embark on a process of codification and progressive development of rules of customary value.

The crisis provoked by the pandemic undermines the previous political consensus for Agenda 2030. SDG 17 could represent a point of departure to build a more concrete legal ground for the rest of Agenda 2030. The international community could use the mandate of the International Law Commission and the SDG 17 framework to build legal ground that keeps the previous consensus and saves the achievement of Agenda 2030.

The codified SDGs as a customary norm, which will be applicable to the international community, could increase the level of compliance of many of the objectives and targets. It will reinforce the work of the UN and other specialized agencies in their mandate on behalf of the international community.

34 Integrating the SDGs through "One Health"

Nicholas A. Robinson

COVID-19 makes an overwhelming case for why all nations should accelerate their implementation of the United Nations (UN) Sustainable Development Goals (SDGs). No nation can be rid of the SARS-CoV-2 virus until all nations unite in a partnership to do so. This chapter explores how the SDGs for health, clean water and sanitation, and restoration of the wild environment, are each called upon to overcome COVID-19. Moreover, since current biodiversity degradation has unleashed microbes capable of infecting humans with the "next" pandemic, countries have persuasive reasons to unite behind attaining the SDGs.

What must be done both to win the battle against COVID-19 and cope with possible reinfections, and does doing so "Strengthen the means of implementation and revitalize the global partnership for sustainable development" to attain SDG 17? This can be done by 2030 within the Agenda for Sustainable Development,[1] and as a key focus for the UN Decade of Ecological Restoration (2021–2030). Having a target of 2030 enables all stakeholders to muster support for action on related SDGs.[2] There are numerous sub-themes that foster implementation of the SDGs.[3] This chapter envisions "One Health" as an integrating and motivational theme linking the SDGs through the lenses of averting pandemics.[4]

One Health may be understood as follows:

> One Health is the universal policy and practice of care for the integrity, stability, resilience and beauty of Earth's biotic community through nurturing the interdependent

---

1 See *Transforming Our World: The 2030 Agenda for Sustainable Development*, United Nations A/RES/70/1 (2015), https://sustainabledevelopment.un.org/content/documents/21252030%20Agenda%20for%20Sustainable%20Development%20web.pdf [hereinafter "Agenda 2030"].
2 See *New UN Decade on Ecosystem Restoration to Inspire Bold UN Environment Assembly Decisions*, UN ENVIRONMENTAL PROGRAM STORY (Mar. 6, 2019), www.unenvironment.org/news-and-stories/story/new-un-decade-ecosystem-restoration-inspire-bold-un-environment-assembly; For this decade, the SDGs most often referenced are 1, 2, 6, 7, 12, 13, 14, 15, and 17.
3 See UN Press Release, *Restoration Offers Unparalleled Opportunity for Job Creation, Food Security and Addressing Climate Change*, UN ENVIRONMENTAL PROGRAM STORY (Mar. 1, 2019), www.unenvironment.org/news-and-stories/press-release/new-un-decade-ecosystem-restoration-offers-unparalleled-opportunity#:~:text=%20New%20UN%20Decade%20on%20Ecosystem%20Restoration%20offers,food%20systems%20can%20be%20the%20common...%20More%20; For example, for the Food and Agriculture Organization (FAO) sustainable food systems are a common thread connecting the many SDGs. FAO is responsible for 21 of the SDGs' indicators and is a contributing agency for a further four. In this capacity, FAO is supporting countries' efforts in achieving both the 2030 SDG Agenda and the Decade of Ecological Restoration.
4 See Nicholas A. Robinson, *The Next Pandemic Is Here*, 37 THE ENVIRONMENTAL FORUM, 30–35 (Nov./Dec. 2020), ISSN 0731–5732, (available at www.eli.org).

health links that are shared among humans, wildlife, domesticated animals, plants, ecosystems, and all nature. One Health transcends and unites the contributions of the life sciences[5] for stewardship of ecosystem integrity and biodiversity to sustain the health and well-being of life on Earth.[6]

Ecological restoration is essential for the world to avert future pandemics, as John Robinson and Federica Pesca explain in their chapter on SDG 15. This is because infectious diseases emerge from areas where unsustainable development has disrupted nature's health. In the process of zoonosis, viruses are shed and infect humans.[7] The SDGs are essential to restoring sustainable patterns of human behavior with nature and each other. Without implementing the SDGs, there is little likelihood that nations can avert the "next" pandemic.

Today, the "next" pandemic is silently among us, hiding in plain sight, but unseen. When it comes to emerging infectious diseases, all nations have a choice: Either endure another pandemic or re-allocate scarce resources in cooperation to avert the next pandemic. A win-win approach to finding resources is to organize international cooperation through a set of thematic practices worldwide. This thematic focus can coordinate and advance implementation of the SDGs because all nations have the same shared stake: All parts of the world share the same issues of human, animal, and ecosystem health. They are also driven by a common anxiety to escape future pandemics. By harnessing a fear of future pandemics with the aspirations of all the SDGs, this "One Health" theme can produce the vibrant partnership called for in SDG 17.

One Health can guide and stimulate implementation of the SDGs before 2030. Embracing One Health will not be easy because "business as usual" priorities crowd out new priorities. Moving One Health precepts from the periphery to the core of governmental decision-making will be problematic. Its success depends on SDG 4 and education about how infectious diseases emerge, on enlightened self-interest, and on invoking ethical roots and human instincts about caring for nature. In the coming years, One Health can mature into a global partnership and become an evolved norm for our times. Humanity has no other choice, beset as we are with the likelihood of more pandemics, unfathomable losses in biodiversity, and unpredictable impacts from climate disruption.

---

5 Life sciences include the disciplines concerned with the study of living organisms, including biology, ecology, botany, zoology, microbiology, physiology, biochemistry, medicine, veterinary science, epidemiology, conservation biology, and related subjects.
6 This definition is supported by the UN Environment Assembly 3 in its endorsement of One Health in 2016, in Part III of UNEA Resolution, UNEP/EA.3/Res.4 , Environment and Health (Dec. 20, 2017), https://wedocs.unep.org/bitstream/handle/20.500.11822/31012/k1709367.english.pdf?sequence=3&isAllowed=y, which provides as follows:"23. Recognizes that biodiversity loss is a health risk multiplier, including by aggravating environmental challenges, and underlines in addition the benefits for health and well-being in protecting and restoring biodiversity, ecosystems and their services;
    24. Also and emphasizes in that regard the value of the "One Health" approach, an integrated approach that fosters cooperation between environmental conservation and the human health, animal health and plant health sectors;
    25. Encourages member States and invites relevant organizations to mainstream the conservation and sustainable use of biodiversity to enhance ecosystem resilience, including by taking actions to halt biodiversity loss, and to promote coordination between policies and actions aimed at improving biodiversity conservation, food safety and human health as an important safeguard for current and future health and human well-being focusing on relevant sectors."
7 DAVID QUAMMEN, SPILLOVER: ANIMALS INFECTIONS AND THE NEXT HUMAN PANDEMIC (W. W. Norton & Company 2012).

Past Pandemics: Precursors Toward One Health

The One Heath leitmotif already permeates such diverse fields as veterinary science, medicine, ecology, environmental law, and ethics. It is a thread that runs, although largely still unacknowledged, through each of the SDGs. All governments currently have in place the policies and tools for implementing One Health albeit not yet deployed to avert newly emerged infectious diseases. If past pandemics are recalled, the logic of doing so becomes clear.

Perhaps conveniently, humanity's collective memory forgets the horrors that historians have recorded about past pandemics. COVID-19, likely shared with humans via bats, was not the first nor will it be the last pandemic people experience. Remember the Brucellosis infections from cows igniting "The Plague of Athens" (430–426 BCE), or the Antonine Plague of 172 killing one of every ten persons in the Roman Empire, or the colonial pandemics that European Conquistadors brought to the Americas killing millions of Indigenous People in the 15th–17th centuries, or the Great Smallpox Epidemic during the American Revolutionary War (1775–82), or the bubonic "Third Plague Pandemic" in China (1855), or the Russian Flu Pandemic (1889–90).[8] Although popular knowledge of former plagues fades, they persist in cultural memory.

The imagery of feared contagions is embedded in folklore and custom. The skeletal specter of Pestilence and Death rides on as one of the Biblical four horsemen of the Apocalypse from Revelations. The Pied Piper beguiles still from the "Great Plague" in 1361 that targeted young children. The plague, pictured as a Piper, first kills the rats before luring off the children to their deaths, eventually killing upward of one-third of all Europeans. Pandemics left popular contrivances to cope. As The Great Plague hit, Venice isolated visiting sailors on a nearby island, for 40 days—*quaranto*. Eight centuries later, the quarantine remains each county's #1 defense against raging epidemics. More recently, recollections of the 1918 Influenza Pandemic, originating in Kansas and killing many more than died in the First World War, are supplanted by memories of the "Great War." The 1918 "flu" virus took up residence among humans, who prosaically learned to live with "the common cold" and their annual "flu shots."

Admittedly, the COVID-19 crises of the moment distract from and obscure the roles that SDGs can serve. But when a pandemic disrupts socio-economic life, receptivity is great for finding effective and easily understood ways to restore social stability and order, as SDG 17 contemplates. Anxiety to avert another pandemic like COVID-19 can awaken decision-makers to their choices, including cooperating under the banner of "One Health." Any vaccine for COVID-19 will likely not provide a defense against other coming pandemics, whose viruses quietly circulate among us already. Having uprooted settled practices everywhere, COVID-19 offers windows of opportunity to establish the SDGs as foundations for managing sustainably those new infectious diseases that are emerging from the animal kingdom. It is in our collective self-interest to act now.

---

8 Owens, Jarus, *20 of the Worst Epidemics and Pandemics in History*, LIVESCIENCE (Mar. 20, 2020), www.livescience.com/worst-epidemics-and-pandemics-in-history.html.

One Health: Coping with Zoonosis

Infectious diseases like COVID-19 emerge through zoonosis, the sharing of the same diseases by humans and mammals. Many illnesses afflict alike humans and wild or domesticated animals, such as tuberculosis. Assorted bacteria or viruses compatibly abide with mammals. Each person's body comfortably hosts more microbes than it has human cells. An individual's microbiome accounts for about three pounds of body weight. Wild and domesticated animals are also hosts for many microbes. When an animal can no longer serve as a healthy host for these microbes, it sheds bacteria and viruses, which can then infect a new host. Humans are infected either directly, as when handling animal meat, or indirectly through intermediate vectors such as other animals or insects like ticks and mosquitos.[9]

Humans first learned about zoonosis through contact with domesticated animals. To their credit, veterinarians first urged an approach to humans and animal health based upon a partnership with medical physicians and public health specialists. Advocates of this initial animal/human variant of One Health have scoped out the need for closer collaboration between medical physicians and veterinarians. It would muster resources for epidemiologists to pinpoint how and where an animal infects a human, enabling governments and animal/human health specialists to build capacity to contain the outbreak in the field. The aim is to limit human to human transmission, and find treatments for ill patients, and start the vaccine search. This initial articulation of One Health is practical and instrumental.

This variant of One Health, however useful, does not get to the heart of the problem, which is preventing the zoonotic spill-over of an infectious disease from an animal in the first place. Coping with new pandemics requires a more holistic framework, engaging with stakeholders from other disciplines. In "*Aëre, Aquis et Locis*" (*Air, Waters and Places/Land*) in 400 BCE, Hippocrates anticipated both medicine and human ecology. In succeeding centuries, these two embryonic fields parted ways. But Hippocrates' early insights carry weight. Health entails a wider focus than just medical concerns for treating illnesses that can infect humans and animals alike. Zoonotic diseases emerge from the animal kingdom, the terrain of countryside, the lands and places of biodiversity. Stewardship of ecosystems and biodiversity is an essential part of One Health. Conservationists, Indigenous Peoples, and protected area managers are partners too. The legal profession is essential too, since the groundwork of environmental laws already serves One Health objectives.

Governments at all levels cannot safely defer implementing a holistic One Health framework because the "next" pandemic is probably already emerging. Since it is not a question of *if* a new pandemic will emerge, but only a question of *when*, much is at stake. For example, six months into the COVID-19 pandemic, the US National Academy of Sciences published a report entitled "Prevalent Eurasian Avian-Like H1N1 Swine influenza Virus with 2009 Pandemic Viral Genes Facilitating Human Infection."[10] Humans working on pig farms are infecting other humans in China with a new virus. Pre-existing immunities appear ineffective against this new infection. The report found that its "infectivity greatly enhances the opportunity for virus adaptation in humans and raises concerns for the possible generation of pandemic viruses."[11] This new G4 EA H1N1 virus is spreading among humans in

---

9 *See generally* MICHAEL T. OSTERHOLM AND MARK OLSHAKER, DEADLIEST ENEMY (2017).
10 *See* Honglei Sun et al., *Prevalent Eurasian Avian-Like H1N1 Swine Influenza Virus with 2009 Pandemic Viral Genes Facilitating Human Infection*, 117 PNAS 17204–10 (Jun. 29, 2020), https://doi.org/10.1073/pnas.1921186117.
11 *Id.*

parallel with a raging animal pandemic of the African swine fever virus (AFS). AFS is forcing Asians to kill their domestic pig herds. AFS is now in 17 European nations and threatens to spread across all continents. No one knows now how to contain the AFS Pandemic among animals. The AFS pandemic in domesticated pigs also threatens the extinction of the remnant wild pig populations in Asia.

Even if public health systems can contain the spread of novel coronavirus G4 EA H1N1, as Ebola has been contained for the moment in Africa, there is always another infectious disease emerging. For the foreseeable future, our reality is to live in an era of escalating numbers of zoonoses. One Health guides governments to realign their programs for ecological well-being to include management of diseases and infections that naturally are transmitted between vertebrate animals and humans.

Increasing Frequency of Infectious Diseases: New Pandemics at Our Doorstep

The frequency of animals shedding viruses onward to infect humans is on the increase. Zoonosis accounts for 61% of all human diseases and 75% of the new infectious diseases of the past decade.[12] Why is this so? Have not humans experienced occasional pandemics for millennia? The answer is evident, considering how pervasively humans now disrupt the ecosystems and displace wild animals. When the Plague of Athens raged or the Roman Empire fell, Earth held only some 190 million people. The 13th century's Great Plague killed 200 million of Earth's then one-half billion inhabitants. By the middle of the 20th century, Earth's population was doubling between 1950 and 1987, from 2.5 to 5 billion people. Demographers estimate that Earth will hold eight billion in 2024. The biomass of humans today is estimated to be ten times that of *all* wild animals.

In the wake of human population growth, homo sapiens negatively impact biodiversity. Twenty percent of the Amazon forests have been lost in the past five decades. Humans grub out forest habitats to harvest timber and minerals, expand agriculture, or invest in development, with scant attention to the fate of wild animals. Half the world's ecosystems are degraded. Populations of mammals, birds, fish, reptiles, and amphibians have, on average, declined by 60% between 1970 and 2014. Dislodged from healthy habitats, distressed animals shed their microbes. Zoonotic spill-over is ever more frequent. Of the millions of viruses yet to be studied, perhaps some 700,000 viruses are capable of zoonosis. There are doubtless many spill-overs to come because the interface between humans and animals has never been greater.

To cope with zoonotic spill-overs, One Heath can differentiate action in each of the three stages of new infectious disease emergence.

Stage One

The pre-emergent stage is when animals live within healthy ecosystems. When nature is protected, microbes are stable within their wild animal reservoirs. A healthy habitat dilutes

---

12 *Zoonoses*, WORLD HEALTH ORGANIZATION (Jul. 20, 2020), www.who.int/zoonoses/diseases/en/; *See also Zoonotic Disease: Emerging Public Health Threats in the Region*, EASTERN MEDITERRANEAN REGIONAL OFFICE OF THE WORLD HEALTH ORGANIZATION, www.emro.who.int/fr/about-who/rc61/zoonotic-diseases.html (last accessed on Dec. 9, 2020).

the risk of spill-overs and human infections because microbes have less exposure to humans. In an intact ecosystem, predators of small mammals keep in check the numbers of wild animals that host microbes. Nature conservation is chronically under-funded, and there is no One Health funding yet for this phase.

Stage Two

The second stage is emergence, the spill-overs resulting from disruptions to wildlife. Humans disrupt animal habitats in much of what they do, such as building new human settlements and roads, clearing land for commercial development and agribusiness plantations, commercial hunting and marketing of wild animals killed for food, harvesting timber, or mining and other natural resources extractions. Encroachments into natural areas disrupt intact ecosystems, fragmenting habitat. Humans find increased numbers of animals with microbes living in their midst. Few, if any, governmental resources are devoted to the health of wild animal habitats to avert or contain spill-overs. Environmental laws are available to manage environmental quality, such as requiring environmental impact assessments (EIAs), but they are rarely deployed to address zoonosis. Governmental capacity in this second stage is weak. There is little funding for surveillance and nearly two-thirds of laboratories capable of identifying zoonotic diseases are in developed nations, with virtually none in the developing countries where many zoonotic diseases are emerging. One Health funding barely exists in this phase.

Stage Three

The third phase, after the spill-over, is rapid spread of the disease among humans, as in the 2003 epidemic of SARS, or as a pandemic. In this phase, travel and trade expand the person-to-person infections world-wide, as in the 1918 Influenza Pandemic, or the still on-going HIV/AIDS or COVID-19 pandemics. Governments concentrate most of their financing on health care and containment of pandemics in this phase.

Preventative measures to find and fend-off the COVID-19 pandemic in its Phase 2 arrived too little, too late. In February of 2018, the World Health Organization (WHO) called for enhanced surveillance to detect next global zoonotic threat, which it labeled virus "X."[13] In 2012, *The Lancet* had published a series on preventing pandemics, emphasizing prediction and prevention of the next pandemic zoonosis.[14] In March of 2019, the WHO and the OiE, the World Organization for Animal Health (formerly *Office international des epizooties*), which since 1924 has led international cooperation on containing zoonoses in farmed and traded animals, joined with the UN Food & Agricultural Organization (FAO) to publish their One Health recommendations in the *Tripartite Guide to Addressing Zoonotic Diseases in Countries*.[15] This *Guide* focuses on cooperation between veterinary and public health authorities, and promotes a One Health approach for establishing cooperation between

---

13 The WHO issued a watch for a new disease, which came to be seen as SARS-CoV-2; *see* Peter Daszak, *We Knew Disease X Was Coming. It's Here* Now, NY TIMES (Feb. 27, 2020), www.nytimes.com/2020/02/27/opinion/coronavirus-pandemics.html.
14 Zoonoses, THE LANCET (2012), www.thelancet.com/series/zoonoses.
15 *Tripartite Zoonoses Guide*, FAO, OIE, WHO (2019), www.who.int/docs/default-source/emergency-preparedness/22211602-tzg-flyer-en-web.pdf?sfvrsn=1ac04d45_2.

agencies responsible for agriculture, food markets, domestic animals, and human health. SARS-CoV-2 spilled over to humans before any of these preventative measures could be implemented.

Preventative measures depend on collaboration across disciplines and agencies. Proposals to establish close collaboration between veterinary science and human medicine date back to 1964 when Dr. Calvin Schwabe, a pioneer of veterinary epidemiology,[16] posited "One Medicine" to unify the science of health and disease in light of the commonality of human and veterinary health interests. "One Medicine" became the basis for the veterinary/public health understanding of One Health.

As new zoonotic infectious diseases emerged, such as Hendra (1994) or Nipah (1998), there were further calls for cooperation between animal and human health sectors. After the SARS epidemic in 2003, the Wildlife Conservation Society launched in 2004 a "ONE WORLD, ONE HEALTH" proposal, with the "Manhattan Principles" for wildlife health.[17] Cooperation among health sectors has progressed haltingly. Most public health departments lack collaboration with veterinary specialists. Financing is inadequate.

One Health for All Phases of Emerging Infectious Disease

For the foreseeable future, the only way to avert new pandemics is to keep wild nature healthy in the first place, thereby minimizing spill-overs of emerging infectious diseases. This is the approach for the pre-emergent Phase One of emerging infectious diseases, to prevent future pandemics, SDG 16. At present, however, the medical One Heath focuses principally on Phases Two and Three, which align with SDG 3 on health and SDG 2 on food safety.[18] It also has not found its links to the other SDGs. The alliance between human medicine and animal veterinary medicine addresses the detection of disease in Phase Two and the issues of pressing mutual scientific and public health concerns in Phase Three. This veterinary/medical One Health approach ignores a century of nature conservation accomplishments, practices, and laws that restore or sustain the health of wild animals and their natural habitats.

Since 1948, the International Union for the Conservation of Nature (IUCN) has provided the focus for nature conservation world-wide. It is unmatched in its members' multi-disciplinary expertise on preservation of ecosystems and habitats. Protected natural areas invariably were "saved" only after experiencing threats or disruptions. IUCN's members are responsible for nature conservation at all levels of government, through national, state, and local parks, wildlife refuges, wilderness areas, wildlife migration corridors, conserved wetlands, forests, and other biomes. Protected areas have kept wild nature healthy across vast areas of the planet. These stewards of natural areas already manage, de facto, the interface between animals and humans, minimizing spill-overs of zoonotic diseases. The IUCN led the establishment of international agreements to back up national conservation,[19] such as the United Nations Educational, Scientific and Cultural Organization (UNESCO) World

---

16 *See* Biography Dr. Calvin Schwabe, *Emerging Infectious Diseases*, CDC, https://dx.doi.org/10.3201/eid1712.1104.
17 *See The Manhattan Principles*, ONE WORLD HEALTH, https://oneworldonehealth.wcs.org/About-Us/Mission/The-Manhattan-Principles.aspx (last accessed on Dec. 9, 2020).
18 *See* Agenda 2030, *supra* note 1.
19 On the IUCN's role, see BARBARA LAUSCHE, WEAVING A WEB OF ENVIRONMENTAL LAW (IUCN 2008), https://portals.iucn.org/library/node/9235.

Heritage Convention,[20] the Ramsar Convention of Wetlands of International Importance,[21] the Bonn Convention on Migratory Species,[22] or the Convention on Biological Diversity (CBD).[23] These agreements are key anchors for attaining SDG 15 and feature significantly in the Decade of Ecological Restoration.

The One Health divide between a veterinarian/public health focus and the nature conservation sector also surfaced in June of 2020 when the UN Environment Programme (UNEP) issued its own zoonosis guide, "Preventing the next pandemic—Zoonotic diseases and how to break the chain of transmission."[24] The UNEP focuses primarily on the health of domesticated animals in close contact with people. The UNEP's guide oddly neglected both the assessments in UNEP's Global Environmental Outlook (GEO-6) on the global crisis in biodiversity,[25] and the third UN Environment Assembly's Resolution 4 of 2016,[26] that endorsed the united, holistic approach to One Health to address zoonotic risks and biodiversity conservation. The UNEP and the IUCN collaborate closely, but do not yet join forces to cope with zoonotic spill-overs in the wild. The Convention on Biodiversity is cooperating with the WHO to advance a One Health approach to containing zoonotic diseases.[27] The CBD's Subsidiary Body on Scientific, Technical, and Technological Advice (SBSTTA) has issued guidance on One Heath also.[28] CBD needs to expand its focus to embrace the holistic definition set out at the start of this chapter.

For its part, the IUCN has been too parochial in focusing on nature conservation without addressing zoonosis. The IUCN's lack of strategic collaboration is short sighted. The Intergovernmental Science Policy Platform on Biodiversity and Ecosystem Services (IPPES),[29] akin to the Intergovernmental Panel on Climate Change, last year reported that zoonotic diseases are significant threats to human health, requiring stronger protection of nature as in Zoonosis Phase One. The IUCN has yet to include pandemic prevention among its traditional conservation missions, although it would have much to contribute.[30] For example, the IUCN's World Commission on Environmental Law has unmatched expertise on the environmental laws in each nation to manage the human interface with nature

---

20 *Convention Concerning the Protection of the World Cultural and Natural Heritage*, Nov. 16, 1972, 1037 U.N.T.S, available at: http://whc.unesco.org/en/conventiontext/.
21 *Convention on Wetlands of International Importance Especially as Waterfowl Habitat*, Feb. 2, 1971, 996 U.N.T.S. 245 (RAMSAR CONVENTION), https://www.ramsar.org/sites/default/files/documents/library/scan_certified_e.pdf.
22 *Convention on the Conservation of Migratory Species of Wild Animals,* June 23, 1979, 1651 U.N.T.S. 356 (BONN CONVENTION), www.cms.int/en/convention-text.
23 *Convention on Biological Diversity*, June 5, 1992, 1760 U.N.T.S. 79, www.cbd.int/convention/text/.
24 UN Environment Programme Report, *Preventing the Next Pandemic—Zoonotic Diseases and How to Break the Chain of Transmission* (Jul 6, 2020), www.unenvironment.org/resources/report/preventing-future-zoonotic-disease-outbreaks-protecting-environment-animals-and.
25 *Global Environmental Outlook 6*, UN ENVIRONMENT PROGRAM (Mar. 4, 2019), www.unenvironment.org/resources/global-environment-outlook-6.
26 UN Environment Assembly, UNEP/EA.3/Res. 4, *supra* note 6.
27 *See Biodiversity and Infectious Diseases: Questions and Answers,* CONVENTION ON BIOLOGICAL DIVERSITY, www.cbd.int/health/infectiousdiseases (last accessed on Dec. 9, 2020).
28 See Guidance Document, *Guidance on Integrating Biodiversity Considerations into One Health Approaches*, CONVENTION ON BIOLOGICAL DIVERSITY, UN Doc. CBD/SBSTTA/21/9 (2017), www.cbd.int/doc/c/501c/4df1/369d06630c901cd02d4f99c7/sbstta-21-09-en.pdf.
29 *See* IPES webpage, https://ipbes.net/.
30 *See* IUCN webpage, www.iucn.org/.

and avert zoonotic spill-overs.[31] The IUCN's World Commission on Protected Areas is pre-eminent in its expertise on protected natural areas, and has long recommended the use of buffer zones to curb human interface with wildlife habitats.[32] In 2014, the IUCN's Species Survival Commission published *Guidelines for Wildlife Disease Risk Analysis* with the OiE, focusing on human–wildlife and domestic animal–wildlife interactions. The narrow scope of this *Guide*, prepared without input from the IUCN's Commissions on Environmental Law or Protected Areas, limits its use in addressing the massive ecological impacts on biodiversity.[33] More expansive collaboration is warranted.

The pathway to unite these still disparate sectors was charted in November of 2019, when the German Foreign Office and the Wildlife Conservation Society (WCS) unveiled a holistic approach to One Health through the "Berlin Principles."[34] They urged an *ecosystem approach* with integration across all sectors. They posit one fundamental premise

> Recognize and take action to retain the essential health links between humans, wildlife, domesticated animals and plants, and all nature; and ensure the conservation and protection of biodiversity, which interwoven with intact and functional ecosystems provides the critical foundational infrastructure of life, health and well-being on our planet.[35]

This is the holistic One Health concept that is congruent with the universality of the SDGs.

Wider international agreement on such a holistic concept of One Health can provide the foundation for restoring international cooperation to cope with COVID-19 and other emerging infectious diseases.[36] Governments can deploy their existing environmental law regimes to implement One Health promptly. Governments could implement the 2017 recommendations of the United Nations Environment Assembly, which stressed that "biodiversity loss is a health risk multiplier" and urged governments to "mainstream the conservation and sustainable use of biodiversity to enhance ecosystem resilience.[37] Once governments appreciate how human, animal, plant, and ecosystem health are all interdependent, they can find that managing zoonotic spill-overs entails a redesign of government architecture and budgets. Inertia and vested interests will doubtless generate resistance. However, pandemics do constitute a non-traditional threat to national security, arguably more important for every nation than military security. The Hobson's choice is evident: "Pay me now or later." Multinational enterprises can understand this. The Global Risk Perception Report 2020 of

---

31 *See* IUCN, www.iucn.org/commissions/world-commission-environmental-law.
32 *See* IUCN, www.iucn.org/commissions/world-commission-protected-areas.
33 GUIDELINES FOR WILDLIFE DISEASE RISK ANALYSIS (IUCN OIE ed. 2014), available at https://portals.iucn.org/library/node/43385.
34 *See The 2019 Berlin Principles on One Health*, ONE WORLD-ONE HEALTH, https://oneworldonehealth.wcs.org/About-Us/Mission/The-2019-Berlin-Principles-on-One-Health.aspx (last accessed on Dec. 9, 2020).
35 *Id.*
36 Nicholas A. Robinson & Christian Walzer, *How Do We Prevent the Next Outbreak?*, SCIENTIFIC AMERICAN (March 25, 2020), https://blogs.scientificamerican.com/observations/how-do-we-prevent-the-next-outbreak/.
37 UN Environment Assembly, UNEP/EA.3/Res. 4, *supra* note 6.

the Davos World Economic Forum for the first time features biodiversity loss among its top five long-term risks.[38]

Public education is well underway in support of all the SDGs.[39] World-wide awareness of both One Health and the SDGs should be aligned closely. Generalized calls for SDG implementation are important, but to generate more robust action to accelerate implementation of the SDGs, a focus on concrete themes will be essential. The pandemic crisis is a catalyst that infuses the SDGs into One Health and vice versa. The holistic One Health approach averts new pandemics through giving strong effect to SDG 15, "Protect, restore and promote sustainable use of terrestrial ecosystems, sustainably manage forests, combat desertification, halt and reverse land degradation and halt biodiversity loss."[40] Moreover, One Health encompasses SDGs 3 and 6 address health and sanitation.[41] Since two billion people lack clean water and soap, and cannot wash their hands to prevent the spread of disease, COVID-19 (or the "next" pandemic virus) will linger in much of the world and be again at the door steps of nations which enjoy sound public health. The FAO has a "One Health, One Water" Programme, which deals with agricultural water pollution, which can grow to support SDG 15.[42]

All governments can manage COVID-19 and avert the "next" pandemic by uniting behind a One Health approach to attaining the SDGs. This thematic focus makes clear that attaining the SDGs is in everyone's self-interest, short-term for COVID-19 and longer-term to prevent another pandemic. All those responsible for implementing SDGs will gain public support by incorporating One Health into their on-going endeavors. This *is* the global partnership that SDG 17 contemplates.

Policy and Legal Instruments to Implement SDGs Through One Health

Governments have ample authority to act now. Beyond enhancing investments to implement the SDGs, governments can use existing international law to establish legal defenses to

---

38 *The Global Risk Report 2020*, WORLD ECONOMIC FORUM (Jan. 15, 2020), www.weforum.org/reports/the-global-risks-report-2020.
39 *See generally* UN Department of Economic & Social Affairs (UN DESA), https://sdgs.un.org/goals; Specifically, *see UN/DESA Policy Brief #78: Achieving the SDGs through the COVID-19 Response and Recovery* (Jun. 11, 2020), www.un.org/development/desa/dpad/publication/un-desa-policy-brief-78-achieving-the-sdgs-through-the-covid-19-response-and-recovery/. *Note*: Policy Brief #78 urges nations to reverse trends in biodiversity degradation (SDG 15) and concludes "The pandemic has generated a pause on 'business-as-usual' activities, forcing us to face terrible human outcomes but also encouraging us to envision a realistic way forward towards achieving the 2030 Agenda and the Paris Agreement on climate change. It has also brought to the fore how central the SDGs are, including past progress on the SDGs, for building resilience against shocks and avoiding backslides into poverty. This brief has indicated strategic objectives that are common across countries. Realizing them is within reach but requires both greater coherence and coordination of national actions, as well as a re-invigorated global partnership for development (SDG 17). The United Nations is committed to facilitating a global response that leads towards this end and turns this moment in history into an inflection point for humanity to overcome hardship and transform together toward a more sustainable future." The "One Health" approach can provide the coherence and coordination of national actions to combat COVID-19 through implementing the SDGs.
40 *See* 2030 Agenda, *supra* note 1.
41 *Id.*
42 See the FAO webinar on this theme, *Seminar "Lessons from COIVD-19 for One Water One Health,"* FAO http://www.fao.org/land-water/news-archive/news-detail/en/c/1272240/.

avert the next pandemic by implementing One Health. Nations can readily incorporate holist One Health standards and implementing measures into the WHO's International Health Regulations, which are binding on all WHO Members.[43] These WHO Regulations can curb zoonotic spill-over through establishing a standard set of actions world-wide and focus programs that build local and regional capacity. Governments have multiple additional opportunities to coordinate such national measures, through the UN General Assembly and the multilateral environmental agreements. For example, the Conference of the Parties of CBD in 2021 will adopt a post-2020 global biodiversity framework as a stepping stone toward the CBD's 2050 Vision of "Living in Harmony with Nature."[44] The CBD's comprehensive and participatory process currently involves stakeholders in preparing the post-2020 global biodiversity framework. In like vein, the nationally determined contributions to implement the 2015 Paris Agreement on Climate Change,[45] might usefully be repositioned more ambitiously around a One Health approach. Moreover, nations can avail themselves of Article XX in the 1947 General Agreement on Tariff and Trade,[46] and the 1998 Agreement on the Application of Sanitary and Phytosanitary Measures,[47] to establish new phyto-sanitary standards to curb the spread of zoonotic diseases in air travel and commerce. States can enforce the 1973 Convention on the International Trade in Endangered Species (CITES),[48] by assigning priority to prevent trade in species that also evidence zoonotic diseases.

National and local governments do not need to wait for any new intergovernmental international developments. They can implement One Heath within their own jurisdictions, and put the SDGs to work. Virtually all these levels of government already have enacted the requisite laws[49] to serve the holistic One Health approach. Governments can deploy three bodies of existing laws to secure the benefits of One Health: (a) laws for nature conservation, (b) for EIAs, and (c) for spatial planning and land use.

Protected areas can be greatly expanded everywhere. World-wide, nations currently protect about 15% of all terrain.[50] The CBD calls for reaching 18% now and proposals seek protection for 30% soon.[51] Dr. Edward O. Wilson has urged maintaining natural areas

---

43 INTERNATIONAL HEALTH REGULATIONS (WHO 3d. 2005), available at https://www.who.int/ihr/publications/9789241580496/en/.
44 *See Preparations for the Post-2020 Biodiversity Framework*, CBD, https://www.cbd.int/conferences/post2020.
45 *Paris Agreement to the United Nations Framework Convention on Climate Change*, Dec. 12, 2015, T.I.A.S. No. 16–1104, https://unfccc.int/files/meetings/paris_nov_2015/application/pdf/paris_agreement_english_.pdf.
46 *See General Agreement on Tariffs and Trade*, Oct. 30, 1947, 61 Stat. A3, 55 U.N.T.S. 187 (GATT Article XX), www.wto.org/english/res_e/booksp_e/gatt_ai_e/art20_e.pdf.
47 *Agreement on the Application of Sanitary and Phytosanitary Measures*, Dec. 15, 1993, GATT Doc. MTN/FA 11-AIA-4 (SPS Agreement), /www.wto.org/english/tratop_e/sps_e/spsagr_e.htm.
48 *Convention on International Trade in Endangered Species of Wild Fauna and Flora*, Mar. 3, 1973, 993 U.N.T.S. 243, https://cites.org/eng/disc/text.php.
49 The Montevideo Programme of the UN Environment Programme, now in its 5th decade, has been building capacity for environmental protections laws in all nations. *See Environmental Rule of Law*, UN ENVIRONMENTAL PROGRAM, www.unenvironment.org/explore-topics/environmental-rights-and-governance/what-we-do/promoting-environmental-rule-law-1 (last accessed on Dec. 9, 2020).
50 *See Mapping the World's Special Places: Opening Access to Data on Global Protected Areas*, UNEP WORLD CONSERVATION MONITORING CENTRE, www.unep-wcmc.org/featured-projects/mapping-the-worlds-special-places.
51 *See Strategic Plan for Biodiversity 2011–2020 and the Aichi Targets*, CBD, UNEP , www.cbd.int/doc/strategic-plan/2011-2020/Aichi-Targets-EN.pdf; Emma Marris, *To Keep the Planet Flourishing, 30% of*

Integrating the SDGs through "One Health" 523

for biodiversity conservation over 50% of the Earth.[52] This is realistic. Humans would still cohabit these areas with flora and fauna, but would have responsibilities to take care that ecological habitats remain healthy. Consider, for example, a state like New York,[53] with an area of 30.2 million acres and a population of 19 million people. Forests in New York cover 18.95 million acres, 63% of land area, or about one acre per resident.[54] Publicly owned forest land is at least 3.7 million acres, and privately owned forest land area is 14.4 million acres or 76% of forest land, owned by 687,000 landowners.[55] New York's carefully managed Adirondack Park and Forest Preserve are larger than the State of Massachusetts. New York meets Wilson's "half Earth" objective. It can now add the One Health mission to care for nature to avert zoonotic spill-overs.

To contribute to building a world with more robust zoonotic defenses, it is in the self-interest of New York and other local authorities to assist other countries to do the same. New York State already cooperates with its adjacent states and provinces. It can do so by supporting UNESCO Biosphere Reserves or World Heritage Parks.[56] Cooperation is essential. No place is secure until all places are safer, since infectious microbes are carried by travelers globally. This message increasingly is understood. For example, the Arbor Day Foundation in Nebraska is planting 1 million trees, of 70 species, across 5,800 acres of the Amazon.[57]

(b) Governments can deploy their EIA procedures to minimize risk of zoonotic spill-overs. Virtually every nation has enacted an environmental impact assessment law.[58] Under international law, nations are legally obliged to implement EIAs.[59] All EIA procedures are essentially the same, but most governments do not rigorously apply EIA. To avert pandemics, every impact assessment could assess the health of natural systems where development is proposed, identify possible pathogens, mandate buffer protections for humans, and establish "One Health" links for continuing stewardship. EIA procedures are properly administered at every level of government and by all agencies. Responsible authorities usually already adapt their EIA procedures to reflect local conditions, and select their most appropriate analytics. For instance, EIA procedures can (i) select site-specific indicators to identify broad health impacts resulting from anthropogenic changes which cause biodiversity loss; (ii) identify indicators of ecosystem degradation, disruption, and fragmentation and human health outcomes; or (iii) designate indicators on the links between biodiversity loss, ecosystem disruption, and zoonotic and vector-borne disease outbreaks. Public participation in the EIA process provides an important educational forum for stakeholders, including scientists,

---

Earth Needs Protection by 2030, NATIONAL GEOGRAPHIC (Jan. 31, 2019), www.nationalgeographic.com/environment/2019/01/conservation-groups-call-for-protecting-30-percent-earth-2030/.
52 EDWARD O. WILSON, HALF EARTH (2017).
53 *See Forests*, NEW YORK STATE DEPARTMENT OF ENVIRONMENTAL CONSERVATION, www.dec.ny.gov/lands/309.html (last accessed on Dec. 9, 2020).
54 *Id.*
55 *Id.*
56 On Biosphere Reserves, see https://en.unesco.org/biosphere/wnbr .
57 *See Arbor Day Foundation Timeline*, ARBOR DAY FOUNDATION, www.arborday.org/media/timeline.cfm.
58 See e.g. EUROPEAN COMMISSION, *Environmental Impact Assessment of Projects, Guidance on the Preparation of the EIA Report* (Directive 2011/92/EU as amended by 2014/52/EU) at https://ec.europa.eu/environment/eia/pdf/EIA_guidance_EIA_report_final.pdf .
59 *Pulp Mills on the River Uruguay (Argentina v. Uruguay)* 2010 I.C.J. (April 20), /www.icj-cij.org/en/case/135/judgments.

policymakers, and decision-makers. When governments weaken EIAs, they heighten the risks of exposing their publics to emerging infectious diseases.

(c) SDG 11 calls for resilient and sustainable cities. The quality of urban life will determine the environmental security of all people. Cities are front lines managing zoonotic diseases since most of the world's people live in cities, as the Global Pandemic Network (GPN), a consortium of leading academics, has made clear.[60] As the Stockholm Resilience Center put it, "If the coronavirus has taught urban planners anything, it is that public access to green areas is more important than ever."[61] Cities and regions can deploy their spatial planning, town and country planning, zoning, and building codes to enhance animal health and manage the interface with humans to minimize zoonotic spill-over risks. Such planning already benefits from environmental best practices, such as "design with nature." The IUCN's 2014 guidelines for urban protected areas expressly addressed "emerging infectious diseases."[62] Urban forestry programs can enhance wildlife corridors, for example by designating overlay zones across suburbia. Urban wetlands and open spaces can have buffer zones to minimize human encroachments and the interface with animals.

Recourse to the tools in these three bodies of environmental law can provide protection against the spread of zoonotic emerging infectious diseases. It is unlikely that an international consensus for One Health can be agreed until after 2022, the 30th anniversary of the 1992 Rio "Earth Summit" and the 50th anniversary of the 1972 UN Stockholm Conference on Human Environment.[63] Since it may well then take a decade for nations to marshal the resources for international cooperation to build the capacity to materially reduce the threats of new pandemics, each step on that pathway should implement the SDGs. As new infections emerge, delaying action is no longer an option. Improvements to sanitation will be needed immediately. Every local government has "self-help" tools with which to cope.

Next Steps

Deploying a thematic approach, One Health to accelerate SDG implementation can materially advance the SDG for Health, for water and sanitation, for terrestrial health and restoration, for food safety, and all other SDGs. These immediate steps are worth pursuing:

(1) Establish a high level One Health coordinating council at each level of government, and supervise an inter-agency or "whole of government" approach to addressing pandemic risks in each of the three phases of zoonotic diseases.
(2) Expand natural areas and ecosystems, with buffer zones, into systems of parks and protected areas, and overlay zones, where wildlife health is protected and monitored.

---

60 *See generally* GLOBAL PANDEMIC NETWORK, www.globalpandemicnetwork.org/ (last accessed on Dec. 9, 2020).
61 *Coronavirus Highlights the Need for Open Green Spaces in Cities*, STOCKHOLM RESILIENCE CENTER, www.stockholmresilience.org/research/research-news/2020-04-21-coronavirus-highlights-the-need-for-open-green-spaces-in-cities.html (last accessed on Dec. 9, 2020).
62 *Urban Protected Area: Profiles and Best Practice Guidelines*, IUCN (2014), https://portals.iucn.org/library/sites/library/files/documents/PAG-022.pdf.
63 During 2019–2021, consultations about such an anniversary are underway in the UN General Assembly pursuant to UNGA Res. 73/333 (2019).

(3) Apply EIA procedures, at all levels of government, to collect data on ecosystem health, vectors for emerging infectious diseases, and to mandate appropriate steps to avert zoonotic spill-over.
(4) Establish education programs for each of the SDGs to explain and highlight their relevance to averting pandemics via the One Health theme.

IV
Conclusions

35 Pathways to 2030

Vesselin Popovski, Narinder Kakar, and Nicholas A. Robinson

The 2030 Agenda for Sustainable Development identified 17 Sustainable Development Goals (SDGs) designed to catalyze action in critical areas of importance to humanity and the planet. Unlike the Millennium Development Goals (MDGs), which are related to developing countries, the SDGs are universal and applicable to all countries. Everybody is obliged to devote resources and energy to the attainment of the goals. Leaving no one behind is not a mere slogan, but it is an inspiration to undertake comprehensive actions toward sustainable human development and to meet the needs of all people deprived of the benefits from the globalization and development processes. The efforts to implement the goals demand a sense of urgency in the face of increasing poverty and growing inequality, gaps in social services, depletion of natural resources, land degradation, rapidly increasing climate change, and all negative effects for the people and the planet.

The challenges are ubiquitous and multi-faceted, and require bold, innovative, and intertwined actions at country, regional, and global levels to attain a healthy, safe, and prosperous future for humanity and the planet. The 2030 Agenda highlighted the inter-dependence of different dimensions of sustainable development; thus, the inter-linkages among the goals are just as important as each individual goal.

Inter-linkages of SDGs

Lack of progress in one goal would adversely affect the progress in others. Poverty remains an endemic problem, inequality not only persists, but is increasing in many countries, climate change is escalating and threatens the existence of the planet, and, not least, conflicts between and within nations continue. The only way to fulfill the 2030 Agenda is to attain all SDGs together, in synergy. It is crucial that the SDGs are implemented in their entirety, instead of approaching individual goals in isolation. The Sustainable Development Report 2018 argued that transitioning toward more sustainable and resilient societies requires an integrated approach. The chart in Figure 35.1 reproduced from the United Nations Economic and Social Commission for Asia and the Pacific (UN ESCAP) Report "Introduction to the 2030 Agenda and the Interconnectedness of the SDGs" shows all interlinkages between the goals.[1]

---

1 Aneta Nikolova, *Introduction to the 2030 Agenda and the Interconnectedness of the SDGs*, UNITED NATIONS ESCAP (Feb. 2019), www.unescap.org/sites/default/files/Introduction%20to%20the%202030%20Agenda%20and%20the%20Interconnected%20SDGs_Eng.pdf.

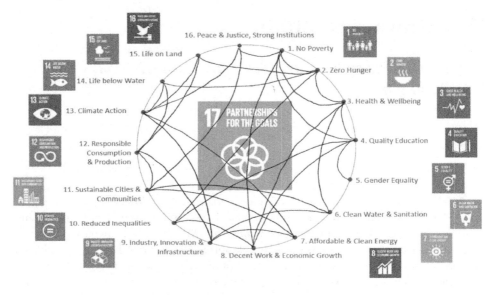

Figure 35.1 Partnerships for the Goals. A diagram showing the web of many interconnections between the Sustainable Development Goals as a demonstration of Goal 17: Partnerships for the Goals. *Introduction to the 2030 Agenda and the Interconnectedness of the SDGs*: UNESCAP Report (Feb. 2019), https://www.unescap.org/sites/default/files/Introduction%20to%20the%202030%20Agenda%20and%20the%20Interconnected%20SDGs_Eng.pdf.

Status of Implementation

Less than ten years remain until the 2030 target of fulfilling the SDGs. How are countries and regions advancing in their actions? What are the challenges, and how can they be addressed? How will the COVID-19 pandemic affect the progress? Our book addresses these questions, provides best practices, and identifies lessons to be learned and gaps to be filled.

The UN Global Sustainable Development Report 2019 gave us a detailed assessment and projected distance from reaching the targets, based on trends at the time.[2] Only three targets: 3.1 (under-5 mortality), 3.2 (neonatal mortality), and 4.1 (enrolment in primary education), were within 5% of the positive prospects to be reached, whereas a much longer list of targets—and worryingly almost all environmental targets—had negative long-term trends.[3] The table in Figure 35.2 gives the whole picture.

This book focuses on the implementation of various targets of each SDG, with relevant case studies from both the developing and developed countries. It was conceived long before COVID-19, and most of the draft chapters were written before the pandemic. With the severity of the disease hitting the world in 2020, accordingly, we had to ask the authors to revise their chapters reflecting on the impact COVID-19 had on the SDGs.

In June 2020, the Sustainable Development Report analyzed the general impact and found it to be "highly negative" for goals 1, 2, 3, 8, and 10; "mixed or moderately negative"

---

2 *The Sustainable Development Goals Report*, UNITED NATIONS (2019), https://unstats.un.org/sdgs/report/2019/The-Sustainable-Development-Goals-Report-2019.pdf.
3 *Id.*

Projected distance from reaching selected targets by 2030 (at current trends)

GOAL	WITHIN 5%	5–10%	>10%	NEGATIVE LONG-TERM TREND
Goal 1		1.1. Eradicating extreme poverty	1.3. Social protection for all	
Goal 2		2.1. Ending hunger (undernourishment)	2.2. Ending malnutrition (stunting); 2.5. Maintaining genetic diversity; 2.a. Investment in agriculture*	2.2. Ending malnutrition (overweight)
Goal 3	3.2. Under-5 mortality; 3.2. Neonatal mortality		3.1. Maternal mortality; 3.4. Premature deaths from non-communicable diseases	
Goal 4	4.1 Enrolment in primary education	4.6 Literacy among youth and adults	4.2. Early childhood development; 4.1 Enrolment in secondary education; 4.3 Enrolment in tertiary education	
Goal 5			5.5. Women political participation	
Goal 6		6.2. Access to safe sanitation (open defecation practices)	6.1. Access to safely managed drinking water; 6.2. Access to safely managed sanitation services	
Goal 7		7.1. Access to electricity	7.2. Share of renewable energy*; 7.3. Energy intensity	
Goal 8			8.7. Use of child labour	
Goal 9		9.5. Enhancing scientific research (R&D expenditure)	9.5. Enhancing scientific research (number of researchers)	
Goal 10			10.c. Remittance costs	Inequality in income*
Goal 11			11.1. Urban population living in slums*	
Goal 12				12.2. Absolute material footprint, and DMC*
Goal 13				Global GHG emissions relative to Paris targets*
Goal 14				14.1. Continued deterioration of coastal waters*; 14.4. Overfishing*
Goal 15				15.5. Biodiversity loss*; 15.7. Wildlife poaching and trafficking*
Goal 16			16.9 Universal birth registration **	

Note: Selected indicators only. SDG 17 is not included as it consists of a wide range of indicators that cannot easily be captured using the methodology for assessing distance from reaching targets. Estimates of the distance from the target by 2030 are based on forecasted value of the corresponding indicator in 2030, relative to target. Forecasts based on best-fit trends of individual indicators, given the available data range.

* Quantitative target for 2030 is not specified in the SDG indicator framework; targets are estimated.

** Assessment is based on indicators outside the SDG indicator framework; inequality in income is based on data from household surveys.

Figure 35.2 Projected distance from reaching selected targets by 2030 (at current trends). A chart demonstrating the likelihood of achieving selected targets of each of the Sustainable Development Goals, except Goal 17 which focuses on partnerships between the remaining goals. The chart measures the distance of current trends from achieving the selected targets by native long-term trends, greater than 10% distance, between 5 and 10% distance, or less than 5% from achieving the selected target. *The Future Is Now: Science For Achieving Sustainable Development*, Global Sustainable Development Report, UNITED NATIONS (2019), https://sustainabledevelopment.un.org/content/documents/24797GSDR_report_2019.pdf.

for goals 4, 5, 6, 7, 9, 11, 16, and 17; and "unclear" for goals 12, 13, 14, and 15.[4] The lack of clarity on the environmental goals 12–15 comes from the fact that the pandemic reduced air travel and industrial activities and initially had a positive effect on the environment. A more recent report, the UN Sustainable Development Goals Report predicted a drop of 6% in CO_2 emissions, but also pointed that to reach the 1.5°C temperature target, an emissions reduction of 7.6% is needed every single year, starting from 2020.[5] We see that the situation is indeed critical; if greenhouse gas emissions cannot even be reduced at the necessary level even during 2020, a year with drastic reduction of industries and air travel, due to the pandemic and the economic recession, it is very unlikely that we can emit less CO_2 in 2021 and every year after, compared to 2020, once the economy and air travel go into full speed. Urgent action to reduce emissions needs to be taken. Climate change disrupts patterns on which current socio-economic relations are based, and all SDGs in turn necessarily adapt to the changing environmental conditions worldwide. One of these is the emergence of zoonotic diseases, which the crisis of biodiversity loss has exacerbated.

The Sustainable Development Report 2020 highlighted that the COVID-19 negative impact will affect almost all the countries, but most adversely the Least Developed Countries (LDCs) and vulnerable populations. It concluded that COVID-19 will have severe negative impacts on most SDGs.[6] Accordingly, efforts are needed to strengthen the resilience of their health systems and prevention programs. International solidarity and partnerships will be crucial to efficiently address and prevent various health, economic, or humanitarian crises. The momentum needed to implement the SDGs should not fade away, as political capital and financial resources get diverted to tackling the pandemic. COVID-19 and its hardships, including an economic recession in many countries, is expected to have adverse effects on the ability and capacity of many countries to implement the SDG targets and needs to be confronted with corrective measures to minimize the effects and build-back-better and greener.

The authors of this book presented the status of implementation of the SDGs five years after their adoption in 2015, demonstrated best practices and lessons learned, and made recommendations on how to speed up the attainment of the goals having in mind the negative effects of COVID-19. Below, we summarize lessons and recommendations for actions. We start with a few general lessons relevant to all SDGs, before we list some more specific recommendations to each goal.

General Lessons

The first general lesson is that managing complexity and building resilience are critical elements of policy-making for sustainable development. Given the sophisticated interactions between various goals and dimensions, it is important to understand the complexity of the entire system and the threshold beyond which the system can unexpectedly fail. Because uncertainty cannot be controlled, the only alternative is to manage complexity. Building resilient societies will be critical to our ability to respond to crises and achieve a sustainable

---

4 *Sustainable Development Report (2020): The Sustainable Development Goals and COVID-19*, at 5, Cambridge University Press (Jun. 2020), https://s3.amazonaws.com/sustainabledevelopment.report/2020/2020_sustainable_development_report.pdf
5 See *The Sustainable Development Goals Report*, UNITED NATIONS (2020), https://unstats.un.org/sdgs/report/2020/The-Sustainable-Development-Goals-Report-2020.pdf.
6 *Id.*

future. While sustainable development is related to the trend behavior of development, resilience is about the fluctuations and the transition toward it, and the dynamic mechanism that keeps us around the sustainable path, with as little well-being loss as possible. A society is resilient when it has the ability to face shocks and persistent structural changes without losing its ability to deliver well-being for its community in a sustainable way.

We also learned that crisis response needs continuous global coordination but also local feedback. Solutions to crises are most effective if globally coordinated and locally informed. The response needs to be multidimensional, swift, and decisive, governed by strong political leadership coupled with the buy-in of the population. It needs to foster public trust, be focused on human value, and be supported by solid institutions, technical skills, and financial resources. Inclusive participation, inter-generational approaches, and co-responsibility at national and international levels are critical.

Another lesson is that Agenda 2030 would be an impossible task if it were not connected to public opinion, to people's needs, to politics and politicians, and to parliaments. A multi-stakeholder approach that includes youth and elders, women, and Indigenous Peoples is a requisite to overcome the disconnection between scales and actors. Social participation in multilateral decision-making should not be seen as a tokenistic, politically correct afterthought, but rather an indicator of impact. For decisions to be effective and transformative, there is a need for social ownership, public engagement, a multi-scale architecture, and a new social contract between society, the economy, and the planet. There has never been so much creativity, talent, think-tanks, mobilized citizens, UN agencies, programs, and regional commissions proposing innovations, alternatives, and options.

The SDGs continue to be a relevant roadmap for the present and the future, perhaps even more than when they were adopted five years ago. COVID-19 requires revisiting our commitments and reasserting their transformative power and relevance. Addressing the immediate response to the current health emergency, we need the same impetus in addressing other related and protracted crises such as poverty, hunger, inequalities, women's rights, climate change, and biodiversity extinction.

The next lesson is that leadership is strongly needed, but it has to come from the whole of society. It is not only governments or messianic leaders, but numerous social activists, women, journalists, opinion-makers, scientists, and indigenous leaders that are needed. Everyone has a role to play in building a new social contract between society, the economy, and nature. And yet another paradox: There is a wealth of ideas and proposals and a shortage of political will and decisions to coordinate, to collaborate, to have a shared vision that leads to transformative action. We need a multilateral system that is inclusive, efficient, relevant, accountable, and truly connected to peoples' needs and expectations. Delivery, Accountability, Relevance, and Efficiency (DARE) are important guidelines. We should be daring, audacious, creative, and seize the moment of transformation for the betterment of our international architecture.

Last but not least, to achieve SDGs, states' actions must be informed by human rights obligations. It includes the whole spectrum of civil and political rights, and economic, social, and cultural rights, but also the already recognized third-generation rights, such as the right to development and the right to a clean environment. Particular attention needs to be paid to protect those who are most vulnerable, including as a result of the COVID-19 pandemic.

Goal-Specific Recommendations

The chapters of our book presented recommendations on how to speed up the implementation of the 17 goals. Below, we make a brief summary of such recommendations.

To fulfill SDG 1, eradication of extreme poverty, it is essential to close the gap between policy and capacity. Sound policies are crucial but are not sufficient to tackle tough challenges in reaching and responding to the poorest communities. Progress requires leadership committed not simply to financial support, but also to robust implementation systems and political accountability. Money is essential, but not enough to end poverty, and it is important to provide not only complementary support, but also an accountable environment to sustain the achievements. The implementation capability in most low-income economies has been stagnant or declining in recent years and more attention needs to go not just to getting policies right, but to building administrative capacity tasked with implementing them.

Protecting and fulfilling the right to food is essential to achieve SDG 2, zero hunger. Progress has mostly been in urban areas. Therefore, ensuring the rights of peasants and people working in rural areas needs to be prioritized. States and non-State actors must invest in a radical transformation of the food system to move away from destructive industrial practices toward more diversified agro-ecological food systems. These transitions must uphold the right of local people to determine food and agricultural systems, such as the right to food sovereignty, which entails advancing just and equitable trade policies and dismantling the corporate capture of the food chain.

SDG 3 on health will face challenges beyond COVID-19 if countries do not move away from a biomedical approach to healthcare and position health at the center of developmental policies to fully capture the social determinants of health. They should develop a policy coherence framework to address the tensions between trade-investment objectives and health promotion and ensure that short-term economic growth does not undermine public health in the long term. Countries need to pursue effective regulatory frameworks to address private sector interests and corporate determinants of health, and steadily increase the health budget to fund the critical components of Universal Health Coverage.

On SDG 4, some good progress has been achieved, though not enough in the LDCs. Developed countries need to eliminate some inefficiencies of their education systems and reduce gaps within and between countries. Real progress in learning can be hidden by enrolment numbers and the narrow focus on achieving a minimum proficiency level. Stronger technical capacity to improve the education data is needed to drive innovation within countries allowing them to adapt and innovate at regional and local levels. Country-level capacity building would benefit if a broader list of competences is included. Governments and formal-sector public and private educational institutions should maintain quality of education through enforcing teachers' certification. SDG 4 should be included in national plans, and constitutional protection for the Right to Education should drive cogent and consistent educational policies. Education for sustainable development should be part of the curricula, strengthened with Science, Technology, Engineering, and Mathematics (STEM) education.

The gender goal SDG 5 requires doubling the efforts and ambitions. Political will is still missing in many countries to implement the targets, and even to adopt legislation to ensure gender justice. Widespread advocacy should be sustained in rural areas and local communities, especially where there is a need for a shift in perception on harmful social practices and stereotypes that impact gender. Capacity building and workshops are essential on gender across all arms of government, including executive, parliamentary, and judiciary, while traditional grassroots and religious leaders remain crucial. Gender studies should be a new curriculum subject in primary education. More profoundly from a young age, students should be taught to recognize and classify traditional notions around gender and educated to understand the influence of gender in socio-political life.

For SDG 6, water pollution prevention, water resources management, sanitation, and conservation of aquatic ecosystem, national integrated plans can be developed to avoid possible conflicts between the different dimensions, especially the use of water as a national resource and the protection of water as an environmental element. Institutional innovations in water management should break the administrative obstacles, for example, setting up cross-regional special administrative departments and special courts for the water basin. Strict responsibility systems and strong incentive mechanisms are needed to explore the potential of local governments. The responsibility systems would externalize the pressure forcing the local governments to focus on sustainable water management. National and local science databases, based on long-term water quality and quantity monitoring, can provide the basis for reasonable policies and regulations.

To meet SDG 7 and achieve affordable and reliable renewable energy, the introduction of carbon pricing would accelerate the cost-efficient provision of clean electricity. It is important to harness and incentivize the potential of centralized and decentralized modern renewable energy solutions. In parallel, phasing out fossil fuel subsidies and coal usage should be a matter of urgency. Clean cooking could also be given higher priority. Global and regional collaboration is needed to reshape the energy systems to transition to a net-zero carbon emittance by 2050. The use of environment-friendly energy sources through transfers of renewable energy technology could be achieved through the promotion of technology bonds, similar to disaster recovery bonds. The UN and the regional development banks can help set multilateral grants to promote renewable energy technology transfers.

To achieve SDG 8 and ensure inclusive and sustainable economic growth, it is crucial to encourage stable planned monetary and fiscal policies based on responsibility, a sound financial system, price stability, maximum output, and full employment. Continuous upholding of the rule of law, property rights, and entrepreneurship are critical for economic growth. Compliance with fair trade of goods and services, borrowing, and lending of assets should be based on a firm legal system that enforces contracts. There is always a positive relationship between the rule of law and good governance indexes and the accumulation of physical and human capital. Other measures needed are the introduction of national minimum wages and incorporating contingency plans into national frameworks to cope with large-scale economic or natural disasters. Economic growth can reduce poverty and generate prosperity; however, it can come at a cost of increased inequality and environmental degradation. Therefore, it is vital that the global community pursues all-inclusive and sustained growth and sustainable development that leaves no one behind through the development of resilient infrastructure, promotion of inclusive and sustainable industrialization, and fostering new technologies.

The progress on SDG 9, decent jobs, has been uneven and slow in terms of including women, and traditionally marginalized groups. COVID-19 exacerbated the challenges and stalled the progress. There is a need to accelerate dissemination of technologies globally and build regional and country-based capacities and skills. Strong government commitment and industrial policies can foster innovative utilization of existing skills and talents. Developing countries often function in instability and uncertainty and are unable to provide funds and expertise for large-scale infrastructure projects. It would be good to encourage small businesses and local credit systems, increase microfinancing, promote entrepreneurship, and reduce the informal labor market. These together with better local financial services would stimulate Foreign Direct Investment (FDI), create more investment opportunities, and accordingly more decent jobs. Entrepreneurial interest to innovate is strongly linked to material incentives and profit opportunities and should be at the center of development strategies. Similarly to other goals, this requires a stable political environment, a sound financial system that channels the funds from lenders to borrowers, a legal framework that protects human rights and property rights, and a government that is committed to inclusion, diversity, and equity.

The implementation of SDG 10 should build upon the fundamental values of equality, non-discrimination, and "leave no one behind." The rising inequality in most regions should serve as an alarm bell, mobilizing force and galvanizing the moment for action. It is crucial to address the root systemic causes of inequality within countries recognizing its broad, cross-cutting, and multi-dimensional nature. Both national and international drivers of inequality should be addressed, together with the necessary institutional requirements for reducing it. Focus needs to be made on healthcare and education as two crucial sectors in reducing inequality. The strengthening of institutions at all levels can also support the reduction of inequality. States should review progress regularly, including through the use of disaggregated data, invite and engage with high-level participatory expertise, and be informed constantly with quality inputs. States need to address immediately tax evasion, illicit financial flows, and money laundering. These are global threats and cannot be solved without close co-operation, information sharing, and robust rules and institutions.

To achieve SDG 11 and make cities inclusive, safe, resilient, and sustainable, the role of citizens is crucially important in policy-making, enforcement, and implementation of city governance. Citizens not only improve the quality of decision-making, but also strengthen the enforceability. New technologies are needed to reduce energy consumption, promote shared transportation, improve the efficiency of urban transportation, and reduce pollutant emissions. Governments should guide the housing plans to improve the overall supply. If the market provides market-oriented housing, the government can be responsible for providing low-rent housing. Slums need to close and people should be given decent housing. More needs to be done to appraise and promote the best practices of urban policy packages and promote the spread of best practices in urban governance around the world.

SDG 12 aims to achieve sustainable consumption and production (SCP) and more resources need to be allocated to increase public awareness and to promote SCP. Attitudinal changes are expected to happen once SCP becomes a mandatory component of education curricula, from primary through tertiary levels. As with other goals, better statistical systems and better reporting are crucial. SCP also needs special financial instruments (similar to Green Bonds and Climate Bonds), especially for the LDCs. Countries should work toward developing national carbon-pricing schemes, as well as carbon-trading programs on regional and international levels and encourage a movement toward a global carbon market.

SGD 13, climate action, continues to be as crucial as ever, and more problematic than it ever was before COVID-19. It is important to acknowledge the definition of "climate victims" and establish legal status for potential climate refugees and grant them the same protections as granted to other refugees. A special fund can be established to help developing nations in creating plans for ameliorating and mitigating extreme weather disasters, especially in rural areas. Subsidizing consumer purchases of hybrid or electric cars would reduce CO_2 emissions, and so would cheap clean stoves for people in LDCs. The Climate Club idea—where members are rewarded for compliance with the Paris Agreement and non-members are sanctioned with tariffs—should be given serious consideration. A carbon tax would be helpful but a targeted approach at high-carbon-using products used against non-compliant countries could also be effective.

The implementation of SDG 14 on oceans can be accelerated by better methods and a holistic understanding of marine pollution at all levels. A global binding instrument on marine plastic pollution can bring robust measures to foster science, provide capacity building and technology transfer, as well as funding for an enabling environment. This is particularly important for Small Island Developing States (SIDS) since they largely depend on marine resources for their economies and disproportionately suffer from marine plastic pollution. Capacity building is of paramount importance to implementing applicable international instruments and facilitating compliance and recommended practices. Most uses of the oceans are approaching unsustainable levels and need to be reassessed. Integrated planning and management of ocean-related affairs at the national level is of major importance.

To achieve SDG 15, more needs to be done to protect, restore, and promote the sustainable use of terrestrial ecosystems. Transformative changes toward sustainability and nature conservation are urgently needed. It is crucial to reduce and even abandon direct pressures, such as habitat conversion, unsustainable harvesting, overhunting, as well as indirect pressures, such as unsustainable production and consumption, rapid demographic growth, unsustainable trade and technological development, poor governance, conflicts, and epidemics, resulting in species extinctions, resource depletion, and ecosystem degradation. To achieve land degradation neutrality, we need a Paris-style agreement that requires States to set nationally determined targets to establish the mandate to control and ecologically manage land degradation. Country-specific indicators, taking into account the physical threats and drivers of land degradation, should be identified as a basis for developing strategies. Legislative provisions can enable participation of stakeholders in the development of policy, guidelines, and standards to enable governments, landowners, and communities to share responsibility, implement policy, develop special codes of practice, land management indicators, physical and ecological limits of land use, etc.

SDG 16, sustainable peace and strong institutions, needs an inclusive and participatory approach to tackle the impact of marginalization and exclusion of certain groups in societies, amidst the continued rise of and risks posed by populism, nationalism, and xenophobia. Accountable and inclusive institutions must live to their responsibility to ensure participatory decision-making and responsive policies that leave no one behind. This includes ensuring unfettered access to justice for all citizens and the rule of law, without which there can be no sustainable development. Improving accountability for action is very important. National governments should report data or take tangible action on the implementation of measures to achieve the targets. Multilateral institutions should develop a system of accountability that considers naming and shaming errant governments for taking actions inconsistent with the targets.

SDG 17 could represent a point of departure to build a solid legal ground for the rest of the 2030 Agenda. Codified SDGs, as customary norms applicable to the international community, could increase the level of compliance with all targets and reinforce the work of the UN and other specialized agencies. The international policy community should create partnerships and agree on a set of investment needs for achieving the SDGs.

Finance and Investments

The international financial community should come to an agreement on a set of institutional and public policy changes that are most needed for sustainable development. One of the key aspects of financing sustainable development is getting the rules of the game right in terms of key fiscal and monetary policies related to sustainable development, namely taxation, increased domestic resource mobilization and carbon pricing, and risk weighting adjustments for high-carbon versus low-carbon assets on bank balance sheets. Financing sustainable development can take advantage of more emphasis on the institutional underpinnings of the real economy and the financial sector that operates within it. The private investment would benefit from more solid standardization that impacts investing. A very important step for the private investment community would be to constructively develop clear, outcome-oriented guidelines and pathways for private investment and sustainable development that have the support of national financial regulators and accounting boards. Public finance should take the lead in building and expanding public financial institutions at the global, regional, national, and local levels. The positive momentum of the past years in growing the capital base of various large development banks and creating new ones like the Asian Infrastructure Investment Bank and New Development Bank should be expanded upon.

One Health Approach

The challenges in protecting healthy lands and seas, and in addressing climate change arise from a failure to manage natural ecosystems and the biosphere. Economic investments to manage and steward natural assets and natural capital already fall far short of what is needed to solve the imbalances in the seas, prevent loss of biodiversity, and address the greenhouse gas emissions. The danger of the COVID-19 pandemic is that, through its very urgency, it may take attention and resources away from the need to massively increase the investments, human and financial, to deliver on the SDGs.

To accelerate SDGs implementation, we should materially advance a common "One Health Approach" to include public health, water and sanitation, terrestrial health and restoration, food safety, and other SDGs. The immediate steps are to create a High-Level One Health Coordinating Council, address pandemic risks in each of the phases, and expand natural areas and ecosystems into a system of parks, protected areas, and over-lay zones, where wildlife health is protected and monitored. Finally, we need education programs for each of the SDGs to explain and highlight their relevance to averting pandemics via the One Health approach.

2022 Anniversaries

As we approach the 50th anniversary of the UN Conference on the Environment in Stockholm and the 30th anniversary of the Rio Earth Summit, it is time for a comprehensive review of the progress made and to assess the extent to which the multilateral system has been able to deal with sustainable development. The challenge is to reconcile the global polarization between the priorities of economic growth and environmental protection, which dominated the debate between rich and poor countries. The multilateral system must recognize that socio-economic development and environmental protection are intimately linked and that effective policy-making must tackle them together.

Yet there is a lingering danger that the 2030 Agenda could fall victim to reluctant governments and resulting inequalities in distribution of incomes and opportunities, deeper division of winners and losers of globalization, lack of effective integration policies for migrants, and escalating climate change.

The assessment provided in this book can serve as a prelude to assess the extent to which the multilateral system has been able to deal with issues of sustainable development. Does the current multilateral framework serve the human development needs of the world's deprived segments of people? Or do we need a re-structuring of the multilateral system to provide development that meets the needs of the present without compromising the ability of future generations to meet their needs? The Summits in 2022 should provide answers and identify pathways to achieve real sustainable human development. Above all, strengthening the multilateral system is certainly the call of the day.

Index

Page numbers in *italics* mark figures or illustrations, while page numbers in **bold** mark tables.

Accra Agenda for Action (2008) 453
Action Plan for the Earth 188–89*n*20
Addis Ababa Action Agenda (AAAA) 433, 451, 453, 462
Adhanom, Dr. Tedros 5, 15
Africa 251, 280–81; and China 214; corruption 411; and COVID-19 220; and extreme poverty 43, 48–50, 53, 56, **58**, 60; and gender discrimination 123; hunting in 387–88; Kenya 216–18; political participation of women 125–26; and SDG9 233–36; *see also* Chololo Ecovillage Project; Nigeria
African Commission of Human and People's Rights 135–36
African Development Bank 434
African Development Fund (AfDF) 42
African Renewable Energy Initiative 268
African swine fever virus (AFS) 516
African Union 'Abuja Declaration' (2001) 70
Agenda 21 170, 188, 227–28, 276, 343–44, 353
Agenda 2030 xxii, 3, 6, 14, 22, 75, 116, 137, 223, 225, 227–28, 253, 270, 274, 276, 281, 283, 287, 290, 321, 358, 367, 371*n*74, 373, 382, 393, 396, 408, 414, 417, 425, 433, 461, 486, 492–93, 504–9, 529, 533; *see also* Sustainable Development Goals (SDGs)
Agenda 2063 280–81
Agreement on Port State Measures 352, 361
agricultural workers 65, 75–76, 78, 126–27
agriculture development 65, 75–77, 81, 85–86, 90–98
agriculture *see* industrial food systems
agroecological food systems 90–98, 491
Aichi Targets 373, **374**, 375, 377–78, 380, 382
alcohol abuse 103–4
Alkirea, Sabina 44

Alliance of Small Island States (AOSIS) 296
Alvaredo, Facundo 243
Annan, Kofi 437
Annual Demographia International Housing Affordability Survey (2020) 156
Arab region 281–82
Areas Beyond National Jurisdiction (ABNJ) 335, 338
armed conflict, and poverty 53
Armenia 122
Arrhenius, Svante 294
Asia 122, 230, 251, 282–83, 388
Asia Indigenous Peoples Pact (AIPP) 492
Asian Development Bank (ADB) 42
Asian Infrastructure Investment Bank (AIIB) 434, 436, 538
Association of South-East Asian Nations (ASEAN) 193, 216
Australia 190, 385
authoritarian governance 407

Banerjee, Abhijit V. 40, 48, 52
banks 431–34
Basel Convention 279, 346, 353–54
bats 385, 387
Bauch, Simone 386
Bauer, Peter 39, 42
BBNJ agreement 330, 334–35, 337–38
Becker, Gary 170
Beijing 155, 163–67; *see also* China
Beijing Consensus 213–14
Beijing Platform for Action 105, **121**
Belgrade Charter: A Framework for Environmental Education (1975) 187
"Berlin Principles" 520
Bezos, Jeff 12
Billion Oyster Project ("BOP") 201–5, *206*, 207, *208*, 209–10
biodiversity 377–78, 382–83, 474, 499, 516; and agroecology 92; and oceans 330, 333,

351; and oysters 202; and the peasant food web 91; recommended conservation amounts 523; and soil 392
black swan events 29
Bobrisky 133–34
Boko Haram 72–74, 131, 135, 417–18
Bolivia 498
Bonn Convention on Migratory Species 519
BOP CCERS Project 201–5, *206*, 207, *208*, 209–10
The Bottom Billion (Collier) 37
Boulton, Matthew 224
Brazil 216, 219–20, 232–33, 236
Brilliant, Larry 29
"Bring Back Our Girls" Movement 134–35
Brownlie, Ian 508
"Brundtland Report" xxi–xxii, 188, 276, 431
Bruno, Simma 504
Buergenthal, Thomas 506
Build, Own, Operate, Transfer (BOOT) structure 235
Bulgaria 46–47
Burkina Faso 126–27, 401
Burundi 175–76
Busan Partnership for Effective Cooperation (2011) 453
"business as usual" xviii, 84, 151, 221, 431, 449, 458, 463, 513, 521*n*39
businesses 428–29; and corporate social responsibility (CSR) 425–26, 437, 439, 442–43; and COVID-19 447; and development aid 457; environmental, governance, and social (EGS) 426, 431–32, 435–36, 438–41; environmental impacts of 440–41; greenwashing vs. sustainability 427; recommendations for 448; sustainable finance 427, 430–32

Cambodia 388
Canada 122, 160, 191, 268–72, 286–88, 497
Canada Infrastructure Bank (CIB) 269
capitalism 240
car-sharing companies 158
carbon dioxide (CO$_2$) 294–95, 300–301, 304, 312, 348–52, 355, 440, 444, 467, 474–75, 532
carbon emission trading 166, 482–83
carbon footprints 444
carbon neutral pledges/goals 324
carbon-pricing/trading schemes 291–92, 309
Caribbean Catastrophe Risk Insurance Facility (CCRIF) 481
Caribbean Community Climate Change Center Plan (2011–2021) 233
Carroll, Dennis 29
cars 157–59
Catastrophe Bonds 481–82
Catastrophe Draw Down Option 481

Chancel, Lucas 243
Chi-Fang, Maria Tiimon 321
child labor 182
child-marriages 131–32
Chile 284
China 160, 213–14, 231, 243, 250–52, 282–83, 388, 469; accountability in 150; and Africa 214; air pollution 165–66; Belt and Road Initiative (BRI) 236; CO$_2$ 229–30, 467, 476; and COVID-19 220, 306; education in 178–79; and extreme poverty 45–46, 57–58, 275; Five Year Plans 164–65; Hubei Province *144*, **145**; infrastructure spending 46; Jiangsu Province *144*, **145**; manufacturing in 229–30; pig farms 515–16; Plan on Implementation of the 2030 Agenda for Sustainable Development 164; river chiefs in *144*, **145**, 147–48; SDG9 231; transportation 158; water management in 137, 143, *144*, **145**, 146–50; *see also* Beijing
Chololo 2.0 (Eco-Act) 95–96
Chololo Ecovillage Project 93–96
chronic hunger 7, 10
clean energy plans 159
Climate Action Tracker (CAT) 305–7
climate change 312, 379–80, 467–68; and displacement 316–17; funding 308; history 294; and national policies 296; recommendations 483–84; and SIDS 311, 315–16; and statehood 317–19; warming temperatures 468, 470–71; and women 322, 326
Climate change and social inequality (Islam and Winkel) 467
"Climate Club" 309, 536–37
climate crisis 6, 59, 257–58, 295; and agriculture 316; and air pollution 160–61; and disasters 62, 64; funding 308; and industrial food systems 77–78; lack of action 11, 303–7, 309; and migrants 469–70; and poverty 53, 62; and SIDs 13; skepticism about 294, 467; *see also* Small Island Developing States (SIDs)
climate refugees 468–71, 484, 494–95
The Closing Circle (Commoner) 5
coal consumption 165, 257, 282–83, 306
Coalition for Epidemic Preparedness Innovations (CEPI) 114
codes of conduct 428–29
Cold War 319
Collier, Paul 37
Colombia 386, 481
Commission on Ending Childhood Obesity 110
Commission on Macroeconomics and Health (2001) 116

Index 543

Commission on Social Determinants of Health (2008) 116
Commission on the Status of Women 122
Committee on World Food Security 88
commodity prices 63, 67
"Common but Differentiated Responsibilities" (CBDR) principle 295
Commoner, Barry 5, 12
communicable disease epidemics, ending 100, 102–3
complexity, importance of managing 30
computational thinking 207
Conard, Edward 242
Conditional Grants Schemes (CGSs), Nigeria 66
Conference of Parties to the United Nations Framework Convention on Climate Change (UNFCCC) (Glasgow) 389
Conference of the Parties of the CBD in Kunming (China) 389
Conference on Sustainable Development, Rio de Janeiro (2012) xxii, 43–44; *see also* Rio+20 Conference
conflict 61, 131, 407–9, 414, 478–79
Consolidated Global Humanitarian Response Plan (GHRP) 115
contraceptives 127–28
Convention for the Protection of the Marine Environment of the North-East Atlantic (OSPAR Convention) 344
Convention on Biological Diversity (CBD) 336, 396, 488–89, 519, 522
Convention on the Elimination of all Forms of Discrimination against Women (CEDAW) (1979) 119, 122, 132
Convention on the International Trade in Endangered Species (CITES) (1973) 522
Convention on the Prevention of Marine Pollution by Dumping of Wastes and Other Matter (1972) 349
cooking 106, 160, 258, 260–62, 266, 268, 270–71, 535
cooperation/coordination, increased need for 54
corporate social responsibility (CSR) 425–26, 437, 439, 442–43
corruption 68, 411, 428–29
Costa Rica 386
Costa Rica Dome 330, 333, 335–37
counter-radicalization 419
country programmable aid (CPA) 456
COVID-19 3, 5–6, 15, 18, 29–30, 50, 215, 306–7, 328, 373, 384, 387, 389–90, 412–14, 462, 511–12, 514; direct impacts on the SDGs 8, 17, 19–20, 22, 24, **25**, 26, *27*, 113–14, 151, 220–21, 223, 270–71, 288–90, 480–81, 532, 538; and education 181–83, 196, 210; environmental impacts of 21, 260, 304–5, 310; and European Union 49; failed preventative measures 517–18; and food insecurity 77–78, 82–84, 97; and gender-based violence (GBV) 133; and gender inequality 8–10, 118; and healthcare disruptions 63–64; and indigenous peoples 487–88, 499; indirect effects on the SDGs 20–22, 24, **25**, 26, *27*; and inequality 5–8, 12, 247–48, 250–51, 253; and land degradation 402; and LDCs 7, 236; and lockdowns 20, 37, 49, 82, 215, 236; and marine pollution 358, 364–65; mortality 50; and the oceans 332–33, 338–39; and One Health 514–15; and poverty 20, **25**, 38, 48–53, 181–82, 394; and recessions 20, 38, 48–49, 63, 220; and resilience building 30; response to 30–31, 113–15, 143, 435–36, 447–48; SDG progress as readiness proxy 21–22; and SDG3 20–22, **25**, 26, 113; and SDG9 **25**, 26, 236–37; and SIDS 314–15; statistics 19–20; and sustainable development financing 434–36; and travel restrictions 414; and unemployment 7; vaccine for 112–14, 116–17; and vaccine shortages 10, 64
COVID-19 Solidarity Response Fund 115
COVID-19 Therapeutics Accelerator 114
Cowie, Annette 403
Crawford, Victoria 304
crisis response 30, 533
crop yields 94–95
Customary International Humanitarian Law 509–10
customary law 504

DAC Untying Recommendation 457–58
Dag Hammarskjöld Foundation 114–15
Dakar Framework for Action 169
DARE (Delivery, Accountability, Relevance, and Efficiency) 16
Darfur 478–79; *see also* Sudan
Dead Aid (Moyo) 39
Deaton, Angus 52
Declaration of Interdependence, Agenda 2030 as 3
Declaration of the International Forum for Agroecology, 2015 92
Declaration on the Elimination of Violence against Women (DEVAW) 119, 121–22
Declaration on the Establishment of a New International Economic Order (NIEO) (1974) 40–41
declarations 503*n*14
deforestation 379, 385–86
democracy 52
Democratic Republic of Congo (DRC) 225, 234–36, 388

deradicalization 419
desertification 377, 393, 421, 469
"Developing Sustainable Industrial Parks in Latin American and Caribbean Countries" initiative 233
Development as Freedom (Sen) 39
Development Finance Institute (FinDev Canada) 269
development rights approaches 245
disaster risk reduction 61–62, 64–65
disaster risks 61
disasters 61–64
disconnects 12–14, 53
diseases 512; emergence of 516–18; preventable 10; zoonotic diseases 18, 22, 384–87, 389, 499, 512–13, 515–16, 522
Djankov, Simeon 42
Do Not Panic: How to End Poverty in 15 Years (2015) 44
Dobson, Andrew 388
Doha Declaration 99, 112
Doha Development Agenda (DDA) 112
Dollar, David 42
domestic violence 7, 118–19, **120**
drylands 377, 400
Dubai 158
Duflo, Esther 40, 48, 52

earnings, women's 131
Earth Charter xxi
Easterly, William 38–39, 42, 52
Eastern Europe 45–46, 49–50, 284–85
Eastern oyster 202
Ebola outbreaks 182–83, 385
Ecologically or Biologically Significant Areas (EBSAs) 336
economic development 39, 214
economic diversification 73, 235, 238
economic growth 212, 237, 454, 535; Brazil 216, 219–20; and economic development 214; and education 168, 171; ex-communist countries 46; Kenya 216–18; LDCs 212; neoclassical theory 212–13, 226; and poverty reduction 38, 211; Singapore 216–17
economic growth contractions 63
economic infrastructure development 228
economic liberalization 46
"Economics of Biodiversity" report 384
ecosystem degradation 385–86
ecosystem services 377
education/education spending 46, 168, 172–73, 272, 534; Burundi 175–76; in China 178–79; and COVID-19 63, 115, 181–83, 196, 210; development aid as 456; on environmental education 193–94; exclusion from 172, 176; green schools 190–91; hands-on 203, 206; improvements in 169–70; learning environments 196; Masters in Environmental Management (MEM) program 196–200; men/boys 130; in Mexico 180–81; in Nigeria 70, 135; peer mentoring 206; PISA tests 173, 181; and poverty 170–71; as right 194; and STEM 201–3; and women's rights 123; *see also* BOP CCERS Project; Education for Sustainable Development (ESD); Environmental Education; teachers
Education for Sustainable Development (ESD) 186, 188–90, 193–96
Education for Sustainable Development Goals–Learning Objectives (2017) 189
Egypt 414
The Elders 114
electricity access 258–68, 271
The Elusive Quest for Growth (Easterly) 38–39
employment 119, 126, 215, 229–30, 233, 246, 292, 441–42, 446–48
The End of Poverty (Sachs) 37, 44
energy consumption levels 259, 286–87
Energy Efficiency Design Index (EED) 348
environmental action 28–29, 222
environmental agreements 11, 303–7, 309, 356; *see also* specific agreements
environmental degradation 59, 77–78, 139–40, 219–20, 275–76, 304, 351; *see also* land degradation neutrality (LDN)
Environmental Education (EE) 186–87, 189–92, 200
environmental governance 159–60
environmental, governance, and social (EGS) 426, 431–32, 435–36, 438–41
Environmental Impact Assessments (EIAs) 496–97, 500, 517, 522–23
environmental risks, deaths from 106–7
environmental treaties 298–99
Ethiopia 46, 126–28, 234, 281, 307, 470
EU-Africa Infrastructure Trust Fund 235
European Commission 49
European Union 45, 49–50, 243, 287–88, 306, 411, 475
EUROSTAT 49
ex-communist countries 45–46
Exclusive Economic Zones (EEZs) 334–35, 337
exporter states 354
extinction crisis 11
extreme poverty 6, 38, 53, 58, 298, 534; and China 45–46, 57–58; declines in 52–53, 57–58, 211, 275; defined 37, 56–57; and Eastern Europe 45–46; and economic diversification 73; and the European Union 45; and ex-communist countries 45; and food insecurity 76; and India 66–67; and industrialization 73; in Nigeria 66–67, **67**, 68; reduction targets 56, 65; and rural lives

65; statistics 37, 43, **44**, 45, 51, 57, **58**, 60, 211; and structural transformation 73; and Sub-Saharan Africa 48; in the US 45; World Bank on 3; *see also* poverty

Factfulness (Rosling) 37
Falk, Richard 297
feedback loops 27–29
female genital mutilation **120**, 132
Figueres, Christiana 307
Financing for Sustainable Development Report 2019 (FSDR 2019) 454–57
Financing for Sustainable Development Report 2020 (FSDR 2020) 454, 456–57
Finland 173–74, 288
First Information and Action Network (FIAN) 85–86, 97
fiscal policy 221
fishing industry 316
"Five-Ps" approach 23–27
flying foxes 385
Food and Agriculture Organization (FAO) 10, 77–78, 83, 91, 97, 110, 123, 139, 142, 376
Food and Land Use Coalition (2019) 390
food insecurity 75–78, 82–84, 97, 402, 488
food loss and waste (FLW) reduction 277, 289
food security 75–76, 86–87, 96
food shortages 3, 6–7, 10, 68, 94
food sovereignty 90
foreign aid 38, 52, 249, 251, 455, 457; *see also* international aid
Foreign Direct Investment 41, 63n57, 110, 216, 226–27, 238, 536
forests 375–76, 379, 381–82, 385, 523
fossil fuels 257, 259, 285, 306, 432
Foster, James 44
Fostering Education & Environment for Development, Inc. (FEED) 192
Fourier, Joseph 294
Free and Prior Informed Consent (FPIC) 488, 494–95
Friendly Relations Declaration 503n14
Fundamental Principles of Official UN Statistics 279
The Future is Now report 403
The Future We Want 350

Garrett, Laurie 29
Gates, Bill 29, 252
GDP 43–44, 49–50, 215
gender 135, 215–16
gender-based violence (GBV) 131–33, 132–34, 136, 322; *see also* domestic violence; sexual violence
gender-based violence (GBV) prevention 119, **120–21**, 130

gender equality 9, 118, 171, 322; funding for 124, 129; laws concerning 122–23, 129; marginalized men 130; and the MDGs 119; and Nike 446; as SDG priority 59; SDG5 targets/indicators **120–21**; and State peacefulness 11; and the UN 119; *see also* Sustainable Development Goal 5; women
gender equity 194
gender gap 7, 9, 177, 215–16, 241, 442–43, 446–47; *see also* women
gender identity 134–36
gender inequality 8–10, 123
General Agreement on Tariffs and Trade (GATT) 459
General Principles for International Remittances Services 250
genetic diversity 378
Gini Coefficient 247, 252
Global Action Program on Education for Sustainable Development (GAP-ESD) 190
Global Alliance for Vaccines and Immunization (GAVI) 102, 114
Global Biodiversity Outlook 5 380
Global Compact 426, 436–37, 441, 443–45, 483–84
Global Education for All Meeting (2014) 170
Global Facility for Disaster Reduction and Recovery 54
Global Goals *see* Agenda 2030; Sustainable Development Goals (SDGs)
"Global Green New Deal" 14
Global Health Security Index (GHSI) 50
Global Impact Investing Network 432
Global Land Outlook 394
Global Pandemic Network (GPN) 524
Global Partnership 449–50
Global Partnership for Effective Development Cooperation (GPEDC) 453, 509
Global Preparedness Monitoring Board 114
The Global Program of Action for the Protection of the Marine Environment from Land-Based activities: A 20 years Perspective on a Unique Program to Advance the Ocean Agenda 345
Global Program of Action for the Protection of the Marine Environment from Land-based Activities (GPA) 344–45
Global Reporting Initiative (GRI) Sustainability Reporting Guidelines (Guidelines) 437–38, 444, 446
Global Schools Program 190
Global Strategy to Accelerate Tobacco Control: Advancing Sustainable Development through the Implementation of the WHO FCTC 2019– 2025 (GS2025) 107–8
global warming 468, 470–71; *see also* climate change; climate crisis

globalization 45, 107, 110, 200, 250–52, 289
Goldstein, Allie 376–77
Gorbachev, Mikhail xxi
government learning 53
grants 456–57, 493–94
green bonds 433–34
Green Climate Fund (GCF) 296, 324–25, 327, 482, 493–94
Green New Deal (GND) (Europe) 306
Green Revolution 76–77
GreenBiz Group's Report (GreenBiz) 439–40
greenhouse gas emissions 159, 257–59, 276, 287, 295, 304, 315, 325, 327–28, 467, 473–74, 480, 532; business-related 440–41; industrial development 229; and industrial food systems 77–78, 91, 379; and maritime traffic 348
greenwashing, vs. true sustainability 427
Growth Facilitation and Identification Framework (GIFF) 73
Guidelines for Wildlife Disease Risk Analysis 520
Guterres, Antonio 325

habitat disruption 517
habitat fragmentation 80, 385
Haiti 477–78
handwashing 21, 139, 151, 413, 521
Hanson, Jeffrey O. 381
harmful cultural practices 118–19, **120**, 131–32, 136
Hasselman, Jan 499
health 99, 115
health-care services 104–6, 108, 116, **121**, 127–28
health issues 80, 93
health spending 63, 70, 108
healthcare disruptions 63–64
Hendra virus 385, 518
Higgins, Rosalyn 502
High Level Political Forum (HLPF) 75, 80, 244–45, 247–48, 277, 279, 299, 303, 305, 331–32, 486
Highly Indebted Poor Countries (HIPC) (1996) 42
Hippocrates 515
HIV/AIDS 102, 116–17
homicide rates 410, 412
Hong Kong 231
housing, unaffordability of 156–57
Human Capital (Becker) 170
human capital investments 421
Human Development Report (HDR) (1994) 41
human rights 41, 86–90, 115–16, 298, 402
Human Rights Committee 495
human rights legal framework 86

human rights violations 421
humanitarian competition 297
hurricanes 61–62, 477
hybrid agreements 302–3
hyperinflation 47

illegal, unreported, and unregulated fishing 329, 331–32, 352, 361
illegal wildlife trade 387
inclusion 13, 214
India 50, 66–67, 159, 174–75, 187–88, 192–93, 236, 243, 251–53, 275, 282–83, 306, 388, 442, 469
Indian Ocean Tsunami Warning and Mitigation System (IOTWMS) 54
indigenous peoples 323, 485–86, 489; and COVID-19 487–88; and the GCF 494; and land grabbing 491–92, 500; and the Nagoya Protocol 488–90, 488–91; in planning 390; and SDG1 486–87; and SIDS 319–21, 326; traditional knowledge 486, 489–91, 494, 497, 499; violence against 487, 491
Indonesia 275, 306, 479–80
industrial food systems 75–80, 91, 379, 390, 441, 534
Industrial Revolution 224, 294
industrialization, and extreme poverty 73
inequality 12, 240–42, 285–86, 402; and COVID-19 5–8, 12, 247–48, 250–51, 253; and discrimination 252–53, 322; growing 240–41, 243–44, 304, 473, 529; North/South 250–52; and SDG9 229–30
inequality reduction 42, 244–50
infant mortality 99, 101–2
Informal Consultative Process (ICP) 345
informal employment 215
information access 412
infrastructure spending 46, 230, 234–35
Integrated Sustainable Development Goals (iSDG) Model 27–28
Integrated Water Resources Management (IWRM) 141–42
integrity pacts 428–29
intergenerational dialog 14
Intergovernmental Oceanographic Commission's Decade of Ocean Science 369
Intergovernmental Panel on Climate Change (IPCC) 92, 312–13, 441
Intergovernmental Science-Policy Platform on Biodiversity and Ecosystem Services (IPBES) (2019) 375, 378, 380–81, 383, 519
interlinkage dynamics 22–23, *27*
Internal Displacement Monitoring Centre (IDMC) 469
international aid 39, 452–53, 455, 458; *see also* foreign aid

International Bank for Reconstruction and Development (IBRD) 43
International Committee of the Red Cross (ICRC) 509–11
International Convention for the Control and Management of Ships' Ballast Water and Sediment (BWM Convention) 349
International Convention on the Control of Harmful Anti-Fouling Systems 348–49
International Convention on the Elimination of All Forms of Racial Discrimination (CERD) 497
International Covenant on Civil and Political Rights 495
International Covenant on Economic, Social and Cultural Rights (ICESCR) 86–88, 116, 194
international customary law 505–6
International Data Bank for SDGs 238
International Development Bank (IaDB) 42
International Energy Agency (IEA) 259, 432
International Environmental Education Program 187
international environmental law (IEL) 486, 488, 498–99; *see also* international law
International Financial Institutions Advisory Commission (IFIAC) 42–43
International Health Partnership Plus (2007) 453
International Health Regulations (IHR) 108–9, 113
international law 13, 297, 301–2, 329, 496, 502–3, 505–8, 510; *see also* international customary law; international environmental law (IEL)
International Law Commission (ILC) 504
international legal discourse 501–5
International Livestock Research Institute (ILRI) 388
International Maritime Organization (IMO) 347–48
International Monetary Fund (IMF) 42, 220, 270–71, 435, 481; and poverty reduction 40; *see also* Poverty Reduction and Growth Facility (PRGF)
international organizations, lack of trust in 12
International Panel of Experts on Sustainable Food Systems (IPES-Food) 93, 96
international poverty line (IPL) 43, 55, 57, 60–61, 66
international trade 212
international treaties 501–2
International Union for the Conservation of Nature (IUCN) xxi, 378, 403, 518–20, 519–20, 524
Iran 413–14
Iron Curtain, fall of 41
Islam, S. Nazrul 467

Japan 307
Jin Gang 148–49
Johannesburg Plan of Implementation (JPOI) 169, 227
Johannesburg World Summit on Sustainable Development (2002) xxii, 227
John Hopkins University (JHU) COVID-19 database 50–51
Joint SDG Fund 115
Jonathan, Goodluck 134
Jones, Kendall R. 381, 384, 399
justice, access to 410–11
justice system reform, in Nigeria 418–19

Kalabia Foundation, "Environmental Education for the Heart of the Coral Triangle" program 193
Kenya 216–18, 234, 262–68, 270–71
Key Biodiversity Areas (KBAs) 381
Kiribati 316–18, 321, 495
Koskenniemi, Martti 507–8
Kremer, Michael 40, 52
Kuznets ratio 473
Kyoto Protocol 295, 299, 302, 475

La Via Campesina 89–90
labor productivity 212, 215
Labour share of GDP 246
Lake Chad Basin 411, 419–21
Lake Chad Basin Commission 419–20
Lamu Port South Sudan Ethiopia Transport (LAPSSET) Corridor Project 234
land 122–24, 392
land degradation 402, 474
land degradation neutrality (LDN) 389, 392, 394–96; implementation 396–401; and the law 402–3; principles 397–98; recommendations 404, 537; scientific framework 396–97, 403; targets 398, 400; *see also* environmental degradation; Sustainable Development Goal 15
land grabbing 491–92, 500
Land Matrix 79–80
land restoration programs 397
Landlocked Developing Countries (LLDCs), and COVID-19 7
Large Marine Ecosystem (LME) Approach 334
Latin America/Caribbean 232–33, 283–84, 388, 412, 477–78, 481; *see also* Costa Rica Dome
leadership, need for 15
learning, by governments 53
Least Developed Countries (LDCs) 212, 225–26, 237, 339; and climate change 471; climate mitigation policies 477–80; and COVID-19 7, 236, 532; development assistance to 455–56; and economic

growth 214, 454; and education 171–72; and employment 212; and the GCF 296; greenhouse gas emissions 467; manufacturing in 229–30; and SIDS 316
Leeds School of Business 445–46
liberalization 226
Lima Declaration: Toward Inclusive and Sustainable Industrial Development 227
literacy 174, 176–77
livestock production 80
Living Breakwaters 208
Living Planet Index 377–78
loans, as ODA 456–57
lockdowns: and COVID-19 20, 37, 49, 82, 215, 236; and gender-based violence (GBV) 133
London Dumping Convention, 1996 Protocol 355
low-carbon economic models 10–11
Low-Income Countries (LICs) 55; and COVID-19 55, 182, 184; disaster-caused economic losses 62–63; education 172–73, 180; financing for 65; and social protection schemes 64; and tobacco control 107–8
Lucas, Robert E. 226

McAdam, Jane 321
Makiguchi, Tsunesaburo 297
malaria 102
Malawi 126–28
Malthus, Thomas 212
Manila Declaration 345
manufacturing 228–30
Marine Environment Protection Committee (MEPC) 348
marine pollution 329–30, 340–41, 352, 357, 357–58n6, 371–72; and Agenda 21 343; and COVID-19 358, 364–65; ecosystem-based approaches 364–65; governance measures 367–69; plastic 366–67; ship-based pollution 347–50, 371; *see also* oceans
marine protected areas 351–52, 361
Marshall, Alfred 225
Marshall Islands 299, 316–17, 319
Martinez, C. 381
Masters in Environmental Management (MEM) program 196–200
material consumption (MC) 279–80, 286–88
material footprints (MF) 276, 281–83, 285
maternal mortality 56, 99–101
Matthyse, Liberty 134
MC Mehta v. Union of India 188, 192
"means of implementation" (MOI) 449–50, 458, 461–62
media 194, 197
Meltzer, Allan 42
men/boys, and toxic masculinity 130

Mendelson, Maurice 507
MERS 387
#MeToo movement 127
Mexico 180–81, 191, 307
Mexico City 159
Micronesia 317
Middle East 243, 411; *see also* specific countries
Middle-Income Countries (MICs) 7, 107–8
migrants 177–79, 178–79, 248–50, 317, 469
migration 468, 470–71, 483
Millennium Declaration 56, 241, 460, 501, 504
Millennium Development Goal 1 43–45
Millennium Development Goal 2 169–70
Millennium Development Goal 3 119
Millennium Development Goals (MDGs) xxii, 40, 55, 59, 66, 99, 119, 122, 169–70, 185, 217, 219, 234, 241, 274, 302, 321–22, 329, 407, 426, 449, 456, 501, 529; and inequality reduction 42, 244; and poverty reduction 42, 58
Millennium Ecosystem Assessment 498
Millennium Promise Alliance 44
Millennium UN Summit (2000) xxii
Millennium Village Projects (MVPs) 56
Minamata Convention on Mercury 346, 353–54
minimum wages 222
minorities 245, 322–23
mobile phones 127
Montgomery, David R. 392
Montreal Guidelines for the Protection of the Marine Environment from Land-based Sources (1985) 344
Montreal Protocol (1987) 297, 472, 483
Moody Stuart, Mark 437
Moon, Ban-Ki 445, 479
Mother Earth 498
mountains 376–77
Moyo, Dambisa 39
Multidimensional Poverty Index (MPI) 44, 49
Multilateral Debt Relief Initiative (MDRI) (1995) 42
multilateralism 6, 15, 325, 430, 483, 502
Muscat Agreement 170
Myanmar 388

Nagoya Protocol on Access to Genetic Resources, and the Fair and Equitable Sharing of Benefits Arising from their Utilization (Nagoya Protocol) 488–90, 495
National Human Rights Institutions (NHRIs) 411–12
National Tariff Lines (NTL) codes 249
National Urban Policies (NUPs) 162
nationalisms xxiii, 407, 410, 430

Nationally Determined Contributions (NDCs) 272
Natsios, Andrew 29
natural capital 378, 392n1, 397, 439–40
natural disasters 51, 53–54, 312–13
natural resource trap 213; *see also* resource extraction
nature 373, 378–79, 383–84
nature conservation 517
Naturebased Solutions (NbS) 389–90
"nature's contribution to people" 383
NCDs 99
Neglected tropical diseases (NTDs) 103
neoclassical theory 212–13, 226
New Development Bank 434, 436, 538
New Growth economic theory 226
New York 523; *see also* United States
New York City 159, 161, 202–3
New York Harbor 202–3, 206–8, 210
New York Harbor School 201, 204
New Zealand 190–91, 495, 498
Nigeria 55–56, 60n27, 66, 68, 413, 417; "Bring Back Our Girls" Movement 134–35; budgets in 71, 73; child-marriages 131–32; and commodity prices 67, 71–72; corruption in 68; counterterroism in 418–19; economic growth in 67, 71; education in 70, 135–36; female genital mutilation **120**, 132; food shortages 68; gender-based violence in 131, 133; health spending 70; justice system reform 418–19; non-binary people in 118, 133–34; Operation Safe Corridor 419; political instability in 72–74; poverty in 66, 67, 68; resource-dependence 67–68; and SDG1 72–74; and the SDGs 420–22; social investment programs 56, 69–70, 73; terrorism in 72, 417–18, 420–21; transgender people in 133–34; unemployment in 68; women's political participation 125–26; *see also* Sub-Saharan Africa
Nike 439, 442–46
Nipah virus 385, 518
non-binary people, violence against 133–34
non-communicable diseases, reducing mortality from 109–11
non-State actors 302–3
Nordhaus, William 309
normative frameworks 449, 461–62
normative systems 502
Norway 497
nuclear waste 319
nuclear weapons 11
Nuorgam, Anne 499

Obama, Barack 476
Ocean Health Index 360
oceans 329, 357, 474, 537; acidification 341, 350–52, 355, 360, 468, 474; and biodiversity 330, 333; and COVID-19 332–33, 364–65; interlinked initiatives 365; *see also* Costa Rica Dome; marine pollution
Official Development Assistance (ODA) 139, 196, 249, 430, 451–57, 462, 482
'Omics Tools 339
One Health 388, 512–13, 515, 538; Berlin Principles 520; implementing 521–25; and new disease emergence 516–18
One Water One Health 142
open public spaces 161–62
Open Working Group on Sustainable Development Goals xxii
Operation Safe Corridor 419
Ordos Declaration (2017) 393
Organization for Economic Co-operation and Development (OECD) 457, 462; Development Assistance Committee (DAC) 452–53, 457, 482; infrastructure spending 46; OECD 2018 Report 454
Organization for Security and Co-operation in Europe (OSCE) 122
orporate Social Responsibility (CSR) 252
Osterholm, Michael 29
Ottawa Charter for Health Promotion (1986) 116
"Our Common Future" (Brundtland Report) xxi–xxii, 188, 276, 431
Oxford Poverty & Human Development Initiative (OPHI) 44
Oyster Restoration field stations (ORS) 203–4
oysters 202

Page, Lucy 53
Pakistan 252
Palau 122
Palestine 413
Pande, Rohini 53
pandemics 49–50, 387, 513–15, 517, 521; *see also* COVID-19
Paris 158
Paris Climate Change accords 257–59, 270, 287–88, 295–303, 325–26, 355, 402, 431, 441, 475–76, 483, 492, 522
Paris Declaration on Aid Effectiveness (2005) 453
Paris Principles 411–12
Parry, Ian 482
partnership (Five Ps) 24, 26
patriarchy, and women's employment 126
payments in kind 131
peace (Five Ps) 24, 26
Peacebuilding Fund 115
peasant agriculture 91
peatlands 479–80
Pellet, Alain 505–6
people (Five Ps) 23, 25

People's Conference on Climate Change and the Rights of Mother Earth (2010) 498
Peru 494
Pesca, Federica 513
PFOA (perfluorooctane sulfonic acid) 354
pharmaceuticals 112
The Philippines 191–92
Philippines 414
Pied Piper 514
Piketty, Thomas 243
planet (Five Ps) 23, 26
plastic-based marine pollution 366–67
Plowright, Raina K. 385
policy coherence 110–11
political instability, in Nigeria 72–74
political representation 11, 118, 123, 125–26
politics, short-term gains in 12
pollution 8, 26, 106–7, 159–61, 163, 282–83, 342n6, 343, 468; *see also* Beijing; marine pollution
Poor Economics (Duflo and Banerjee) 48, 52
population growth 211–12, 275
populist political parties 29
Port State Agreement 352, 361
Potapov, Peter 376
Pouillet, Claude 294
poverty 28, 53, 211, 529, 534; and armed conflict 53; capability poverty 57; and the climate crisis 53; and climate inaction 14; and COVID-19 20, **25**, 38, 48–52, 181–82, 394; defined 57; and economic development 39; and education 170–71; income poverty 57; and inequality 242; measuring 40; and natural disasters 51, 53, 62–63; and Russia 47; and social cohesion 68; as social phenomenon 39–40; *see also* extreme poverty
"Poverty Dimensions and Trends: A Race against the Poverty Clock" 71
poverty gap 43–44
poverty reduction 38, 275; and conflict 61; and COVID-19 51–52; debt relief 44; and economic growth 38; and economic liberalization 46; in ex-communist countries 45–46; and foreign aid 38; International Monetary Fund (IMF) 40; and the MDGs 42; monetization of 39–40; targets 56, 65; *see also* Sustainable Development Goal 1
Poverty Reduction and Growth Facility (PRGF) 42–43; *see also* International Monetary Fund (IMF)
Poverty Reduction Strategy Papers (PRSP) 42
Pradhan, Prajal 383
preparedness/prevention 54
principle of PIC 489–90
Principles for Responsible Investing (PRI) 432, 438

procedural rights 87–88
productivist paradigm 85
Programme of Action of the International Conference on Population and Development 105, **121**
Prokopijević, Miroslav 42
prosperity (Five Ps) 23; and COVID-19 26
protected areas 380–81, 389–90, 522–23
Protected Planet report 381
Protocol Concerning Marine Pollution from Land-Based Sources and Activities (Wider Caribbean) (1999) 347, 354–55
Protocol for the Protection of the Marine Environment against Pollution from Land-Based Sources (1990) 347
Protocol for the Protection of the Mediterranean Sea against Pollution from Land-Based Sources and Activities (1980) 346, 354
Protocol for the Protection of the South-East Pacific against Pollution from Land-Based Sources (1983) 347, 354
Protocol on Protection of the Black Sea Marine Environment against Pollution from Land-Based Sources (1992) 347, 354
public transportation 157–59
Pulp Mills on the River Uruguay 496

quarantines 514

Ramsar Convention of Wetlands of International Importance 519
recessions 20, 38, 48–49, 63, 220; *see also* 2008 recession
refugees 408–9, 413, 468, 495; *see also* climate refugees
relationship inequality 131
Remdesivir 333
renewable energy 258–60, 263–68, 270, 272, 284, 286–88, 304, 324, 432, 444–45, 475–76
Report on the Fragmentation of International Law 507
research/development, investment in 228, 230–33
resilience building 217, 222–23, 337, 533; for climate change 481; and COVID-19 30, 532; and diversified agroecology 92; and the ocean 351
resilience dynamics 21–22
resource-dependence 67–68, 234–35, 373
resource depletion 275–76, 283
resource efficiency 275
resource extraction 280, 283, 378, 468; *see also* natural resource trap
Reversals of Fortune 53
Ricardo, David 212, 225

right to development 449, 458–60
right to education 194, 534
right to food 86–90, 402
Rio Declaration on Environment and Development xxii, 227, 460
Rio+10 Summit 187
Rio+20 Conference 56, 227, 350; *see also* Conference on Sustainable Development, Rio de Janeiro (2012)
Rivett-Carnac, Tom 307
road traffic accidents 104
Robinson, John 513
Robinson, Mary 114
Romer, Paul 226
Rosling, Hans 37–38
Rostow, Walt W. 225–26
Rotterdam Convention 279, 346, 353–54
rule of law 222, 410–14
rural communities 75–76, 78–79, 130, 177
Russia 47, 50, 213, 225, 243
Rwanda 125, 128

Sachs, Jeffrey 12, 37, 44
SAFER initiative 103–4
SARS 387, 518
savings/investments 39, 226
Schwabe, Dr. Calvin 518
SCP 274–77, 279, 282, 285, 289–93, 536
SDG Compass 446
SDGs Progress Reports 21–22
sea-level rises 216, 312–13, 315, 317, 352, 379, 469
self-employment 246, 292
Sen, Amartya 39, 52
Sendai Framework for Disaster Risk Reduction 2015–2030 62, 64–65
sexual violence 9, 131, 322
Shaikh, Alanna 29
Shekau, Abubakar 135
Shen Kunrong 148–49
Shimray, Gam 492, 498
Singapore 216–17, 231
Slaughter, Anne-Marie 297
slums 156, 177, 536
Small Island Developing States Accelerated Modalities of Action (SAMOA) Pathway 273, 323–24
Small Island Developing States (SIDs) 311, 328, 339, 371; and the climate crisis 64, 312–13, 322–23, 470–71; and COVID-19 7, 314–15; development aid to 455; and education 172; and fresh water 316, 318, 321; and the GCF 296; and indigenous peoples 319–21, 323, 326; and loss of statehood 317–18; in the Pacific 315–17; and SDG13 targets/indicators 323–26; and SDG14 360, 537; *see also* climate crisis

Smith, Adam 212, 225, 251
social contracts 14
Social Institutions and Gender Index (SIGI) report (2019) 122–23
social norms 136; and gender 118; and harmful practices 129; *see also* harmful cultural practices
social protection systems 56, 59–60, 64, 69–70, 73
soft law 88, 297–98, 301–3, 341, 343–45, 502, 507, 510
soil 392, 394, 400
"SoiLEX" 400–401
Solomon Islands 317
Solow, Robert 226
South Asia 49
South Korea 225, 231–32
Sowell, Thomas 39
Spencer Report 477
Spotlight Initiative 115
"State of Food Security and Nutrition in the World" (SOFI) reports 81–82
statehood 317–18
statistics: air pollution 160; Arab region 282; Beijing 163–64; Bulgaria 46–47; Burundi 175; child-marriages 131–32; chronic hunger 10, 488; communicable diseases 102; conflict 407–9; corruption 411; COVID-19 19–20, 48, 480–81; deaths and environmental risks 106–7; discrimination 245; DMC 286; domestic violence 118; drylands 377, 400; ecosystem services 377; ecovillage project 94–95; education 135, 172–73, 176, 203; ESG 432, 440; extreme poverty 37, 43, **44**, 45, 51, 57, **58**, 60, 211; forests 375–76, 381, 523; GDP 49–50; gender-based violence 131; green bonds 433; greenhouse gas emissions 467, 474; handwashing 21; indigenous peoples 485, 488; information access 412; literacy 174; manufacturing 228–29; marine protected areas 351–52, 361; material consumption (MC) 280; mobile phones 127, 228; mountains 376–77; Nigeria 68, 417; non-communicable diseases 109; ODA 455–57; pandemic GDP declines 49–50; plastic pollution impacts 366; political representation 11, 118, 125; refugees 408–9; Russia 47; sexual violence 9, 131; teachers 179–80; threatened species 378; transportation 158–59; unpaid labour 124–25; urbanization 156; water 139–40; wetlands 376; wilderness 375; women 9, 11, 123–28
Statute of the International Court of Justice (ICJ) 502, 505–6

Stiglitz, Joseph 241
Stockholm Conference on the Human Environment (1972) xxi, 186, 279, 341, 510, 524, 538
Stockholm Convention on Persistent Organic Pollutants (POPs) (2001) 346, 353–54
Stockholm Declaration on the Human Environment 186
Stockholm Resilience Center 524
Strong, Maurice xxi
structural transformation 73
stunting 82
Sub-Saharan Africa 49–50, 56, 258, 473; Burundi 175–76; and communicable diseases 102; and COVID-19 50, 63; and domestic violence 118; education 176, 179–80, 183; electricity 258–59; and extreme poverty 48, 61; Kenya 216–18; slums 156–57; and social protection schemes 64; transportation 158–59; water in 139–40; *see also* Nigeria
substance abuse, prevention/treatment of 103–4
Sudan 414, 478–79
supply chain disruptions 20–21, 77
Suriname 299
sustainability 425, 427, 436
Sustainability Accounting Standards Board (SASB) 438
sustainable development 14, 229, 431, 533; and climate-related vulnerability 61; and disaster risk reduction 61; financing 430–36, 450–51, 458, 537–38; and indigenous peoples 492; and plastic pollution 367
Sustainable Development Goal 1 48, 55, 170, 242, 277, **278**, 298, *531*, 534; and businesses 439, 443, 446–48; and COVID-19 20, **25**, 38, 48–52, 151; in feedback loops 28; and indigenous peoples 486–87, 492; Latin America/Caribbean 232; in Nigeria 72–74; and social protection schemes 59–60, 64; targets/indicators 59–63, 65, 69–73, 314, 363; *see also* extreme poverty; poverty reduction
Sustainable Development Goal 2 75, 85, 87, 96–98, 115, 171, 242, 277, **278**, 339, 382, 402, *531*, 534; and COVID-19 20, **25**, 26; in feedback loops 28; HLPF review (2017) 75, 84; and indigenous peoples 486; interdependence of 80–81, 115, 277, **278**; and One Health 518; targets/indicators 81, 83–84, 88–89, 363
Sustainable Development Goal 3 99, 115, 143, 171, 242, 277, **278**, 339, 382, *531*, 534; and COVID-19 20–22, **25**, 26, 113, 151, 314; in feedback loops 28–29; and One Health 518, 521; targets 99–109, 111–12, 116, 363, 530

Sustainable Development Goal 4 115, 168–69, 176, 178, 183–86, 197, 209, 242, 272, 277, **278**, *531*, 534; and COVID-19 20, **25**, 181–82; in feedback loops 28; and indigenous peoples 486; targets 171–72, 174, 179–80, 182–83, 189, 194, 363, 530
Sustainable Development Goal 5 119, 128–30, 136, 171, 228, 242, 269, *531*, 534–35; and businesses 439, 441–43, 446–47; and COVID-19 **25**, 26, 447; in feedback loops 28; funding for 129; and gender minorities 134; indicators 118–19, **120–21**, 124–28, 131, 446; and indigenous peoples 487; targets 104–5, 119, **120–21**, 122, 129, 363, 441–42, 446; *see also* gender equality
Sustainable Development Goal 6 137, 151–52, 171, 277, **278**, 382, 402; and businesses 439, 441; constraints on 141; and COVID-19 21, **25**, 151; in feedback loops 28; handwashing 139, 151; and One Health 521; progress 138–41, *531*; recommendations 143, 535; targets 138, 363; and uncertainty 150–51
Sustainable Development Goal 7 143, 171, 228, 257, 269, 277, **278**; and COVID-19 270–71; in feedback loops 28; implementation 260–70, *531*; recommendations 271–73, 535; targets 258, 363
Sustainable Development Goal 8 143, 209, 211–12, 214, 221, 223, 228, 269, 272, 277, **278**, 339, *531*; and Brazil 219–20; and businesses 439, 443, 446–48; and COVID-19 20, **25**, 26, 151, 220, 223, 314; in feedback loops 28–29; and Kenya 216–18; Latin America/Caribbean 232; recommendations 221–23, 535; and Singapore 216–17; targets 214, 216–17, 363
Sustainable Development Goal 9 171, 225, 228, 237; and Africa 233–36; and COVID-19 **25**, 26, 236–37, 535; inequality 229–30; Latin America/Caribbean 232–33; progress 228–36, *531*; recommendations 238–39, 535–36; South Korea 225, 231–32; targets/indicators 228, 234, 363
Sustainable Development Goal 10 171, 228, 241, 243, 252, 272, 473, 481, 497, *531*; and businesses 439, 443; and COVID-19 **25**, 26, 247–48, 314; in feedback loops 28–29; and indigenous peoples 494; opposition to 241–42; recommendations 253–54, 536; targets/indicators 244–50, 363, 472–73
Sustainable Development Goal 11 143, 155, 167, 171, 209, 339, 524, *531*, 536; and COVID-19 22, **25**, 26, 29, 163; and slums 156, 536; targets 155, 163, 363

Sustainable Development Goal 12 171, 228, 274, 340, 497, *531*; and COVID-19 **25**, 26, 29, 288–90; interdependence of 277, **278**; recommendations 290–92, 536; targets/indicators 277, **278**, 279–88, 282, 363

Sustainable Development Goal 13 143, 171, 228, 272, 295, 302–3, 311, 317–19, 382, 472, 480, 483–84; and businesses 439; and COVID-19 **25**, 26, 304–5; in feedback loops 29; and indigenous peoples 488, 492–93; lack of progress 303–9, *531*; and the Paris Agreement 298–302; recommendations 308–9, 326–27; targets/indicators 295–96, 323–26, 363, 493

Sustainable Development Goal 14 210, 277, **278**, 329, 352, 358, 472, 474, 500; commitments to 330–31; and COVID-19 **25**, 26, 359–60; in feedback loops 29; and indigenous peoples 488; progress 330–33, *531*; recommendations 337–40, 369–70, 537; targets/indicators 329–30, 333–35, 337, 340, 352, 360–61, 363, 366–67; and UNCLOS 329–30, 334, 342

Sustainable Development Goal 15 171, 277, **278**, 373, 393, 402, 473–74; and COVID-19 22, **25**, 26; in feedback loops 29; and indigenous peoples 488, 490–91; lack of progress 373, 388–89, *531*; and One Health 521; recommendations 390–91, 537; targets/indicators 363, **374**, 375, 377, 379–84, 387–88, 397, 400; *see also* land degradation neutrality (LDN)

Sustainable Development Goal 16 171, 272, 407–8; and COVID-19 22, **25**, 26, 412–14; in feedback loops 28; and indigenous peoples 487–88, 492; and One Health 518; progress on 408–12, 414–15, *531*; recommendations 416, 537; targets/indicators 363

Sustainable Development Goal 17 210, 427–28, 509–10, *531*, 537; and business 446, 448; and COVID-19 **25**, 26; and partnerships 428–30; targets/indicators 363, 450, 452, 455

Sustainable Development Goals (SDGs) 55, 58–59, 75, 87, 137, 185, 225, 295, 321, 398, 407, 501, 505, 529, 533; and businesses 425–26, 438–39, 445; costs 428; and COVID-19 response 31, 143, 514; direct impacts of COVID-19 8, 17, 19–20, 22, 24, **25**, 26, *27*, 113–14, 151, 220–21, 223, 288–90, 480–81, 514; implementation of 59, 398–99, 426, 449, 502, 521, 530, *531*; and inequality reduction 42, 241–42; interdependence of 14, 22–24, *27*, 59, 80–81, 115, **278**, 362–64, 382–83, 401, 426, 529, *530*; as international law 505–8, *507*; MOI 450, 452–53, 458; and poverty reduction 42; progress on 472–74, *531*; relevance of 6, 15; and the right to development 460–62; rights-based approaches to 87; and SCP 277; targets 450; and uncertainty 150–51; *see also* Agenda 2030; specific goals

Sustainable Development Report 2019 62, 140, 215, 257, 351–53, 359–62, 394–95, 430, 454–55, 487, 530

Sustainable Development Report 2020 7–8, 305, 358–61, 371, 434, 454, 487, 530, 532

Sustainable Development Reports 100–101, 305, 529

sustainable finance 427, 430–34, 537–38

sustainable natural resource management 381–82

Taki, Hiroshi 508–9
Tanzania 93–96
Target Gender Equality (TGE) 447–48
Tata, Ratan 252
Tbilisi Declaration 187
teachers 179–80, 196; BOP Project 204, 206–7; Burundi 175–76; in Finland 173; in Mexico 181; *see also* education/education spending
technology, and SDG5 129
terrorism, in Nigeria 72, 134–35, 417–18
The International Convention for the Prevention of Pollution from Ships (MARPOL) 73/78 348, 355
Thomson, Peter 331
"The Threat of Growing Inequalities: Building More Just and Equitable Societies to Support Growth and Sustainable Development" 241
tobacco control 107–8
Tomuschat, Christian 503
Tong, Anote 318
Tonga 315
toxic masculinity 118, 130
traditional knowledge 486, 489–91, 494, 497, 499
traffic 157–59
transgender people, violence against 133–34
transportation 157–59
Treaty on Environmental Education for Sustainable Societies and Global Responsibility (2011) 187
TRIPS Agreement 111–12
Trump, Donald 475–76, 483
trust crisis 13
Tunisia 122
turberculosis 102–3
Turkmenistan 45
Tuvalu 316, 318

554 *Index*

2019 6
2004 earthquake/tsunami 54
2008 recession 44–45, 213, 217, 247; *see also* recessions

Uber 158
UN Conference on Environment and Development (Earth Summit), Rio de Janeiro (1992) xxii, 227, 276, 510, 524, 538; *see also* Agenda 21
UN Convention to Combat Desertification 389, 393, 396–400, 402
UN COVID-19 Response and Recovery Fund 115
UN Decade of Ecological Restoration (2021–2030) 390, 512
UN Declaration on the Right to Development 115–16, 459–60, 504
UN Declaration on the Rights of Indigenous Peoples (UNDRIP) 485
UN Declaration on the Rights of Peasants and Other People Working in Rural Areas (UNDROP) 88–89
UN Development System 114
UN Environment 2017 369
UN Global Compact 426–27
UN-Habitat 157
UN Permanent Forum on Indigenous Issues (UNPFII) 487
UN Resolution 74/270 314
UN Sustainable Development Solutions Network—Youth Initiative (SDSN Youth) 190
UN Women 9, 447–48
unemployment 7, 28, 68, 131, 215, 219
unemployment payments 51*n*108
UNESCO Global Education Monitoring Report (2019) 172
UNESCO-Japan Prize on ESD 193
UNFCCC Local Communities and Indigenous Peoples Platform (LCIPP) 493
United Arab Emirates (UAE) 414
United Kingdom 190, 224, 307
United Nations Charter 38, 241, 327, 460, 502–4
United Nations Children's Fund (UNICEF) 3
United Nations Commission on the Status of Women (CSW) 9
United Nations Conference on Environment and Development (UNCED) 344
United Nations Conference, San Francisco (1945) 9
United Nations Convention on the Law of the Sea (UNCLOS) 329–30, 342–50, 353, 356–57
United Nations Development Program (UNDP) 245–46, 473, 477–78
United Nations Economic and Social Council (ECOSOC) 299
United Nations Economic and Social Council (ESC) 49; July report 51
United Nations Educational, Scientific and Cultural Organization (UNESCO) World Heritage Convention 518–19
United Nations Environment Assembly (UNEA) 367–68, 519
United Nations Environment Program (UNEP) 187, 189, 192–93, 344, 346, 388, 440, 491, 519
United Nations Framework Convention on Climate Change (UNFCCC) 295, 301–2, 324, 350, 389, 396, 488, 492–93, 495
United Nations General Assembly (UNGA) 8, 88, 119, 299, 344–45, 395–96, 501, 503–4, 506–07, 509
United Nations Ocean Conference (2017) 330–31
United Nations Ocean Conference (2020) 330, 332–33
United Nations Population Fund (UNFPA) 105
United Nations Principles for Responsible Management Education (UN PRME) 445–46
United Nations (UN) 8–9, 13, 16, 113–14, 119, 408–9
United Nations World Summit for Social Development, Copenhagen (1995) 41
United Nations World Water Development Report 2020 137
United States 122, 286–88; CO_2 467, 475–76; and COVID-19 50, 220, 236, 306, 499; Dakota Pipeline 496–97; education 201; emissions in 306, 483; environmental education 191; extreme poverty in 45; hurricanes 61–62; inequality in 243–44, 251–52; nationalism 410; nuclear waste 319; President's Council of Advisors on Science and Technology (PCAST) 201–2; STEM jobs in 201; *see also* New York City; New York Harbor
Universal Declaration of Human Rights (UNDHR) 9, 38, 86, 194
universal health care (UHC) 105–6, 108, 116
unpaid work: and COVID-19 7; and women 7, **120–21**, 123–25, 131, 177
urban development 64, 159, 162
urban greening 159
urban populations 409
urban public creative spaces (UPRS) 161
urbanization 156–57, 162–63
Uzbekistan 45

vaccines 10, 64, 102, 112–14, 116–17
Vanuatu 315
Venezuela 481
veterinary specialists, and One Health 516–18
Vienna Declaration (1993) 460

Vienna Programme of Action for Landlocked Developing Countries 273
Viet Nam 260–62, 271
violence 412, 434, 487, 491; *see also* domestic violence; gender-based violence (GBV); sexual violence
viruses 384–87, 389, 516; *see also* COVID-19
Voluntary Guidelines on the Responsible Governance of Tenure of Land, Fisheries and Forests (Tenure Guidelines) 88
voluntary national reviews (VNRs) 332

Washington Consensus 40–43, 47, 213
Washington Declaration 344–45
water 137, 139, 316, 318, 321, 440–41
water management 137, 141–43, *144*, **145**, 146–50, 262–63
water pollution 441
Water Pollution Prevention Act (China) 143, 150
water quality 139–40
Watson, James 375
Watt, James 224
Watt, Sir Arthur 504
Webster, Robert G. 29
wetlands 376
The White Man's Burden (Easterly) 39
WHO Coronavirus Disease (COVID-19) Dashboard 50
WHO-UNICEF Declaration of Alma-Ata on Primary Health Care (1978) 116
Wibowo, Ignatius 214
wild meat 386–88
wild species 377–80
wilderness 375
Williamson, John 213
Wilson, Dr. Edward O. 522–23
Winkel, J. 467
Wolfe, Nathan D. 387
Wolferson, James 42
women 28; Chololo Ecovillage Project 95; and climate change 322, 326; with disabilities 129–30; discrimination against 245–46, 446; earnings 131, 446–47; education 123, 174, 177, 194; employment 119, 126, 215, 229–30, 233, 441–42, 446–48; as farmers 79, 81, 126–27; in healthcare 7; and mobile phones 127; political participation 11, 118, 123, 125–26; in rural communities 130; and sexual/reproductive choices 127–28; and sexual violence 9, 131; statistics 9; and unpaid work 7, **120–21**, 123–25, 177; violence against 408; *see also* gender equality; gender gap
women's empowerment 59, 119
women's rights 122–24
Women's Rights Agenda 8–9
Woods Hole Oceanographic Institute 333
World Bank 3, 39–40, 42, 48, 57, 218, 250, 252, 267, 271, 289, 481
World Bank Poverty and Shared Prosperity (PSP) Report 2018 52, 470
World Commission on Environment and Development xxi
World Conservation Strategy xxi
World Development Report (WDR) (1990) 40
World Development Report (WDR) (1997) 42
World Development Report (WDR) (2006) 43
World Economic Forum, Davos (2014) 241, 437, 520–21
World Food Programme (WFP) 3, 82–83
World Health Assembly 111
World Health Organization (WHO) 101, 106; air pollution 160, 166; and COVID-19 21, 99, 113–15; funding for 114; Global Action Plan for the Prevention and Control of NCDs 109–10; Global Strategy on Human Resources for Health: Workforce 2030 108; and One Health 519, 522; and tobacco 100, 107–8
World Inequality Report (WIR) (2018) 243–44
World Summit for Social Development (1995) 57
World Trade Organization (WTO) 111–12, 430
World Water Council 139

Yett, Sheldon 314
Yong, Li 227–28

Zero Hunger Goal *see* Sustainable Development Goal 2
zero net land degradation 393, 400
zoonotic diseases 18, 22, 384–87, 389, 499, 512–13, 515–16, 522

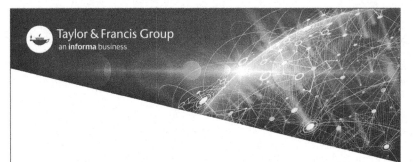

Made in the USA
Coppell, TX
22 January 2025

44784776R00319